Pearson New International Edition

Fundamentals of Clinical Supervision

Janine M. Bernard Rodney K . Goodyear

Fifth Edition

PEARSON®

Pearson Education Limited
Edinburgh Gate
Harlow
Essex CM20 2JE
England and Associated Companies throughout the world

Visit us on the World Wide Web at: www.pearsoned.co.uk

PEARSON®

ISBN 10: 1-292-04207-9
ISBN 13: 978-1-292-04207-7

British Library Cataloguing-in-Publication Data
A catalogue record for this book is available from the British Library

ARP Impression 98
Printed in Great Britain by Clays Ltd, St Ives plc

Table of Contents

Introduction to Clinical Supervision

Introduction to Clinical Supervision

Many professions have a *signature pedagogy* (Shulman, 2005a), a particular instructional strategy that typifies the preparation of its practitioners. In medicine, for example, a team of physicians and medical students visit a prescribed set of patients during clinical rounds, discussing diagnostic and treatment issues related to each patient, along with what has happened since the team last discussed that patient. In law, students come to class prepared to be called on at any moment to describe the essential arguments of a particular case, or to summarize and respond to the arguments another student has just offered. During these interactions, their professor engages them in a type of Socratic dialogue.

Clinical supervision is the signature pedagogy of the mental health professions (Barnett, Cornish, Goodyear, & Lichtenberg, 2007; Goodyear, Bunch, & Claiborn, 2005). Like the signature pedagogy of other professions, it is characterized by (a) engagement, (b) uncertainty, and (c) formation (Shulman, 2005a): *engagement* in that the learning occurs through instructor–learner dialogue; *uncertainty* because the specific focus and outcomes of the interactions typically are unclear to the participants as they begin a teaching episode; and *formation* in that the learner's thought processes are made clear to the instructor, who helps shape those ideas so that the learner begins to "think like a lawyer (Shulman, 2005b, p. 52), a physician, a psychologist, and so on. In this text, we also are concerned with a higher level shift, which is to that of thinking like a supervisor (cf. Borders, 1992).

> *Shulman (2005a) notes that signature pedagogies are "pedagogies of action, because exchanges typically [end] with someone saying, 'That's all very interesting. Now what shall we do?'"* (p. 14)

Clinical supervision qualifies as a signature pedagogy against all these criteria; criteria that underscore both supervision's importance to the mental health professions and its complexity. This text is intended to address that complexity by providing the technical and conceptual tools that are necessary to supervise.

We assert that every mental health professional should acquire supervision skills, because virtually all eventually will supervise others in the field. In fact, supervision is one of the more common activities in which mental health professionals engage. For example, in each of the three surveys conducted over a 20-year span (summarized by Norcross, Hedges, and Castle [2002]), supervision was the third most frequently endorsed professional activity (after psychotherapy and diagnosis/assessment) by members of the American Psychological Association's Division of Psychotherapy. Surveys of counseling psychologists (e.g., Goodyear et al., 2008; Watkins, Lopez, Campbell, & Himmell, 1986) show similar results.

This is true internationally as well. In a study of 2,380 psychotherapists from more than a dozen countries, Rønnestad, Orlinsky, Parks, and Davis (1997) confirm the commonsense relationship between amount of professional experience and the likelihood of becoming a supervisor. In their study, the number of therapists who supervised increased from less than 1% for those in the first 6 months of practice to between 85% and 90% for those who have more than 15 years of practice.

In short, this text is for all mental health professionals. Its focus is on a training intervention that is not only essential to, but also defining of those professions; an intervention that has developed in a complementary way to psychotherapy and so now has more than a 100-year history (Watkins, 2011).

FOUNDATIONAL PREMISES

One challenge in writing this text has been our recognition that almost anyone who reads it does so through a personal lens that reflects beliefs, attitudes, and expectations about supervision that they have formed through their own experiences as supervisees; perhaps also as supervisors. Such foreknowledge can make the reading more relevant and personally meaningful, but it can also invite critical responses to material that readers find dissonant with their beliefs. We hope readers who have that experience find we have presented material in a manner that is sufficiently objective so that they may evaluate dispassionately any dissonance-producing content or ideas.

Three premises are foundational to what follows:

- *Clinical supervision works*. As we discuss later, the data show that supervision has important positive effects on the supervisees and on the clients they serve.
- *Clinical supervision is an intervention in its own right.* It is possible, therefore, to describe issues, theory, and technique that are unique to clinical supervision. Moreover, as with any other psychological intervention, the practice of supervision demands that those who provide it have appropriate preparation.
- *The mental health professions are more alike than different in their practice of supervision, regardless of discipline or country.* Most supervision skills and processes are common across these professions. There are, of course, profession-specific differences in emphasis, supervisory modality, and so on. These might be considered the unique flourishes each profession makes on our common signature pedagogy, but we assume there are core features that occur (a) whether the supervision is offered by psychologists, counselors, social workers, family therapists, psychiatrists, or psychiatric nurses and (b) regardless of the country in which it is offered (see, e.g., Son, Ellis & Yoo, in press). Therefore, we have drawn from both an interdisciplinary and international literature to address the breadth of issues and content that seems to characterize clinical supervision in mental health practice.

In keeping with our interdisciplinary focus, we most often use the term *clinical supervision* (versus such alternatives as *counselor supervision, psychology supervision,* or *social work supervision*). Figure 1 draws from Google's database of more than 5.2 million scanned books spanning 200 years (available through ngrams.googlelabs.com) and depicts the relative frequency with which *clinical supervision* and several alternatives have been used as a term in English-language books between 1940 and 2009. Because the black and white rendering of this graphic makes it difficult to differentiate categories, we note that *clinical supervision* is depicted in the top line, showing it to be the most widely used term. Notable too is the slow linear growth in the use of the term between the mid-1940s and the late 1960s, when the frequency of its use began to increase substantially (interestingly, it also shows some dropoff in the past several years).

Our Convention on the Use of Key Words

We use *counseling, therapy,* and *psychotherapy* interchangeably, because distinctions among

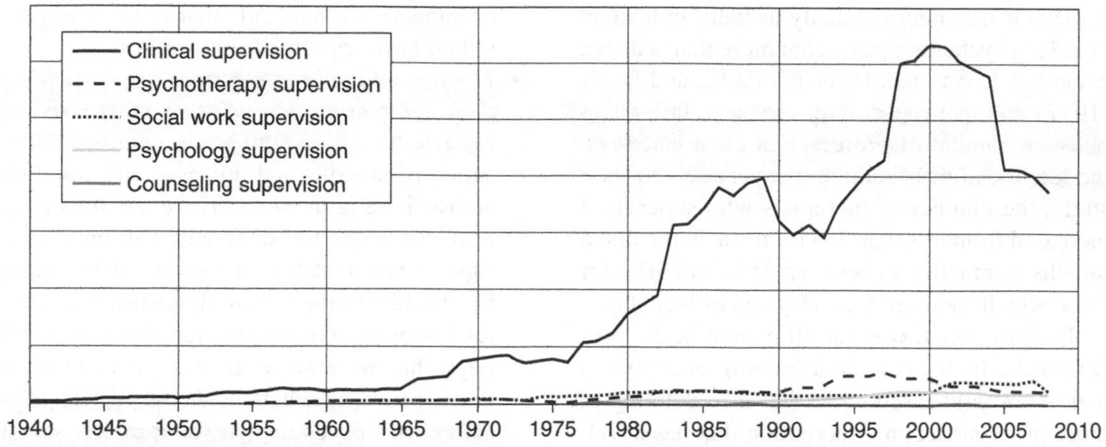

FIGURE 1 Occurrence of *clinical supervision* and related terms in English-language books: 1940–2008

these terms are artificial and serve little function. We also follow the convention first suggested by Rogers (1951) of referring to the recipient of therapeutic services as a *client*.

We distinguish between supervision and training as well. *Training* differs from *supervision* in being "structured education for groups of trainees . . . [and] involves a standardized set of steps" (Hill & Knox, in press, msp. 3). The trainer's primary role is that of teacher (see our discussion later in this chapter distinguishing the roles of *teacher* and *supervisor*).

Paralleling this *training-versus-supervision* distinction is the one that we make between *trainee* and *supervisee*. We believe that *supervisee* is the more inclusive term—that is, *trainee* connotes a supervisee still enrolled in a formal training program and so seems less appropriate for postgraduate professionals who seek supervision. In most cases, we use *supervisee*.

SUPERVISION'S CENTRALITY TO THE PROFESSIONS

Supervision's crucial role in the preparation of professionals has been recognized for thousands of years, as is suggested in the first few lines of the famous Hippocratic Oath:

> *I swear by Apollo the physician, and Asclepius, and Health, and All-heal, and all the gods and goddesses, that, according to my ability and judgment, I will keep this Oath and this stipulation—**to reckon him who taught me this Art equally dear to me as my parents, to share my substance with him, and relieve his necessities if required; to look upon his offspring in the same footing as my own brothers.*** (Hippocrates, ca. 400 BC, from Edelstein, 1943; bold ours for emphasis)

In this oath, the veneration being accorded a teacher or supervisor is clear; moreover, the comparison of that teacher to one's parents suggests the power and influence the neophyte physician cedes to the teacher. To appreciate that power and influence requires an understanding of the nature of the professions (see, e.g., Goodyear & Guzzardo, 2000), especially of the ways in which they are distinct from other occupations. Those distinctions include that (a) professionals work with substantially greater autonomy; (b) professionals need to make judgments under conditions of greater uncertainty (Sechrest et al., 1982), an attribute of the work that Schön (1983) vividly characterized as "working in the swampy lowlands" (p. 42) of practice (this is in contrast to technicians who work from a prescribed protocol on situations that typically are carefully constrained); and (c) professionals rely on a knowledge base that is sufficiently specialized so that the average person would have difficulty grasping it and its implications (Abbott, 1988).

Because of these qualities of professions, it is generally understood that laypersons would not have the knowledge necessary to oversee them, and so society permits the professions to self-regulate. The implicit contract, however, is that this self-regulation is permitted in return for the assurance that this profession will place the welfare of society and of their clients above their own self-interests (see, e.g., Schein, 1973; Schön, 1983). This self-regulation includes controlling who is admitted to practice, setting standards for members' behavior, and disciplining incompetent or unethical members.

Within the mental health professions, three primary mechanisms of self-regulation are (a) regulatory boards, (b) professional credentialing groups, and (c) program accreditation. Supervision is central to the regulatory functions of each, because it provides a means to impart necessary skills; to socialize novices into the particular profession's values and ethics; to protect clients; and, finally, to monitor supervisees' readiness to be admitted to the profession. In short, "supervision plays a critical role in maintaining the standards of the profession" (Holloway & Neufeldt, 1995, p. 207).

Regulatory Boards

State and provincial—and in some countries (e.g., Australia, England, Korea), national—regulatory boards codify the practice of supervision. They often stipulate (a) the *qualifications* of those who supervise; (b) the *amounts* of supervised practice that licensure or registration candidates are to accrue; and (c) the *conditions* under which this supervision is to occur (e.g., the ratio of supervision to hours of professional service; what proportion of the supervision can be in a group format; who can do the supervising; as an example, see the practicum supervision guidelines adopted by the Association of State and Provincial Psychology Boards, www.asppb.net/files/public/Final_Prac_Guidelines_1_31_09.pdf). Some require that members of a particular profession who wish to supervise obtain a separate license in order to do so (e.g., Alabama licenses counseling supervisors).

Professional Credentialing Groups

Independent groups, such as the Academy of Certified Social Workers (ACSW), the American Board of Professional Psychology (ABPP), the National Board for Certified Counselors (NBCC), the American Association for Marriage and Family Therapy (AAMFT), the British Association for Counselling and Psychotherapy (BACP), and the Korean Counseling Psychology Association (KCPA) also credential mental health professionals, usually for advanced practitioners and to certify competence above the minimal level necessary for public protection (the *threshold level of competence for licensure* is the reasonable assurance that the person will do no harm). Like the regulatory boards, these credentialing groups typically stipulate amounts and conditions of supervision a candidate for one of their credentials must have. In some countries (e.g., Korea), these groups serve as de facto regulatory boards.

Some groups (e.g., AAMFT, NBCC, BACP) also have taken the additional step of credentialing clinical supervisors. In so doing, they make clear their assumption that supervision is based on a unique and important skill constellation.

Accrediting Bodies

Whereas licensure and credentialing affect the individual professional, accreditation affects the training programs that prepare them. Each mental health profession has its own accreditation body, and their guidelines address supervision with varying degrees of specificity. For example, the American Psychological Association (APA, 2008) leaves it to the individual training program to establish that supervised training has been sufficient. However, other groups are very specific about supervision requirements. For example, any graduate of an AAMFT–accredited program is to have received at least 100 hours of face-to-face supervision, and this should be in a ratio of at least 1 hour of supervision for every 5 hours of direct client contact (AAMFT, 2006). The Council for Accreditation of Counseling and Related Educational Programs (CACREP, 2001) requires that a student receive a minimum of 1 hour per week of individual supervision and 1.5 hours of group supervision during practicum and internship; CACREP doctoral program standards also specify requirements for supervision-of-supervision.

FOSTERING SUPERVISEES' PROFESSIONAL COMPETENCE

Our remarks thus far speak to the role supervision plays in the professions and to the broader society they serve. This section addresses supervision as a mechanism to ensure that supervisees develop necessary competencies, as well as to the less-direct effects of supervision that occur through supervisees' exercise of those competencies.

Integration of Research and Theory with Practice

During their training, novice mental health professionals obtain knowledge from (a) formal theories and research findings, and (b) the practice-based knowledge of expert practitioners. However, there is a third type of knowledge as well—about themselves. For example, they identify aspects of their own personality and interpersonal behavior that affects their work as professionals. Skovholt (2012) refers to this last as an inevitable "loss of innocence" (p. 286).

Clinical supervisors are key to the integration of these several types of knowledge. Supervised practice provides the crucible in which supervisees can blend them, and it is the supervisor who can help provide a bridge between campus and clinic (Williams, 1995), the bridge by which supervisees begin to span what often is a "large theory–practice gulf" (Rønnestad & Skovholt, 1993, p. 396).

Practice is absolutely essential if supervisees are to develop professional skills. This is Peterson's (2002) point when he tells the joke about a New York City tourist who, lost, stops a cabbie and asks, "How can I get to Carnegie Hall?" The cabbie's response is, "Practice, practice, practice!" Peterson notes that this joke's punch line is significant in that the cabbie does not say, "Read, read, read!"

However, practice alone is an insufficient means to attain competence: Unless it is accompanied by the systematic feedback and guided reflection (the operative word being *guided*) that supervision provides, supervisees may gain no more than the illusion that they are developing professional expertise. Dawes (1994) asserts:

> *Two conditions are important for experiential learning: one, a clear understanding of what constitutes an incorrect response or error in judgment, and two, immediate, unambiguous and consistent feedback when such errors are made. In the mental health professions, neither of these conditions is satisfied.* (p. 111)

Dawes' assertions about the two conditions necessary for experiential learning are compelling. Yet we believe his assertion that *neither* condition is met in the mental health professions is overstated. We predicate our writing of this text on the assumption that supervision can satisfy these and other necessary conditions for learning.

It is true a *supervisor* (by whatever name) may be unnecessary for attaining many motor and performance skills. In these domains, simply performing the task may provide sufficient feedback for skill mastery. Learning to type is one example. Learning to drive an automobile is another (Dawes, 1994): When driving, the person who turns the steering wheel too abruptly receives immediate feedback from the vehicle; the same is true if he or she is too slow applying the brakes when approaching another vehicle. In these and other ways, experience behind the wheel gives the person an opportunity to obtain immediate and unambiguous feedback. Driving skills are therefore likely to develop and improve simply with the experience of driving.

However, psychological practice skills are of a different type. These skills require complex knowledge for which experience alone is rarely able to provide either of the two conditions that Dawes stipulated as necessary for experiential learning to occur. Practitioner skill development requires intentional and clear feedback from another person, such as is available through supervision. Research data confirm that unsupervised counseling experience does not accelerate the clinical progress of trainees (Hill, Charles, & Reed, 1981; Wiley & Ray, 1986), a conclusion complemented by that of educational psychologists who examined the broader domain of instruction (see especially Kirschner, Sweller, & Clark, 2006).

COMPETENCE TO SUPERVISE

Whereas the literature gives a great deal of attention to fostering the competence of new professionals, a great deal less attention has been given to the development of competence in the supervisors themselves. Milne and James (2002) comment that this has been something of a paradox that the field must address.

Developing supervisor competence implies systematic training. It was disappointing, therefore, to see that internship supervisors responding to the Rings, Genuchi, Hall, Angelo, and Cornish (2009) survey gave only lukewarm endorsement for the two items, "Supervisor has received supervision of his or her supervision, including some form of observation (audio or video) with critical feedback," and "Supervisor has completed coursework in supervision." In contrast, Gonsalvez and Milne (2010) note that "expert opinion is unanimous in identifying the need for supervisor training, often in forceful terms" (p. 234). It is increasingly rare to encounter people who believe that being an effective therapist is a sufficient prerequisite to being a good supervisor; analogous, we believe, to assuming that if a person is a good athlete, she or he inevitably will make a good coach or sports announcer.

Research literature that focuses on the effectiveness of supervisor training is still small and developing. Importantly, though, it does document positive outcomes.

Availability of Training for Supervisors

In the early 1980s, several authors (e.g., Hess & Hess, 1983; McColley & Baker, 1982) comment on what seems the limited availability of supervision training for mental health professionals. Fortunately, circumstances have changed quite significantly since then (except, perhaps in the case of psychiatry; e.g., Rodenhauser, 1996). Accrediting bodies (i.e., APA, CACREP, and AAMFT) have been important in this shift, through their stipulations that students in doctoral programs they accredit should receive at least some preparation to supervise.

Some organizations also have specified levels and type of training for those mental health professionals who do move into supervisory roles. For example, the Association for Counselor Education and Supervision (ACES) endorses Standards for Counseling Supervisors (ACES, 1990), a variant of which later was adopted by the Center for Credentialing and Education as the basis for its Approved Clinical Supervisor credential. AAMFT, too, has a supervisor membership category that requires specified training.

Regulatory boards also are beginning to require that mental health professionals who provide supervision receive supervision training. For example, psychologists licensed in California who want to supervise must to participate in one 6-hour supervision workshop during every 2-year licensure cycle; at this writing, several other state and Canadian provincial psychology boards either mandate some level of supervision training or are considering doing so (Janet Pippin, personal communication, September 13, 2011). Sutton (2000) reports that 18% of counselor licensure boards require a course or its equivalent for persons providing supervision, and another 12% require training in supervision.

Similar trends in supervision training are evident in other countries as well. For example, programs accredited by the Canadian Psychological Association are to provide supervision training. In Britain, supervision training is readily available to qualified professionals through a number of freestanding training "courses" (i.e., programs), and the National Health Service's Improving Access to Psychological Therapies (IAPT) group developed a proposal to create structures to permit briefer (e.g., 5–7 day) supervision training (IAPT, 2011); to inform that training, it also commissioned the development of a document to identify supervision competencies (Roth & Pilling, 2008). Korean counselors and psychologists often can obtain supervision training in their academic programs, although not universally (see Bang & Park, 2009).

The Competence Movement and Its Implications for Supervisor Training

Regulatory boards always have been concerned that the practitioners they certify for practice are competent. A relatively recent development, however, has been the attention being given to operationalizing, training for, and assessing competencies. The emergence of what has been called "the competence movement" (Rubin et al., 2007, p. 453) roughly coincides with the increasing demands for accountability seen in higher education in, for example, U.S. accreditation and in Europe's Bologna Process (Adelman, 2008). Essential to that movement is some common working definition of *competence.* It is useful, then, to consider the definition put forth by Epstein and Hundert (2002):

> *the habitual and judicious use of communication, knowledge, technical skills, clinical reasoning, emotions, values, and reflection in daily practice for the benefit of the individual and community being served; [it relies on] habits of mind, including attentiveness, critical curiosity, awareness, and presence.* (p. 227)

Their definition of *medical competence* has been sufficiently useful to have been embraced as well in the mental health professions (see, e.g., Rubin et al., 2007). It makes clear that competence is not merely a disparate collection of knowledge and skills, but rather something that requires the exercise of judgment. It seems highly similar to Aristotle's concept of *phronesis,* or practical wisdom, which "concerns how individuals 'size up' a situation and develop and execute an appropriate plan of action" (Halverson, 2004, p. 94).

The 2002 Competencies Conference (Kaslow et al., 2004) was something of a watershed in U.S. psychology. Although competencies had been an explicit aspect of the National Schools of Professional Psychology's training model (Peterson, Peterson, Abrams, & Stricker, 1997), this conference signaled broad embrace of competencies. Important to note is that there was clear consensus among conference attendees that *supervision* is a core competence of psychologists. In fact, a task group of supervision experts attending that conference articulated competencies they believed supervisors should attain and demonstrate (Falender et al., 2004).

However, all conceptions of competence are grounded in expert opinion, and these opinions can differ across groups of experts or across time within a group of experts, and so are inherently value laden. Understandably, then, authors have varied some in the focus and specificity with which they have addressed competencies (see, e.g., Falender et al., 2004; Roth & Pilling, 2008; Tebes et al., 2010).

Deist and Winterton's (2005) assertion that *competence* is a fuzzy concept seems borne out to some extent in these several conceptions of supervision competence. This is not to say that these conceptions are contradictory or unimportant; in fact, despite its fuzziness, we absolutely embrace the importance of competence as a central focus of this text.

DEFINING SUPERVISION

We assume that anyone reading this text is bringing some understanding of what *supervision* is. However, an important next step is to provide a more formal definition, and then to address the aspects of this definition.

In parsing the term, it is possible to infer that its practitioners exercise *super vision.* In fact, supervisors have the advantage of a clarity of perspective about counseling or therapy processes precisely because they are not an involved party. Levenson (1984) speaks to this when he observes that, in the ordinary course of his work as a therapist, he spends considerable time perplexed, confused, bored, and "at sea," but, "When I supervise, all is clear to me!" (p. 153).

Levenson (1984) also reports finding that theoretical and technical difficulties were surprisingly clear to him. Moreover, he maintains that people he supervised and who seemed confused most of the time that they were supervisees reported that they attained a similar clarity when they were supervising. He speculates that this is "an odd, seductive aspect of the phenomenology of the supervisory process itself" (p. 154) that occurs at a different level of abstraction than therapy. Perhaps this is the perspective of the "Monday-morning quarterback."

The Merriam-Webster (n.d.) online dictionary reports, however, that the etymological definition of *supervision* is simply "to oversee," from the Latin word *supervises,* and that the first known use of the term in English occurred in about 1645. *To provide oversight* is a key function of supervisors in virtually *any* occupation or profession. Yet as important as this is, it is an insufficiently precise description of what occurs during the clinical supervision of trainees and practitioners in the mental health professions.

Definitions of *supervision* offered by various authors differ from one another as a function of such factors as the author's discipline and training focus. Our intent is to offer a definition that is specific enough to be helpful, but at the same time broad enough to encompass the multiple roles, disciplines, and settings associated with supervision.

We have offered, with only the slightest of changes, the following working definition of *supervision* since the first edition of this text (Bernard & Goodyear, 1992):

> Supervision *is an intervention provided by a more senior member of a profession to a more junior colleague or colleagues who typically (but not always) are members of that same profession. This relationship*
>
> - *is evaluative and hierarchical,*
> - *extends over time, and*
> - *has the simultaneous purposes of enhancing the professional functioning of the more junior person(s); monitoring the quality of professional services offered to the clients that she, he, or they see; and serving as a gatekeeper for the particular profession the supervisee seeks to enter.*

The earlier version of this definition has been informally adopted as the standard in both the United States and the United Kingdom (see, e.g., Milne, 2007). In this edition, we make two changes to that definition:

1. Whereas the definition we use in prior editions asserts that supervision is a relationship between two people of the same profession, this revised definition acknowledges that this is not always true.
2. Whereas the final clause stipulates that supervisors serve as gatekeepers for those *entering* the profession, the revised version acknowledges that gatekeeping can occur at other points as well.

Because this definition is succinct, it merits further explication. Each of the following sections addresses a specific element of this definition.

Supervision Is a Distinct Intervention

Supervision is an intervention, as are teaching, psychotherapy, and mental health consultation. There are substantial ways in which supervision overlaps with and draws from these other interventions (see, e.g., Milne, 2006), yet still remains unique. Table 1 summarizes what we believe to be the most salient similarities and differences.

Teaching versus Supervision. Teaching is central to supervision, and the supervisee's role of learner is suggested in the title of the classic supervision book, *The Teaching and Learning of*

TABLE 1 Supervision versus Teaching, Counseling, and Consultation

	SIMILARITIES	DIFFERENCES
Teaching	• Both have the purpose of imparting new skills and knowledge. • Both have evaluative and gatekeeping functions.	• Whereas teaching is driven by a set curriculum or protocol, supervision is driven by the needs of the particular supervisee and his or her clients.
Counseling or Therapy	• Both can address recipients' problematic behaviors, thoughts, or feelings.	• Any therapeutic work with a supervisee must be only to increase effectiveness in working with clients. • Supervision is evaluative, whereas counseling is not. • Counseling clients often have a greater choice of therapists than supervisees have of supervisors.
Consultation	• Both are concerned with helping the recipient work more effectively professionally. For more advanced trainees, the two functions may become indistinguishable.	• Consultation is a relationship between equals, whereas supervision is hierarchical. • Consultation can be a one-time event, whereas supervision occurs across time. • Consultation is more usually freely sought by recipients than is supervision. • Supervision is evaluative, whereas consultation is not.

Psychotherapy (Ekstein & Wallerstein, 1972). Teaching and supervision also have in common an evaluative aspect reflected in their gatekeeping functions, regulating who is legitimized to advance further into training or into the workplace.

Teaching, however, typically relies on an explicit curriculum with goals that are imposed on everyone uniformly. However, even though the focus of supervision at its broadest level might seem to speak to common goals (i.e., to prepare competent practitioners), the actual intervention is tailored to the needs of the individual supervisee and the supervisee's clients. Eshach and Bitterman's (2003) comments about the challenges in preparing physicians to address the needs of the individual—and therefore about the need for an educational context that is flexible and adaptive to the needs of the trainee and the person she or he is serving—apply just as well to the training of mental health practitioners (and, notably, have the characteristics of a signature pedagogy).

> *The problems are often poorly defined. . . . The problems that patients present can be confusing and contradictory, characterized by imperfect, inconsistent, or even inaccurate information. . . . Not only is much irrelevant information present, but also relevant information about a case is often missing and does not become apparent until after problem solving has begun.* (Shulman, 2005a, p. 492)

Counseling versus Supervision. There are elements of counseling or therapy in supervision—that is, supervisors often help supervisees examine aspects of their behavior, thoughts, or feelings that are stimulated by a client, particularly as these may act as barriers to their work with the client. As Frawley-O'Dea and Sarnat (2001) observe, maintaining "a rigidly impenetrable boundary between teaching and 'treating' in supervision is neither desirable nor truly achievable" (p. 137).

Still, there should be boundaries. Therapeutic interventions with supervisees should be made only in the service of helping them become more effective with clients; to provide therapy that has broader goals than this is ethical misconduct (see, e.g., Ladany, Lehrman-Waterman, Molinaro, & Wolgast, 1999; Neufeldt & Nelson, 1999).

It also is worth noting that clients generally are free to enter therapy or not, and usually have a voice in choosing their therapists. However, supervision is not a voluntary experience for those who have committed to a training program, and they often have scant voice in whom their supervisor is to be. Given this circumstance, it is salient to note that Webb and Wheeler (1998) found in their study that supervisees who had chosen their own supervisors reported being able to disclose to their supervisors more information of a sensitive nature about themselves, their clients, and the supervisory process than supervisees who had been assigned a supervisor.

Page and Woskett (2001) differentiate supervision from counseling according to their respective *aims* (in counseling, to enable a fuller and more satisfying life, versus in supervision, to develop counseling skills and the ability to conceptualize the counseling process); *presentation* (clients present material verbally, whereas supervisees present in multiple ways, including not only verbally, but via audio and videotape, live observation, etc.); *timing* (clients choose the pace, whereas supervisees often must have new understanding or skills in time for their next counseling session); and *relationship* (in counseling, regression may be tolerated or even encouraged, whereas that is not so in supervision; although some challenging of boundaries is expected in counseling, there is no such expectation in supervision).

The single most important difference between therapy and supervision, however, may reside in the supervisor's evaluative responsibilities. This can create challenges to supervisors.

Consultation versus Supervision. For more senior professionals, supervision often evolves into consultation—that is, the experienced therapist might meet informally on an occasional basis with a colleague to get ideas about how to handle a particularly difficult client or to regain needed objectivity. We all encounter blind spots in ourselves, and it is to our benefit to obtain help in this manner.

Consultation, however, is more likely than supervision to be a one-time-only event, and the parties in the consultation relationship often are not of the same professional discipline (e.g., a social worker might consult with a teacher about a child's problem; Caplan, 1970). Two other consultation–supervision distinctions echo distinctions already made between *therapy* and *supervision.* One is that *supervision* is more likely imposed, whereas *consultation* typically is freely sought. More significantly, whereas evaluation is one of the defining attributes of supervision, Caplan and Caplan (2000) observe that consultation

> *is non-hierarchical. Our consultants reject any power to coerce their consultees to accept their view of the case or to behave in ways the consultants may advocate. . . . consultants have no administrative power over the consultees or responsibility for case outcome.* (pp. 18–19)

In summary, specific aspects of teaching, therapy, and consultation are present as components of supervision. Supervision should be thought of as an intervention composed of multiple skills, many of which are common to other forms of intervention. Yet their configuration is such as to make supervision unique among psychological interventions. Moreover, there is at least one phenomenon, that of *parallel* or *reciprocal processes* (e.g., Doehrman, 1976; Searles, 1955), that is unique to supervision and distinguishes it from other interventions .

Typically a Member of the Same Profession

The widely acknowledged purposes of supervision are to facilitate supervisees' development and to protect clients. It is possible to accomplish these purposes when the supervisory dyad is composed of members of two different disciplines (e.g., a marital and family therapist might supervise the work of a counselor). In fact, almost all supervisees will be supervised by someone outside their immediate profession.

However, supervision also serves a professional socialization function missing in cross-disciplinary supervision dyads. Ekstein and Wallerstein (1972) speak to this when they note that it is possible for a training program to prepare its supervisees with all the basic psychotherapeutic skills, but that "what would still be missing is a specific quality in the psychotherapist that makes him [or her] into a truly professional person, a quality we wish to refer to as his [or her] professional identity" (p. 65). Crocket et al. (2009) found that supervisors who were providing interdisciplinary supervision reported many positive features of this arrangement, but also note the difficulties of working from different ethics codes and of having too-limited knowledge of the professional culture of the supervisee. Kavanagh et al. (2003) found that Australian public mental health workers perceived that the extent of supervision they received was related to its impact on them, but *only* when the supervisor was of the same profession.

In a cautionary tale concerning the use of members of one profession to supervise neophyte members of another profession, Albee (1970) invokes the metaphor of the cuckoo: The cuckoo is a bird that lays its eggs in the nests of other birds, which then raise the offspring as their own. His case in point was U.S. clinical psychology, which had used the Veterans Administration system as a primary base of training in the decades following World War II. From Albee's perspective, the clinical psychology fledglings were put in the nest of psychiatrists, who then socialized them into their way of viewing the world. Albee asserts that one consequence is that clinical psychology lost some of what was unique to it, as its members began incorporating the perspectives of psychiatry.

Notably, Gabbard (2005) expresses concern about social workers and psychologists supervising psychiatry residents. He acknowledges that they can be excellent therapists, but then observes that:

> *Children become what their parents do more than what their parents say. The same can be said of psychiatric residency training. If their professional role models treat psychotherapy as a marginal endeavor taught by allied professionals, residents will assume that psychiatrists are not really psychotherapists.* (p. 334)

In short, counselors and psychotherapists are supervised by people from different professions and often receive excellent training from them. Our point is not to argue against that practice, but rather to suggest that for the sake of professional identity development, it is important that the majority of supervision be done by someone who is in the profession that the supervisee is preparing to enter.

Supervision Is Evaluative and Hierarchical

We mentioned previously that evaluation stands as one of supervision's hallmarks, distinguishing it from both counseling or therapy and consultation. Evaluation is implicit in the supervisors' mandate to safeguard clients, both those currently being seen by the supervisee and those who would be seen in the future by the supervisee if he or she were to finish the professional program.

That supervisors have an evaluative function provides them with a tool, giving them an important source of interpersonal influence. For example, although most supervisees have a very high degree of intrinsic motivation to learn and to use feedback to self-correct, evaluation can provide supervisees with an additional, extrinsic motivation to use supervisory feedback.

However, despite its importance as a component of supervision, both supervisor and supervisee can experience evaluation with discomfort. Supervisors, for example, were trained first in the more non-evaluative role of counselor or therapist. Indeed, they may well have been attracted to the field because of this feature of counseling. The role of evaluator therefore can be not only new, but uncomfortable as well.

> *The role of evaluator also affects the trainee's perception of the supervisor. Students are not only taught psychotherapy by their supervisors, they are also evaluated by them. . . . Supervisors are thus not only admired teachers but feared judges who have real power.* (Doehrman, 1976, pp. 10–11)

Supervision's evaluative function means that the relationship is hierarchical. To the extent that hierarchy recapitulates issues related to ethnicity and gender, this can be problematic. Feminists, for example, have wrestled with the best means by which to balance their collaborative stance of work between two equals with the fact of hierarchy in supervision (see, e.g., Prouty, Thomas, Johnson, & Long, 2001). Some (e.g., Edwards & Chen, 1999; Porter & Vasquez, 1997), in fact, suggest the term *covision* as an alternative to *supervision* to signal a more collaborative relationship. Yet hierarchy and evaluation are so intertwined with supervision that to remove them makes the intervention something other than supervision.

Evaluation is, then, an important and integral component of supervision, but it is one that often is the source of problems for supervisors and supervisees alike. Although there is no way in which evaluation could (or should) be removed from supervision, there are ways to enhance its usefulness and to minimize problems attendant to it.

Supervision Extends over Time

A final element of our definition of *supervision* is that it is an intervention that extends over time. This distinguishes supervision from *training,* which might be brief, for example, in a short workshop intended to impart a specific skill; it distinguishes supervision, too, from *consultation,* which might be very time limited, as one professional seeks the help of another to gain or regain objectivity in his or her work with a client.

The fact that it is ongoing allows the supervisor–supervisee relationship to grow and develop. Indeed, many supervision theorists have focused particular attention on the developing nature of this relationship.

Purposes of Supervision

Our definition suggests that supervision has two central purposes:

1. To foster the supervisee's professional development—a supportive and educational function
2. To ensure client welfare—the supervisor's gatekeeping function is a variant of the monitoring of client welfare

Vespia, Heckman-Stone, and Delworth (2002) show how central supervisors find these two purposes. When supervisors rated the extent to which each of 53 supervisee behaviors characterized individuals "who use supervision well" (p. 59), two of the three highest rated items corresponded to one of these purposes: "Implements supervisor's directives when client welfare is of concern to the Supervisor" and "Demonstrates willingness to grow." Each is an essential focus, although it is possible for a particular supervisor to emphasize one more heavily than the other. For example, a student working at a field placement might have both a university-based and an on-site supervisor. In this situation, it is possible for the university-based supervisor to give relatively greater emphasis to the teaching–learning goals of supervision, and the on-site supervisor to give relatively greater emphasis to the client-monitoring aspects. Feiner (1994) alludes to this dichotomy of goals when he suggests the following:

> *Some supervisors assume that their most important ethical responsibility is to the student's patient. This would impel them to make the student a conduit for*

> *their own expertise. Others make the assumption that their ultimate responsibility is to the development of the student.... Their concern is the possible lowering of the student's self-esteem when confronted by the supervisor and his rising fantasy that he should become a shoe salesman.* (p. 171)

It is important to acknowledge other possible purposes for supervision. For example, Proctor (1986) asserts that supervision serves three purposes that she labeled (a) *formative,* equivalent to our teaching–learning purpose; (b) *normative,* generally equivalent to ensuring client welfare; and (c) *restorative,* providing supervisees the opportunity to express and meet needs that will help them avoid burnout (see Hyrkäs, 2005, for results that provide preliminary support for this function). Howard (2008) extends the restorative purpose by drawing from positive psychology to suggest as well that supervision should also have the goals of enhancing work engagement, "flow" (see Csikszentmihalyi, 1990), and resilience.

Occasionally, too, supervision is mandated as a method to rehabilitate impaired professionals (see, e.g., Frick, McCartney, & Lazarus, 1995). This overlaps with both the training and client-protective purposes of supervision, but really should be considered an additional purpose. Although we do not specifically address this purpose of supervision in this text, interested readers might consult discussions by Cobia and Pipes (2002) and Walzer and Miltimore (1993).

Both the restorative and rehabilitative purposes of supervision are important. Knudsen, Ducharme and Roman (2008) found, for example, that being supervised reduced substance abuse counselors' emotional exhaustion and job turnover. However, restorative and rehabilitative purposes are not common across *all* supervision, whereas the two purposes that are part of our definition of supervision (i.e., client protection and development of supervisee competence) are. Each is addressed in turn in the two subsections that follow.

Before turning to those discussions, however, we add one additional, ultimate goal, which is to prepare the supervisee to self-supervise (Dennin & Ellis, 2003). At the point of licensure, practitioners, at least in the United States, no longer are required to be supervised and so must be able to monitor their own work, knowing how to learn from it and also when to seek consultation. Supervisees work with a number of supervisors; a psychologist will work with about eight supervisors prior to obtaining a doctorate (M. V. Ellis, personal communication, August 31, 2006, from data obtained as part of an instrument validation study). In the process of that work, they should develop a sort of *internal supervisor* that incorporates what they have learned from each of their supervisors.

Fostering the Supervisee's Professional Development. We state the teaching–learning goal simply as "to enhance professional functioning." This is a pragmatic definition that meets our need to provide a succinct and generally applicable definition of supervision. It is silent about any performance criteria that supervisees are to meet or even about the content of learning. To that end, however, the APA's competency benchmark task group (Fouad et al., 2009) performed important work in articulating those expected performance criteria, breaking them out by level of training.

To enhance professional functioning speaks to the development of supervisee competence. The form of that competence typically derives from some combination of the supervisor's own theory or model, the supervisee's particular developmental needs, and the supervisee's expressed wishes.

In addition, the supervisor almost certainly wants the supervisee to develop skills and competencies necessary for eventual licensure or certification. This utilitarian goal has the virtue of specificity—that is, supervisors generally know what competencies the supervisee must demonstrate for licensure, at least in his or her own state. Moreover, this is a logical target in that to attain licensure is, at least in the United States, the point at which the supervisee makes the transition to an autonomously functioning professional who no longer has a legal mandate to be supervised.

The truth is that no one knows or tracks in any systematic way what transpires between therapist and client once the therapist escapes the onus of training and supervision, and unlike most medical procedures of significant consequence, there's generally no one present to observe other than the provider and the recipient—neither of whom is apt to be vested with an unbiased view or recollection. (Gist, 2007, personal communication via email)

The assumption undergirding this right to practice without supervision is that the person has developed *metacompetence* (Roth & Pilling, 2008), or "the ability to assess what one knows and what one doesn't know" (Falender & Shafranske, 2007, p. 232). It is a professional's metacompetence that allows him or her to seek consultation when faced with an issue beyond his or her expertise; to engage in the self-supervision to which we alluded earlier.

In a now-famous statement to the press, U.S. Secretary of Defense Donald Rumsfeld (2002) describes "known knowns," "known unknowns," and "unknown unknowns." Metacompetence reduces the number of "unknown unknowns" a professional will face; however, until they develop it, they must rely on their supervisors. We suppose it should go without saying that it is essential that supervisors' own metacompetence is an important means of helping to ensure that supervisees develop that in themselves.

Whereas it is the norm in the United States to permit licensed professionals to work without formal supervision, this is not true in other countries, which may be wise given Gist's observation earlier. In the United Kingdom, for example, many mental health professionals are expected to continue receiving supervision throughout their professional lives (West, 2003). This is codified in the British Association for Counselling and Psychotherapy's (BACP) ethical code, which stipulates: "There is an obligation to use regular and ongoing supervision to enhance the quality of the services provided and to commit to updating practice by continuing professional development" (BACP, 2007, p. 3). BACP expectations are that practitioners will participate in supervision at least 1.5 hours per month. Australia has a similar rule (see Grant & Schofield, 2007). This convention recognizes that professional development is ongoing and extends even after a professional develops expertise; supervision in this context is understood to have more than a training function.

Fried (1991) offers the folk wisdom that it takes 10 years to become a really good psychotherapist. In fact, Hayes (1981) estimates that it requires about 10 years to become an expert in *any* skill domain, an assertion that others (e.g., Ericcson & Lehmann, 1996) document as well. Yet, for many professionals, time alone is insufficient to attain expert status or clinical wisdom. However, even if a mental health professional attains expertise or wisdom, it still is useful for him or her to have continuing supervision to foster lifelong learning and help address our field's knowledge half-life (see, e.g., Lichtenberg & Goodyear, 2012).

In fact, many—perhaps most—postgraduate, credentialed practitioners *want* and do continue some level and type of supervision, even if it is not mandated (see, e.g., Borders & Usher, 1992; McCarthy, Kulakowski, & Kenfield, 1994; Wiley, 1994). This is good not only for them, but for their clients as well. Slater (2003, p. 8) states: "I remember a patient once asking me, 'Who do you talk about me with?' He wasn't asking out of fear, but hope. What suffering person doesn't want many minds thinking about how to help?"

Monitoring Client Care. In addition to their responsibilities to the supervisees' professional development, supervisors must also ensure that supervisees are providing adequate client care. In fact, this was the original purpose of clinical supervision. Supervision in the mental health disciplines almost certainly began with social work supervision, which "dates from the 19th-century Charity Organization Societies in which paid social work agents supervised the moral treatment of the poor by friendly visitors" (Harkness & Poertner, 1989, p. 115). The focus of this supervision was on the client.

Eisenberg (1956) notes that the first known call for supervision to focus on the professional, rather than exclusively on the client, was in 1901 by Zilphia Smith. This supervisory focus became more prominent two decades later, when, as Carroll (2007) observes, "Max Eitington is thought to be the first to make supervision a requirement for those in their psychoanalytic training in the 1920s" (p. 34).

However, the need to ensure quality of client care is one job demand with particular potential for causing dissonance in the supervisor. Most of the time, supervisors are able to perceive themselves as allies of their supervisees. Yet they also must be prepared, should they see harm being done to clients, to risk bruising the egos of their supervisees or, in extreme cases, even to steer the supervisee from the profession—an ethical obligation we have to the public.

PERSON-SPECIFIC UNDERSTANDINGS OF SUPERVISION

A formal definition of *supervision* is important, but it is inevitable that supervisors and supervisees also will operate according to their own idiosyncratic and personally nuanced definitions. Because these more individualized—and usually implicit—definitions can affect supervision processes in important ways, they too should be acknowledged as complements to the more formal definition.

To consider these nuanced definitions, it is useful to invoke the concept of the *schema* (in the plural, *schemata*) that Bartlett (1932, 1958) introduces and that now is widely used among cognitive psychologists and mental health professionals. A *schema* helps us interpret our world by providing a mental framework for understanding and remembering information. More formally stated, a *schema* is a knowledge representation based on our past experiences and inferences that we use to interpret a present experience. In short, people have a tendency to understand one domain of life experience in terms of another. Our perceptions and responses to a new situation are organized and structured as they were in a previous similar situation.

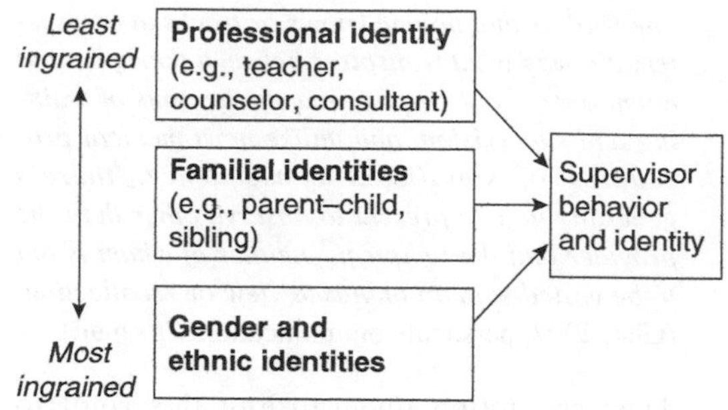

FIGURE 2 Life and Professional Roles That Affect Supervisory Role Behavior

Because of their apparent similarities, we respond to the new situation as if it were the earlier one. Moreover, the more ingrained the particular role we have learned, the more it is likely to intrude on later learned roles. The schema people develop for supervision is shaped in this manner. Figure 2 shows, for example, that gender and ethnicity roles are among the most ingrained, and therefore permeate much of our behavior, including supervision.

Professional roles are learned later and are therefore less an ingrained part of ourselves. Yet, even so, earlier learned professional roles (such as that of counselor) are likely to affect later learned professional roles. For those taking on the later learned roles, it is natural, perhaps inevitable, to attempt to understand them in terms of things we do know. It is merely human to attempt to understand that which is new in terms of that which is familiar.

It should be no surprise, then, that the roles of supervisor and supervisee are at least partially understood as metaphoric expressions of other life experiences. Proctor (1991), for example, invokes the concept of *archetypes,* which actually could be understood as *schemata:*

> *A number of my colleagues asked me what archetypes went into taking the trainer role; we immediately identified a number. There are the Guru, or Wise Woman, from whom wisdom is expected, and the Earth Mother—the all-provider, unconditional*

positive regarder. In contrast there is the Clown or Jester—enjoying performance, and cloaking his truth in riddles, without taking responsibility for how it is received. The Patriarch creates order and unselfconsciously wields power. The Actor/Director allocates roles and tasks and holds the Drama; the Bureaucrat demands compliance to the letter of the law. The Whore gives services for money, which can be indistinguishable from love, and re-engages with group after group. There is even the Warrior—valiant for truth; and of course the Judge—upholding standards and impartially assessing. The Shepherd/Sheep-dog gently and firmly rounds up and pens. (p. 65)

These are some possible metaphors for the supervisor. There also are metaphors that speak to the process or experience of supervision, independent of other life roles. Therefore, a supervisee (or supervisor) might understand supervision as akin to a lighthouse beacon that provides one with bearings in often foggy situations. Participants in workshops led by our colleague, Michael Ellis, describe *supervision* as a shepherd and flock, as an oasis in the desert, and (more ominously) as going to the principal's office. Milne and James (2005) use the metaphor of supervision as tandem bicycle riding.

We believe that these metaphors exist at various levels of awareness, but they are often present and affect participants' expectations and behaviors. The following discussions of more frequently occurring metaphors are therefore in the service of making them available for consideration.

Family Metaphors

Family metaphors (middle of Figure 2) seem especially common in supervision. The most basic of these is that of the parent–child relationship. Lower (1972), for example, uses this metaphor in alluding to the unconscious parent–child fantasies that he believed are stimulated by the supervisory situation itself. In fact, Itzhaky and Sztern (1999) caution supervisors against allowing themselves to behave without awareness of what they term a *pseudo-parental role* (p. 247).

Of course, many theorists use this metaphor of parent–child relationship as a way to think about therapy. As it may apply to supervision, the metaphor is simultaneously both less and more appropriate than for therapy. On the one hand, it is *less* apt in that personal growth is not a primary goal of the intervention, as it is in therapy, but rather is an instrumental goal that works in the service of making the supervisee a better therapist. It is *more* apt, on the other hand, in that supervision is an evaluative relationship, just as parenting is—and therapy presumably is not.

Just knowing that they are being evaluated is often sufficient to trigger in supervisees an expectation of a guilt–punishment sequence that recapitulates early parent–child interactions. Supervisors can, through their actions, intensify such transference responses among supervisees, triggering perceptions of them as a good or bad parent. We have heard, for example, of instances in which supervisors posted publicly in the staff lounge the names of supervisees who had too many client "no-shows." The atmosphere created in situations such as this can easily establish supervisory staff as "feared parents."

Still another parallel between parent–child and supervisor–supervisee relationships is that status, knowledge, maturity, and power differences between the participants eventually begin to disappear. The parties who today are supervisor and supervisee can expect that one day they might relate to one another as peers and colleagues.

The parent–child metaphor is suggested, too, in the frequent use of developmental metaphors to describe supervision.

A second family metaphor that can pertain to supervision is that of older and younger siblings. For many supervisory dyads, this probably is more apt than the parent–child metaphor. The supervisor is further along on the same path being traveled by the supervisee. As such, she or he is in a position to show the way in a nurturing and mentoring relationship. However, as with siblings, issues of competence can sometimes trigger competition over who is more skilled or more brilliant in understanding the client.

The older–younger siblings metaphor is structurally similar to the relationship between master craftspersons and their apprentices. Such relationships have existed for thousands of years and are perpetuated in supervision. In these relationships, master craftspersons serve as mentors to the people who aspire to enter the occupation, showing them the skills, procedures, and culture of the occupation. In this manner, too, master craftspersons help perpetuate the craft. Eventually, after what is usually a stipulated period of apprenticeship, the apprentices become peers of the craftspersons.

These metaphors, particularly those of parent or sibling, occur at fundamental and often primitive levels. Because they influence in an immediate and felt way, they have a special and probably an ongoing influence on the supervisory relationship. Moreover, such metaphors probably operate outside the awareness of the supervisor.

If it is true that supervision is a unique intervention, then one might reasonably infer that there is a unique role characteristic of supervisors in general. In a broad sense, this is true, and we can identify at least two major components of this generic supervisory role. The first of these is the perspective from which the supervisor views his or her work; the second pertains to the commonly endorsed expectation that the supervisor will give feedback to the supervisee.

Liddle (1988) discusses the transition from therapist to supervisor as a role-development process that involves several evolutionary steps. An essential early step is for the emerging supervisor to make a shift in focus—that is, the supervisor eventually must realize that the purpose of supervision is neither to treat the client indirectly through the supervisee nor to provide psychotherapy to the supervisee, a point which Borders (1992) also makes. She maintains that the supervisor-to-be must make a cognitive shift as he or she switches from the role of counselor or therapist. To illustrate how difficult this often is for new supervisors, she gives the example of a neophyte supervisor who persisted for some time in referring to his supervisee as "my client." Until he was able to label the supervisee's role correctly in relation to himself, his perceptual set remained that of a therapist.

This shift, then, requires the supervisor to give up doing what might be thought of as *therapy by proxy, therapy by remote control,* or what Fiscalini (1997) calls *therapy by ventriloquism.* We would note, however, that the pull to doing this may always remain present, even if unexpressed in practice. In part, this is reinforced by the supervisor's mandate always to function as a monitor of client care and remain vigilant about how the client is functioning. Similarly, the longer the person has functioned as a therapist, the harder it may be for the supervisor to make the necessary shift in perspective. It is interesting to note, for example, that Carl Rogers talked about having occasionally experienced the strong impulse to take over the therapy of a supervisee, likening himself to an old fire horse heeding the call (Hackney & Goodyear, 1984).

Borders (1992), in fact, observes that untrained professionals do not necessarily make this shift on their own, simply as a result of experience as a supervisor. As a matter of fact, some "experienced" professionals seem to have more difficulty changing their thinking than do doctoral students and advanced master's students in supervision courses.

A CONCEPTUAL MODEL OF SUPERVISION

The conceptual model depicted in Figure 3, an adaptation of the competencies cube developed by Rodolfa and colleagues (2005), provides a complementary perspective that influenced our organization of this text. This is a three-dimensional model in which the three dimensions are what we have labeled *Parameters of Supervision, Supervisee Developmental Level,* and *Supervisor Tasks.*

Parameters of Supervision

The *parameters of supervision* are the features of supervision that undergird *all* that occurs in supervision, regardless of the particular supervisory function or the level of the supervisee. For example, the supervisor's model or theory is a factor at all times, as is the supervisory relationship and each of the other of the parameters listed in the figure.

Supervisee Developmental Level

We assume that supervisees need different supervisory environments as they develop professionally and that the manner in which supervisors intervene differs according to supervisee level. As well, the expression of each parameter (e.g., relationship, evaluation) is affected by the *supervisee's developmental level.*

Different supervision theorists suggest a different number of stages through which the supervisee progresses. Figure 3, however, is drawn in a way to suggest that we do not take a stand on exactly how many of these stages there actually are. We believe it is sufficient here simply to make clear that developmental processes affect all that we do as supervisors.

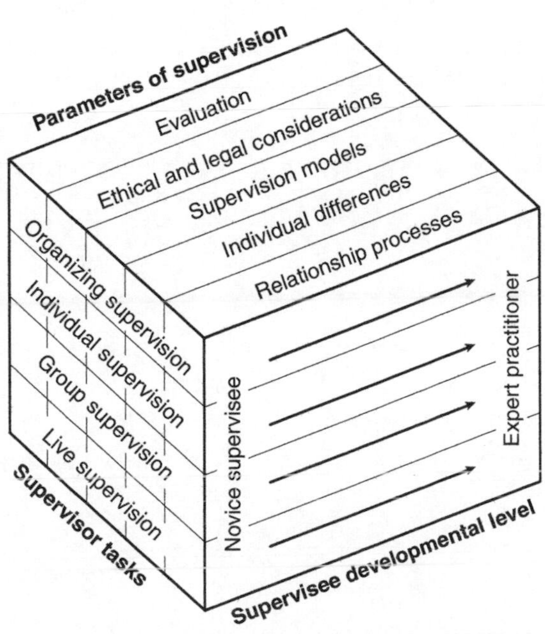

FIGURE 3 Conceptual Model of Supervision

Supervisor Tasks

Supervisor tasks are the actual behaviors of the supervisors. We discuss the four tasks depicted in Figure 3 (i.e., organizing supervision, individual supervision, group supervision, and live supervision). It is possible, of course, to think of more, but we believe these four are the most frequently used.

Using the Model

We assume that the three dimensions interact with one another. To illustrate, consider the supervisor using individual supervision: He or she does so within the context of a relationship, and that work is guided by the supervisor's particular theory or model, attention to supervisee's individual differences (e.g., ethnicity, gender), and ethical and legal factors; the fact of evaluation affects it as well. The developmental level of the supervisee, then, moderates each of these things.

We should note that we are not attempting in this model to capture *all* that occurs in supervision. This is especially true with respect to our discussion of supervisor tasks. We recognize, for example, that individual, group, and live supervision are not the only modalities. Kell and Burow (1970), for example, discuss the use of conjoint treatment as a supervision modality. However, although this is not a modality included in Figure 3, it is easy enough to see how conjoint treatment might fit into the conceptual model.

CONCLUSION

We hope we have been effective in establishing the basis for and importance of supervision by offering a formal definition of supervision and considering possible idiosyncratic definitions of supervision that occur at less manifest levels. We also hope our conceptual model will be useful in thinking about supervision and the ways its various aspects relate to one another.

We also addressed the historical context, importance, and prevalence of supervision. We then considered definitions, both formal and more personal. We concluded by presenting the conceptual model that both informs our understanding about supervision and guides the organization of this text.

We alluded early in the chapter to the two realms of knowledge (Schön, 1983) that are the basis of professional training: the theory and research that are the focus of university training and the knowledge derived from practitioners' experience. We asserted, too, that these actually are complementary knowledge domains (e.g., Holloway, 1995). Because of this conviction, material in this text is drawn from both realms of knowledge, with the belief that each informs the other. That is, in the course of our work, we draw both from theoretical and empirical literature as well as from literature that describes the insights and practices of supervisors themselves.

Supervision Models

The supervisor who is learning to venture out on his or her own has, in the core model, a safe and certain "parent" to return to and look back upon when a steadying presence is needed. Beginning supervisors will inevitably lose their footing on occasion and need to know that when this happens they can fall back on and be guided by a tried and trusted model. (Woskett & Page, 2001, p. 14)

There is a classic East Indian story of six blind men who, encountering an elephant for the first time, attempted to understand it. Each, having touched a different part of the elephant, made his own inferences about its nature—for example, the man who touched its side likened the elephant to a wall, the man who touched its tusk likened it to a spear, the man who touched its knee likened it to a tree, and so on (Saxe, 1865).

Both Woskett and Page's comments and the parable of the six blind men and the elephant are relevant to our discussion of supervision models. In fact, models fulfill the function of grounding the supervisor (the certain *parent*); at the same time (not unlike parents), the models give one perspective well to the exclusion of other important perspectives. We hope in this chapter to discuss both of these characteristics of models.

Models of supervision provide a conceptual framework(s) for supervisors. As such, they help make supervision cohesive and guide supervisors toward providing supervision that addresses their supervisees' needs. They can also attend to the organizational contexts as well as societal and professional contexts. Models have also been developed that attend to supervision of therapy with specific client populations. Because of the complexity of both psychotherapy and supervision, no one model could succeed in addressing all of these important areas lest it topple from its own weight. Therefore, as the specialty of supervision evolved, models that attend to different aspects of supervision emerged.

Garfield (2006) reports that there were more than 1,000 approaches to counseling and psychotherapy described in the mental health literatures. As noted in the early 1980s, the area of supervision tends to follow the lead of psychotherapy (Leddick & Bernard, 1980) in terms of theoretical development (e.g., postmodern approaches), professional development (e.g., ethical codes), and key issues (e.g., expertise in multicultural therapy and supervision). Although we are not yet approaching the millennial mark for supervision models, it is the case that new models continue to appear and older models continue to be refined. Our goal in this

From Chapter 2 of *Fundamentals of Clinical Supervision,* Fifth Edition. Janine M. Bernard and Rodney K. Goodyear.

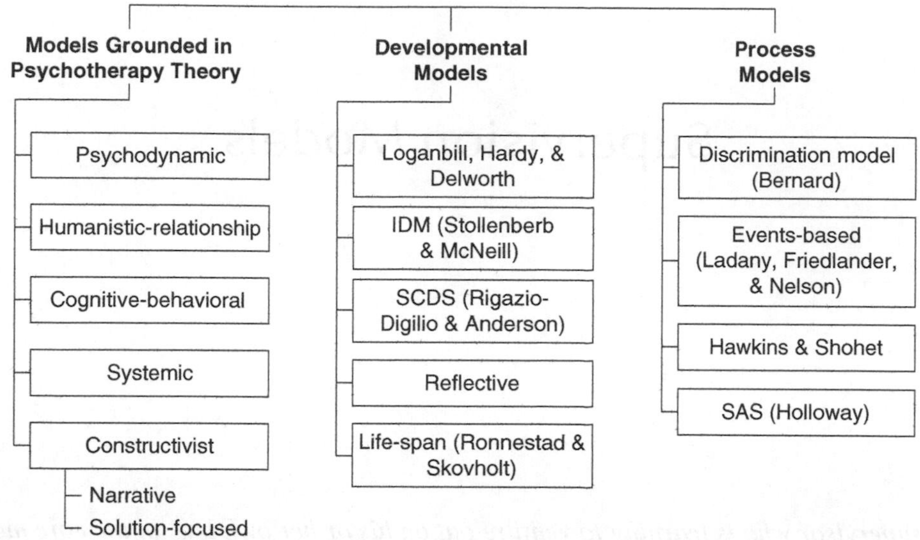

FIGURE 1 Major Categories of Clinical Supervision Models

chapter is to offer the reader an organizational map for models and to explain some of the key characteristics of each category of models. We also provide a more detailed description of particular models. Before we begin, we define some key terms and also express our belief about how supervisors are informed by various supervision models.

We prefer the word *model* to *theory* when describing supervision. Whereas all *theories* of counseling and psychotherapy attempt to cover fairly comprehensive worldviews of problem etiology, maintenance, and resolution, *models* of supervision can be simple or complex, and may not be intended as stand-alone entities. Therefore, the word *model* seems to be a better fit and is most commonly used in the supervision literature. We also choose to veer away from the word *integrate* when discussing the practice of combining models of supervision (which we believe is common), as *integrating* and *integrationist,* as well as *eclectic,* are generously used to describe psychotherapy and counseling approaches. Therefore, we use the term *integrate* only when referring to combining psychotherapies, not in reference to supervision.

Our organization, as depicted in Figure 1, recognizes three broad categories of supervision models: the first category of models is composed of those based on *psychotherapy theories*; the second category depicts *developmental models* as well as empirical contributions regarding the development of cognitive complexity in supervisees; and the final major category is that of *supervision process models,* those models that attempt to explain the activity of supervision itself from a variety of vantage points. Once we describe several leading models in each of these categories, we move on to what we call *second-generation models* because they are more recent and because they tend to draw from the work of those listed within the major categories. These second-generation models include combined models, target models, and common factors models. *Combined models* combine two established models either from the same category or across two categories. *Target models* are those that have been developed to focus on important issues such as multicultural expertise. They may or may not infuse an existing model from a primary category. Typically, these models are not meant to be used exclusively by supervisors but are to be included in their conceptual repertoire so that they can offer supervision that does justice to a specific issue. *Common factors models* are proposed by those who attempted to look at major supervision models to determine what characteristics they all have in common.

Having introduced our categories for positioning models and before we embark on further description of each, we suggest that, in practice, supervisors do not practice *within* categories but *across* categories, often interfacing aspects of models from all three categories. Our defense of this position is as follows: Just as all counseling and psychotherapy reflects theory, so too does supervision of that therapy. In other words, good supervision must include the oversight of whether the counseling or therapy being offered is theoretically grounded. Therefore, despite how a supervisor describes him- or herself, he or she is, at some level, supervising in a manner consistent with a psychotherapy-based supervision model. In addition, intentionally or not, supervisors often rely on their own theoretical orientation to understand their supervisees and to arrive at supervision interventions. In a similar manner, every supervisor makes an assessment of where her or his supervisee is situated developmentally. Training programs understand that students enrolled in a first practicum are different in their supervision needs that those in a final internship. It would be folly to ignore developmental level when conducting supervision. Therefore, even if one describes oneself as a cognitive–behavioral supervisor (or another primary identity), he or she is borrowing from the decades of work of those who have focused on developmental models. Finally, increasingly more supervisors, especially those trained in clinical supervision, also adopt a supervision process model that gives them insight into the choices they have as supervisors regarding the focus of a particular session, the interventions available to them, the context within which supervision operates, and so forth. In summary, as noted previously, at this point in the evolution of supervision knowledge and practice, we believe most trained supervisors interface models across categories to arrive at a supervision practice that attends to psychotherapy theory, development, and supervision process. This position is argued by others (e.g., Watkins, 2011) as well.

The rest of this chapter describes each of the three primary categories more fully, giving examples of these from the literature; we also give examples of the three second-generation categories we have identified.

Finally, before beginning our discussion of the models, we believe it important to note that whereas entire books are devoted to some of these models, our space is limited to such an extent that we are able to cover each of these at only a relatively general level. With this disclaimer, we begin our overview with those models that most directly tie supervision to therapy.

PSYCHOTHERAPY-BASED MODELS OF SUPERVISION

Clinical supervisors first were counselors or therapists. It is almost inevitable, then, that the lens they learned to use in understanding their work in that role would generalize to their work in the role of supervisor as well. By many estimates, there are several hundred such lenses (i.e., theories) through which to view therapy. Supervision has been described from a number of these perspectives, including Adlerian (e.g., Kopp & Robles, 1989), reality (e.g., Smadi & Landreth, 1988), Gestalt (Hoyt & Goulding, 1989; Resnick & Estrup, 2000), and Jungian (Kugler, 1995). In the interest of space, however, we cover six psychotherapy-based models of supervision: psychoanalytic, client-centered, cognitive–behavioral, systemic, constructivist, and integrative models.

Before discussing these models, it is important first to contextualize this discussion, beginning with the inevitable continuity in how supervisors conceptualize their work as therapists versus work as supervisors. As Shoben (1962) argues and others (e.g., Arthur, 2000; Topolinski & Hertel, 2007) since have corroborated empirically, therapists work from an implicit theory of human nature that also must influence how they construe reality, including interpersonal behavior, normal personality development (or family development), and abnormal or dysfunctional development. Friedlander and Ward (1984) refer to this as the *assumptive world* of the therapist, and propose that this affects the therapist's choice of theory.

It is reasonable to assume that this assumptive world is constant across situations. Therefore, it would be manifest in professionals' work as both therapist *and* supervisor (see, e.g., data from Friedlander & Ward, 1984; Goodyear, Abadie, & Efros, 1984; Holloway, Freund, Gardner, Nelson, & Walker, 1989). Moreover, many of the techniques used in therapy are used in supervision as well.

In their survey of 84 psychology interns from 32 sites, Putney, Worthington, and McCulloughy (1992) document the extent to which theories of therapy affected supervisors' focus and behavior. They found that supervisees perceived cognitive–behavioral supervisors to use a consultant role and to focus on supervisees' skills and strategies more than humanistic, psychodynamic, and existential supervisors (see, also, Goodyear & Robyak, 1982). Supervisees perceived supervisors who adhered to these latter models, however, as more likely to use the relationship, to use something of the therapist role during supervision, and to focus on conceptualization of client problems. Thus, it appears that the theory of the supervisor does indeed affect supervision.

Maher's (2005) discovery-oriented (constructivist) model of supervision is one exception; this model focuses on helping supervisees discover their own implicit models of practice. This is a minority position—and one that would be absolute anathema to adherents of evidence-based practice whose focus usually is on helping the supervisee learn to deliver a particular treatment with fidelity. Interestingly, however, Maher was able to locate a statement from Rogers (1957) that is consistent with his position.

> *I believe that the goal of training in the therapeutic process is that the student should develop his own orientation to psychotherapy out of his own experience. In my estimation every effective therapist has built his own orientation within himself and out of his own experience with his clients or patients.* (p. 87)

The constructivists adhere to the position stated in this quote, but that position is unique among the psychotherapy-based models we cover in this chapter.

We begin our coverage of the psychotherapy-based models of supervision with psychodynamic supervision. We then cover, in turn, humanistic-relationship oriented, cognitive–behavioral, systemic, constructivist, and integrative approaches.

Psychodynamic Supervision

Psychoanalytic conceptions of supervision have a long history. Arguably, these conceptions have affected supervision theory and practice more than those of any other model. For example, the two psychodynamically derived concepts of working alliance and parallel processes are dominant supervision concepts that have informed the work of supervisors of all orientations.

Freud seems to deserve credit not only for developing the *talking cure,* but also for being the first psychotherapy supervisor. Freud supervised actual therapeutic practice and reports that supervision began in 1902 with "a number of young doctors gathered around me with the express intention of learning, practicing, and spreading the knowledge of psychoanalysis" (Freud, 1914/1986, p. 82).

Frawley-O'Dea and Sarnat (2001) note that

> *Freud was the first supervisor and thus represents the archetypal supervisor to whom we all maintain a transference of some kind. In his model of supervision, he combined a positivistic stance analogous to his model of treatment with a personal insistence on maintaining a position as the ultimate arbiter of truth, knowledge, and power.* (p. 17)

Supervision soon became an institutionalized aspect of the psychoanalytic enterprise and enjoyed a long and rich history of advancement. Caligor (1984) notes that as early as 1922, the International Psychoanalytic Society adopted formalized standards that stipulated formal coursework and the treatment of several patients under supervision.

During the 1930s, two competing views developed concerning the place of *control analysis,* the psychoanalytic term for supervision. One group (the Budapest School) maintained that it should be a continuation of the supervisee's personal analysis (with the same analyst in each case) with a focus on transference in the candidate's therapy and countertransference in his or her supervision. The other group (the Viennese School) maintained that the transference and countertransference issues should be addressed in the candidate's personal analysis, whereas supervision itself should emphasize didactic teaching.

Ekstein and Wallerstein (1972) were the first to articulate a model of supervision that most psychodynamic (and many other) supervisors accepted. They portray supervision as a teaching and learning process that gives particular emphasis to the relationships between and among patient, therapist, and supervisor and the processes that interplay among them. Its purpose is not to provide therapy, but to teach, and the reason for working closely with the supervisee is to have him or her learn how to understand the dynamics of resolving relational conflicts between supervisor and supervisee (cf. Bordin, 1983; Mueller & Kell, 1972) for the benefit of future work with clients.

Because of the diversity within the psychoanalytic perspective and the richness of its conceptualizations, it has continued to provide ideas and concepts that have been infused throughout supervision. Psychoanalytic writers have been prolific contributors to the supervision literature. This continues as psychodynamic supervision evolves (Frawley-O'Dea & Sarnat, 2001; Gill, 2001; Jacobs, David, & Meyer, 1995; Rock, 1997; Sarnat, 2010, 2012) and attempts to grapple with a fundamental challenge—as stated by Tuckett (2005)—to identify a framework for supervisees that is broad enough and sensitive enough to "take cognizance of the twin facts that there is more than one way to practice psychoanalysis and that it is necessary for the legitimacy of the field to avoid an 'anything goes' stance" (p. 31). Building on Tuckett's work, Sarnat (2010) identified four categories of supervisee competence that supervisors must promote:

1. The ability to be in relationship with clients and, by inference, with supervisors, "because a psychodynamic psychotherapist views the relationship as the crucible of psychotherapeutic change, not just as a preliminary to effective interventions, relationship competency implies developing relationship skills that go beyond these capacities" (p. 23).
2. The ability to self-reflect, which includes "a highly developed capacity to bear, observe, think about, and make psychotherapeutic use of one's own emotional, bodily, and fantasy experiences when in interaction with a client" (p. 23).
3. Assessment and diagnosis from a psychodynamic framework
4. Interventions that are theoretically consistent and in keeping with the centrality of the therapeutic relationship

Knowing what supervisees must learn is only half the equation. Frawley-O'Dea and Sarnat (2001) articulate a supervision model that describes key supervisory dimensions that serve as the context for psychodynamic supervision.

To set the stage for their model, Frawley-O'Dea and Sarnat reviewed the development of psychodynamic supervision. They observe, for example, that the earliest supervision was *patient-centered,* focusing on the client's dynamics and employing a didactic role. Later psychodynamic supervisors, beginning with Ekstein and Wallerstein (1972), began to conduct *supervisee-centered* supervision, giving greater attention to the supervisee's dynamics.

Both types of supervision place the supervisor in the role of an *uninvolved expert* on theory and technique. In contrast, the relational model proposed by Sarnat (1992) and further developed by Frawley-O'Dea and Sarnat (2001) allows the supervisor to focus either on the therapeutic or on the supervisory dyad. The supervisor's authority stems less from the role as expert on theory and practice and more from the role "as an embedded participant in a mutually influencing supervisory process" (p. 41). In this manner, these authors are modeling a key competence (relationship) that they consider foundational for psychodynamic therapy.

Frawley-O'Dea and Sarnat propose three dimensions as the context for psychodynamic supervision:

***Dimension 1:* The nature of the supervisor's authority in relationship to the supervisee.** Supervisors' authority can be understood as existing somewhere on a continuum between two poles. On one end is authority that derives from the knowledge that the supervisor brings to supervision. His or her stance is that of the objective and uninvolved expert who helps the supervisee know "what is 'true' about the patient's mind and what is 'correct' technique" (p. 26). On the other end of the continuum is authority that derives from the supervisor's involved participation. He or she certainly has more expertise than the supervisee, but makes no absolute knowledge claims. His or her authority resides in supervisor–supervisee relational processes. Frawley-O'Dea and Sarnat clearly endorse this end of the continuum. Sarnat (2010, 2012) reiterates the importance of being in relationship with the supervisee, including appropriate self-disclosure and open discussion of countertransference.

***Dimension 2:* The supervisor's focus.** This concerns the relevant data on which supervision is based. Specifically, the supervisor can focus attention on (a) the client, (b) the supervisee, or (c) the relationship between supervisor and supervisee.

***Dimension 3:* The supervisor's primary mode of participation.** This final dimension concerns roles and styles that supervisors might adopt. Among those that the authors describe are didactic teacher, Socratic "asker of questions," a container of supervisee affects, and so on. More recently, Sarnat (2012) argues for a relational approach to supervision over the didactic.

It should be noted that the influence of supervision process models is clearly evident in Frawley-O'Dea and Sarnat's model in that they have moved beyond a focus on transmitting the execution of a theory and are considering the dynamics and processes of supervision per se.

In summary, it is safe to assert that psychoanalytic or psychodynamic models have influenced supervision as have no other. They certainly have historical importance. However, they have also served as a rich source of observations and as a springboard for various conceptions of supervision.

Humanistic-Relationship Oriented Supervision

Models such as that of Frawley-O'Dea and Sarnat (2001) stand as evidence of the influence of humanistic- and relationship-oriented tenets across all schools of psychotherapy. Central to humanistic-relationship approaches is increasing experiential awareness and using the therapeutic relationship to promote change. Supervision, therefore, focuses on helping the supervisee to expand not only their knowledge of theory and technique, but also their capacity for self-exploration and their skill in the use of self as a change agent (Farber, 2010, 2012). *Use of self* includes their ability to be fully present, transparent, genuine, and accepting with their clients.

No other theorist is more identified within this theoretical school than Carl Rogers. Supervision was a central and long-standing concern of Rogers, as it was for those who later identified with his person-centered model. Rogers (1942) and also Covner (1942a, 1942b) were among the very first to report the use of electronically recorded interviews and transcripts in supervision. Until then, supervision had been based entirely on self-report of supervisees, as it still often is in psychoanalytically oriented supervision, despite appeals for change in that regard (Sarnat, 2012).

Rogers (1942) concluded from listening to these early recordings of therapy interviews that mere didactic training in what then was called *nondirective methods* was insufficient. Only when students had direct access to the content of their interviews could they identify their natural tendencies to provide advice or otherwise control their sessions. This is consistent with Patterson's (1964) contention two decades later that client-centered supervision was an influencing process that incorporated elements of teaching and therapy, although it was neither.

Rogers's own conception of *supervision* leaned more toward therapy and is in line with current understanding of humanistic–existential supervision. In an interview with Goodyear, he states:

> *I think my major goal is to help the therapist to grow in self-confidence and to grow in understanding of himself or herself, and to grow in understanding the therapeutic process. And to that end, I find it very fruitful to explore any difficulties the therapist may feel he or she is having working with the client. Supervision for me becomes a modified form of the therapeutic interview.* (Hackney & Goodyear, 1984, p. 283)

Later, when he was asked how he differentiated supervision from therapy, Rogers answers:

> *I think there is no clean way. I think it does exist on a continuum. Sometimes therapists starting in to discuss some of the problems they're having with a client will look deeply into themselves and it's straight therapy. Sometimes it is more concerned with problems of the relationship and that is clearly supervision. But in that sense, too, I will follow the lead, in this case, the lead of the therapist. The one difference is I might feel more free to express how I might have done it than I would if I were dealing with a client.* (p. 285)

It is clear from Rogers's words that his counseling theory informed his supervision in a relatively direct way. He believed the facilitative conditions (e.g., genuineness, empathy, warmth) were necessary for supervisees and clients alike. Rice (1980) describes person-centered supervision as relying on a theory of *process* in the context of *relationship*. The successful person-centered supervisor must have a profound trust that the supervisee has within himself or herself the ability and motivation to grow and explore both the therapy situation and the self. This is the same type of trust that the therapist must have (Rice, 1980). Patterson (1983, 1997), too, emphasizes the similarity between the conditions and processes of therapy and those that occur during supervision.

Patterson and Rice both outline the attitudes toward human nature and change and the attitude toward self that the supervisor must model for the supervisee. More recently, these have been echoed by Farber (2010, 2012). First and foremost is the supervisor's basic respect for the supervisee as an individual with unique learning needs. This is communicated by a supervisory stance that is collaborative, relational, and emphasizes the development of the person of the supervisee (Farber, 2012). According to Farber, such a supervisory context "offers the trainee an experiential reference point for cultivating skill in the use of self in psychotherapy to support and encourage change in the client" (p. 175).

With a few notable exceptions (Bryant-Jeffries, 2005; Farber, 2010, 2012; Lambers, 2007; Tudor & Worrall, 2004, 2007), humanistic-relationship oriented approaches to supervision are more often blended with other constructs to provide a combined model (e.g., Pearson, 2006) or infused into a supervision process model (e.g., Ladany, Friedlander, & Nelson, 2005) than advanced as a singular approach to supervision. Still, the impact of especially the Rogerian perspective on mental health training programs has been profound and enduring. All training programs that introduce students to basic interviewing skills are using procedures that have a direct lineage to Rogers. Rogers and his associates (e.g., Rogers, Gendlin, Kiesler, & Truax, 1967) developed rating scales to assess the level at which therapists demonstrated use of Rogers' (1957) relationship variables. To operationalize these relationship attitudes or conditions then enabled two of Rogers's research associates, Robert Carkhuff and Charles Truax, to propose procedures to teach these relationship attitudes as specific skills (e.g., Carkhuff & Truax, 1965). This skill-building approach and its variants are now in nearly universal use.

Cognitive–Behavioral Supervision

Behavioral therapy and the rational and the cognitive therapies had separate origins. Behavioral therapy focused on observable behaviors and a reliance on conditioning (classical and operant) models of learning; rational and cognitive therapies were concerned with modifying clients' cognitions, especially those cognitions that were manifest as *self-talk* (e.g., Beck, Rush, Shaw, & Emery, 1979; Ellis, 1974; Mahoney, 1974, 1977; Meichenbaum, 1977). As the models have become more blended (see, e.g., most of the chapters in Barlow, 2001), the convention has become one of grouping them into the broader category of *cognitive–behavioral therapy* (CBT) models. Among the psychotherapy-based supervision models, CBT supervision has experienced the most continual development and expansion (Milne, 2008; Milne, Aylott, Fitzpatrick, & Ellis, 2008; Pretorius, 2006; Reiser & Milne, 2012; Rosenbaum & Ronen, 1998).

Cognitive–behavioral therapists operate on the assumption that both adaptive and maladaptive behaviors are learned and maintained through their consequences. It is probably no surprise that behavioral supervisors have been more specific and more systematic than supervisors of other orientations in their presentation of the goals and processes of supervision (Pretorius, 2006). Specifically, CBT supervisors are advised to set an agenda for each supervision session, set homework collaboratively with the supervisee, and assess what has been learned from session to session continuously (Beck, Sarnat, & Barenstein, 2008; Liese & Beck, 1997; Newman, 2010; Pretorius, 2006; Reiser & Milne, 2012; Rosenbaum & Ronen, 1998).

Common to most CBT supervision is a list of propositions first articulated by Boyd (1978):

1. *Proficient therapist performance is more a function of learned skills than a "personality fit." The purpose of supervision is to teach appropriate therapist behaviors and extinguish inappropriate behavior.*
2. *The therapist's professional role consists of identifiable tasks, each one requiring specific skills. Training and supervision should assist the trainee in developing these skills, applying and refining them.*
3. *Therapy skills are behaviorally definable and are responsive to learning theory, just as are other behaviors.*
4. *Supervision should employ the principles of learning theory within its procedures. (p. 89)*

The following structure for CBT supervision first suggested by Liese and Beck (1997) continues to serve as a template for CBT supervisors:

- *Check-in.* This serves as an ice-breaker and offers a personal link.
- *Agenda setting.* The supervisee is first asked what they would like to work on; the supervisor may add to the agenda.
- *Bridge from previous supervision session.* The supervisor asks what the supervisee learned from the last supervision session, and may ask how this was helpful.
- *Inquire about previously supervised therapy cases.* This brief step serves a case management function.
- *Review of homework.* This is considered a key aspect of CBT supervision. Supervisees and supervisors assign homework collaboratively for the supervisee between each session, and reviewing the outcome of this homework, which may include attempting new techniques, is essential.
- *Prioritization and discussion of agenda items.* The majority of CBT supervision revolves around this item. Supervisors are encouraged to listen to recordings of the supervisee's work prior to supervision, and engage in direct instruction, role-playing, and soliciting supervisees' questions and concerns at this time.
- *Assign new homework.* Based on what has transpired thus far, the supervisor attempts to identify what might be fruitful homework for the supervisee.
- *Supervisor's capsule summaries.* This serves as an opportunity for the supervisor to emphasize important points, summarize, and reflect on the session.
- *Elicit feedback from the supervisee.* Although supervisors seek feedback throughout the session, this is a final opportunity to make sure that the supervisee's questions have been answered and their opinions heard.

Despite the focus on overt behavior, didactic learning, and cognition, the supervisee's affect is also addressed within CBT supervision. As with the therapy model, irrational or unhelpful thoughts (e.g., "I must be the best counselor in my supervision group") are addressed in supervision for the stress and negative emotions they produce and the effect they have on the supervisee's ability to accomplish learning goals (Liese & Beck, 1997). Newman (2010) underscores the importance of creating a safe environment for supervisees, thus reflecting the development of CBT supervision to, as noted by Safran and Muran (2000), include working alliance assumptions. This, it seems to us, is an example of supervision models influencing each other in ways that make each tradition richer. More recently, Reiser and Milne (2012) call for more integration of, for example, developmental models with CBT supervision.

The evolution of CBT (therapy, and by extension, supervision) does not nullify its emphasis on assessment and close monitoring. CBT dominates the list of empirically validated treatments (see, e.g., Chambless & Ollendick, 2001), all of which use treatment manuals. CBT manuals tend to be much more specific and detailed than those of other models (cf. Barlow, 2001) because the essential premise of these models is that specific interventions result in specific client outcomes. Treatment fidelity (i.e., whether the therapist is adhering to what the manual dictates) is a very important matter. For this reason, CBT authors suggest that supervisors listen to recordings of entire sessions of their supervisees' therapy (Liese & Beck, 1997; Newman, 2010). Therefore, in a wide range of contexts, CBT supervisors are more engaged in assessment and monitoring than supervisors overseeing other therapies. It also might be suggested that, because of this, the distinctions between training and supervision can become more blurred in this form of supervision than in others.

In summary, behavioral supervisors define the potential of the supervisee as the potential to learn. Supervisors take at least part of the responsibility for supervisee learning, because they are the experts who can guide the supervisee into the correct learning environment. Perhaps more than most supervisors, they are concerned about the extent to which supervisees demonstrate technical mastery and that their work has fidelity to the particular mode of treatment being taught.

Systemic Supervision

Systemic therapy is virtually synonymous with *family therapy*. As is the case with individual psychotherapy, family therapy is characterized by a number of different theoretical approaches, including the structural, strategic, Bowenian, and experiential schools. Early on, systems supervision was therapy-based, that is, supervision paralleled the particular tents of the therapy being used. Therefore, the structural family therapist supervisor would assist the supervisee to establish a clear boundary between parents and children and would also maintain a clear boundary between him- or herself and the supervisee (McDaniel, Weber, & McKeever, 1983). The more recent trend has been for integration in family therapy theory and therefore also in supervision and training (Beck, Sarnat, & Barenstein, 2008; Celano, Smith, & Kaslow, 2010; Fraenkel & Pinsof, 2001; Kaslow, Celano, & Stanton, 2005; Lee & Everett, 2004; Storm, Todd, & Sprenkle, 2001). Our discussion here follows this trend in our reference to *systemic supervision* rather than any reference to a particular therapy approach.

All systems therapies are characterized by attention to interlocking system dynamics. A particular contribution of systems therapy is the understanding that therapists and their supervisors are "active agents of the system in which they are intervening" (Beck et al., 2008, p. 80). As systems specialists, supervisors stay attuned to dynamics within the family system, between the family and the therapist (supervisee), and within the supervisor–supervisee dyad. If supervision involved a reflecting team doing live supervision, the system dynamics become more complex and the supervisor's responsibility is expanded.

Celano et al. (2010) describe the essential components of integrated couples and family therapy supervision as follows:

1. Developing a *systemic formulation* (i.e., conceptualizing the problem in terms of recursive family processes)
2. Helping the supervisee forge a *systemic therapeutic alliance* (i.e., a working alliance with each member of the family)
3. Introducing and reinforcing the process of *reframing* (to relabel or redefine problems so that they can be resolved more productively)
4. Assisting the supervisee in managing negative interactions that occur within therapy, building cohesion among family members, and assisting with family restructuring and parenting skills
5. Understanding and appying existing evidence-based family therapy models

One additional hallmark of systemic supervision is the focus on the supervisee's family-of-origin issues (Celano et al., 2010; Storm, McDowell, & Long, 2003). In fact, Montgomery, Hendricks, and Bradley (2001) elaborate on that point, noting that

> *[t]he activation of family-of-origin dynamics is a supervision issue because they affect the degree of objectivity and emotional reactivity that counselors have with their clients and hence their therapeutic capabilities. . . . Therefore, supervision should provide trainees with opportunities to attain higher levels of differentiation and emotional maturity.* (p. 310)

This focus seems a more specific instance of the broader issue of whether supervisees should themselves participate in therapy as a means of better understanding themselves (cf. Orlinsky, Botermans, & Rønnestad, 2001). It also raises the sometimes-tricky issue of where the boundary is or should be between supervision and therapy for the supervisee (Thomas, 2010).

Several other hallmarks of systemic supervision have been incorporated into the broader domain of clinical supervision. The constructivist approaches to supervision discussed in the section that follows often are embedded in a family-therapy supervision context.

Constructivist Approaches

A significant development in the human sciences has been the emergence of a worldview that has been characterized as *postmodern, postpositivist,* or *constructivist.* The terms are not completely synonymous, but have in common the position that reality and truth are contextual and exist as creations of the observer. For humans, *truth* is a construction grounded in their social interactions and informed by their verbal behavior (Philp, Guy, & Lowe, 2007).

Constructivism has been adopted as an approach to science, but also increasingly informs thinking about psychotherapy. George Kelly (e.g., 1955) generally is credited as having developed the most formal expression of constructivism in psychotherapy. However, more recently, a number of other models have been developed that are informed by a constructivist perspective.

> *What joins constructivists is their commitment to a common epistemology, or theory of knowledge. . . . [C]onstructivists believe that "reality" . . . lies beyond the reach of our most ambitious theories, whether personal or scientific, forever denying us as human beings the security of justifying our beliefs, faiths, and ideologies by simple recourse to "objective circumstances" outside ourselves.* (Neimeyer, 1995, p. 3)

In short, "knowledge is not only *shared* in interaction, it is *created* in interaction" (Whiting, 2007, p. 141; italics in original). Counselors and therapists must engage with clients to help them construct what is true and accurate for them, including their cultural reality. Both problem identification and therapeutic goals must remain faithful to these constructions.

Common among constructivist approaches to supervision is a heavy reliance on a consultative role for the supervisor, an attempt to maintain relative equality between participants (i.e., a downplaying of hierarchy; Behan, 2003), and a focus on supervisee strengths. Whiting (2007) includes the following admonition:

> *For example, there is irony in a supervisor who expertly dispenses knowledge about how to be collaborative and non-directive. Also, the power difference of supervision makes it tempting for supervisors to become recruited into trying to sound smart, or dazzle underlings with elegant postmodern philosophical pronouncements about the family. More commonly, supervisors may inadvertently recruit the therapist to one "right way" of seeing.* (p. 142)

Narrative and solution-focused approaches fall under the larger constructivism umbrella. In the sections that follow, we briefly summarize each.

Narrative Approaches to Supervision. Therapists who work from a narrative model perspective assume that people inherently are "storytellers" who develop a story about themselves that serves as a template both to organize past experience and to influence future behavior (Bob, 1999; Parry & Doan, 1994; Polkinghorne, 1988). This story is populated with characters who are chosen for, or who are influenced to perform, certain roles in the story.

Parry and Doan (1994) developed what may be the most fully articulated version of the narrative approach. Clients come to therapy with a story about themselves that they have developed over a lifetime. The therapist's role is to help the person to tell his or her story, while being careful not to "be violent" with the client by insisting that she or he accept a particular point of view. The therapist serves as a story "editor." In this role, the therapist is careful to ask questions in the subjunctive ("As if") rather than the indicative ("This is the way it is") mode.

Although clients generally have a developed story of self that they are seeking to modify, supervisees are just beginning to develop their own stories of self-as-professional. The supervisor's role, then, is both to assist supervisees in the editing of clients' stories and also to help them to develop their own professional stories. Supervisors, therefore, must also substitute a stance of *knowing* (which is manifest as straightforward declarations of fact) with a stance of *curiosity* (which is expressed in a questioning or wondering way). For example, "At that moment with the client, you seemed to be feeling overwhelmed" (knowing) versus "I am wondering what you were feeling at that moment with the client" (curiosity). As Whiting (2007) notes, this posture of curiosity requires that the supervisor forfeit much of his or her expert status; this can be a challenge for some supervisors. It may also frustrate a novice supervisee, as we discuss when we cover developmental supervision models.

Solution-Focused Supervision. *Solution-focused therapy* (e.g., Molnar & de Shazer, 1987) focuses on enabling clients to get what they want, rather than on what is wrong with them. It is grounded in the assumptions that

1. Clients know what is best for them.
2. There is no single, correct way to view things.
3. It is important to focus on what is possible and changeable.
4. Curiosity is essential.

One of the best-known features of the model is what its adherents call the *miracle question,* which has this basic form: "Imagine that a miracle has occurred: the problems for which you are seeking treatment magically disappear. What, specifically, will you notice that will tell you that this has occurred? What else? (and so on)." This question has both a goal-setting intent and a focus on the positive.

An increasing number of authors have begun to discuss *solution-focused supervision (SFS)* (see, e.g., Gray & Smith, 2009; Hsu, 2009; Juhnke, 1996; Presbury, Echterling, & McKee, 1999; Rita, 1998; Thomas, 1996; Triantafillou, 1997; Wasket, 2006). Hsu's qualitative study of SFS identified seven components of SFS:

1. A positive opening followed by a problem description.
2. Identifying positive supervision goals.

3. Exploring exceptions for both supervisees and clients.
4. Developing other possibilities by discussing hypothetical situations with the supervisee as well as considering what meaning is embedded in supervisee's worries about worst case scenarios.
5. Giving feedback and clinical education.
6. Assisting the supervisee in forming the first little step for their upcoming counseling session.
7. Following up in subsequent supervision sessions about changes that occurred for both client and supervisee based on solution-focused techniques and philosophy.

These components are consistent with what others have identified as key SFS approaches, including the importance of focusing on small incremental steps rather than more radical ones.

As with the narrative approach, the supervisor uses a consultant role (e.g., using questions to guide interactions) and gives particular attention to language usage. Presbury et al. (1999) distinguish between *subjunctive language* and *presuppositional language. Subjunctive language* supposes a possibility (e.g., "Can you think of a time when you were able to be assertive with your client?"), whereas *presuppositional language* supposes an actuality (e.g., "Tell me about a time when you were able to be assertive with your client"). Supervisees are less likely to dismiss the latter. As well, in their use of presuppositional language, supervisors convey an assumption of the supervisee's competency.

Presbury et al. (1999) provided some possible examples of questions that a solution-focused supervisor might ask a supervisee. For example, in an effort to direct discussion toward supervisee achievements and competencies, the supervisor might ask, "What aspect of your counseling have you noticed getting better since we last met?" or, "Tell me the best thing you did with your client this week" (p. 151). Should the supervisee focus too heavily on problems that she or he is experiencing with the client, the supervisor might ask, "As you begin to get better at dealing with this situation, how will you know that you have become good enough at it so that you can take it on your own?" and then, later, "What will you be doing differently?" or, "When you get to the point at which you won't need to deal with this issue in supervision any more, how will you know?" (p. 151).

Integrative Supervision

Integrative supervision is used here as it is primarily used in the professional literature, that is, the supervision of integrative therapy (e.g, Boswell, Nelson, Nordberg, McAleavey, & Castonguay, 2010; Foy & Breunlin, 2001; Norcross & Halgin, 1997; Scaturo, 2012; Tennen, 1988). Therefore, it is a psychotherapy-based model, as its primary focus continues to be on the mentoring of the supervisee toward competence in a theoretical context, albeit a flexible theoretical context.

Boswell et al. (2010) suggest that supervisees be mentored to conceptualize a case from a particular theoretical perspective, one that is tailored for the case. If that approach must be adjusted or supplemented as therapy proceeds, it is important that supervision include oversight of the implications of integration of concepts or techniques from another theoretical perspective and the compatibility of such to the original conceptualization. Therefore, a necessity for integrative supervision is the ability and desire to supervise from multiple perspectives as well as a commitment to devote the time necessary to assist supervisees in understanding the constraints and implications of integration. Addressing integrative supervision from a family-therapy perspective, Foy and Breunlin (2001) note, "Therein lies one of the real treasures of integrative work: Each case is uniquely defined by the subtle interaction of the family and the therapist and by the many decisions they address to make therapy successful" (p. 394).

Norcross and Halgin (2005) assert that integrative work is more imaginative and adventurous, but that this can cause perplexity and anxiety as well as satisfaction. They warn that integrative supervisors should be prepared for a wide range of emotions from supervisees, who may become more frustrated that they would be in learning one approach to therapy. They suggest that a cost–benefit analysis be conducted for each supervisor and supervisee to determine if the gratification of integration outweighs the anxiety it produces, especially for novice supervisees who, as noted by Scaturo (2012), may view adherence to one theoretical approach as a "theoretical life preserver" (p. 190).

In summary, true theoretical integration is far more challenging than technical eclecticism. Therefore, integrative supervisors may need to be prepared to spend more time with their supervisees discussing theory than those who choose to supervise within one theoretical orientation.

Conclusions about Psychotherapy-Based Supervision Models

Supervision clearly found its beginnings within the various schools of therapy theory. Despite the growth of supervision in a variety of directions, any reference to resistance in supervision or reinforcing a supervisee's good work harks clearly back to psychotherapy roots. The primary advantage of leaning toward a psychotherapy-based model in one's supervision is the modeling it provides supervisees who wish to master a particular theoretical approach to therapy. Also, because supervisees "experience" the theory in supervision, their understanding of their clients' reaction to similar interventions increases.

Concerns about using psychotherapy-based supervision include the possible theoretical foreclosure of a supervisee if supervision requires them to commit to one theoretical approach (Bernard, 1992). Also, as noted by Thomas (2010), such supervision may blur the boundary between therapy and supervision, possibly causing confusion for the supervisee about the nature of the supervisory relationship.

DEVELOPMENTAL APPROACHES TO SUPERVISION

Developmental conceptions of supervision are not at all new. In fact, some date to the 1950s and 1960s (e.g., Fleming, 1953; Hogan, 1964). They were moved to center stage, however, in the early 1980s with the work of Stoltenberg (1981) and Loganbill, Hardy, and Delworth (1982). These authors and others (e.g., Blocher, 1983; Littrell, Lee-Bordin, & Lorenz, 1979) struck a resonant chord in the supervision community, which responded enthusiastically.

By 1987, Holloway was able to comment: "[D]evelopmental models of supervision have become the Zeitgeist of supervision thinking and research" (p. 209). That same year, Worthington (1987) performed a literature review that found 16 models of counselor–supervisee development; in a later expansion of this review, Watkins (1995d) identified 6 more. That level of interest could not be sustained, of course. In fact, with few exceptions (e.g., Lambie & Sias, 2009; Young, Lambie, Hutchinson, & Thurston-Dyer, 2011), attention to the topic of developmental models has dropped off considerably since. In part, this has much to do with the quality of extant models; in addition, developmental constructs have been infused into other models of supervision.

Developmental models are not all of the same type. Some draw heavily on psychosocial developmental theory (e.g., Loganbill et al., 1982); others appear to be more Eriksonian by offering discrete, primarily linear stages of development (e.g., Stolenberg, 1981). Stoltenberg and McNeill (2010) include cognitive learning theory, interpersonal influence and social learning, motivation theory, and models of human development, as all contributors of their integrative developmental model (IDM). This list may be adequately comprehensive to appreciate the underpinnings of developmental models of supervision. Said as succinctly as possible, all development models are organized around the needs of the supervisee based on some assessment of his or her status of professional development relative to some standard(s) of performance.

In the following pages, we describe five developmental models: Loganbill et al.'s (1982) model; integrative developmental model (Stoltenberg & McNeill, 2010); systemic cognitive–developmental supervision model (Rigazio-DiGilio, Daniels, & Ivey, 1997); reflective developmental models; and lifespan developmental models. In addition, we report some of the research on supervisee development that has both informed and supported these models.

The Loganbill, Hardy, and Delworth Model

Holloway (1987) observes that Loganbill et al. (1982) probably were the first to publish a comprehensive model of counselor development. Although there has been scant research follow-up on that model, it is sufficiently unique and important to warrant coverage.

Loganbill et al. chose Chickering's (1969) developmental tasks of youth and redefined them into professional issues for those training to be therapists: competence, emotional awareness, autonomy, professional identity, respect for individual differences, purpose and direction, personal motivation, and professional ethics. For each issue, the trainee might be at one of three stages—stagnation, confusion, or integration—or in transition between stages. The stages are as follows:

Stagnation Stage. For more novice supervisees, stagnation is characterized by unawareness of deficiencies or difficulties. The more experienced supervisee, however, is more likely to experience this stage either as stagnation (or "stuckness") or as a blind spot concerning his or her functioning in a particular area. The supervisee at this stage is likely to engage in cognitively simple, black-and-white thinking and to lack insight into his or her impact on the supervisor or client. He or she also may experience counseling as uninteresting or dull.

Supervisees at this stage may exhibit one of two patterns during supervision. In one, the supervisee is especially dependent on the supervisor and idealizes him or her. Alternatively, the supervisee may view the supervisor as somewhat irrelevant, at least with respect to the issue with which the supervisee is dealing. The tone, however, more likely is one of neutrality or unawareness.

Confusion Stage. The onset of the confusion stage can be either gradual or abrupt. Its key characteristics are "instability, disorganization, erratic fluctuations, disturbance, confusion, and conflict," and in which the supervisee "becomes liberated from a rigid belief system and from traditional ways of viewing the self and behaving toward others" (Loganbill et al., 1982, p. 18). This can be troubling, because the supervisee realizes that something is wrong, but does not yet see how it will be resolved.

In this stage, the supervisee recognizes that the answer will not come from the supervisor. The dependency that characterized the earlier stage is replaced by anger or frustration toward the supervisor, who either is withholding or incompetent, depending on the supervisee's particular perception.

Integration Stage. This stage, the "calm after the storm," is characterized by "a new cognitive understanding, flexibility, personal security based on awareness of insecurity and an ongoing continual monitoring of the important issues of supervision" (Loganbill et al., 1982, p. 19). At this stage, the supervisee sees the supervisor in realistic terms, as a person with strengths and weaknesses. The supervisee takes responsibility for what occurs during supervision sessions and has learned to make the best use of the supervisor's time and expertise. His or her expectations are consistent with what is possible from supervision.

The three supervisee stages and their relationships with each other are depicted in Figure 2.

In contrast to other developmental models, which assume a more linear progression across stages, this model assumes that the counselor cycles and recycles through the stages, increasing their levels of integration at each cycle. To explain, Loganbill et al. used the metaphor of changing a tire:

> *One tightens the bolts, one after another, just enough so that the wheel is in place; then the process is repeated. Each bolt is tightened in turn until the wheel is entirely secure. In a similar way, stages of*

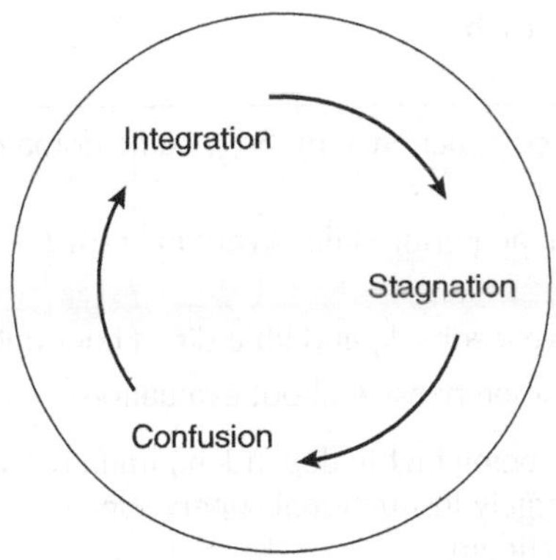

FIGURE 2 The Three (Repeating) Stages of Development (Loganbill et al., 1982)

> *the process can be gone through again and again with each issue receiving increasing thoroughness.* (p. 17)

What makes the model complex is that Loganbill et al. asserted that for any of the eight developmental issues to which the supervisor should be attentive, the supervisee could be at any one of the three stages. The supervisor's role is to assess each supervisee's standing on each of the eight issues and attempt to move the supervisee to the next stage of development. This requires the supervisor to track the supervisee's progress through 24 different positions with respect to the model (8 issues × 3 stages). No one has tested supervisors' ability to do that; our understanding of the limits of working memory (see, e.g., Miyake & Priti, 1999) suggest that it would be difficult. It is more likely that a supervisor will attend more selectively to a few of the eight issues in any given period.

The supervisory interventions that Loganbill et al. (1982) described were adopted by Stoltenberg and McNeill (2010) for their IDM and are described next.

The Integrated Developmental Model

The *integrated developmental model (IDM)* (Stoltenberg, McNeil, & Delworth, 1998; Stoltenberg & McNeill, 2010) is the best known and most widely used stage developmental model of supervision. It has the virtue of being both descriptive with respect to supervisee processes and prescriptive with respect to supervisor interventions.

Stoltenberg's (1981) initial four-stage model was an integration of two others: Hogan's (1964), concerning stages through which supervisees progress; and Harvey, Hunt, and Schroeder's (1961) conceptual level model. Stoltenberg and his collaborators have continued to refine the model (Stoltenberg & Delworth, 1987; Stoltenberg et al., 1998; Stoltenberg & McNeill, 2010). The IDM still has a cognitive basis, but one that is less prominent and relies instead on Anderson's (1996) work on the development of expertise, as well as on others who have conceptualized the development of schemas, rather than assumptions about conceptual level that were used in the original 1981 model.

The IDM describes counselor development as occurring through four stages, each of which is characterized by changes on "three overriding structures that provide markers in assessing professional growth" (Stoltenberg & McNeill, 2010, pp. 23–24):

- *Self–Other Awareness: Cognitive and Affective*—"[W]here the person is in terms of self-preoccupation, awareness of the client's world, and enlightened self-awareness. The cognitive component describes the content of the thought processes characteristic across levels, and the affective component accounts for changes in emotions such as anxiety."
- *Motivation*—"[R]eflects the supervisee's interest, investment, and effort expended in clinical training and practice."
- *Autonomy*—Reflects the degree of independence that the supervisee is manifesting.

Table 1 summarizes the manner in which these three structures are reflected for the four supervisee developmental levels. Supervisors interested in assessing their supervisees' level of functioning on these three structures have available

TABLE 1 Supervisee Characteristics and Supervisor Behavior for Each of the Four IDM-Specified Supervisee Developmental Levels

Level 1. These supervisees have limited training, or at least limited experience in the specific domain in which they are being supervised.

Motivation: Both motivation and anxiety are high; focused on acquiring skills. Want to know the "correct" or "best" approach with clients.

Autonomy: Dependent on supervisor. Needs structure, positive feedback, and little direct confrontation.

Awareness: High self-focus, but with limited self-awareness; apprehensive about evaluation.

Level 2. Supervisees at this level are "making the transition from being highly dependent, imitative, and unaware in responding to a highly structured, supportive, and largely instructional supervisory environment" (p. 64); usually after two to three semesters of practicum.

Motivation: Fluctuating, as the supervisee vacillates between being very confident to unconfident and confused.

Autonomy: Although functioning more independently, he or she experiences conflict between autonomy and dependency, much as an adolescent does. This can manifest as pronounced resistance to the supervisor.

Awareness: Greater ability to focus on and empathize with client. However, balance still is an issue. In this case, the problem can be veering into confusion and enmeshment with the client.

Stoltenberg et al. note that this can be a turbulent stage and "supervision of the Level 2 therapist . . . [requires] considerable skill, flexibility, and perhaps a sense of humor" (p. 87).

Level 3. Supervisees at this level are focusing more on a personalized approach to practice and on using and understanding of "self" in therapy.

Motivation. Consistent; occasional doubts about one's effectiveness will occur, but without being immobilizing.

Autonomy: A solid belief in one's own professional judgment has developed as the supervisee moves into independent practice. Supervision tends to be collegial as differences between supervisor and supervisee expertise diminish.

Awareness: The supervisees return to being self-aware, but with a very different quality than at level 1. Supervisees at this level are able to remain focused on the client while also stepping back to attend to their own personal reactions to the client, and then to use this in decision making about the client.

Level 3i (Integrated). This level occurs as the supervisee reaches level 3 across multiple domains (e.g., treatment, assessment, conceptualization). The supervisee's task is one of integrating across domains. It is characterized by a personalized approach to professional practice across domains and the ability to move easily across them. This supervisee has strong awareness of his or her strengths and weaknesses.

to them the Supervisee Levels Questionnaire–Revised (McNeill, Stoltenberg, & Romans, 1992).

Stoltenberg and McNeill (2010) also specified eight domains of professional functioning in which the supervisee develops:

1. *Intervention skills competence*—confidence and ability to carry out therapeutic interventions
2. *Assessment techniques*—confidence and ability to conduct psychological assessments
3. *Interpersonal assessment*—extends beyond the formal assessment period and includes the use of self in conceptualizing client problems;

its nature varies according to theoretical orientation

4. *Client conceptualization*—diagnosis, but also pertains to the therapist's understanding of how the client's circumstances, history, and characteristics affect his or her functioning
5. *Individual differences*—an understanding of ethnic and cultural influences on individuals
6. *Theoretical orientation*—pertains to the level of complexity and sophistication of the therapist's understanding of theory
7. *Treatment plans and goals*—how the therapist plans to organize his or her efforts in working with clients
8. *Professional ethics*—how professional ethics intertwine with personal ethics

The supervisor interventions adopted for the IDM are those originally described by Loganbill et al. (1982), who in turn had adapted them from the work of Blake and Mouton (1976). Interestingly, Heron (1989) also adapted Blake and Mouton's organization-level interventions to the individual level. The Heron and the Loganbill et al. interventions differ somewhat, but because of the general similarity of their work and because Heron's (1989) six-category system of interventions has been widely adopted in Great Britain (Sloan & Watson, 2001) to conceptualize the work of both therapists and supervisors, we summarize Heron's, which features two broad classifications of interventions, each with three specific interventions.

Facilitative interventions—enable the client (or, in supervision, the supervisee) to retain some control in the relationship. The three specific interventions in this category are:

- *Cathartic*—interventions that elicit affective reactions
- *Catalytic*—open-ended questions intended to encourage self-exploration or problem solving (e.g., Supervisor: "What keeps you from acting on what you are understanding about this client?")
- *Supportive*—interventions that validate the supervisee

Authoritative interventions—provide more relational control to the therapist or supervisor. The three specific interventions in this category are:

- *Prescriptive*—giving advice and making suggestions
- *Informative*—providing information
- *Confronting*—pointing out discrepancies the supervisor observes between or among supervisee (a) feelings, (b) attitudes, and/or (c) behaviors

We should note that Loganbill et al. and Stoltenberg and McNeill do not discuss using the catalytic or informative interventions. Also, they suggest one intervention that is missing from the Heron (1989) model: that of *conceptual interventions,* which help the supervisee link theory to practice. Loganbill et al. suggest that there are two primary ways to do this, depending on the learning style of the supervisee: (a) watch for the supervisee's use of a particular strategy, then help him or her develop a conceptual frame for what was just done; or (b) present the model, then suggest an intervention based on it.

Johnson and Moses (1988) also followed Loganbill et al. (1982) and relied on Chickering's (1969) vectors as the criteria for supervisee development. Rather than the interventions proposed by Loganbill et al. and later revised by Stoltenberg and McNeill, however, Johnson and Moses reduce supervisor input to either *challenge* or *support.* If the supervisor offers too little challenge, the supervisee might slip into stagnation (borrowing from the Loganbill et al. model); with too much challenge and too little support, the supervisee may get discouraged or defensive. The choice between challenge and support is seen by Johnson and Moses as the most critical decision that the supervisor makes. Once this decision is made, Johnson and Moses refer to the Bernard (1979, 1997) schema of roles (i.e., teacher, consultant, and counselor) as being the primary choices for the supervisor to help the supervisee to attain the desired growth. Although Johnson and Moses do not imply that either support or challenge interventions should constitute the majority of supervisor interventions, McCarthy, Kulakowski, & Kenfield, (1994) found that the most frequent supervisor technique was the offering of support and encouragement, whereas confrontation and the assignment of homework were rarely used. Supervisors, therefore, must reflect on their own work to determine if their avoidance of confrontation is meeting their own needs or that of their supervisees.

Finally, we underscore a part of the IDM that provides an additional anchor for supervisor and supervisee alike. As a way to understand how supervisees develop useful schemata for conducting counseling or therapy, Stoltenberg and McNeill use concepts proposed by Schön (1987). *Knowing-in-action (KIA)* reflects actions that are automatic for the supervisee. When client responses surprise the supervisee, there is a possibility of *reflection-in-action (RIA)*—that is, the supervisee notices what is occurring that is different from other interpersonal interactions or what has occurred with other clients. Between sessions, *reflection-on-action (ROA)* can occur based on RIA and supervisor encouragement—that is, if RIA did not occur in a session, the supervisor can use recordings of the counseling session to stimulate ROA. Through this process, schema are refined and development can occur leading to more complex RIA in session and an expanded repertoire of KIA behaviors. These conceptual tools assist the supervisory dyad both within and across levels.

Systemic Cognitive–Developmental Supervision Model

Rigazio-DiGilio and her colleagues extended the earlier work of Ivey (1986) to develop a model that encourages supervisors to track and intervene with supervisees based on the cognitive style of the supervisee (Rigazio-DiGilio, 1997; Rigazio-DiGilio & Anderson, 1994; Rigazio-DiGilio et al., 1997). Although the *systemic cognitive–developmental supervision (SCDS)* model is referred to as a developmental model using Piagetian terms to describe different types of learners (supervisees), there is no assumption within the model that one type of learner is superior to another. Rather, each of the four cognitive orientations has its advantages and disadvantages for conducting therapy. The task of the supervisor is to identify the primary orientation(s) of each supervisee and to assist each supervisee to become more flexible and to see the world from additional orientations to the one(s) that comes naturally. When supervisees can access all four orientations, they can shift gears when necessary during therapy, thus enabling them to offer assistance that is more likely to be on target. Therefore, although the reader may view other developmental models presented in this section in a vertical fashion, this model is primarily horizontal because supervisees are assisted in expanding their conceptual and experiential capabilities while not forfeiting their original "natural" style. What follows is a description of each cognitive orientation as described by Rigazio-DiGilio (1995). For each orientation, we include the strengths of the supervisee if they are able to use the orientation competently, as well as the deficits if the supervisee is limited or constrained by this orientation.

The first type of orientation described by Rigazio-DiGilio (1995) is the *sensorimotor*. These supervisees are affected emotionally, if not viscerally, by their experiences. Those who are skilled in this orientation can identify feelings easily and process them, permitting them to work through issues of transference and countertransference. If constrained by this orientation, supervisees can be overstimulated by their emotions, and this can interfere with their conceptual skills. They may also rely on "what feels right" as the basis for interventions, rather than solid treatment planning. Rigazio-DiGilio suggests that the supervisor working with the sensorimotor supervisee use a directive style that provides the supervisee with a safe environment to explore sensory data. The goal is to help the supervisee translate an abundance of emotional data into a viable framework for conducting therapy.

The second cognitive style is *concrete,* and these supervisees see the world (and their clients) through a linear, cause–effect lens. The concrete learner can describe the events described by the client, often in the same order as the client presented them. Because of their if–then reasoning ability, concrete thinkers can anticipate patterned behavior of their clients. At the same time, supervisees with a concrete orientation can foreclose regarding their understanding of the client and can have difficulty seeing alternative perspectives. They also have difficulty moving from the specific to the more nuanced in understanding potential directions of counseling or therapy.

Rigazio-DiGilio's (1995) third orientation is the *formal.* These supervisees analyze situations from multiple perspectives and are naturally reflective. They modify their treatment plans easily based on supervisory feedback. They have no difficulty linking a specific session to larger themes in therapy. If the formal orientation is too dominant, however, supervisees have difficulty translating their understanding of client themes to actual practice. They can also underestimate the role of feelings and behavior in counseling. Because they see their analytical abilities as their strength, they may have difficulty when these are challenged.

Finally, Rigazio-DiGilio (1995) describes the *dialectic* orientation as one in which supervisees challenge their own assumptions that inform their case conceptualization. In other words, these supervisees are drawn to think about *how* they think. Because of their tendencies to conceptualize broadly, dialectic thinkers are more likely to consider the broader environment, including historical and cultural contexts. The supervisee with a strong dialectic orientation can become overwhelmed by multiple perspectives, unable to commit to one because competing perspectives appear equally valid (or invalid). Clients may have a difficult time integrating the complex thinking of a dialectic therapist.

In discussing supervision environments, Rigazio-DiGilio and Anderson (1994) suggest that supervisors first match supervisees' orientation and assist them in becoming more competent (i.e., less restrained) with their primary orientation. Once this has been achieved, the supervisor can begin to mismatch orientations to assist supervisees in expanding their competence across orientation. The ultimate goal is for supervisees to be able to move in and out of the four orientations, even though they may continue to be grounded in a particular orientation.

Although the SCDS model has not been widely adopted, it continues to provide an excellent way to assess supervisee's primary way of experiencing and conceptualizing their work. It also provides a developmental model that can be relevant to therapists at any level, especially when they have been "activated" by a client to revert to a safer, primary orientation.

Reflective Developmental Models

Dewey (1933) is credited with the first formal statement about the use of reflection to improve practice. Many others—including, particularly, Schön (1983, 1987)—offer more contemporary statements about reflection, yet all continue to describe it as Dewey originally had. Reflection is a process that begins with a professional practice situation that is somehow upsetting, surprising, or confusing; Holloway (in Neufeldt, Karno, & Nelson, 1996) refers to this as a *trigger event* that sets in motion a critical review of the situation that results in a new and deeper understanding of that situation. It is assumed that the person will implement this new understanding when similar situations arise in the future.

Hinett (2002) observes that those who discussed reflection in professional practice emphasize that, unlike reflections that provide an exact image, reflection in professional practice goes beyond the original to shed light on what might be. In this way, reflection is inherently developmental.

Figure 3 graphically depicts the basic process of reflection as it occurs in supervision. The trigger event can be related to the supervisee's skills, to issues related to his or her personhood

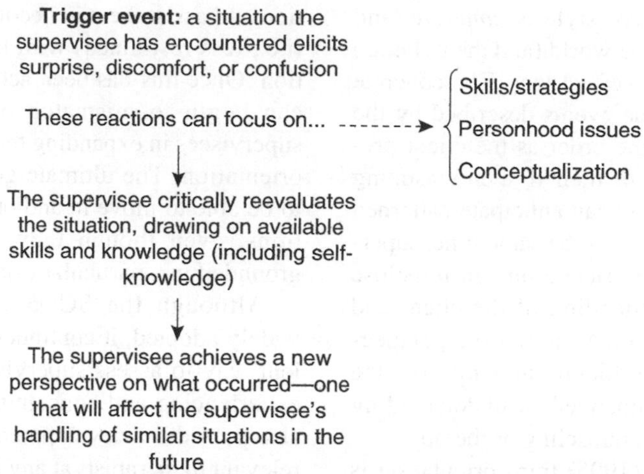
Trigger event: a situation the supervisee has encountered elicits surprise, discomfort, or confusion
These reactions can focus on...
Skills/strategies
Personhood issues
Conceptualization
The supervisee critically reevaluates the situation, drawing on available skills and knowledge (including self-knowledge)
The supervisee achieves a new perspective on what occurred—one that will affect the supervisee's handling of similar situations in the future

FIGURE 3 The Reflective Process in Supervision

(e.g., countertransference), or to the way the supervisee conceptualizes the client or the therapeutic process. These are the foci of supervision Bernard (1979, 1997) proposes (discussed later). For example, a supervisee might try an intervention with a client that does not work, even though he or she had been sure it would; the supervisee might wonder what there is about a particular client that is so irritating; or, the supervisee might find that what she or he had understood to be going on with the client was simply wrong. Each of these is an example of a trigger event that might set in motion a reflective process that the supervisor would facilitate.

Authors such as Ward and House (1998), Driscoll (2000), Guiffrida (2005), and Frølund and Nielsen (2009) discuss reflective approaches to supervision. The qualitative study by Neufeldt et al. (1996), based on interviews with prominent experts on reflective practice, provides important understandings of the nature of reflection as well. Various interventions and techniques have been developed to assist the supervisor in promoting supervisee reflectivity and are used by a broad swath of supervisors (i.e., not only those who work primarily from a developmental stance).

We close this brief discussion of reflective processes in supervision with three observations. First: We reiterate that it is likely that all supervisors facilitate some level of reflective processes with their supervisees. Second: As supervisors facilitate supervisees' work-related reflections, they are also teaching those supervisees an important skill that they eventually can use on their own. This skill in reflecting on their work—paired with the related ability to self-monitor—becomes an important method of self-supervision (cf. Goodyear, 2006). Once a mental health professional is licensed, he or she typically no longer required to be supervised formally (at least in the United States). It is important, therefore, that she or he be able to self-supervise (see also Dennin & Ellis, 2003).

Our third observation is that reflection should be more than simply "discovery learning" (see, e.g., Kirschner, Sweller, & Clark, 2006). Otherwise, each of us might discover something quite unique, and that discovery might or might not correspond to what others understand to constitute good practice. The supervisee's reflections certainly should involve his or her own internal processes (e.g., confusions, discomforts), but ultimately should be linked to some externally

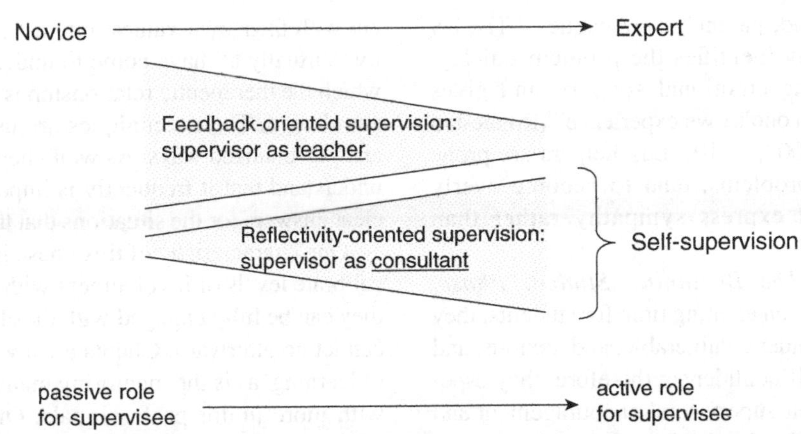

FIGURE 4 A Developmental Conception of the Reflective Process in Supervision

validated understandings of good professional practice as well. Therefore, the supervisee's level of experience affects (a) the extent to which reflection is used as a supervisory process and (b) the quality of the reflections.

Figure 4 suggests how we believe these assumptions translate to practice. It shows, for example, that some level of reflection always is a part of supervision, but that supervision of a more-novice supervisee has a greater teaching component. The intent is to help the supervisee accrue and master the essential practice skills and to develop an appreciation for what constitutes a good or effective skill or way of thinking. Gradually, however, the proportion of time focused on teaching drops as the proportion of time devoted to fostering reflection increases. The ultimate outcome is the ability to use those reflective skills to self-supervise.

The Rønnestad and Skovholt Lifespan Developmental Model

Although most models of counselor development focus primarily on the period of graduate and internship training, professional development no more stops at graduation than does our personal development. The work of Rønnestad and Skovholt (1993, 2003; Skovholt & Rønnestad, 1992b) is therefore important for its articulation of the ways that therapists continue to develop across their professional lifespan.

This model is based on interviews with 100 counselors and therapists who ranged in experience from the first year of graduate school to 40 years beyond graduate school. In their initial analyses of their qualitative data, Rønnestad and Skovholt identify 8 stages of therapist development, each of which might be characterized along a number of dimensions (e.g., style of learning). They also identify 20 themes that are not specifically stage related, but that characterize therapist development across time.

In their later work, Rønnestad and Skovholt (2003) offer a more refined and parsimonious model, based on reinterviews with some therapists, feedback obtained over the previous decade, and their own reanalyses of the data. They collapse the model so that there now are only 6 *phases* (a term that they now believe is more technically accurate than *stages*) of development and 14 themes. Because of the importance of this model, we summarize these phases and then the themes. It is useful to note that the early phases correspond well to stages described by Stoltenberg and McNeill (2010).

Phase 1: The Lay Helper Phase. Novices already have had the experience of helping others (e.g., as a friend, parent, or colleague). "The lay helper typically identifies the problem quickly, provides strong emotional support, and gives advice based on one's own experience" (Rønnestad & Skovholt, 2003, p. 10). Lay helpers are prone to boundary problems, tend to become overly involved, and express sympathy rather than empathy.

Phase 2: The Beginning Student Phase. Although this is an exciting time for students, they often feel dependent, vulnerable, and anxious, and have fragile self-confidence; therefore, they especially value their supervisors' encouragement and support. Perceived criticism from either their supervisors or their clients can have a severe effect on their self-confidence and morale. They actively search for the "right" way to function, looking for models and expert practitioners to emulate.

Phase 3: The Advanced Student Phase. These students, usually at the advanced practice or internship stage, have the central task of functioning at a basic established, professional level. They feel pressure to "do it right" and therefore have a conservative, cautious, and thorough style (versus one that is relaxed, risk-taking, or spontaneous).

The opportunity to provide supervision to beginning students "can be a powerful source of influence for the advanced student" (Rønnestad & Skovholt, 2003, p. 15), who are able both to see how much they have learned and to consolidate that learning.

Phase 4: The Novice Professional Phase. The years immediately postgraduation can be a heady time, because the person now is free of the demands of graduate school and the constraints of supervision. Still, many find that they are not as well prepared as they had imagined. The new therapist increasingly integrates his or her own personality in treatment. As this occurs, the therapist becomes more at ease. He or she also uses this period to seek compatible work roles and environments.

Phase 5: The Experienced Professional Phase. Counselors and therapists with some years and types of experience have the core developmental task of finding a way to be authentic—specifically, developing a working style that is highly congruent with their own values, interests, and personality. Virtually all have come to understand ways in which the therapeutic relationship is crucial for client change. Their techniques are used in flexible and personalized ways. As well, they have come to understand that it frequently is impossible to have clear answers for the situations that they encounter.

One characteristic of this phase is the ability to calibrate levels of involvement with clients so that they can be fully engaged with the clients, but then can let go afterward. Clients are a valuable source of learning, as is the mentoring many therapists do with more junior professionals. Often they also begin looking outside the profession to areas such as religion or poetry, or even theater or cinema to expand their knowledge of people.

Phase 6: The Senior Professional Phase. These professionals, usually with more than 20 years of experience, typically have developed very individualized and authentic approaches. Despite their felt competence, they generally have become more modest about their own impact on clients. They also tend to have become skeptical that anything really new will be added to the field. Loss is a prominent theme in this phase. This is both anticipatory, as they look toward their own retirements, and current, for "their own professional elders are no longer alive and same age colleagues are generally no longer a strong source of influence" (Rønnestad & Skovholt, 2003, p. 26).

Woskett and Page (2001) observe that it might be possible to think of the first phases as ones that, together, make up a broad *learning* phase, and that the last of the phases might, together, make up a broad *unlearning* phase. Significantly, this latter phase lasts for most of the practitioner's professional life! Most supervision literature focuses on the learning phase, with much less written about the supervision of experienced professionals. The Skovholt and Rønnestad model, however, suggests that the focus of this supervision is less on established models of practice and more on the individualized work of the particular practitioner.

Rønnestad and Skovholt's 14 themes are summarized in Table 2. When the label is not sufficient to fully express its meaning, we add

TABLE 2 Rønnestad and Skovholt's 14 Themes of Therapist–Counselor Development

1. *Professional development involves an increasing higher-order integration of the professional self and the personal self.* Across time, a professional's theoretical perspective and professional roles become increasingly consistent with his or her values, beliefs, and personal life experiences.
2. *The focus of functioning shifts dramatically over time, from internal to external to internal.* During formal training, a person drops an earlier ("lay helper") reliance on an internal and personal epistemology for helping in order to rely on the professionally based knowledge and skills that guide practice. Later, during postdegree experience, professionals gradually regain an internal focus and, with it, a more flexible and confident style.
3. *Continuous reflection is a prerequisite for optimal learning and professional development at all levels of experience.* A straightforward observation, but its implications for supervision are substantial. It implies, for example, that supervisees should be taught self-reflection and self-supervision (cf. Dennin & Ellis, 2003).
4. *An intense commitment to learn propels the developmental process.* Importantly, Rønnestad and Skovholt found that, for most of their respondents, enthusiasm for professional growth tended not to diminish with time.
5. *The cognitive map changes.* Beginning practitioners rely on external expertise; seasoned practitioners rely on internal expertise. Early on, supervisees seek "received knowledge" of experts and therefore prefer a didactic approach to supervision. They later shift increasingly to developing "constructed knowledge" based on their own experiences and self-reflections.
6. *Professional development is a long, slow, continuous process that also can be erratic.*
7. *Professional development is a lifelong process.*
8. *Many beginning practitioners experience much anxiety in their professional work.* Over time, anxiety is mastered by most.
9. *Clients serve as a major source of influence and serve as primary teachers.*
10. *Personal life influences professional functioning and development throughout the professional life span.*

    Family interactional patterns, sibling and peer relationships, one's own parenting experiences, disability in family members, other crises in the family, personal trauma and so on influenced current practice and more long term development in both positive and adverse ways. (Rønnestad & Skovholt, 2003, p. 34)

11. *Interpersonal sources of influence propel professional development more than "impersonal" sources of influence.* Growth occurs through contact with clients, supervisors, therapists, family and friends, and (later) younger colleagues. Rønnestad and Skovholt found that, when asked to rank the impact of various influences on their professional development, therapists ranked clients first, supervisors second, their own therapists third, and the people in their personal lives fourth.
12. *New members of the field view professional elders and graduate training with strong affective reactions.* It is likely that the power differences magnify these responses, which can range from strongly idealizing to strongly devaluing teachers and supervisors.
13. *Extensive experience with suffering contributes to heightened recognition, acceptance, and appreciation of human variability.* Through this process, therapists develop wisdom and integrity.
14. *For the practitioner, there is realignment from Self as hero to Client as hero.* Over time, the client's contributions to the process are better understood and appreciated, and therapists adopt a more realistic and humble appreciation of what they actually contribute to the change process.

    If these "blows to the ego" are processed and integrated into the therapists' self-experience, they may contribute to the paradox of increased sense of confidence and competence while also feeling more humble and less powerful as a therapist. (Rønnestad & Skovholt, 2003, p. 38) explanatory text. Together with the 6 phases, these themes provide supervisors with an important career cognitive map. Like the other models, this suggests the importance to beginning students of having clear and direct models for practice and supervision that include didactic approaches, but it also adds support for providing a supervision course during graduate training (i.e., as a source of development for the supervisor-in-training) and makes clear how the mentoring of newer professionals is a source of professional development to therapists at phases 5 and 6.

In short, this is a unique and important model. Its applications to supervision, however, are not as direct as is true with some other models. It was developed through a research study of therapist development and therefore remains more descriptive than prescriptive.

The 14 themes vary in their level of implication for supervisors. For example, whereas theme 3, concerning self-reflection, has very important and direct implications for supervisors (who can design interventions to foster the self-reflective process), other themes are more distantly related to supervision. As a final note, it is our impression that the themes could be collapsed in the interest of simplifying. Goodyear, Wertheimer, Cypers, and Rosemond (2003) demonstrate, for example, that it is possible to refine these 14 themes into 6 themes.

Research on Cognitive Development

Thus far, we have presented key developmental models in the supervision literature, yet, there is a body of empirical work that also addresses supervisee development and should be considered as the supervisor implements any of the models we have covered. Some research results may cause the supervisor to modify his or her application of a model; other results confirm the developmental model assumptions. We begin our review with studies concerning the relationship between cognitive complexity and cognitive development, followed by the relationship between experience and development. We end with a discussion of the research that addresses those factors that moderate the relationship between experience and development.

Cognitive Complexity and Cognitive Development. We have ample evidence that trainees with high cognitive complexity are more capable of several of the tasks of counseling, such as increased empathy and less negative bias (Stoppard & Miller, 1985), more sophisticated descriptions of client characteristics (Borders, 1989a), more parsimonious conceptualization of specific counseling situations (Martin, Slemon, Hiebert, Hallberg, & Cummings, 1989), and better ability to stay focused on counseling and less on themselves (Birk & Mahalik, 1996). Because of this, the mental health professions have been invested in determining (or confirming) how cognitive development can be nurtured so that supervisees attain the desired level of conceptual competence by the end of their formal training and be poised for additional development after training.

Simultaneously, the supervision literature has been dominated by developmental assumptions about training and supervision, most of which assume that experience under supervision and cognitive development enjoy a symbiotic relationship. In the following pages, we attempt to answer the following questions: How and to what extent are cognitive complexity and cognitive development related? To what extent does cognitive development occur during training programs? How does it occur? Is supervised experience the most potent training variable for assuring or accelerating cognitive development?

Although it is impossible to isolate these variables entirely, we begin this section with a brief discussion of the relationship between cognitive complexity and cognitive development, and follow with a more elaborate discussion of the role of experience in supervisee development.

As is stated earlier, cognitive complexity has been found to be correlated with competencies that are important to successful counseling. The assumption of the mental health professions has been that training and supervision stimulate cognitive development among trainees that culminates in increased cognitive complexity by the end of training. In recent years, empirical scrutiny has found that, whereas development does indeed seem to occur as a result of training (e.g., Duys & Hedstrom, 2000), training cannot be described as uniformly robust, nor does it stimulate all aspects of cognitive complexity (Fong, Borders, Ethington, & Pitts, 1997; Granello, 2002; Lovell, 1999; Stein & Lambert, 1995). In fact, to date, there is little to challenge the work of Skovholt and Rønnestad (1992a), who conclude that the majority of cognitive development for mental health practitioners occurs after formal training.

What is unknown at this point is the relationship between baseline cognitive complexity and cognitive development that occurs through training and supervision. In other words, although there is an assumption that higher cognitive complexity at the beginning of training is an advantage, little is known about its lasting advantage throughout training and beyond. Stoltenberg and McNeill (2010) assert that, whereas all trainees begin at level 1 of their developmental model, the speed of transition between levels depends to some extent on the cognitive growth that they have attained in their individual lives.

As Stoltenberg (1981) implies in his earlier work, Granello (2002) speculated that persons of higher cognitive complexity must "re-progress" (p. 292) through earlier stages of development as they conceptualize the intricacies of counseling, but that the learning for trainees of high cognitive complexity may be more accelerated. Although these assumptions make intuitive sense, Lovell (1999) found that the amount of supervised clinical experience accounted for more cognitive development than individual cognitive complexity, although the latter also contributed significantly. Similarly, Granello (2002) found that the bulk of cognitive development occurs between the midpoint and end of training for persons seeking a master's degree in counseling—that is, during the time that the trainee is under supervision. This finding is consistent with the study conducted by Fong et al. (1997). A study that considers counselors over a longer segment of their professional lifespan (Welfare & Borders, 2010b) found that experience in the profession, including postdegree experience and involvement in teaching of counseling, was related to increased cognitive complexity about counseling. Considering these studies together, we may surmise that supervision is critical to stimulate cognitive development, but that persons who are beyond training may indeed be reflecting Rønnestad and Skovholt's lifespan model.

In addition to the obvious benefits of conceptualizing clients in a more complex manner, Ramos-Sánchez et al. (2002) found that higher cognitive developmental levels for supervisees were correlated with stronger working alliances with supervisors and more satisfaction with supervision. Thus, the costs for stalled cognitive development could be significant.

Experience as an Indicator of Developmental Level. The supervisee's level of experience has been one of the more broadly researched areas of counselor development. Although there are a few exceptions (e.g., Friedlander & Snyder, 1983), the great majority of empirical studies suggest that supervisees have different characteristics and different abilities based on the amount of supervised experience that they have accrued (e.g., Borders, 1990; Burke, Goodyear, & Guzzardo, 1998; Cummings, Hallberg, Martin, Slemon, & Hiebert, 1990; Granello, 2002; Ladany, Marotta, & Muse-Burke, 2001; Lovell, 1999; Mallinckrodt & Nelson, 1991; McNeill, Stoltenberg, & Pierce, 1985; McNeill et al., 1992; Murray, Portman, & Maki, 2003; Olk & Friedlander, 1992; Shechtman & Wirzberger, 1999; Swanson & O'Saben, 1993; Tracey, Ellickson, & Sherry, 1989; Tracey, Hays, Malone, & Herman, 1988; Wiley & Ray, 1986; Williams, Judge, Hill, & Hoffman, 1997; Winter & Holloway, 1991). Other reviewers of the empirical literature (Goodyear & Guzzardo,

2000; Holloway, 1992, 1995; Stoltenberg, McNeill, & Crethar, 1994) also identify experience level as an important point of departure for understanding the developmental needs of the supervisee.

Several authors (Ellis & Ladany, 1997; Fong et al., 1997; Granello, 2002) echo Holloway's (1992) earlier caution, however, that there are multiple problems in interpreting the results of most developmental studies, one of these being the lack of longitudinal studies. That is, without tracking the same supervisees over time, it is very difficult to discern whether the significant results of various studies depict true *development* or cohort effects. Yet even without this and other issues fully resolved, there is still ample empirical evidence to support an examination of the supervisee's experience level as one indicator of developmental level.

Researchers examined the relationship between amount of training and supervisee behavior. Looking at the beginning practicum student, Borders (1990) found significant change in supervisee self-reports for self-awareness, dependency–autonomy, and theory–skills acquisition over one semester. McNeill et al. (1985) obtained similar results when they compared beginning trainees to intermediate trainees. Examining prepracticum student growth over a period of one semester, Williams et al. (1997) found that trainees at the end of the semester decreased in anxiety and were better at managing their own transference and countertransference reactions.

Studies that considered larger experience differences have reported inconsistent and more complex results. Cummings et al. (1990) and Martin et al. (1989) found that experienced counselors were more efficient in their conceptualization, using well-established cognitive schemata to conceptualize clients, although novice counselors seemed to require much more specific information about the clients to conceptualize the problem; they were more random in their information seeking, and their ultimate conceptualizations were less sophisticated. Welfare and Borders (2010b) found that counseling experience, supervisory experience, counselor education experience, and advanced degrees all predicated higher cognitive complexity for their sample that included master's level supervisees, doctoral students, practicing counselors, and counseling faculty.

Other researchers have also looked at a broader continuum of experience. Tracey et al. (1988) studied counselor responses across three experience levels: beginning counselors (0 to 1 year of practicum), advanced counselors (graduate students with more than 1 year of practicum), and doctoral counselors (at least 2 years of postdoctoral experience). When supervisee interventions (i.e., dominance, approach–avoidance, focus on affect, immediacy, breadth versus specificity, meeting client demands, verbosity, and confrontation) were compared across groups, doctoral-level counselors were less dominant (yet confronted more), were less verbose, and yielded less to client demands than non-doctoral-level counselors.

Burke et al. (1998) investigated the working alliance of 10 supervisor–supervisee dyads in terms of events that "weakened" and interventions that "repaired" the alliance. Even though all their supervisees had master's degrees in a mental health discipline, experience effects were found in the types of issues that were raised in supervision, as well as in the supervisee's approach to supervision. Less-experienced supervisees (i.e., 1 year or less of postdegree experience) raised issues that revolved around the development of professional skills (e.g., definitions of diagnostic terms, delivery of particular techniques). They also devoted considerable time to a single case, and often did not meet previously established supervision goals. However, more-experienced supervisees were more active in prioritizing the supervision agenda, and also tended to treat their supervisors more as consultants. When issues emerged, they tended to be around differences in theoretical orientation, presentation style, and treatment planning. The Burke et al. (1988) results, therefore, support several assumptions of developmental models of supervision.

Finally, an investigation conducted by Ladany et al. (2001) involved supervisees who were seeking master's degrees in counseling and supervisees seeking doctoral degrees in a mental health discipline. Ladany et al. sought to determine if general experience (i.e., length of time engaged in the practice of counseling) was related to cognitive complexity, or if number of clients seen was a better predictor. Results indicated that experience alone accounted for cognitive complexity around diagnostic and treatment conceptualization. Seeing a greater number of clients over a shorter time span did not produce similar gains in cognitive development. The authors hypothesized that too many clients may discourage the supervisee from reflective activity, or may mean that supervision is less intensive for any particular case, either of which might account for the diminished returns.

A final comment regarding experience is in order before we proceed. Most studies that demonstrate supervisee development over time have confounded experience with training. It is important, therefore, that some researchers have investigated post-training development (e.g., Cummings et al., 1990, Martin et al., 1989; Welfare & Borders, 2010b), as we presently have only modest evidence that experience alone leads to developmental gains. Yet the changes observed within trainees under supervision are promising, and provide evidence that supervision within training is of paramount importance and may serve as a catalyst for lifespan professional development, only to be enhanced by post-degree supervision.

Experience Level and Moderating Variables. We indicated earlier that cognitive complexity interacts with experience; that is, the trainee who has attained high conceptual ability advances more quickly. Winter and Holloway (1991) found that less-experienced trainees were more likely to focus on conceptualization of the client, whereas more-advanced trainees were more likely to focus on personal growth. Trainees with higher conceptual levels were more likely to request a focus on the development of counseling skills and to request feedback, thus indicating less concern about evaluation. Both level of experience and conceptual level (cognitive complexity), therefore, produced significant results in this study.

Swanson and O'Saben (1993) report that supervisees' Myers–Briggs Type Indicator (MBTI) profile, amount of practicum experience (ranging from prepracticum to 15 completed semesters of practicum), and type of program (i.e., counseling psychology, clinical psychology, or counselor education) all produced significant differences in terms of supervisee needs and expectations for supervision. Program membership was the least-dramatic predictor of differences, and level of experience produced the greatest differences. Level of experience differences produced results similar to other experience studies, indicating that supervisees with less experience expected more supervisor involvement, direction, and support.

Finally, whereas Granello (2002) found evidence of cognitive development with experience, she also found that program concentration was a moderating variable. Granello used an instrument that tapped Perry's (1970) model of cognitive development. As expected, beginning counselors-in-training demonstrated dualistic thinking, whereas more-advanced trainees demonstrated multiplistic thinking. (As in Perry's 1981 research, relativistic thinking was not demonstrated.) However, in contrast to students majoring in mental health counseling, rehabilitation counseling, or marriage and family therapy, students majoring in school counseling became *more* dualistic in their thinking over the course of their training, not less. Granello also found that experience in human services prior to the training program, age, or GPA accounted for no differences in cognitive complexity.

Supervision Environment. Much research interest has been shown in the relative importance of matching supervisee developmental level with the appropriate supervisory conditions, typically referred to as the *supervision environment.* The assumptions regarding the appropriate environment have been based primarily on the work of early counselor development theorists, especially Stoltenberg and his colleagues (Stoltenberg, 1981; Stoltenberg & Delworth, 1987; Stoltenberg & McNeill, 2010). As described earlier in this chapter, the model asserts that during the initial stages of supervision, the supervisee should be offered significant structure, direction, and support to assure movement in a positive direction. As supervisees gain some experience, expertise, and confidence, they are ready to have some of the structure diminished, to be challenged with alternative conceptualizations of the cases that they have been assigned, to be given technical guidance as needed, and to begin to look at personal issues that affect their work. In short, to accommodate the different developmental needs of supervisees, supervisors alter their interventions or the supervision environment.

By and large, research has supported, or partially supported, the supervision environment premises of counselor developmental models (Bear & Kivlighan, 1994; Borders & Usher, 1992; Dodenhoff, 1981; Fisher, 1989; Glidden & Tracey, 1992; Guest & Beutler, 1988; Heppner & Handley, 1982; Heppner & Roehlke, 1984; Holloway & Wampold, 1983; Jacobsen & Tanggaard, 2009; Krause & Allen, 1988; Lazar & Eisikovits, 1997; Miars, Tracey, Ray, Cornfield, O'Farrell, & Gelso, 1983; Murray, Portman, & Maki, 2003; Rabinowitz, Heppner, & Roehlke, 1986; Reising & Daniels, 1983; Stoltenberg, Pierce, & McNeill, 1987; Usher & Borders, 1993; Wetchler, 1989; Wiley & Ray, 1986; Williams et al., 1997; Winter & Holloway, 1991; Worthington & Stern, 1985). The questions that have driven this body of research include: Has the matching of environment to development level of supervisee significantly enhanced supervisee learning, and do supervisees prefer a supervision environment that is developmentally appropriate?

The assumptions underlying these questions have received some support, although there certainly have been mixed results when the literature is examined closely. A study conducted by Ladany, Walker, and Melincoff (2001) produced results that challenged developmental models. As part of their research, Ladany et al. hypothesized that a relatively low level of cognitive complexity, limited experience, and unfamiliarity with a particular type of client would lead supervisees to seek supervision that was more task focused. Instead, they found that all supervisees wanted supervisors to be moderately high on all supervision environments. Ladany et al. concluded that "the theoretical assumption that beginning supervisees need more structure is an overgeneralization or a misguided view based more on clinical lore than on research, which specifically attends to changes in trainees' conceptual understanding of clients" (p. 215). Jacobsen and Tanggaard (2009) found that the subjects in their qualitative study reflected the assumptions of developmental models by and large. However, they also note that major individual differences emerged. Specifically, some novice supervisees found the frustration they encountered when not being offered as much advice and guidance as they wished from their supervisors, and the manner in which they handled that frustration, ended up being among their most memorable learning experiences in supervision. Sumerel and Borders (1996) also found that, contrary to assumptions of developmental models that novice supervisees are reluctant to discuss their personal issues and that supervision should focus on techniques and didactic information, the subjects in their study showed no significant difference when compared to more advanced trainees. These authors concluded that it may not be the supervision environment (intervention) per se that matters, but the style of delivery. Although inexperienced supervisees are expected to find a focus on personal issues to be less helpful, Sumerel and Borders suggest that, when this is done in a manner that is warm, supportive, and instructional, supervisees can benefit. Barrett and Barber (2005), however, argue that the novice supervisee's inability to integrate emotional experience in a way that promotes growth is more to the point. Such integration takes insight and tolerance for ambiguity, both signs that the counselor has reached a higher level of development.

Despite arguments to the contrary, it seems that moderating variables operate to change the needs of trainees, making them occasionally inconsistent with the assumptions of developmental models. A case in point is an interesting study conducted by Tracey et al. (1989), in which they considered the interaction of level of experience (beginning or advanced counseling psychology doctoral students), reactance potential (an individual's need to resist or comply with imposed structure), supervision structure (low structure or high structure), and content of supervision (crisis or non-crisis) using Brehm's (1966) concept of reactance potential. The authors found that advanced trainees with high reactance (i.e., high need to resist structure) preferred supervision with less structure than did advanced trainees with low reactance. In non-crisis situations, beginning trainees preferred structured supervision, whereas more experienced trainees preferred less structure. However, in crisis situations, *all* trainees preferred structured supervision, regardless of their level of experience or reactance.

This last finding is reinforced by Zarski, Sand-Pringle, Pannell, and Lindon (1995), who note that supervision must be modified based on the severity of individual cases. For supervisees working with difficult or volatile situations (e.g., family violence), more structure may be needed for advanced supervisees until they have attained a necessary level of comfort and competence. Similarly, when Wetchler and Vaughn (1992) surveyed marriage and family therapists at multiple levels, supervisor directiveness was the most frequently identified supervisor skill that therapists thought enhanced their development. This result may indicate that more advanced supervisees take more difficult cases to supervision, thus requiring more direction from the supervisor around these identified cases.

In summary, although supervisors seem to offer different environments when supervisees' developmental differences are pronounced, empirical findings do not as yet support some of the finer distinctions made by developmental theorists. It is difficult to determine if the problem is in the design of particular studies or with the developmental models themselves (Ellis & Ladany, 1997). It is important to recall, however, that development is multifaceted, and the ability to address different levels of competence at any one point in the supervision process is challenging indeed. In addition, we do not know what stage of development might take precedence at any measuring point. It is likely that supervisees master particular aspects of the therapeutic process, thus reflecting more advanced developmental characteristics around these, while still faltering with other aspects of skill development. One group of supervisees, therefore, may represent several levels of development when measured on one variable; if multiple variables are considered, each supervisee may offer a developmental profile in which the supervisee is more advanced on some variables than on others, consistent with development as proposed by Stoltenberg and McNeill (2010). If differing developmental levels require different supervision interventions, each supervisee may need a variety of interventions offered in a discriminating fashion. In short, it is probably best if the supervisor considers both development and environment to be dynamic and fluid, requiring astute observation and flexibility during all levels of training and for post-training supervision as well.

Implications of Research. As noted earlier, although there is still much about developmental models that we do not know, there is a body of research that informs us to some extent. We conclude this section by highlighting some of those findings as well as report the assessment of others regarding research on developmental models.

- *Cognitive complexity matters.* High cognitive complexity (or conceptual level) is an important predictor of success for key counseling tasks, such as offering increased empathy (Deal, 2003; Stoppard & Miller, 1985) and developing accurate conceptualizations of client situations (Martin et al., 1989). Supervisees with low cognitive complexity need assistance in forming cognitive maps that can be used to assess client issues and in goal setting and strategy selection. Supervision interventions that challenge these supervisees to conceptualize in highly abstract ways will be counterproductive.

Supervisees with high cognitive complexity appear more confident and ask for more feedback to improve counseling skills, and thus seemingly are less concerned about evaluation. It is likely that the process of counseling is more exciting to supervisees with high cognitive complexity because they are able to produce and weigh more options and choose the most appropriate intervention (Gordon, 1990; Holloway & Wampold, 1986).

• *Experience under supervision matters.* Because of the field-specific nature of conceptual level, Stoltenberg (1981) and Blocher (1983) are among those who initially suggested that, at least for novices, experience and conceptual level are highly correlated. Indeed, they suggest that it is possible to predict conceptual level from experience. It is not surprising, then, that much of the development of clinical supervision practice has been informed by this assumption.

Although we have a substantial body of research that supports the claim that supervised experience results in developmental advances for supervisees, the research has its critics (e.g., Ellis & Ladany, 1997). As discussed earlier, the discourse regarding the relative strength of experience to increase the supervisee's competence has become more complicated and more interesting.

• *Experience may be trumped by circumstances.* As discussed earlier, despite the fact that research suggests consistently that the more advanced supervisee wants or requires less structure in supervision, several variables can change this prediction, including a crisis situation (Tracey et al., 1989) or a particularly difficult client population (Zarski et al., 1995). This leads us to the conclusion that supervision of an advanced supervisee is more idiosyncratic than supervision of a novice supervisee. In other words, the novice supervisee most likely needs some structure across his or her client load, whereas the advanced supervisee may benefit from more autonomy with some clients, more structure with others, support with difficult clients, and challenge with those clients who may push the supervisee's personal buttons.

• *Experience level is typically paired with certain developmental characteristics. Supervisors should know these.* With experience, the supervisee should exhibit an increase in: (a) self-awareness of behavior and motivation within counseling sessions, (b) consistency in the execution of counseling interventions, and (c) autonomy (Borders, 1990; McNeill et al., 1992). If these developmental characteristics are not forthcoming, supervisors must ask what might be blocking learning (e.g., cognitive complexity, intrapersonal issues, cultural insensitivity on the part of the supervisor) and to consider this more carefully.

With experience, it is expected that supervisees will develop more sophisticated ways to conceptualize the counseling process and the issues that their clients present, and be less distracted by random specific information (Cummings et al., 1990). Novice supervisees are more rigid and less discriminating in their delivery of therapeutic interventions. An *exaggerated forcefulness* (Tracey et al., 1988) in the delivery of an intervention may indicate that the supervisee is at the front end of a learning curve regarding this intervention. A hallmark of more advanced supervisees is that they are more flexible and less dominant when delivering interventions such as confrontation or addressing cultural differences in counseling.

• *Supervision environment matters.* Supervisee characteristics and developmental agendas must be met with appropriate supervisor interventions in order for growth to occur. Although there are a plethora of supervision techniques to consider, these must be used in ways that are appropriate to the developmental stage of the supervisee. To date, the research supports using experience level as a determinant for supervision environment, at least initially. At the same time, research has found that it is overly simplistic to view experience level as a sole criterion for intervention.

- *Development only begins during formal training; it doesn't end there.* In their seminal longitudinal study of professional development (Skovholt & Rønnestad, 1992a) and in a more recent reformulation (Rønnestad & Skovholt, 2003), Skovholt and Rønnestad established that development for the mental health professional was a long road, with many intriguing complexities along the way. They also established that most of the development for serious professionals occurred after formal training. Similarly, Granello's study (2002) found that counselor (cognitive) development occurred only in the latter half of training programs. All this underscores the importance of clinical supervision beyond training and the early years in the field.

As a concluding comment about the research focused on developmental models, Stoltenberg et al. (1994) assert: "[E]vidence appears solid for developmental changes across training levels" (p. 419). They also note that, whereas experience alone is a relatively crude measure of "development," it has been used in most studies. For this reason and given that most of this research had focused on a restricted range of experience (e.g., first practicum versus second practicum versus internship), Stoltenberg and colleagues found that "it is remarkable that so many differences have been found among trainees based on this categorization" (p. 419).

Yet Ellis and Ladany (1997), echoing Holloway's (1987) conclusion a decade earlier, characterize their rigorous review of the developmental literature as "disheartening." In particular, they found that methodological problems and failures to eliminate rival hypotheses have so characterized this area of research that "data from these studies are largely uninterpretable" (p. 474).

Probably the safest conclusion at this point is that there is some evidence to support some aspects of stage developmental models. Furthermore, anecdotal reports of untold numbers of supervisors attest to professional development of their supervisees, even if this development does not fall in line with development as it has been conceived. Additional research in this area of supervision is sorely needed.

Conclusions about Developmental Models

Development is endemic to supervision. If supervisors did not believe that supervisee development would occur under supervision, then supervision would be reduced to its gatekeeping function only. Therefore, despite one's primary approach to supervision, all supervisors share some assumptions with those who have focused on supervisee development. The advantage of working primarily from developmental models is that it keeps the supervisor attuned to the different needs of supervisees at different levels in their training. Because developmental models are pantheoretical, the supervisee is not asked to commit to a particular psychotherapy theory too early in the training process.

Potential disadvantages of adhering primarily to developmental models is their relative weakness in describing different learning styles within any stage of development, as well as their relative silence about divergent learning paths. Discussions of supervision environments needed at different levels of experience also give inadequate attention to cultural differences among supervisees.

SUPERVISION PROCESS MODELS

Our final major category of models is supervision process models. These models emerged from an interest in supervision as an educational and relationship process. In fact, although it represents somewhat of an overstatement, one way to describe the three major categories of supervision models is that psychotherapy-based models are primarily centered around passing on one therapy approach, developmental models are centered on the intricacies of the learning process for the supervisee, whereas supervision process models primarily step back to observe the supervision process itself. These models can be either simple or complex, depending on how much of the process they attempt to describe as well as how many systemic levels. We describe four supervision process models: the discrimination model (Bernard, 1979, 1997); the Ladany, Friedlander, and Nelson (2005) model that focuses on critical events; the Hawkins and Shohet (2000) model; and Holloway's (1995) systems approach to supervision.

The Discrimination Model

Bernard's (1979, 1997) discrimination model (DM) is often considered one of the most accessible models of clinical supervision. It was created in the mid-1970s to assist supervisors-in-training to discriminate among the various choices they had when choosing how to interact with their supervisees. The DM is an eclectic model with the virtues both of parsimony and versatility. It is often the first model novice supervisors encounter.

The DM attends to three separate foci for supervision as well as three supervisor roles:

Foci—Supervisors might focus on any or all of a supervisee's following skills:

- *Intervention*—what the supervisee is doing in the session that is observable by the supervisor, what skill levels are being demonstrated, how well counseling interventions are delivered, and so on
- *Conceptualization*—how the supervisee understands what is occurring in the session, identifies patterns, or chooses interventions, all of which are covert processes
- *Personalization*—how the supervisee interfaces a personal style with counseling at the same time that he or she attempts to keep counseling uncontaminated by personal issues and countertransference responses

Lanning (1986) adds a fourth focus area to the DM, that of *professional issues*. This added focus area is helpful for supervisors when monitoring their supervisees beyond their counseling interactions with clients.

Roles —Once supervisors have made a judgment about their supervisee's abilities within each focus area, they must choose a role or posture to accomplish their supervision goals. These roles change the manner in which the supervisee is approached by the supervisor. These roles include

- *Teacher*—a role assumed when the supervisor believes that the supervisee needs structure and includes instruction, modeling, and giving direct feedback
- *Counselor*—a role assumed when the supervisor wishes to enhance supervisee reflectivity, especially about their internal reality rather than cognitions
- *Consultant*—a more collegial role assumed when the supervisor wishes for supervisees to trust their own insights and feelings about their work, or when the supervisor believes it is important to challenge supervisees to think and act on their own

As a consequence, the supervisor might be responding at any given moment in one of nine different ways (i.e., 3 roles $\times$ 3 foci). Table 3 illustrates how the model might operate in practice. We should note, however, that it is unlikely that the cells of this table are used uniformly. For example, the teacher role for a focus on personalization issues is less likely than the counselor role for personalization issues. However, there are instances when any of the nine choices are the best fit for the supervision task, and supervisors should consider all choices.

The model is *situation specific,* meaning that the supervisor's roles and foci should change not only across sessions, but also *within* a session. Supervisors should attend to each focus as appropriate. The problems arise either when the supervisor attends to one focus at the expense of the supervisee's more salient needs or, in a more-related version, when the supervisor is rigid in a

TABLE 3 Examples of Focus and Role Intersections of Bernard's Discrimination Model

FOCUS OF SUPERVISION	*Teacher*	*Counselor*	*Consultant*
Intervention	Supervisee struggles to exhibit immediacy with clients	Supervisee appears unable to challenge one of her clients	Supervisee is intrigued by the prospect of using music in his counseling with middle-school children
	Supervisor not only models how the supervisee might use immediacy with one of supervisee's clients, but models immediacy in the supervision session	Supervisor asks supervisee to reflect on the fact that she communicates a desire to help her client, but is not doing what is needed for the client to achieve insight and change behavior	Supervisor provides supervisee with the resources for using art forms in child counseling, and offers to help him brainstorm how he might apply what he has learned to his counseling
Conceptualization	Supervisee does not identify the crux of the client's presenting concern	Supervisee assesses a young Black male client at a drug rehab unit as being hostile and resistant	Supervisee shares that he would like to know more about Motivational Interviewing (MI)
	Supervisor requires the supervisee to prepare a transcript of the session and uses it to review client statements, identifying the statements that are directly related to the client's presenting concern and those that are not	Supervisor reflects the supervisee's fears in working with this client as one intervention to help the supervisee understand what is blocking her empathy for her client, and thus making it unlikely that she will understand his behavior within a larger systemic context	Supervisor assists the supervisee in identifying resources and also discusses the possibility of using some of the principles of MI in goal setting for one of his clients
Personalization	Supervisee treats his older female client in a manner that the supervisor finds condescending	Supervisee's desire to avoid making any mistakes leaves her distant and overcontrolling in her counseling sessions	Supervisee shares that she is attracted to one of her clients
	Supervisor reviews videotape of session with supervisee and gives him feedback about one such exchange, pointing out how this is different from his usual demeanor	Supervisor reflects the supervisee's feelings of anxiety and need to be perfect, and asks supervisee to consider how her needs and the behaviors that follow might be affecting her clients	Supervisor offers herself as a sounding board for the supervisee while communicating assurance that the supervisee is handling the issue appropriately and professionally

preference for one particular focus or role. There are many reasons to choose a particular focus or role, but the worst reason is habit or personal preference independent of the supervisee's needs.

Theory and research concerning developmental approaches suggest that supervisors are more likely to use the teaching role with novice supervisees and the consultant role with those who are more advanced. Also, supervisors of beginning supervisees might expect to focus primarily on intervention and conceptual skills, whereas supervisors of more advanced students might expect to spend more of their time focusing on personalization issues.

However, these are general predictions of what a supervisor might do. Bernard (1979, 1997) argues that the effective supervisor is prepared to use all roles and address all foci for supervisees at any level. Still, it is important for supervisors to be aware that too early a focus on personalization may "freeze" one novice supervisee, and too constant a focus on interventions may bore another novice supervisee. The model is only the beginning of truly discriminating supervision.

Russell, Crimmings, and Lent (1984) correctly note that very little research has tested models of supervision that suggest supervisor roles. Their observation remains true today. However, a strength of the DM is that it is among the most researched of these models. A number of studies either explicitly have tested the DM or used it as a way to frame research questions (e.g., Ellis & Dell, 1986; Ellis, Dell, & Good, 1988; Glidden & Tracey, 1992; Goodyear et al., 1984; Goodyear & Robyak, 1982; Lazovsky & Shimoni, 2007; Luke, Ellis, & Bernard, 2011; Stenack & Dye, 1982; Yager, Wilson, Brewer, & Kinnetz, 1989). The model seems generally to have been supported in the various findings of the research to date.

Interestingly, the role of consultant has remained somewhat elusive in these studies. For example, Goodyear et al. (1984) found that a sample of experienced supervisors was able to differentiate among the supervision sessions of four major psychotherapy theorists according to their use of the teacher and counselor roles, but not the consultant role. Similarly, the counselor and teacher roles were validated, but the consultant role was not, in a factor analytic study by Stenack and Dye (1982). In multidimensional scaling studies by Ellis and Dell (1986) and Glidden and Tracey (1992), the teaching and counseling roles were found to anchor opposite ends of a single dimension; the consultant role did not emerge clearly from their data.

This is curious, because the idea of the consultant role for supervisors is intuitively appealing, especially in work with more advanced supervisees. One possible explanation is that the consultant role is "fuzzier" than the others. Although it is frequently endorsed, there is not the common understanding of it that is true of the counselor and teacher roles. In addition, supervisors may indeed find it more difficult than they espouse to remain outside of their *expert* or *therapist* status. Both teacher or counselor postures may be more inherently familiar to supervisors than that of consultant.

Styles versus Roles. Friedlander and Ward (1984) equated supervisory styles with supervisory roles. In fact, their Supervisory Styles Inventory (SSI) measures three styles that correspond roughly to Bernard's three roles (i.e., teacher—task oriented; consultant—attractive; and counselor—interpersonally sensitive). The fairly substantial literature on the SSI therefore reasonably can be understood to have clear implications for the DM as well.

Hart and Nance (2003) offer a framework of supervisory styles that could be understood according to a 2 (high versus low direction) by 2 (high versus low support) framework. That framework, depicted in Table 4, is a potentially useful way to consider supervisory roles. In this framework, there are two variants of the teacher role: although they can be differentiated from one another by their level of support, both are high in direction. In contrast, the other two of the DM's roles are characterized by low direction, although the counselor role has high support and the

TABLE 4 Hart and Nance's Framework for Supervisory Styles

	HIGH SUPPORT	LOW SUPPORT
High Direction	Supportive Teacher	Directive or Expert Teacher
Low Direction	Counselor	Consultant

consultant role low support. Interestingly, these researchers found that supervisors tended to approach supervision with a goal of being high on support but low on direction; their supervisees (fourth-semester master's students), however, approached supervision hoping that their supervisors would be high on support and high on direction. These conflicting agendas may also add some insight into the mixed results regarding the consultant posture within the DM.

In summary, the DM has been adopted widely by supervisors primarily as a tool to consider options within the supervision process. It also provides language to describe supervision that is helpful for novice supervisors and their supervisees alike (Ellis, 2010). Finally, the DM offers supervisors a relatively straightforward way to assess both successful and unsuccessful supervision interactions and identify, if needed, a different focus/role combination for a subsequent supervision session.

Events-Based Supervision Model

Ladany, Friedlander, and Nelson's (2005) Events-Based Model (EBM) is grounded in the premise that most supervision focuses on the "smaller" events in the supervisee's work. They focus on the supervisor's handing of specific events as they occur, drawing on the strategy of task analysis used by some psychotherapy researchers (e.g., Greenberg, 1984). It is because of their focus on task analysis rather than a sole emphasis on the reflective process that we place the model here rather than as a developmental model.

An event has an identifiable beginning, middle, and end. Although it often occurs within a particular session, it might also extend across sessions. In addition, there can be events within events. In all cases, however, an event begins with a *Marker*. This can be the supervisee's overt request for a specific kind of help, or it might be subtler and something the supervisor notices. Markers span all areas of supervisee development, including skill deficits, intrapersonal issues, and issues specific to supervision. Furthermore, Markers may point to more than one issue.

> *Although different Markers suggest similar problems, different problems can manifest themselves with similar Markers. As an example, role conflict . . . can be marked by prolonged silence or missed appointments. These same Markers might also reflect the supervisee's crisis in confidence . . . [T]he Marker phase of the event continues until it is clear to the supervisor precisely what needs addressing* (Ladany et al., 2005, p. 14).

Once the Marker has been assessed, supervision shifts to the *Task Environment,* which might consist of any number of what Ladany et al. (2005) refer to as *interaction sequences.* These are "comprised of various supervisor operations (interventions or strategies) and supervisee performances or reactions" (p. 14). Depending on the situation, these interaction sequences might include, but are not limited to: (a) focus on the supervisory alliance; (b) focus on therapeutic process; (c) exploration of feelings; (d) focus on countertransference; (e) attention to parallel process; (f) focus on self-efficacy; (g) focus on skill; (h) assessment of knowledge; (i) focus on multicultural awareness; and (j) focus on evaluation.

Any given Task Environment is likely to involve the use of multiple interaction sequences. Ladany et al. (2005) gave the example of the Marker as the supervisee reporting feelings of sexual attraction for the client, and then suggest, "The Task Environment proceeds through four stages: (a) exploration of feelings, (b) focus on the supervisory alliance, (c) normalizing experience, and (d) exploration of countertransference" (pp. 16–17).

Although many types of events can become the focus of supervision, Ladany et al. focused on the seven they believe occur most commonly, devoting one chapter to each: (a) remediating skill difficulties/deficits; (b) heightening multicultural awareness; (c) negotiating role conflicts; (d) working through countertransference; (e) managing sexual attraction; (f) repairing gender-related misunderstandings; and (g) addressing problematic thoughts, feelings, behaviors (e.g., crisis in confidence, vicarious traumatization, impairment).

The progression of the supervisory event depends on such factors as the supervisee's readiness to address the issue, his or her level of development, the supervisor's interventions, and the supervisee's response to them. The end point is the *Resolution,* which Ladany et al. suggest is ideally an increase in one or more of the following: supervisee knowledge, supervisee skills, supervisee self-awareness, or supervisory alliance.

In summary, the Events-Based Model offers rich opportunities for the supervisor to identify supervisee struggles and multifaceted avenues for intervention. Also, it labels many of the particular crises of personalization only alluded to globally in the Discrimination Model. Furthermore, whereas the DM attends only to the supervisor approach in a one-approach-per-incident manner, the EBM does more to explain the multiple steps required to resolve any supervision critical event. This model, then, is particularly helpful when an issue emerges that is derailing the supervisee's development.

The Hawkins and Shohet Model

The orienting metaphor for Hawkins and Shohet (2006) is that of the "good enough" supervisor. The supervisor is there not only to offer support and reassurance, but also to contain the otherwise overwhelming affective responses the supervisee might have. Theirs is a Supervision Process Model that includes not only the supervisory dyad in their schema, but organizational and social contexts as well. Hawkins and Shohet also devote relatively more attention to the focus of supervision than to supervision roles or styles. Although theirs is clearly a supervision process model, much of their description of key supervisory moments reflects a psychodynamic theoretical orientation.

Hawkins and Shohet (2006) developed seven possible supervisory phenomena on which supervisors might focus at any given moment. This, which they describe colorfully as the *seven-eyed model of supervision,* is depicted in Figure 5. They refer to theirs as being a *double-matrix model* that reflects two primary ways that supervisors conduct supervision. The first is to pay attention to the supervisee–client matrix; the second is to attend to this matrix through the supervisee–supervisor matrix using immediacy techniques. These two matrices exist within wider contexts that impinge on and have the power to alter them. The seven eyes, then, are the choices (modes) by which the supervisor navigates the different relationships and perspective within each matrix.

Mode 1: Focus on the client and what and how they present. Attention to the supervisee's narrative about the phenomena of the therapy session, including clients' verbal and nonverbal behaviors; examining how material from one session is related to that of other sessions.

Mode 2: Exploration of the strategies and interventions used by the supervisee. Attention to the supervisee's interventions with clients.

Mode 3: Focusing on the relationship between the client and the supervisee. Attention to the system the supervisee and client create together, rather than on either as an individual.

Mode 4: Focusing on the supervisee. Attention to the internal processes of the supervisee, especially countertransference, and their effects on the counseling.

Mode 5: Focusing on the supervisory relationship. Attention to parallel processes as well as all ways that the supervisor can model what he or she is expecting of the supervisee.

Mode 6: The supervisor focusing on his or her own process. Attention to the supervisor's own countertransference reactions to the supervisee.

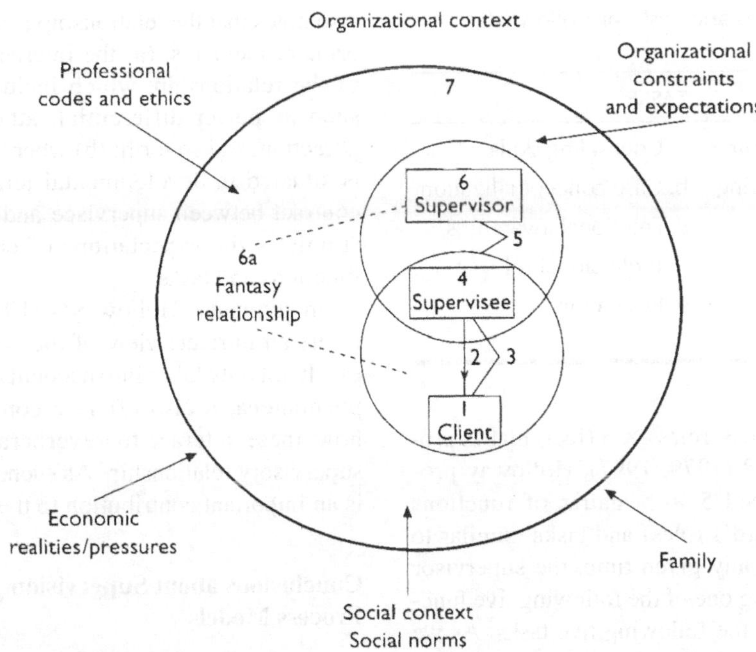

FIGURE 5 Seven-Eyed Model of Supervision

Source: From *Supervision in the Helping Professions, Third Edition,* by P. Hawkins & R. Shohet, 2006. London, UK: McGraw-Hill Education/Open University Press. Reprinted by permission.

Mode 6a: The supervisor–client relationship. Attention to fantasies the supervisor and client have about one another.

Mode 7: Focusing on the wider context. Attention to the professional community of which the supervisor and supervisee are members. This includes the organization in which they work, as well as their profession. Hawkins and Shohet then stipulated that this mode includes considerations of the context of each person in the supervisory system (i.e., client, supervisee, and supervisor) as well as the context of each relationship and that of the supervisee's work in the context of his or her profession and organization of employment or training.

Attention to focus is central to the Hawkins and Shohet model. It is not, however, the only feature of the model. In addition, they introduce five factors that serve as an additional layer to their model: (a) the style or role of the supervisor; (b) the stage of development of the supervisee; (c) the counseling orientation of both the supervisor and supervisee; (d) the supervisor–supervisee contract; and (e) the setting, or what we would call *modality* (e.g., individual, group).

The Hawkins and Shohet model provides a more expansive picture of supervision and their factors include references to both theory and development. The strength of this model is its delineation of seven distinct entry points for the supervisor to consider when conducting supervision.

The Systems Approach to Supervision Model

Like Hawkins and Shohet, Holloway's Systems Approach to Supervision (SAS) model offers a more faceted view of supervision. Unlike Hawkins and Shohet, Holloway does more to weave together her various model elements to portray the systemic reality that each element is related to all others in a cybernetic fashion.

TABLE 5 Functions and Tasks of Holloway's SAS Model

FUNCTIONS	TASKS
1. Advising/instructing	a. Counseling skills
2. Supporting/sharing	b. Case conceptualization
3. Consulting	c. Emotional awareness
4. Modeling	d. Professional role
5. Monitoring/ Evaluating	e. Evaluation

Rather than the 3 (roles) × 3 (foci) matrix proposed by Bernard (1979, 1997), Holloway provided an expanded 5 × 5 matrix of functions (similar to Bernard's roles) and tasks (similar to foci). That is, at any given time, the supervisor may be performing one of the following five functions with one of the following five tasks. As we noted previously regarding Bernard's model, Holloway (1997) commented that "hypothetically a supervisor may engage in any [task] with any [function, but] . . . realistically there probably are some task and function matches that are more likely to occur in supervision" (p. 258). Functions and tasks of the SAS model are listed in Table 5.

Functions and tasks are but two of the seven components of the SAS model. Four of the components are what Holloway terms *contextual factors,* which include not only the three principals in the supervisory relationship (the supervisor, the supervisee, and the client), but the institutional context in which supervision is occurring as well. For the persons involved, these factors can include personal history, cultural dimensions, professional training for the therapist and supervisor, and, for the client, the identified problem. For the institution, *context* includes things like organizational structure and work environment.

The seventh component of the SAS model, the *supervision relationship,* is placed at the core of the model. Thus, Holloway proposes that the relationship is the most important aspect of supervision and it is within the supervisory relationship that all other components are experienced. She also notes that the relationship is affected by three primary elements: (a) the interpersonal structure of the relationship, which includes dimensions such as power differential, attachment issues, attraction, and so forth; (b) where the relationship is situated in developmental terms; and (c) the contract between supervisee and supervisor that stipulates the expectations of each in terms of functions and tasks.

In summary, Holloway's (1995) SAS model offers an intricate view of the supervision process. It not only takes into account a number of key phenomena, it also offers a conceptual map of how these interact to reverberate through the supervisory relationship. As such, the SAS model is an important contribution to the literature.

Conclusions about Supervision Process Models

Supervision process models add more description about the supervision process than do models in the other two principal categories of models. Whether simple or complex, their contribution is, in part, the fact that they can be used within any psychotherapy theory orientation, and are also compatible with developmental models. Process models are also valuable to the supervisor because they counteract stagnation by giving the supervisor a new lens to use in deconstructing supervision.

Although we believe process models are valuable tools, they could be criticized for not placing adequate attention on theory or, for that matter, development. However, these criticisms are only of concern if the supervisor adhered to a supervision process model only.

This discussion of supervision process models completes the triangle of theory, development, and process that most supervisors consult in developing their own supervision approach. As we stated at the outset of this chapter, although most supervisors identify more strongly with one category than the others, it is likely that their supervision is influenced by the other two. It is perhaps for this reason that what we discuss as combined models have been proposed by some authors.

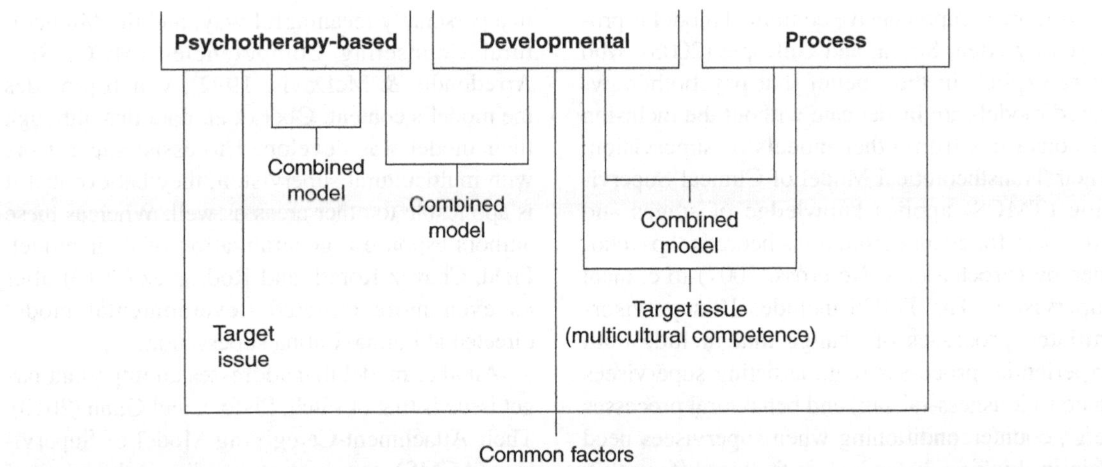

FIGURE 6 Examples of Second-Generation Supervision Models

SECOND-GENERATION MODELS OF SUPERVISION

Because therapy and supervision are so closely linked, developments in psychotherapy theory inevitably will affect supervision models (cf. Milne, 2006). Psychotherapy theory itself is changing. Almost none of the larger-than-life proponents of their own psychotherapy theories are still living. A decade ago, Norcross (Lilienfeld & Norcross, 2003) observed that there is not a new generation of "giants" to replace persons like Rogers, Perls, Bateson, and Haley. Instead, we are in a second or even third generation of psychotherapies, and these tend to be more integrative and evidence-based than the first generation. Norcross concluded that this follows the predictable evolution of a science-practitioner field.

In a similar fashion, the discipline of supervision appears to have settled in with three major categories of supervision models. Those models that have been proposed in more recent years are either models that combine aspects of models from the primary groups or are models with a particular target for supervision. A third second-generation group is made up of those models that attempt to identify common factors that cross all models. Figure 6 depicts the relationship of second-generation models to the original three categories.

Combined Models

Combined models are either relatively simply or highly complex. Pearson (2006) proposes a blending of the Discrimination Model with psychotherapy-based models demonstrating how this would be operationalized for CBT, humanistic, and systems-based supervision. James, Milne, Marie-Blackburn, and Armstrong (2006) suggest a particular emphasis on Vygotsky's (1978) Zone of Proximal Development to enhance CBT supervision, thus blending constructs from psychotherapy-based supervision and developmental supervision. Callaghan (2006) combines behavioral supervision with an interpersonally based approach to form Functional Analytic Supervision, a model that draws primarily from within the psychotherapy-based supervision category. Young, Lambie, and Thurston-Dyer (2011) offer a model that infuses the concepts of reflectivity into Stoltenberg and McNeill's (2010) IDM, thus offering a combined model within the developmental camp.

A more comprehensive combined model is proposed by Aten, Strain, and Gillespie (2008), who were explicit in their belief that psychotherapy-based models are inadequate without the inclusion of constructs from other models of supervision. Their Transtheoretical Model of Clinical Supervision (TMCS) applies knowledge of stages and processes for change from transtheoretical psychotherapy (Prochaska & Norcross, 2007) to clinical supervision. The TMCS includes 10 supervisor-initiated processes of change that include both experiential processes (e.g., assisting supervisees in consciousness-raising) and behavioral processes (e.g., counterconditioning when supervisees need help in thinking, behaving, or feeling differently). By combining elements from various perspectives, Aten et al. hope to offer supervisors a model that meets most—if not all—supervision needs. To this point, they suggest that, because of its complexity, their model can be used to address diversity issues more successfully than others.

Target Issue Models

Another indication that we are well within the second generation of supervision model development is the appearance of models that target a particular supervision issue. Because more-generic models are well established, these newer models can draw from them as needed, yet also apply developments from supervision research or place in the foreground a critical issue for successful supervision.

One target issue model was developed by Ober, Granello, and Henfield (2009) to address multicultural competence among supervisees. Their Synergistic Model for Multicultural Supervision (SMMS) draws from three sources to provide a structure for process and content of supervision. The first of the three is Bloom's Taxonomy (Bloom, Engelhart, Hurst, Hill, & Krathwohl, 1956), a model to promote cognitive development; the second is the Heuristic Model of Nonoppressive Interpersonal Development (HMNID; Ancis & Ladany, 2001), which assists supervisees in learning about multiculturalism and relevant skills in a personally meaningful way; and the Multicultural Counseling Competencies (MCC; Sue, Arredondo, & McDavis, 1992), which provides the model's content. Ober et al. note that although their model was developed to assist supervisors with multicultural supervision, they believe that it is applicable to other areas as well. Whereas these authors espouse a generalization of their model, Field, Chavez-Korell, and Rodriguez (2010) offer an even more targeted developmental model directed at Latina–Latina supervision.

Another model that addresses an important target issue is that of Fitch, Pistole, and Gunn (2010). Their Attachment-Caregiving Model of Supervision (ACMS) stresses the centrality of the relationship to supervision. Specifically, the ACMS describes the normative activation of supervisees' attachment systems and the necessary deactivation in order for supervisees to explore new learning. Within their model, the supervisors provide the necessary safe haven through their responsiveness and flexibility, and later as an anchor and source of guidance for the supervisee once they have arrived at a secure base in the relationship. Fitch et al. assert that their model is additive and designed to be used with other supervision approaches.

Combined models of supervision and target issue models are a predictable development in the evolution of clinical supervision and continue to appear in the professional literature. They enhance our understanding of the primary categories from which they draw, and they have the capacity to spotlight essential components of the supervision process. As such, they represent an important contribution and, we suspect, will be a growing phenomenon.

We end this discussion of second-generation models by considering common-factors models. Authors of these models attempted a different sort of analysis—that of finding themes that cut across all extant models.

Common-Factors Models

Although there is frequent reference to similarities among supervision approaches, there is little published literature on the topic. Because a common-factors approach is another avenue for working across model categories, we cover the two published contributions here. We also refer the reader to Milne, Aylott, Fitzpatrick, and Ellis (2008), who offer a complex best-evidence synthesis derived from supervision research since the late 1980s to construct a model based on common factors.

Lampropoulos (2003) uses the broad conceptualization of human change encounters to identify common factors in supervision that parallel those in counseling and teaching and, in fact, all human relationships that are hierarchical and where some *deficiency* (i.e., for supervision, lack of mastery of counseling skills) is evident. Lampropoulos proposes the following common factors:

- *The supervision relationship,* which includes facilitative conditions for the supervisee and adjustment of the relationship to attend to the supervisees' needs; establishing a working alliance; and readiness to attend to transference and countertransference issues.
- *Support and relief from tension, anxiety, and distress,* which alerts that, although supervisees are different from each other, all experience some anxiety because of their lack of expertise, which must be woven into a supervision agenda.
- *Instillation of hope and raising of expectations,* which includes not only encouragement, but also setting attainable goals and normalizing developmental challenges that supervisees face.
- *Self-exploration, awareness, and insight,* which Lampropoulos notes is crucial for supervisee development.
- *Theoretical rationale and a ritual,* which simply is a testament that all supervision models include a philosophy or theory and a methodology for implementing the model.
- *Exposure and confrontation of problems,* which points to the inevitability that learning the complex set of skills required for counseling includes rough patches.
- *Acquisition and testing of new learning,* which is, of course, the purpose of all clinical supervision.
- *Mastery of the new knowledge,* which is a final step in order for supervisees to attain self-efficacy as a counselor. This final factor is one that supervisors monitor carefully in light of other factors (e.g., anxiety), and repeat often as new skills and reflective abilities emerge.

Morgan and Sprenkle (2007) conducted a comprehensive review of supervision models in the mental health professional literatures and identified several domains (objectives) that cut across models as well as 48 broad categories of supervision activity. *Domains* include assisting supervisees with the development of clinical skills, acquiring clinical knowledge, learning to function as a professional, personal growth, and achieving some level of autonomy and confidence. Another important domain of supervision models is monitoring and evaluating supervisees. Morgan and Sprenkle identify three constructs that capture the variability of model domains and activities. All three are described as *continua.* The first of these is *emphasis,* with models falling somewhere on a continuum from an *emphasis on clinical competence* (and virtually no emphasis on professional competence) to an *emphasis on professional competence* (with little emphasis on clinical competence). The second construct is *specificity,* with the opposing ends of the continuum being *the idiosyncratic/the particular* and the other end being *nomothetic/general.* The authors describe these extremes as a focus on one supervisee only and his or her clients on one end of the continuum, and the welfare of the profession as a whole on the other. The third construct identified was *relationship,* and the two poles are *collaborative* and *directive.*

Morgan and Sprenkle derived four supervisor roles based on the *specificity* and *emphasis* dimensions of a model: *Coach* (high clinical competence and idiosyncratic emphases); *Mentor* (high professional competence and idiosyncratic emphases); *Teacher* (high clinical competence and general emphases); and *Administrator* (high professional competence and general emphases). This three-dimensional model offers supervisors a template to assess their own supervision model and appreciate their alternatives.

Evidence-Based Supervision

Evidence-based supervision derives its mandate from evidence-based psychotherapy, which is a call to design therapeutic approaches to reflect research that supports their efficacy. Who, after all, could argue otherwise? When we see our physicians, we want to believe that they are making decisions based on the best available evidence. And the people who seek our services as mental health professionals expect the same.

But matters are not always as straightforward as they might seem. For example, Wampold (2001) vividly illustrates the sometimes-heated controversies that exist with respect to what should count as evidence. As Wampold, Goodheart, and Levant (2007) observe:

> *Evidence can be thought of as inferences that flow from data. These data may be of various types but are derived from observations, in the generic sense of the word (e.g., they may be "observed" by a machine and transformed before being processed by the human brain, or they may be sensory experiences transformed during self-observation). The data become evidence when they are considered with regard to the phenomena being studied, the model used to generate the data, previous knowledge, theory, the methodologies employed, and the human actors.* (pp. 616–617)

As a consequence, the variants of what gets labeled *evidence-based therapy* and *evidence-based supervision* have their advocates and their skeptics (cf., Milne & Reiser, 2012; Osborn & Davis, 2009). For supervision in particular, there is concern that the development of the supervisee may be placed on the back burner if supervision becomes little more than oversight of the extent to which the supervisee is adhering to a specific treatment protocol (see, e.g., Henggeler, Schoenwald, Liao, Letourneau & Edwards, 2008). That said, the focus of authors such as Falender and Shafranske (2007) to identify supervisor competencies may serve as an antidote to such concerns.

Although Milne (2009) argues that evidence-based supervision is a model within which to operate, we choose not to include it as such in our present schema. Instead we argue first that virtually all models of supervision might, hypothetically, be evidence based if adequate research was conducted; therefore, it is not a separate model of supervision. Our second point is that rather than offering us an additional conceptual model, evidence-based supervision as a construct is, instead, an overarching evaluation movement with enormous positive implications for the field if the concerns of its critics are addressed adequately.

CONCLUSION

We cover a great deal of ground in this chapter. Novice supervisors may be as flummoxed considering their choices as counseling and therapy trainees reading their first theories of psychotherapy text. We end this chapter as we began—by claiming that good supervisors incorporate tenets from psychotherapy theory, an awareness of supervisee development, and an appreciation for supervision process in their approach to supervision. Beyond that, we hope this chapter stimulates the reader to investigate distinct models and their offshoots further.

As we conclude this chapter, we also stress that one's model is only the conceptual map for supervision; there is much more that must be addressed in terms of the supervisory relationship, interventions, evaluation plan, ethics, and so forth.

Processes and Issues of the Supervisory Triad and Dyad

Processes and Issues of the Supervisory Triad and Dyad

I believe that good supervision happens with supervisors who are genuine about themselves, and therefore, genuine, real, present, and honest with the person they are supervising. I don't think that it is all that different than the kind of process that goes on in therapy. The flow of both processes is about a good relationship. (Majcher & Daniluk, 2009, p. 66)

This quote is effective in capturing the general consensus of supervision researchers and theorists that "good supervision is about the relationship" (Ellis, 2010, p. 106). Above all, a trusting human relationship is essential to supervision's various teaching and learning functions (e.g., Ramos-Sánchez et al., 2002; Rønnestad & Skovholt, 1993; Worthen & McNeill, 1996). However, poor supervisory relationships can not only impair learning, but also may have deleterious effects on the supervisee. Nelson, Barnes, Evans and Triggiano (2008) point out that there are "iatrogenic effects of mishandled supervisory relationships . . . including supervisee loss of self-efficacy, mistrust of counseling and/or psychology as a profession, and chronic extreme stress" (p. 173).

Gelso and Carter's (1985) definition of therapeutic relationship that applies also to supervisory relationships. They argue that relationships concern "the feelings and attitudes that [supervision] participants have toward one another, and the manner in which these are expressed" (p. 159). Relationships are not static; nor are they the same across any two subsets of people.

In fact, supervisory relationships are multilayered and complex and to examine them is akin to scanning a forest through a telescope: Each focal range will reveal different aspects and details of that forest. Fiscalini's (1997) term *supervisory ecology* (p. 43) suggests the complexity of the interactions among people and phenomena that can be observed at the various focal ranges.

In examining the figurative forest that is supervision, we focus our telescope at three different ranges:

1. Supervision as a triadic system (the broadest focal range)
2. The supervisory dyad
3. Individual participants' contributions to the relationship (the most restricted range)

In this chapter, we focus on the first two of these focal ranges.

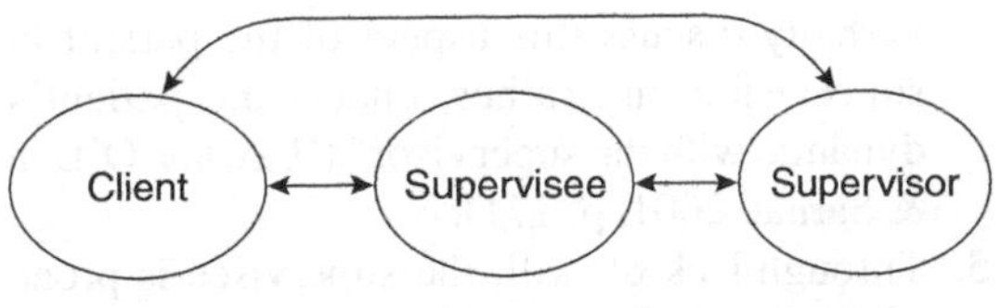

FIGURE 1 Supervisee as Relational Pivot Point in the Supervisory Triad

SUPERVISION AS A THREE-PERSON SYSTEM

> *In pyramid fashion, the supervisory relationship is a relationship about a relationship about other relationships.* (Fiscalini, 1997, p. 30)
>
> *It is important to be aware that the supervisory room is crowded with all sorts of "persons" who create anxieties for both the supervisor and the supervisee. It is often more crowded than the analytic one.* (Lesser, 1983, p. 126)

The preceding two observations underscore the complexity of the supervisory relationship system. Not only does that system involve the supervisor, supervisee, and client, but it also is possible for other people in the client's life to have effects that reverberate throughout the system. However, to keep our discussion manageable, we limit it to only the three principals in the supervisory relationship: the client, the therapist/supervisee, and the supervisor. This triadic relationship is illustrated in Figure 1, which makes clear that the supervisee is the pivot point in this system (Frawley-O'Dea & Sarnat, 2001). It shows that there are two manifest relationships (i.e., client–supervisee and supervisee–supervisor), and that the person common to both those relationships is the supervisee, who serves as a conduit of both information and processes between the dyads.

Figure 1 seems simple, but the processes it encompasses can be complex, because each of the three involved parties influences the other two. This chapter is about that complexity. In the section that follows, we discuss supervision as a three-person system, addressing first parallel processes and isomorphic phenomena, and then triangulations that occur among the members of the supervisory triad.

Parallel Processes and Isomorphism

Friedlander, Siegel, & Brenock (1989) describe *parallel process* as a phenomenon in which "supervisees unconsciously present themselves to their supervisors as their clients have presented to them. The process reverses when the supervisee adopts attitudes and behaviors of the supervisor in relating to the client" (p. 149). It is a reenactment in one dyad (supervisor–supervisee or supervisee–client) of processes occurring in the other.

Parallel processes have their conceptual roots in psychodynamic supervision (Friedman, 1983; Gediman & Wolkenfeld, 1980; Grey & Fiscalini, 1987; Schneider, 1992). Searles (1955), apparently the first to write about the phenomenon, describing it as the *reflection process* between therapy and supervision. Others (e.g., Ekstein & Wallerstein, 1972; Mueller, 1982; Mueller & Kell, 1972) began soon after to use the concept, but using the current term, *parallel process,* instead. This now has become perhaps the best-known phenomenon in supervision; perhaps even the signature phenomenon.

Structural and strategic family therapists have employed the related concept of isomorphism, for which Haley (1976) has been given credit (Liddle & Saba, 1983). In choosing the term *isomorphism,* systemic supervisors have focused on the interrelational and structural similarities between therapy and supervision.

These concepts initially were described and promoted by adherents of specific models of treatment (i.e., *parallel process* by psychodynamic supervisors; *isomorphism* by family systems theorists), but are not model-specific. They seem in many respects, however, to be two sides of the same coin. Abroms (1977) came as close as anyone to blending the concepts of parallel process and isomorphism in his introduction of the term *metatransference:* "To think in terms of metatransference is to think in parallel structures at different levels of abstraction, that is, to recognize the multilevel, isomorphic mirroring of interactional processes" (p. 93).

Nevertheless, these two phenomena are distinct enough to warrant separate treatment. We discuss each in the sections that immediately follow.

Parallel Process. Russell, Crimmings, & Lent (1984) suggest two ways that parallel processes can be useful in supervision:

> *First, as the supervisee becomes aware of the parallels in the relationships with the client and the supervisor, understanding of the client's psychological maladjustment is increased. Second, the supervisee's understanding of the therapeutic process grows in that the supervisee learns how to respond therapeutically to the client just as the supervisor has responded to the supervisee.* (p. 629)

Initially, supervisors assumed that parallel process was a bottom-up phenomenon in which some characteristic of the client is displayed by the supervisee during supervision. Therefore, a supervisee working with a depressed client might present in supervision in an uncharacteristically depressed manner, or the supervisee working with a particularly confused client might present in supervision in an uncharacteristically confused manner.

Parallel process dynamics have been explained in various ways. The following explanations all emphasize a bottom-up process that (a) is triggered either by the client or by some aspect of the client–supervisee relationship; (b) occurs outside awareness of the participants; and (c) for which the supervisee serves as the conduit of the process from the client–therapist relationship to that of the supervisor–supervisee:

1. Because of their identification with their clients, supervisees produce reactions in their supervisors that they themselves had felt in response to their clients (Russell et al., 1984).
2. The parallel the supervisee (unconsciously) chooses to exhibit reflects the initial impasse formed between the client and the supervisee (Mueller & Kell, 1972).
3. The supervisee selects part of the client's problem that parallels one that the supervisee shares (Mueller & Kell, 1972).
4. The supervisee identifies unconsciously with some aspect of the client's psychological functioning. Because the supervisee is unaware of this identification, she or he "cannot verbally discuss this aspect of the patient in supervision but, rather, enacts the patient's dynamic with the supervisor" (Frawley-O'Dea & Sarnat, 2001, p. 171).
5. Through lack of skill, the supervisee is prone to those aspects of the client's problem that parallel the supervisee's specific learning problems in supervision (Ekstein & Wallerstein, 1972).
6. Parallel process has "similarities with the repetition compulsion, namely, that what is not understood is enacted" (Arkowitz, 2001, p. 53).
7. When supervisor, therapist, and/or client represent different cultural backgrounds, some parallel processes are likely to reflect cross-cultural issues (Vargas, 1989).

Ekstein and Wallerstein (1972) comment that parallel process is a "never-ending surprise" based on the "irrational expectation that the teaching and learning of psychotherapy should consist primarily of rational elements" (p. 177). The flavor of their comment, however, is that the supervisee is the root of that irrationality—the bottom-up perspective to which we already have alluded; what Frawley-O'Dea and Sarnat (2001) characterize as the traditional view of parallel processes.

The more contemporary view of parallel processes is that the supervisor is as likely to initiate a dynamic that is then played out in the supervisee's therapy as is the reverse. This expanded perspective began with Doehrman's (1976) dissertation research findings that parallel processes were bidirectional. For example, she observes that a supervisor–supervisee relationship impasse was mirrored by a supervisee–client impasse; when the supervisor–supervisee impasse was resolved, so too was that between supervisee and client.

Frawley-O'Dea and Sarnat (2001) discuss this bidirectional conception as "symmetrical parallel processes":

> *The central conceptualization of symmetrical parallel process is that a transference and countertransference configuration arises in either the*

supervised treatment or the supervision. At this point, the relational pattern in play is out of the conscious awareness of the members of the dyad. It is not available for conscious elaboration, discussion, meaning making, or negotiation because it has not been linguistically formulated yet by either party to the dyad. The supervisee, however, the common member of both dyads, nonverbally exerts relational pressure on the member of the other dyad to enact a similar transference and countertransference matrix with the supervisee, in the often unconscious hope that someone can contain, enact, process, and put words to what is transpiring now in both dyads. The key to symmetrical parallel processes is that both the treatment and the supervisory dyads play out similar relational constellations. (p. 182)

Addressing Parallel Processes in Supervision. Virtually all theorists who discuss parallel processes now embrace this more contemporary and symmetrical view of parallel processes. Yet most discussions of possible interventions for the supervisor focus only on the traditional view, in which the supervisee is transmitting client material to the supervisory dyad. It may be that this is because it is easier for the supervisor to observe this phenomenon than it is to observe phenomena that originate with him or her. Heidegger's observation that "Fish are the last ones to discover water" perhaps is apt in this situation.

Neufeldt, Iverson, and Juntunen (1995) point out that, whereas a supervisor might anticipate many interventions in advance, opportunities to address parallel processes typically occur serendipitously. They also note that, whereas psychodynamic supervisors often point out or interpret parallel processes to more-advanced supervisees as they observe them, less-advanced supervisees can be confused by this. As well, for a supervisee simply to be made aware of a particular parallel process does not make it disappear (Carroll, 1996).

Neufeldt et al. (1995) recommends instead that the supervisor respond less directly and serve as a model for the supervisee about how to respond to the client issues that the supervisee is mirroring in the supervisory sessions. For more intractable situations, Carroll (1996) recommends that the supervisee role-play the client in order to gain a clearer perspective.

McNeill and Worthen (1989) caution that too much focus on the process of supervision might become tiresome for supervisees and that, in general, more advanced supervisees are most likely to benefit from a discussion of transference and countertransference.

It is important as well to acknowledge that parallel processes can manifest in supervision-of-supervision as well (Ellis & Douce, 1994). In this case, the supervisory relationship system involves four people: client, supervisee, supervisor, and the supervisor's supervisor. Despite the added complexity of this situation, the material we cover in this section should extrapolate readily to it.

Research Concerning Parallel Processes. Two circumstances hamper research on parallel processes: One is that the concept is sufficiently "fuzzy" that it has been a challenge to operationalize meaningfully; the other is that it is hard to predict when parallel processes will manifest themselves and therefore be available for study. Therefore, the few studies of parallel processes mostly have used case-study designs (e.g., Alpher, 1991; Doehrman, 1976; Friedlander et al., 1989; Jacobsen, 2007) that have varied in sophistication. Those who reviewed that literature (e.g., McNeill & Worthen, 1989; Mothersole, 1999) express concern about the nature and extent of this empirical support for parallel processes. Recent work by Tracey, Bludworth, and Glidden-Tracey (2012), however, provides what is the most robust empirical demonstration of parallel processes to date. They focus on 17 supervisory triads to examine a sequence of one therapy session, a supervision session that focused on that session, and then the subsequent therapy session. Each interaction in each session (therapy or supervision) was coded on level of dominance and affiliation using Strong, Hills, and Nelson's (1988) coding manual. Tracey et al. observed parallel processes occurring with respect to

> *both dominance and affiliation. So if a client tended to act in a distrustful and self-effacing manner (submissive-critical) in the prior session and the therapist complemented this by acting in a critical manner in therapy, then the therapist in the role of trainee would enact some of the distrustful client behavior in the subsequent supervision session. The supervisor would also demonstrate this parallel process by acting in a manner similar to how the therapist acted in the previous therapy session; in this example, the supervisor would become more critical than typical. This is clear evidence for parallel process in supervision.* (p. 339)

Less-direct support for parallel processes has come from research links processes occurring in both the supervisory and therapy dyads. For example, Patton and Kivlighan (1997) found that the week-to-week fluctuations in the quality of the supervisor–supervisee working alliance predicted the week-to-week fluctuations in the supervisee–client working alliance. Williams (2000) found that the greater the supervisors' affiliative interpersonal style, the less controlling or dominant the supervisees' style in their work as therapists with their clients.

Some researchers began with the premise that parallel processes do exist, and then examine which supervisors attend to them and how they perceive its effects. Perhaps unsurprisingly, Raichelson, Herron, Primavera, and Ramirez (1997) confirm that psychodynamic supervisors and supervisees were more likely than their rational—emotive or cognitive—behavioral counterparts to recognize the existence and importance of parallel processes. In a qualitative study, Ladany, Constantine, Miller, Erickson, and Muse-Burke (2000) found that supervisors of unspecified theoretical orientations frequently identified parallel processes as sources of countertransference reactions that they had experienced toward supervisees.

Concluding Comments about Parallel Processes. Sometimes parallel processes have been presented as a nearly mystical phenomenon. McWilliams (1994) acknowledges that this apparent mysticism can be particularly troublesome for someone with the skepticism of the scientist–practitioner. She suggests, however, that parallel processes become more comprehensible when one realizes that in the earliest years of life, most communication with others is both nonverbal and complex, and that we then continue to use this mode throughout life without necessarily understanding the extent to which we do so.

Whereas she was arguing against a too-skeptical perception of parallel processes, the complementary issue is that of invoking it too frequently and uncritically. Mothersole (1999), for example, describes a type of *pseudo-parallel,* in which either unresolved problems or lack of skills in the supervisee are "'beaming out' in both directions and affecting the therapeutic and supervisory relationships" (p. 118). Schimel (1984) similarly observes that parallel processes can be invoked in an irresponsible and possibly trivial manner to frame in psychological terms a matter that actually is one of skill and competence.

> *The basic observation is a simple one. The patient wants something from the therapist that is not forthcoming. He or she is displeased. This troubles the therapist, who, in turn, looks to the supervisor for help that may or may not be forthcoming. The therapist is displeased with the supervisor, who, in his turn, may be troubled and displeased with the supervisee and himself. This is a common situation. One has reason to expect, however, that with the increasing skill of the supervisee and the accumulating experience of the supervisor that this kind of situation will be recognized early and dealt with by putting it into an appropriate perspective.* (p. 239)

Feiner (1994) is another who urges caution with respect to invoking parallel processes as a concept:

> *The supervisor is allegedly "put" (not deliberately) in the position of a proxy therapist with the supervisee playing the part of the patient. Although out-of-awareness, the enactment is not taken by sophisticated supervisors as a simple, mechanistic repetition, but as more likely representing some sort of homology. It's as though the student were saying, "Do it with me and I'll know what to do with my patients." But . . . while the issues that belong to the patient may seem similar to the issues that the therapist-as-student brings into supervision . . . the similarity is more apparent than real.* (pp. 61–62)

Feiner points out that one risk of a too-heavy reliance on parallel-process thinking is that it may ignore, obscure, or even deny the supervisor's or the supervisee's own contributions to the interactions occurring between them.

Isomorphism

> Isomorphism *refers to the phenomenon whereby categories with different content, but similar form, can be mapped on each other in such a way that there are corresponding parts and processes within each structure. When this occurs, these parallel structures can be described as isomorphic, and each is an isomorph of the other. Therefore, when the supervisory system is mapped onto the therapeutic system, the roles of supervisor and supervisee correspond to those of the therapist and client, respectively.* (White & Russell, 1997, p. 317)

For systems therapists, *isomorphism* refers to the "recursive replication" (Liddle, Breunlin, Schwartz, & Constantine, 1984) that occurs between therapy and supervision. The focus is interrelational and not intrapsychic. As Liddle and Saba (1983) suggest, the two fields (therapy and supervision) constantly influence and are influenced by each other; both are interpersonal systems with properties of all systems, including boundaries, hierarchies, and subsystems, each with its own distinct characteristics. There is no linear reality in this construct, only reverberation. Content is important, but not nearly as important as repeating patterns.

Because supervision is viewed as an isomorph of therapy, Liddle et al. (1984) suggest that many of the same rules, such as include the need to join with both clients and supervisees, the need for setting goals and thinking in stages, the importance of appreciating contextual sensitivity, and the charge of challenging realities, apply to both. "It suggests that trainers would do well to understand and intentionally utilize with their supervisees the same basic principles of change employed in therapy" (Liddle et al., 1984, p. 141).

The supervisor who is aware of this process watches for dynamics in supervision that reflect the initial assessment that the supervisor has made about what is transpiring in therapy. In this way, the assessment is either verified or called into question. Because the client (family) is usually a group, and because many systemic supervisors prefer team supervision, the interactions are easily replicated. One example is when an overwhelmed parent appeals to the supervisee for help (while other family members sit expectantly), followed by an overwhelmed supervisee appealing to the supervisor for help (while other team members sit expectantly). When using isomorphism to guide interventions into the therapeutic system (supervisee plus family), it is important that there be consistency down the hierarchy. For example, Haley (1987) recommends that if the goal is for the parents to be firm with their teenager, the therapist must be firm with the parents. And to complete the isomorph, the supervisor must be firm with the therapist.

Liddle and Saba (1983) argue that live supervision, by requiring risk taking and experiential behavior on the part of the therapist, parallels structural family therapy, during which family members are actively put in direct contact with each other. Therefore, live supervision is an isomorphically correct form of supervision for structural family therapy.

White and Russell (1997) found that authors who had written about isomorphism had focused on four phenomena, or *facets,* related to it:

Facet 1: *Identifying repetitive or similar patterns*: the replication of patterns across systems. Often, this is the replication from another system (e.g., client–therapist system; family of origin for either the supervisor or supervisee) into the supervisory system, but it also can manifest as a replication of supervisor–supervisee pattern onto other systems, especially the therapist–client system. White and Russell (1997) note that the concept of parallel processes could just as well describe this facet of isomorphism.

Facet 2: *Translation of therapeutic models and principles into supervision*: As we note in chapter "Multicultural Supervision," it is impossible for a person's therapeutic model not to affect his or her approach to supervision. To the extent that this occurs, this facet of isomorphism is operating.

Facet 3: *The structure and process of therapy and supervision are identical:* Certainly, there are many structural similarities between supervision and therapy, at least with respect to individual therapy. For example, both typically involve two people isolating themselves in a room with a closed door to discuss sensitive material in private; in both, one person is to disclose material to another whose task is to examine and perhaps take action on some aspect of that material.

Facet 4: *Isomorphism as an interventive stance:* The supervisor can alter the sequences in supervision with the purpose of influencing a corresponding alteration of sequences within therapy.

The following illustrates the first of these four facets of isomorphism between therapy and supervision, the facet that is most difficult to differentiate from parallel process (White & Russell, 1997).

> *Ted is seeing the Doyles for marital therapy with a supervision team observing the session. The Doyles, married for 20 years, have no children and Mr. Doyle has fought depression most of his adult life. Mrs. Doyle reports how hard it has been to help him, only to have her efforts go nowhere, and she cries intermittently. It is obvious watching Ted that he is feeling this couple's plight. In the supervision room, there is virtually no movement. The team mirrors the sadness and despair of the couple. Half way through the session, Ted excuses himself to consult with the team. . . . As Ted is seated, JoAnn turns around and says, "Boy, what do you do for them at this point?" Ted shrugs and looks around for help.*

In summary, given the potential utility of the concept, isomorphism seems a useful tool for supervisors. At the same time, supervisors should be aware of the caution by Storm, Todd, and Sprenkle (2001) that a too-heavy emphasis on it can obscure the important differences between therapy and supervision.

Interpersonal Triangles

Bowen (e.g., 1978) did a great deal to sensitize mental health professionals, especially family therapists, to the notion that the interpersonal triangle actually is the more fundamental unit of relationship than the dyad. This conception has important implications for how supervisors, supervisees, and clients interact with one another.

Since at least the 1890s there have been theorists who have maintain that triangles constitute a type of social geometry (Caplow, 1968). Within any given triangle, two members tend to be in a coalition, with the third either more peripheral or even perceived as antagonistic to them. Triangles occur in many ways in our day-to-day lives. Psychoanalytic therapists are concerned with Oedipal triangles and family therapists are concerned with the broader spectrum of possible triangles that can occur in a family system. We all can describe childhood (and perhaps current!) relationships in which, within a group of three friends, there were two who were particularly close: During times of tension between these two, however, the less-involved third member was drawn into an alliance with one of those two; the other then becomes more peripheral.

One especially interesting characteristic of triangles is that they seem to have a catalytic effect on participants' behavior—that is, although coalitions can occur between two members of a triangle without the third member present, that third member's presence almost always modifies the relationship of the other two. To illustrate, Caplow offered as an example the common playground situation in which the presence of a mutual antagonist enhances (a) the affection between two friends and (b) their felt hostility toward the antagonist. It is not difficult to see how variants of this same scenario play out in the professional lives of adults as well.

One manifestation of a coalition (and therefore of triangulation) is the circumstance of two people secretly discussing a third. Most of us also have experienced this in our families and in work settings, but this occurs in counseling as well. For example, triangulation is one reason it is so difficult for counselors to begin with an individual client and then later to include that person's spouse in the treatment. The initial client already has already discussed ("in secret") the spouse with the counselor, who almost inevitably has adopted at least some of that person's perspective about the spouse. This situation has all the characteristics of the coalition of which Bowen (1978) spoke, making it very difficult for the spouse to enter a neutral situation.

Interpersonal Triangles in Supervision. In supervision, the most obvious triangle is that of the client, counselor, and supervisor. This particular triangle has characteristics that constrain the possible coalitions that occur. Two of these are (a) the way in which power is arrayed (the least powerful member of this group is the client; the most powerful, the supervisor) and (b) the fact that the supervisor and client rarely have an ongoing face-to-face relationship with each other.

Within this triangle, the discussion between two people of the third person most often occurs between supervisee and supervisor. This, of course, suggests a counselor–supervisor coalition with the client as the third member. It is possible, however, for the counselor and client to discuss the supervisor. In this instance, it is possible to develop a coalition between counselor and client against the supervisor.

Strategically oriented family therapists sometimes use this latter coalition possibility to their advantage, using the supervisory relationship for therapeutic purposes. The supervisor is deliberately set up in the "oppressor" role as a means to catalyze the client–counselor bond and steer the client toward a desired behavior. For example, the supervisor might direct the counselor to say something like this to the client: "My supervisor is convinced that your problem is ____________ and that I should be doing ____________ about it. Just between us, though, I think she's off base. In fact, I think she's pretty insensitive to the issues you are facing." The goal of such a strategy is for the client to improve in order to prove the supervisor wrong.

However, because supervision occurs in a larger context, not all the possible triangles of which the supervisor and supervisee might be a part necessarily involve the client. For example, the supervisee might "triangle in" another current or past supervisor by saying to his or her supervisor something like this: "I'm feeling confused: You're telling me this, but the supervisor I had last semester [or, the supervisor I have in my other setting] has been telling me something really different."

Such a statement establishes a coalition between the supervisee and another supervisor who may not even realize that he or she has become a member of this particular triangle. Coalitions—even with a phantom member such as this—redistribute power. Whether or not the supervisee is doing this with deliberate intent, it has the effect of putting the current supervisor in the situation of being "odd person out."

Baum (2011) invokes the concept of interpersonal triangles to examine the circumstance of a supervisor having multiple supervisees. She found that supervisees monitor not only the quality of their own relationships with the supervisor, but the relationships of other supervisees who are working with that supervisor as well. Most supervisees reported observing qualitative differences in these relationships.

In summary, interpersonal triangles are ubiquitous in human interactions. It is unsurprising, then, that they occur between and among professionals. Our intent in this discussion was not to suggest that triangles are necessarily always to be avoided. We are convinced, however, that it is essential for supervisors to be aware of interpersonal triangles and their effects. With this knowledge, supervisors are better equipped to avoid problematic triangles and to manage others in a strategic manner.

Lawson (1993) makes helpful suggestions about how supervisors might assist supervisees to avoid being triangulated. He notes Bowen's position that the more *differentiated* (roughly equivalent to being emotionally autonomous) the supervisee, the less likely she or he will be vulnerable to being triangulated. This suggests the importance of providing opportunities for the supervisee's personal growth so that they can increase their levels of differentiation. And, more simply, Lawson suggests teaching supervisees about triangles as a way to help negotiate them successfully.

SUPERVISION AS A TWO-PERSON SYSTEM

In the first part of this chapter, we set our figurative telescope at a focal range that permitted the broadest view of the supervisory relationship: that of a three-person system composed of the client, supervisee, and supervisor. In the remainder of the chapter, we restrict our telescopic range to focus on the two-person system of supervisor and supervisee.

The Working Alliance as a Means to Frame the Supervisory Relationship

A number of ideas and constructs have been adapted from counseling or therapy to inform our understanding of supervision (Milne, 2006). Among those has been the ways we understand supervisory relationships. Early on, for example, supervisory relationships were viewed through a psychodynamic lens; then, for a period in the late 1960s and 1970s, a Rogerian-influenced lens (see Lambert & Ogles, 1997). But since the early 1980s, Bordin's (1979, 1983) working alliance has become increasingly central in conceptualizing not only therapeutic relationships, but supervisory ones as well. Bordin's 1983 article, for example, is the third-most cited article in the supervision literature.

Quality of the client–therapist working alliance predicts therapeutic outcomes consistently (see, e.g., Norcross & Wampold, 2011). In fact, Castonguay, Constantino and Holtforth (2006) observe that

> *Empirically, the alliance appears to be the most frequently studied process of change. . . . Clinically, the alliance occupies such an important place in our conceptualization of what good therapy entails that not paying attention to its quality during practice or supervision could be viewed as unethical.* (p. 271)

This is consistent with Ladany, Ellis, and Friedlander's (1999) suggestion that the alliance is "potentially one of the most important common factors in the change process of supervision" (p. 447). Inskipp and Proctor (2001) inextricably linked the the alliance and supervision when they defined supervision as "A working alliance between the supervisor and counsellor" (p. 1).

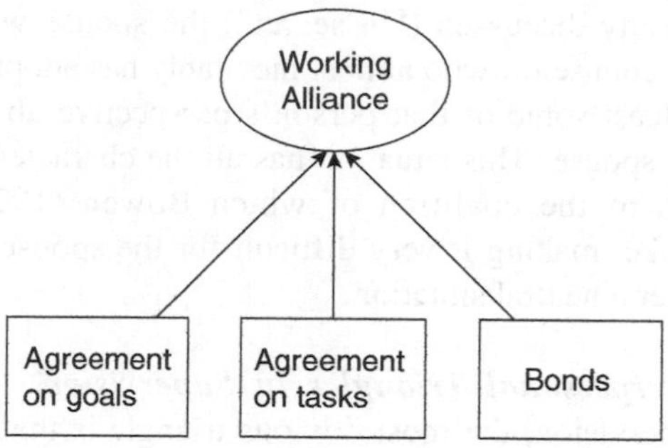

FIGURE 2 Bordin's Model of the Working Alliance

Initial theorizing about the working (or *therapeutic*) alliance came from a psychodynamic tradition. Bordin, however, argues that it should be understood as a pantheoretical construct; that it is a "collaboration to change" (1983, p. 73) composed of (1) the extent to which the therapist and client agree on *goals,* (2) the extent to which they agree on the *tasks* necessary to reach those goals, and (3) the affective *bond* that develops between them (Figure 2). Bordin (1983) asserts that relational bonds develop as a result either of working together on a common task to achieve shared goals or on the basis of shared emotional experiences. These bonds "center around the feelings of liking, caring, and trusting that the participants share" (p. 36).

Angus and Kagan (2007) make the point that some alliance processes are not the same in therapeutic and supervisory alliances. They provide evidence, for example, that

> *clients initial disclosures of personal information and emotionally-salient stories seem to contribute to the rapid development of a shared affective bond between therapist and client in good outcome therapy dyads [whereas] . . . the discussion of supervisee personal issues, during initial therapy supervision sessions, has been found to occur more often in low alliance dyads and may be linked to weaker supervisory alliances* (p. 375)

This underscores the importance of reviewing factors that specifically affect the supervisory alliance, which we do in the material that follows.

Research on any construct depends on the availability of psychometrically sound measures. Fortunately, those have been available for studying *therapeutic* alliances (see, e.g., Tichenor & Hill, 1989), although the most frequently used seems to have been the Working Alliance Inventory (WAI; Horvath & Greenberg, 1989). Studies of *supervisory* alliances used slight modifications of the WAI (e.g., substituting *supervisor* for *therapist* in the items; see Bahrick, 1990; Baker, 1990). A number of supervision researchers also have used the measure that Efstation, Patton, and Kardash (1990) developed specifically for supervision.

Other promising new supervisory alliance scales are being developed, including, for example, those of Rønnestad and Lundquist (2009). Most of the studies we review here, however, have used those of either Bahrick (1990) or Efstation et al. (1990).

Antecedents of Effective Supervisory Alliances

> *We propose that a key task in early supervision is building a strong working alliance (Bordin, 1983) that can serve as a base from which future dilemmas in supervision can be managed. Ongoing maintenance of the alliance should be the supervisor's responsibility throughout the course of the relationship.* (Nelson, Gray, Friedlander, Ladany, & Walker, 2001, p. 408)

Maintaining the quality of the *supervisory working alliance (SWA),* however, requires that the supervisor appreciate the variables that affect the alliance. These are summarized in the left portion of Figure 3 and in the discussion that follows.

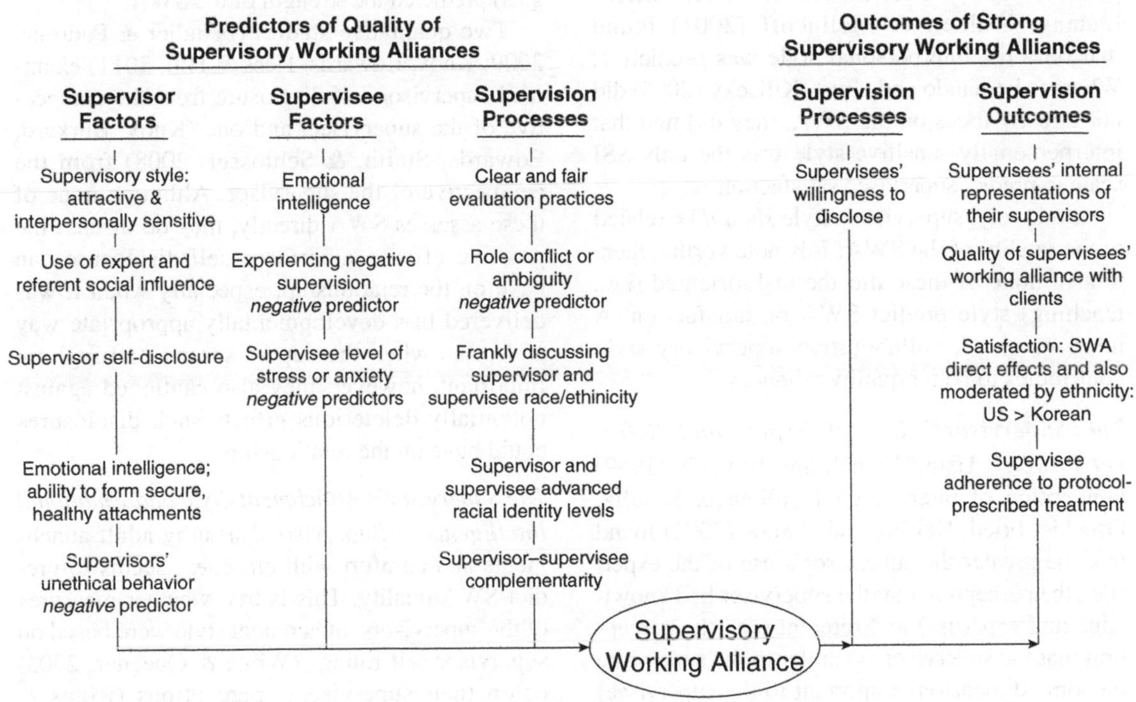

FIGURE 3 Antecedents and Consequences of Positive Supervisory Alliances

Those discussions are, respectively, of (a) supervisor, (b) supervisee, and (c) supervisor x supervisee factors that influence the SWA.

Supervisor Factors Affecting Quality of Supervisory Alliance. Five supervisor attributes or behaviors have been shown to affect the supervisory alliance: the supervisor's (a) style, (b) use of expert and referent power, (c) use of self-disclosure, (d) attachment style and emotional intelligence, and (e) ethical behavior.

The Supervisor's Style. Friedlander and Ward's (1984) Supervisory Styles Inventory (SSI) advanced our understandings of supervisory style by both operationalizing it and providing a method for assessing (and was used in the four studies we cite in this subsection). In fact, in two studies (Chen & Bernstein, 2000; Spelliscy, Chen, & Zusho, 2007) found that the interpersonally sensitive (consultant) and attractive (counselor) styles predicted one or more aspects of SWA, whereas Ladany, Walker, & Melincoff (2001) found that only the interpersonal style was predictive. Whereas Fernando and Hulse-Killacky (2005) did not directly focus on the SWA, they did find that interpersonally sensitive style was the only SSI scale to predict supervisee satisfaction

Intuitively, supervisory style *should* be related to the quality of the SWA. It is noteworthy, then, that in none of these did the task-oriented (i.e., teaching) style predict SWA or satisfaction. A more involved, collaborative supervisory style contributes to better quality alliances.

The Supervisors' Use of Expert and Referent Power. Using French and Raven's (1959) conception of interpersonal influence, Schultz, Ososkie, Fried, Nelson, and Bardos (2002) found that the greater the supervisor's use of the expert (i.e., the perception that the supervisor had knowledge and expertise) and referent (i.e., the perception that the supervisor is similar to the supervisee on some dimensions important to the supervisee) power bases, the stronger the SWA. This seems generally consistent both with the social influence research (e.g., Heppner & Claiborn, 1989), which shows that referent power—also referred to as *attractiveness*—is related to the client's liking of the therapist as well as with supervisory style, as just discussed.

The Supervisor's Use of Self-Disclosure. Hill and Knox (2002) concluded from their review of the literature that, whereas there were relatively few studies of the immediate outcomes of self-disclosure in therapy, moderate levels of therapist self-disclosure tended to have a positive effect on the therapeutic relationship. Because supervisors are better known to their supervisees than counselors are to clients, and because they serve as professional role models, it stands to reason that supervisor self-disclosures would have at least as great an impact. In fact, Ladany and Lehrman-Waterman (1999) found that level of supervisory disclosures (which primarily concerned personal issues, neutral counseling experiences, and counseling struggles) predicted the strength of the SWA.

Two qualitative studies (Feindler & Padrone, 2009; Knox, Edwards, Hess & Hill, 2011) examined supervisor self-disclosure from the perspective of the supervisee, and one (Knox, Burkard, Edwards, Smith, & Schlosser, 2008) from the perspective of the supervisor. Although none of these assesses SWA directly, they do discuss the positive effects supervisor self-disclosure can have on the relationship, especially when it was delivered in a developmentally appropriate way and often when the supervisee was struggling. Important, however, they also cautioned against potentially deleterious effects such disclosures could have on the relationship.

The Supervisor's Attachment Style and Emotional Intelligence. Supervisors' healthy adult attachments and comfort with closeness seems to predict SWA quality. This is true whether measures of the supervisors' attachment style were based on supervisor self-ratings (White & Queener, 2003) or on their supervisees' perceptions (Riggs & Bretz, 2006).

Emotional intelligence is not the same as attachment, of course, but because both have relational implications, we note here that Cooper and Ng (2009) found that supervisors' level of emotional intelligence predicts SWA quality.

The Supervisor's (Un)Ethical Behavior. Ladany, Lehrman-Waterman, Molinaro, and Wolgast (1999) examine the prevalence of 15 supervisor ethical behaviors. Ladany, Lehrman-Waterman et al. (1999) found that the greater the frequency with which supervisees reported unethical behaviors by their supervisors, the lower the supervisees rated the SWA and their level of satisfaction with supervision.

To put this in a more colloquial way, the more the supervisor had let down the supervisee, the weaker the supervisee felt a connection to the supervisor. This is supported by the Ramos-Sanchez et al. (2002) finding that the more negative events supervisees experienced in supervision, the lower their ratings of the SWA.

Supervisee Factors Affecting Quality of Supervisory Alliance. The supervisor has the greater responsibility for maintaining the alliance, and so it probably is fitting that less attention has been given to supervisee variables. Nevertheless, we find it surprising that there have been so few. To date, only two have been investigated: the supervisee's attachment style and experience of negative supervision.

The Supervisee's Attachment Style and Emotional Intelligence. Renfro-Michel (2006) found that a secure attachment style predicted SWA, whereas White and Queener (2003) found no relationship between supervisee attachment style and working alliance. Therefore, as intuitive as that relationship might seem, the findings so far are mixed with respect to the connection between supervisee attachment style and SWA.

We noted in our earlier discussion of supervisor factors that supervisor emotional intelligence predicted SWA. That same study (Cooper & Ng, 2009) found that supervisees' emotional intelligence did as well.

The Supervisee's Experience of Negative Supervision. An important subset of studies have been concerned with what constitutes supervision that is good, bad/harmful, or both. Ramos-Sánchez et al. (2002) confirm the intuitive link between negative supervisory experiences and the resulting, weaker supervisory alliances. From a national sample of supervisees, they compared those who reported at least one negative supervisory event with those who had not. The former group reported weaker alliances. Also, those who reported negative experiences reported (1) being less satisfied with supervision, (2) being at a lower developmental level as measured by the Supervisee Levels Questionnaire–Revised (SLQ–R; McNeill, Stoltenberg, & Romans, 1992), and (3) having less positive relationships with their clients.

There are many ways, of course, for the supervisory experience to be made negative for the supervisee. Magnuson, Wilcoxon, and Norem (2000) and Nelson (2002) catalog ways for supervisors to provide what they term "lousy" supervision. Table 1 lists the 22 ways Nelson found in her review of the literature. Regardless of how obvious items on this list might seem, to have this list in writing provides an important reminder to supervisors of behaviors to avoid.

Supervisee Stress and Coping as Predictors of Alliance. Supervisees' level of stress-in-general (Gnilka & Chang, 2012) or workplace related stress (Sterner, 2009) predicted lower levels of WA, as did levels of supervisee anxiety (Mehr, Ladany, & Caskie, 2010). Conversely, higher levels of supervisees' coping resources predict better-quality SWAs. It is important to note, though, that these data were correlational, and so causal directions might run the other way (i.e., anxiety might have been the result of poorer SWA).

Supervision Processes Affecting Quality of Supervisory Alliance. Five processes that involved both supervisor and supervisee interactions have been found to be related to working alliance. Each is discussed individually next.

TABLE 1 How to Be a Lousy Supervisor: Lessons from the Research

From Worthen and McNeill (1996)

1. Don't establish a strong supervisory alliance with your supervisee.
2. Don't reveal any of your own shortcomings to your supervisee.
3. Don't provide a sense of safety so that your supervisee can reveal his or her doubts and fears about competency.

From Kozlowska, Nunn, and Cousins (1997)

4. Place the importance of service delivery above your supervisee's educational needs.
5. Ignore your supervisee's need for emotional support in a new and challenging context.

From Wulf and Nelson (2000)

6. Involve your supervisee in the conflicted dynamics among professional staff in your setting.
7. Don't support your supervisee's strengths; point out weaknesses only.
8. Don't take an interest in your supervisee's interests.
9. Talk mostly about your own cases in supervision.

From Nelson and Friedlander (2001)

10. Don't conduct a role induction process with your supervisee that involves being explicit about his or her and your own expectations about how supervision will proceed.
11. Allow yourself to feel threatened by your supervisee's competencies.
12. Retaliate against your supervisee for being more competent than you are in one or more areas or more mature than you are chronologically.
13. Insist that your supervisee work from the same theoretical orientation that you do.
14. Demand that your supervisee "act like a student rather than a colleague."
15. Criticize your supervisee in front of his or her peers.
16. Deny responsibility for interpersonal conflicts that arise between you and your supervisee.
17. If you sense the presence of conflict in the relationship, don't bring it up.
18. If your relationship with your supervisee becomes difficult, don't consult with someone else about it. It might reveal your lack of competence.
19. Treat your supervisee as a confidante. Use her or him as your counselor.
20. Be sexist, ageist, multiculturally incompetent, and the like.
21. Don't take your supervisee's expressed concerns about any of the above issues seriously.
22. Reveal intimate details about your own sexual experiences to your supervisee.

Source: From table based on a paper, *How to Be a Lousy Supervisor: Lessons from the Research*, by M. L. Nelson, October, 2002, presented at the convention of the Association for Counselor Education and Supervision, Park City, UT.

The Supervisor's Evaluative Practices. Ladany, Lehrman-Waterman, et al. (1999) found that a third of the ethical violations that supervisees reported concerns with how open and fair the evaluative processes of their supervisors. The level of this concern corroborates just how important it is for supervisors to be clear about expectations and evaluative processes and to be perceived as fair in how feedback and evaluation was handled.

It is important, then, that Lehrman-Waterman and Ladany (2001) report the development of a measure to assess evaluation practices in clinical supervision, the Evaluation Process within Supervision Inventory (EPSI). Two EPSI scales were used:

1. *Goal Setting—Sample items: The goals my supervisor and I generated for my training seemed important; My supervisor and I created goals that were easy for me to understand.*
2. *Feedback—Sample items: My supervisor welcomed comments on his or her style as a supervisor; The feedback I received was directly related to the goals we established.*

This was an instrument-development study, but, as part of the validation process, Lehrman-Waterman and Ladany compared scores on the new measure with scores on measures that would be linked theoretically. Scores on both EPSI scales predicted supervisees' ratings of supervisory alliance (all three alliance dimensions: tasks, goals, and bonds). As well, scores on these scales predicted satisfaction with supervision. It is logical to wonder about the extent to which the EPSI's Goal Setting Scale and the Goal Scale of the Working Alliance Inventory might actually be measuring the same construct (e.g., the correlation between the two was .78).

Reasonably, the clearer and fairer the evaluative process is perceived to be, the less supervisee anxiety and greater the level of trust. Both have positive effects on the SWA. A complementary perspective is that the stronger the SWA, the better able the supervisee to receive and use difficult feedback productively (Hoffman, Hill, Holmes, & Freitas, 2005).

Role Conflict and Ambiguity. Drawing from the organizational psychology literature, Olk and Friedlander (1992) identified role conflict and role ambiguity as a source of difficulty for supervisees. It is important to note that levels of role conflict and role ambiguity have been shown to be negatively related to the quality of the SWA (Ladany & Friedlander, 1995; Son, Ellis, & Yoo, 2007).

Ladany and Friedlander (1995) make the point that role *ambiguity* occurs when the supervisee is uncertain about the role expectations that the supervisor and/or agency has for him or her. Role *conflict* occurs one of two instances:

- supervisees are required to engage in two or more roles that may require inconsistent behavior (e.g., being required to reveal personal weaknesses and potential inadequacies while *also* needing to present themselves to the supervisor as competent so that they will pass the practicum; here the conflict is between the supervisee-as-client and supervisee-as-counselor); or,
- supervisees are required to engage in behavior that is incongruent with their personal judgment (e.g., being given directives to behave in a manner that is inconsistent with the supervisee's ethical or theoretical beliefs—the conflict is between the roles of supervisee-as-student and supervisee-as-counselor).

Olk and Friedlander (1992) developed the Role Conflict and Role Ambiguity Inventory (RCRAI) in order to operationalize and measure those two constructs. They found that whereas many supervisees reported no role difficulties, those who did were more likely to report work-related anxiety and dissatisfaction as well as dissatisfaction with supervision. They also found that supervisees reported less role ambiguity when they perceived that their supervisors offered clear statements about their expectations for supervision (one useful means to do this is a supervision contract).

SWA was not an explicit focus of Nelson and Friedlander's (2001) qualitative study of supervisees who had experienced conflictual supervision, but they found clear evidence that role conflict and ambiguity negatively affected those supervisees' relationships with their supervisors. Notably, all but 1 of the 13 supervisees they interviewed scored substantially above the norm group means for both role conflict and role ambiguity. As well, these supervisees rated their supervisors substantially below norm group means for the Attractive and Interpersonally Sensitive scores on the SSI (Friedlander & Ward, 1984), which, as we discuss earlier, predict SWA.

Often role conflict and ambiguity occurs when the supervisor provides mixed or unclear messages. But to the extent that these are a function of ignorance of the supervisory process—as with very novice supervisees—role induction strategies can be useful. The effectiveness of using this educative strategy has been demonstrated with therapy clients (see, e.g., Garfield, 1986; Strassle, Borckardt, Handler, & Nash, 2011). In applying that approach to supervision, Bahrick, Russell, and Salmi (1991) developed a 10-minute audio-taped summary of Bernard's (1979) supervision model and then presented it to supervisees at one of several points in the semester. After hearing the tape, supervisees reported having a clearer conceptualization of supervision and being more willing to reveal concerns to their supervisors. This effect occurred regardless of when in the semester supervisees heard the tapes. More recently, Ellis, Chapin, Dennin, and Anderson-Hanley (1996) found that a role induction procedure that they used decreased supervisee anxiety significantly in comparison to a control group.

Role induction, however, need not rely on audio or video tapes; for example, assigned readings can be used. At least one book now available to supervisees has a role-induction intent (Carroll & Gilbert, 2005), and a chapter in Holloway and Carroll (1999) speaks to how to prepare supervisees for their role. Another potentially useful supervision strategy would be to assess and then discuss participants' expectations. Supervisors might, therefore, find two scales useful: The scale created by Ellis, Anderson-Hanley, Dennin, Anderson, Chapin, and Polstri (1994) is a 52-item scale (one for supervisees, another for supervisors) for examining expectations for supervision; the scale developed by Vespia, Heckman-Stone, and Delworth (2002) is a 50-item Supervision Utilization Rating Form (SURF), which they explicitly suggest as a role induction/clarification tool.

Racial Identity Matching. In examining the effects of racial identity matching, Ladany, Brittan-Powell, and Pannu (1997) found that supervisors and supervisees who shared higher levels of racial identity attitudes had stronger SWAs.

Discussions of Racial and Ethnic Differences. Racial identity matching focuses on attitudes and beliefs, but not on supervisory behaviors. Gatmon et al. (2001) found that those supervisor–supervisee dyads who had frank discussions of similarities and differences in their ethnicity had stronger SWAs. Interestingly, frank discussions of neither gender nor sexual orientation predicted SWA, although it did predict satisfaction with supervision (whereas discussion of ethnicity did not).

Supervisor–Supervisee Complementarity. *Complementarity* is based on two assumptions: (a) in any relationship, there are power inequities; and (b) relationships are smoother when each person's behavior complements the other on that power dimension. An example of a complementary interaction sequence is when one person requests help, and the other person responds by providing that help. In short, they can be thought of as "cooperating" in their interactions with one another.

Tracey (1993) proposes that the level of therapist–client complementarity in successful therapy is likely to vary by stage of counseling, although this stage hypothesis for complementarity was not borne out in a study of supervision (Tracey & Sherry, 1993). Chen and Bernstein (2000) did find that when they compared two supervisory dyads, the one with the higher level of complementarity had the stronger SWA.

Quarto (2002) used a questionnaire to examined supervisory dyads that were conflictual, or noncomplementary (sample item: "My supervisor/supervisee and I do not follow one another's leads when discussing issues in supervision"), versus those who were not. Perhaps unsurprisingly, level of conflictual/noncomplementary interactions had a strong negative correlation with SWA.

The Effects of Supervisory Alliance on Supervision

We have been discussing supervisor and supervisee attributes and behaviors that predict strong or effective SWAs. Now, we shift our attention to some of the processes and outcomes that are predicted by quality of the alliance. These are highlighted on the right side of Figure 3.

Working alliances receive so much attention in therapy because they predict therapeutic outcome (e.g., Horvath & Symonds, 1991; Norcross & Wampold, 2011; Orlinsky, Grawe, & Parks, 1994); the alliance is not an end in itself. It also is true in supervision that an effective relationship is not the *purpose* of supervision; rather, the SWA is an important a mechanism to effect positive change in processes and certain outcomes.

Supervisory Alliance Effects on Supervision Processes The research has focused on one supervision process—supervisees' willingness to disclose to their supervisors.

SWA's Effect on Process: Supervisees' Willingness to Disclose. Supervisors assume that supervisees withhold at least some information (Reichelt et al., 2009). Slavin (1994) poses this rhetorical question: "How often have we heard clinicians joke, privately and guiltily, about what they don't tell their supervisors?" (p. 256). In so doing, he highlights a significant problem in supervision: Supervisees vary in their willingness to reveal both what Sarnat and Frawley-O'Dea (2001) playfully call "crimes and misdemeanors" as well as more personal material.

However, to the extent that supervisees withhold relevant information, clients are put at risk—and, by extension, put the supervisor at legal risk, for he or she is liable if the supervisee is engaged in unethical or illegal activities or simply malpractice. As well, supervisees limit what they can learn. For these reasons, the study by Ladany, Hill, Corbett, and Nutt (1996) of what supervisees failed to disclose to their supervisees and why should rank as among the more important in the supervision literature. Their results are summarized in Table 2.

As these results indicate, supervisees report a number of reasons for having failed to disclose material, but half the supervisees reported that poor alliance was one of the reasons. However, studies that have explicitly examined the link between nondisclosures and SWA have found that the two are negatively related: the higher the

TABLE 2 What Supervisees Fail to Disclose and Why

In their sample of supervisees, Ladany et al. (1996) found the following:

What they had failed to disclose

- Negative feelings toward a supervisor (90% of supervisees who had failed to disclose material)
- Their own personal issues (e.g., thoughts about themselves; experiences; problems) (60%)
- Clinical mistakes (44%)
- Uneasiness or concerns about the supervisor's evaluations of them (44%)
- General observations about the client (e.g., diagnosis; appearance; interventions; counseling process) (43%)
- Negative (critical, disapproving, or unpleasant) reactions to the client (36%)
- Thoughts or feelings of attraction toward the client (25%)
- Positive feelings toward the supervisor (23%)
- Countertransference reactions to client (22%)

Why they had not disclosed

- Perceived to be too personal (73%)
- Perceived to be unimportant (62%)
- Negative feelings such as shame, embarrassment, or discomfort (51%)
- Feelings of deference (i.e., it was not the supervisee's place to bring up material that would be uncomfortable to the supervisor) (55%)
- Poor alliance with the supervisor (50%)
- Impression management (i.e., to avoid being perceived negatively) (46%)

Note: Percentages were of those supervisees who reported having failed to disclose material. Supervisees could indicate multiple categories of what they had or had not disclosed this material.

level of nondisclosure, the lower the quality of the SWA (Mehr, Ladany, & Caskie, 2010; Webb & Wheeler, 1998). Although SWA was not an explicit variable in Yourman and Farber's (1996) study, they found that nondisclosures were related to lower levels of satisfaction with supervision. As well, relationship quality was underscored in the findings by Hess et al. (2008) about psychology interns' nondisclosures: "We were struck by the fact that so many interns . . . despite their advanced levels of training and clinical experience, reported negative personal feelings (e.g., anxiety, doubt, confusion) that contributed to nondisclosure" (p. 408).

Finally, we note that a consistent theme across these studies is that one important area about which supervisees withhold information is their perceptions of the supervisor and of the supervision itself. To the extent this is true, there is a sort of vicious cycle in which relationship problems affect supervisees' willingness to discuss those problems—which then do not get resolved unless the supervisor is attentive to the cues suggesting a relationship breach (see the upcoming discussion of relationship ruptures and repairs) and is able to intervene constructively.

Supervisory Alliance Effects on Supervision Outcomes. Supervision is a complex endeavor, and so its "outcomes" can be conceptualized at several levels. That is true here with respect to the following four outcomes of a quality alliance.

SWA's Outcomes: Internalizing the Supervisor. In an intriguing study, Geller, Farber, and Schaffer (2010) examine the extent to which supervisees' internally represent their supervisors, the occasions in which the invoke those representations, how this is helpful to them, and how they experience the embodiment of their supervisors. Whereas Geller et al. use no direct measure of alliance in this study, they ground this work conceptually in the alliance.

Geller et al. found that "93% of our sample reported that they were aware of experiencing the felt presence of their supervisor a few times per month; 47% indicated that this experience occurred 2–3 times per week" (p. 215). Supervisees responded to questions about the ways in which such internal representations are helpful to them (items they rated highly include "Recapture what we talked about in supervision," and, "Confront the patient or take up a painful issue"), the extent to which they experienced the felt-presence of their supervisor during particular occasions (items they rated highly include "When my patient confirms my supervisor's views," and, "When preparing process notes"), and how they experienced the felt-embodiment of their supervisor (items they rated highly include "I imagine a particular quality to the sound of my supervisor's voice," and, "I think of my supervisor as making specific statements to me").

SWA's Outcomes: Therapeutic Alliances of Supervisees with Their Clients. Patton and Kivlighan's (1997) findings about the correspondence between fluctuations in the supervisory and therapeutic alliances are important in having established an inferential link between quality of supervision and client outcomes—that is, (1) client–therapist working alliances have been shown to predict therapeutic outcome (Horvath & Symonds, 1991; Norcross & Wampold, 2011; Orlinsky et al., 1994); (2) the Patton and Kivlighan study established a link between supervisory and therapeutic alliance; and (3) it is possible, therefore, to infer that supervisory alliances indirectly affect client outcomes through the therapeutic alliances between supervisee and client.

SWA's Outcomes: Satisfaction. It is intuitive to believe that a better supervisory alliance predicts greater satisfaction with supervision. At least two studies have found this to be the case. In fact, in the Ladany, Lehrman-Waterman, et al. (1999) study, measured satisfaction correlated so highly with all three (i.e., task, goals, and bond) scales of the Working Alliance Inventory (*r*s of .88, .87, and .78, respectively) that they seemed to be measuring a common construct. In another study, however, Ladany, Ellis, et al. (1999) found that only supervisees' level of emotional bond predicted satisfaction.

Son et al. (2007) found that the relationship between working alliance and satisfaction was stronger for American than for Korean supervisees. This finding provides a useful reminder that the predictors and outcomes of supervisory working alliance that are depicted in Figure 3 were obtained in Western—primarily American—studies, and so should be generalized with caution to supervisory relationships in Eastern (especially Confucian) and other cultures.

SWA's Outcomes: Adherence to Treatment Protocols. Manualized treatments have been greeted with suspicion by many mental health professionals who regard adherence to a protocol as an unnecessary constraint on their use of professional judgment and creativity. However, for some mental health professionals (see, e.g., Roth, Pilling, & Turner, 2010), one important purpose of supervision is to increase the level of fidelity between the treatment supervisees are offering and the protocols that are specific to that model of treatment. Even for those who do not insist on such close adherence, treatment manuals provide an important means by which supervisees can learn about a particular approach (Lambert & Arnold, 1987). Significantly, then, Holloway and Neufeldt (1995) suggest that the quality of the supervisory relationship should affect the level of supervisees' adherence to a treatment manual.

Therefore, the results of Patton and Kivlighan's (1997) study are significant. In their examination of supervisees' adherence to a particular treatment model—Strupp and Binder's (1984) time-limited psychodynamic therapy—they found that week-to-week fluctuations in the supervisory alliance accounted for a substantial portion of the week-to-week fluctuations in adherence to general psychodynamic interviewing skills. The supervisory alliance did not, however, predict the use of specific manualized techniques.

Managing Alliance Fluctuations: Addressing and Resolving Conflict

> *Sullivan's statement, "God keep me from a therapy that goes well!" can be extended to "Keep me from a supervisory relationship that goes well!" Going well may mean that there is more superficiality in the relationship, but less anxiety; a more comfortable atmosphere, but limited interpersonal engagement; a greater sense of certainty, but complexities are dissociated; more interpretations, but little structural change in the relatedness between the participants . . . disappointments and struggles have more likely been avoided, but the potential richness and joy of a significant relationship [are] lost.* (Lesser, 1983, p. 128)

The material we have just covered documents that there are some factors that contribute to a good supervisory relationship and, in turn, a good supervisory relationship makes positive contributions to supervision processes and outcomes. This picture would remain incomplete, however, if we did not address (a) fluctuations that occur in the quality of supervisory relationships over time, and (b) supervisors' responses to them.

In the language used by working alliance theorists, relationships undergo a continual *weakening and repair* (also referred to as *tear–repair, rupture–repair,* or *disruption–restoration*) process (Bordin, 1983). Safran, Muran, and Eubanks-Carter (2011) define a *rupture in the therapy alliance* as

> *a tension or breakdown in the collaborative relationship between patient and therapist . . . ruptures vary in intensity from relatively minor tensions, which one or both of the participants may be only vaguely aware of, to major breakdowns in collaboration, understanding, or communication.* (p. 80)

Conflict, or *breakdown in collaboration* (Safran et al., 2011), occurs in all relationships, whether personal or professional. How and whether the parties are able to resolve these conflicts affects the relationship's growth or stagnation. This was a central theme in Mueller and Kell's (1972), now-classic book, *Coping with Conflict.* Nelson, Barnes, Evans, and Triggiano (2008) put it well when they observe that "numerous investigations of negative supervision events have indicated that major difficulties arise when supervisors either neglect or mishandle conflict" (p. 172).

It is likely that most weakenings or conflicts in relationships are resolved within a single supervision session, but some last longer. In a relatively informal study of supervision with psychiatric residents, Nigam, Cameron, and Leverette (1997) examine supervisory *impasses* as stalemates that lasted at least three to four weeks. Interestingly, 40% of the respondents reported having experienced at least one such impasse as supervisees. The usefulness of this descriptive study is in its cataloging of types of interpersonal problems between the supervisor and supervisee that led to impasses including boundary violations, lack of acceptance of a supervisee's sexual identity, and inhibition of disclosure of pertinent information.

Finally, we should note that a few supervisor–supervisee conflicts are never resolved. When these are of a serious nature, the supervisee can suffer lasting consequences (cf. Nelson & Friedlander, 2001) and clients, too, can be affected. Arkowitz (2001), invoking a parallel process framework, notes that, "A supervisee injured in supervision will act out these injuries with the patient, in confused attempts to repair them" (p. 59). Ramos-Sánchez et al. (2002) provide some support for this in their finding that supervisees who experienced problematic supervision experienced less-strong relationships with their clients.

Figure 4 visually models how the resolution—or non-resolution—of episodes of conflict cumulatively affects the quality of the supervisory relationship across time. If the conflict is resolved, the relationship is strengthened and grows; if the conflict is *not* resolved, the relationship suffers and is diminished. Because there are likely to be multiple conflictual episodes, there will be multiple opportunities to strengthen or weaken the relationship. In one way, this is a hopeful model

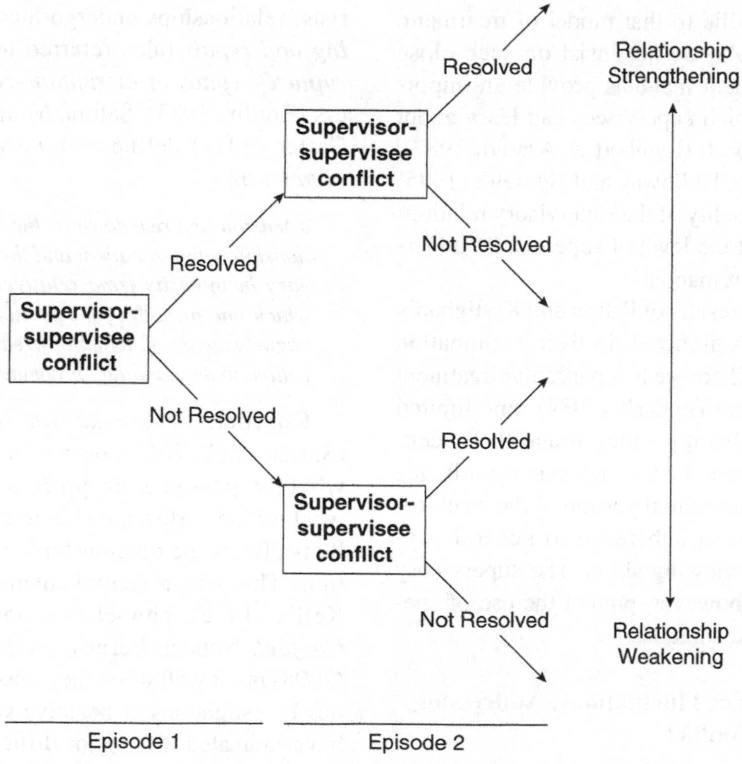

FIGURE 4 Relationship Trajectory as Conflictual Episodes Are Resolved or Not Resolved

in that it shows that if one episode is not resolved well, there likely will be other episodes that provide the opportunity to correct the trajectory of the relationship.

Figure 4 oversimplifies, of course, for it is unlikely that a supervisor–supervisee conflict will be resolved or not in a dichotomous manner. In real life, the resolution can be understood as occurring in some degree. But this figure is useful in making the point that relationships have a history of a series of conflict-resolution sequences and that the overall course of a particular supervisory relationship will be affected by the successes in resolving these conflicts. Ladany (2007) refers to data obtained in an earlier study (Ladany, Ellis, & Friedlander, 1999) that were obtained from supervisees at two points, at least six weeks apart. He notes: "[T]here is some evidence to suggest that at least in the realm of supervision, the alliance changes a third of the time for the better, does not change a third of the time, and changes a third of the time for the worst" (p. 395).

Conflict Origins and Type. Supervisee–supervisor conflicts can arise from many sources, some of which are more problematic than others. It is useful to consider them as types that occur on a continuum from (a) those that occur as a function of either a supervisor mistake or a miscommunication between the two, (b) those that occur because of normative processes, and (c) those that occur as a function of interpersonal dynamics and expectations of the supervisee. Each provides a learning opportunity. In the section that follows, each of these types is discussed in turn.

Conflicts Arising from Miscommunications or Mismatched Expectations. Evaluative feedback seems to make the supervisory relationship particularly vulnerable to conflict (Robiner, Fuhrman, & Ristvedt, 1993) and sensitive to potential ethical implications (Ladany, Lehrman-Waterman, et al. 1999). Moreover, the clearer the evaluation process (Lehrman-Waterman & Ladany, 2001) and expected supervisor roles (Ladany & Friedlander, 1995; Son et al., 2007), the better the supervisory relationship and the lower the supervisee anxiety.

These findings were confirmed in the only study yet to examine the weakening–repair process in supervisory alliances. In their observations of within-session tear–repair processes within 10 consecutive sessions of 10 supervisory dyads, Burke, Goodyear, and Guzzardo (1998) found that the more affect-arousing and difficult to repair weakenings occurred as supervisors assumed evaluative roles. They also observe that the type of weakening events varied according to the experience level of the supervisees. For example, alliance-weakening events with more advanced supervisees were more likely to involve disagreements about theoretical or treatment-planning issues.

Safran and Muran (2000) discuss interventions that the therapist (or supervisor) could use in response to these misunderstandings or disagreements. Among them were:

- *Direct intervention:* involves (a) clarifying to the client (or supervisee) the rationale for the intervention, and (b) addressing any misunderstandings that he or she might have.
- *Indirect intervention:* gives particular attention to the tasks and goals that have relevance to the client (or supervisee), rather than trying to address the underlying conflict.

In supervision, direct intervention is the better option in most cases in which a supervisory conflict has arisen because of either a misunderstanding or incongruent expectations. For example, and Safran, Muran, and Eubanks-Carter (2011) discuss metacommunicating about the processes occurring between therapist and client (or, in this case, the supervisor and supervisee); that is, to use the skill of immediacy. This also has the important advantage of helping model the resolution of relationship conflicts the supervisees inevitably will have with their clients.

Normative Conflicts. Some supervisee–supervisor conflict is normative and occurs in response to the supervisee's developmental level. In particular,

Rønnestad and Skovholt (1993) suggest that both supervisor–supervisee tension and dissatisfaction with supervision may be at its greatest with more advanced students. Like most adolescents, supervisees at this level vacillate between feelings of confidence and insecurity. Rønnestad and Skovholt note, "The student has now actively assimilated information from many sources but still has not had enough time to accommodate and find her or his own way of behaving professionally" (p. 400). This is not, in itself, a matter for concern, particularly if the supervisor is able to understand and anticipate this particular developmental phenomenon.

Conflicts Arising from Participants' Interpersonal Dynamics. Safran and Muran's (1996, 2000) is probably the best-known research program to focus on the resolution of therapeutic alliance ruptures. Many of their observations apply as well to supervisory alliances, with one important caveat: In most cases, the maladaptive interpersonal cycle to which they refer is less prominent in supervision. That is, most supervisees have less rigid or negative expectations about others than do clients, and therefore are less likely to elicit a complementary response from their supervisors.

With this caveat, it is useful to consider Safran and Muran's observations. Although we use their language and discuss client–therapist interactions, it is reasonable in most cases to understand that these same observations apply as well to supervisee–supervisor interactions.

Safran and Muran note that there are two major subtypes of alliance ruptures, although they often work in some degree of combination with one another. In one, the *confrontation rupture,* the client directly expresses unhappiness or even anger at some aspect of the therapy or the therapist. In *withdrawal ruptures,* the client disengages from the therapist or some aspect of the therapeutic process.

Therapists' initial attempts to resolve the ruptures often are complementary to the client's response, putting them into the role of perpetuating the "maladaptive interpersonal cycle" (Safran & Muran, 2000, p. 240)—that is, therapists often respond to confrontation ruptures defensively or with their own anger, and to withdrawal ruptures with their own controlling behavior. These responses generally replicate those of other people in the clients' lives.

To be effective, it is essential that the therapist be (a) aware of his or her own reactions that the client has elicited, and then (b) rather than participating further in the maladaptive interpersonal cycle, begin metacommunicating.

> *The process of extricating oneself from the dysfunctional dance that is being enacted is facilitated by inviting the client to take a step back and join with the therapist in a process of examining or metacommunicating about what is currently going on between them. The therapist's task is to identify his or her own feelings and to use these as a point of departure for collaborative exploration.* (Safran & Muran, 2000, p. 238)

The therapist's purpose is to help clients to learn that they can express their needs without endangering the therapeutic alliance. To do this, therapists have at least the following options in metacommunicating about an alliance rupture for tailoring their response to the specific client.

- Share his or her personal reactions and feelings by giving specific examples of client behaviors that might elicit them. "I feel dismissed or closed out by you, and I think it's because you don't seem to me to pause and reflect in a way that suggests you are really considering what I am saying" (Safran & Muran, 2000, p. 238). The therapist should then follow up with an inquiry such as, "How does this match your perceptions?" to elicit the client's response.
- In response to the client's withdrawal or confrontation, offer an empathic statement as means both to convey understanding and to invite the client to explore the issue.
- Offer a more interpretive response, especially to clients who have limited access to their inner experience or who find it too anxiety provoking or chaotic to explore.

These seem useful strategies for the supervisor as well. Of the three, the last strategy is least likely to be of use in supervision to resolve impasses. That is, we can assume that most supervisees have reasonable access to their inner experience.

Mental health professionals generally acknowledge that therapists may not be expected to form an effective working relationship with every client they see: Why should we have a different expectation for supervision? In the (fortunately rare) cases of intractable personality conflicts, the responsible supervisor transfers the supervisee to another supervisor or otherwise works to protect the supervisee's interests. However, to be sensitive to the issues we raise here is likely to minimize the frequency with which such conflicts happen.

Preparing Supervisees to Address Alliance Ruptures

Next we discuss two-person systems, focusing primarily on the relationship between supervisor and supervisee, but it is important in this case to address the other two-person system of supervisee and client. As already noted, the data are convincing that the working alliance predicts treatment outcome. The supervisor, therefore, is responsible for helping ensure good alliances.

The quality of the supervisory alliance affects that between supervisee and client, as Patton and Kivlighan (1997) demonstrate. And to the extent that the supervisor is attentive to and addresses relationship ruptures with the supervisee, important modeling is occurring that serves the supervisee well in work with the client.

Yet this is an indirect approach. Supervisors also more directly help supervisees monitor and resolve their relationship ruptures with clients. In fact, there have been some structured supervision programs designed explicitly for this purpose (e.g., Bambling, King, Raue, Schweitzer, & Lambert, 2006; Hilsenroth, Ackerman, Clemence, Strassle, & Handler, 2002). Safran et al. (2011) conducted a metaanalysis of nine of those programs and conclude that "rupture resolution training/supervision leads to small but statistically significant patient improvements relative to treatment by therapists who did not such training" (p. 84). Therefore, this is an area that seems to merit additional attention by supervision practitioners and scholars.

CONCLUSION

This chapter demonstrates just how complex the supervisory relationship is. That complexity is most evident when the relationship is considered as a three-person system, with its attendant parallel processes, isomorphism, triangulations, and so on. But even when supervisory relationships are scrutinized at the level of a two-person system, with only the supervisor and supervisee interactions, there is ample complexity. In short, this material illustrates how important it is that supervisors receive the formal training that helps them address this complexity.

In summary, conflict occurs in any relationship, including that between supervisor and supervisee. The manner in which it is resolved affects the overall course and strength of the relationship, and also provides useful learning opportunities for both supervisor and supervisee.

Supervisee and Supervisor Factors Affecting the Relationship

Supervisee and Supervisor Factors Affecting the Relationship

The supervisory relationship is the pillar that supports everything else about supervision. Therefore, it has a presence—even if only implied—in virtually *all* that we cover in this text. However, there are some aspects of the relationship that require direct and specific attention. We turn the spotlight on them in this chapter.

This chapter focuses on the two-person system, but directs attention to factors at the individual level that affect the supervisory relationship. Figure 1 visually depicts the supervisor and supervisee behaviors and attributes that affect relationship quality. Each of the two major sections of this chapter address one side of Figure 1. We begin with supervisee factors, depicted on the left side.

FACTORS AFFECTING SUPERVISEE ENGAGEMENT

Supervision involves both teaching and learning, but these processes are only imperfectly related, as Berliner (2012) illustrates by making a deliberately absurd assertion that "I spent all day yesterday teaching my dog to whistle"—to no avail. His point is that in order for what we teach to have its intended effects, the learner must be both (a) capable of developing the desired skill or knowledge *and* (b) motivated to do so. In what follows, we assume supervisees are capable of learning and so focus on motivational factors. Our particular concern is with supervisee engagement with the supervisor and in the supervision process.

To be engaged is integral to the "collaboration for change" (Bordin, 1983, p. 35) so definitive of the working alliance. Therefore, in giving attention to supervisee engagement and the factors that affect it, our discussion here concerns the relationship rupture-and-repair processes.

We begin with a discussion of supervisee resistance; then, we discuss, in turn, attachment style, shame, anxiety, concerns about competence, and transference.

Supervisee Resistance

Our understandings of supervisee resistance extrapolate from what we know of client resistance to therapy. As Beutler, Moleiro, and Talebi (2002a) observe:

> *While they disagree with one another in many ways, the 400+ theories of psychotherapy that are practiced in contemporary society converge on the curious observation that some painfully distressed*

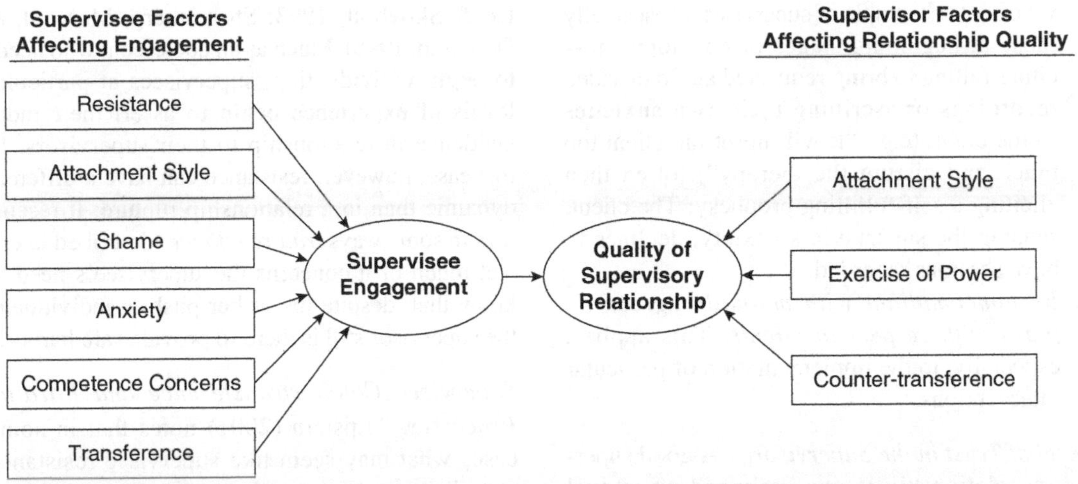

FIGURE 1 Supervisee and Supervisor Factors That Affect the Nature and Quality of the Supervisory Dyad

patients seeking assistance from expensive and highly trained professionals reject their therapists' best advice, fail to act in their own best interests, and do not respond to the most effective interventions that can be mustered on their behalf. . . . [But whereas] the descriptions offered of resistant behavior by different theories are similar, they offer dramatically different explanations and intervention methods. (p. 207)

Supervision has an educational rather than a therapeutic purpose, but these observations about resistance in therapy generalize as well to supervision (see, e.g., Bradley & Gould, 1994; Pearson, 2000). McColley and Baker (1982) found, in fact, that most novice supervisors identified their primary difficulty to be that of not knowing how to intervene effectively to reduce or minimize supervisee resistance. Resistance is antithetical to engagement, and so minimizing it is a supervisor priority.

To frame any supervisee behavior as *resistance* risks blaming the supervisee for what can be healthy response to perceived threat (Liddle, 1986). For the supervisor to adopt such a stance—however subtle it might be—can blind him or her to other causes for the supervisee's resistant behavior, including possible roles they may be playing to elicit it (see, e.g., Beutler, Moleiro, & Talebi, 2002b).

Ways Supervisees Reduce Their Engagement through Resistance. *Resistance* implies that something is being resisted; but what that is and how supervisees express it can vary. The following four (overlapping) types of resistance are among the more frequent of these.

1. *Resist the supervisor's influence.* This can occur, for example, by withholding or distorting information during sessions (e.g., Hess et al., 2008; Ladany, Hill, Corbett, & Nutt, 1996; Mehr, Ladany, & Caskie, 2010; Webb & Wheeler, 1998; Yourman & Farber, 1996); by deflecting discussions away from particular topics, or from a focus on some aspect of his or her behavior; or by engaging in power struggles with the supervisor.
2. *Resist the supervisory experience itself.* This category sometimes may be difficult to differentiate from the preceding one. Perhaps it is best exemplified by Epstein's (2001) comment that "I operate on the assumption that persisting negative behaviors, such as lateness or missing sessions, are resistances signifying negative reactions to supervision" (p. 150).
3. *Be noncompliant with tasks related to the supervisory process.* This is a more specific instance of the second category. To illustrate,

we offer the example of supervisees—especially those at beginning stages of development—either failing to bring requested audio or video recordings or ascribing their own anxieties to the client (e.g., "It will upset the client too much and disrupt the therapy"), often then eliciting a self-fulfilling prophesy: The client, sensing the supervisee's anxiety, declines to have sessions recorded.

4. *Be noncompliant with mutually agreed on plans with respect to clients.* This applies, especially, to the implementation of particular interventions.

Level of Trust in the Supervisor. A good supervisory relationship is one grounded on mutual trust (Scaife, 2001). That trust means that each person finds the other to be dependable. In a supervisory context, it means that the supervisee can relax energy-consuming vigilance against any supervisor actions that could be considered exploitive or intended to meet his or her own needs at the supervisee's expense (see, e.g., Strong, 1968).

In general, the more trusting a supervisee is of his or her supervisor, the more engaged she or he is in the process. However, trust always exists in some degree, rather than as a categorical, all-or-nothing phenomenon. Moreover, trust is earned over the course of many interactions and shared interpersonal risks. An important implication for supervisors, then, is that they should remain sensitive to relationship ruptures and have the skills to resolve them when they occur.

Level of Agreement with the Supervisor about Tasks and Goals. Dissonant goals and expectations about tasks are one source of relationship ruptures. Therefore, we simply acknowledge it here to underscore just how important it is for the supervisor to identify and then resolve these disagreements.

Supervisee Developmental Level. Various models predict that supervisees will differ from one another in their levels of resistance according to their levels of development (see, e.g., Rønnestad & Skovholt, 1993; Stoltenberg, McNeill, & Delworth, 1998). Much as an adolescent who needs to begin individuating, supervisees at particular levels of experience begin to assert their independence in relationship to their supervisors. In this case, however, resistance can have a different dynamic than in a relationship rupture: It resembles in some ways *trait reactance* (described later). Yet much of it concerns the supervisee's need to know that, despite his or her push to individuate, the supervisor still is there to provide safe harbor.

Supervisee Countertransference and Parallel Processes. Epstein (2001) notes that in some cases what may seem like supervisee resistance actually may be a manifestation of other processes. For example, it could be that the supervisee's failure to carry through with agreed-on interventions with the client stems from some particularly strong countertransference reaction to the client. In this case, the supervisor's intervention is one of helping the supervisee identify and address those reactions.

In a similar vein, Ekstein and Wallerstein (1972) observe that resistance may arise through the enactment of parallel processes—that is, supervisee resistant behavior occasionally occurs as a mirroring of the client's attitudes and behaviors.

Supervisor Style. A supervisor's style sometimes can trigger supervisee resistance (Quarto, 2002). This can be illustrated, for example, by considering Proctor and Inskipp's (1988) *must* versus *can* supervisory interventions.

- *Must interventions* are ones supervisors use when they want to ensure that the supervisee takes some very specific action, for the welfare of the client as well as other reasons.
- *Can interventions* are ones in which the supervisee has the choice about whether and when she or he might take a particular action.

Of the two, *must interventions* are the more likely to elicit resistance. This is especially true when the supervisee does not understand or agree with the rationale for the intervention and therefore perceives it as arbitrary. Must interventions also are likely to elicit resistance from supervisees who have high trait reactance, which Dowd (1989) describes as a hypersensitivity to losses of freedom with correspondingly high levels of vigilance in the presence of people of authority. This is consistent, for example, with the findings of Tracey, Ellickson, and Sherry (1989) that, among more advanced trainees, higher levels of reactance predicted supervisees' preference for less structured supervision.

Of the several supervisory styles or roles (Bernard, 1997) discusses (i.e., consultant, counselor, and teacher), that of the consultant is probably least threatening and maximizes supervisees' sense of control. Interpersonal process recall (IPR; Kagan & Kagan, 1997) for example, is a technique that is almost entirely consultative in style and therefore useful in minimizing resistance. Also, Borders (2009) discusses what she terms *subtle messages* in supervision. This means, for example, using a discovery-oriented approach to learning, which is the essence of the IPR model as well.

Supervisor Focus. Supervisors make constant choices about where they will focus attention during their work with supervisees. Those choices can affect supervisees' felt-vulnerability—and, in turn, their levels of resistance. Supervisees tend to feel least vulnerable, for example, when their supervisors focus on client dynamics, and most vulnerable when the focus is on some aspect of the supervisee's personhood (see Bernard, 1979). Therefore, one response to supervisees who seem especially anxious or vulnerable is to give greater *initial* attention to case conceptualization, thereby directing attention away from the supervisee. Epstein (2001) seems to be speaking of a similar strategy when he comments

> *I favor, whenever possible, the use of what Spotnitz (1969) has termed "object-oriented questions" as contrasted with "ego-oriented questions." These questions direct the supervisee's attention to faults of the other, to myself, or to the patient rather than to his own faults. This technique might appear to further the supervisee's tendency to externalize responsibility for his own contribution to the failure of the supervision or of the treatment situation. Actually, it has the opposite effect. Object-oriented questions establish an atmosphere in which the supervisee becomes increasingly free, with a minimal sense of risk, to contact and directly communicate all of his feelings vis-à-vis both the supervision and his patient.* (p. 298)

Summary Comments About Supervisee Resistance. Supervisee resistance can be thought of as the supervisee applying the brakes when he or she perceives the vehicle that is supervision to be moving too fast, or in the wrong direction, or on a too-bumpy road. In most instances, the resistance is akin to gently tapping the brakes. But there also are some instances in which a supervisee will figuratively "lock-'em-up." For the supervisor to be effective, she or he should create a climate that minimizes supervisees' felt need to put on the brakes. As well, she or he must be alert to instances of resistance and then make informed decisions about the best response. In general, the best supervision is that in which the supervisee is least resistant.

For the remainder of the first portion of this chapter, we address specific supervisee factors that affect resistance and therefore the quality of the dyad relationship. We begin with attachment and then examine, in turn, shame, anxiety, the need for competence, and finally, transference.

Supervisee Attachment

"The need to belong is a powerful, fundamental, and extremely pervasive motivation" (Baumeister & Leary, 1995, p. 497). To use a computer analogy, people are "hardwired" to be relational, but they differ in how they enact their relationships needs. Attachment theory has been helpful in understanding these differences.

Bowlby (1977), who did the seminal work in attachment theory, stated, "Briefly put, attachment behavior is conceived as any form of behavior that results in a person attaining or retaining proximity to some other differentiated and preferred individual, who is usually conceived as stronger and/or wiser" (p. 203). Bowlby (1977, 1978) describes two primary pathological attachment patterns or styles. One is anxious attachment; the other, compulsive self-reliance. A third, which is something of a variant on the second, is compulsive caregiving (whereas subsequent theorists also are concerned with secure attachment, they show some variability in the numbers of and labels given to the variant attachment styles; see, e.g., Bartholomew & Horowitz, 1991).

Bowlby argues that a person's style (i.e., the way he or she approaches and maintains relationships) is learned during childhood, through experiences with parents and other caregivers. That style tends to be maintained throughout life in that person's relationships with important others, enduring across people and situations and predicting which social information a person encodes (see, also, Dykas & Cassidy, 2011).

Watkins (1995c) and Pistole and Watkins (1995) observe that the supervisory relationship is an adult–adult relationship with many similarities to parent–child relationships and, therefore, that it might be usefully thought of as an attachment process that involves the development and eventual loosening of an affectional bond. They suggest, for example, that a supervisee with an anxious attachment style is likely to be dependent and even "clingy," to call the supervisor constantly for help, to want to be the supervisor's favorite, and to resent the supervisor for not needing him or her in a reciprocal way.

However, a supervisee who is a compulsive caregiver is likely to "rescue" clients, working to lessen their concerns and problems immediately (often at the expense of letting them fully grapple with and find resolution to their issues); this supervisee also is likely to be uncomfortable and even anxious in the supervisory context where she or he is the recipient of the supervisor's help and support. And a compulsively self-reliant supervisee is likely to refuse, resist, or even resent the supervisor's attempts to help.

A few studies now have examined the relationship between supervisee attachment and the working alliance. Renfro-Michel (2006) found a link between supervisee attachment and supervisory alliance, as did Bennett, Mohr, BrintzenhofeSzoc, and Saks (2008); however, two others (Dickson, Moberly, N. J., Marshall, Y., & Reilly, 2011; White & Queener, 2003) did not. Clearly, this is an area warranting more research attention.

Foster, Lichtenberg, and Peyton (2007) found that supervisors and supervisees have differential perceptions of supervisees' attachment style and its relationship to supervisee development. Specifically, they found that whereas supervisees' fearful, preoccupied, or dismissive attachment styles predicted lower self-ratings of professional development, that relationship was not upheld with respect to supervisor ratings of their development.

Supervisee Shame

Guilt and shame are self-conscious emotions. Because it sometimes is difficult to distinguish between them, it is useful to begin this section with Lewis's (1971) suggestion that in *shame,* the focus of evaluation is the self (i.e., "I am flawed"), whereas in *guilt,* it is some act, thought, or feeling (i.e., "I have done something wrong").

> *[I]n guilt, behavior is evaluated somewhat apart from the self. There is remorse or regret over the "bad thing" that was done and a sense of tension that often serves to motivate reparative action. . . . Whereas guilt motivates a desire to repair, to confess, apologize, or make amends, shame motivates a desire to hide—to sink into the floor and disappear.* (Tangney, Wagner, Fletcher, & Gramzow, 1992, pp. 669–670)

Supervision has the potential to elicit shame because of its evaluative components, the requirement that supervisees expose themselves and their work, and supervisees' inevitable ego investment in the work they are doing. As well, shame has two other attributes that are particularly important to supervision: (a) it involves a sense of exposure or of being exposed; and (b) for it to occur, there must be some level of bond between the person and the "observing other" (Retzinger, 1998).

Yet, as Hahn (2002) points out, only a little (e.g., Alonso & Rutan, 1988; Lidmila, 1997) has been written about the role of supervisee shame in supervision. Because of its potentially detrimental effects on both the supervisee and the supervisory relationship, supervisee shame warrants more attention than it has so far received

Supervisee Responses to Shame or the Threat of Shame. Gilbert (1998) suggests that when people experience shame, it is possible for them to respond either submissively or aggressively. Hahn (2002) draws from Nathanson (1992) to identify four common supervisee reactions to shame, which we summarize next. Consistent with Gilbert, the first two of these could be characterized as *passive,* and the second two as *aggressive* (significantly, too, these all could describe supervisee resistance, as discussed earlier).

Passive Response: Withdrawal. Withdrawal can occur as a momentary response to shame (e.g., pulling back, breaking eye contact). However, depending on the strength and pervasiveness of the shame reaction, supervisees can manifest their withdrawal as forgetfulness, coming late to sessions, and even the adoption of a passive and noncurious style of interaction with the supervisor.

Passive Response: Avoidance. "Avoidance reactions are relatively active efforts to prevent exposure and condemnation" (Hahn, 2002, p. 276). Among the many avoidance strategies that supervisees might use are diverting the supervisor's attention away from their mistakes and failures, and encouraging the supervisor to provide his or her own observations and wisdom about a particular case (versus exposing their own knowledge, feelings, or skills). In fact, shame can prompt supervisees to withhold information from their supervisors (e.g., Yourman, 2003).

Aggressive Response: Attack on Others. This externalizing behavior can vary in intensity from mild dismissiveness and devaluing of the supervisor (Yerushalmi, 1999) to more overt and hostile criticism. It is most likely to occur as a response to shame that has been triggered by feeling devalued or in some way diminished by the supervisor (a feeling that can be based on an actual supervisor behavior, or by some supervisee's unmet expectation of which the supervisor is unaware).

Aggressive Response: Attack on Self. This internalizing behavior "occurs on a continuum and may be manifested as deference on one end of the continuum to excessive self-criticism on the other" (Hahn, 2002, p. 280). Hahn notes that in supervision, this defensive style can be used as a "preemptive strike": By criticizing him- or herself, the supervisor is deflected from doing so. McWilliams (1994) describes such a strategy:

> *Therapists in training who approach supervision in a flood of self-criticism are often using a masochistic strategy to hedge their bets: If my supervisor thinks I made a major error with my client, I've already shown that I'm aware of it and have been punished enough; if not, I get reassured and exonerated.* (p. 263)

The Supervisor's Role in Minimizing Supervisee Shame. To the extent that supervisors can create a climate of trust and respect, supervisees develop a sense of security and dignity, enabling them to examine "secret failures that [they otherwise would be] too horrified to admit" (Alonso & Rutan, 1988, p. 580). It also is important that supervisors offer supervisees consistent support and backing (Alonso & Rutan, 1988) and provide them with performance feedback in ways that least likely to be shame-invoking (see, e.g., the Claiborn, Goodyear, & Horner, 2002, review of feedback in psychotherapy and the Hoffman, Hill, Holmes, & Freitas, 2005, study of supervisors' perspective on the feedback they provide).

Bridges (1999) suggests as well that supervisors can create a "shame-free learning milieu" by normalizing "the trainee's shame, powerlessness, and self-consciousness about not knowing, being a trainee, and [struggling] with personal, painful feelings" (p. 220). Echoing a similar suggestion by Alonso and Rutan (1988), Bridges suggests that the supervisor be willing to share his or her own "mistakes, humiliating clinical moments, and examples of countertransference domination with attention to how to understand and manage these dilemmas" (p. 220).

Yet even supervisors' best efforts to optimize environments cannot head off all supervisee shame. This means that supervisor should be alert to signs of shame so that they can respond constructively. For this, an awareness of these four major supervisee responses to shame, described earlier, provides a useful conceptual tool to guide their attention. Also, some supervisees are more prone to feel shame than others, and so supervisors should be alert to supervisees who might function with higher levels of that variable. Notably, Bilodeau, Savard and Lecompte (2012), for example, found that shame-prone supervisees experienced successively lower supervisory working alliances across the five supervisory sessions that they examined.

Supervisee Anxiety

Many aspects of the training experience can elicit supervisee anxiety. In fact, one of the really striking findings in Skovholt and Rønnestad's (1992a, 1992b) qualitative study of therapists across the lifespan was that graduate students experience intense anxiety. It is interesting, too, that Skovholt and Rønnestad were less able to access this anxiety from their graduate student informants than they were from more senior practitioners, who were reflecting back on their experiences in graduate school.

Anxiety may be common supervisee response, but they express it in multiple ways and in response a number of circumstances. What adds even more complexity to the picture is that supervisees' anxiety can be moderated by such factors as the supervisee's maturity, experience level, personality, and relationships with clients and the supervisor. In the material that follows, we address, in turn, the effects of supervisee anxiety, its sources, and possible supervisor responses to it.

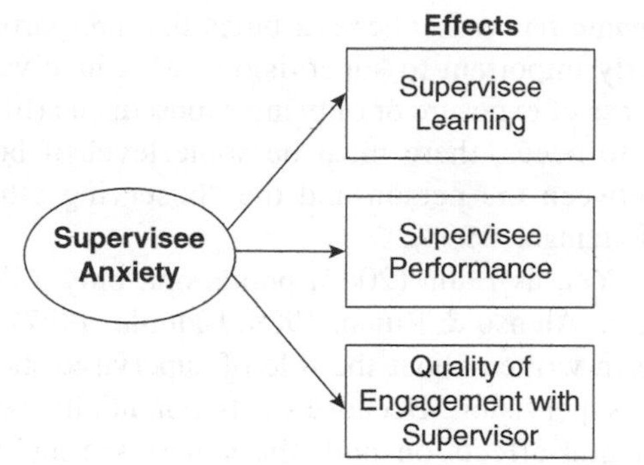

FIGURE 2 Consequences of Supervisee Anxiety

Effects of Anxiety on the Supervisee. In general, supervisee anxiety can affect the supervisee's ability to learn, ability to demonstrate already-present skills, and interactions with the supervisor. This is depicted visually in Figure 2. We discuss all three in turn.

The first two of these—ability to learn and ability to demonstrate already-present skills—have no direct effects on the supervisory relationship, which is the focus of this chapter. However, they *are* important to the supervisee, and so discussing them warrants a short digression from the chapter's central theme.

Anxiety Affects Supervisee Learning. Too much anxiety reduces what supervisees notice and encode (Dombeck & Brody, 1995); however, this is not to suggest that supervisee anxiety is always to be warded off. As counselors or therapists, we know that much of the time it is unhelpful to rush in with attempts to diminish a client's anxiety. The same pertains to supervisors' response to supervisee anxiety. Within limits, the more anxiety counselors are able to allow themselves, the more they learn (Rioch, Coulter, & Weinberger, 1976). In part, this is because being able to "stay with" anxiety can be useful in identifying problem areas,

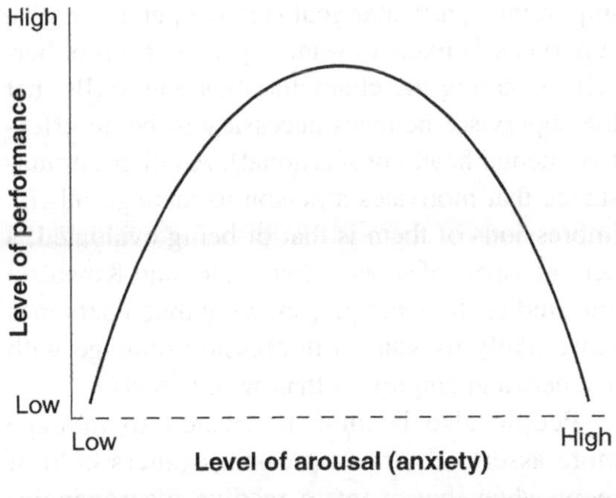

FIGURE 3 Depiction of the Yerkes–Dodson Inverted-U Hypothesis Regarding the Relationship Between Level of Arousal and Level of Performance

either in what the client is presenting or in the supervisee's own history and characteristic ways of responding.

Anxiety Affects Supervisee Performance. Supervisee performance is concerned with what the supervisee actually has learned and can demonstrate in practice. Perhaps unsurprisingly, Friedlander, Keller, Peca-Baker, and Olk (1986) found that supervisees' performance was inversely related to their anxiety levels. However, repeating our earlier point concerning supervisee learning, this is not to suggest that supervisee anxiety always is to be minimized.

Yerkes and Dodson's (1908) inverted-U hypothesis, shown in Figure 3, is a useful way to think about anxiety, despite some conceptual and empirical questions (e.g., Matthews, Davies, & Lees, 1990; Neiss, 1988). This is one of psychology's most famous hypotheses: Anxiety is an arousal state that, in moderate amounts, motivates the individual and facilitates his or her task performance. Yet an individual's performance suffers when he or she experiences either *too little* or *too much* anxiety: too little, and one lacks sufficient motivation to perform; too much, and one is debilitated.

Given the hypothesis that there is an optimal range of anxiety within which supervisees best function, then supervisors logically have the simultaneous goals of helping keep their supervisees from engaging in anxiety-avoidant behaviors, and helping keep supervisee anxiety in bounds so that it works in the service of performance. Kell and Burow (1970) note, for example, that they worked as supervisors "not only to facilitate . . . an awareness of the anxiety associated with the seriousness of learning, but also to leaven and help control the anxious experience" (p. 184).

One important source of supervisee anxiety is that their work is observed and evaluated continually. Social facilitation theory, which "focuses on changes in performance that occur when individuals perform in the presence of others versus alone" (Aiello & Douthitt, 2001, p. 163), is useful to understand the effects of observation and evaluation on performance. Although this theory has a history of more than a century, Aiello and Douthitt credit Zajonc (1965) for developing its contemporary version. Zajonc distinguishes between *dominant responses* (those it is easiest for the person to perform) and *non-dominant responses* (those that are part of the person's skill repertoire, but are less likely to be performed). He notes that increases in arousal facilitate performance of dominant responses, but impede performance of non-dominant responses.

Athletics performance provides useful illustrations of this effect. On one extreme, Olympic athletes have over-learned their particular athletic skill through thousands of hours of practice, to the point that these skills have become dominant responses. Under conditions of competition and close scrutiny, their performance is enhanced and may even attain record-breaking levels. In contrast, however, people who still are working to master their skills are much more prone to "clutching" when they are being observed. Supervisees are akin to these beginning athletes in that they still are working to develop skills that have not yet become automatic (e.g., Bargh & Chartrand, 1999). When observed or monitored by a supervisor, their performance is vulnerable to deterioration.

We should note that only a relatively few supervisees may experience these consequences. On the basis of data from several studies (e.g., Chapin & Ellis, 2002; Ellis, Krengel, & Beck, 2002), Ellis (personal communication, October 15, 2002) concludes that the role of supervisee anxiety may have been overstated in the supervision literature. He asserts: "It looks like less than 10 percent report even moderate anxiety in high anxiety supervision or training situations (e.g., first videotape review supervision in pre-practicum)." It appears, therefore, that more research is needed. In the meantime, it is useful for supervisors to be sensitive to the possible effects of observation on the supervisee.

Anxiety Affects Quality of Engagement with the Supervisor. Supervisees' anxiety affects how they relate to their supervisors, including how much they withhold (Hess et al., 2008; Ladany, Hill, Corbett, & Nutt, 1996; Mehr, Ladany, & Caskie, 2010; Webb & Wheeler, 1998) or distort (Yourman & Farber, 1996). Rønnestad and Skovholt (1993) note that "the anxious student may tend to discuss in supervision only clients who show good progress, choose themes in which he or she is functioning well, or choose a mode of presenting data that allows full control over what the supervisor learns" (p. 398). They suggest that the supervisor may therefore, in the beginning, allow the student to select or even distort data until some of that anxiety dissipates.

We are all concerned about how others perceive us (e.g., Schlenker & Leary, 1982). We want to convey certain impressions of ourselves, but worry about how well we are doing it. Social psychologists have discussed the strategies people use to address these concerns as *impression management* (or *strategic self-presentation*). This is the person's attempt to deliberately project a certain image. It is possible to think of any person's social behavior as being a performance intended to create desired effects on others.

A number of factors can motivate a person to more assertively manage impressions others have of them (Leary & Kowalski, 1990). One is how important a particular goal is to the person (e.g., a supervisee is likely to want to present him- or herself as having the characteristics and skills that the supervisor believes necessary to be an effective mental health professional). Another circumstance that motivates a person to manage others' impressions of them is that of being evaluated; a central aspect of supervision. Leary and Kowalski cite studies, for example, showing that a person is more likely to want to impression manage with teachers and employers than with friends.

People also become motivated to manage more assertively the impressions others hold of them when they want to resolve discrepancies between their desired image and the image others currently have of them. This is especially true when their social image has been damaged and people want to gain respect and admiration. Therefore, when individuals believe they have failed at an important task (e.g., receiving negative evaluations of their work), they tend to behave in a more self-enhancing manner in order to repair their image (Schlenker, 1980).

Despite the clear relevance of the concept of impression management to supervision, only a couple of studies so far have examined directly supervisees' self-presentation motivations and impression-construction strategies (Friedlander & Schwartz, 1985; Ward, Friendlander, Schoen, & Klein, 1985). Yet a number of supervision studies that have not been explicitly framed as studies in impression management actually have implications for that model. Several studies of what supervisees choose not to disclose (e.g., Hess et al., 2008; Ladany et al., 1996; Mehr et al., 2010; Webb & Wheeler, 1998) provide excellent examples as they found that a very frequent motive to withhold information from their supervisor was to manage impressions.

In summary, we all have certain ways we would like to be seen by others. This certainly is the case with supervisees who, in addition to the wish that most of us have to be seen as likeable and so on, also have strong practical reasons to wish to be perceived as competent. Supervisors should remain alert to how these motives to present themselves in a certain light might be activated when supervisees are anxious about how they are being seen and how that, in turn, may affect how supervisees relate to them.

Supervisor Management of Supervisee Anxiety. Supervision itself reduces supervisee anxiety. In fact, Whittaker (2004) found in a meta-analysis that the average effect of supervision on supervisee anxiety was .46, which approximates the .5 level that Cohen (1992) identifies as a "medium" effect size in the social sciences. Given this evidence that supervisors can reduce supervisee anxiety, it is useful to consider specific strategies they might use to enhance that effect.

Normalizing Anxiety and Giving Permission to Make Mistakes. Borders (2009) suggests that supervisors make it clear to supervisees that they have permission to take risks and make mistakes. She suggests, too, that supervisors normalize anxiety: "A good thing to say is, 'I expect you'll be a little anxious about some of your new experiences here. That's perfectly normal, and I want to help'" (pp. 202–203).

Optimizing Levels of Supervisor-Offered Support and Challenge. Good supervision involves providing supervisees with an optimal balance between *support* (including structure) and *challenge* (Blocher, 1983; reflected as well in the factor analysis of supervisor behaviors discussed in Worthington & Roehlke, 1979). Too much support and too little challenge robs the supervisee of initiative and the opportunity to try new behaviors; too little support and too much challenge and the supervisee may become overwhelmed and incapacitated. This is confirmed by Lizzio, Wilson, and Que (2009), who found that level of support supervisees perceived their supervisors to offer was inversely related to their anxiety levels, whereas the level of challenge they perceived their supervisors to offer was directly related to their anxiety level.

The level of structure that supervisors provide during sessions with their supervisees can affect the support supervisees experience. In fact, theory (e.g., Stoltenberg & Delworth, 1987) and research (e.g., Tracey et al., 1989) both suggest that supervisees desire more structure when they are experiencing greater anxiety (e.g., when the context of counseling arouses anxiety, when the client presents "in crisis," when the supervisee is relatively inexperienced). Freeman (1993) observes that supervisors can decrease supervisee anxiety by providing structure, and she suggests, along with others (e.g., Friedlander & Ward, 1984; Sansbury, 1982; Usher & Borders, 1993), that the provision of structure is more important to the inexperienced counselor than to one who is more advanced (e.g., Heppner & Roehkle, 1984; McNeill, Stoltenberg, & Pierce, 1985; Reising & Daniels, 1983; Stoltenberg, Pierce, & McNeill, 1987; Tracey et al., 1989; Wiley & Ray, 1986).

Interestingly, Lichtenberg, Goodyear, and McCormick (2000) found no relationship between supervisee anxiety and level of session structure. Perhaps the reason for this seemingly discrepant finding can be ascribed to differences in how structure has been operationalized across studies. Lichtenberg et al. define *structure* in terms of moment-to-moment verbal interaction patterns. Most others who have written about structure, however, have operationalized it in terms of supervisor directiveness and control of session content and process. Perhaps it would be useful for the field to develop a general understanding of this commonly used term.

Role Induction. Uncertainty about role and performance expectations that their supervisors have for them creates an almost-inevitable—and *unnecessary*—source of supervisee anxiety. It is important that supervisors address these expectations early and directly, whether through dialogue with the supervisee, a written contract, or audio- or videotape modeling. *Role induction,* has had demonstrated effectiveness with preparing clients for counseling. For example, in a meta-analysis of 28 studies, Monks (1996) found that role induction had significant positive effects on clients' treatment outcome, attendance, and drop-out rates.

Less research has been done on role induction in supervision. However, that which *has* been done has shown positive effects. For example, Bahrick, Russell, and Salmi (1991) presented a 10-minute audiotaped summary of Bernard's (1979) supervision model to supervisees at one of several points in the semester. After supervisees heard the tape, they reported having a clearer conceptualization of supervision and being more willing to reveal concerns to their supervisors. This effect occurred regardless of when in the semester they heard the tapes.

Ellis, Chapin, Dennin, and Anderson-Hanley (1996) found that a role induction that they conducted significantly decreased supervisee anxiety compared to a control group. More recently, Chapin and Ellis (2002) again confirmed the utility of role induction. Moreover, they found in their multiple case-study design that a role-induction workshop interacted with supervisee level—that is, practicum students showed a decrease in anxiety following a role-induction procedure, whereas interns either showed no difference or a brief *increase* in anxiety before it again decreased.

A promising supervision tool is Vespia, Heckman-Stone and Delworth's (2002) 48-item Supervisory Utilization Rating Form (SURF). They propose its use as a systematic means for structuring initial discussions about expectations; perhaps also, to help supervisory dyads that are having difficulties to identify sources of their mismatched expectations.

Supervisees' Need to Feel and Appear Competent

Our field has a very strong current emphasis on the development and demonstration of professional competence (e.g., Kaslow, Grus, Campbell, Fouad, Hatcher, & Rodolfa, 2009). Yet even as supervisees are in the process of developing actual competence, they are motivated (like everyone) to *feel* competent; a motivation that varies according to the supervisee's level of (professional) development. This is explicit in Loganbill, Hardy, and Delworth's (1982) developmental model. And Rabinowitz, Heppner, and Roehlke (1986) found that beginning-practicum students, compared to intern-level supervisees, rated as significantly more important to them this issue: *Believing that I have sufficient skills as a counselor or psychotherapist to be competent in working with my clients.*

Bordin (1983) notes that, when he contracted with supervisees about goals that they wished to accomplish during supervision, he found that their overt request typically was for fairly limited and focused goals, such as "Learning to deal more effectively with manipulative clients" or "Becoming more aware of when my own need to nurture gets in my way of being therapeutic." Yet he found that his supervisees' unspoken agenda almost always seemed to be the wish for him to provide global feedback about their overall level of functioning.

> *At first, I thought that this goal would be satisfied by the feedback I was giving in connection with the more specifically stated ones. But I soon learned such feedback was not enough. Despite our reviews of what the therapist was doing or not doing and of its appropriateness and effectiveness, the supervisee seemed uncertain how I evaluated him or her. Only as I offered the remark that I saw him or her as typical of (or even above or below) those of his or her level of training and experience was that need satisfied.* (p. 39)

Stoltenberg (1981) hypothesizes that supervisees at level 2 (of his four-level model, in which level 4 is the most advanced) move from the strong dependency that is characteristic of beginning-level supervisees to a dependency–autonomy conflict. Correspondingly, he observes that "there is a constant oscillation between being overconfident in newly learned counseling skills and being overwhelmed by the increasing responsibility" (p. 62). This is very similar to the struggle that adolescents experience as they enter the middle ground between childhood and adulthood. Kell and Mueller (1966) vividly capture this struggle around adequacy by using what they refer to as a topographic analogy, characterizing the supervisee's struggle as

> *an effort to stay on a highway which is bordered on one side by the beautiful and inviting "Omnipotence Mountains" and on the other side by terrifying "Impotence Cliff." Clients can and often do tempt counselors to climb to the mountain tops. Sometimes the counselor's own needs and dynamics can push him into mountain climbing. More often, the complex, subtle interaction of counselor and client dynamics together lead to counselor trips into the rarified mountain air. Yet the attainment of a mountain top may stir uneasy and uncomfortable feelings. From a mountain top, what direction is there to go except downward? The view to the bottom of the cliff below may be frightening and compelling. The trip down the mountain may well not stop at the highway. The momentum may carry our counselor on over the cliff where he or [she] will experience the crushing effects of inadequacy and immobilization. . . . It seems that either feeling state [omnipotence or impotence] carries the seeds of the other. . . . Rapid oscillation between the two kinds of feeling can occur in such a short time span as a five minute segment of an interview.* (pp. 124–125)

Another competence-related supervisee phenomenon is that of experiencing themselves as impostors (Harvey & Katz, 1985) who are vulnerable to being found out. This occurs when their level of actual competence exceeds that of their felt competence: they behave as therapists, but worry that they are acting a charade; that it is only a matter of time before they are found out to be the impostors that they believe themselves to be. Significantly, then, Kell and Mueller (1966) contend that supervision is "a process of mobilizing [the supervisee's] adequacy" (p. 18). To the extent that they feel competent, supervisees will be less vulnerable to feeling like imposters—or to experience the demoralization that can occur (Watkins, 2012).

Another way to frame this discussion of competence is in terms of *self-efficacy,* which Bandura (1994) defines as "people's beliefs about their capabilities to produce designated levels of performance that exercise influence over events that affect their lives" (p. 71). *Self-efficacy* usually is understood to be domain specific, so that one of us might have high self-efficacy for one thing (say, our athletic ability) but low self-efficacy for another (say, singing).

Larson has been central to the work on self-efficacy in counselor supervisees. She and her colleagues (Larson, Suzuki, Gillespie, Potenza, Bechtel, & Toulouse, 1992) developed the Counseling Self-Estimate Inventory, which has been perhaps the most widely used instrument in studying counselor self-efficacy. With Daniels (Larson & Daniels, 1998), she reviewed the 32 studies on counselor self-efficacy that then were available, establishing that it is a crucial variable in understanding supervisee development.

Authors such as Barnes (2004) have described specific strategies supervisors might use to increase supervisor self-efficacy. Whittaker's (2004) meta-analysis of the several available studies shows that supervision's impact on supervisee self-efficacy has a robust effect size of .65.

Supervisee Transference

In a nontechnical sense, *transference* is a phenomenon in which a person transfers to someone in the present the responses and feelings that that person has had to someone in the past. It is understood that clients develop transferences to their therapists. However, supervisees develop transference-based responses to their supervisors as well (cf. Fiscalini, 1985). To illustrate, consider Lane's (1986) example of how supervisee transference can affect the supervisory process:

> *The supervisor becomes the father who died or who left them or the mother who was never there for them, and is accused of taking something from them. This gives them the right of refusal to take in anything from the supervisor parent.* (p. 71)

Supervisee transference can take numerous forms. At the broadest level, they can be categorized as either negative or positive. To illustrate the former, the supervisee can develop a negative transference in which he or she perceives the supervisor to be more critical or punitive than actually is the case. Lewis (2001) suggests that one mechanism by which this occurs is the supervisee's projection of their own punitively self-critical evaluations of themselves onto the supervisor.

A frequently occurring positive transference is that in which supervisees idealize their supervisors (Allphin, 1987). To do so can fill an important need, especially at the very early stages of training. Specifically, it can be important for the neophyte to have a relationship with someone who seems more competent and therefore capable of guiding their learning and development, someone to serve as a model.

Sexual attractions can constitute a specific type of positive transference. Attractions toward the supervisor can have various origins, including such reality-based considerations as having shared interests. Such feelings, however, often derive at least in part from supervisee transference (Frawley-O'Dea & Sarnat, 2001).

Frawley-O'Dea and Sarnat (2001) also assert that at least some supervisee transference can originate in parallel processes. This speaks to the origin rather than the valence of the transference. The following example that they gave is one of negative transference, but positive ones are just as possible.

> *For example, a patient may experience his male therapist as a persecutory, demanding father who is never pleased. The therapist who is uncomfortable with the patient's transference may not become consciously aware of it and therefore ignores [it]. . . . Rather than consciously working with the patient's transference, the therapist resists awareness of it and instead begins to experience the supervisor as a persecutory figure who never can be satisfied.* (p. 173)

Implications for Supervisors. In therapy, transference is most likely to occur when the therapist remains relatively anonymous to the client. In his discussion of transference in supervision, Lewis (2001) contrasts supervision with therapy, noting that in the former,

> *you are not anonymous or abstinent. Here you are a real person. Here you show your warmth and openness and acceptance. Here you praise, support, encourage, and advise. Here you show empathy to the vulnerability of the learner. Here you share your own experiences, your own mistakes. Here you share your own doubts and anxieties as a learner.* (pp. 76–77)

This is consistent with Carl Rogers's observation that in supervision, he shared more of his own thoughts and reactions than when he was in the role of therapist (Hackney & Goodyear, 1984). To the extent that the supervisor is known as a "real" person, supervisee transference is minimized.

Supervisee transference is yet another reason for supervisors to avoid providing therapy to their supervisees. To blur this *teach versus treat* distinction not only is ethically problematic (Ladany, Lehrman-Waterman, Molinaro, & Wolgast, 1999; Neufeldt & Nelson, 1999), but also invites supervisee transference.

Yet even in an optimal supervisory environment, supervisees still develop transference reactions to their supervisors. How to handle them depends on the nature, intensity, and origin of the transference. For example, with idealizing transference, the supervisor should steer a careful course. It can be important to respect the supervisee's need to idealize the supervisor (e.g., it can be very important to the supervisee to be reassured with the "knowledge" that the supervisor has it all under control), but the flip side is to not allow the idealization of the supervisor to cheat the supervisee of the chance to develop his or her own sense of competence. In addition, the type and timing of supervisor interventions in the face of supervisee idealization should be moderated by the supervisee's developmental level (e.g., Stoltenberg, McNeill, & Delworth, 1998).

Negative transference responses can be more difficult, both because of the greater difficulty in addressing them productively and because of their consequences to the supervisory relationship and to supervisee learning. To address them can be one avenue.

SUPERVISOR FACTORS

In the first part of this chapter, we discuss supervisee factors and dynamics that affect their level of engagement and, therefore, the quality of the supervisory relationship. We now shift our focus to the supervisor, using the right side of Figure 1 to organize our discussion.

Before addressing the supervisor factors in Figure 1, we must acknowledge two other factors that we addressed with respect to supervisees but that also have application to supervisors.

- We discuss supervisee trust, which is important to the supervisor as well: Unless the supervisor can trust that supervisees are being honest and straightforward about material from their work with clients, he or she will be especially vigilant because of liability and other issues. This can lead to attempts to constrain supervisee behaviors in a way that affects not only their relationship, but also the supervisee's learning.
- We also discuss supervisee anxiety and its effect on the supervisory relationship at some length, but the supervisor's anxieties also are a factor in supervision. Lesser (1983) discusses possible sources of supervisor anxiety, including the anxieties that arise in evaluation and the feelings of responsibility both to supervisees and to the public that they will serve if successful in training; anxiety can arise when a client is in crisis and the supervisor has some doubts, however small, about the supervisee's ability to handle it (that the supervisor is vicariously liable certainly can amplify this feeling); and anxieties can occur at times when the supervisor may feel no longer needed.

Although we were not able to give more space to matters of supervisor trust and anxiety, they are sufficiently important to at least have been acknowledged. In the remainder of the chapter, we address, in turn, supervisor attachment style, their comfort with and use of power, and countertransference.

Supervisor Attachment Style

Earlier in this chapter we address supervisee attachment and its possible effects on the supervisory relationship; but supervisors, too, have particular relational styles that they bring to supervision. White and Queener (2003) did not find that supervisees' attachment styles predicted either supervisor or supervisee ratings of the supervisory working alliance. Interestingly, however, *supervisors'* attachment styles predicted strength of alliance, as rated by both supervisor and supervisee. The authors concluded, "This study suggests that supervisors' ability to make positive–affiliative attachments with others play[s] an important role in understanding the supervisory relationship" (p. 214). More recently, two additional studies (Dickson et al., 2011; Riggs & Bretz, 2006) found a relationship between supervisor attachment style and the supervisory alliance when supervisors' attachment style was assessed on the basis of their supervisees' perceptions (versus the supervisors' own self-ratings).

Foster, Heinen, Lichtenberg, and Gomez (2006) found that supervisors with a preoccupied attachment style were more likely to give their supervisees lower professional ratings than their colleagues with other attachment styles—that is, their accuracy in evaluating supervisees seemed to be impaired.

Although we have only these studies so far, their results are important and are showing results consistent enough to suggest that supervisor attachment is important. Not only does supervisor attachment seem to predict the quality of the supervisory alliance, but it could affect how supervisees are evaluated. This seems to suggest the importance of supervisors' having enough self-awareness about their attachment style that they can be especially vigilant for ways in which it may affect their work.

Interpersonal Power

Supervisory relationships are characterized by asymmetry in power. The supervisor's greater power can be problematic if the supervisor is oblivious to it, abuses it, or (more typically) has difficulty assuming it comfortably. Indeed, learning to handle that power confidently and effectively is an essential task for new supervisors to master (Heid, 1998); learning, for example, to address the issues related to power openly with their supervisees (see Nelson, Barnes, Evans, & Triggiano, 2008).

One challenge for supervisors in becoming comfortable with power is that

> *In the helping professions, power often has been viewed pejoratively because the concept of control and dominance has seemingly been antithetical to the tenets of mutuality and unconditional positive regard. This interpretation limits the ability of power in constructing a mutually empowering relationship.* (Holloway, 1995, p. 43)

Moreover, having status and power actually permits supervisors to be more flexible in how they respond to their supervisees. Moskowitz (2009), for example, cites research showing that

> *When individuals are in a high status position, they have greater freedom to be responsive to the other person. Thus, there is more change in behaviour in association with variations in the other person's behaviour for a supervisor than for a coworker or a supervisee.* (p. 36)

In this section, we focus on power that derives from the supervisory role. We want, however, to acknowledge Ryde's (2000; 2011) observation that supervisors also can derive power via two other pathways: (a) the force of his or her own personality; and (b) what she terms *cultural power:* the type of power that can come with being male, heterosexual, a member of the dominant racial or ethnic group, and so on. Both of these are important.

There are many ways to conceptualize power in supervision. It is, for example, a central issue in feminist supervision (see, e.g., Falender, 2009; Green & Dekkers, 2010; Szymanski, 2003). In what follows, we focus on two conceptions of interpersonal power that have been especially important for supervisors and supervision researchers: social influence theory and the interactional perspective.

Social Influence Theory. *Power,* which can be understood as the ability to influence others' behaviors and attitudes, is a social psychological construct. Heppner and Claiborn (1989) assert that literature applying social psychological concepts of interpersonal influence and attitude change to counseling and therapy probably began with the publication of Frank's (1961) *Persuasion and Healing*. Goldstein, Heller, and Sechrest (1966) and Strong (1968) also have done important work in extending social psychology to the mental health arena. In fact, Strong's article presenting a two-stage model of change probably was most directly instrumental in stimulating what became a large research literature.

In Strong's view, we impart *interpersonal power* (i.e., the ability to influence us) to those in our lives whom we perceive to have the resources necessary to meet our needs. This is consistent with social exchange theory, which posits that if *A* has what *B* wants, *A* has power over *B*. The extent of this power depends on the access that *B* has to alternative resources.

Strong (1968) adopted three of French and Raven's (1959) five types of interpersonal power to conceptualize counselors' influence. Strong asserts that a counselor has interpersonal power or influence to the extent that the client perceives him or her to have *expertness, attractiveness* (e.g., perceived similarities in values, goals), and *trustworthiness*. This same model applies as well to supervision.

During the first of Strong's posited two stages, the supervisor's task is to establish him- or herself to the supervisee as a credible resource (i.e., a person who is perceived to possess the requisite expertness, attractiveness, and trustworthiness). Once the supervisor establishes credibility, the second stage is one in which he or she begins using these sources of power to influence the supervisee to make behavioral or attitudinal changes. This is the actual social influence process.

Appropriately, Strong (1968) had not used in his model of counseling a fourth of French and Raven's types of interpersonal power, that of *coercion.* This type of "power is based on H's ability to punish T for failure to conform to H's wishes" (Turner & Schabram, 2012). In this case, *punishment* occurs through negative reviews of supervisees' work when supervisors perform their obligatory evaluative function. Therefore, supervisors *do* have coercive power, whereas counselors do not. However, although this type of power is theirs to exercise—a fact of which their supervisees are keenly aware—supervisors' primary identity is as counselors or therapists, and so having this type of power can feel uncomfortable.

Corrigan, Dell, Lewis, and Schmidt (1980), Heppner and Dixon (1981), and Heppner and Claiborn (1989) all provide important reviews of counseling-related research based on Strong's model; Dixon and Claiborn (1987) review that supervision-specific research on that model. With a few exceptions, most of this research has been analog in nature. The real-life applications that exist suggest that *attractiveness* (which we understand as *relational bonding*) probably is the most robust of the French and Raven power sources from which Strong extrapolated.

Petty and Cacioppo's (1986) elaboration likelihood model (ELM) is a more recent and complex model of attitude change and might be considered the "second-generation" social influence model. This model suggests that people can be influenced through two information-processing routes: either *central* (involving an effortful elaboration of information) or *peripheral* (greater reliance on cues or on simple rules) for information processing. Influence that occurs through the central route is considered more enduring and has more effect on subsequent behaviors.

However, the route by which persuasion occurs depends on characteristics of the person who is the source of the information (e.g., credibility and attractiveness), message variables (i.e., the subjective strength of the arguments supporting a position), and recipient characteristics (e.g., degree of motivation to process the message). When people are motivated and able to consider messages that they perceive to have compelling arguments, they can then be influenced by a central route; otherwise, influence might occur through more peripheral means, such as the perceived expertness of the communicator. Claiborn, Etringer, and Hillerbrand (1995) and Stoltenberg, McNeill, and Crethar (1995) have discussed the promise of the ELM for research in supervision. Significantly, also, is that Stoltenberg et al. attempt to incorporate what we already know about supervisee development into applications of the ELM.

Both the Strong/French and Raven and the Petty and Cacioppo models of social influence use a more formal *scientific* language and structure than much of what we discuss in this text (see Blocher, 1987, and Martin, 1988, for discussions of distinctions between models to guide practice versus those to guide inquiry). However, they are important models for supervisors to understand because they provide supervisors with valuable explanations of how power operates in their relationships with supervisees. Supervisors interested in learning more about their practice implications should consult articles such as those of Claiborn et al. (1995), Kerr, Claiborn, and Dixon (1982), and Stoltenberg et al. (1995).

An Interpersonal Perspective. A second perspective on interpersonal power is more explicitly interactional. It is concerned especially with the dynamic give and take between people and is grounded in the assumption that people always are negotiating their status (i.e., relative power) with respect to one another.

Gregory Bateson and Timothy Leary made two of the seminal contributions to this perspective. Bateson (1936/1958) proposed that *status* (which also has been referred to variously as *dominance, control,* or *power*) influences all human relationships and communication. Leary (1957) later used Sullivan's (1953) interpersonal theory of personality to develop a circumplex model in which behavior can be plotted according to its placement on a circle with two orthogonal dimensions. One of those dimensions is that of *power* (dominance versus submission). In this way, his model is similar to that of Bateson.

However, Leary's inclusion of *affiliation* as the second dimension (i.e., hostility versus nurturance) was a significant additive step. Leary's assumption that any given behavior can be described according to how it maps on these two dimensions has come to inform a great deal of current personality research. The model has proved to be robust (cf. Tracey, Ryan, & Jaschik-Herman, 2001); most people tend to organize their perceptions of their interpersonal worlds along those two dimensions.

This model can be used to describe the characteristic interpersonal behavior of any one person, often in ways that correspond to diagnostic categories. However, the model also provides a way of understanding how any two people might interact with one another.

Bateson (1936/1958) proposed that interpersonal interactions can be characterized as of two basic types:

> complementary *(where there is an unequal amount of status) and* symmetrical *(where there is equal status). In a complementary interaction, each person is agreeing on the relative status positions (i.e., who determines what is to occur and who is to follow along). If the behaviors of the actors complement each other, there is a smooth interaction that is productive as the dyad agrees on what is to be done. In essence, one actor initiates and the other follows. However, if the behaviors of the two actors indicate equal status, resulting in a symmetrical interaction, there is more tension in the interaction and there is less accomplished.* (Tracey, 2002, p. 268)

Tracey (2002) characterizes the degree of complementarity in a relationship as one index of *between-participant harmony.* It indicates that the two individuals are similarly defining their relative power within that relationship. Variants of Leary's circumplex model (e.g., Benjamin, 1974; Carson, 1969; Kiesler, 1983; Strong & Hills, 1986; Wiggins, 1985) have been used in studies of complementarity. For example, Figure 4 reproduces the Tracey, Sherry, and Albright (1999) variant.

The interpersonal perspective assumes that "every behavior carries information regarding how the other should respond, and thus, each behavior elicits or constrains subsequent behavior from others" (Markey, Funder, & Ozer, 2003, p. 1083); that is, any behavior will elicit a reciprocal (complementary) response from the person with whom we are interacting. Complementarity occurs if, for example, a supervisor were to make a leading statement (e.g., "Would you turn on your tape so that we can listen to some of what you have been describing?") to which the supervisee responds with a docile behavior (e.g., "Sure, let me pull out my tape recorder"). As Figure 4 indicates, leading behaviors are high on dominance, whereas docile behaviors are low; both leading and docile behaviors are moderate in level of friendliness. The figure also indicates that nurturant behavior elicits cooperative behavior; self-enhancing behavior elicits self-effacing behavior; and critical behavior elicits distrustful behavior.

One variant of Leary's model that has been especially important to supervision researchers is that of Penman (1980). Although not organized as a circumplex, this model uses the same two dimensions of *power* and *involvement* to characterize interpersonal behaviors. At least four studies (Abadie, 1985; Holloway, Freund, Gardner, Nelson, & Walker, 1989; Martin, Goodyear, & Newton, 1987; Nelson & Holloway, 1990) used Penman's system to analyze supervisory interactions. This model was useful, for example, in the Nelson and Holloway (1990) finding that supervisors were more likely to reinforce high-power statements by male supervisees than those by their female counterparts, thereby demonstrating that gender role affects how power is used in supervision. Holloway's (1995) model of supervision is grounded in this interplay between the dimensions of supervisor power and involvement.

Drawing from his and others' research, Tracey (1993) proposes a three-stage model of counseling based on the notion of complementarity. In the initial phase, level of therapist and client complementarity is high; in the middle or working phase, it becomes lower as the relationship becomes more

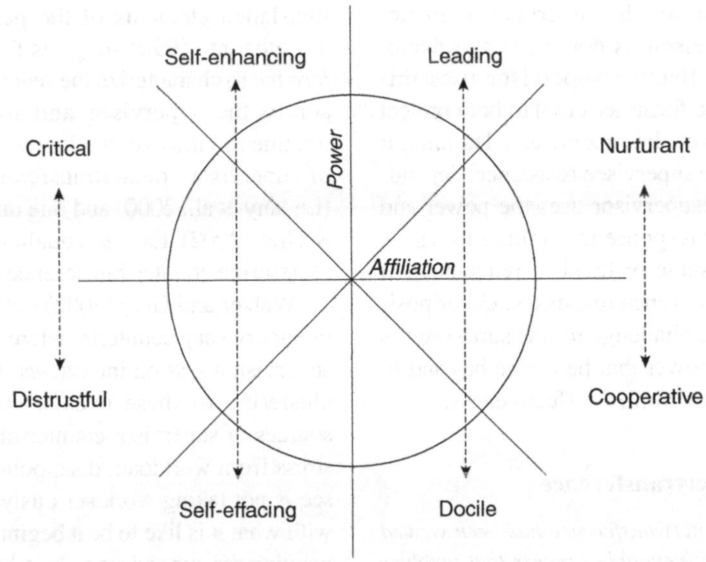

FIGURE 4 Complementary Behaviors of the Interpersonal Circle
Note: Arrows Connect Behaviors Hypothesized to Be Complements.
Source: From "The Interpersonal Process of Cognitive–Behavioral Therapy: An Examination of Complementarity Over the Course of Treatment," by T. J. G. Tracey, P. Sherry, & J. M. Albright. 1999, *Journal of Counseling Psychology*, 46, pp. 80–91. Copyright 1999 by the American Psychological Association.

conflictual; and in the final stage, the relationship returns to a situation of higher complementarity. Yet, although there seems to be generally solid support for this model in therapy, the one supervision study of this type (Tracey & Sherry, 1993) found no support for it. The authors speculate that their results might call into question the application of therapy models to supervision. It was, however, only a single study, so the question about whether Tracey's (1993) stage model of counseling applies to supervision is yet to be fully considered.

Implications for Supervisors. Power often is thought to involve dominance or control by one person over the other. But to use social psychological conceptions of power as the social influence by one person of another importantly broadens understandings of it. All behavior is communication, and communication is an act of influence (Watzlawick & Beavin, 1976). This perspective allows for mutual influence: the supervisor and supervisee each influence the other, although the supervisor has the greater role-based power and, therefore, the greater influence.

We once heard a conference presenter assert that the person with greater power in a relationship is able to define reality for the other person. This does seem strong as an absolute statement. Yet, through the types of power we discuss in this section (i.e., expertness, attractiveness, and trustworthiness), the supervisor is able to persuade the supervisee to look through a particular theoretical lens to evaluate behavior and to adopt particular attitudes. In this sense, the supervisor is using interpersonal power to define (or at least shape) the supervisee's reality.

It is likely that the person with less power in the relationship will be more conscious of this fact. Yet, precisely because of his or her greater power, the supervisor has a responsibility to be aware of it and to use it both effectively and without abusing it.

In short, the fact of the supervisor's greater power in the relationship is not in itself problematic. In fact, the effective supervisor uses this power in its multiple forms as a tool to both protect the client and enhance the supervisee's learning. It can, however, invite supervisee resistance, depending on (a) how the supervisor uses the power and (b) the supervisee's response to it (either by virtue of developmental stage or level of reactance). It also can invite transference responses, either positive or negative. The challenge for the supervisor is to be aware of the power that he or she has and to use it in a way that maximizes effectiveness.

Supervisor Countertransference

> *[S]upervisor countertransference has been viewed as a complex and inevitable process that involves unconscious and exaggerated reactions stemming from a supervisory interaction customarily related to the supervisor's unresolved personal issues or internal conflicts.* (Ladany, Constantine, Miller, Erickson, & Muse-Burke, 2000, p. 102)

Strean (2000) notes that mental health professionals generally recognize that therapist countertransference is as ubiquitous as client transference. He then suggests that, by analogy, supervisor countertransference is likely as ubiquitous as supervisee transference. Ekstein and Wallerstein (1972) note that the mutual evaluation and reevaluation that occur in supervision do not occur at a strictly intellectual level. They are "accompanied by interactions on every level, which would be described, were they to occur in a therapeutic context, as transference reactions of the one and countertransference reactions of the other" (p. 284).

Literature on this topic is relatively scarce. Ladany et al. (2000) note that Balint (1948) and Benedek (1954) apparently were among the earliest authors to acknowledge supervisor countertransference and its potentially harmful effects on supervisees. A number of authors offer their observations about supervisor countertransference. For example, Lower (1972) observes that "the learning alliance . . . is threatened continuously by resistances that derive from immature, neurotic, conflict-laden elements of the personality" (p. 70). Teitelbaum (1990) suggests the term *supertransference* to characterize the reactions of the supervisor to the supervisee and to the supervisee's treatment. However,we know of only two studies of supervisor countertransference, one published (Ladany et al., 2000) and one unpublished (Walker & Gray, 2002). Each is a qualitative study designed to describe countertransference events.

Walker and Gray (2002) obtained 144 instances of supervisory countertransference during 70 post-supervision session interviews. In their preliminary clustering of these events, they identified four sources of supervisor countertransference: external stress from workload; disappointment that supervisee is not taking work seriously; overidentification with what it is like to be a beginning counselor; and wanting the supervisee to be a better therapist.

An important aspect of this work is that the authors not only were interested in problematic countertransference reactions, but also in those that in one way or another, they facilitated the supervision. Other work treats countertransference almost exclusively as problematic. For example, even positive countertransference is considered problematic when it has erotic overtones (e.g., Ladany et al., 2000).

Ladany et al. (2000) conducted the single published investigation of supervisor countertransference. Their findings provide the most comprehensive knowledge to date about this phenomenon. Therefore, we devote more space than usual to summarizing this study's findings. Theirs was a qualitative study of 11 supervisors at university counseling center internship sites. Raters coded the structured interviews with these participants, all of whom believed that this had affected the supervisory relationship in either positive or negative ways. Ladany et al. (2000) found that most supervisors reported the countertransference lasted more than 2 months. To deal with it, most reported having pursued one or both of two courses: (a) consulting with a colleague (e.g., coworker, the training director, a supervision group) or (b) discussing it with the supervisee as it was appropriate. A few reported using either personal therapy or developing increased awareness through self-reflection as a means to resolve it.

A particularly useful feature of the Ladany et al. (2000) study was their examination of cues that led the supervisor to become aware of his or her countertransference. There was no single cue that all 11 supervisors reported, but more than half reported each of the following types of cues:

- Having particularly strong positive or negative feelings when they interacted with the supervisee
- Experiencing feelings toward the supervisee that were uniquely different from those toward other supervisees with whom she or he had worked
- Experiencing a gradual change in feelings toward the supervisee or their sessions together
- Discussions with colleagues (especially their own supervisors)

Ladany et al. (2000) were able to identify six sources of supervisor countertransference, of which the following two were reported by all respondents:

1. *Countertransference triggered by the interpersonal style of the supervisee.* In some cases, this was a defensiveness or guardedness; in others, an assertiveness; in still others, passivity, shyness, or vulnerability; and finally, such positive qualities as warmth and being engaging (this last was especially true for erotic countertransference).
2. *Countertransference stemming from some aspect of the supervisor's own unresolved personal issues.* In some cases, this concerned personal and family issues; in others, concerns about his or her competency; his or her own interpersonal style (e.g., having unduly high self-expectations; strong need to be liked); or experiences in the past from work with other supervisees.

To have these two sources identified through an inductive and empirical technique is important. However, because this literature still is small, we also summarize next the four categories of supervisor countertransference that Lower (1972) suggested some years ago.

1. *Countertransference stemming from general personality characteristics.* This type of countertransference stems from the supervisor's own characterological defenses, which then affect the supervisory relationship.
2. *Countertransference stemming from inner conflicts reactivated by the supervisory situation.* Lower's (1972) first category of supervisor countertransference focused on supervisors' characteristic ways of expressing themselves. The second category focused on supervisors' inner conflicts that are triggered by the supervision. Although some of the supervisor behaviors might resemble those of the first category, they have different origins.

   The following list of other supervisor responses suggests the myriad ways that supervisors' own inner conflicts can be manifest in supervision. Lower (1972) suggests that they may

   - Play favorites with the supervisees
   - Covertly encourage the supervisee to act out his or her own conflicts with other colleagues or encourage rebellion against the institution
   - Compete with other supervisors for supervisees' affection
   - Harbor exaggerated expectations of the supervisee that, when unmet or rejected by the supervisee, lead to frustration and perhaps even aggression
   - Have narcissistic needs to be admired that divert the supervisor from the appropriate tasks of supervision

3. *Reactions to the individual supervisee.* The types of supervisor countertransference discussed so far have been triggered by the supervisor's response to the supervisory situation. In addition to these, there may be aspects of the individual supervisee that stimulate conflicts in the supervisor; for example, if the supervisee seems brighter (or more socially successful, or financially better off, etc.) than the supervisor.

Sexual or romantic attraction is a specific instance of this type of supervisor countertransference (Frawley-O'Dea & Sarnat, 2001). Ellis and Douce (1994) argue that issues of supervisor attraction to supervisees have been too little emphasized during supervision training.

Another specific instance of this type of supervisor countertransference (i.e., reaction to the individual supervisee) is cultural countertransference. Vargas (1989) differentiates between this and prejudice: "Whereas *prejudice* refers to an opinion for or against someone or something without adequate basis, the sources and consequences of cultural countertransference are far more insidious and are often repressed by the therapist" (p. 3).

Vargas (1989) notes that cultural countertransference reactions can originate in either of two ways:

- The first, and more common, instance, occurs when the supervisor has limited experience with members of the ethnic minority group to which the supervisee belongs.
- The second is the consequence of potent feelings associated with nonminority people in the supervisor's past with whom the current minority supervisee is associated.

Regardless of the source, however, these cultural countertransference reactions, like many social perceptions, occur at an automatic level, outside the observer's awareness (see, e.g., Bargh & Chartrand, 1999). Research such as that of Abreu (1999) illustrates how this applies in a mental health context using *subliminal priming* (i.e., words flashed at 80 milliseconds, a speed that precludes conscious recognition of them), using 16 words or stereotypes ascribed to African Americans (e.g., Negroes, Blacks, lazy, blues, rhythm), therapists rate a client described in a vignette as more hostile, even though most indicated that they understood the client probably was White. This suggests the importance of ongoing attention to cultural sensitivity, even when at a conscious level the supervisor is not aware of stereotyping.

4. *Countertransference to the supervisee's transference.* Perhaps the area in which supervisors are at the greatest risk of experiencing countertransference reactions to the supervisee is when the supervisee manifests transference responses to the supervisor. As a vivid illustration, Lower (1972) offers the following example:

> *A resident had been working in psychotherapy with a . . . young woman for about six months when a new supervisor questioned his formulations and treatment goals and suggested that they follow the patient in supervision over a period of time. The resident responded as though the supervisor were intruding on his relationship with the patient and became more and more vague in his presentation of material. In reaction, the supervisor became increasingly active in suggesting what the therapist should pursue with the patient and at last asked to see the patient together with the resident in order to make his own assessment. Only after the supervisor began the interview by asking the patient, "Well how are you and Doctor what's his name here getting along?" did he recognize the Oedipal conflict within both himself and the resident that had interfered with the learning alliance.* (p. 74)

CONCLUSION

Each of the several factors we address in this chapter has implications for, or even direct influence on, the dyadic supervisory relationship. Our intent in presenting these factors is to better equip supervisors with knowledge that permits greater sensitivity to these features in the supervisory process and allows them to offer more prescriptive intervention (e.g., to minimize supervisee anxiety or transference or supervisors' countertransference).

We also are aware that the factors we present in this chapter do not exhaust the range of individual factors and characteristics that might affect supervision; however, they are those that have received particular emphasis in the supervision literature.

Organizing the Supervision Experience

Organizing the Supervision Experience

We appreciate that most supervisors envision themselves *conducting* individual, group, or live team supervision when they think of delivering supervision, not *planning* for the experience. However, we want to begin the section where we believe supervision must begin, with a process of assuring that supervision is organized with clear parameters and expectations. We begin by looking at the available data that underscore the importance of organized or intentional supervision. We then consider institutional characteristics that are supervision friendly, primarily through discussion of some of the activities and tools that add consistency and predictability to supervision. We see the content of this chapter as including many of the activities that often get neglected in supervision or are performed in a pro forma manner. Although nothing in the chapter deals with the essence of clinical supervision (e.g., relationship issues, intervention selection, supervision models), the topics discussed here create the framework that makes it easier to attend to issues such as these. We refer to much in the chapter as the *organizational responsibilities* of the supervisor (which we sometimes refer to as *managerial competence*). We include what we consider essential for the process of mapping out the supervision experience before it begins, and monitoring the experience for the duration of the relationship.

Traditionally, roles and responsibilities held by supervisors have been described as either administrative or clinical. Although there is almost always some overlap—and, indeed, some supervisors fulfill both clinical and administrative duties for the same supervisees—these terms help differentiate supervisory functions within an organization. The clinical supervisor has a dual investment in the quality of services offered to clients and the professional development of the supervisee; the administrative supervisor, although obviously concerned about service delivery and staff development, must also focus on matters such as communication protocol, personnel concerns, and fiscal issues. By necessity, the administrative supervisor must view supervision in the larger context of institutional expediency (Falvey, 1987; Tromski-Klingshirn, 2006); the clinical supervisor views supervision and service delivery quite differently. In fact, the argument has been made that the tasks demanded of each role are divergent enough to make them essentially incompatible (Erera & Lazar, 1994).

Our position is that there is a strong and necessary component to clinical supervision that is managerial in nature, thus requiring organizational skills that are similar to those used by administrative supervisors. It is difficult to accept the information presented without recognizing that these issues must be managed adequately within the supervisory relationship. Therefore, our goal in this chapter is to address some of the most essential managerial aspects of clinical supervision.

We have chosen the words *managerial* and *organizational* in order to avoid the word *administrative*. Borders and Fong (1991) use the term *executive* to refer to the same set of behaviors and skills. All these terms imply some choreography within an institutional system(s) to achieve clinical supervision goals.

At least two matters complicate a discussion of the organizational tasks of clinical supervision. The first is a bias among many mental health practitioners (clinical supervisors included) that such matters are tiresome—a necessary evil that detracts from, rather than enhances, one's clinical supervision. This bias is supported, in part, by Kadushin and Harkness (2002), who report results from an earlier study conducted by Kadushin that the most highly ranked source of dissatisfaction reported by clinical supervisors was "dissatisfaction with administrative 'housekeeping'" (Kadushin & Harkness, 2002, p. 316). In addition, Kadushin (1992a, 1992b, 1992c) sampled a large number of social work supervisors and supervisees about supervisor strengths and shortcomings. Both supervisors and supervisees identified enacting managerial responsibilities as the major shortcoming of supervisors.

The second complicating factor to our discussion is the reality that in some organizations there is no distinction between clinical supervision and administrative supervision. Supervisors are asked to cover both sets of responsibilities without the luxury of a clear focus in either direction. Several authors have commented on the inherent challenges of blending administrative and clinical supervision (Erera & Lazar, 1994; Henderson, 1994; Kadushin, 1992a; Kadushin & Harkness, 2002; Rodway, 1991; Tromski-Klingshirn, 2006; Tromski-Klingshirn & Davis, 2007). We acknowledge this real dilemma, and hope that having some clarity about the types of managerial activities that affect clinical supervision directly will somehow help those supervisors in this situation be more intentional when carrying out their clinical supervisory duties.

With these complications in mind, we begin by arguing for the importance of managerial–organizational competence in the delivery of clinical supervision. We then underscore the importance of understanding a particular institution's culture and how this can provide either a positive or negative context for clinical supervision. We follow with a consideration of the differences when supervision is offered within a graduate program (i.e., on campus) versus when supervision is conducted in the field. An examination of various tasks follows and a variety of tools to assist with those tasks are described. Finally, we suggest some ways to assist a clinical supervisor in achieving organizational competence.

THE IMPORTANCE OF COMPETENCE IN ORGANIZING SUPERVISION

Even though there are many references to the importance of being organized in one's delivery of clinical supervision, until recently there has been little empirical support for the importance of organizational skills for clinical supervisors. Perhaps because the field has only recently begun to address and codify ineffective, conflictual, or "lousy" supervision, the importance of managing clinical supervision remained in the background. Although the centrality of the supervision relationship to satisfactory supervision is clear (e.g., Magnuson, Wilcoxon, & Norem, 2000; Nelson & Friedlander, 2001; Worthen & McNeill, 1996), it is equally apparent that a significant amount of dissatisfaction can result from supervision that is poorly organized.

Nelson and Friedlander (2001) found that supervision had a negative impact when supervisees entered the relationship without a clear sense of what was expected of them or how supervision would proceed. They also found that unstable relationships between the site and home program had negative consequences. Gross (2005) also found that a sizable number of supervisees had negative feelings about their practical experiences because they were not what the supervisees had expected, as did those subjects in a study conducted by Ramos-Sanchez et al. (2002), who report negative supervisory events that included unclear expectations. Kozlowska, Nunn, and Cousins (1997) surveyed psychiatric trainees and found that they were dissatisfied when their educational needs were neglected by their supervisors, pointing to supervision that is reactive, rather than organized and deliberate.

A key study indicating the importance of organizational factors in supervision came from Magnuson, Wilcoxon, and Norem's (2000) qualitative study of "lousy" supervision. Although the number of supervisees interviewed was small ($N = 11$), organizational–administrative issues emerged as one of three general spheres of lousy supervision (the other two being technical–cognitive and relational–affective). Specifically, subjects reported six areas in which organizational–administrative competence was lacking to their detriment:

1. Failure to clarify expectations
2. Failure to provide standards for accountability
3. Failure to assess the supervisee's needs
4. Failure to be adequately prepared for supervision
5. Failure to provide purposeful continuity
6. Failure to provide an equitable environment in group supervision

Reporting from the vantage point of graduate students, Martino (2001) similarly found undesirable supervisor behaviors to include lack of interest in the supervisee's professional development, lack of availability, unreliability, and lack of structure in the supervisory process.

From the site supervisor's perspective, Bennett and Coe (1998) found that satisfaction with their role was significantly related to both quality and frequency of contact with the program liaison and to their agencies, providing adequate release time for conducting supervision. Similarly, in a study of social-work field supervisors in Israel, Peleg-Oren and Even-Zahav (2004) found that the primary reason for field supervisors dropping out of supervision was less-than-functional communication with the graduate training program.

Other studies have indicated that a lack of regular supervision during field placements is a common problem (Giddings, Vodde, & Cleveland, 2003; Gross, 2005; Ramos-Sanchez et al., 2002; Sommer & Cox, 2005), that orientation to sites is often neglected (Gross, 2005), that supervision is sometimes not performed by the site supervisor identified by the training program (Gross, 2005), and that field sites are often unclear about the training program's expectations (Lewis, Hatcher, & Pate, 2005). We should note that the research that reports negative supervision experiences also finds that most supervisees are satisfied with the supervision they have received. However, it is clear that some of the negative experiences have had lasting effects on those who have experienced them. One exception to supervisee angst was reported by Giddings et al. (2003), who found that social work supervisees in their study were not particularly concerned by the lack of overall supervision on-site. The authors found this alarming, and stated, "[S]tudents are not in a position to evaluate the potential impact of a lack of supervision on their careers, the profession, or future clients" (p. 209).

We do not assume that the situation exposed by any of these research findings were the result of intentional malice on the part of supervisors; rather, it seems it is the result of structures that have not been thought out thoroughly for the purpose of providing adequate supervision. It is also not lost on us that the importance of organizational or management skills for the practice of clinical supervision becomes evident through a negative lens, rather than a more affirming lens. Our hypothesis is that well-organized supervision allows for other aspects of supervision to emerge; therefore, the organizational backdrop is likely to remain invisible. When a supervisee is given clear guidelines for supervision by a well-prepared supervisor, this is experienced as the norm. If, however, the supervisor confuses the supervisee, offers little or no structure for the experience, and seems unable to manage supervisory duties, the supervisee is more likely to become aware of the organizational skills requisite for good supervision.

Another body of literature that indicates the importance of well-managed supervision is that of practitioner burnout (again, a view of organizational skill through a negative lens). Several authors have asserted that practitioner burnout may indeed be related not only to service demands, but also to a poor administrative structure (Bogo, 2005; Brashears, 1995; Hyrkäs, 2005; Kaslow & Rice, 1985; Malouf, Haas, & Farah, 1983; Murphy & Pardeck, 1986; Raiger, 2005; Sommer & Cox, 2005; Stoltenberg & Delworth, 1987). Murphy and Pardeck note that either authoritarian or laissez-faire styles of management (supervision) add to burnout, and that burnout may be more organizational than psychological. They assert the importance of appreciating that "a lack of planning is not understood to be the only method for encouraging individualism" (Murphy & Pardeck, 1986, p. 40). Brashears similarly notes that, when the administrative tasks of supervision are viewed as too distinct from service delivery, this false dichotomy contributed to job stress, burnout, and turnover.

We wish to underscore the idea that burnout may be organizational as well as, if not rather than, psychological. From the supervisee's perspective, it makes intuitive sense to us that the best of supervisory relationships or the finest of clinical insights can be sabotaged by weak managerial skills (Bernard, 2005). This can be seen in training situations or in work situations when supervisees are no longer patient or tolerant of inconveniences or frustrations caused by the supervisor who cannot maintain some level of mastery of the supervisory plan. Supervisees often realize that a lack of organization leaves not only them vulnerable, but also leaves the client and agency vulnerable as well. When messages are inconsistent, communication is erratic, procedures are unclear or not adhered to, and weekly conferences are rushed, the entire experience of service delivery under supervision becomes compromised. Because of lack of experience, supervisees or new employees are hard-pressed to distinguish their feelings about service delivery from their feelings about supervision. Supervisors must realize, therefore, that signs of frustration or burnout may be feedback *to* the supervisor rather than *about* the supervisee.

Finally, certain supervisory functions are inextricably tied to managerial competence. Specifically, evaluation of supervisees and maintaining a clinic or agency that meet minimal ethical standards require organizational skill. Because a deficit in these areas can become threatening to supervisors and supervisees alike, we hope that the importance of organizational competence becomes self-evident. However, with the minimal attention given to this topic in clinical supervision literature, it is understandable that these skills remain underdeveloped.

Once the supervisor appreciates the importance of supervision that is thoughtful, organized, appropriate for the supervisee, and well executed, the supervisor also appreciates the importance of a work environment that supports exemplary supervision. Even if the environment is one in which supervision is expected to be an integral part, the institutional culture plays a role—often an enormous role—in either assisting or hampering the supervisor. It is important, then, to assess institutional culture as one task in managing clinical supervision.

THE ROLE OF INSTITUTIONAL CULTURE

Supervision is an integral and time-consuming aspect of the delivery of mental health services. When taken seriously and conducted properly, clinical supervision demands institutional support. It behooves supervisors to assess the culture of the organization to determine if it is supervision-friendly; otherwise, the most organized supervisor with the best-laid plans will soon be frustrated by an institutional culture that works against supervision goals. Furthermore, because supervisors are persons of some authority, they have an opportunity and a responsibility to influence their organization's culture if it reflects characteristics that are anathema to clinical supervision. This is so whether their organization is a training program, a school or university, or a mental health agency. Therefore, we hope to provide some food for thought as supervisors assess their institutions and the underlying characteristics of those institutions.

Osborn (2004) uses the acronym STAMINA (Selectivity, Temporal sensitivity, Accountability, Measurement and management, Inquisitiveness, Negotiation, and Agency) to describe a series of characteristics or behaviors that can assist counselors to remain fully engaged in the demanding contexts within which they find themselves. Emphasizing the positive, she encourages mental health professionals to develop stamina rather than "resisting burnout." Using Osborn's acronym, we next look at institutional culture and describe some of the essentials that must be in place if clinical supervision is to be managed optimally.

Selectivity

Organizations cannot be all things to all constituents. Clinical supervision is often squeezed out because organizations are overburdened with heavy client loads, grant applications, new programs, and bureaucratic demands. For clinicians to become increasingly competent (and more valuable to the organization), clinical supervision must be *selected* in, not out. When this is the case, it is unlikely that supervisees will feel like a supervisee interviewed by Sommer and Cox (2005) who stated, "My supervisor is just being pulled in too many directions with too many responsibilities, so I'm just put on a list of things to do" (p. 129).

Temporal Sensitivity

Osborn describes the characteristic of *temporal sensitivity* as both a realistic understanding of the limits of time and a respect for the time that one is given. Organizations that value clinical supervision demonstrate this value by allocating the precious resource of time to it. There is no apology necessary in a supervision-friendly organization when adequate time is blocked out for supervision. Furthermore, this commitment to supervision is viewed as seriously as commitments to clients. Kadushin and Harkness (2002) report a study of 885 supervisors and supervisees and found the time given to supervision to be a serious problem. Both supervisors and supervisees complained that there was too little time to conduct adequate supervision. Inadequate amounts of time committed to supervision leading to reports of dissatisfaction with supervision is a theme that continues to be reported in the literature (Bogo, 2005; Giddings et al., 2003; Gross, 2005; Ramos-Sanchez et al., 2002; Sommer & Cox, 2005). It is impossible to discern whether the problem is too little time to do too much, or the status of supervision among competing duties. Regardless, supervisees across several mental health disciplines report feeling shortchanged in their field placements.

Just like individuals, organizations that are effective and efficient about time can accomplish more. These organizations are less likely to be experienced as frenetic, a characteristic more often associated with institutional cultures in which time is perceived as the enemy and often managed poorly.

Accountability

Osborn was quick to state that she did not use the term *accountability* in its more reactive sense—that is, as an admonition with the potential to stifle creative practice. Rather, consistent with Osborn's definition, the organization that values accountability is credible, both internally and to its constituents. Implicit in this kind of accountability is some ownership of the work that takes place within the organization and a keen desire to improve. Used in this way, clinical supervision is key to accountable counseling and therapy. Organizations that welcome accountability embrace the evaluative and developmental aspects of clinical supervision. Copeland (1998) states that organizations that create a context conducive to supervision expect more accountability from the supervisor. If framed in the way Osborn framed the term, this could only be a good thing.

Measurement and Management

As used by Osborn, *measurement and management* come closest to describing the kinds of activity necessary to organize effective supervision. Although *selectivity* more broadly defines the mission of the organization, *measurement and management* reflect the day-to-day operations and the skills necessary to complete them effectively. An organization with this characteristic is clear about assigned roles, has good record-keeping practices, and so on. It is a real advantage for the supervisor when clinical supervision is grounded in efficient and effective measurement and management.

Inquisitiveness

Osborn states that the importance of a spirit of inquisitiveness for the long-term stamina of the individual counselor cannot be overstated. If one does not remain curious about one's work, stagnation can quickly set in. As an organizational trait, *inquisitiveness* is often translated as a respect for professional development and is viewed as essential for building and maintaining vibrant organizations (Frohman, 1998; Hawkins & Shohet, 2000). Clinical supervision is integral to professional development. Barretti (2009) found that supervisees recognize and value inquisitiveness (defined as continued interest) in their supervisors. Ongoing supervision can enhance the process of *reflectivity* (a form of inquisitiveness) that Skovholt and Rønnestad (1995) found was essential for professional development. Furthermore, the organization that reflects inquisitiveness encourages professional development for the supervisor as well as for supervisees.

Negotiation

Osborn's inclusion of negotiation is essential for the supervisor-friendly organization. In this context, *negotiation* is defined as the ability to give and take without giving in. In other words, organizations that reflect the value of negotiation give their members voice. Others refer to the importance of trust and collegiality within an organization (e.g., Frohman, 1998; Raiger, 2005; Sparks & Loucks-Horsley, 1989). Clinical supervision is highly sensitive to relationship. Although a positive supervisory relationship can limp along within a caustic institutional context, it is unlikely that this could be sustained indefinitely. Organizations that value negotiation and collegiality are a great support to clinical supervisors.

Agency

Finally, Osborn advanced the concept of *agency*, which she defines as "an intangible, dynamic force" (p. 326). She views agency as coming close to the essence of stamina and including several empowering characteristics, such as having a sense of one's impact and being aware of one's resourcefulness. Translated to the institution, *agency* is a quality of those organizations that refuse to be dragged down by complications, unresponsive bureaucracies, or demanding client loads. These organizations are fed by their work, not depleted by it. They are the organizations that view clinical supervision as a building force, not a time drain. In short, they are defined by a vision that is fundamentally optimistic.

Although these descriptions of organizational stamina may not include all that is necessary in an institution to support the functions of clinical supervision, they give the clinical supervisor one viable frame for such an assessment. In addition, they can provide a handle for the supervisor in determining what feels wrong in an organization when attempting to meet supervisory responsibilities. For example, Congress (1992) notes that ethical decision making is controlled by agency culture, rather than individual input (perhaps reflecting the agency's view of accountability and management). The supervisor who has not attempted to evaluate organizational context may be unprepared for a discrepancy between a supervision goal and the culture within which supervision is occurring. Without a systemic intervention, it is most likely the supervision, not the culture, that will be compromised when there is such a discrepancy.

THE ESSENTIAL INGREDIENT: A SUPERVISION PLAN

Before we look at the places in which supervision occurs and the tasks that must be accomplished, we must stress the importance of arriving at a general framework for supervision even before one meets the supervisee for the first time. In fact, it could be argued that the source of all sustained influence is planning and foresight (Covey, Merrill, & Merrill, 1994), and that these allow for other dimensions of supervision to emerge, such as the supervisory relationship (Bernard, 2005). To some extent, *planning* includes methods for assuring accountability, and we cover the importance of recordkeeping later in this chapter. However, the driving force for the supervisor should be to plan an effective and efficient supervision experience that culminates in the emergence of a capable and grounded practitioner, while safeguarding client welfare (Giddings, Cleveland, & Smith, 2006). This goal will be frustrated if supervision is random or repetitious—in other words, the antithesis of planning occurs when a supervisor accepts a supervisee, sets weekly appointments with the supervisee, and lets things just happen; or when a university instructor places students in field sites and then conducts weekly group supervision sessions that are based on self-report and little else. In both of these instances, there is no evidence of an awareness of supervisees' developmental needs or of the desirability for some variety of learning methods. This is *supervision as you go,* not *planned supervision.*

In preparation for supervision, therefore, the supervisor might be well advised to answer the following questions:

- What do I know about the supervisee I will work with? How do learning style, cultural worldview, experience level, and so on, affect my thinking about working with this supervisee?
- In light of what I know about my supervisee, is there any additional preparation I must do in order to be most helpful to this person?
- As I understand the supervisee's goals, which are more likely to be met in this experience? Which are less likely to be met? Is the supervisee clear about this?
- What supervision methods are available to me? Can I supplement those that are provided by the organization? What is my rationale for beginning where I intend to begin? What supervision schedule will we adhere to?
- How and when will I orient the supervisee to the organization within which clients will be treated? How will I determine if the supervisee is adequately aware of ethical and legal imperatives? When will I introduce my evaluation plan?
- Have I structured matters adequately to ensure client flow for my supervisee? Have I made plans for other important experiences, including integration into the organization?
- Knowing the institution as I do, what are the predictable challenges that the supervisee will face? How can I make these productive learning opportunities?
- To whom will I turn for consultation when I am challenged in my work with this supervisee?

With a general idea of the importance of organizational skill, institutional culture, and a framework that defines clinical supervision broadly, we can now turn to more specific topics. We begin by looking at two different contexts within which supervision occurs.

CONTEXTS FOR SUPERVISION: TWO DIFFERENT WORLDS

Outside of private practice, there are two different contexts for supervision: graduate programs and agencies (used generically to include schools, hospitals, mental health agencies, etc.). The fundamental difference between these two contexts, of course, is that one is organized around education and the other is organized around service delivery. Most students in graduate training programs receive clinical supervision within the training context and in a field site (i.e., an agency) where they complete clinical hour requirements. Postdegree supervision is more contained (and therefore less complicated) within the agency. The challenges for postdegree supervision are discussed later when we refer to field sites as the context for supervision. This section, however, focuses primarily on counselors and therapists in training and the contexts within which they receive their clinical experiences.

The Graduate Program as Context for Supervision

Although navigating back and forth between the graduate training program and the field site is normative for most graduate students, some training programs run counseling centers or other service delivery training clinics on campus so that students receive clinical supervision and didactic education within the same context (Myers, 1994). Graduate programs often prefer such a setup for the very reasons that we discuss here: It is much easier to negotiate one system than it is to react to two. Furthermore, because these training clinics exist for the purpose of training, supervision is central to their culture. As a result, neither faculty nor students must spend time advocating for the importance of clinical supervision, leaving more time for the process itself.

Because of the educational advantages of program-based training clinics, these are usually viewed enviably by supervisors working in contexts with less of an emphasis on supervision. Beavers (1986) notes that training clinics were usually less hurried and supervisees could expect individual attention, facilities that are usually more than adequate, and supervisors that are typically well grounded theoretically. With pressures at universities increasing (Bogo, 2005), these conditions may be less ideal than imagined from the outside, even though it is still likely that they are more controlled than in agencies without a primary training function. Although they tend to offer strong organizational structures for training, training clinics have unique challenges as well, and include balancing training responsibilities with the responsibilities of service delivery (Bernard, 1994b; Myers & Hutchinson, 1994); identifying, or perhaps recruiting, appropriate clients and matching clients with supervisees (Leddick, 1994; Scanlon & Gold, 1996); managing client expectations (Leddick, 1994); bridging the gap between the academic calendar and client needs (Scanlon & Gold, 1996); and clarifying roles of professional staff, especially when a tiered system exists—that is, master's-level students supervised by doctoral students who are themselves supervised by faculty supervisors (Dye, 1994; Scanlon & Gold, 1996; West, Bubenzer, & Delmonico, 1994).

As what we state implies, there may be downsides to being supervised in a training facility. Beavers (1986) notes that, even though the staff may attempt to recruit a wide range of clients, it is most often the case that university settings offer a rather narrow and limited client population. In addition, university supervisors may have less clinical experience than supervisors found in off-campus settings and are not as "street savvy"—in other words, university settings may confront the supervisee with fewer dilemmas resulting from bureaucratic protocol, but this can be reframed as offering the supervisee fewer experiences in negotiating complex systems to achieve service delivery and professional development goals. This view is echoed by Gross (2005), who notes that the shortfalls of field sites might indeed help students come to terms "with the realities of service provision and training in the imperfect world of mental health" (p. 304).

The Field Site as Context for Supervision

Often, the supervisee in a graduate training program completes clinical experiences off campus and is supervised by a site supervisor; this, of course, is by design. Departments of social work and psychiatry were perhaps the first to realize the importance of field instruction to supplement academic instruction. Counseling, psychology, and marriage and family therapy, as well as a host of other clinical professions, also require the student to complete a supervised field experience successfully while still in a degree program. The site supervisor typically accepts the supervisee because the supervisor enjoys the supervision process (Globerman & Bogo, 2003), including influencing trainees about real client issues and agency circumstances (Copeland, 1998; Holloway & Roehlke, 1987). Often, the site supervisor would also like to influence the training program in terms of the preparation offered to trainees prior to field experience. Therefore, each context has an investment in the other that is both practical and educational. Yet the differences between these two types of organizations and their separate goals are often not acknowledged in a way that allows the principals to work through them (Peleg-Oren & Even-Zahav, 2004), and communication between the two is often perceived as inadequate (Bogo, Regehr, Power, & Regehr, 2007; Elman, Forrest, Vacha-Haase, & Gizara, 1999; Holtzman & Raskin, 1988; Igartua, 2000; Kahn, 1999; Lewis et al., 2005; Olsen & Stern, 1990). We address goals and communication separately.

Goals. Dodds' (1986) delineation of the major difference between the training institution and the service delivery agency as a difference in population to be served remains unchanged. As depicted in Figure 1, the training institution is invested in the education and training of its students, whereas the mental health agency is primarily invested in the delivery of quantity and quality services to a target population. Dodds warns, however, that to

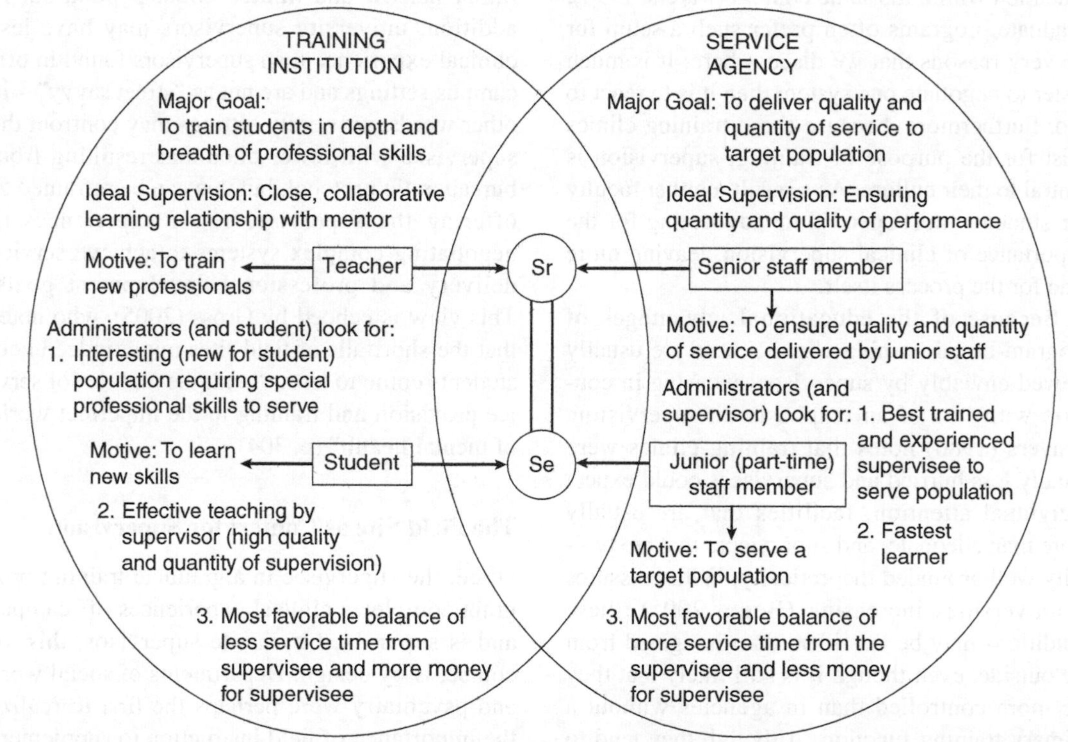

FIGURE 1 Overlapping Systems of a Training Institution and a Service Agency

Note: Sr: supervisor; Se: supervisee

Source: From "Supervision of Psychology Trainees in Field Placements," by J. B. Dodds, 1986, *Professional Psychology: Research and Practice, 17,* pp. 296–300. Copyright © 1986 by the American Psychological Association.

stereotype each system by these goals is to lose sight of each unit's investment in the other's mission. That notwithstanding, the basic goals of each system drive some of the decision making within the system. As Figure 1 illustrates, the university and site supervisors have the responsibility for interfacing these two systems. However, if they default on this responsibility because of time constraints, disinterest, or the absence of managerial acumen, it is left to the supervisee to interface the two systems. When difficulties emerge, this leaves the least powerful individual (in both organizations) to negotiate and attempt to find a resolution.

As an example of one of the many differences that grow out of each system's goals, Dodds (1986) notes the "common source of stress [that] arises when the student participates simultaneously in two institutions with differing time rhythms" (p. 299). For instance, the trainee must perform the role of junior staff member on the agency's timetable, turning in reports and so on, regardless of whether the training institution is on semester break. Furthermore, the regularity of demands at the site are not sensitive to pressure increases from the training institution, such as during midterm or final exams.

Although Dodds' (1986) depiction of the influence of each system is equal, often the systems are unequal in the influence or pressure they place on the supervisee or supervisor. As Stoltenberg and McNeill (2010) argue, expectations from a training program may take precedence, or the reverse may also be true. One way that this occasionally plays out is that the supervisee is given a caseload to meet academic requirements, sometimes outside of typical site protocol and without the kind of thoughtful support that avoids ethical dilemmas. Or conversely, when a site's expectations take precedence and the supervisor is employed by the site, the supervisee may be viewed only within the context of the site and not as a professional-in-training who may end up working elsewhere with different contextual demands. If site and program are not fairly well in tune with each other, supervisees are bound to feel system stress. Supervisors in both settings have the power and obligation to attend to such cross-system issues. A primary strategy for reducing problems either within each system or—especially—between them is to increase the quantity and quality of communication.

Communication. The university supervisor is often very clear about what kinds of communication are expected from the site supervisor; however, a reciprocity of information often is lacking. Authors of empirical studies report frustration among field site supervisors when expectations of training programs exceeded what was initially understood (Shapiro, 1988) or when expectations in general are not clearly communicated (Lewis et al., 2005; Peleg-Oren & Even-Zahav, 2004). Another error both sides make is to keep information too limited in its focus. For example, there can be ample information about placement expectations from both sides. However, university programs do not always keep their field sites current with program growth or curriculum changes, and agencies do not let university programs know when administrative, fiscal, or programmatic changes are being planned or implemented. Programs do not always communicate clearly about the evaluation criteria that they adhere to (Elman et al., 1999). The result of such incomplete communication can be conflict that could have been avoided, or two systems growing increasingly less relevant to each other without being aware of it. We consider the types of communications that are desirable between graduate program and field site later in the chapter.

The remainder of this chapter outlines some of the tasks of supervision and some of the issues that can either enhance or detract from the goal of offering exemplary clinical supervision. We attempt to delineate which tasks are primarily the responsibility of the training program supervisor and which fall to the site supervisor. We also caution the reader that, in and of itself, well-organized supervision is not necessarily good supervision. Yet if clinical supervisors have addressed the tasks that follow, they can have some confidence that supervisory efforts will not be undermined by a crumbling structural base (Bernard, 2005).

FOUNDATIONAL TASKS FOR ORGANIZING SUPERVISION

Although we have discussed several ways in which supervisors prepare themselves to approach a productive supervision experience, we now turn our attention to tasks that involve the supervisor with the supervisee. Whereas much of our discussion focuses on the trainee in a graduate program, many of the tasks outlined can be applied to all supervision relationships. As with many enterprises, it is also the case that most of the organizational activity is concentrated at the front end of the supervisory relationship. The reward for getting organized comes later, when supervision is well under way.

Initial Communication between Graduate Program and Site

It is up to the university supervisor, not the student, to communicate the program's expectations to the site supervisor (Lewis et al., 2005). Under the best of circumstances, this is done both in writing and in person. Manzanares, O'Halloran, McCartney, Filer, Varhely, and Calhoun (2004) describe the development of a CD-ROM for site supervisors that included key information about the training program, training expectations, and video clips of the faculty. Face-to-face contact allows the university supervisor to determine whether there is any resistance to meeting the program's requirements. It has been our experience that student supervisees are typically not good judges of a site when the site is ambivalent about meeting program requirements. Perhaps they are too eager to find an appropriate site to be discriminating. Even when they do discern ambivalence, they are in a vulnerable position regarding the site and are uncertain about asserting themselves with potential site supervisors. Clearly, this is something the university supervisor can and should do. Although we believe it is primarily the graduate program's responsibility to orient the site to the program's expectations, Roberts, Morotti, Herrick, and Tilbury (2001) address the site's responsibility and urge site supervisors to seek full clarification of what is expected of them when they agree to take a supervisee.

Once a site has been chosen, it is important that the campus supervisor stay in touch with the site supervisor. A phone call or e-mail a couple of weeks after the student has been placed is a good idea to be sure that things are going reasonably well. In addition, there should be a plan for formal contacts in order to evaluate the student's progress. The site supervisor should know when these will occur and what form they will take (i.e., face-to-face meeting or written evaluations).

The Interview

The goal of the university training program is to place all students; the goal of the site supervisor is to make a judgment about the individual student's fit with the goals and work of the agency. Although background information is sometimes requested, the basis for the decision is usually the placement interview. It is essential that the site supervisor has a grasp of the attributes that are necessary for the student to take full advantage of the placement.

The interview may also serve as a metaphor for the agency. In other words, if the agency is unstructured and requires a great deal of creativity from staff, the interview should mirror this situation. If, however, the agency is highly structured with clear guidelines for each staff member's role, the interview should be handled similarly. This type of consistency serves two purposes: it becomes a first-level orientation for the student to the agency and its expectations, and it allows the site supervisor the opportunity to gain relevant data about the student on which to base a decision.

Trainees should receive feedback about this interview regardless of whether the site accepts them. Hearing the supervisor's perception of why one was seen as appropriate is a good beginning for a working relationship with the site supervisor. When the trainee is not accepted, it is important to know if the decision was made based on a negative evaluation of the student's competence or because of a perceived lack of fit. If the feedback is not given directly to the student, it should at least be given to the campus supervisor.

Orientation

Because of the relatively short duration of both practicum and of many internship situations, the trainee must be oriented to the site as efficiently as possible. There are some lessons that only a learn-as-you-go approach can accomplish. However, many more things can be learned through an orientation. Unfortunately, many trainees believe that they are just getting a handle on procedures and policy issues as they wrap up their field experience. At least some of this can be attributed to an inadequate orientation process.

If an agency accepts trainees on a regular basis, the site supervisor would be wise to develop a trainee manual covering the major agency policies that must be mastered. (A good resource for such a manual is the trainees who are at the end of their field experience; they can usually be precise about what information would have made their adaptation easier.) If written orientation materials are not available, the site supervisor might schedule more intensive supervision the first week or so to cover orientation matters with the trainee.

The Supervision Contract

Supervision contracts or agreements of understanding have traditionally been good-faith documents between the training institution and the field site, stipulating the roles to be played by the supervisee, the program supervisor, and the field site supervisor. Such agreements also spell out the responsibilities for all parties and the opportunities that afforded to the supervisee for the duration of the contract. Although such contracts are not binding in a legal sense, they serve the purpose of increasing accountability for those concerned.

More recently, emphasis has been placed on the supervision contract as a supervisory intervention (e.g., Studer, 2005). These more individualized supervision contracts should be created (usually with the supervisee) by the supervisor (either program or field) who will be the primary supervisor. The supervision contract typically acts not only to orient the supervisee to supervision, but as a method of ensuring informed consent (Thomas, 2007). Hewson (1999) also hypothesizes that contracts can have the positive effects of increasing mutuality of goals between supervisee and supervisor and minimizing covert agendas. Smith and Pride (2011) advocate for reciprocal supervision agreements that ensure the inclusion of discussions about diversity in supervision. Even so, supervision contracts can lean toward agency structure (i.e., how the supervisee must conform in order to be successful), toward reducing legal vulnerability by outlining in detail ethical mandates and recordkeeping imperatives (Falvey, 2002; Sutter, McPherson, & Geeseman, 2002), or toward the developmental learning goals of the supervisee (i.e., how supervision will be organized to encourage supervisee professional development).

Munson (2002) offers a supervision contract outline that reflects an emphasis on agency structure, and suggests that contracts include reference to the following:

1. *Timing element.* Frequency of supervision, length of session, and the duration of the supervision experience should be made clear.
2. *Learning structure.* Items that fall under this heading have to do with approaches that the supervisor might use to enhance learning, including audiovisual techniques, co-therapy, assigned reading, and the like.
3. *Supervision structure.* Munson suggests that a contract include not only supervision modality (e.g., individual supervision, group supervision, a combination), but also clear information about any change of supervisor, required

rotation through different agency units, and explicit information about lines of authority.
4. *Agency conformity.* Items such as work hours, dress codes, agency rules regarding sharing phone numbers or e-mails, and recordkeeping format should be covered in this section.
5. *Special conditions.* Finally, Munson suggests that any requirements unique to a particular site should be delineated, as well as how the agency expects the supervisee to acquire the knowledge and skills listed. Such requirements might include familiarity with a particular assessment tool, or familiarity with certain medications.

Osborn and Davis (1996) and Luepker (2003) developed contract guidelines that veer more toward the supervisee's professional development while still covering necessary structural elements. Osborn and Davis argue that contracts not only help clarify the supervision relationship, but, as later asserted by others (Luepker, 2003; Thomas, 2007), can also be used to promote ethical practice by itemizing important ethical standards (e.g., informed consent) and their implementation within supervision. Osborn and Davis suggest that supervision contracts include the following:

1. *Purpose, goals, and objectives.* This includes the obvious purpose of safeguarding clients, as well as promoting supervisee development. Putting this in writing, however, is an important ritual for both supervisor and supervisee. In addition, the more immediate goal of, for example, completing the clinical requirements for a training program is listed as well. Luepker (2003) suggests that a category such as this also include the type of clients needed for the supervisee's professional goals to be attained.
2. *Context of services.* The contract must include where and when supervision will take place, what method of monitoring will be in place, and what supervision methods will be used.
3. *Method of evaluation.* Both formative and summative evaluation methods and schedules should be included. Any instrument to be used for evaluation should be given to the supervisee at this time.
4. *Duties and responsibilities of supervisor and supervisee.* In this section, both persons outline the behaviors that they are committed to in order that supervision evolves successfully. For the supervisor, this may include challenging the supervisee to consider different treatment methods; for the supervisee, this may include coming to each supervision session with a preset videotaped sample of his or her use of a particular technique.
5. *Procedural considerations.* Part of the contract must address issues such as emergency procedures and the format for recordkeeping required by the agency. Osborn and Davis also advise that the contract include a procedure to be followed if either party believes that a conflict within supervision has not been resolved.
6. *Supervisor's scope of practice.* Finally, Osborn and Davis suggest that the supervisor's experience and clinical credentials be listed to "make explicit to themselves and their supervisees their professional competence" (p. 130).

Supervisee Bill of Rights

Although supervision contracts establish tasks and responsibilities for both supervisees and supervisors, documents described as supervisees' bill of rights (Giordano, Altekruse, & Kern, 2000; Munson, 2002) have emerged in professional literature and clearly places the supervisee at the center of the contractual relationship. Whereas these documents can include responsibilities of supervisees, they emphasize the rights of supervisees to be the recipients of quality supervision. For example, Munson (2002) includes five conditions in the bill of rights for the supervisee:

1. A supervisor who supervises consistently and at regular intervals
2. Growth-oriented supervision that respects personal privacy

3. Supervision that is technically sound and theoretically grounded
4. Evaluation based on criteria that are made clear in advance, and evaluations that are based on actual observation of performance
5. A supervisor who is adequately skilled in clinical practice and trained in supervision practice (p. 43)

Giordano et al. (2000) developed a comprehensive supervision document that outlines the nature of the supervisory relationship and clarifies expectations as part of the bill of rights. This is followed by an enumeration of relevant ethical standards that regulate supervision. The authors subsequently offer a supervision contract template based on the bill of rights and an evaluation form to document the extent to which the supervisee experienced supervision as consistent with the bill of rights. Giordano et al.'s contribution offers a synthesis of intent and outcome that is still relatively rare in the profession.

Professional Disclosure Statements

Although statements about the supervisor's credentials, supervision approach, experience, and the like, are often included in supervision contracts (e.g., Giordano et al., 2000; Osborn & Davis, 1996; Thomas, 2007), some supervisors develop separate statements to educate the supervisee about them and about their supervision. This practice of preparing professional disclosure statements has become more common as states have increasingly required them for mental health practitioners. Because therapists have experienced the advantage of preparing such statements for their clients, they began preparing statements specific to supervision for their supervisees.

Professional disclosure statements provide a slightly different slant than the supervision contract. Because they tend not to be individualized for each supervisee, they provide a look at the constants that a particular supervisor offers. If they go beyond the "nuts-and-bolts" type of statements, they can also be used as a handout to help to orient the supervisee to a particular supervisor. Doing so also is often more productive than attempting to convey an equal amount of information verbally.

A professional disclosure statement is required as part of the application process for the Approved Clinical Supervisor (ACS) credential (Center for Credentialing and Education [CCE], 2001). CCE, an affiliate of the National Board for Certified Counselors, Inc., requires that applicants for the ACS submit a professional disclosure statement that addresses the following:

1. Name, title, business address, and business telephone number
2. A listing of degrees, credentials, and licenses
3. General areas of competence in mental health practice in which the applicant can supervise
4. A statement documenting training in supervision and experience in providing supervision
5. A general statement addressing a model(s) of or approach to supervision, including the role of the supervisor, objectives and goals of supervision, and modalities
6. A description of the evaluation procedures to be used in the supervisory relationship
7. A statement indicating the limits and scope of confidentiality and privileged communication within the supervisory relationship
8. A statement, when applicable, indicating that the applicant is under supervision and that the supervisee's actions may be discussed with the applicant's supervisor
9. A fee schedule (when applicable)
10. A way to reach the applicant in an emergency situation
11. A statement indicating that the applicant follows a relevant credentialing body's Code of Ethics and CCE's Standards for the Ethical Practice of Clinical Supervision.

What we have discussed thus far is foundational—that is, these aids help lay the groundwork for supervision that is not distracted by the "white noise" of a chaotic supervisory context (Bernard, 2005). It is very difficult later in a supervisory relationship to recover from a disorganized beginning. The few tasks that follow fall in the category of maintenance, and are much less onerous when foundational tasks have received adequate attention.

ONGOING ORGANIZATIONAL TASKS

Communication, Communication, Communication

When trainees are involved, the need for communication does not end once the student has begun a practicum or internship. "Communication is the heart and soul of the counseling profession, yet, too often, communications among site supervisor, the intern, and the [training] program get garbled" (Roberts et al., 2001, p. 211). As we mention at the beginning of this chapter, the need for increased communication between the field and graduate programs has been echoed by others as well (Bogo, 2005; Bogo et al., 2007; Emmons, 2011; Kahn, 1999; Lee & Cashwell, 2001; Lewis et al., 2005).

The Internet has significantly reduced the effort that must be expended to keep everyone informed. A site supervisor listserv allows the training program to communicate efficiently regarding program developments (an area that almost always gets neglected, at least in the short run). A listserv can also be used to alert site supervisors to web-based resources (Mangione, 2011). Chat rooms could invite site supervisor input for campus supervisory discussions. With very little technological expertise, the communication between the training program and site could be vastly improved.

Although technology serves an important purpose in communication, it cannot replace site visits or, at the very least, contact by phone. Meetings on campus for site supervisors are also essential in allowing a forum for discussion and professional development. Training programs should attempt to communicate new developments in the area of supervision to their site supervisors. Although site supervisors have a wealth of practical knowledge, traditionally they have not stayed as current as university types in terms of the research on supervision, new models and techniques, and supervision literature in general. Therefore, in-service training for site supervisors or seminars in which both campus and site supervisors share their ideas and experiences make up a special kind of communication activity (Beck, Yager, Williams, Williams, & Morris, 1989; Brown & Otto, 1986; Roberts et al., 2001).

Just as it is critical for the university supervisor to keep the site supervisor abreast of programmatic developments, it is equally important for the site supervisor to keep the university current. Political, organizational, and fiscal developments may affect trainees in both their field experiences and employment search. When campus supervisors are kept current, they are better able to advise students about the professions that they are entering.

Finally, as specified by Hardcastle (1991), the site supervisor must organize communication within the agency to benefit the trainee. It happens occasionally that a trainee has contact only with the supervisor and feels isolated from the rest of the agency. In some instances, trainees are made to feel disloyal if they happen to ask advice from another employee other than their primary supervisors. This always leads to a negative outcome. The supervisor should have a plan as to how the trainee will be integrated into the agency, including attendance at staff meetings and joint projects with other staff members.

Communication and Evaluation. It is the prerogative and responsibility of the university supervisor to develop an evaluation plan and to conduct all summative evaluations that lead to course grades. The extent to which the site is being asked to evaluate the supervisee must be communicated clearly (Bogo et al., 2007; Olsen & Stern, 1990). As Rosenblum and Raphael

(1987) note, however, site supervisors often dread evaluating university students. Kadushin (1992c) offered empirical support that evaluation was among field supervisors' least favorite responsibilities. When the site supervisor's experience with a trainee has been positive, evaluation tends to be glowing; when the trainee has not met expectations, the evaluation is sometimes avoided. Therefore, it is important for site supervisors and campus instructors to stay in touch as the summative evaluation approaches and for specific behavioral descriptions of supervisee work to be used as the basis for a final grade.

The above notwithstanding, occasionally the site supervisor alerts the training program about some conflict with the supervisee or concern about the performance of the supervisee during the clinical experience (Elman et al., 1999; Igartua, 2000; Leonardelli & Gratz, 1985). It is important that training programs encourage sites to contact the training program if a supervisee shows any signs of unprofessional behavior, problems with professional competence, or developmental stagnation. It goes without saying that training programs must be responsive to such contact. Peleg-Oren and Even-Zahav (2004) found that a primary reason for site supervisors discontinuing their service as site supervisors was disenchantment over the lack of a functional way to negotiate with the training program when there were differences of opinion about a student. In addition, field supervisors interviewed for Bogo et al.'s (2007) qualitative study reported feeling isolated in their roles as gatekeepers and were not confident that academic programs would in fact support their negative evaluations of trainees when these occurred.

Occasionally, it is the supervisee who raises concerns with the training program about the site. Although it is important for students to have experience in resolving conflict, the power differential between them and their site supervisors may make this difficult. In such instances, the program supervisor has a legitimate role to play.

Supervisor as Agency Representative. Another communication function, but one that the site supervisor is less likely to perceive as such, is to serve as a liaison or advocate between supervisees and agency administration. (Even if the supervisor wears two hats, when in the role of clinical supervisor, the supervisor must communicate administrative parameters to trainees.) This function is unique enough to be addressed separately and is critical to the trainee's professional development. Often, the site supervisor fulfills this role in an informal manner, sharing bits and pieces of both spoken and unspoken rules, agency politics, and the like. When done in an informal fashion, however, the trainee is more likely to get incomplete information and/or become triangulated in organizational power struggles. It is far better for the interface between service delivery and organizational realities to be covered in supervision in a deliberate way. Perhaps part of each supervision session could be reserved for "organization as system" discussions, not as a gripe session, but as a learning process.

Another liaison function of the site supervisor is to structure some way that other agency personnel can give input about the performance of the trainee. Again, it is common for this to occur informally and therefore inconsistently. The site supervisor can devise a short form and ask colleagues to complete it once or twice during the field placement. This kind of overture can have several positive effects.

1. It lessens the trainee's isolation by involving additional personnel in the trainee's experience.
2. It can provide the trainee with additional feedback from different perspectives or role positions.
3. It can confirm or confront the supervisor's own evaluation of the trainee.

Managing Time

Time management has become a cliché, even as the challenge to "find time" seems to increase. Supervisors are busy people. Whether at the university or in the field, many obligations compete with supervision. Because supervision is an enjoyable role for many professionals, they often take it on when they really have little extra time. Yet almost without exception, those studies that have surveyed supervisees about past unsatisfactory supervision found having insufficient time for supervision as a primary complaint.

Time management, therefore, becomes a crucial skill for clinical supervisors, one that must be exercised and modeled for supervisees who themselves are juggling several roles. Falvey (1987) lists several simple time-management strategies for administrative supervisors, which include coordinating activities to maximize one's productivity (e.g., tackling difficult tasks when one's energy is high), avoiding escapist behaviors (e.g., doing an unpleasant task first thing in the morning, rather than allowing it to weigh on one's mind all day), and dividing difficult tasks so that they do not appear overwhelming.

A central time-management skill is the ability to set priorities and keep to them. It is virtually impossible to end one's workday with absolutely no work leftover for the following day. Rather, supervisors who can manage time have addressed the most important concerns immediately and have learned to pace themselves in accomplishing less-pressing tasks. For some supervisors, it is a seemingly natural ability to take control of one's schedule; for others, it is a constant struggle that can be supplemented by time-management strategies suggested in the literature. Covey et al. (1994) warn against falling into an *urgency mentality*—that is, what is immediate is always treated as urgent, even when it is not. They also caution against using time-management strategies to fit an unreasonable amount of activity into one's schedule, a sentiment echoed by Osborn (2004); in other words, time management can become part of the problem, not the solution. Regardless of how the supervisor accomplishes the goal of finding and protecting time for supervision, the supervisor must realize that making time must be a deliberate choice, and is not something that will take care of itself.

Time Management and Choosing Supervision Methods. There are a variety of ways in which the process of supervision can be conducted. Deciding on the form that supervision will take and implementing the desired process can be an organizational task as well. For example, the supervisor might decide that using live supervision is desirable with a particular supervisee because of difficulties the supervisee is having with one of her clients. Using this method, however, requires a coordination of schedules and reserving an appropriate space. It is understandable, although regrettable, that supervisors often default on their supervision plans because the method that supervision should take requires the time to plan ahead. If the supervisor is convinced that a particular process is important for the supervisee's learning, it is incumbent on the supervisor to work out the logistical details in advance. This is even more the case when using technology for distance supervision (e.g., Schultz & Finger, 2003; Watson, 2003). When supervisors continue to put aside their teaching instincts because of the time and care required, the quality of supervision eventually deteriorates. Perhaps there is no organizational responsibility so essential to clinical supervision as the choreography required to ensure that the method of supervision matches the learning needs of supervisees.

Record Keeping

In a litigious era, the process of record keeping has gained in importance for helping professionals of all disciplines. Falvey and Cohen (2003) assert that from a legal perspective, "if it isn't documented, it didn't occur" (p. 77). Other researchers concur that good clinical records serve as a desirable defense against litigation (Brantley, 2000; Snider, 1987; Soisson, Vandecreek, & Knapp, 1987; Swenson, 1997; Thomas, 2010).

Whether supervising from campus or on site, it is the supervisor's responsibility to be sure that client records are complete. Most agencies and university professors have established recordkeeping procedures that have evolved over time, but with an ever-changing professional and legal climate, the wise supervisor reviews the recordkeeping system occasionally to be sure that it is current with national trends.

Research conducted by Worthington, Tan, and Poulin (2002) underscores the wisdom of supervisor vigilance regarding supervisee documentation of work with clients. Of the behaviors viewed by supervisees and supervisors as unethical, one of the most frequently committed (as reported by supervisees about their own behavior) was failure "to complete documentation of client records within the required time frame" (p. 335). In addition, although both supervisors and supervisees found this behavior to be problematic, supervisees found it less so than supervisors. The authors concluded that

> *documentation is one of the most important protections against legal liability because of its importance in establishing whether a given liability claim meets the criteria for malpractice, and failure to complete documentation may increase exposure to liability if harm comes to a client—a set of circumstances that may be more salient to supervisors than it is to supervisees.* (p. 345)

Most supervisors are far more careful about client records than about supervision records. Yet, as the Tarasoff case points out (*Tarasoff* v. *Regents of the University of California,* 1976), supervision records can be equally important in a malpractice suit. On a more optimistic note, supervision records discipline supervisors to pause and consider their supervision with each supervisee, offering moments of insight that might not otherwise occur. Luepker (2003) found parallel benefits between good psychotherapy records and good supervision records—that is, just as psychotherapy records help therapists approach their work in a more intentional manner, so too do supervision notes assist the supervisor to do the same. They also provide a record of progress (or lack thereof) regarding the supervisee. Luepker (2003) also makes the point that records can establish that the supervision provided met professional standards for supervision within the relevant professional community. In summary, then, for legal, instructional, and best-practice reasons, supervisors are strongly encouraged to keep accurate and complete supervision records.

Munson (2002) suggests that supervision records include seven components, and Luepker (2003) added an eighth component:

1. The supervisory contract, if used or required by the agency
2. A brief statement of supervisee experience, training, and learning needs
3. A summary of all performance evaluations
4. Notation of all supervisory sessions
5. Cancelled or missed sessions
6. Notation of cases discussed and significant decisions
7. Significant problems encountered in the supervision and how they were resolved, or whether they remain unresolved and why (Munson, 2002, p. 256)
8. Appropriate consent forms (informing clients and supervisees of supervision parameters) (Luepker, 2003)

Although Thomas (2010) does not delineate what records should include, she states multiple purposes for supervision records that might add to this list. In addition to ensuring client welfare, tracking supervisee development, and risk management, Thomas suggests that supervisors document conflicts and impasses that occur between the supervisor and supervisee, as well as evidence that supervisees complied with requirements of either a training program or a regulatory board. Her intent is clearly to create supervision records that assist the supervisor beyond the requirements of a subsequent supervision session.

Supervision risk management issues can include a host of topics, including a need for parental consent, risk of harm, concerns about substance abuse, need for medical consultation, possible boundary issues, suspected abuse, and required supervisee or supervisor expertise (Falvey, Caldwell, & Cohen, 2002). Once risk management issues are identified, it is incumbent on the supervisor to document interventions that have been executed to address these issues.

Planning for the Exceptions

It is frustrating, if not frightening, for a trainee to face an emergency with a client—for example, the need to hospitalize—and have no idea how the situation is to be handled. Although it may be the supervisor's intention or assumption that a supervisee will never handle an emergency alone, the unexpected happens, and emergency procedures should be in written form, given to the trainee during orientation, and placed in a convenient place for reference should an emergency occur.

Planning ahead is also crucial is when the supervisor will be away. For example, it is not unusual for all clinical supervisors in a training program to attend the same conference, leaving a university-based clinic either in the hands of doctoral students or fill-in supervisors. With the rush to prepare the paper to be presented at the conference or the arrangements that must be made to cover one's classes, it can happen that a colleague from the field or another department is asked to cover supervision with little or no information about the operations of the clinic, the status of any worrisome clients, or the student staff. This could easily be a case for which the lack of managerial foresight takes on the characteristics of questionable ethical practice.

By *planning ahead,* we do not mean to suggest that the supervisor compulsively worry about every possible way that things may go wrong. "The sky is falling" is not a productive supervisory posture. Rather, we urge supervisors to take reasonable care regarding their responsibilities and, especially, to give themselves the time to plan well and to put their plans into action.

EVALUATION AND DEBRIEFING

Devising an evaluation plan is a major organizational task that should also be considered at the outset of supervision. There are many ways to organize the evaluative aspect of supervision, and these should be reflected in the supervision contract and the recordkeeping system.

Although most supervisees receive some sort of final evaluation, many do not experience a quality debriefing of their time under supervision. This is unfortunate, because many worthwhile insights could be offered by both supervisor and supervisee during a debriefing session. In fact, debriefing is a perfect context for the supervisor to receive feedback about the supervision package that was offered to the supervisee, including how well supervision was organized, and can also include comments about how the supervisee might approach future supervision experiences in ways that build on the experience just ended.

SOME FINAL THOUGHTS

Short of receiving training in time management or developing training manuals, what can the clinical supervisor do to achieve organizational competence? (Not that the former wouldn't be a good idea!) This chapter presents many of the goals that the clinical supervisor might set for him- or herself. The following are five additional guidelines that can be of use as one sets out to achieve these goals.

Get Support

Before clinical supervisors commit themselves to the substantial task of supervising either on or off a university campus, they should be sure that they have administrative support for this responsibility, because without it, they are vulnerable to a host of difficulties that are bound to affect their supervision (Copeland, 1998; Globerman & Bogo, 2003; Sommer & Cox, 2005). The greater the support offered by superiors, the more that can be accomplished and the better the quality of the supervision. If support is limited, the clinical supervisor must decide if minimal standards can be met. If they cannot, the supervisor should decline an offer to supervise on ethical grounds.

Know Yourself

As simple as it sounds, there seems to be a relatively high degree of unawareness among clinical supervisors about their ability to organize themselves and those under their supervision. Perhaps supervisors assume that they should already have the organizational skills to manage the supervisory process and therefore resist admitting that this is an area in which they need to grow.

Organization comes far more naturally to some than to others. When supervisors believe that they fall in the latter category, they should find a member of their staff or a professional colleague whom they believe can help to develop—or more likely, help implement—a plan. The beginning of implementation is a critical juncture that calls for different abilities than those required for arriving at the original plan. This is the point at which many clinical supervisors could use assistance.

Gather Resources

There is nothing particularly virtuous about reinventing the wheel. As supervisors approach the prospect of supervising, they might contact other training programs or agencies and ask for samples of policy statements, supervision forms, and other materials relevant to their tasks. When a specific issue arises, consulting with colleagues and determining how they managed a similar issue is a sound strategy. Isolating oneself is a common supervisor flaw. Supervisors have a tremendous amount to learn from each other, and they must model for their supervisees the ability to consult with others as part of good clinical practice. Supervisors who intend to continue in this role may save valuable time with the development of a supervision portfolio of criteria for evaluation and templates for supervision contracts, recordkeeping, and the like.

Get Feedback

Any new procedure should be considered a pilot study of sorts. An organizational strategy may work well from the supervisor's vantage point, but be untenable for supervisees. The competent supervisor knows how to manipulate procedures to work for people and the program or agency, not the other way around, and part of this competence is demonstrated by seeking the opinions of others. The result is an organizational style that is always being fine-tuned without continually starting over from scratch.

Be Intentional

One way to avoid having to scrap one plan for another (and thereby keeping those under supervision in a state of turmoil) is for supervisors to give themselves permission to build their organizational plan slowly, but deliberately. No one who is supervising for the first time will be totally organized in the first year. Rather, one should begin with those aspects of supervision that are most critical for ethical and safe practice, and eventually pay heed to items that add to convenience and expediency of communication and a variety of training goals, among other things. In addition to being practical, being intentional encourages the supervisor to immediately home in on those things that are absolutely essential to any supervisory operation. Discriminating between issues that are essential and those that are desirable is the beginning and the core of organizational competence.

CONCLUSION

Although organizational issues tend to fall to the bottom of the list of motivational forces for clinical supervisors, the manner in which they are handled may be as predictive of long-term success as a supervisor as clinical expertise. Organizational tasks are tedious only when they are viewed as distracters. When viewed as building blocks for the essential work of supervision, organizational challenges can tap the energy typically reserved for such activities as establishing a working relationship with a supervisee. Paradoxically, the energy invested in the organization of clinical supervision may produce the greatest payoff in terms of protecting time and providing a context for exemplary supervisory practice.

Individual Supervision

Having described the major models of supervision and the supervisory relationship, we are prepared to consider the delivery of supervision interventions. Individual differences, interpersonal issues, ethical dilemmas, delivering evaluative feedback—all require specific supervision interventions. This chapter on individual supervision looks at supervision interventions and so serves a more targeted purpose, a template so to speak, for how supervision takes place in a one-on-one context.

Individual supervision is still considered the cornerstone of professional development. Although most supervisees experience some form of group supervision in their training, and some may have an opportunity to work within a live supervision paradigm, virtually all supervisees experience individual supervision sessions. Whether these individual conferences produce memories and insights that linger long into the supervisee's career or frustrate, bore, or even outrage the supervisee has something to do with the supervisor's skill in choosing and using a variety of supervision methods. At this point in the history of the helping professions, there are many different interventions or methods from which the supervisor can choose to conduct an individual case conference. This chapter describes the most common of these assorted approaches and discusses their advantages and occasional disadvantages. Although all the supervision interventions described in this chapter are appropriate for individual conferences, many also could be applied within a group supervision context. It is possible to conduct supervision using a great many different formats without stepping back to consider the bigger picture—a conceptual base, an evaluation plan, ethical constraints, cultural differences, and so on.

INITIAL CRITERIA FOR CHOOSING SUPERVISION INTERVENTIONS

A supervisor's initial choice of method is influenced by a number of factors, both rational and irrational in nature. The supervisor might believe that without an audio or video recording of counseling or therapy, there is no real way to know what has transpired between supervisees and their clients. Or the supervisor might be adamant that the use of reflective techniques is the only form of supervision that provides a glimpse into the supervisee's internal reasoning. The list can, and indeed does, go on. Borders and Brown (2005) list six reasons for choosing specific supervision methods:

1. Supervisor preferences (influenced by worldview, theoretical orientation, and past experience)
2. Supervisee developmental level
3. Supervisee learning goals
4. Supervisor goals for the supervisee
5. Supervisor's own learning goals as a supervisor (which may include becoming more comfortable with a particular supervisory intervention)
6. Contextual factors (e.g., site policies or facility capabilities, client difficulty)

Each of these criteria and all of them in unison will influence the choice of a supervision method.

As just one example of how interventions reflect different agendas, a supervisor who favors Stoltenberg and McNeill's (2010) developmental model will use different methods with a level 1 supervisee than a level 2 supervisee. However, if the supervisor is intrigued with web-based supervision, she or he may investigate ways to use such with each. Furthermore, because it is known that the particular level 2 supervisee is struggling with use of self in counseling, Interpersonal Process Recall (IPR; Kagan, 1980) may be planned as a regular intervention for this supervisee.

Methods and techniques, therefore, must be malleable and conducive to reaching a variety of supervision goals. Technical eclecticism may be as important to supervisors as it has been argued to be for therapists. Supervisors (and supervisees) may be best served when creative alternatives are used to accomplish immediate goals, as well as goals that are more long range.

Finally, an additional frame for deciding what method to use in a given situation is to determine the function of supervision at a given point in time. There are three general functions of supervision interventions (Borders et al., 1991):

1. *Assessing* the learning needs of the supervisee
2. *Changing, shaping,* or *supporting* the supervisee's behavior
3. *Evaluating* the performance of the supervisee

Although the majority of supervision falls within the second function, supervisors are continually reassessing their supervisee's learning needs and evaluating their progress. As these separate functions are being addressed, the supervisor might find that different methods serve one function better than others; for example, a supervisor might choose to watch a video of a supervisee to assess that person's skills, but rely on process notes to accomplish the second function of attempting to change, support, or redirect the supervisee's work.

STRUCTURED VERSUS UNSTRUCTURED INTERVENTIONS

Much of the literature addressing developmental issues, cognitive style of the supervisee, and numerous other topics refers to the relative need for structure in supervision. Rarely, however, do authors describe specifically what is meant by structure or the lack of it. Highly structured supervision can be viewed as an extension of training, whereas unstructured supervision can be viewed as approaching consultation. Although methods of supervision are often associated with a particular degree of structure, it is the supervisor's use of the method that will determine the level of structure. For example, Rigazio-DiGilio and Anderson (1994) note that a structured use of live supervision might entail the use of the "bug-in-the-ear," thus coaching the supervisee through a therapy session, whereas a less structured form might rely on presession planning, midsession consultation, and postsession debriefing. Similarly, individual supervision based on audio recording may be directed by the supervisor and follow the supervisor's instructional agenda, or the use of audio may be used to encourage the supervisee to reflect on a moment in a counseling session that appears to have had special meaning for the supervisee.

In short, structure or the lack of structure is not dictated by the method used. Rather, structured interventions are supervisor directed and involve a reasonably high amount of supervision control; unstructured interventions may be supervisor or supervisee directed and require more discipline on the part of the supervisor to allow learning to take place without directing it. For the supervisor who is impatient or who dislikes ambiguity, unstructured interventions are more challenging; for the supervisor who has difficulty planning ahead and organizing learning, structured interventions are more challenging. The great majority of supervisees benefit from both types of interventions at different junctures in their professional development.

METHODS, FORMS, AND TECHNIQUES OF SUPERVISION

With technology and computer capabilities becoming more sophisticated every day, and with the helping professions exhibiting a heightened interest in supervision, different techniques, methods, and paradigms for conducting supervision continue to evolve. Because of the dynamic nature of the field, therefore, we do not presume to present an inclusive list of supervision interventions; rather, we hope to reflect the diversity of choices that has been spawned as clinical supervision continues to develop, to give some rationale for using different methods, and to report the findings on their frequency of use and relative strengths and weaknesses.

The remainder of this chapter has been designed to review supervision methods, advancing from those methods that use little technology to those that require more sophisticated tools. Therefore, self-report begins our list as a supervision format that relies on the supervisee's recollections of counseling or therapy as the source of information to be used for supervision.

Self-Report

Although it is a simple form of supervision in one sense, we consider self-report to be a difficult method to perform well. In fact, some of the best as well as some of the worst supervision can be found within the domain of self-report. Under the best of conditions, supervisees are challenged conceptually and personally and learn a great deal. Many supervisors relying on self-report, however, have fallen into stagnation; supervision becomes pro forma, with little difference evident from session to session or from supervisee to supervisee. Also, much of what is viewed in the field as self-report supervision is, instead, restricted to case management.

Professional literature has given relatively little attention to self-report in the recent past, focusing much more on forms of supervision that include direct samples of the supervisee's work. Self-report, however, continues to be a commonly used form of supervision, both during training and for postgraduate supervision (e.g., Amerikaner & Rose, 2012; Goodyear & Nelson, 1997; Magnuson, 1995). At its best, self-report is an intense tutorial relationship in which the supervisee fine-tunes both case conceptualization ability and personal knowledge as each relates to therapist–client and supervisor–supervisee relationships. At its worst, self-report is a method where the supervisee *distorts* (rather than *reports*) his or her work, whether or not this is conscious (Haggerty & Hilsenroth, 2011; Noelle, 2002), leading Ellis (2010) to assert that it is a myth of supervision that supervisors can do their job adequately using self-report only. Because novice supervisees are more likely to be overwhelmed by the amount of data available to them in their sessions with clients, self-report is viewed as far less appropriate for them (e.g., Holloway, 1988; Thomas, 2010). In short, self-report is only as good as the observational and conceptual abilities of the supervisee and the seasoned insightfulness of the supervisor. It seems, therefore, that self-report offers too many opportunities for failure if it represents the complete supervision plan.

Campbell (1994) supports this contention on ethical and legal grounds. He refers to an early study conducted by Muslin, Thurnblad, and

Meschel (1981) in which more than 50 percent of the important issues evident in videotapes of therapy sessions of psychiatric supervisees were not reported in supervision; furthermore, some degree of distortion characterized more than 50 percent of supervisees' reports. Campbell describes such supervision as *supervision in absentia,* and states that

> *As a result of their inexperience, trainees find it difficult to comprehend the problems of their clients. Because they do not observe trainees, supervisors find it difficult to correct their errors. Thus, trainees struggle with what they do not understand; and supervisors labor with what they cannot see.* (p. 11)

A more recent study further indicts the memories of therapists when a group of licensed psychologists was asked to recall the molar (main) and molecular (supporting) ideas from specific segments of actual therapy sessions. Wynne, Susman, Ries, Birringer, and Katz (1994) report only a 42 percent recall rate for molar ideas and 30 percent recall for molecular ideas. It seems reasonable to ask whether such a rate is adequate for the purposes of supervision.

Despite these issues, self-report as a supervision method is alive and well. Studies that investigate the frequency of methods used in supervision find self-report to be a relatively dominant—and often, the most frequently used—method (Amerikaner & Rose, 2012; Anderson, Schlossberg, & Rigazio-DiGilio, 2000; Borders, Cashwell, & Rotter, 1995; Coll, 1995; Romans, Boswell, Carlozzi, & Ferguson, 1995; Wetchler, Piercy, & Sprenkle, 1989). When these same supervisees (and sometimes supervisors) were asked to identify the most valuable form of supervision, self-report dropped in its primacy (e.g., Wetchler et al., 1989). In a study that compared perceptions of best and worst supervision, Anderson et al. (2000) found that their subjects were far more likely to consider self-report as representing their worst supervision experiences than their best. Supporting a cautious stance toward self-report as the supervision method of choice, Rogers and McDonald (1995) found that when supervisors used more direct methods of supervision, they evaluated their supervisees as less prepared for the job than when they used self-report. As a parallel concern, Amerikaner and Rose (2012) found that supervisees whose supervisors had not used more direct methods of supervision believed that their supervisors were very knowledgeable of their clinical functioning. Together, such results make the regular use of self-report highly suspect, especially for novice supervisees. Finally, an interesting investigation conducted by Wetchler and Vaughn (1992) homed in on the supervision method used during what, in retrospect, was identified as a critical supervisory incident that had a positive developmental impact on the supervisee. For both supervisors and supervisees, the method most frequently noted was an individual conference without reference to the use of any technology. Although this study may seem to contradict other findings, it may be viewed as underscoring our earlier statement that self-report includes some of the best as well as some of the worst supervision experiences. When a situation is highly charged for the supervisee, it may take the more open-ended context of a conference based on self-report to help the supervisee process the meaning of what is occurring, because the supervisee has processed it internally. At times, information does not enlighten, but rather detracts from the issues. (Our discussion of encouraging reflective practice later in this chapter returns to this theme.) Knowing when to limit the information flow in order to take a more introspective approach to supervision requires both experience and a posture of keen attentiveness on the part of the supervisor.

Process Notes and Case Notes

Process notes are the supervisee's written explanation of the content of the therapy session, the interactional processes that occurred between supervisee and client, the supervisee's feelings about the client, and the rationale and manner of intervention (Goldberg, 1985). As such, process notes can be very extensive and, therefore, time consuming. Outside of social work, where process notes are the norm, it is unlikely that a supervisor would require

TABLE 1 Leads to Assist the Supervisee in Preparing for the Supervision Case Conference

1. A. [a]Briefly describe the client's presenting problem.
   B. What were your objectives for this session?
2. Describe the dynamics in the session (your own reactions to the client and the interactions between you and the client). Be sure to attend to dynamics that may be based on cultural differences/ similarities.
3. A. Describe other important information that was learned during the session, including contextual information.
   B. Summarize key issues discussed during the session.
4. Describe relevant cultural or developmental information as it relates to the presenting problem(s).
5. A. What is your initial conceptualization of the client's issue(s)? (Be sure that your comments are theoretically sound.)
   B. Explain changes (or expansions) of your conceptualizations of the presenting problem(s).
6. List relevant diagnostic impressions, including DSM[b] code and axis.
7. A. To the extent possible, describe initial treatment plan for this client.
   B. Explain changes (or expansions) of your treatment plan for this client.
8. Based on your treatment plan, what are your objectives for the next session?
9. To what extent were your objectives for this session met?
10. Does any aspect of this case raise ethical concerns for you?
11. Share any personal reflections on the session.
12. What specific questions do you have for your supervisor?

[a]Leads relevant to (A) initial counseling session and (B) subsequent counseling sessions.

[b]DSM: *Diagnostic and Statistical Manual, 4th edition, Text Revision.*

complete process notes for each session that a supervisee conducts. They may, however, be a worthwhile endeavor on occasion, especially if the supervisor believes that the supervisee would benefit from a more intensive review of supervisee–client interactions and the outcomes of these.

Case notes, however, are a normative aspect of counseling and supervision. Case notes should include all pertinent information from a counseling session, including the interventions used. As such, case notes are the professional, institutional, and legal record of counseling. This being said, case notes can also be used deliberately as part of the supervision conference. Although some information should be apparent in all therapy case notes, a supervisor may ask the supervisee to reflect on and answer specific questions that meet supervision goals. For example, questions could be posed to assist the supervisee in a reflective process (discussed later in this chapter), to assist the supervisee in linking conceptualization to intervention, or to be vigilant regarding cultural dynamics. When used in this way, case notes become a supervision intervention that can direct the conference. Case notes can and perhaps should be used in conjunction with any other supervision modality. Table 1 shows sample case conference leads that may be helpful to supervisees in preparing for supervision.

Live Observation

Live observation is a relatively frequent form of supervision in graduate programs with in-house training clinics; it is used less frequently in the field because of scheduling difficulties and structural constraints. In their study that reviewed supervisor activity across master's, doctoral, and postgraduate supervisees in psychology, Amerikaner and Rose (2012) report that direct observation represented a very small percentage of supervisor activity (approximately 4 percent). We differentiate between live observation and live supervision, the former being a method of observing the supervisee, but not interacting with the supervisee during the session (except in the case of an emergency) and the latter being a combination of observation and active supervision during the session.

Live observation offers three advantages over all other forms of supervision, with the exception of live supervision. First, there is a high safeguard for client welfare because the supervisor is immediately available to intervene in case of emergency. Second, live observation affords the supervisor a more complete picture of clients and supervisees than is attainable through the use of audio or video. Even when using video, the camera position is typically fixed throughout a session, giving only side views of both client and supervisee, or focusing on one or the other exclusively. Supervisors who have used both live observation and recordings can certainly attest to the more firsthand experience that live observation provides. Finally, when supervisors observe regularly, they are more engaged in determining what cases are discussed in supervision. By contrast, Amerikaner and Rose (2012) found that 80 percent of the supervisees in their study primarily or exclusively chose what case material to discuss in supervision. Although this may be argued by some as appropriate, it is fraught with the problems we discuss under the Self-Report heading.

Audio and Video Recordings

Although live observation and video recording have led to some of the more dramatic breakthroughs in the supervision process, the audiotape was the first to revolutionize our perceptions of what could be accomplished in supervision, and Rogers (1942) and Covner (1942a, b) are attributed with this development (Goodyear & Nelson, 1997). Without the facilities of a training clinic to observe directly, audio or video recordings allow supervisees to transport an accurate sample (albeit partial when audio only) of counseling or therapy to a supervisor who was not present at the time that the session occurred. Until the emergence of devices that have made video recording easy, the audio recording was the most widely used source of information for supervisors who wanted to have some sort of direct access to the work of their supervisees (e.g., Borders et al., 1995; Coll, 1995). Furthermore, this supervision method has found support among those who investigated its effectiveness. As one example, when Magnuson, Wilcoxon, and Norem (2000) asked experienced counselors to reflect on exemplary supervision that they had received, the review of audio or video recordings with their supervisors surfaced as examples of supervision that led to strong positive recollections.

When an audio or video is first required of supervisees (especially if they have been relying on self-report or process notes), there is often some resistance that takes the form of "My clients won't be comfortable." This reaction is occasionally echoed at practicum or internship sites when a training institution asks for recordings of the supervisee's clinical work. Although client resistance to recording may be real and must be addressed in a sensitive and ethical manner, it is often not the client but the supervisee who is experiencing the greatest amount of discomfort at the prospect of being recorded (and therefore scrutinized). In truth, the majority of clients are open to having their sessions recorded if the supervisee's demeanor is professional when presenting the topic of recording and they have an assurance that confidentiality will not be compromised. In addition, once over their initial reactions, Ellis, Krengel, and Beck (2002) found that recording (audio or video) did not cause significant anxiety in supervisees. In fact, any aversive reactions to recording as a supervision method were negligible.

Planning Recording-Based Supervision. The least productive way to use a recording in supervision may be that which is depicted in the following example: The supervisee arrives with two or three recordings of recent counseling sessions, without having reviewed any of them privately. Because the supervisee has made no decision about which session to discuss during supervision, the supervisee spends several minutes telling the supervisor about the different cases represented in the recordings. The supervisor eventually picks one session. The counseling session is played from the beginning until something strikes the supervisor as important.

Our point is simple: The process of supervision must be based on a plan, and it is the supervisor's responsibility to outline that plan. We do believe that spontaneity is important, but it is unlikely to emerge when the supervision process is tedious. Listening to or watching a recording for 20 minutes with a supervisee saying, "Gee, I guess the part I was talking about was further into the session than I realized," is one sure way to add to the tedium factor.

Recorded segments of counseling can be used in several ways for supervision. West, Bubenzer, Pinsoneault, and Holeman (1993) note that delayed reviews of recordings are best used to facilitate the supervisee's perceptual–conceptual skills. Goldberg (1985) identifies several teaching goals that can be accomplished using recordings, including focusing on specific therapy techniques, helping the supervisee see the relationship between process and content, focusing on how things are said (*paralanguage*), and helping the supervisee differentiate between a conversational tone and a therapeutic one. Sobell, Manor, Sobell, and Dum (2008) found that requiring supervisees to self-critique their audio recordings of counseling using motivational interviewing principles prior to supervision resulted in less defensive reactions to supervisor critical feedback.

Our previous comments notwithstanding, Huhra, Yamokoski-Maynhart, and Prieto (2008) advise supervisors to tailor recording reviews to the developmental level of the supervisee. Using IDM as their developmental model (Stoltenberg, McNeill, & Delworth, 1998), they suggested that supervisors require supervisees to watch their sessions prior to supervision in order to become accustomed to the anxiety of reviewing their own work. This is done with the hope that it allows level 1 supervisees to be able to focus more on the client during supervision. Huhra et al. also suggest that supervisors share their observations about the client as the recording is reviewed with a level 1 supervisee rather than ask probing questions. They note that level 1 trainees are easily overwhelmed by the amount of information available in a session, and supervisors can assist by modeling what is important to attend to and what is inconsequential. Only once the supervisor sees development in the supervisee's ability to recognize relevant material can the focus shift to the therapeutic use of that material.

During the initial phase of a supervision relationship, it may be advisable for the supervisor to listen to or watch an entire counseling session prior to supervision in order to get an overview of the supervisee's ability and to have control over what segment of the recording is chosen for supervision (Borders & Brown, 2005). It is important also to help the supervisee understand the rationale behind the choice of a recorded segment if this is not apparent. Preselected segments can be chosen for a variety of reasons, as follows:

1. To highlight the most productive part of the session
2. To highlight the most important part of the session
3. To highlight the part of the session where the supervisee is struggling the most
4. To underscore any number of content issues, including metaphors and recurring themes
5. To ask about a confusing part of the session, perhaps because paralanguage or nonverbal behavior contradicts content
6. To focus attention on the point in the session where interpersonal or cross-cultural dynamics were either particularly therapeutic or particularly strained, or where cultural encapsulation is evident (Cashwell, Looby, & Housley, 1997)

In other words, supervisors almost always have a teaching function in mind when they select a section of a recording for supervision. In addition, such supervisor goals help novice supervisees who are more likely to be tuned into the content of the session than the process (Maione, 2011).

This process should evolve, however, as the supervisee develops in conceptual ability and experience. Relatively quickly, the supervisee can select the section of a session that determines the direction of supervision. Often, supervisees are just asked to choose a part of the session where they felt confused, lost, overwhelmed, or frustrated. The supervisor then listens to or watches the segment with them and proceeds from there. If this format is used, the supervisee should be prepared to do the following:

1. State the reason for selecting this part of the session for discussion in supervision
2. State briefly what transpired up to that point
3. Explain what he or she was trying to accomplish at that point in the session
4. State clearly the specific help desired from the supervisor

Any format used repeatedly may contribute to supervision becoming stagnant. When the supervisee is asked repeatedly to select a troublesome session segment, for example, the supervision may become skewed toward problems in counseling sessions, with little opportunity for the supervisee to enjoy successes in supervision.

As an alternative method for using recordings, the supervisor might assign a theme for the next session and ask the supervisee to be responsible for producing the segment. For example, the supervisor might suggest that reframing would be of great help for a particular client or family, and that the supervisee should try to reframe as often as possible in the next session and choose the most successful of these attempts to present in the next supervision session. In addition to using supervision to sharpen a skill, this strategy also allows the supervisor to connect technique to a counseling situation and to get data on the supervisee's self-evaluation ability. The types of assignments that can direct the use of recordings are potentially limitless and can focus on the process of therapy, the conceptual issues in therapy, personal or interpersonal issues, and ethical dilemmas, among others; assignments should also reflect different supervisee developmental levels. In summary, careful selection of a recorded segment is perhaps most crucial in making the recording a powerful supervision tool.

Although the use of direct supervision methods is not as associated with psychodynamic approaches to supervision as other theoretical approaches, Aveline (1992) and Brandell (1992) address the unique advantages of using recorded segments in psychodynamic supervision. In a particularly adroit description of the benefit of hearing a supervisee's session, Aveline states:

> *I am stimulated by the way in which words are used, the metaphors deployed and the images evoked. Snatches of interaction often vividly illustrate the central dilemmas of a person's life. . . . The medium is particularly well placed to identify such phenomena as the patient filling all the space of [the] session with words so as to leave no room for the therapist to say anything for fear that what might be said will disrupt the inner equilibrium; the nervous laugh that as surely indicates that there is an issue of importance at hand as does the bird with trailing wing that the nest is nearby; the therapist whose words of encouragement are belied by his impatient tone or gesture; and the patient whose placatory dependence is shot through with hostility.* (p. 350)

Despite his convincing and poetic arguments in favor of the use of recordings for supervision, Aveline also cautions that there are significant disadvantages. Primarily, Aveline argues that a recording device always has an effect on therapy, and its meaning to the client (and the therapist) must be explored. He cautions that recording might even be abusive to a client who is in too weak a position to refute its use. Similarly, Aveline saw the possibility that recording could hurt the supervisory relationship if the exposure that the recording allowed led to humiliation for the therapist. In all cases, Aveline stressed that the supervisor must be willing to address the consequences that the recording produces. Aveline's insights notwithstanding, we assert that in some instances, direct samples of supervisee work may be an ethical necessity, and most assuredly is so for the novice supervisee. We further assert that recording technology has become much more intertwined in our professional and personal lives than when Aveline made this cautionary statement. There is no question that we are a more recording-tolerant culture than we were even a decade ago.

Written Feedback. For supervisees who are more visual than auditory, the supervisor can add written feedback to individual supervision, either as a reaction to a recording or after a supervision session. Many supervisors choose to listen to recordings between supervision sessions rather than during them. This is especially so during the beginning stages of supervision. Rather than taking notes to use in a subsequent supervision session, the supervisor can write feedback regarding the session that can be given to the supervisee. This exercise forces the supervisor to conceptualize the feedback before the supervision session. In addition, the critiques automatically become a record of supervision; they allow the supervisee to review comments made by the supervisor, and they can become a way of coordinating supervision if other supervisors are involved (e.g., a site supervisor could be sent a copy of the feedback prepared by the university supervisor). Desmond and Kindsvatter (2010) refer to such feedback as *letters* that can exhibit one of Bernard's (1979, 1997) Discrimination Model roles of teaching, counselor, or consultant, depending on the needs of the supervisee and the goals of the supervisor. They use such letters as a supplement to individual supervision, and stress their utility in underscoring particular developmental goals, addressing intrapersonal issues, and so forth.

Transcripts. Supervisors occasionally ask supervisees to transcribe their recordings and submit these for supervision. Arthur and Gfoerer (2002) argue that transcripts were especially helpful for supervisees in early stages of training (e.g., a first practicum).That is, because the sessions are in print form, it is more likely that supervisees will be able to notice faulty interventions, such as multiple questions or a run of incomplete statements, than might be possible using the recording alone. This, then, allows supervisees greater opportunity to critique their own work (at this early stage) than recording alone might afford. In addition, because transcripts use a more familiar educational modality (a written document), it may be helpful for supervisees who seem to be having a particularly difficult time making the transition from traditional classroom contexts to clinical supervision.

Arthur and Gfoerer (2002) gathered survey data from 30 graduates of a training program, all of whom had been supervised by the same supervisor using transcription as the focus of supervision. For the questions regarding the value of the transcripts, 11 of 12 were answered positively by the vast majority of the respondents. Only the item "The use of transcripts made me anxious" caused mixed results. Although 16 of the 30 disagreed with this statement, 13 agreed; 1 gave no response. It is unknown, however, if those who found this form of supervision anxiety provoking would have found another form to be less so.

Arthur and Gfoerer (2002) also asked their respondents to identify positive and negative attributes that they associated with transcript use in supervision. Positive attributes included that the supervisor reviewed the whole session; that transcripts gave supervisees a visual reminder of the session; and that transcripts were concrete and allowed for equally concrete examples of what they needed to work on, thus making it easier for them to critique their own work. Negative attributes associated with the transcripts were that they were so time consuming for both intern and supervisor, that nonverbal cues and all paralanguage were not included in supervision, that mistakes were even more visible than they may have been through other supervision methods, and that they were too focused on the content of a session, rather than the overall development of the supervisee.

Transcripts of counseling sessions provide an enormous amount of material for a subsequent supervision session. They seem to result in several positive outcomes, at least for novice interns. In light of the time-consuming nature of this form of supervision, however, as well as its other limitations, perhaps an intermittent or abbreviated (i.e., transcription of a certain number of minutes of a session) use of this supervision method represents its optimal use.

Issues Specific to Video Recordings. Munson (1983) makes an observation that still merits consideration. He speculates that the associations that supervisees may make between video-recorded supervision and commercial television can present a problem (perhaps even more so now with the growth of reality TV). Because television connotes entertainment, Munson saw the dual problem of observers not finding others' sessions entertaining enough, and supervisees feeling they must "perform" on video, thereby suffering from excessive "performance anxiety." The supervisor's role, according to Munson, includes structuring supervision so that observers are stimulated cognitively (usually by means of a specific task related to the video-recorded segment), while at the same time attempting to safeguard the integrity of the supervisee. Munson's admonition has been supported by empirical findings that video recording review of counseling sessions caused a shift from positive mood about a counseling session to a lowered mood for therapists and therapists-in-training after video review (Hill et al., 1994). It seems, therefore, that the obvious advantage of video can become a liability and must be monitored carefully by the supervisor. As one of our supervisees put it, "[V]ideo is a little like some hotel room mirrors; the reflection is *too* accurate."

Despite valid cautions regarding the use of video in supervision, there is no question that our knowledge base and intervention alternatives have increased greatly as a result of this technology. With video, supervisees can literally see themselves in the role of helper, thus allowing them to be an observer of their work, which is not possible with audio alone.

In an excellent discussion of the use of video in the supervision of marriage and family therapy, Breunlin, Karrer, McGuire, and Cimmarusti (1988) argue that video supervision should not only be focused on the interaction between supervisee and clients, but also on the far more subtle internal processes experienced by the supervisee during both the therapy session and the supervision session. To focus on one to the exclusion of the other is an error, according to Breunlin et al. Furthermore, they state that therapists can never be objective observers of their own roles separate from the family (or individual) client, as this is an interactional impossibility. Breunlin et al., therefore, recommended six guidelines for working with both the cold accuracy of the video and the dynamic reality experienced by the supervisee. These guidelines, when followed, help alleviate some of the dangers noted by Munson (1983) and Hill et al. (1994). (Note, however, that the guidelines outlined by Breunlin et al. also apply to other methods of supervision.)

1. *Focus video supervision by setting realistic goals for the supervised therapy session.* This has two advantages: It reduces the sense of information overload by narrowing down the field to those interventions that are connected to goals, and it increases the possibility that the supervisee will emerge from the session moderately satisfied because realistic goals are attainable.

2. *Relate internal process across contexts.* The point here is that what the supervisee experiences in the session is important to discuss in supervision. Furthermore, Breunlin et al. emphasize that supervisors should allow supervisees to disclose their perceptions first, rather than supervisors offering their observations, which contradicts Huhra and co-authors' (2008) advice. Most important, however, is the issue of validating the internal processes of the supervisee, rather than forfeiting such a discussion in favor of "strategy review." Interpersonal process recall (Kagan, 1976, 1980; Kagan & Kagan, 1997), described later in this chapter, is an excellent technique for meeting this guideline.

3. *Select tape segments that focus on remedial performance.* The authors explain this guideline as providing corrective feedback about performance that the supervisee has the ability to change. In other words, focusing on aspects of the supervisee's personal style or on skills that are too complex for immediate attainment will be nonproductive.

4. *Use supervisor comments to create a moderate evaluation of performance.* The authors rely on Fuller and Manning's (1973) research to arrive at this guideline. Fuller and Manning found that a moderate discrepancy between performance and the target goal is optimal for learning; therefore, the supervisor must find video segments that are neither exemplary nor too far from the stated goal. We can begin to appreciate the kind of supervisor commitment that is required to use Breunlin et al.'s (1988) suggestions.

5. *Refine goals moderately.* This guideline underscores the fact that video review must be seen in the larger context of supervisee development. Sometimes the multitude of possibilities that a review can generate are irrespective of the skill level of the supervisee. In addition, Breunlin et al. remind us that what appears easy when viewing a session can be far more difficult to pull off in therapy. Small increments of improvement, therefore, should be targeted by the supervisor.

6. *Maintain a moderate level of arousal.* The authors posit that attending to the first five guidelines will take care of the sixth. The supervisor, however, must always be cautious that the supervisee is stimulated to grow without becoming overly threatened. Therefore, the supervisor, as always, must be alert to multiple levels of experience.

Also addressing supervisee internal processes, Rubinstein and Hammond (1982) maintain early on that the supervisor who uses video must have a healthy respect for its power. There is no hiding from the stark reality of one's picture and voice being projected into the supervision room. Therefore, they caution that video should not be used unless there is a relatively good relationship between supervisor and supervisee. We concur, to a point, but also postulate that a good relationship can be formed in the process of using video with sensitivity. In addition, the supervisee will be far less camera-shy if video was used in training prior to supervision. Rubinstein and Hammond also make one excellent suggestion: Supervisors should appear on video prior to having their supervisees do the same. Kaplan, Rothrock, and Culkin (1999) also suggest this kind of modeling. Providing samples of one's own counseling can serve many purposes, but especially attractive is dispelling the myth that supervisors conduct perfect therapy sessions. As all supervisors know, the insight and cleverness evidenced in supervision are rarely matched in one's own therapy, at least not without the occasional misstep.

Finally, Rubinstein and Hammond suggested that the use of video remain technologically simple. They are not in favor of split screens, superimposed images, or other such equipment capabilities, believing that it detracts from the lifelike experience of watching the recorded session. Of course, decisions about using video reflect the supervisor's comfort, or lack thereof, with this type of technology, as well as the supervision goals. And yet, as we state earlier, supervisor comfort and technological expertise may need to increase as the present technological revolution continues. Each supervisor ultimately finds a viable comfort level with technological advances, but the supervisor is still wise to remember Rubinstein and Hammond's caution lest technology and its multiple uses become the center of supervision.

Interpersonal Process Recall. Perhaps the most widely known supervision method using video is *interpersonal process recall (IPR)* (Kagan, 1976, 1980; Kagan & Kagan, 1997; Kagan & Krathwohl, 1967; Kagan, Krathwohl, & Farquahar, 1965; Kagan, Krathwohl, & Miller, 1963). An earlier national survey of counselor education programs (Borders & Leddick, 1988) found that, at that time, IPR was one of only two clearly delineated methods of supervision taught in supervision courses, the other being live supervision. IPR began as a therapy model and occasionally is still used as such; for our purposes here, however, we confine ourselves to the use of IPR in supervision. Kagan (1980) asserts that there are many psychological barriers to open and honest communication, and that these operate in counseling and therapy as they do in other daily interactions. Primary among these is the strongly socialized habit of behaving diplomatically. As a result, much of what a supervisee thinks, intuits, and feels during counseling and therapy is disregarded almost automatically, because allowing such perceptions to surface would confront the predisposition to be diplomatic.

The purpose of IPR, then, is to give the supervisee a safe haven for these internal reactions. Kagan (1980) strongly maintains that all persons are "the best authority of their own dynamics and the best interpreter of their own experience" (pp. 279–280). Starting with this assumption, therefore, the supervisor's role becomes that of a facilitator to stimulate the awareness of the supervisee beyond the point at which it operated during the counseling session.

The process of IPR is relatively simple. The supervisor and supervisee view a recorded video of a counseling session together. Any point at which either person believes that something of importance is happening in the session, especially something that is not being addressed by either the supervisee or the client, the video is stopped (dual controls are helpful, but it is easy enough to signal the person holding the controls to stop the recording). If the supervisee stops the recording, the supervisee speaks first, saying, for example, "I was getting really frustrated here. I didn't know what she wanted. We had been over all of this before. I thought it was resolved last week, but here it is again." At this point, it is essential that the supervisor refrain from adopting a teaching role to instruct the supervisee about what might have been done. Rather, the supervisor must allow the supervisee the psychological space to investigate internal processes to some resolution. At the same time, the good facilitator, or *inquirer,* as Kagan prefers to call the role, can ask direct questions that are challenging to the supervisee. Some possibilities for this example include: "What do you wish you had said to her? How do you think she might have reacted if you said those things to her?" "What kept you from saying what you wanted to say? If you had the opportunity now, how might you tell her what you are thinking and feeling?" Once it is believed that the dynamics for the chosen session segment have been reexamined sufficiently, the recording is allowed to continue.

Table 2 lists a variety of lead statements that reflect different supervision goals. Specifically, leads are listed that inspire affective exploration, check out unstated agendas, encourage cognitive examination, get at images, or help to search out expectations. As one can certainly discern, this process is slow. Only a portion of a therapy session can be reviewed in this manner unless supervision is extended significantly. Therefore, choosing the most interpersonally weighted or most metaphorically meaningful segment of the video will be most productive for supervision purposes.

One caution is advisable: Because IPR often puts interpersonal dynamics under a microscope, it is possible that they will be magnified to the extent of distortion (Bernard, 1981). In other words, what is a perfectly functional helping relationship can come to look somehow dysfunctional when overexposed, and as all persons in the helping professions know, some relationship dynamics are best left underexposed. We need not be in perfect sync with all our clients to be of help to them. The clinical skill comes in determining which interactions are important and which are not. IPR is not a method to guide what is to be examined. For this reason, Huhra et al. (2008) suggest that IPR be used primarily with supervisees who have reached IDM Level 2—that is, those who are advanced enough to be able to differentiate important dynamics from those that are less consequential. For supervisors, the following

TABLE 2 Supervisor Leads for Use with Interpersonal Process Recall

Leads That Inspire Affective Exploration
- How did that make you feel?
- How did that make you feel about him or her?
- Do you remember what you were feeling?
- Were you aware of any feelings?
- What do those feelings mean to you?
- Does that feeling have any special meaning to you?
- Is it a familiar feeling?
- What did you do (or decide to do) about that feeling you had?
- Did you want to express that feeling at any time?
- Did you have any fantasies of taking any risk?

Leads That Check Out Unstated Agendas
- What would you have liked to have said to her or him at this point?
- What's happening here?
- What did you feel like doing?
- How were you feeling about your role as counselor at this point?
- What had that meant to you?
- If you had more time, where would you have liked to have gone?

Leads That Encourage Cognitive Examination
- What were you thinking at that time?
- What thoughts were you having about the other person at that time?
- Something going on there?
- Anything going on there?
- Had you any ideas about what you wanted to do with that?
- Did you fantasize taking any risks?
- Were you able to say it the way you wanted to?
- Did you want to say anything else then?
- Did you have any plan of where you wanted the session to go next?
- Did you think that the other person knew what you wanted?
- What kind of image were you aware of projecting?
- Is that the image you wanted to project?
- Can you recall what effect the setting had on you or the interaction?
- Can you recall what effect you thought that the setting had on the other person?
- Did the equipment affect you in any way?
- (If reaction to the recorder) What did you want, or not want, the recorder to hear from you?

Leads That Get at Images
- Were you having any fantasies at that moment?
- Were any pictures, images, or memories flashing through your mind then?
- What was going on in your mind at that time?
- Did it remind you of anything?
- Did you think that you had "been there before"? Is that familiar to you?
- Where had that put you in the past?

Leads That Explore Mutual Perceptions between Client and Counselor
- What did you think that she or he was feeling about you?
- How do you think that she or he was seeing you at that point?

(*Continued*)

TABLE 2 Supervisor Leads for Use with Interpersonal Process Recall (*Continued*)

- Do you think that she or he was aware of your feelings? Your thoughts?
- What message do you think that she or he was trying to give you?
- Did you feel that he or she had any expectations of you at that point?
- What did you think that she or he wanted you to think or feel or do?
- Do you think that your description of the interaction would coincide with her or his description?
- Was she or he giving you any cues as to how she or he was feeling?
- How do you think that she or he felt about talking about this problem?
- How do you think that she or he felt about continuing to talk with you at this point?

Leads That Help Search Out Expectations

- What did you want her or him to tell you?
- What did you want to hear?
- What would you have liked from her or him?
- Were you expecting anything of her or him at that point?
- Did you want her or him to see you in some particular way? How?
- What do you think that her or his perceptions were of you?
- What message did you want to give to her or him?
- Was there anything in particular that you wanted her or him to say or do or think?
- Was she or he "with you"? How did her or his responses hit you?
- What did you really want to tell her or him at this moment? What prevented you from doing so?
- What did you want her or him to do?
- Did you want her or him to do something that would have made it easier for you?
- What would that have been?

two questions may be useful in selecting segments for IPR:

1. From what I can observe, does this interaction seem to be interrupting the flow of counseling?
2. From what I know of the supervisee, would focusing on this interaction aid in his or her development as a mental health professional?

Finally, it is important that the supervisor refrain from asking questions to make statements. Loaded questions are very quickly discerned by the supervisee and most assuredly shut down the process as it was intended. For this reason, it is not advisable to use IPR when direct feedback is warranted. As an example, cultural encapsulation may need to be addressed in a different manner. Once a learning goal around cultural competence has been established, IPR can serve the purpose of assisting the supervisee to process internal filters operating during a counseling session.

Methods to Stimulate Reflection

Developmental models include those that focus on the growth that occurs as a result of supervisee reflection. Although reflection per se may not be the centerpiece of other models of supervision, encouraging reflective practice is an overriding supervision goal. Here we discuss specific methods a supervisor can use to encourage reflection in supervisees.

Neufeldt, Karno, and Nelson (1996) provide the following description of the reflective process:

> *The reflective process itself is a search for understanding of the phenomena of the counseling session, with attention to therapist actions, emotions, and thoughts, as well as to the interaction between the therapist and the client. The intent to understand what has occurred, active inquiry, openness to that understanding, and vulnerability and risk-taking, rather than defensive self-protection, characterize the stance of the reflective supervisee.*

> *Supervisees use theory, their prior personal and professional experience, and their experience of themselves in the counseling session as sources of understanding. If they are to contribute to future development, reflections must be profound rather than superficial and must be meaningful to the supervisees. To complete the sequence, reflectivity in supervision leads to changes in perception, changes in counseling practice, and an increased capacity to make meaning of experiences.* (p. 8)

Nelson and Neufeldt (1998) emphasize the short amount of time that supervisors typically have with supervisees and the importance, therefore, that reflective tools are established so that supervisees can contribute to their own subsequent development. They also specify what must happen in order for reflection to occur:

> *[T]here must be a problem, a dilemma—something about which the learner feels confusion or dissonance and intends to search for a solution. The problem should revolve around an issue of consequence, one that is important to good practice. Reflection occurs in a context of the learner's capacity to tolerate the ambiguity of not knowing and an educational setting in which the learner has space to struggle with ideas as well as the safety to experience not knowing as acceptable.* (pp. 81–82)

Therefore, the first task of the supervisor is to establish a context for reflection. To do this, they must at the very least provide time, encouragement, and psychological space for this activity, as well as a supervisory relationship that is built on trust (Nelson & Neufeldt, 1998; Orchowski, Evangelista, & Probst, 2010; Osborn, Paez, & Carribean, 2007; Ward & House, 1998). Several authors offer suggestions for interventions that encourage supervisee reflection (Borders, 2006; Deal, 2003; Griffith & Frieden, 2000; Guiffrida, 2005; Knowles, Gilbourne, Tomlinson, & Anderson, 2007; Koch, Arhar, & Wells, 2000; Moffett, 2009; Neufeldt, 1999; Orchowski et al., 2010). What follows highlights some of these suggestions.

Griffith and Frieden (2000) argue the usefulness of four supervision interventions to facilitate reflective thinking among supervisees, all of which have been supported by others as well. The first of these is Socratic questioning, emphasizing the role of the supervisor as the source of important questions, rather than the source of all the answers. This age-old method of stimulating reflection is highly relevant to clinical contexts. Griffith and Frieden encourage primarily *How* and *What* questions to help dualistic thinkers to broaden their horizons. Whereas Socratic questioning may be best used in group supervision contexts, it certainly has a place in individual supervision as well. Guiffrida's (2005) Emergence Model of counselor development seems to support a Socratic approach as a process for helping supervisees identify their instincts and existing knowledge as it relates to their present interventions with clients. Deal (2003) concurs that the quality of supervisor questions is key to supervisee development as reflective and discriminating thinkers.

A second suggestion is that supervisors require supervisees to engage in journal writing (Griffith & Frieden, 2000; Guiffrida, 2005; Knowles et al., 2007; Orchowski et al. 2010). Although journals are often used early in the training program, they are less likely to be used as part of supervision. The advantage of journaling is that it not only helps supervisees evaluate their counseling and external conditions critically, but it also helps them focus on their internal reality, including painful emotional experiences that are stimulated by either the therapeutic or supervisory context. In addition, journal writing can be used to assist students to move beyond a description of events in counseling to identifying themes and patterns, thus assisting them in the necessary cognitive development from concrete thinking to that which is more complex and abstract (Rigazio-DiGilio, Daniels, & Ivey, 1997). Finally, journaling can simulate the kind of reflection required of most trainees in their multicultural training and, thus, assist in keeping culture front and center as an area of reflection in supervision as espoused by Orchowski et al. and others.

The third strategy suggested by Griffith and Frieden (2000) and Orchowski et al. (2010) is IPR, already described in this chapter. These authors agree with Kagan that well-constructed reflective probes could stimulate new insight for the supervisee regarding internal processes that may have been outside the supervisee's consciousness, but nevertheless influenced the direction of counseling.

Griffith and Frieden's last strategy is the use of a *reflective team* (Anderson, 1987), which they describe within a group supervision format. The reflective team technique is primarily used during live supervision. However, Stinchfield, Hill, and Kleist (2007) describe the use of a reflective process for triadic supervision.

Although presented for implementation as a group supervision activity, Koch et al. (2000) describe an approach to engaging students in reflective practice that spans an entire semester of supervision. Each supervisee is first invited to reflect on a dilemma that resonates for them, consistent with Nelson and Neufeldt's (1998) conditions for reflectivity. Typical examples include: "How can I prevent clients from manipulating me?" "How do I keep focused on a client's concerns and keep my personal issues from clouding my judgment?" "How can I know when racism is affecting my behavior?" Once they have been challenged to reflect, supervisees are asked to spend a couple of weeks identifying their own dilemma while the supervisor stays alert to the same for them during supervision. Several weeks into the semester, supervisees are asked to present their dilemma to their peers. The other students in the supervision group are advised to ask open-ended questions to gain clarity (and are discouraged from giving advice). Following this session, which includes debriefing for the supervisee involved, the supervisee is asked to develop an action plan to help him or her to address the dilemma. Koch et al. cautions that supervision after this point must continue to encourage reflectivity through assignments such as a reflection journal. They also emphasize the importance for the supervisee to follow contemplation with "making informed decisions and taking action in a way that addresses the dilemmas in a socially and ethically responsible manner" (pp. 263–264). In this way, the supervisee experiences a complete process from problem identification through reflection and growth to some resolution. Supervisees should also be aware that this process can and should be revisited at more profound levels.

Inspired by the work of Skovholt and Rønnestad (1995), who determined the importance of continuous professional reflection, Neufeldt (1999) advances the importance of helping supervisees learn to self-reflect. Supervisees are directed to respond to a number of questions (Table 3) immediately after a session in which they encountered a puzzle or dilemma. Although time consuming, challenging supervisees to complete such an assessment independently is essential for helping them claim ownership of reflective skills. Of course, this exercise can become the subject of a subsequent supervision session as well. Similarly, Moffett (2009) suggests that supervisors generate a list of questions on which supervisees who are about to work with an unfamiliar population could reflect. Moffett bases this suggestion on his experiences with novice supervisees that the unknown is often feared and laden with inaccurate assumptions. Moffett also notes that supervisors can use this exercise to assist supervisees with rather predictable challenges when working with special populations. He also stresses that it is important that supervisees know that they will not be asked to share their reflections so that self-censorship can be avoided. Moffett further emphasizes that honest self-reflection is paramount for self-supervision; therefore, such an activity can assist supervisees in developing such a habit. Of course, it is also hoped that supervisees will be open to bringing some of the concerns their reflections raise into their current supervision.

Finally, Borders (2006) and Borders and Brown (2005) advance a supervisor approach that she describes as *thinking-aloud.* In this approach, the supervisor models a reflective, decision-making process that can occur during a counseling session. Borders emphasizes the importance that supervisors "think aloud" in ways that are

TABLE 3 Self-Reflection Activity: Questions to Answer Regarding a Therapy Session Dilemma

1. Describe the therapy events that precipitated your puzzlement.
2. State your question about these events as clearly as you can.
3. What were you thinking during this portion of the session?
4. What were you feeling? How do you understand those feelings now?
5. Consider your own actions during this portion of the session. What did you intend?
6. Now look at the interaction between you and the client. What were the results of your interventions?
7. What was the feel, the emotional flavor, of the interaction between you? Was it similar to or different from your usual experience with this client?
8. To what degree do you understand this interaction as similar to the client's interactions in other relationships? How does this inform your experience of the interaction in session?
9. What theories do you use to understand what is going on in session?
10. What past professional or personal experiences affect your understanding?
11. How else might you interpret the event and interaction in the session?
12. How might you test out the various alternatives in your next counseling session? (Be sure to look for what confirms and what disconfirms your interpretations.)
13. How will the clients' responses inform what you do next?

Drawn from "Training in reflective processes in supervision," by S. A. Neufeldt, 1999, in *Education of Clinical Supervisors* (pp. 92–105), by M. Carroll & E. L. Holloway (Eds.), London: Sage Publications.

developmentally appropriate for the supervisee, and challenge the supervisee to stretch their thinking about clients and about their work with them. Supervisor's statements often include observations regarding the client; reflections about the client's behavior across sessions; awareness of the supervisee's internal processes in reaction to the client; a willingness to test out a hypothesis about a client's dilemma rather than having to figure it out before acting; and some attempt to integrate the information presented to the supervisee, including information that has been presented to them as well as insights that have surfaced from their own internal processes (Borders & Brown, 2005). This technique provides a mirror to IPR in that the supervisor offers reflective observations for the benefit of the supervisee rather than asking questions in a manner that requires the supervisee to reflect on their internal reality. Osborn et al. (2007) concur that this modeling of reflective thinking by supervisors is very important for supervisees to experience.

Nonlinear Strategies. In recent years, a subset of the literature has emerged that we refer to as *nonlinear strategies.* Those authors who describe the use of nonlinear strategies for supervision consistently claim that they increase reflectivity (Dean, 2001; Fall & Sutton, 2004, 2006; Guiffrida, Jordan, Saiz, & Barnes, 2007; McNamee & McWey, 2004; Mullen, Luke, & Drewes, 2007; Sommer & Cox, 2003, 2006; Ward & Sommer, 2006). For example, the use of the sandtray technique (Dean, 2001; Fall & Sutton, 2004, 2006; Guiffrida et al., 2007; Mullen et al., 2007) allows the supervisee to represent counseling dynamics symbolically using a variety of small figures in sand. The choice of figures to represent each person in the counseling system and the use of space to depict relationship dynamics often offer insights that were beyond the supervisee's awareness when describing a case verbally. Additional insights are possible if the technique is used by someone else listening to the supervisee's case presentation (either the supervisor or a peer). And the creative use of the figurines to symbolize people, events, and relationship dynamics give the supervisee a great deal of "new" information on which to reflect. In the same way that "a picture equals a thousand words," drawing a "picture" of dynamics using a variety of symbols can be profound for some supervisees. For this reason, Dean (2001) suggests that the technique be used only after a comfortable relationship between supervisor and supervisee has been established.

Sommer and colleagues (Sommer & Cox, 2003, 2006; Ward & Sommer, 2006) describe the use of the rich themes of mythology and fairy-tales to help supervisees make meaning of their own development as counselors and of the supervision process. They argue that stories ranging from classics to children's stories can be chosen by supervisors to address a multitude of developmental tasks, thus bringing home the universality of issues that supervisees often believe are unique to them. In short, just as film and literature has been used to embellish counseling, Sommer and colleagues argue that the arts can assist supervisees in reflecting on their development within supervision.

Guiffrida et al. (2007) reviewed the use of metaphor in supervision to assist the supervisee in understanding the process of becoming a mental health professional and to facilitate case-conceptualization skills. They conclude that it was important for supervisees to be amenable to activities such as using metaphoric drawing activities in order for them to be effective, and that the success of such techniques also depends on supervisor comfort in using them. Guiffrida et al. also report that, to date, the efficacy of such techniques is primarily anecdotal. Still, it seems to us that the use of metaphor is probably underused in most clinical supervision. Although a direct question such as, "How do you experience your client?" may have a brief impact on the supervisee, a question such as, "If you were to describe your experience of your client from the animal kingdom, would she be an opossum, a porcupine, a kitten, a tiger, or yet some other animal?" might not only open up new insights but linger beyond a supervision session. When creative juices are activated, their life span can be longer than their more logical counterparts.

We conclude this section on reflective practice by referring to Carroll's (2001) use of the concept of the *philosophy of supervision.* Carroll draws a distinction between *functional supervision* (supervision as technology) and a philosophy of supervision that focuses on the being of people and the meaning *supervision* has for the supervisor—that is, supervision is not something someone does, but something that someone is. In short, supervisors who have a philosophy of supervision reflect on their supervision; they view reflective behavior as something to engage, not something to teach. Only through their own reflection can the supervisor continue to pair functional supervision with a maturing philosophy of supervision. Clearly, Carroll implies that a nonreflective supervisor would be hard-pressed to create a reflective context for others. Perhaps concerning this issue, more than around many other activities, "Do as I do" is the only credible posture.

Technology and Supervision

Generally speaking, there are three different uses of technology within clinical supervision:

1. To provide the supervisor with samples of the supervisee's work
2. To bridge distance between the supervisee and the supervisor
3. To influence the process of supervision

Until now, we discussed technology as a means of providing the supervisor with samples of the supervisee's work (e.g., use of audio or video recording; capability for live observation). And as we stated, even the most commonplace form of technology (e.g., audio) should be used with its advantages and disadvantages in mind.

Using technology to bridge distance between the supervisee and the supervisor is, in effect, using technology to conquer geography (Bernard, 2005), and this is where the field is developing quickly (Abbass et al., 2011). Several authors report the use of technology for this purpose (e.g., Chapman, Baker, Nassar-McMillan, & Gerler, 2011; Court & Winwood, 2005; Dudding & Justice, 2004; Kanz, 2001; Panos, 2005; Schultz & Finger, 2003). Among the many arguments made for using technology to bridge distance include serving rural and other sparsely populated areas, providing supervision within specific clinical settings that are not replicated nearby, serving the needs of international students who are completing internships in their home countries, supplementing supervision in settings where within-agency supervision may be inadequate or where a particular expertise is missing, and serving supervisees with disabilities.

Following the lead of McAdams and Wyatt (2010), we use the term *technology-assisted distance supervision (TADS)* to include all the innovative ways being tested for use in supervision. Because of the growing capacities of cell phones, iPads and other notebooks, and services such as Skype, synchronous (i.e., real time) TADS does not hold the exotic place in clinical supervision that it held just a decade ago. Also, although attempting TADS a decade ago meant a sizable infrastructure investment, this is simply no longer the case (Abbass et al., 2011). We refrain from offering any concrete software or hardware information here, as it would most likely be outdated by the time this book is in print. Therefore, we concur with Abbass et al. that persons wanting to engage in TADS must be willing to either become educated about operating systems, their strengths and their flaws, or find good support (which can include courses, tutorials offered on web sites, and YouTube) before launching into TADS. They must also be willing to develop the habit of securing updates for whatever systems they use. Reading their excellent "nuts-and-bolts" article that includes the use of video recordings of therapy sessions during web-conference supervision sessions may be a good place to begin to test one's TADS IQ.

Despite the principal goal of serving broader audiences, some have reported advantages of using distance technology that goes beyond reaching supervisees in other vicinities. For example, Dudding and Justice (2004) reports that some speech–language pathology students were more positively disposed toward videoconferencing than face-to-face supervision, finding it led to "a greater sense of autonomy and control when the supervisor was not physically present" (p. 149). Participants in this study also commented that videoconferencing was less intrusive and that they found the supervisor more transparent when using this form of supervision. Perhaps most important, students reported no differences in what they gained from supervision when using videoconferencing versus being in face-to-face supervision. These findings are similar to psychotherapy research reported by Day and Schneider (2002), who found that clients actually had higher scores on activity level, trust, spontaneity, and disinhibition when psychotherapy was offered using distance technologies. Furthermore, no significant treatment differences were found overall when contrasting face-to-face therapy with distance modalities.

Advantages of TADS notwithstanding, there are still barriers to their use, including uneven technological expertise among supervisees, cost for the supervisee of supervisor-preferred equipment, incompatible operating systems, inconsistent broadband connections, informed consent issues, and different state laws regulating the acceptability and the parameters of using TADS for supervision. In addition, using TADS in, for example, email loses valuable nonverbal cues, and all TADS methods are vulnerable to breaches of confidentiality and technological failure. (We refer the reader to several resources that embellish on the advantages and disadvantages of TADS: Dudding & Justice, 2004; Jerome, DeLeon, James, Folen, Earles, & Gedney, 2000; Kanz, 2001; McAdams & Wyatt, 2010; Olson, Russell, & White, 2001; Panos, 2005; Panos, Roby, Panos, Matheson, & Cox, 2002; Powell & Migdole, 2012; Sampson, Kolodinsky, & Greeno, 1997; Schultz & Finger, 2003; Vaccaro & Lambie, 2007; Watson, 2003).

The third use of technology is to influence the process of supervision directly. A good example of this is live supervision, which relies on technology as endemic to its process. The literature that addresses technology for the purpose of changing or supplementing supervision exclusively is modest, especially for individual supervision (as opposed to group or live supervision). However, that which exists is research-based and is as follows.

Graf and Stebnicki (2002) initiated a thread of research using email as a supplemental supervision intervention. They conducted a pilot study with three practicum students in a rehabilitation counseling program. These students were asked to communicate by email at least once weekly with the practicum instructor. Messages were analyzed and found to fall into messages about clients, messages about the on-site supervisors, and messages about themselves. Although messages about clients stayed positive throughout the practicum, messages about the site supervisors seemed to follow a more predictable developmental path, moving from highly positive to becoming more critical and ending with a more balanced view of their supervisors. The students' messages about themselves reflected the following pattern: an initial sense of anticipation and lack of confidence; a period of boredom when responsibility was withheld from them; increased confidence paired with increased responsibility; a sense of frustration over inability to make sufficient changes; and, finally, a more reflective place of increased awareness and more realistic goals. Interestingly, these results are reflective of supervisee development described by Stoltenberg and McNeill (2010). It is impossible to know the role that email played for these supervisees relative to individual and group supervision, which they also were receiving.

Clingerman and Bernard (2004) also tracked the use of email with practicum students. Specifically, the authors asked whether email would encourage a personalization (intrapersonal) focus and if this would increase over the course of one semester. Nineteen students in three sections of practicum (taught by three different instructors) were asked to email their instructor once a week, in addition to the individual and group supervision they were receiving. Instructors were asked to respond to each email, but to refrain from responding in a way that encouraged a follow-up email. Once the 15-week practicum was over, all messages were divided into three time periods (i.e., first 5 weeks, second 5 weeks, and final 5 weeks) and trained raters coded each message using the Discrimination Model (Bernard, 1979, 1997) and Lanning's (1986) additional focus area of professional behavior. Messages were coded as *addressing interventions, conceptualizations, personalization, professional behavior having to do with the practicum class,* and *professional behavior having to do with the practicum off-campus site.* The question regarding the fit between email and a personalization focus was answered in the affirmative. A full 40 percent of all student messages addressed a personalization focus and this pattern was maintained across all three time periods. The second most-frequent category, professional issues having to do with the practicum class, accounted for another 24 percent of the messages. Unlike the students monitored by Graf and Stebnicki (2002), only 7 percent of messages dealt with the site or the site supervisor, and patterns were the same for students in all three sections of practicum. Clingerman and Bernard conclude that further investigation is warranted regarding the benefit of email for tapping personalization issues. However, their results are consistent with research reported by others that supervisees feel freer to express themselves through technology than in a face-to-face context (Yeh et al., 2008).They also note that their data did not offer insight about the degree of reflectivity embedded in personalization comments sent by students; that is, no judgment was made about emails regarding their relative superficiality or depth. Because reflectivity is regarded as an essential developmental issue for persons in supervision, the compatibility of email with a reflective process is worthy of further investigation.

Chapman et al. (2011) extended this research and compared *asynchronous* (delayed time) to *synchronous* (real time) TADS methods for students enrolled in practicum. All students involved in their study volunteered to use a TADS format for supervision rather than a face-to-face format. Using discussion threads, email, VHS video, and text chats as the TADS methods, the authors collected end-of-practicum data on supervisee competence, confidence, and attitudes toward TADS. Their results found no difference between synchronous and asynchronous experiences. These students were not compared to students who had chosen a face-to-face supervision experience. Despite positive results, these authors caution that all supervisors and supervisees involved were interested in TADS and relatively competent with technology to begin with. They also raise the question whether supervisors who have not conducted face-to-face supervision should engage in TADS as their initial supervision experience. Luke and Gordon (2012) used discourse analysis methods to analyze email communications between supervisees and supervisors during internship. They studied the specific language used by supervisors, referred to as *re-authorship,* to affect and shape supervisee experience. The three specific types of re-authorship that occurred were *reinforcement* (basically offering agreement of assurance to the supervisee), *reframing* (offering another way to think about an experience that the supervisee shared), and *advice-giving* (e.g., offering a direct suggestion regarding how to address an issue that has emerged in counseling). All three types of supervisor responses were plentiful, with advice representing a slightly larger percentage of responses than the other two. Although all three are familiar supervision interventions, it is unlikely that most supervisors are aware of their relative use of each or its effects in their supervision. Such discourse analysis, therefore, holds promise for increased understanding of the importance of the specific language supervisors use in their supervision.

Finally, Guth and Dandeneau (2007) report on a technological advance for clinical supervision based on the Landro Play Analyzer (LPA), a sophisticated software package originally designed to assist football coaches to review and analyze game videos. The LPA requires digital video capability and an adequate technological infrastructure, and allows supervisors and supervisees to analyze counseling sessions on a multitude of dimensions. Using such a system virtually eliminates randomness from session review. Although start-up costs are high, the system can be designed to fit different developmental levels of supervisees, to reflect any conceptual model the supervisor adopts, and offers a multitude of possibilities for process research.

In conclusion, the explosion of technological capacity has affected and continues to affect supervision. The benefits of using technology appear to outweigh their constraints, as long as supervisors use technology in a manner that enhances learning, protects the supervisory working alliance, and is performed within ethical and legal parameters.

Timing of Supervision

Regardless of the methods used to produce the material for the case conference, an additional matter—the timing of the conference—should be considered. Little has been said in professional literature about the timing of supervision, except to warn that supervision that is scheduled for convenience only (e.g., every Tuesday at 10:00 for 1 hour) may invite legal liability if there are no provisions for the occasion when the supervisee experiences a more pressing need for supervision (Disney & Stephens, 1994).

A single study (Couchon & Bernard, 1984) examined how several variables were influenced by the timing of supervision. Among the variables considered were supervisor and counselor behavior in supervision, follow-through from supervision to counseling, client and counselor satisfaction with counseling, and counselor satisfaction with supervision. Three treatments were introduced: supervision within 4 hours prior to an upcoming counseling session, supervision the day before a specified counseling session, and supervision occurring more than 2 days before a specified counseling session.

Some provocative results emerged from this study. Perhaps the most surprising result was that the timing of supervision seemed to affect supervisor behavior in the supervision session more so than counselor behavior. Supervision the day before a specified counseling session was very content oriented. The supervisor was more likely to adopt an instructional mode, and transmitted a robust amount of information in these sessions. Interestingly, counselor follow-through to the subsequent counseling session was low; in other words, strategies discussed and approved by the supervisor in the supervision session were not acted on in counseling to any significant degree. Supervision conducted within 4 hours of a subsequent session was very different. With the press of the upcoming session, the supervisor was far less likely to offer content and, instead, adopted a more consultative role. Fewer strategies were discussed, more of the strategies were offered by the counselor than by the supervisor, and those that were suggested met with supervisor approval. Furthermore, there was far more follow-through from supervision to counseling for this treatment condition. The third time frame for supervision, more or less midway between counseling sessions, had no strong effects. Because other counseling sessions with other clients intervened and there was no immediate pressure to prepare for an upcoming session, the supervision conference was simply more diffuse in its content and follow-through.

The counselors in the Couchon and Bernard (1984) study were equally satisfied with supervision regardless of when supervision was offered. (Timing also did not affect client or counselor satisfaction with counseling.) It should be noted, however, that an important time for supervision, immediately after counseling, was not studied. We hypothesize that if there is a time that would get an elevated satisfaction rating, it is immediately after counseling, when the supervisee might benefit from support and reinforcement. This hypothesis is supported by Ray and Altekruse (2000). Although we know that supervisee satisfaction is high when feedback is delivered immediately, the amount and kind of learning resulting from this timing of supervision is still unknown. Additional research regarding the effects of the timing of supervision is warranted.

TRIADIC SUPERVISION

We place our discussion of triadic supervision near the end of our discussion of individual supervision because in many ways and as we will describe, triadic supervision is a bridge modality between the two. *Triadic supervision* has become the trade term for supervision with one supervisor and two supervisees. This has been an acceptable form of *individual supervision* for AAMFT marriage and family therapists since the inception of their standards. For the counseling profession, triadic supervision first became an acceptable form of individual supervision in 2001 (Council for Accreditation of Counseling and Related Educational Programs, CACREP, 2001). This development has spawned significant research interest within the counseling profession since the turn of this century.

Triadic supervision takes two forms that have been described as *split-focus* or *single-focus* (Nguyen, 2004). *Split-focus* divides the available time between the two supervisees; when using *single-focus,* one supervisee presents his or her work for the entire time and supervisees alternate roles from week to week. Both methods have, to date, been found to produce positive outcomes (Nguyen, 2004), which include supervisees reporting higher working alliance ratings when experiencing triadic supervision than when in individual supervision (Bakes, 2005).

Despite its viability as a supervision method, several researchers have uncovered themes that make triadic supervision a challenging method for conducting supervision when it is meant to replace individual supervision, as well as some clear benefits (Borders et al., 2012; Hein & Lawson, 2008, 2009; Lawson, Hein, & Getz, 2009; Lawson, Hein, & Stuart, 2009; Oliver, Nelson, & Ybañez, 2010; Stinchfield, Hill, & Kleist, 2007, 2010). We begin with benefits of the method and follow with challenges.

Benefits Associated with Triadic Supervision

When triadic supervision is working well, supervisees have found it to be more relaxed, comfortable, and psychologically safer than individual supervision, in part because each supervisee is not the sole focus of the supervisor (Lawson, Hein, & Getz, 2009). Supervisees also report that they value the special relationship that can form with one other supervisee from their cohort within triadic supervision (Lawson, Hein, & Stuart, 2009). In addition, triadic supervision allows for more diversity of perspectives as the supervisee presents cases (Hein & Lawson, 2009). Finally, supervisees report that they benefit from vicarious learning when one of their peers is the focus of the session (e.g., Borders et al., 2012; Lawson, Hein & Stuart, 2009).

Supervisors also report advantages that resonate with those mentioned by supervisees, such as a more relaxed atmosphere and increased diversity (Hein & Lawson, 2008, 2009). Supervisors also report that the nonpresenting supervisee can occasionally offer feedback that stimulates their own thoughts. At the very least, they find that the input from the peers gives them breathing room to formulate their own supervision. Supervisors also found that the presence of another supervisee helped normalize some of the developmental challenges each supervisee is bound to encounter.

Challenges Associated with Triadic Supervision

As an alternative to individual supervision, triadic supervision poses challenges as well, with the two most frequently cited by time constraints and compatibility of the supervision pair (Borders et al., 2012; Lawson, Hein, & Stuart, 2009). If supervision is limited to 1 hour, it stands to reason that supervisees will not have as much time as they would in individual supervision. Thus, research finds that both supervisees and supervisors are very time conscious during triadic supervision, and experience time often as working against them. Lack of time can translate to lack of opportunity to go deeper with supervisees, whether it is to challenge their conceptual take on a particular case or to invite them to take the time to reflect in supervision.

As important as time management—indeed, if not more so—is the compatibility of the supervision peers (e.g., Hein, Lawson, & Rodriguez, 2011). Researchers report that this compatibility can refer to developmental level and ability to articulate helpful feedback as well as more personal attributes such as ability to empathize, warmth, and so on. We add attachment style, anxiety level, and image management as other compatibility issues. Although not studying triadic supervision per se, Baum (2010) found that cosupervisees at field sites reported many of the behaviors and feelings association with siblings, including sharing emotional difficulties, learning from or wanting to serve as a model for the other, desiring to differentiate from the other, as well as feelings of envy and competitiveness. Baum implies that trainees who are professional "adolescents" may be more prone to have feelings that are similar to adolescent siblings. Whether or not that is the case, Baum's discussion strikes a note with us that it might be useful to discuss supervisees' sibling relationships as part of orientation to triadic supervision.

When the pair is not functional, it appears that much of what supervision should be is lost in triadic supervision. The context becomes less safe, peer feedback is constrained, and self-disclosure and immediacy are less likely (Lawson, Hein, & Stuart, 2009). It is important to note that an incompatible pair affects not only the supervisees' behavior, but the supervisors' as well. Supervisors reported that their feedback was more restrained when pairs were incompatible. They found themselves worrying about not only how the subject of their feedback would respond but also the peer, regardless of whether the feedback was critical or positive (Hein et al., 2011). Without adding too much interpretation, it appears that supervisors had to settle for a blander middle ground, because moving toward challenge or praise seemed fraught with unintended complications.

These challenges emerge from deficits; however, triadic supervision also poses challenges that are similar to group supervision; that is, the process of triadic supervision must be managed in way that makes the experience meaningful for both supervisees, regardless of which person is presenting his or her work. Therefore, although there were times that supervisors found triadic supervision to be more relaxed than individual (because of less intensity), they also reported that it could be more taxing and required different preparation and different skill sets (e.g., Borders et al., 2012).

Methods for Conducting Triadic Supervision

A defining aspect for successful triadic supervision is to assure that the nonpresenting supervisee has an active role. Lawson, Hein, and Getz (2009) suggest that supervisors using the single-focus form of triadic supervision use methods developed for group supervision, such as asking the peer to adopt the perspective of the client and track thoughts and feelings as the session is being presented (see Borders, 1991). Lawson et al. also suggest the use of Wilbur, Roberts-Wilbur, Hart, Morris, and Betz's (1994) Structured Group Supervision to elevate the role of the nonpresenting peer and allow that person to make a significant contribution to the process. Finally, Lawson et al. note that the use of role-plays can be richer within triadic supervision, allowing, for example, the presenting supervisee to observe how the supervisor might introduce an intervention in counseling with the peer playing the role of the client. Just as triadic supervision allows for some creative downtime for the supervisor, it can also do the same for the presenting supervisee who can observe a skill that must be learned and reflect on it before having to engage in practice him- or herself.

Stinchfield, Hill, and Kleist (2007, 2010) describe a process that uses a split-focus format within 90-minute supervision sessions. The goal of their method is to increase the opportunity for each person to engage in both inner dialogue to stimulate reflection, and outer dialogue that contributes to their own learning and that of their peers. During the first half of the supervision session, a supervisee presents a recording of a counseling session for review and receives direct supervision from the faculty supervisor. While this is occurring, the peer adopts an Observer–Reflector role, engaging in silent reflection and inner dialogue as both counseling and supervision are observed. This is followed by the peer then engaging in outer dialogue with the supervisor about what was reflected. Simultaneously, the presenting supervisee moves into the Reflective Role and is required only to listen and reflect on the outer dialogue taking place. This process is then repeated, with supervisees switching roles for the second half of the supervision session. Stinchfield et al. (2010) found that supervisees who engaged in this process reported positive outcomes, including a distinct value to sharing the developmental process with a peer. This process shares some aspects of the Reflecting Team approach to live supervision.

Favorable Conditions for Triadic Supervision

Oliver et al. (2010) report that when it is working well, triadic supervision displays systemic engagement (i.e., a spontaneous and functional flow of information among all three participants), synergy (i.e., enjoying an impact greater than could be achieved alone, or even within a dyad), and community (i.e., allowing for a safe place to air ignorance within an atmosphere of mutual accountability), among other attributes. From the research to date, we have some evidence that controlling a few factors can greatly enhance the possibility that triadic supervision may achieve the kind of training context described by Oliver et al.

Time Allotted. Several authors note that the typical 60 minutes per week is not adequate for triadic supervision, especially if one uses a split-focus form. Rather, 90 minutes appears to be the recommended span for productive triadic sessions (Borders et al., 2012; Lawson, Hein & Getz, 2009; Stinchfield et al., 2010).

Choosing Pairs Carefully. Another strong theme across the research is that much of the success of triadic supervision is dependent on the compatibility of the supervisees paired together. Although "perfect" pairing is probably rare in training programs, it appears that the pair must at least fit the definition of "good enough" across several dimensions.

Having a Distinct Role for the Nonpresenting Supervisee. It is clear from the literature that triadic supervision is much more than having two supervisees present while the supervisor focuses on one of them at a time. Complaints from supervisees that they didn't get the time they needed in supervision most likely come from situations where they were observing passively and not engaged in the process.

Orienting Supervisees. Another emergent recommendation is that supervisees receive an orientation to triadic supervision so that they can be better prepared for its unique opportunities and challenges (Hein & Lawson, 2008). As noted previously, this includes specific orientation for when the supervisee was in the nonpresenting role. We make the point here that orienting supervisees to any form of supervision is good practice.

Supplementing with Individual Supervision. The *raison d'être* for triadic supervision, at least originally, was to offer a more efficient way to cover the responsibility of individual supervision; yet, all who engage in triadic supervision clearly note that it does not replace individual supervision (e.g., Borders et al., 2012 Oliver et al., 2010). Some supervisees are struggling too much to be a good peer in this model. In addition, some personal growth issues are more appropriately addressed in individual supervision. Finally, evaluation must be addressed privately. For these and other reasons, triadic supervision should not be viewed as a standalone method.

Training Supervisors. Oliver et al. (2010) stress that supervisors trained only in individual supervision need additional training to conduct triadic supervision. Supervisors must be able to engage more than one person in the process, keep in the forefront the needs of more than one supervisee, choose strategies with flexibility and often creativity, and so forth.

Concluding Comments

The increased interest in triadic supervision is a clear example of how accreditation decisions can influence research. As a result, persons wishing to engage in triadic supervision have some good information to draw from as they implement this method. As we note at the beginning of this section, triadic supervision appears to fit between individual and group supervision, sharing some characteristics from each. Although it is viewed as a replacement for individual supervision, it seems that this is less the case than its potential as a supplement to group supervision. Group dynamics are a critical element of group supervision. We wonder if these might be improved if the group were made up of peers who had an occasional opportunity to work in the triadic format. This speculation is supported by the research conducted by Borders et al. (2012).

PUTTING IT ALL TOGETHER

Reviewing each supervision method is a bit like reviewing theories of psychotherapy. While in the process of considering a particular method, it may seem attractive and worthwhile; however, like psychotherapy, the use of supervision formats and techniques requires an acceptable level of expertise and a sound rationale that is compatible with the supervisor's vision and the supervisee's needs. In general, technical eclecticism among supervisors is desirable, because it allows the supervisor to help a variety of supervisees attain a variety of supervision goals.

At the beginning of the chapter, we discussed initial criteria for choosing an intervention. Here, we attempt to draw on the information in this chapter, as well as broader topics, to form a list of questions to ask when selecting format and technique within individual and triadic supervision.

1. *How will this method of supervision be received?* No method is appropriate if the supervisee cannot become more expert as a result of the method. At times, this may be a developmental issue only. For example, a supervisee may be too novice or too concrete to be able to benefit from the advantages of self-report. Occasionally, a particular method of supervision may simply be a bad fit for the supervisee as an individual. For example, is e-supervision a perfect fit for an introvert supervisee, or a method that will retard growth? Not only developmental level and learning styles, but also temperament and cultural norms determine the receptivity to particular supervision delivery systems.

2. *Am I being true to my beliefs about how one learns to be a mental health practitioner?* As stated earlier, if the supervisor believes that reflectivity is the cornerstone to becoming an expert therapist, then the supervision method must achieve reflectivity. In such cases, supervisee behaviors are viewed in the context of the larger dynamics of interpersonal or intrapersonal processes and meaning, not the other way around. Other supervisors assume that supervisees become more competent with a series of successes, and therefore focus more on therapeutic interventions. The larger point is that, if the supervisor doesn't accept the outcome of a supervision method as crucial to the supervisee's development, the method will most likely be used in a perfunctory manner.

3. *Am I considering the three functions of supervision (i.e., assessing learning needs; changing/shaping/supporting; and evaluating performance)?* Using a different format to evaluate clinical competence from one used to promote supervisee development may make the supervision process clearer to the supervisee. Furthermore, a change of method can help the supervisor maintain boundaries between different supervisor roles.

4. *Am I considering the timing or relative structure of my supervision?* Busy professional schedules often dictate the timing of supervision. However, for the supervisee who is floundering, timing may be a relatively easy and potentially important variable to manipulate to assist a breakthrough in learning. Similarly, the relative use of structure may be manipulated to allow a different and potentially potent learning opportunity for the supervisee.

5. *Are administrative constraints real, or am I not advocating with a strong enough voice?* It is not uncommon to hear that a piece of media equipment is too expensive or that a method of supervision is too time consuming for a particular setting. Yet, a strong supervision program can energize a setting so that what is accomplished is more efficient and of higher quality. Supervisors must advocate for the kind and level of supervision they believe must be present. As models to supervisees, it is imperative that supervisors work in ways that are productive and credible.

6. *What does this particular supervisee need to learn next? Am I using the best method for this purpose?* There are times when the supervisor must realize that the method being used is simply not accomplishing the desired outcome. One supervisor reported that, after spending several frustrating weeks in supervision with the supervisee making little progress conceptualizing client issues, the supervisor began to assign homework that required the supervisee to come to the conference with three different avenues to take with each client to be discussed, one of which had to be unconventional. This assignment seemed to energize the counselor, and she started to make significant gains in her area of weakness.

What the supervisee needs may also challenge the comfort level of the supervisor. It may be more comfortable to remain supportive when the supervisee needs to be challenged. It may be more natural to continue a highly structured approach to supervision when the supervisee is ready for the supervisor to be more of a consultant in approach. If supervision is fairly standard from supervisee to supervisee, the supervisor should question whether it is the supervisor that needs to be stretched.

7. *Am I skilled in the use of this particular method or technique?* Ultimately, supervision falls flat if the method is used poorly. IPR is a good example of a technique that can deteriorate quickly if the supervisor is not skilled at asking probing questions without loading them with the supervisor's opinion. As we stated earlier, self-report can be a highly charged method of supervision, but only when the supervisor is expert and knows how to use the method to challenge the supervisee. Or some form of e-supervision may be attempted before the supervisor is adequately skilled, leading to frustration and failure.

8. *Have I considered ethical safeguards?* Supervision is based on the premise that the supervisee is not yet expert enough to handle a wide range of clients autonomously. An important criterion for choosing a method of supervision, therefore, must be some judgment about the level of competence of the supervisee. This is one reason why self-report is considered foolhardy for novice counselors. The ethics of supervision also include the supervisor's responsibility to the supervisee. Supervision that does not assist the supervisee in learning the helping process could be considered unethical. As was stated earlier, technology introduces a whole new array of ethical concerns (Vaccaro & Lambie, 2007).

9. *Is it time to try something new?* Even if the supervisor is adamant about the centrality of one aspect of therapeutic practice (e.g., establishing an empathic relationship with the client), there are different ways to help the supervisee to reach the goal. For example, Sterling and Bugental (1993) suggest using role-play to help the supervisee to make phenomenological gains, Guiffrida et al. (2007) reviewed different techniques using metaphor to assist in conceptualization, and Deacon (2000) advocates the use of visualization to help supervisees to think more creatively. Training literature is replete with examples of specific techniques to arrive at a variety of areas of competence. Trying something new is as important for the supervisor as the supervisee. The goal is to stay fresh or to use a new method or technique to stimulate new and sometimes unexpected learning.

10. *Can I document the success of my method?* It would be nice if supervisors had hard data to support their work with each supervisee. (Some methods—e.g., transcription, taping, e-supervision—lend themselves to the possibility of data collection.) In the absence of data, it is still important that the supervisor glean a sense of accomplishment from the method or techniques being used. Each method chosen translates to alternative methods rejected. Therefore, supervisors must seek some justification for the continuation of a particular approach to supervision. At the very least, supervisors should seek feedback from supervisees about what they experienced as most helpful to their learning.

11. *Am I willing to confront my own assumptions?* Good supervisors can revisit familiar tenets with new scrutiny. No vision is complete. No supervision method has been found to be indispensable. Supervision at its best is a healthy balance of authority and humility. Supervisors who opt for confusion over stagnation model the essence of professional growth for their supervisees.

CONCLUSION

As the supervisor conducts individual supervision, many options are available regarding the form that supervision will take. Much of this is determined by prior experience, interest in experimenting with different methods, and perceived supervisee need. All methods carry with them opportunities—and opportunities bypassed. The quality of supervision we offer is intimately related to the decisions we make about methods. However, presently, there is insufficient empirical evidence to either encourage or reject the use of any of the available methods for any particular supervisee. Clearly, supervisors must not only expand their repertoire, but also study their methods systematically, to examine both the process and meaning of what they do (Carroll, 2001; Holloway & Carroll, 1996). In this way, they can best serve both their supervisees and their profession.

Group Supervision

Group Supervision

Most mental health professionals' first thought of clinical supervision is of *individual* supervision. Yet much supervision also occurs in a group format; so much so that eventually, virtually all supervisees will have participated in group supervision.

University training programs across mental health professions typically use group supervision at some point in their curricula. The Council for the Accreditation of Counseling and Related Education Programs (CACREP) stipulates conditions for group supervision in their standards (CACREP, 2009). Furthermore, pre-doctoral psychology internship site supervisors (Riva & Cornish, 1995), university counseling center supervisors (Goodyear & Nelson, 1997), and family therapy supervisors (Lee & Everett, 2004) all report group supervision as a close second to individual supervision as a modality of choice.

In their review of research on group supervision, Mastoras and Andrews (2011) found that group supervision was beneficial, especially when certain conditions were met. These authors offered several suggestions to group supervisors based on the research, and these suggestions are interspersed throughout this chapter. Significantly, several studies that compare group supervision to individual supervision directly do not shown one to be superior to the other with respect to training outcomes (Averitt, 1989; Lanning, 1971; Ray & Altekruse, 2000). Studies that attempt to determine supervisees' preferences for one over the other have produced contradictory findings (Borders et al., 2012) Nielsen et al., 2009; Ray & Altekruse, 2000), although it seems that individual supervision has an edge in this regard.

Neither supervision modality has any historical advantage over the other, and in fact, both can claim origins with Freud. With respect to group supervision, Rosenthal (1999) reports

> *The Wednesday Evening Society, which met weekly in Freud's home from 1901 to 1906 (and then became the Vienna Psychoanalytic Society), has been identified as the first recorded instance of analytic group psychotherapy. . . . However, since its members had avowedly gathered around Freud for instruction in psychoanalysis and for supervision on their cases, this historic group might more fittingly be seen as constituting the first recorded example of group supervision. Members presented their cases, their ideas, and their written papers to Freud and to each other. The final comments in any discussion were always reserved for Freud.* (p. 197)

In short, group supervision is prevalent, appears to rival individual supervision's effectiveness, and is a long-established form of supervision. The litmus test for good group supervision, however, is that it offers opportunities that offset the lack of individual attention that is the cornerstone of individual supervision. The remainder of this chapter builds on these grounding observations to address definitional, conceptual, and practical issues related to group supervision.

DEFINITION, ADVANTAGES, AND LIMITATIONS OF GROUP SUPERVISION

The definition of *supervision* applies to all formats of supervision. However, the group format warrants its own, more-specific definition to complement that more generic one. We suggest that *group supervision* is the regular meeting of a group of supervisees (a) with a designated supervisor or supervisors; (b) to monitor the quality of their work; and (c) to further their understanding of themselves as clinicians, of the clients with whom they work, and of service delivery in general. These supervisees are aided in achieving these goals by their supervisor(s) and by the feedback from and interactions with each other.

Another more colorful (pun intended) description of group supervision is offered by McMahon (2002), who notes that it is "both similar to and different from group therapy and individual supervision. . . . The red of supervision and the yellow of group bring about the orange of group supervision" (p. 56). McMahon captures both the essence and the challenge of group supervision. Functionally, its goals are not very different from individual supervision; however, the processes for achieving these goals are quite distinct.

Neither of these definitions suggests how many supervisees might constitute a group; nor do they consider a closed versus an open group. Both the size of a group and the membership (constant vs. changing) greatly affect group dynamics that are an endemic aspect of group supervision. This chapter uses as its model a closed supervision group (which is most likely within a training program and less the case in the field) and a group of 5 to a maximum of 10 supervisees. Groups that differ from these parameters are cautioned to consider how the uniqueness of their group alters the experiences of those involved. That being said, the single available study of the differential training effects of supervision group size (supervisor: supervisee ratios of 8:1 vs. 4:1; Ray & Altekruse, 2000) was inconclusive.

Benefits and Limitations of Group Supervision

As with any supervision format, there are both benefits and limitations to group supervision. We address some of the more important ones here.

Benefits. A number of authors (e.g., Carroll, 1996; Fleming, Glass, Fujisaki, & Toner, 2010; Hawkins & Shohet, 1989; Hayes, 1989; Jacobsen & Tanggaard, 2009; Linton & Hidstrom, 2006; Proctor, 2000; Proctor & Inskipp, 2001; Riva & Cornish, 1995, 2008; Tebb, Manning, & Klaumann, 1996) discuss the advantages and limitations of a group format for supervision. From these contributions and our own experience, we begin with benefits and give particular emphasis to the following:

1. *Economies of time, costs, and expertise.* Perhaps the most obvious advantage of group supervision is that it offers many of the same economies that are afforded by group counseling or therapy, particularly those of time, costs, and expertise.

2. *Opportunities for vicarious learning.* Important vicarious learning can occur as supervisees observe peers conceptualizing and intervening with clients. In fact, Proctor and Inskipp (2001) suggest that "Perhaps the true 'economy' of group supervision lies in the 'free learning' opportunity of observing and participating in the supervision of other supervisees" (p. 160).

It is significant to note that novices who observe their peers performing a particular skill are more likely to exhibit skill improvement and increased self-efficacy than those who instead observe an expert (Hillerbrand, 1989). *Vicarious learning* also can include personal insights, as other group members discuss their experiences and reflections.

3. *Breadth of client exposure.* During group supervision, supervisees are exposed to and learn about the clients with whom the other group members are working. This enables them to learn about a broader range of clients than any one person's case load would afford.

4. *Supervisee feedback of greater quantity and diversity.* Other supervisees can offer perspectives that are broader and more diverse than those a single supervisor could provide. The range of life experiences and other individual and cultural differences represented within the group can enrich the feedback supervisees receive. Supervisors in a study conducted by Riva and Cornish (2008) claimed that multicultural dynamics are discussed in their supervision groups. Kaduvettoor, O'Shaughnessy, Mori, Beverly, Weatherford, and Ladany (2009) found that attending skillfully to multicultural events in a group supervision format led to vicarious multicultural learning for supervisees as well as higher group engagement. (Of course, they found the reverse to be true as well. When events were managed poorly, learning did not occur and group conflict increased.)

Counselman and Gumpert (1993) note that parallel processes can be especially transparent in groups: "Group member reactions such as boredom, anger, anxiety, and excessive helpfulness can serve as important clues to the case dynamics" (p. 26). Moreover, they suggest that for a supervisee to receive feedback about these processes from a number of peers often has more impact than similar feedback delivered by a single supervisor.

5. *A more comprehensive picture of the supervisee emerges.* The group format expands the ways the supervisor is able to observe a supervisee. For example, a particular supervisee might seem blocked when discussing his or her own work, and yet be an intelligent and insightful contributor to group discussions. The opportunity to see this can allow the supervisor to view the supervisee's difficulties in a different way (e.g., as a function, perhaps, of individual differences within individual supervision) than might be the case if the supervisee were seen only in individual supervision. This feature of the group format also can moderate potentially deleterious countertransference reactions the supervisor might develop (Aronson, 1990).

6. *The opportunity for supervisees to learn supervision skills.* It is very important that mental health professionals be formally prepared to provide supervision. Participation in supervision groups should not substitute for that formal training, but it can play a significant role in preparing mental health professionals for a supervisory role. In the group, they have an opportunity to observe both the supervisor and other group members provide supervision and actually to engage in it themselves.

7. *Normalizing supervisees' experiences.* Supervisees can find themselves troubled by a number of experiences, including their own feelings of anxiety and doubt and their personal reactions to client material. To know that they are not alone in those reactions can be important and reassuring.

8. *Learning specific to group process.* A final advantage pertains specifically to the supervision of supervisees who are offering counseling or therapy in a group format. Supervisees can benefit by having a supervision format that mirrors that of the treatment being supervised. This benefit, however, only holds when supervisors are expert at the facilitation of the supervision group.

Limitations. The advantages of group supervision outweigh the limitations—otherwise, there would be no reason to provide group supervision! Nevertheless, there are limitations to be considered.

1. *The group format may not permit individuals to get what they need.* This can occur for several reasons. For example, supervisees with heavier caseloads may not have sufficient time to review their caseloads adequately. In groups that are heterogeneous with respect to group members' skill levels, the less-skilled members may receive attention at the expense of their more-skilled peers. Also, if time is not managed well, some members may find during any particular session that the time has run out before they are able to get necessary feedback. Finally, time may be devoted to issues that are perceived as irrelevant or extraneous to the supervision needs of some group members.
2. *Confidentiality concerns.* Confidentiality is less secure in group supervision with respect

to (a) the clients who are the focus of attention and (b) the supervisees in the group. Most supervisees readily understand the issues related to client confidentiality, but they may be less clear about the importance of protecting the privacy of their fellow supervisees. In university training programs, supervisees interact with one another in multiple contexts. Therefore, they may be in a supervision group during the morning, then in the afternoon sitting in a class that includes group members, and then in the evening participating in social events with them. Although confidentiality about other supervisees can be difficult to maintain, it is an important rule to impress on all members of the group.

3. *The group format is not isomorphic to individual counseling.* We already noted that it is an advantage that the group supervision of group counseling or therapy is isomorphic with what is being supervised. However, most group supervision focuses on individual counseling, and so has the opposite problem: The form and structure of the supervision does not mirror that of the treatment being supervised, and therefore there is more limited opportunity for supervisees to learn from the supervisory interventions they observe.
4. *Certain group phenomena can impede learning.* Some group phenomena, especially between-member competition, insensitivity to individual and cultural differences, and anxiety that translates into "hiding," can impede learning. It is even possible for one or more of the supervisees to experience harm in the face of these phenomena.

GROUP SUPERVISION: A UNIQUE BLEND OF SUPERVISION AND GROUP DYNAMICS

Each form of supervision emphasizes particular strategies to stimulate learning and ways to address relationship dynamics. In this section, we consider key variables that must be considered when conducting group supervision. These variables include the style, experience, and goals of the supervisor, the developmental stage(s) of the supervisees, and the stage of the supervision group itself.

Style, Experience, and Goals of the Group Supervisor

Prior to discussing styles, experience, or goals, we believe it necessary to state the obvious—that group supervision involves multiple participants and, therefore, requires group leadership from the supervisor.

With increased frequency, authors emphasize how essential it is that the group supervisor possess group facilitation skills (e.g., DeStefano, D'Iuso, Blake, Fitzpatrick, Drapeau, & Chamodraka, 2007; Fleming, Glass, Fujisaki, & Toner, 2010; Kuechler, 2006; Reichelt et al., 2009). Although one may think that this goes without saying, many supervisors who engage in group supervision are much more comfortable with the "supervision" part of their task than the "group" part. Similarly, many supervisors understand the importance of helping the supervisee who is struggling in individual supervision; yet, they do not have the same level of expertise when working in a group context.

Proctor and Inskipp (2001) identify three essential supervision styles that vary in the extent to which the group itself is used as part of the supervisory process. (They identify peer-group supervision as a fourth style, but we do not include it here because it does not involve a formal leader.) The supervisor who uses *authoritative supervision* conducts supervision *in* the group rather than *with* the group (Proctor & Inskipp, 2001), and applies an individual supervision template to his or her work. This minimizes the extent to which other supervisees participate in the supervision. This can occur, for example, with supervisors who are newer to the group supervision format (Mastoras & Andrews, 2011).

Proctor and Inskipp note that an authoritative style has some important advantages, including the greater ease it affords in managing group time and the sense of safety it can afford those members who distrust groups; however, there are significant disadvantages to this style as well. In particular, the expertise remains with the supervisor and the other members are neither used nor given the opportunity to develop their own feedback or group skills. Furthermore, the safety promoted by having the supervisor in charge does not include safety with one's peers that grows over time when peers support each other. Also, depending on the supervisor, an authoritative style may zero in on any one group member in a way that leaves the supervisee feeling both exposed and unprotected.

Supervisors who use the second style, *participative supervision,* capitalize on the richness of the group as they encourage members to participate actively. It is a style that fosters commitment to a shared task, and therefore promotes interest and even excitement among its members. Its disadvantages include the possible change of focus from client issues to group process and the difficulties the supervisor can have in managing either the equitable sharing of time or the maintaining of reflective space within the group. For some members, it can feel unsafe, and therefore cause them to monitor too carefully what they tell the group.

The third style is *cooperative supervision*, in which the group itself provides supervision. The supervisor's tasks are to facilitate the group and share the actual supervision. For supervisees who are experienced practitioners, this style offers both a collegial experience and the opportunity to receive supervision informed by a variety of therapy models and styles. Proctor and Inskipp (2001) note that the "freer interaction allows for serendipity—parallel process, group surprises" (p. 104). This third style of group supervision requires both the supervisor and the group members to have higher skill levels. There also are some risks, because even though the group members may be experienced practitioners, they may not have well-developed group skills; in addition, because the group processes are riskier, some members may feel unsafe. Also, it is more difficult to keep the group focus on supervision versus on group processes and between-member interactions.

Grigg (2006) notes that some styles of group supervision are far better suited for a focus on content, whereas others are more likely to stimulate personal development and self-awareness. Grigg proposes that without being so labeled, many supervision groups operate as psychoeducational groups with a fixed process more appropriate for learning content. Instead, Grigg argues that the better model for group supervision is that of a counseling group in which goals include the personal development of the supervisee. The rationale for this assertion is that skill acquisition should not be divorced from personal awareness if supervisors believe that the person of the therapist is a vital part of the therapeutic process. Interestingly, Ögren, Jonsson, and Sundin (2005) found that a theory and conceptualization focus in group supervision was least predictive of students' self-reported learning, adding support to Grigg's argument that conceptual learning is only part of what should transpire in group supervision. And to this end, Grigg states, "[T]here are some things you can only know about yourself from being in group" (p. 116). He also notes that group supervision that mirrors group counseling calls for a skilled group facilitator in the person of the supervisor. Reinforcing this point, Nielsen et al. (2009) found that supervisees became less open over time when they perceived their group supervisor as unskilled in group facilitation. In addition, group supervision that uses group counseling as a referent also requires careful boundary negotiation, adequate informed consent, and clear group ground rules.

In summary, the style of the supervisor often reflects his or her experience with group facilitation as well as his or her supervision goals. Another important factor for the supervisor to consider in selecting an approach to group supervision is the developmental stage of supervisees as well as their group experience(s).

Supervisees' Developmental Levels

An important dimension of group supervision is assessing the supervisees' developmental levels as mental health practitioners or practitioners-in-training, and their developmental levels with group work. Both either expand or restrict the supervisor's choices of interventions and focus.

Supervisees in their first clinical course, for example, are looking for direction and affirmation from their supervisors. They are likely to be relatively unsure of themselves as clinicians, and sensitive to their relative place within their cohort of peers. In this context, the group supervisor must establish a sense of safety by, at the very least, normalizing developmental challenges and offering direction for novel situations. Furthermore, the supervisor must model helpful feedback when a supervisee is the focus of the group, and invite peers to follow the supervisor's lead. A psychoeducational focus is often appropriate with novice supervisees, with encouragement over time to increase self-awareness and engage in more immediacy within the group. Using Discrimination Model (Bernard, 1979, 1997) nomenclature, it is common to see group members assist each other with a focus on conceptualization and intervention, and slowly move to more sharing regarding personalization.

In addition to developmental level as a counselor or therapist, experience with group work is highly relevant for the group supervisor to assess. Within training programs, the supervisor usually has a good idea of the experience level of supervisees, although the experiences of supervisees with each other in a group context may not be known to the supervisor. In the workplace, group supervisors can make fewer assumptions, because some supervisees may have had relatively strong training in group process and facilitation, whereas the training of others may have been limited to being a member of a group only. In the worst case, a supervisee may have experienced only one group that was led poorly, and in which he or she did not feel safe to share personal insights.

As noted earlier, supervisees often come into group supervision with various interpersonal experiences with other members of the group. A good strategy for a group supervisor is to take inventory of these experiences as one of the first discussions in the group. If five of seven supervisees have prior group experience with each other, for example, the supervisor can give them an initial task of pulling in the other two. The supervisor may also have less experience with the "in" group than they do with each other. Another good strategy is to ask the group supervision members who have had other experiences with each other to form a fishbowl and discuss what they know about each other that is relevant to group supervision. Those outside the fishbowl can then process what they hear in light of their own membership in the group.

Group supervision of advanced trainees is more likely to mirror group counseling as suggested by Grigg (2006). Group members are more helpful to each other and more willing to share their insights—unless their efforts are frustrated by a group supervisor with poor facilitation skills. Advanced trainees have typically run groups themselves and may have assisted in group supervision of novice trainees; therefore, they may be capable of Proctor and Inskipp's (2001) cooperative supervision, and would benefit most by a supervisor who can use this style.

Group Stages and Group Supervision Processes

Some group process experts would assert that there is little support for the generally held assumption that groups follow a predictable, linear sequence. Nevertheless, the linearity assumption can provide a useful heuristic to therapists and supervisors. Tuckman's (1965) (later refined by Tuckman & Jensen, 1977) is the best-known model of group processes. Tuckman's model suggests that groups of any type proceed through five stages, each with characteristic goals for its members:

1. *Forming.* Members work to become comfortable with one another.
2. *Storming.* Members work to resolve issues of power; in a supervisory context, this is the stage at which between-member competitiveness is likely to be in its most direct and obvious form. Jacobs, Masson, Harvill, and Schimmel (2012) argue that the storming stage in particular is not always evident, and may be as much a result of poor group leadership as a part of the normative development of the group.
3. *Norming.* Members work to set norms for appropriate within-group behavior. *Norms* concern what is expected of those who are participating in the group. Although these norms may develop and function outside group

members' conscious awareness, they still exert powerful influences on behavior. Sanctions for their violation can be strong. Supervisors have a particular responsibility to both (a) be aware of emerging norms and (b) shape them by, for example, modeling behaviors that should become normative (e.g., starting the group on time) and helping the members identify the norms that are developing.

4. *Performing.* This is the group's most productive stage, when members tackle work-related tasks.
5. *Adjourning.* Members work on saying goodbye to one another.

For our purposes here, we discuss the forming, norming, performing, and adjourning of supervision groups. Storming is not discussed as a stage; rather, we infuse issues that can hinder group supervision throughout the remainder of this chapter.

Forming Stage. During this initial stage, the supervisor has a particular responsibility to establish expectations (i.e., a contract) with respect to group rules and structure. In doing so, the supervisor communicates a sense of command that many supervisees find comforting in a new situation. Establishing a contract with supervisees, whether done formally or informally, makes the management of the group easier; it minimizes supervisee role conflict and ambiguity, which has been shown to have deleterious effects on supervisees (cf. Nelson and Friedlander, 2001); it also goes a long way toward establishing the sense of safety and trust so essential in group supervision (see, e.g., Sussman, Bogo, & Globerman, 2007).

A useful contract covers both the supervisees' and the supervisor's expectations and responsibilities. Supervisees should have the opportunity to state their expectations for the group, which can include expectations about both process (e.g., how members behave toward one another) and outcomes (e.g., what each person hopes to leave the group having gained).

It is useful to preface discussions of supervisee expectations, however, with a statement of the supervisor's own expectations, because these can have a real effect on what the supervisees then state as their own. The supervisor should make clear his or her preferred or intended style (i.e., authoritative, participative, or cooperative), a rationale for the style, and the implications of that style for expected member behavior. The supervisor's expectations also include an articulation of the ground rules that guide group and individual behavior.

Ground rules include, of course, expectations about supervisee (a) participation (sharing their own material, but also giving honest feedback to others), (b) confidentiality, and (c) boundaries. Ground rules also concern such matters as frequency of meetings, attendance, and manner of case presentation; we discuss each in turn. Although we attempt to convey what we understand to be conventional clinical wisdom with respect to these matters, we realize that not all supervisors may agree on these points. What is important, however, is that supervisors are clear about how they intend to handle these matters and how they convey that clearly to group members.

Frequency of Meetings. How often the group meets affects group process; meeting once a month, for instance, might make it difficult to develop a viable atmosphere, whereas, at the other extreme, to meet twice a week might be untenable for some members. Marks and Hixon (1986) found that members of groups that met weekly (as opposed to biweekly) had greater trust of other members and less anxiety. By contrast, groups that met biweekly were more cognitive and formal.

Attendance. Regular attendance is an especially important expectation to convey and enforce. Absences affect the group in multiple ways, including members' sense of cohesion, as well as the energy experienced during the meeting. Group members essentially are committing to be there for one another; therefore, members attach meaning to absences of other supervisees. For example, the supervisee who does not come the week after she presents a difficult case might cause others to worry that their feedback was too confrontational. This not only affects the group session with the missing member, but, if not addressed in the group, affects the quality of feedback given to this member when she returns.

Manner of Case Presentation. It is important to have ground rules concerning the manner of case presentation, and can include rules regarding confidentiality and each member's expected responsibilities and level of participation. (How clinical material is presented and processed is covered under the performing stage.) Still, Munson (2002) suggests that supervisors are well advised to present the first case, modeling not only the procedure the supervisor wants all to use, but also an attitude of openness. By contrast, Munson also suggests that ground rules include things to avoid, such as discussing several cases in a short amount of time.

Norming. The transition from forming to norming is fluid, as both lead to the "work" of supervision. By imposing an optimal level of structure, the supervisor provides group members with the sense of safety they need in order to risk exposing their clinical work—and themselves—to their peers. Yet the key word here is *optimal,* because if structure is too rigid, it can create its own tension by stifling spontaneity. The supervisor, therefore, must not only create an initial structure, but must also monitor its effect on the group, and be prepared to alter or abandon part of the group's structure based on group dynamics and on group feedback. Processing what the supervisor and others observe during early case presentations is an important aspect of norming. Norming is an evolving process that takes more or less time, based on the type of group the supervisor hopes to facilitate, the developmental level of the supervisees, and other factors unique to the particular supervision group.

Another way to view norming is that the group culture is being formed at this time. Shulman (2010) argues that the supervision group's culture is an important phenomenon to keep in mind. The culture is the gestalt that makes the group "feel" different from all other groups; these are the systemic norms and rules that the group adopts. Many of these are outside of members' conscious awareness, but powerful nevertheless. One such rule might be, "Give feedback, but don't make anyone uncomfortable." Although such a rule might be benign enough in the initial stages of group supervision, it may adversely affect the work of the group if it were to persevere and override the injunction to be honest and promote growth.

It is rewarding when supervisees call into question nonproductive aspects of the supervision group's culture. However, should this not occur, it ultimately is up to the supervisor to be aware of and confront the limitations brought about by certain aspects of the group's culture. Mastoras and Andrews (2011) note that anxiety was a frequently raised concern for supervisees across the research. How anxiety is addressed and managed by the supervisor as, for example, a normative part of the developmental process, contributes to a culture of learning through trial and error rather than a culture of avoiding shame.

Performing. Keith, Connell, and Whitaker (1992) suggest that group supervisors initially adopt a "maternal" role—providing nurturance, being solicitous of supervisees' feelings, and inviting supervisees to be comfortable. The supervisor gradually then shifts to a "paternal" role, setting limits on topics and making demands on supervisees. Then, as the supervisees' emotional investment in the group increases, the supervisor gradually turns increasingly more responsibility over to them. Keith et al. note, however, that

> *the supervision group passes through similar stages, but the maternal and paternal periods are usually brief. And to the extent the supervisor is either maternal or paternal, the parenting model is that of parent and older teenager; that is, it is very limited, acknowledging the freedom and maturity of the second generation. . . . The early 4 to 6 sessions require guidance; like learning to drive a car. Then the teacher becomes less active . . . (the driving instructor chooses to move to the back seat).* (p. 98)

This observation suggests, then, that Keith et al. expect the supervision group to be into the performing stage by the fourth to the sixth session. In what they describe, the supervisor uses Proctor and Inskipp's (2001) *participative* style of supervision. We expect that the developmental level of members within such a supervision group is relatively advanced as well.

Whether the supervision group is taking the reins by the fourth session or not, the performing stage is the point at which norms have been established and the supervision group is more or less predictable. Whatever roles have been encouraged by the supervisor should begin to bear fruit at this time. In the most effective supervision groups, members assume appropriate levels of shared responsibility for the group and for one another. Individually, they begin to trust and become energized by a commitment to explore and examine their own therapeutic efforts. Supervisees present cases that show them stretching the upper limits of their skill, rather than cases that either are too clear or are too impossible to elicit critical comments.

During the performing stage, the supervisor continues to have issues and tasks to address, although these are of a somewhat different nature than was true in the earlier stages. The supervisor is watching, for example, for signs of *nonwork:* if this occurs, the supervisor changes direction, asks the group for feedback, or offers the group some process feedback. However, the supervisor must understand the importance of recycling some issues in order to permit them to be understood and confronted at new levels. What might feel like an old theme revisited might be a theme that finally is understood. Several models have been proposed to be used either to assist supervision groups in arriving at the performing stage, or as part of this stage. These models are particularly useful for a supervisor with limited group supervision experience, or for work with relatively novice supervisees. We discuss a few of these next.

Group Supervision Models

Borders' Structured Peer Group Supervision Model. Borders (1991) describes a structured group format, the *structured peer group supervision (SPGS)* model, that can be used to enhance group supervision. Although described as a peer group supervision model, SPGS is used primarily under the direction of a supervisor. This approach relies on direct samples (preferably a video recording) selected by a supervisee for presentation to the group. The supervisee is expected to be prepared to offer a brief summary of client and therapy issues with enough context for peers to have a sense of the case prior to watching the recording. The supervisee also asks specific questions related to the case and his or her counseling.

Peers then choose or are assigned specific tasks for their focus as they observe the recording. These may include *focused observations* on a skill, such as how well the counselor executes a confrontation, or one aspect of the session, such as the relationship between the counselor and client, the nonverbal behavior between the two, and so forth. Borders points out that a particular observation task could be used to develop specific skills of the observer. For example, the observer who has a tendency to quicken the pace of his or her sessions might be asked to observe the pace of the recorded session.

Another assigned task is *role taking.* An observer might be asked, for example, to take the perspective of the counselor, the client, or even some significant person in the client's life (e.g., a parent, a spouse). For family sessions, the assignment could be to represent the family member who refuses to come to therapy. After the video has been shown, the observer gives feedback from the perspective of the person that he or she represents.

A third task is to observe the session from a particular *theoretical orientation.* One observer could be assigned this task, or several observers could be asked to look at a session from different theoretical perspectives. Not only does this exercise help supervisees apply theory to practice, but it also helps them elicit underlying assumptions about problem formation and resolution.

The fourth task is for an observer to watch the session with the assignment of developing a *descriptive metaphor.* Borders reports that this approach has been particularly helpful when the issue is the interpersonal dynamics between the client and counselor, or the counselor feeling "stuck." For example, an observer is asked to think of a road map and describe the direction that counseling is taking, or to view the counselor–client relationship within the context of a movie and describe each person's part in the drama. Fall and Sutton (2004, 2006) expand this last task by using the *sandtray technique,* wherein a peer watches and listens to a case presentation and the discussion that ensues and uses play figures in sand to create a metaphor for one or several dynamics being discussed. This can focus on the most salient relationship discussed within the counseling session, for example, or on layers of interest from the counseling session to the supervision group itself. Because this activity is, by its nature, typically nonlinear, it offers an important dimension to the Borders exercise. Fall and Sutton (2006) also note that the use of different-size figures, metaphorical figures (e.g., a knight; a threatening animal), and the sand itself (e.g., almost covering an object/figure; providing safety), provides context that verbal feedback cannot. In addition, Dean (2001) found that feedback provided in this way was received less defensively by supervisees. Sandtray techniques can also be used in individual supervision.

Lassiter, Napolitano, Culbreth, and Ng (2008) also expanded the Borders format to include a *multicultural-intensive observer role.* The supervisee assigned this role focuses on cultural matters as they are represented in the session, including issues of cultural differences and assumptions, privilege, and power differentials. Lassiter et al. argue that, along with other supervisor interventions, an explicit role to track cultural phenomena is key in enhancing multicultural competence among supervisees.

After tasks have been assigned for SPGS, supervisees view the selected segment of the counseling session and offer feedback specific to their assignments. The supervisor serves as *moderator* for the group and ensures they stay on task. Then the supervisor adopts the role of *process commentator* for the group and offers feedback about group dynamics. For both roles, Borders emphasizes the need for the supervisor to be cognizant of the developmental level of supervisees (e.g., novice counselors needing more direction and structure; more advanced supervisees being able to take on more responsibility). The model, therefore, requires a good deal of supervisor flexibility. Finally, the supervisor summarizes the initial feedback and the discussion that followed, and asks the presenting supervisee if her or his supervision needs were met.

Structured Group Supervision. Wilbur and Roberts-Wilbur (1983), followed by Wilbur, Roberts-Wilbur, Hart, Morris, and Betz (1994), devised a structure that, in our experience, works well with supervision groups in which participation has been uneven. Their *structured group supervision (SGS)* model begins with a supervisee making a "plea for help" that includes relevant information about the case, often with a sample recording from the session. The supervisee then states specifically what they need help with.

Following the plea, the supervision group members ask the supervisee questions about the information that has been presented so that any faulty assumptions are cleared up, missing information is added, and so forth. During this step, it is important for the supervisor to monitor the group so that no one slips into offering premature feedback. Rather, one by one, group members are allowed to ask informational and clarifying questions (but not "Have you tried . . .," types of questions). The process is repeated until no one has additional questions.

The next step of the SGS model is feedback or consultation from group members to the supervisee. The supervisor asks the group members to take a few minutes to formulate some thoughts about how they would handle whatever it is that constitutes the plea for help. Then, again, in orderly fashion, each member offers their thoughts, typically beginning with, "If this were my client, . . ." or "If I had your concern, ..." During this step, the supervisee remains silent but may take notes regarding the comments or suggestions. The process is repeated until there is no additional feedback.

Wilbur et al. (1994) suggest a pause or break of 10–15 minutes following feedback. They also stipulate that group members should not converse with the supervisee during this break. Rather, the supervisee should be allowed this time to reflect on the group's feedback and prepare for the next step.

After the break, the supervisee responds to the group. This time, the group members remain silent while the supervisee, again in an orderly fashion, responds to each group member's feedback. The supervisee is instructed to tell members what feedback was helpful, what was not helpful, and why feedback was helpful or not. We have found that the use of the verb *resonate* is pertinent at this stage. When supervisees are asked to tell the group what resonated with him or her, it become less about right or wrong and more about therapeutic style, perspective, cultural fit, and history with the case.

Depending on the supervisor's preference and often because of the developmental level of the supervisees involved, the supervisor may add a last step of discussing the process that unfolds. At times, the supervisor may want to underscore some feedback or even reframe an issue so the group may look at it differently, but must be cautious not to undercut the process by critiquing the feedback that was delivered. However, comments about group dynamics and those about the case that could be framed as "Additional food for thought" may be received well. Finally, supervisees who have taken full advantage of the process, have allowed themselves to be vulnerable, and have been open to feedback should be affirmed for their efforts.

Edwards and Hashmati Model of Group Supervision. Edwards and Hashmati (2003) offer an outline of *phases* for group supervision of beginning marriage and family therapists. Among their stated goals is to "provide space for multiple voices to be heard and appreciated. A major challenge with any group is building tolerance for diversity of thought" (p. 296). Their phases have a good deal of similarity with Wilbur et al.'s (1994) steps and include

1. Checking in
2. Case presentation
3. Questions from the audience
4. Video review
5. Commentator reflections
6. Audience reflections
7. Postsupervision supervisor reflections

The last three phases are described next, because they are more distinct from other models.

The *commentator* is a key role in Edwards and Heshmati's model, is chosen from among supervisees not involved with the case presentation, and is required to watch the video of the session prior to supervision. In fact, it is the commentator, not the clinician, who picks out about a 10-minute segment for the group to watch, often including a part of the session that went well. After the video has been seen by everyone, the commentator offers her or his reflections about what was seen. The supervisor most often has provides an outline for commentators to follow regarding their feedback. Edwards and Heshmati suggest a three-part outline: (a) Aspects of the work the commentator sees as helpful; (b) aspects of the work that raise concerns or questions; and (c) future directions the presenter may want to consider in their work with the client. Once the commentator has finished, the presenter responds to the feedback, and a discussion between the two follows as others observe.

This controlled process between the two members of the supervision group, as well as the video that was shown, is now open for reflection from the rest of the group. The supervisor facilitates the discussion and continues to focus on making space for each voice in the group. Finally, the last phase of this model is unique in that it is a private, one-way interaction from the supervisor to the presenter. After supervision is over, the supervisor sends the presenter a write-up of his or her thoughts about the case, which undoubtedly includes more-refined reflections than those offered by peers. The supervisor takes this opportunity to embellish any points regarding the direction of the case, and makes sure that all of the supervisee's questions about the case are answered. This last phase is an interesting departure from the typical norms of group supervision. The authors state that presenters appreciate receiving this more-detailed review of their session fairly soon after supervision is over, but did not comment on any negative group dynamics caused by this last phase.

Collective Group Reverie. Berman and Berger (2007) offer a complex discussion of group supervision, and note the chronic problem for some group supervision in that supervisees often feel more vulnerable and exposed than they do even in therapy. Epstein (1986), speaking from the supervisory position, says, "I also learned that the more I follow the practice of explaining and formulating whatever it is that I might feel like formulating and explaining, the more I will be admired by the group members yet the worse they will feel about themselves" (quoted in Berman & Berger, 2007, p. 238). By contrast, and especially for more advanced supervisees, Berman and Berger argue that the most worthwhile material supervisees can offer each other is their internal emotional experiences. They note that each member brings assets and liabilities to the group, but by sharing their inner worlds, they broaden the horizon of the emotional range of the group as a whole.

To this end, Berman and Berger suggest that after a group member presents a case, the remaining supervisees tune in to their inner worlds and become aware of unique emotional responses. They do not ask questions about the case or the approach the presenter has taken, and are free from "any need to support or criticize the presenter" (p. 245). Instead, once time has been given for reflection, supervisees are invited to share whatever they choose about their sensations, feelings, memories, and thoughts while they were listening to the presenter for the wisdom contained in those internal experiences. For groups who have become too cerebral or who appear to be resistant to engaging at a more personal level, this exercise may be worth using.

Additional Thoughts about "Performing" Group Supervision. The models we present for group supervision are options a supervisor may consider; however, there is abundant excellent supervision that occurs outside of such structure. What is essential is that the group dynamics are facilitated in a manner that is productive to the individuals involved, and that supervisees are increasing their clinical skills as a result of the group supervision format. Although we offer some overarching maxims for group supervision in what follows, we believe that it is necessary to highlight two observations here as particularly relevant for the performing stage.

The first observation is that, although the supervisor should be open to feedback from the group members in all stages of the group, it is especially relevant that the supervisor request input about his or her facilitation at this stage. This allows the opportunity to change course if necessary, but also provides an important experience for the supervisees:

> *Therapists tend to have perfectionistic defenses that are reinforced by regular admonitions about appropriate behavior and professional responsibility. They need models and mentors who can keep their self-esteem despite acknowledged limitations and who concede that some clinical situations are inherently defeating, regardless of good intentions and proper training.* (McWilliams, 2004)

Furthermore, Reichelt et al. (2009) provide evidence that supervisees are reluctant to offer critical feedback to supervisors. Therefore, supervisors must strive to make constructive feedback the norm for all group members, including themselves.

Second, we wish to underscore the importance of mutual trust and support among group members for productive supervision to occur during the performing stage (Fleming et al., 2010). Earlier, we mentioned the importance of balancing challenge and support, and we emphasize the support side of that equation here.

Keith et al. (1992) and Nicholas (1989) suggest that the supervisor provide *nurturant* energy in the early stages of the supervision group. As group members begin to invest emotionally in the group and in each other, primary responsibility for this nurturant energy shifts from the supervisor to the group members. This process corresponds with the development of group cohesiveness, which Yalom (1985) asserts is the group equivalent of empathy.

These processes, then, lead to an atmosphere of support between and among group members. And as support levels increase, so too do levels of between-member trust and, therefore, the extent to which supervisees are willing to become vulnerable with one another and to reveal their mistakes and weaknesses. All this contributes to the increasing value of the supervisory group to members (Fleming et al., 2010; Jacobsen & Tanggaard, 2009). Fleming et al. found perceived group safety to be a critical element in group supervision, and that supervisees' ability to manage anxiety was a necessary condition for learning within the supervision group. They suggest that supervisors engage in open discussions of anxiety and couple this with the expectation that everyone learns from mistakes, both their own and those of others. Finally, support might be understood as a counterbalance to between-member competitiveness. In fact, competition typically is more manifest in the early stages of the group, but then becomes moderated as group cohesiveness and mutual support develop.

Adjourning. Most supervision groups probably are time limited; some, however, are ongoing. Therefore, it is appropriate to discuss the termination processes of each type of group separately.

The Time-Limited Group. Training calendars determine the time frames for many supervisory relationships. These calendars typically are linked to a semester, an academic year, or an internship rotation. For practicum and internship groups, the supervision experience can be one of weeks, rather than months or years. Especially when the life of the supervision group is across a single semester, the ending of the group may feel premature to almost everyone. In addition, toward the conclusion of the semester, the urgency that supervisees may experience in managing the termination of their clients might override any consideration of the closure issues in the group itself. It would be a mistake, however, to end a supervision group without allowing the group to process this phase. Moreover, because the ending of the supervisees' therapeutic relationships usually coincide with the ending of the supervisory group, the parallels become a useful tool and provide important material to process.

Virtually all brief therapy models have a particular structure, an emphasis on a treatment plan, and a particular emphasis on the process of termination. In a sense, this is a model that applies as well to time-limited supervision in any format. The goals of the supervision group should be specific enough that supervisees notice when those goals have been achieved so that they can feel a sense of accomplishment. At the same time, the supervisor must help supervisees contextualize their learning—especially among less-experienced supervisees—to help allay panic at finding that they still are not the totally competent practitioners that they imagined they might or should be by the end of this group supervision experience.

A time-limited experience inherently limits what supervisees have the opportunity to learn. It is important, therefore, that they leave the supervision experience with a plan for self-improvement. One part of this plan for each supervisee is most likely the securing of additional supervision. An important culminating experience, therefore, is to crystallize what can be learned from supervision and how one goes about securing this type of supervision for oneself.

One aspect of time-limited supervision that can be frustrating for the supervisor is the nearly universal tendency of supervisees to begin withdrawing from the group when the end is in sight. Supervisees who are simultaneously approaching closure with their clients may complain that their clients have stopped working. Often, these same supervisees are unaware that, in a type of parallel process, they are working less with each other in the supervision group. The need for psychological distance in order to cope with the loss, both of people and of a valuable process, is important to address in the group as supervisees handle multiple closure experiences.

The Ongoing Supervision Group. A danger of the ongoing supervision group is that it might fizzle out, rather than end in a clear fashion. Like a relationship that fizzles out, the group that terminates in this manner is left with more unfinished business and perhaps an inadequate understanding of what caused the ending. One strategy to avoid this is to schedule an ending from the outset of the group. Like all social systems, groups need markers in order to appreciate their development. An ending can provide this kind of marker, even if the group should reconstitute itself immediately with no change of membership.

The kind of ending that we suggest may be an appointed time when the group reviews the assumptions and decisions that were made before the formation of the group. It is a time when as many things as possible become negotiable, including ground rules and the process of supervision itself. The ending allows supervisees to evaluate their individual development and their level of commitment and contribution to the goals of the group. Also, it is a time for the supervisor to evaluate the amount of responsibility that has been shared with group members, the process that has been in place, and the feasibility of continuance.

Endings can be added to the life of a group in several ways. One way is to freeze membership for a certain amount of time, say 1 year, at the end of which some members might leave and others might enter. In a sense, the change of membership gives the group a chance to start over. Another way is for the process of the group itself to change. For example, a supervisor might decide that it is time for the group to change from a supervisor-led group to a peer-supervision group. This juncture could be planned as an ending.

Time can also be manipulated to produce a marker. A break of a couple of weeks could be planned to occur every 6 months to encourage an evaluation and renegotiation period prior to or immediately after the break. Each group finds its own way to end once it appreciates the importance of such markers.

Evaluation of the Supervisory Experience. The ending of the group also presents an opportunity for both supervisees and supervisor to evaluate the experience. One key focus should be on what new knowledge and skills each supervisee obtained from the experience (from both their own and the supervisor's perspective), linking this to the contract that was developed at the outset. It is equally important to assess what each supervisee expected to get, but did not—and why they believed that was the case.

This is an opportunity, too, for the supervisor to obtain feedback about how the group perceived his or her work. If the group is offered as a practicum class, most universities ensure that students complete end-of-term course evaluations. However, these typically indicate more global information, such as how much the students learned and how prepared they believed the instructor to have been. Course evaluations typically do not provide information specific to effectiveness in supervising a group. The supervisor should be prepared to ask specific questions that yield the type of feedback that will be helpful to him or her.

Researchers are beginning to recognize the need for instruments that help provide group supervisors with more systematic feedback. Among those available to supervisors are the *Group Supervisory Behavior Scale* (White & Rudolph, 2000), the *Group Supervision* Scale (Arcinue, 2002), and the *Group Supervision Impact Scale* (Getzelman, 2004). To have group members use instruments with established psychometric qualities to provide their supervisor with feedback about his or her performance can be very useful, not only during the adjourning stage of the group, but at other points as well.

PEER-SUPERVISION GROUPS

Peer supervision has an important role in the lifelong development of mental health professionals. Anyone who has been in the helping professions for a while knows—either firsthand or through observations of others—about problems of isolation and practitioner burnout, as well as that of becoming stale in one's work.

We include peer supervision in its own section because it has unique features that set it apart from supervisor-led groups. Most important, it is not hierarchical and includes no formal evaluation. In this sense, it really is consultation rather than supervision (see, e.g., McWilliams, 2004). However, at the same time, it is ongoing, and group members feel more accountable to each other than they might in a consulting relationship. Wilkerson (2006), addressing the need for peer supervision among school counselors, describes it as follows:

> *Peer supervision is a structured, supportive process in which . . . colleagues (or trainees), in pairs or in groups, use their professional knowledge and relationship expertise to monitor practice and effectiveness on a regular basis for the purpose of improving specific counseling, conceptualization, and theoretical skills.* (p. 62)

However defined, peer supervision seems to be a growing phenomenon and an important ingredient to the vitality of the mental health professions. Therefore, it is an important topic to address.

Until recently, peer supervision received only modest coverage in the professional literature (Hilmes, Payne, Anderson, Casanova, Woods, & Cardin, 2011). However, peer supervision is not new as a forum for professional development. Lewis, Greenburg, and Hatch (1988) found, at least among psychologists in private practice, that 23 percent of a national sample were currently members of peer supervision groups, 24 percent belonged to such a group in the past, and 61 percent expressed a desire to belong to a group if one were available. Among the reasons for joining peer groups (in rank order by importance) were as follows:

1. Receiving suggestions for problem cases
2. Discussing ethical professional issues
3. Countering isolation
4. Sharing information
5. Exploring problematic feelings and attitudes toward clients
6. Learning and mastering therapeutic techniques
7. Receiving support for stress in private practice
8. Countering burnout
9. Gaining exposure to other theoretical approaches

Wiley (1994) found that counseling psychologists who were 8 to 15 years postdoctorate were the most likely to be participating in peer supervision (38 percent), with only a slight dip after 15 years of experience (32 percent).

Peer supervision groups can either evolve from supervisor-led groups to peer groups or can be conceived as peer supervision groups from the outset. In either case, at the point that peers attempt to offer each other supervision, certain conditions must exist if the process is to be successful. Chaiklin and Munson (1983) note that a sincere desire to improve one's clinical skills is, of course, the primary condition for peer supervision. They also found that administrative backing was essential for those working in mental health agencies or institutions. If administrators do not view peer supervision as valuable and cost-effective, and if this is not communicated by the provision of space and time to conduct supervision meetings, the within-agency peer group will certainly falter (Chaiklin & Munson, 1983; Marks & Hixon, 1986).

In their review of the professional literature, Hilmes et al. (2011) report that conditions that are highly desirable for peer supervision to be successful include participants who engage in the process with respect for their peers and their values, openness to learning from peers, an investment in identifying and achieving personal and professional goals, an inclination toward teamwork, an assertive communication style, the ability to self-reflect, and a willingness to engage in emotional expression.

The independent peer group (i.e., outside any employment setting) has probably the greatest potential for compatibility among its members because such a group tends to be formed by professionals who already know and respect each other. For the peer group formed within an institution, there may be some history to overcome among some of the members, such as political entanglements, competitiveness, or personality issues (Hamlin & Timberlake, 1982). In addition, lack of homogeneity of experience is far more likely for the within-agency group, which means that the group will most likely veer toward either the more-experienced or least-experienced members, to the potential frustration of the other members of the group.

Regardless of the initial compatibility of the peer group, group stages outlined earlier in this chapter still occur and need attention. It is a common error of professionals who are already comfortable with one another to forego the planning stage for the group until issues begin to arise. Another potential for all supervision groups, but more so with peer groups, is differential contact among its members outside supervision. It may be necessary to outline the ground rules regarding any discussion of supervision outside the group so as not to drain off energy that legitimately belongs within the group.

The Process of Peer-Supervision Groups

Peer supervision groups tend to be more informal than other types of supervision groups (Lewis et al., 1988). This, however, might be an error, at least in the beginning. Without the direction of a designated leader, structure can give the group some measure of stability while it is finding its particular rhythm. In fact, Counselman and Weber (2004) insist that a contract is essential in a peer supervision group.

Part of the structure must be, in fact, a plan for handling the leadership of the group. Although peer supervision groups are leaderless by definition, to ignore the issue of leadership gives rise to competitiveness and conflict (Hilmes et al., 2011; Schreiber & Frank, 1983). Therefore, many groups rotate the leadership role, with one person directing each meeting. The leader may concern him- or herself with group leadership issues only, or may also be asked to take responsibility for secretarial issues arising as a result of the meeting, including communicating with absent members about the next meeting, keeping records of supervision meetings and actions taken, and so on.

On the other hand, Counselman and Weber (2004) present an alternative view:

> *We believe that the successful, truly leaderless PSG shares the tasks of leadership. These include adherence to contract, gatekeeping and boundary management, and working with resistance. A successful PSG stays on task; i.e., it does not deviate from the original idea of being a PSG. . . . A PSG does not allow a de facto leader to emerge [nor do we] . . . recommend appointing a leader for each meeting. We believe in the value of everyone having equal responsibility for the group process.* (p. 133)

The process of peer group supervision also includes a plan for case presentation. Typically, one or two cases are the maximum that can be reasonably discussed at one meeting. Marks and Hixon (1986) suggest that the presenter come prepared with two or three questions about the case to direct the group's discussion. They also suggest that a process observer be appointed (different from either the presenter or the designated leader). This person gives feedback at the end of the supervision meeting about the group process that he or she observed, including "a statement regarding the group's ability to stay task-oriented, its adherence to ground rules, what group building may have occurred and the participation level of the group members" (p. 421). Also, we recommend a consideration of the models of supervision presented earlier in this chapter that could be adapted easily for peer group supervision.

Advantages and Disadvantages of Peer-Supervision Groups

Those practitioners who participate in peer supervision groups tend to rate them very favorably. There is every reason to assume, therefore, that the number of peer supervision groups will grow. Among the advantages ascribed to peer-supervision groups are the following (Counselman & Weber, 2004; Hamlin & Timberlake, 1982; Lewis et al., 1988; Marks & Hixon, 1986; Schreiber & Frank, 1983; Wendorf, Wendorf, & Bond, 1985):

1. They help clinicians remain reflective about their work and offer options beyond their individual frameworks. Skovholt and Rønnestad (1992b) found in their qualitative study of therapists across the life span that one theme that predicted therapists' ongoing professional development was their willingness to engage in reflective activity. Peer-supervision groups serve this purpose.
2. They offer the type of environment that is especially attractive to adult learners.
3. They provide a forum for the reexamination of familiar experiences (e.g., early terminations; working with one particular cultural group).
4. They provide a peer-review process that maintains high standards for practice, thus reducing the risk of ethical violations.
5. They provide a forum for transmitting new information, thus providing continuing education for members.
6. They provide the continuity necessary for serious consultation.
7. They can provide some of the therapeutic factors often attributed to group process, including reassurance, validation, and a sense of belonging. As a result, they can reduce the potential for burnout.
8. They enable clinicians to become more aware of countertransference issues and parallel process.
9. Because peers, rather than experts, offer feedback, supervision is less likely to be compromised by conflicts with authority figures.

The major limitation reported by members of peer supervision groups came from within-agency groups (Marks & Hixon, 1986), because group members might form their own coalitions and interagency communication might not be facilitated. Also, when group members must work with each other outside the group, they may be reticent to self-disclose and are less trustful in the group.

However, for some group members, the peer supervision group can be a vehicle for obtaining support or even some level of therapy. Counselman and Weber (2004) note that "one reason many therapists join a PSG is because they feel isolated in their professional lives" (p. 135), and so it is important that the group provide a mechanism to permit socializing, but not at the expense of the overall task, which is case presentation and discussion.

Evaluation of Peer-Group Supervision

The evaluation of peer-group supervision is mostly neglected except for vague statements about a need to make sure that the group is functioning. Žorga, Dekleva, and Kobolt (2001), by contrast, offer a serious discussion of evaluation of peer-group supervision, including the idea that outside consultants may be invited on occasion to review the efficacy of the peer group. Within the group, Žorga et al. repeat many of the conditions for evaluation of supervision in general, including the premise that evaluation can occur only within positive working relationships. For groups that want to take stock of their performance, Žorga et al. offer the following questions, which we believe will be helpful to most groups:

1. What have I learned during the process of peer supervision for myself and for my future work performance? What was the outcome of the goals I set down at the beginning of the peer-supervision process? What are my strengths and weaknesses? Which style of working in the group was most productive for me? What is my style of working?

2. What was the role of the group in my learning process? What did I learn from the other participants in the group (from each one separately)? How did I experience each individual participant and the group as a whole? What was my contribution to the group? What could others learn from me? Is this a group in which I could learn, and what exactly do I need to learn here? What do I expect from others, and what don't I desire from them?
3. How has the group developed? Where is it now, and what do we expect in the future? What was the group dynamic like? What were the rules that were developed in the group, and is there any need to change them?
4. What was good about the peer-supervision process, and what could be better? What are my goals for the future so that I may continue my learning process? How can the others from the group help me reach these goals? What else could the others learn in the future, and what could they improve? What am I willing to offer them? (p. 157)

TECHNOLOGY AND GROUP SUPERVISION

Technology has made its mark on supervision processes. In some cases, the use of technology is perceived not only as adequate but even preferred to face-to-face contact. Conn, Roberts, and Powell (2009) studied school counseling interns and divided their sample of 76 into those who received only face-to-face group supervision and those who received a hybrid model (i.e., 5 face-to-face sessions and 10 technology-mediated supervision sessions using WebCT). No differences were found regarding quality of supervision. Interestingly, satisfaction with supervision scores was higher for those in the hybrid group than the face-to-face only group.

Using a much smaller sample size of six students divided into two groups of three, Nelson, Nichter, and Henriksen (2010) compare the experience of students assigned to a face-to-face group supervision experience and those who volunteered to be in an online supervision group. Occasionally, the two groups met together for face-to-face supervision. For the online group, only audio was available because not all students had video capacity. Both groups reported a positive experience, and all students enjoyed their small-group meetings over the larger-group meeting. The recommendations made by the authors as a result of their experience include giving students a choice (if possible) between face-to-face and online group supervision, being clear about the technology required for students to engage in online supervision, and having a backup plan should technological problems occur. The authors note that it was also advantageous if interns and faculty had a relationship with each other prior to engaging in online supervision.

Yet another group of researchers (Yeh et al., 2008) looked at the benefits of technology for counseling interns who formed an online peer-supervision group to supplement their individual supervision. In this study, interns were allowed to use aliases and used a Web site throughout their 30-week experience to pose questions to each other and receive interpersonal support and guidance. It should be noted that the purpose of this study was to determine if the typical processes found in face-to-face group supervision could occur online, not to determine the quality of peer input (although the interactions were tracked by two psychologists for ethical reasons). Interestingly, the subjects reported that the anonymity they were afforded encouraged them to disclose more. Nielson et al. (2009) note a lack of self-disclosure as being a hindrance to good group supervision. Therefore, this finding alone may encourage a serious consideration of the place of technology for group supervision.

Technology may be especially suited for post-training peer-group supervision. Cummings (2002) studied the use of an email case presentation, followed by 60 minutes of supervision from three peers in a text-based chat room. The participants reported a positive experience that included support, challenge, and feedback that assisted them in their clinical work. They also reported that the disinhibition effect of online contact allowed them to be more honest that they might have been in person. The chat room used in Cummings' research may be an essential element for success. A similar study of several peer groups consisting of four supervisees each that used email but no time-limited chat room (McMahon, 2002) found the lag time between case presentations and feedback to be a concern. Still, McMahon's participants were more positive than negative, and found the use of the Internet to be a viable way to offer and receive peer supervision.

SUMMARY: WHAT ENHANCES—AND WHAT HINDERS—GROUP SUPERVISION

We have considered the types of group supervision, their stages, and their different processes. We end this chapter by summarizing some key principles that several authors have addressed and should be considered when conducting group supervision. These principles stress not only what supervisors must be prepared to do, but also include pitfalls to avoid. In addition to our own observations, the following draws from the work of Boëthius, Sundin, and Ögren, 2006; Carter, Enyedy, Goodyear, Arcinue, and Puri, 2009; DeStefano et al., 2007; Ellis, 2010; Enyedy, Arcinue, Puri, Carter, Goodyear, and Getzelman, 2003; Kaduvettoor et al., 2009; Kuechler, 2006; Mastoras and Andrew, 2011; Melnick and Fall, 2008; Skjerve et al., 2009; and Sussman, Bogo, and Globerman, 2007.

1. Supervisors must understand that their management of group process is as important as their supervisory insights about the supervisee and the case that is presented. *Group process facilitation* includes building relationships among group members so that trust emerges and anxiety is diminished, as well as the management of the various and different histories between and among group members so that relationships are "evened out" to the extent possible before the work of supervision begins. Group supervisors must also stay attuned to various cultural assumptions exhibited in the group, and how these influence both group dynamics and case discussions. Finally, management includes such issues as scheduling of case presentations and allowing adequate time for group process around individual presentations and group dynamics.
2. Supervisors must facilitate supervision that is developmentally appropriate for persons in the group. Typically, supervisees are, more or less, a homogeneous group in this regard (at least in training settings). Still, within each group, there are stronger and weaker members. Supervisors must use interventions and group supervision models that allow space for each person to work productively in the group. In addition, they must challenge groups made up of more advanced supervisees to risk more in the group than they might more fledgling supervisees in order to enhance their development.
3. Supervisors must understand group stages and do what is stage-appropriate, such as establishing ground rules early on and having a clear agenda for the group (which includes having each member establish his or her own learning goals). Unstructured group supervision using a *laissez faire* leadership style rarely works, and is more likely to lead to unnecessary storming than would be the case when group supervisees are members of a well-conceived group facilitated by a competent supervisor with adequate structure (Jacobs et al., 2012).
4. Supervisors must remain vigilant about the continua of safety to risk-taking, disclosure to nondisclosure, anxiety to comfort, and ebb and flow. At times, supervisors use their observations to enhance group safety by perhaps sharing a vulnerable clinical moment of their own, or introducing a relatively safe group exercise to enhance relationships among members. At other times, they bring their observations to a group they consider strong enough to process the group dynamics. It is important for supervisors to recognize any increasing inhibition among group members as a need for more facilitation toward group

safety. Finally, good group supervisors model validation, challenge, and immediacy to assist supervisees in doing the same.

5. Supervisors must offer feedback. Although research indicates that supervisors may not be prepared to offer some feedback in a group context that they would offer in individual supervision (Skjerve et al., 2009), supervisors must remember that feedback and evaluation are endemic to supervision. A primary ethical complaint from former supervisees is the lack of adequate feedback and evaluation from their supervisors (Ladany, Lehrman-Waterman, Molinaro, & Wolgast, 1999). Group supervision does not get a "pass" on this crucial dimension. That said, supervisors must balance their ultimate role as evaluator with their goal of having group members take more ownership of the process over time. Although this is not essentially different from the developmental goals of individual supervision, it is more complicated when working with a group. Whenever there is the threat of a negative evaluation from a supervisor for any individual within a group, it affects not only that individual, but also the group as a whole. To some extent, this is unavoidable; however, it is still important for the supervisor to be ever cognizant and sensitive to the power differential between him or her and the group supervisees. If supervisors create a group supervision context that is appropriately safe, the challenging feedback and evaluation components of the experience are far more likely to be accepted favorably by supervisees.
6. Supervisors must be highly engaged with the group in order to recognize and capitalize on key moments, which include cultural misunderstandings as indicated in a case presentation, feedback among group members that must be reframed to be useful or to achieve an important learning goal, and opportunities to link or contrast group members' styles or conceptualizations for working with similar clients. Each group session offers opportunities that pull from the clients being presented, the people in the room, and the innumerable ways to conceptualize or experience what is going on. What appears to distinguish good group supervisors from those who are not is their willingness to invest in the process, their skills as group facilitators, their commitment to each person's professional development (which necessitates giving feedback), and their ability to model the kind of personal attributes that engender trust and confidence in others.

CONCLUSION

Group supervision is an effective form of supervision that offers the supervisee the benefits of peer relationships, exposure to a greater number of cases, and vicarious as well as direct learning. It also affords supervisees a role in each other's development not afforded them in individual supervision. Successful group supervisors are skillful in capitalizing on the advantages of this modality while minimizing any disadvantages. At present, group supervision is most often a supplement to individual supervision in training programs. Its potential as a standalone modality is greater postdegree. Despite the context of its use, group supervision is here to stay as a fruitful and engaging form of supervision.

Live Supervision

From Chapter 9 of *Fundamentals of Clinical Supervision,* Fifth Edition. Janine M. Bernard and Rodney K. Goodyear.

Live Supervision

A significant number of supervisors rely on and often prefer the use of live supervision interventions. For obvious reasons, live supervision is especially popular in training programs where facilities are more conducive to its application (Carlozzi, Romans, Boswell, Ferguson, & Whisenhunt, 1997; Kolodinskey, Lindsey, Young, Lund, Edgerly, & Zlatev, 2011), although some argue for its importance in the field as well (e.g., Beddoe, Ackroyd, Chinnery, & Appleton, 2011).

Live supervision represents a paradigmatic shift from either individual supervision or group supervision; therefore, it cannot be considered a subgroup of either. This shift essentially consists of two components: (a) the distinction between counseling or therapy and supervision is less pronounced in live supervision than in traditional supervision, and (b) the role of the supervisor is significantly changed to include both coaching and cotherapist dimensions. As a result of these essential differences, the process of live supervision and its advantages and drawbacks are different from other forms of supervision. This chapter addresses the evolution of live supervision, describes its process both with and without a supervision team, notes the advantages and disadvantages for these two forms of live supervision, and addresses the available empirical findings about its effectiveness.

At one time, live supervision was considered the "hallmark of family therapy" (Nichols, 1984, p. 89). Marriage and family therapy training programs are still more likely to use live supervision than their sister disciplines (Nichols, Nichols, & Hardy, 1990; Wark, 2000), but its use has infiltrated other mental health professions (Bubenzer, West, & Gold, 1991; Carlozzi et al., 1997; Champe & Kleist, 2003; Evans, 1987; Haber, Marshall, Cowan, Vanlandingham, Gerson, & Fitch, 2009; Kivlighan, Angelone, & Swafford, 1991; Kolodinskey et al., 2011; Saltzburg, Greene, & Drew, 2010), and Saba (1999) reports the use of live supervision in medical training. Live supervision began as an intensive method for working with an individual supervisee (or perhaps two supervisees working as cotherapists). More recently, the team form of live supervision has gained in momentum, especially what is known as the *reflecting team* (Anderson, 1987; Chang, 2010). The team is a group of therapists (with or without a supervisor) or supervisees (with a supervisor) who work together on their cases. Because of the significantly different dynamics between live supervision without a team and team supervision (Clarke & Rowan, 2009), we begin with live supervision without a team and address team supervision later in this chapter. Furthermore, because "the literature suggests that the one-way mirror may be as basic to family therapy as the couch was to psychoanalysis" (Lewis & Rohrbaugh, 1989, p. 323), our discussion follows suit and assumes, in most cases, that the client is a family.

Live supervision was initiated by Jay Haley and Salvadore Minuchin (Simon, 1982) in the late 1960s as a result of a rather singular project. At the time, both were invested in treating low-income families, but were not enamored with the idea of trying to teach middle-class therapists what it was like to be poor. Therefore, they decided to recruit people with no more than a high-school education from the communities being served and train them to work with other similar families. Because of the legitimate need to protect the families being treated from inexperienced "therapists," Haley and Minuchin devised a live supervision model in which they could guide these inexperienced and untrained therapists as they worked. Haley described the result: "Actually they did very well. We worked with them in live supervision, 40 hours a week for two years. Nobody has ever been trained that intensely" (Simon, 1982, p. 29).

Live supervision combines direct observation of the therapy session with some method that enables the supervisor to communicate with and thereby influence the work of the supervisee during the session. Therefore, the supervisor is simultaneously in charge of both training the therapist and controlling the course of therapy (Lewis, 1988). Because of the dual agenda of both observing and interacting with the supervisee, much has been written about the methods of live supervision, especially about different methods for communicating with the supervisee. We begin, therefore, by reviewing the different methods used to communicate with the supervisee(s); we also consider the messages given by the supervisor during live supervision, as well as the function of pre- and postsession deliberations. Once we have explored how live supervision is conducted, we back up to consider some of the guidelines for the use of live supervision.

METHODS OF LIVE SUPERVISION

Bubenzer, Mahrle, and West (1987) list six methods used to conduct live supervision: (a) bug-in-the-ear, (b) monitoring, (c) in vivo, (d) walk-in, (e) phone-in, and (f) consultation. We explain each of these briefly, as well as consider the use of computer and interactive television technology to communicate with the therapist.

Bug-in-the-Ear

The *bug-in-the-ear (BITE)* consists of a wireless earphone worn by the supervisee through which the supervisor can coach the supervisee during the therapy session. It has three major advantages: First, it allows the supervisor to make minor adjustments (e.g., "Get them to talk to each other") or to briefly reinforce the therapist (e.g., "Excellent job of pulling in Dad") without interrupting the flow of the therapy session. In fact, much of what can be communicated through BITE might not warrant a more formal interruption of the session. Second, it has been established that BITE works as a behavioral strategy on the part of the supervisor to increase supervisee behaviors through such reinforcement (Gallant, Thyer, & Bailey, 1991). Third, BITE protects the therapy relationship more fully than other live supervision technologies because clients are unaware which comments are the direct suggestions of the supervisor (Alderfer, 1983, as cited in Gallant & Thyer, 1989). BITE also has been found to be effective even when delivered through teleconferencing (Smith et al., 2007).

The disadvantages of BITE emerge from its advantages: Because BITE is seemingly so nonintrusive, it can be overused by the supervisor, and can be a distraction to the supervisee who is trying to track a therapy session, as well as take in advice from the supervisor (Smith, Mead, & Kinsella, 1998). Similarly, there is a danger of "echo therapy" (Byng-Hall, 1982, as cited in Adamek, 1994): The supervisee simply parrots the words of the supervisor with little or no assimilation of the therapeutic implications of what is being said, thus encouraging supervisee dependence. Finally, because it is a less visible form of live supervision, it can produce awkward moments. For example, the supervisee who is attempting to listen to a supervisor comment might need to interrupt the family in order to focus on the supervisory input. Furthermore, because family members do not know when the supervisee is receiving input, the device itself can produce ambivalent feelings because of the secrecy it symbolizes.

Monitoring

Monitoring, the process whereby the supervisor observes the session and intervenes directly into the session if the therapist is in difficulty (Minuchin & Fishman, 1981), is used minimally. By implication, therefore, monitoring can be either a way to safeguard client welfare (in which case it is really not live supervision per se, but something that many supervisors might do if they felt a sense of urgency), or a form of live supervision that is less sensitive to the dynamics between therapist and clients. Conversely, an advantage of monitoring, assuming that the supervisor takes over when entering the room, is that it allows the supervisor to experience the family dynamics directly while allowing the supervisee to benefit from the modeling provided by the supervisor working with the family.

For more experienced therapists, supervisors can be called into an ongoing case as a consultant–supervisor (Richman, Aitken, & Prather, 1990). The supervisor is briefed ahead of time about the case and the difficulties that the therapist is having. The supervisor then conducts a session with the therapist present, typically referring particularly to the impasse being faced in therapy. Richman et al. note that using supervision in this way models and normalizes appropriate help-seeking behavior for the clients, as well as providing a helpful alteration to the therapy system that has been established.

In Vivo

In vivo has some similarity to monitoring in that it allows clients to see the supervisor in operation. Rather than taking over for the therapist, however, the supervisor consults with the therapist in the presence of the clients. With *in vivo supervision,* there is an assumption that the family deserves to have access to all information, including a discussion of interventions. Seen from a different angle, the conversation between supervisor and therapist can itself constitute an intervention by heightening the family's awareness of particular dynamics, especially when dynamics are reframed therapeutically for the benefit of the family. In vivo supervision has some similarity to the reflecting team discussed later in the chapter.

The Walk-In

In another form of live supervision, the *walk-in,* the supervisor enters the room in order to interact with both the therapist and the clients, and then leaves. The walk-in does not imply an emergency, nor does it imply the kind of collegiality that is evident with in vivo supervision. A walk-in, therefore, can be used to redirect therapy and establish certain dynamics between the supervisor and the family or the therapist and the family. As a result, it can be viewed as more of a therapy intervention than either monitoring or in vivo supervision. All three methods of supervision that involve having the supervisor enter the therapy room are more intrusive in the therapy relationship than the methods that follow; therefore, they do not represent the norm.

Phone-Ins and Consultation Breaks

The most common forms of live supervision are phone-ins or consultation breaks. These methods are similar in that both interrupt therapy for the therapist to receive input from the supervisor. There is little opportunity for the therapist to react to the intervention, however, when it is *phoned in* using some sort of intercom system. In the *consultation break,* the therapist leaves the therapy room to consult with the supervisor when the supervisor alerts the therapist by, for example, knocking on the door when the therapist feels the need to consult, or at a predetermined point in the therapy hour. The therapist then has an opportunity to clarify what the supervisor is suggesting prior to returning to the therapy room. Although both methods have documented training and supervision advantages, they have the disadvantage of altering the therapy flow by virtue of the interruption.

Using Computers, Interactive Television, and Notebooks for Live Supervision

First coined as a *bug-in-the-eye* by Klitzke and Lombardo (1991), this alternative to BITE uses a monitor in the therapy room in a fashion similar to how Teleprompters are used in broadcast journalism. Rather than speaking into the ear of the supervisee, supervisors can unobtrusively make suggestions by typing them from a keyboard in the observation room to be read on the monitor placed behind the client. Proponents of this method argue that it retains all the advantages while eliminating the disadvantages of BITE (Miller, Miller, & Evans, 2002). Because the supervisee controls when it is an opportune time to read the supervisor's message, the supervisee feels less distracted by the method. Supposedly, this translates to a smooth session from the client's perspective. Neukrug (1991) adds that the ability to save supervisor feedback on a disk to print out later is another advantage that allows the supervisee to review the feedback (along with an audio or video recording of the session), or allows the supervisor and supervisee to discuss the feedback at length in supervision.

Rosenberg (2006) developed a system where text-based feedback is sent to supervisees observing a session while this same feedback is recorded on the session video recording (in a manner similar to subtitles) for the therapist to review after the session. The immediate beneficiaries of this method, therefore, are the peers of the therapist supervisee.

Finally, Yu (2012) developed a method of interacting with supervisees using iPads that supervisees hold in their laps. The observing supervisor uses Google doc (or a similar service) that has been set up for supervisor and supervisee ahead of time and allows comments to be communicated to the supervisee. As sessions are video recorded, these comments are also available to the supervisee after the fact for review against the video. More recently, Yu (personal communication, 2012) developed www.iSupeLive.com which allows the user to bypass Internet programs such as Google and offers a timestamp for future review of supervisor feedback against a recording, as well as other shortcuts and touch features that make the process easier and richer. As increasingly more students acquire notebooks, the kind of set up described by Yu goes far to eliminate any sense that this form of live supervision is exotic.

Using Distance Technologies for Live Supervision

As *technologically assisted distance supervision (TADS)* has grown, it should not be surprising that some supervisors are interested in using TADS for live supervision. Rousmaniere and Frederickson (2012) used webcam to transmit live video of a therapy session to the supervisor. The interventions to the supervisee are delivered over a laptop placed adjacent to the client, thus providing feedback in a way similar to what Klitzke and Lombardo (1991) and Yu (2012) propose. Rousmaniere and Frederickson suggest that supervisor comments be restricted to client comments (i.e., statements that the therapist might make to the client) or process comments (i.e., observations about what is transpiring in therapy), and also recommend the use of remote live supervision for postgraduate supervisees for ethical reasons in light of the geographic distance between supervisor and supervisee/client.

Although some supervisors are firmly committed to one method of live supervision, most of the literature on live supervision downplays the method while focusing on guidelines for the intervention or directive, parameters that must be respected when using live supervision, the acculturation of supervisees and clients to live supervision, and supervisee issues while working within the live supervision framework.

THE LIVE SUPERVISION INTERVENTION

Supervisor to supervisee communications during live supervision are typically referred to as the *supervisory intervention* or *supervisor directives.* For our purposes here, the terms are interchangeable. We discuss interventions delivered by means of the bug-in-the-ear, phone-ins, and consultation breaks, as these are the most commonly used methods of live supervision. Consultation breaks, also a commonly used intervention when a team is involved in live supervision, is discussed later in the chapter.

Prior to implementing a live supervision intervention, the supervisor should ask:

1. Is redirection necessarily called for in the session?
2. Might the therapist redirect the session without an intervention?
3. Will the therapist be able to carry out the intervention successfully?
4. Is the driving force of the intervention to attend to the needs of the therapist and the client, or is it the supervisor's desire to do cotherapy?
5. Can the intervention be communicated briefly and succinctly? (Frankel & Piercy, 1990; Haber et al., 2009; Heath, 1982; Liddle & Schwartz, 1983)

In addition, the supervisor must consider the strengths and limitations of the intervention modality to be used.

Bug-in-the-Ear Interventions

There is no question that the BITE form of sending a supervision directive is the most limited for the reasons already discussed. In particular situations and for specific reasons, however, BITE may still be the intervention method of choice, and is especially recommended for novice supervisees (Adamek, 1994) when relatively frequent, yet brief, suggestions are warranted. The new supervisee may also benefit from the reinforcing potential of BITE (e.g., "Nice question") that might be lost using other methods of supervision. It stands to reason that the use of BITE implies that the supervisor will focus on basic observable skills during the therapy session. In addition, it follows that if BITE is the method of delivering interventions, the major part of supervision must occur either before or after the session. Finally, because BITE is inherently distracting, the supervisor must be sensitive to its effect for each supervisee. There may be instances, for example, when the use of BITE has no benefits at all because of the reactivity of the supervisee to the supervisor's interventions.

It might be appropriate to use BITE for a more advanced supervisee if the supervisee has a specific goal for a particular session. For example, if a supervisee has been consistently sidetracked by a particular client, the supervisor could alert the supervisee when this was occurring in the session using BITE. As this example demonstrates, BITE interventions take the form of *coaching,* whether they are delivered to novice supervisees or more experienced therapists.

Phone-In Interventions

Unlike BITE, phone-in interventions have the advantage of stopping the therapy session. This allows the supervisee to listen to the directive without having to attend to the client at the same time. The phone-in has another advantage in that the client is alerted simultaneously that the therapist is being advised and may be prepared for a change in direction in the session. Furthermore, because the client knows that the therapist is receiving feedback, the supervisor directive can be the intervention itself. For example, if the supervisor believes that a member of the family is getting lost, the therapist might be advised to continue the session with, "My supervisor thinks that we women [referring to herself and the mother] have been doing all the talking and we're not letting John [the father] have a say. My supervisor would like to hear what you [John] think is going on between your wife and your son."

As is the case for all live supervision interventions, telephone directives should be used conservatively; furthermore, they should be brief, concise, and generally action oriented (Haley, 1987; Lewis & Rohrbaugh, 1989; Mauzey & Erdman, 1997; Rickert & Turner, 1978; Wright, 1986). Depending on the developmental level of the supervisee, a verbatim directive might be given (e.g., "Ask the mother, 'What is your worst fear about Thomas if he continues with his present crowd?'"), or, for the more advanced supervisee, a more flexible directive might be given (e.g., "Reframe Mom's behavior as concern") (Rickert & Turner, 1978; Wright, 1986). Other generally accepted guidelines when phoning in interventions include avoiding process statements (or keeping them very brief) and refraining from complex directives, not exceeding two instructions per phone-in, being sensitive to the timing of the intervention and avoiding interventions during the first 10 minutes of the therapy session, limiting phone-ins to a maximum of five per therapy session, and communicating that it is the supervisee's decision when a suggestion can be worked into the session (unless the supervisor has clearly stipulated a time for the intervention) (Frankel & Piercy, 1990; Lewis & Rohrbaugh, 1989; Wright, 1986).

Wright also asserts that it is sometimes strategically wise to begin an intervention with positive reinforcement of what has transpired in the session up to the present. In other words, taking the time to say, "You're really doing a terrific job keeping Dad from taking over" might be worth the time and increase the supervisee's investment in carrying out future interventions. This advice was supported by research that found that supervisees experienced phone-ins that included support components as "most effective"; conversely, supervisees were twice as likely as their supervisors to judge phone-in interventions without support as "least effective" (Frankel, 1990). Unfortunately, Frankel found that supervisors using phone-ins used supportive interventions only about one third as often as they used directive behaviors.

Mauzey and Erdman (1997) conducted a phenomenological study of the effect of phone-in interventions on supervisees that confirmed these earlier suggestions as valid. In addition, they found that well-received phone-ins focused on the welfare of the client more than on training, were on track rather than suggesting that therapy go in a new direction, flowed from a trusting relationship with the supervisor, and considered both the anxiety and the developmental levels of the supervisee.

In summary, the phone-in is a sound live supervision method when the message is relatively brief, uncomplicated, and action oriented; however, it is less effective for more complicated process issues. When the supervisee needs more clarification than can be provided with a phone directive, the supervisee should leave the room for a consultation break (Haley, 1987).

Consultation Break Interventions

Even if BITE or a phone system is available to the supervisor, a consultation break may be the intervention method of choice. In addition to the supervisee's need for clarification, consultation may be preferred if it is the opinion of the supervisor that

1. The intervention may be lengthy, and the supervisee may need some extra time to absorb it (Rickert & Turner, 1978).
2. The supervisee may need a rationale for the intervention, which is not accomplished well using the phone-in (Rickert & Turner, 1978).
3. The supervisee may profit from the opportunity to react to the intervention, perhaps to be sure that it is understood or compatible with how the supervisee is experiencing the family.
4. There is a need to check out some impressions with the supervisee as part of forming the intervention.

When consultation is used, it is essential that the supervisor attend to the amount of time that the conference takes away from therapy. There is a momentum to the therapy session that is diluted by a live supervision conference. This momentum must be considered to be part of the formula for successful live supervision. If the therapist remains out of the therapy room too long, the intervention that is carried back to the client might be moot. A partial exception to this admonition is if the client system has been forewarned that a lengthy consultation is part of the therapy hour. In fact, when strategic family therapy is being implemented, the consultation break may be substantial, and the supervisee might return to the session only to deliver a final directive, usually in the form of a homework assignment. That being said, several researchers (Hunt & Sharpe, 2008; Locke & McCollum, 2001) have found that clients are satisfied with live supervision as long as its perceived helpfulness outweighs its perceived intrusiveness. Therefore, a conservative approach to within-session consultations is warranted.

In summary, during-session interventions are far more complex than they may appear. A good directive must be succinct and add clarity, not confusion, to the supervisee's deliberations. Even consultation breaks must be efficient in their use of therapy time and should focus primarily on the supervisee's executive (behavioral) skills (West, Bubenzer, Pinsoneault, & Holeman, 1993). In addition, supervisees must experience live supervision as constructive, not critical, if the interventions are to be successful. For the supervisee to have an opportunity to process more reflectively, thus developing perceptual and cognitive skills, both presession and postsession conferences are requisite.

PRESESSION PLANNING AND POSTSESSION DEBRIEFING

Although the interaction between the supervisor and the therapy system is the crux of live supervision, what comes before and after are the foundation for the successful implementation of the model. Especially because of the level of activity involved in live supervision, there is a necessity for groundwork to be done in order for the activity during the session to remain meaningful.

As one might suppose, the goal of the presession is to prepare the supervisee for the upcoming therapy session. There will be some speculation about what the family might bring to this session. The supervisor will have two goals in the presession: to prepare the supervisee for the upcoming session and to focus on the supervisee's own learning goals as they pertain to the upcoming session (Haber et al., 2009). Piercy states that he wants his supervisees to show evidence of having a *theoretical map,* and then to be able to "tie it to a practical understanding of how to bring about change" (West, Bubenzer, & Zarski, 1989, p. 27). In addition, supervisees are often asked to attempt a particular technique (e.g., to raise the intensity of the interactions between family members), or they may be asked if they have something particular that they would like the supervisor to observe. In other words, it is important that both the supervisee and supervisor complete the presession with some clarity about their roles for the therapy session.

However, Okun argues that family therapy "cannot be organized like a lesson plan" (West et al., 1989, p. 27). Families force both supervisees and supervisors to be spontaneous even if they are adequately prepared for the session. The developmental level of the supervisee must be reflected in presession planning. The supervisor will be more active with the novice supervisee in terms of both helping to provide a conceptual overview and planning for immediate interventions. Once the supervisee has gained experience, it is expected that the supervisor will take a more consultative position (West et al., 1989, 1993).

The postsession debriefing allows the supervisee and the supervisor to discuss what transpired in the session. Because they were both involved in the therapy but held different vantage points, this is an important time to share perceptions, review the effectiveness of interventions, offer feedback, and address any unfinished business from the session as a precursor to planning the next session.

If homework has been assigned to the family, this is also a time to consider ways in which the family might respond to the assignment and to begin to consider future interventions based on the family's response. In other words, the successful postsession leaves the supervisee with some food for thought to consider prior to the next presession (West et al., 1989).

Although the presession conference is an important coaching session, the postsession debriefing is the optimal time for the conceptual growth of the supervisee. This conference, therefore, should not be rushed. If there is no opportunity to meet immediately after the therapy session, it should be scheduled at another time, but far enough prior to the next therapy session so it does not feel like another presession conference.

IMPLEMENTING LIVE SUPERVISION

In his seminal article, Montalvo (1973) lists six guidelines for live supervision that continue to be relevant today:

1. *Supervisor and supervisee agree that a supervisor can either call the supervisee out, or that the supervisee can come out for feedback when he or she wishes.* Elizur (1990) asserts that supervisees must buy into the model before its use, suggesting that this be negotiated as part of a supervision contract.

2. *Supervisor and supervisee, before settling down to work, agree on defined limits within which both will operate.* For example, the supervisor outlines under what conditions, if any, the supervisee can reject the supervisor's intervention.

3. *The supervisor endeavors not to inhibit the supervisee's freedom of exploration and operation too much, but, if the supervisor does so, the supervisee is expected to let the supervisor know this.*

4. *The mechanism for establishing direction is routine talks before and after the session.* Montalvo (1973) believes strongly that the family should not be privy to these discussions and that efforts to "democratize" the therapy process have not proved useful. Anderson (1987) came to a very different conclusion, and developed the reflecting team approach to live supervision.

5. *The supervisor tries to find procedures that best fit the supervisee's style and preferred way of working.*

6. *The beginning supervisee should understand at the start that he or she may feel as if he or she is under remote control.* (adapted from Montalvo, 1973, pp. 343–345)

The wisdom of Montalvo's guidelines lies in both their clarity regarding the supervision hierarchy and their respect for the integrity, if not the ego, of the supervisee. Insufficient attention to one of these issues can result in an unsatisfactory experience with live supervision. More recently, Lee and Everett (2004) compiled their own list of conditions for effective live supervision. Reflecting the increasing focus on relationship variables within supervision, their admonitions are paraphrased as follows:

1. Supervisors, respecting the presence of isomorphism, must attend to the supervisory relationship and relate to their supervisees as they would have their supervisees relate to their clients.
2. Supervisors must use active listening with their supervisees, validate them, and remain flexible as part of live supervision.
3. Supervisors should understand that offering criticism in a live setting, particularly with other supervisees present or in front of a clinical family, can be emotionally devastating to the supervisee.
4. Supervisors should not offer directions that are inappropriate to the supervisee's level of development, and should take into account the supervisee's ability to tolerate risks in this public setting.
5. Supervisors should be personable, acknowledge their mistakes, use concrete suggestions, explain the rationale for their suggestions, and be open to supervisee feedback.

6. Supervisors should demonstrate respect, support, and—when appropriate—humor, enthusiasm, and humility.
7. Supervisors should remember that when supervisee anxiety gets too high or if criticism is combined with disrespect, the entire training experience can become toxic (p. 71).

McCollum (1995) addresses the supervisor's own anxiety during live supervision and poses the following question: "How do I keep my own anxiety under control and curb my own oldest-brother wish to take over and make things 'right' versus letting the [supervisee] and clients stew with their troubles?" (p. 4).

Bubenzer et al. (1987) make four suggestions to help desensitize supervisees to live supervision. Using phone-ins as their method, they suggest that supervisors first show new supervisees videotapes of family sessions during which the phone rings and the session is interrupted. By doing this, supervisees observe how clients react when the phone rings and how things proceed afterward, often one of the first concerns for new supervisees. Second, new supervisees are allowed to be observers while live supervision is being conducted with other counselors and are encouraged to ask the supervisor any questions as things proceed. Third, hypothetical cases are presented to the supervisees for them to practice the consecutive stages of pretreatment (or presession planning), counseling during session, and post-treatment (or postsession debriefing). At this time, the possible use of phone-ins is discussed. Finally, again through role-play of hypothetical cases, the supervisees conduct sessions, following through on their plans and experiencing phone-ins during the session, as previously discussed. With the amount of anxiety that can surround supervision of any type, the idea of allowing a trial run as described by Bubenzer et al. makes intuitive sense and has been implemented elsewhere (e.g., Neukrug, 1991). It should also be noted that this type of careful and caring orientation to the use of live supervision is consistent with the comments made by supervisees in the Mauzey and Erdman (1997) study when describing positive experiences with live supervision.

Once the therapist becomes used to the idea of the inevitability of being interrupted during therapy and knows what form this will take, the pressure is on the supervisor to be concise and helpful. Berger and Dammann (1982) offer two astute observations about the supervisor's reality versus the supervisee's reality during live supervision. Because of the one-way mirror separating them, the supervisor "will see patterns more quickly and will be better able to think about them—to think meta to them—than the therapist will" (p. 338). Second, "the supervisor will lack accurate information as to the intensity of the family affect. This becomes readily apparent if the supervisor enters the room to talk with the family" (pp. 338–339).

There are outgrowths to each of these perceptual differences. Because of the advantage that the supervisor enjoys by being behind the one-way mirror, a common reaction for the therapist, according to Berger and Dammann (1982), is to "feel stupid" (p. 338) once something is called to the therapist's attention. The reason, of course, that the supervisee feels stupid is because what is pointed out seems painfully obvious, but is something that eluded the supervisee during the therapy session. The wise supervisor prepares supervisees for this reaction, and allows them opportunities to experience firsthand the cleverness that comes from being at a safe distance from the therapy interaction.

Regarding the intensity issue, the supervisee might rightfully believe that the supervisor does not understand the family if the supervisor is underestimating the intensity of family affect. It is for this reason—that is, the direct contact with the family experienced primarily by the supervisee—that Berger and Dammann (1982) support others who believe that, except for an emergency, "the supervisor proposes and the therapist disposes" (p. 339).

Gershenson and Cohen (1978) also note that, during live supervision, the relationship between supervisee and supervisor can begin on rocky ground because of the vulnerability—experienced as anxiety and resistance, persecutory fantasies, and anger—felt by the supervisee. It could be conjectured that at this stage the supervisee is reacting to the unfair advantage of the supervisor (behind the one-way mirror), along with extreme embarrassment at the mediocrity of his or her own performance. Fortunately, this initial stage seems to be short-lived for most supervisees, and indeed, Mauzey, Harris, and Trusty (2000) found that both anger and anxiety diminish with more exposure to live supervision. According to Gershenson and Cohen, a second stage follows, characterized by having high emotional investment in the process, and perceiving the supervisor as a supporter rather than as critic. We can assume that this stage also represents a heightened dependence on the supervisor. Finally, a third stage emerges, in which "the directions of our supervisor became less important as techniques to be implemented and instead served as a stimulus to our own thinking . . . [we] reached a point at which we were able to initiate our own therapeutic strategies" (p. 229).

ADVANTAGES AND DISADVANTAGES OF LIVE SUPERVISON

Advantages

The advocates of live supervision have been ardent (Bubenzer et al., 1991). The well-documented advantage of live supervision is that through this form of coaching by a more experienced clinician, there is a much greater likelihood that counseling and therapy will go well. There is also an assumption and some empirical evidence (Bartle-Haring, Silverthorn, Meyer, & Toviesse, 2009; Kivlighan et al., 1991; Landis & Young, 1994; Storm, 1994) that the supervisee learns more efficiently and, perhaps, more profoundly as a result of these successful therapy sessions. To return to our coaching metaphor, it is better to be coached and win the game than to be playing independently and suffer defeat.

In addition to the training function of live supervision, there is a built-in safeguard for client welfare. Because the supervisor is immediately accessible, clients are protected more directly. This also allows trainees to work with more challenging cases, which might be too difficult for them if another form of supervision were being used (Cormier & Bernard, 1982; Jordan, 1999; Lee & Everett, 2004; Yu, 2012). Of course, the difficulty of the case must be considered carefully. One that is too difficult means that the trainee is simply the voice of the supervisor and little more. The supervisor must be astute regarding the developmental level of the trainee and determine which cases are within the trainee's grasp (Lee & Everett, 2004).

A similar advantage to live supervision is that the supervisee is more likely to risk more in conducting therapy because of the knowledge that the supervisor is there to help with interventions (Berger & Dammann, 1982). Furthermore, because of the direct involvement of the highly skilled supervisor, clients assigned to supervisees receive better treatment (Rickert & Turner, 1978).

Another set of advantages related to live supervision has to do with the supervisee's relationship with the supervisor. Because the supervisor often shares responsibility for interventions, the supervisor is far more active than in other forms of supervision. This level of involvement increases the credibility of the supervisor because supervisees experience the clinical skills of the supervisor directly (Lee & Everett, 2004). Furthermore, because the supervisor's assistance is direct and immediate, there is great potential for enhancement of the supervisory working alliance (Dickens, 2011).

The supervisee's view of the process of therapy is also affected by live supervision, because it should unfold more systematically as a result of the supervisor's input. When the supervisor gives a rationale for an intervention, predicts reactions, and proves to be right, the supervisee experiences firsthand the predictability of some client patterns. This is an exciting moment for the supervisee; fortunately, it is balanced by those moments when clients react unpredictably, thus ensuring a sense of our fallibility as helpers.

Finally, supervisors often enjoy supervision more when engaged in live supervision (Lee & Everett, 2004). Because supervisor investment is central to good supervision, this advantage is a powerful one.

Disadvantages

The most noted disadvantages of live supervision are the time it demands of supervisors (Bubenzer et al., 1991; Lee & Everett, 2004; Yu, 2012), the cost of facilities, the problem of scheduling cases to accommodate all those involved, and the potential reactions of clients and supervisees to this unorthodox form of supervising (e.g., Anonymous, 1995). In addition, Schwartz, Liddle, and Breunlin (1988) return to one of Montalvo's (1973) initial concerns and alert supervisors to the tendency of *robotization* in using live supervision. Unless the supervisor is highly systematic in giving the supervisee increasingly more autonomy, live supervision can produce clinicians who show little initiative or creativity during therapy and who conceptualize inadequately. This potential disadvantage of live supervision has been echoed by others (e.g., Adamek, 1994; Kaplan, 1987; Lee & Everett, 2004; Lee, Nichols, Nichols, & Odom, 2004; Montalvo, 1973; Rickert & Turner, 1978; Storm, 1997; Thomas, 2010; Wright, 1986). Lee et al. (2004) speculate that the practical challenges endemic to live supervision, as well as some pedagogical concerns, might have contributed to its relative decline in recent years.

> *Because live supervision historically has been highly associated with directive models of therapy, such as structural and strategic, the postmodern and integrative movements may be a contributing factor to the increasing use of other modalities. The decline of live supervision and the popularity of videotape and case presentation methods also may be a combination of the practical difficulties and financial costs of getting supervisor, therapists, and clients together in the same time and place, and the fact that live approaches, for all their benefits, do not address important training needs.* (pp. 67–68)

Lee and Everett (2004) also view the potential of stalling the supervisee's self-sufficiency and self-confidence as a disadvantage of live supervision. In addition, they underscore a concern that focusing on the present session to the exclusion of all else can endanger a broader assessment of clients, as well as limit the supervisee's theory development and professional growth.

Focusing on the supervisor's influence on the supervisee, Moorhouse and Carr (2001) found that isomorphism between the behavior of the supervisor and that of the therapist was met with resistance more often than cooperation from the client. They hypothesize that if therapist and supervisor were highly attuned to one another, they may generate more creative and novel interventions, thus stimulating resistance in their clients. Therefore, Moorhouse and Carr seem to suggest that, although the professionals take pleasure in their ingenuity, they may lose sight of the immediate needs of the clients or their readiness to engage in challenging strategies.

Finally, there is virtually no evidence in professional literature that skills learned within a live supervision context generalize to other counseling situations (Gallant et al., 1991; Kivlighan et al., 1991). This is a serious gap in our knowledge for both supervisee and client welfare, especially in cases for which supervision is limited to the live supervision modality.

TEAM SUPERVISION

To this point the focus has been on the supervisor–therapist (supervisee) relationship in live supervision. Increasingly, however, *live supervision* has become synonymous with *team supervision*—that is, live supervision with other supervisees (in addition to the supervisor) behind the one-way mirror and involved in the supervision. Although team therapy was originally developed by seasoned practitioners (peers) as a means to study and improve their trade, it has become increasingly popular as a method of training even novice practitioners (e.g., Haley, 1987;

Heppner et al., 1994; Landis & Young, 1994). Briefly, the process of team supervision involves both the supervisor and a group of supervisees present behind the one-way mirror during the therapy session, while another supervisee serves as the therapist with the clients. As with supervisor-only live supervision, the technology most frequently used in team supervision is the phone, although consultation in the observation room is also common.

Therefore, while the therapist is working with the family, the team is observing family interactions, metacommunication, places where the therapist appears to be stymied, and so on, to arrive at some sort of decision regarding the direction that therapy should go and what might be helpful to the therapist. The observation room is as busy—if not busier—than the therapy room. The team members have the luxury of being one step removed, allowing them to see the entire therapeutic system, including the therapist. The assumption is that this more objective posture aids the conceptualization process, as does the synergy of ideas as the family is discussed. Team supervision also allows the supervisor to do a good deal of teaching while therapy is being conducted and to culminate an important clinical lesson with a timely intervention sent into the therapy room. Team supervision, therefore, becomes therapy, supervision, and classroom all in one.

To facilitate the activity and efficiency of the team or for broader educational reasons, it is sometimes helpful to assign specific tasks to different team members (Bernstein, Brown, & Ferrier, 1984; Lowe, Hunt, & Simmons, 2008; West et al., 1989). These tasks can be assigned by the supervisor or, if the therapist is looking for specific feedback, by the therapist. For example, the therapist–supervisee who is concerned about his or her ability to maintain appropriate boundaries within the session might ask one team member to observe only this aspect of the session. Lowe et al. (2008) describe a model in which the team is divided into a Treatment Team and an Observing Team. The teams are then assigned competing theoretical perspectives (e.g., modern vs. postmodern). Only the Treatment Team is involved directly during the session, but the Observing Team weighs in during the postsession conference. The goal of this approach is to increase trainee sophistication regarding multiple theoretical perspectives and to discourage overidentification with one. At the same time, it attends to the caution articulated by Cade, Speed, and Seligman (1986) that the team offering interventions should demonstrate theoretical cohesion so as not to confuse the therapist or the client.

From a more pragmatic perspective, Bernstein, Brown, and Ferrier (1984) present a model describing what they consider essential roles in team supervision: the *therapist:* the person who sits with the family during the session and remains attuned to the mechanics of running the session; the *taskmaster:* the member of the team assigned to direct the conference and keep the team from deviating from the previously agreed-on structure for analyzing the information being produced by the family, while ensuring an atmosphere conducive to creativity and spontaneity; and the *historian:* the person responsible for maintaining the threads of continuity across and within treatment sessions.

The supervisor can organize the team to accomplish any number of goals. One member could be asked to observe one member of the family or one relationship (e.g., father–child), or to track one theme, such as what happens in the family when feelings are introduced. Such assignments allow the supervisor to teach the importance of particular dynamics for progress in therapy. Furthermore, the supervisor can assign tasks to specific team members that represent their unique training goals; for instance, the team member who has a difficult time joining with children in counseling sessions can be asked to observe another supervisee's joining style with children. The team, therefore, offers not only the advantage of in-session assistance, but also numerous and rich possibilities for learning and postsession feedback.

The Reflecting Team

In his seminal work, Anderson (1987) describes a novel team approach to working with families. His *reflecting team* represents a way to demystify the team approach to therapy for the family. Rather than leaving the family to their conjectures when the therapist joins the team for consultation, Anderson proposes that light and sound be switched from the therapy room to the observation room, and that the family and therapist listen to the team reflect on what they have heard during the session to that point. Anderson suggests that the team's reflections could either be sought by the therapist (e.g., "I wonder if the team has any ideas that might be helpful at this point") or could be offered by the team (e.g., "We have some ideas that might be useful to your conversation").

By having the team's deliberations observed by the family, a certain egalitarianism is added to the live supervision model that seems to be an advantage in accomplishing therapeutic goals. Rather than receiving one central message delivered by a spokesperson for the team, the family is able to hear the deliberations themselves and draw from them as they wish. Reflections could represent competing—yet equally sound—alternatives that allow the family to reflect on others' impressions of their options. The input from the team, therefore, is far richer from the family's perspective.

For the team, the reflecting team model makes all deliberations public. Because there are no throwaway comments within this model, team members are more attentive as observers and more disciplined in their reflections. Guidelines for framing comments become more important than with confidential consultation breaks. Chang (2010) admonishes practitioners to stay faithful to Anderson's original intent of careful deliberations and offering diverse perspectives from which clients may choose, and not to allow the reflecting team to be diminished to simply a "technique."

Anderson suggests that three team members participate in the model (not counting the therapist who stays with the family); this way, a third person can react to the deliberations of the other two. If the team is larger than this, Anderson advises that additional members be observers, participating only if called on by the team. In addition, Anderson notes that persons may change rooms if it is not possible to reverse lights and sound within a facility. In the original discussion of reflecting teams, supervisees are mentioned only tangentially. Anderson states that supervisees are invited to participate as reflecting team members as they believe themselves to be ready, and most become increasingly active with experience.

Since Anderson's introduction of the reflecting team approach, the model has received attention as a supervision model (e.g., Chang, 2010; O'Connor, Davis, Meakes, Pickering, & Schuman, 2004; Roberts, 1997; Shilts, Rudes, & Madigan, 1993; Young et al., 1989). Young et al. offer a strong rationale for the reflecting team based on the disadvantages of the more standard live supervision team. According to Young et al., there are at least four disadvantages of nonreflecting teams:

1. Regardless of the espoused support of the team, the supervisee in the room filling the role of therapist feels anxious and on the spot, not only with the family, but also in relation to the observing team. By contrast, the reflecting team spreads out the spotlight. The therapist is no longer the sole representative of the team of experts. The experts can speak for themselves and may look no more impressive than the therapist.

2. Supervisees find it very difficult to disengage from the family, join the team in any meaningful way, and reengage with the family in the short time available for consultations. With the reflecting team, the therapist stays with the family, both physically and systemically. The therapist hears the team's thoughts as the family does, and is in a position to facilitate the family's response to the team's comments from the vantage point of a neutral position.

3. The message delivered back to the family in traditional team approaches is often construed under time pressures and with uneven contributions from team members. With the reflecting team, the reflections themselves become the intervention, and therefore need only develop as far as they can in the time allotted. The value is in the insightful musings themselves as team members attempt to view the family's situation from different angles. Also, because of the structure of the team, the likelihood that one member will dominate is greatly diminished.

4. Young et al. cite the relationship between clients and the team as a problem that the reflecting team addresses. In the more traditional model, the team becomes a cause for suspicion, "spies" from on high, persons of dubious motives. This apprehension is erased when clients hear the team members firsthand, not with slick interventions to transmit, but with their unrehearsed interactions on the family's behalf.

Despite Young et al.'s optimistic view, O'Connor et al. (2004) found some therapists and clients were overwhelmed by the amount of information generated by reflecting teams. Similarly, Chang (2010) recounts one client who reported that listening to the team's reflections was like "trying to drink from a fire hose" (p. 41). Therefore, it may be safe to say that reflecting teams that get overstimulated by therapy data may suffer from diminishing returns at some point in the reflection process.

Young et al. (1989) suggest the following guidelines for all comments made by reflecting team members:

1. *All remarks or comments are made in terms of positive connotations and genuine respect for family members.*
2. *Ideas and speculations are put in terms of the family's beliefs, not the team member's beliefs.*
3. *The team's beliefs about the family's beliefs are couched in "possibilities" or "maybes."*
4. *As a result, as many sides as can be seen of a situation are argued by different team members.*
5. *Team members should enjoy trust and respect for each other.* (p. 70)

Young et al. (1989) sought feedback from supervisors, supervisees, and clients about the use of the reflecting team. Supervisors expressed initial nervousness that team members would say negative and unhelpful things (as they had done in confidential team meetings). When this did not occur, they found themselves trusting the process more, and ultimately feeling liberated. Supervisees felt rudderless at the thought of the process, but found the experience itself to be affirming. Of 20 responses received from clients, 18 found the reflecting team to be either extremely or moderately helpful; the remaining 2 were unsure of their reactions. In a separate study of clients' reaction to the reflecting team, Smith, Yoshioka, and Winton (1993) found that clients also reacted positively to the reflecting team's ability to offer them multiple perspectives. They determined that these multiple perspectives were most helpful "when they contained dialectic tensions. Clients who are confronted with two or more credible explanations of the same event benefited from teams able to articulate the differences between positions and hence their dialectic" (p. 40).

In spite of the many strengths claimed about reflecting teams as a therapy model and method of supervision, some reasonable questions may be posed. Is the egalitarianism this model espouses an evolution of training and supervision (Hardy, 1993), or is it a model that fuses therapy and supervision to a point that supervision is compromised? Does the model diffuse individual contributions in its focus on the collective? Does the therapist lose the feeling of control over the outcome of therapy (Young et al., 1989)? Does the model produce too much information for the supervisee therapist to process with the family in the limited time available (Kruse & Leddick, 2005)? Chang (2010) makes three suggestions to counter the vulnerabilities of the reflective team format:

1. Teams should be encouraged to focus on common factors that enhance the outcomes of therapy, primarily the therapeutic alliance. The team's reflections are always secondary to the relationship between the therapist and the client.

2. Supervisors should ensure that clients are prepared for and comfortable with the reflecting team format.

3. Trainees should be instructed to focus on the postreflection portion of the therapy session, when the primary therapist and the client discuss the reflections. If clients do not feel heard by the team, one of the fundamental underpinnings of the reflecting team has been violated.

Team Dynamics

A team approach to live supervision involves some initial issues and complications not typically associated with other forms of supervision. Because the team is a group, the dynamics associated with groups must be addressed. Yet, this is often not the case, and issues including competition, power dynamics, conflict, and group roles go unaddressed by the supervisor (Clarke & Rowan, 2009; Fine, 2003). Fine also notes that clients can exacerbate group dynamics when reflections made by certain team members are not acknowledged or are openly rejected; or, by contrast, if particular team members are "sanctioned" when their reflections are chosen consistently by the client. It is important, therefore, to integrate an awareness of group dynamics into team discussions. Some authors (e.g., Roberts, 1997; Wendorf, 1984) stress the importance of group building prior to working as a team so that issues among group members are less likely to influence the direction and quality of therapy being offered.

In-Session (Midsession) Dynamics. The therapist's right to accept or reject the intervention (i.e., supervision) is a chronic supervisory issue and one that is exacerbated with a team. Unlike the situation with a solitary supervisor, for which a supervisee might be asked to carry out an intervention even though not totally committed to it, the dynamic is more complicated when a group of peers is primarily responsible for the intervention. Even if the supervisor is supportive of the team's direction, it is more important for the supervisee to be in agreement with the directive than it is when no team exists. If not, the therapist eventually feels manipulated by his or her peers, and team dynamics might eventually override the goal of providing sound therapy. This concern is supported by Mauzey and Erdman (1997), who found that directives initiated by the supervisor were received more favorably by supervisees than directives coming from team members.

Heath (1982) asserts that it is the supervisor's responsibility to choreograph the input from the team to the therapist and to be sure that the intervention is compatible with the therapist's style "unless the style has become part of the problem" (p. 192). Similar to Fine's (2003) position, Heath also acknowledges that prior to the in-session conference, the supervisor may be confronted with competitiveness among team members, an understandable phenomenon when the role of therapist is curtailed in favor of the team approach to therapy and training. As one matter of choreography, Fine advises that team members remain silent behind the mirror in order to enhance each member's individual creativity and minimize distraction. We also suggest that silence is a form of respect for clients and therapist while they are working.

A final issue in planning for midsession intervention is which and how many team members are allowed to formulate interventions for the therapist during the session. When consultation is the method used, this is less of an issue, especially if there is a designated taskmaster to translate the group discussion into an intervention. However, when directives are phoned in or the therapist is called into the consultation room to receive the directive rather than to confer with the team, are several members of the team allowed to be involved in the exchange, or only one? This may seem like a minor issue, but it is probably one of the most critical process issues for a team if relations between therapist and team are to remain intact and to avoid having the therapist become overwhelmed by a barrage of team opinion (O'Connor et al., 2004). Once again, it is up to the supervisor to monitor the activity level of the observation room and the readiness of individual team members to participate in a more direct fashion.

Pre- and Postsession Dynamics. Because of the complexity and intensity of team supervision during the therapy session, planning and debriefing sessions are vital. Liddle and Schwartz (1983) maintain that the presession conference should address family, supervisee, relationship, and teaching considerations. If the team goes into the session knowing fairly well what is to be accomplished with the family and what the supervisee will be working on personally, the during-session consultations should serve the function of "midcourse corrections to the general session plan" (p. 478). In addition, giving presession time to team dynamics, taking time to convey a respect for the position and perspective of the therapist, and addressing how this particular session reflects overall training goals prepare the team for the intensity and activity of team supervision.

The postsession conference is equally important. Regardless of the amount of planning that has occurred, team members, especially the therapist, have a need to debrief. Furthermore, Adams (1995) reports that supervisees ask their best questions during the postsession. Heath (1982) suggests that the supervisor allow the therapist to suggest a format for the discussion. In addition to a general discussion of the session, including a discussion of hypotheses and goals, the postsession should include some feedback to both the therapist and the team. Heath also maintains that emotional reactions on the part of different team members can be addressed appropriately if they enhance the process, but that criticism should be offered only if paired with alternative action. In a similar vein, Cade et al. (1986) state:

> *The therapist will often need time to "disengage" mentally and emotionally from the family before feeling able to consider what the team has to offer. The advantages of multiple perspectives can become a disadvantage if the therapist becomes swamped with ideas, particularly where these are conflicting ideas arising out of conflicting frameworks.* (pp. 112–113)

Once more immediate session issues have been processed, the supervisor should help the team address the session that just occurred as it fits in the larger context of training (Adams, 1995; Liddle & Schwartz, 1983; Lowe et al., 2008) and direct team members' thinking for the next scheduled presession. As stated earlier, if the supervisor is attempting to broaden the theoretical approaches of therapists-in-training, the postsession is the time for divergent input to be presented (Lowe et al., 2008).

Advantages and Disadvantages of Team Supervision

Advantages. We stated earlier that advocates of live supervision tend to be enthusiastic in their support; this is true of working with the team model of live supervision as well. Among the advantages enumerated are the following (Cade et al., 1986; Elizur, 1990; Fine, 2003; Hardy, 1993; Landis & Young, 1994; Lowe et al., 2008; Quinn, Atkinson, & Hood, 1985; Speed, Seligman, Kingston, & Cade, 1982; Sperling et al., 1986):

1. Teamwork appears to be highly satisfying. "Family therapy is always difficult, sometimes nerve-wracking and sometimes depressing; working in teams can be creative, highly supportive, challenging and very often fun" (Speed et al., 1982, p. 283).
2. When a crisis occurs within a case, the therapist can attend to the immediate needs of the client while the team wrestles with conceptual issues.
3. As with other forms of group supervision, the therapeutic team reinforces the value of case consultation. Because the team must brainstorm during the session, the criticism that live supervision is primarily a model for executive skill development is canceled.
4. The model requires that team members work on their feet, thus training them to arrive at therapeutic interventions more quickly.
5. The team model automatically multiplies the numbers of interesting cases with which each team member has the opportunity to work.
6. The team itself can be used to enhance therapeutic goals. For example, a team split can be

used as the intervention (Sperling et al., 1986). Using this intervention, the team is said to be in disagreement behind the mirror and sends in two opposing courses of action. This allows the therapist to stay in a neutral position and help the family look at alternatives while acknowledging that there is more than one valid way to proceed.

7. Because the team presents different cultural backgrounds, the therapy process is more likely to reflect a sensitivity to culture, as does training (Hardy, 1993).
8. A group of therapists is more likely to take greater risks and operate at a more creative level than is an individual therapist. For highly intransigent cases, if the client system is to improve, creative approaches to intervention are called for.
9. When the supervisor is clearly directing the team and the team is stuck, the supervisor must assess whether he or she is part of the problem (Elizur, 1990). As a result, supervisors are less insulated from their own blind spots, and team members benefit from realizing that challenge is part of therapy, regardless of the expertness of the therapist.

Disadvantages. Although the team model is intriguing and dynamic, certain disadvantages and pitfalls must be considered and avoided (Cade et al., 1986; Clarke & Rowan, 2009; Fine, 2003; Kruse & Leddick, 2005; O'Connor et al., 2004; Smith et al., 1998; Todd, 1997; Wendorf, Wendorf, & Bond, 1985):

1. Because of the intensity of the team's efforts, the team can become more involved in its own processes than what is transpiring in therapy.
2. It is very difficult for competitive team members to resist using the therapy sessions to prove their conceptual superiority. This not only means that team members are competing with each other instead of supporting each other, but also that sometimes interventions sent in to families are unduly complicated or clever, and not necessarily the most productive for accomplishing therapeutic goals.
3. Team supervision may not prepare therapists adequately for other, more common forms of supervision. Therefore, team supervision may inadvertently contribute to a difficult transition from a training to a practice setting.
4. Because of the high level of group cohesiveness that typically is associated with therapeutic teams, members can become overprotective and fail to challenge each other. For peer team groups, members might drop from the team, rather than pursue a different line of thinking.
5. Teams can produce too much information in a limited amount of time for the supervisee therapist or the family to assimilate in a productive manner.
6. If a team is a subunit of an agency or a training program, the members of the team can pose a threat to other staff members. "A mystique can develop around what a particular team is 'up to.' Other staff feel 'put down' or patronized when in discussion with team members who can somehow convey that they are in possession of 'the truth'" (Cade et al., 1986, pp. 114–115). At the very least, team members share a common experience not available to others, thus promoting an atmosphere of an *in group* and an *out group*.
7. For a team that has a long span of time to work together, there is a danger of the team becoming the "other family." We believe, as do Cade et al., that every group has a limited creative life span, at least without the impetus of new members or a change of context. Supervisors must be sensitive to systemic and developmental dynamics within teams as well as within client groups.
8. For some cases, the team approach is more intensive than is needed and may distort client dynamics through unnecessary scrutiny. One way to compensate for this pitfall is to vary one's approaches to supervision. We think the Quinn et al. (1985) "stuck-case clinic" is an excellent approach to team supervision. Rather than having the team consider all cases (and thereby running the risk of overkill for some

cases), each team member is charged with bringing his or her most difficult case to the team. As a result, the team's time is spent efficiently, and the risk of client distortion is diminished.

9. Finally, it seems to us that team supervision is as much a closed system as some other forms of supervision. By this, we mean that there is definitely some self-selection among those supervisors who choose team supervision as their method of choice. They might, for example, be somewhat more theatrical than other supervisors, or perhaps they enjoy therapy more than supervision. Whatever the reasons, training programs that wed themselves entirely to team supervision might be discriminating against some of their trainees unknowingly—trainees who are equally talented but more traditional in their approach to therapy. Supervisors should be challenged to vary their approaches to supervision, just as trainees are challenged to vary their approaches to therapy.

RESEARCH RESULTS AND QUESTIONS

Although live supervision has received adequate treatment in the training literature, especially in marriage and family therapy training literature, empirical work continues to be very modest. Because of the interface of therapy and supervision caused by live supervision models, many questions emerge. This section examines the extant research, as well as some questions that remain to be investigated.

Live supervision breaks many normative canons of psychotherapy having to do with privacy and the centrality of relationship to therapy; therefore, there has been a good deal of interest in the reaction of clients and supervisees to the model. Piercy, Sprenkle, and Constantine (1986) conducted a follow-up study of both groups and found that almost one third (32%) of trainees would have preferred no observers to their therapy, and family members report discomfort with the model in certain situations. Although comfort level was impeded, it is important to note that for these therapists and families, the outcome of therapy did not seem to be affected by their negative feelings. Liddle, Davidson, and Barrett (1988) found that novice supervisees were most sensitive to evaluation issues during live supervision, whereas more experienced therapists focused on power and control issues. Reactions of both groups, however, minimized with continued use of live supervision, a result supported by Wong's (1997) subsequent research.

Using hierarchical linear modeling, Bartle-Haring et al. (2010) asked whether live supervision over a six-session span made a difference to either supervisees or clients in terms of problem resolution. Supervisees reported that even one live supervision session during that time had a positive impact; however, clients did not report equal optimism. The authors wonder if live supervision is used for more difficult client cases, which may help to explain the disparity between therapist and client perceptions. However, without data regarding client difficulty, this speculation may be misleading.

The more common studies seeking client input while in therapy have been satisfaction studies. Locke and McCollum (2001) found that clients were satisfied with live supervision as long as perceived helpfulness outweighed perceived intrusiveness. Denton, Nakonezny, and Burwell (2011) question whether introducing the supervision team to a client in the first session would make them more satisfied with therapy. Using a mixed linear model of analysis of covariance, these authors found no significant difference between clients who met the team and those who did not. In fact, their results showed a trend toward lower satisfaction for clients who met the team, leaving the authors to conclude that it is important for therapists to leave this decision up to clients. Finally, Smith et al. (1993) conducted a qualitative study to determine client reactions to reflecting teams. Clients were asked about their reactions at three different times during therapy (i.e., fourth week, seventh week, and eighth week), and the questions became more sophisticated as the clients gained more experience with the model. The results indicated that clients had a reasonable grasp of the process, found much of the process to be beneficial, and were able to articulate some limitations (e.g., feeling overwhelmed by the additional team members, the team going off on its own tangent, the abruptness experienced when a session had some emotional content and the team interrupted). Interestingly, O'Connor et al.'s (2004) qualitative study tracking therapists' reactions to using reflecting teams revealed the same range of responses—that is, from exciting and challenging to overwhelming. One therapist in their study noted that, as an introvert, it was particularly difficult to use the team's insights without having an opportunity to process them. We are aware of no research that has attempted to investigate the fit for individuals having any particular personality characteristics with the use of different forms of live supervision.

Perhaps because of the labor intensity of live supervision, the relative frequency of the use of this method of supervision has received empirical attention (Carlozzi et al., 1997; Lee et al., 2004; Lewis & Rohrbaugh, 1989; McKenzie, Atkinson, Quinn, & Heath, 1986; Nichols et al., 1990). Although marriage and family therapy supervisors in particular often defend live supervision as the most productive form of supervision, its actual use has peaked and waned over the years. Lee et al. (2004) conducted a survey of American Association for Marriage and Family Therapy (AAMFT)–approved supervisors in 2001 that used the same methodology as studies conducted in 1976 and 1986. Although live supervision was only beginning to be used in 1976 (6 percent of the time), it rose to the most regularly used method by 1986 (26 percent of the time). However, as we noted earlier, the method has declined in its use since then, and in 2001 was the third most-frequently used method (15 percent of the time) after video recordings and process reports.

Carlozzi et al. (1997) tracked methods of supervision in Council for the Accreditation of Counseling and Related Educational Programs (CACREP)–accredited counseling programs and programs accredited by the Commission on Accreditation for Marriage and Family Therapy Education (COAMFTE). Programs with either accreditation relied most heavily on video recording review for supervision. Live supervision was the second most-frequent supervision modality for marriage and family therapy programs and the third most-frequent for CACREP programs. The difference between this study and that conducted by Lee et al. (2004) is easily explained by the populations studied. Lee et al. investigated supervision of supervisors who practiced both in the field and in training institutions, whereas Carlozzi et al. surveyed only accredited graduate training programs. Live supervision is a more realistic supervision modality for graduate programs than for clinical settings because of the presence of training facilities.

Taking a slightly different approach, Anderson et al. (2000) surveyed marriage and family therapists regarding the modality used for their best and worst supervision experiences. Similar to the frequency studies, video recordings and live supervision were most often referred to for best supervision experiences. Because of their frequency, they were also frequently referred to as the modality for worst supervision, although self-report led in this category. Therefore, it seems that modality per se is independent from the factors that determine whether supervision is viewed as exemplary or deficient.

As live supervision has become less novel to the mental health professions and as its overall tenability as a supervision modality has been established, there has been more interest in understanding the discrete contributions of different aspects of this supervision approach. Mauzey et al. (2000) investigated the power of delayed supervision, phone-ins, or the bug-in-the-ear to increase supervisee anxiety and anger. Their results indicate that modality was not correlated with these affective states; rather, having a predisposition to anxiety or anger was predictive of having these states increase during the initial stages of supervision.

We have already reported Frankel's (1990) and Frankel and Piercy's (1990) work that investigates types of supervisor directives and their different effects. Kivlighan et al. (1991) conducted a similar study that focused on supervisee intentions, rather than supervisor intentions. Supervisees in this study were learning an interpersonal–dynamic approach to individual psychotherapy. Kivlighan et al. were interested in the difference between supervisees exposed to live supervision versus those using video recording supervision. The dependent variable was the intention motivating each therapist response. Overall, the intentions for those in the live supervision treatment were consistent with the interpersonal approach to therapy (i.e., more support and relationship intentions); therefore, the authors conclude that the live supervision approach allows supervisees to learn more quickly. In addition to types of intentions, the authors hypothesize that live supervision leads to stronger working alliances with clients and to therapy sessions that were deeper and rougher (i.e., more uncomfortable and difficult) (Stiles, Shapiro, & Firth-Cozens, 1988). The working alliance was considered stronger by clients for the live supervision condition than for the video recording condition, and sessions were viewed as rougher. Sessions were not experienced as deeper, however, a characteristic typically associated with interpersonal–dynamic therapy.

Although Lee (1997) found that therapist cooperation increased when phone-ins were longer than 30 seconds, Moorhouse and Carr (1999) found that frequency of phone-ins seemed to be more important than length in relation to particular supervisor and therapist behaviors. Fewer phone-ins led to more collaboration between supervisor and therapist, and more cooperation (less resistance) from clients. (One assumes that a collaboration posture takes more than 30 seconds to establish, thus supporting Lee's earlier findings.) Moorhouse and Carr also found that fewer phone-ins led to a less collaborative interaction between therapist and client. Therefore, although clients cooperated with therapy goals, therapists did not engage them as often in collaborative discourse. A separate analysis of these same interactions (Moorhouse & Carr, 2001) found that isomorphism between supervisor and therapist (i.e., therapist using the same style with the client as had been used by the supervisor with the therapist) led to decreased client cooperation. Moorhouse and Carr's results raise interesting questions about the supervisory system and the relationships within it (i.e., therapist and supervisor, therapist and client, supervisor and client). Obviously, more research is required before we can come to any definitive conclusions concerning these important relationship matters.

Although the research base regarding live supervision is growing, it is still relatively small. There are many questions to be asked, including the following:

1. Thus far, most live supervision experiences and observations have been done with supervisees conducting family therapy. Although live supervision has become popular outside family therapy, we know very little about its utility across theoretical approaches (Bubenzer et al., 1991). The requisite interruptions of therapy when conducting live supervision may discourage levels of the interpersonal depth required of some therapies.
2. Some authors argue for an increased egalitarianism within live supervision (e.g., Hardy, 1993; Moorhouse & Carr, 1999; Woodside, 1994). The relationship between egalitarian supervision and the ability of the supervisor to evaluate supervisees must be measured.
3. There has been virtually no study of the generalizability or continuity of the therapist behaviors exhibited as a result of live supervision (Gallant et al., 1991; Kivlighan et al., 1991).
4. Hardy (1993) proposes that live supervision may change dramatically to reflect changes in our understanding of cultural variables, especially as they relate to power. To date, these variables have not been isolated within live supervision research.
5. Finally, with the exception that BITE is best used with more novice supervisees, the developmental level of the supervisee has received

little empirical attention within live supervision research. Especially in terms of team activity, the developmental needs and abilities of supervisees are unknown.

CONCLUSION

The use of live supervision represents a blending of skills training and the more contemplative forms of clinical supervision. Its primary advantage is the closing of the gap between the supervisee's experience and the supervisor's review of that experience; the assumed outcome of this advantage is accelerated learning and improved service to clients. The disadvantages of the model revolve around the time commitment required of the supervisor, the need for specific facilities, and the intrusion into the therapy relationship. Team approaches to live supervision offer additional training possibilities, as well as additional challenges and potential disadvantages. The reflecting team moves live supervision to a point down the supervision–consultation continuum that it may be viewed more accurately as live consultation (Lewis, 1988).

Live supervision has evolved from its identity as a family therapy training model exclusively to increased use within the other mental health professions (Carlozzi et al., 1997; Champe & Kleist, 2003; Heppner et al., 1994; Schroll & Walton, 1991). Empirical investigation of live supervision has commenced and shows promise of ultimately assisting clinical supervisors in determining the optimal conditions for the use of live supervision, as well as its most necessary components.

Evaluation

Evaluation

Evaluation could be viewed as the nucleus of clinical supervision. In fact, evaluation is a defining aspect of supervision. Supervisors direct and encourage, but also monitor, those who enter the helping professions. Many of the more direct methods for conducting clinical supervision have developed, in part, as a response to a need for better data for the evaluation process.

As central as it is to proper functioning of clinical supervision, many supervisors struggle with their responsibility to evaluate, at least occasionally. For novice supervisors, this responsibility is almost always a challenge, because it puts them juxtaposed (or so it feels) from where they sit. Whether an experienced a supervisor or someone new to the role, the struggle becomes more pronounced when overall competency of supervisees comes into question (Brear & Dorrian, 2010; Jacobs et al., 2011; Nelson, Barnes, Evans, & Triggiano, 2008). Because clinical supervisors were first trained as counselors or therapists, their values often lie within that domain. Therapists are taught to accept their clients' limitations and respect their clients' goals. Like good parents, good therapists learn to respect the boundary between clients' ambitions for themselves and therapists' ambitions for them. The good therapist is a facilitator of another's change, not a decision maker about what change is necessary.

Many of the working conditions within supervision reflect those for therapy or counseling. Yet there is an essential and paradigmatic difference: The supervisor might want to use the supervisee's progress as the critical criterion for evaluation, but responsibility to the profession and to the supervisee's future clients preclude this (referred to as the *gatekeeping function*). The supervisor is charged to evaluate the supervisee based on an established external set of criteria that must meet institutional as well as professional standards of practice (Fouad et al., 2009; Robiner, Fuhrman, Ristvedt, Bobbitt, & Schirvar, 1994).

An essential assumption underlying evaluation is that the criteria chosen or derived from professional standards reflect competent practice. Herein lies the first major obstacle in conducting sound evaluation. Robiner, Fuhrman, and Ristvedt (1993) describe *clinical competence* as a "moving target with an elusive criterion" (p. 5). Although there has been significant progress in identifying and assessing professional competence (e.g., Engels et al., 2010; Kaslow, Celano, & Stanton, 2005), the research continues to challenge the assumption that particular types of therapist knowledge, skill, or level of experience determine client outcome (e.g., Nyman, Nafziger, & Smith, 2010). Reviews of the outcome literature produced mixed results (e.g., Pinsof & Wynne, 1995; Shaw & Dobson, 1988), and some continue to support the notion that nonspecific factors such as the counselor's personal characteristics might be the more predictive of successful outcome with clients than specific knowledge or skill sets (Herman, 1993; Orlinsky, Grawe, & Parks, 1994; Shaw & Dobson, 1988). Because of this, helping professionals have not yet determined definitively the educational experiences that yield competent practitioners, nor have they developed performance measures that distinguish competent from incompetent practitioners reliably (Robiner et al., 1993).

In spite of our imperfect present position on the evolutionary path of the helping professions, there is evidence, even in the absence of conclusive data, that training and experience matter and that there are specific knowledge and skill sets that professionals must possess. Clinical supervisors, therefore, are responsible for monitoring supervisees' development of knowledge, skills, and professionalism. The helping professions continue to seek better research to indicate which aspects of training are especially important (e.g., Binder, 2004); in the meantime, it is safe to assume that supervisors will continue to evaluate supervisees based on their own interpretation of what is understood in their professional community to constitute acceptable standards of practice.

Given the consistent finding that personal characteristics of therapists are highly predictive of success (Herman, 1993; Jennings, Goh, Skovholt, Hanson, & Banerjee-Stevens, 2003; Sakinofsky, 1979), it may be of some comfort to clinical supervisors that the personal characteristics of supervisees and supervisors alike have always been considered relevant to supervision. However, these same personal characteristics often lead to some of the most difficult evaluation moments, as we review later (Elman & Forrest, 2007; Forrest, Elman, Gizara, & Vacha-Haase, 1999; Jacobs et al., 2011; Johnson, Elman, Forrest, Rodolfa, Schaffer, & Robiner, 2008; McAdams, Foster, & Ward, 2007; McCutcheon, 2008). Finally, this is a time when the call for more rigorous evaluations has increased as a result of legal accountability (e.g., McAdams et al., 2007). In summary, then, clinical supervisors must evaluate within present (and imperfect) professional guidelines; be sensitive to the importance of supervisees' personal characteristics, including cultural characteristics (Hansen et al., 2006; Forrest, Elman, & Shen-Miller, 2008, that interface with training; and remain cognizant of an increasingly litigious society. They often do this in the absence of any comprehensive understanding of what exactly contributed to their own competence, as either a counselor/practitioner or a supervisor. This combination of factors can lead to considerable dissonance when supervisors are required to evaluate. Supervisors have two choices for managing this dissonance: They can throw up their hands and minimize the function of evaluation in their supervision, or they can work to counteract their dissonance by thoughtful planning, structuring, intervening, and communicating. The rest of this chapter can be viewed as an outline of topics for consideration by those who choose to face evaluation responsibly and attend to its requirements to the best of their ability, even in light of imperfect or incomplete criteria, within a social context that exhibits greater demands for accountability.

The first step for the supervisor is to recognize a clear distinction between formative and summative evaluation. Robiner et al. (1993) describe *formative assessment* as the process of facilitating skill acquisition and professional growth through direct feedback. As such, they contend that formative evaluation causes little discomfort for clinical supervisors. This assumption does not necessarily hold when formative feedback is particularly challenging (Jacobs et al., 2011), discussed later. Still, it is probably accurate that formative evaluation does not necessarily feel like evaluation because it stresses the process and progress of professional competence, rather than outcome. Nevertheless, it is important to remember that there is an evaluative message in all supervision. When supervisors tell supervisees that an intervention was successful, they are evaluating. When supervisors say nothing, supervisees may decide that their performance was either exemplary or too awful to discuss. In other words, by virtue of the nature of the relationship, evaluation is a constant variable in supervision (Briggs & Miller, 2005). Some of the supervisor's evaluative comments are deliberately sent (encoded) by the supervisor to the supervisee; others are received (decoded) by the supervisee and may or may not be an accurate understanding of the supervisor's assessments, especially in light of individual and cultural differences. Because we are always communicating, an evaluative message can always be inferred.

Summative evaluation, however, is what many of us mean when we discuss evaluation, and it causes far more stress for both supervisors and supervisees. This is the "moment of truth," when the supervisor steps back, takes stock, and decides how the supervisee measures up. To do this, supervisors must be clear about the criteria against which they are measuring supervisees. Furthermore, the supervisee should possess the same yardstick.

In truth, summative evaluations are too often stressful. Because of lack of organization, lack of a clear set of standards, lack of a positive working relationship, or lack of good communication skills, summative evaluations are disappointing and occasionally surprising or highly distressing. This may be true not only for the supervisee, but for the supervisor as well. Robiner et al. (1993) postulate that the stress of summative evaluation may lead supervisors to view it defensively with disdain, "despite its central importance in the supervisory process" (p. 4). Because summative evaluations are those that influence major educational, regulatory, and administrative decisions, such disdain is highly problematic. The chief antidote to summative evaluation disdain is the amount of time and care invested in the formative evaluation process. However, before any evaluation begins, the difficult task of identifying criteria must be addressed.

CRITERIA FOR EVALUATION

Establishing criteria for evaluation is much easier said than done. As noted earlier, the science of the mental health professions does not yet offer the kind of specificity that lends itself to ease of assessment. Over time, a combination of research and practice has culminated in professional standards for all mental health professions. Standards for clinical practice are remarkably similar across these professions and include theoretical grounding, diagnostic assessment skills, skills in establishing a therapeutic relationship with clients, skills in attending to individual and cultural characteristics in an appropriate and sensitive manner, skills in establishing appropriate goals, and intervention skills to help clients reach these goals. Although this list is not exhaustive to each profession, it is relatively generic to them all.

Beginning at the turn of this century, there was a push to be more explicit regarding criteria. Building on earlier initiatives for the professional of psychology (e.g., Rodolfa, Bent, Eisman, Nelson, Rehm, & Ritchie, 2005), Fouad et al. (2009) developed a list of 15 competencies that encompassed 7 core *foundational* competencies (i.e., Professionalism, Reflective Practice/Self-Assessment/Self-Care, Scientific Knowledge and Methods, Relationships, Individual and Cultural Diversity, Ethical Legal Standards and Policy, and Interdisciplinary Systems) and 8 *functional* competencies (i.e., Assessment, Intervention, Consultation, Research/Evaluation, Supervision, Teaching, Management, and Advocacy). For each competency, they not only enumerated subcompetencies but also described how each should be understood at the point the supervisee was ready for practicum, ready for internship, and ready for entry to practice. In addition, the authors created rubrics with behavioral descriptors for each developmental level. Table 1 shows a description of one of the subcompetencies (skills) under the

TABLE 1 Subcompetency of "Skills" as Described by Fouad et al. (2009)

Readiness for Practicum	Readiness for Internship	Readiness for Entry to Practice
Essential Component: Basic helping skills Behavioral Anchor • Demonstrates helping skills, such as empathic listening and framing problems	Essential Component: Clinical skills Behavior Anchor • Develops rapport with most clients • Develops therapeutic relationships • Demonstrates appropriate judgment about when to consult supervisor	Essential Component: Independent intervention planning, including conceptualization and intervention planning specific to case and context Behavior Anchor • Develops rapport and relationships with wide variety of clients • Uses good judgment about unexpected issues, such as crises, use of supervision, and confrontation • Delivers intervention effectively

From Fouad et al. (2009). Competency benchmarks: A model for understanding and measuring competence in professional psychology across training levels. *Training and Education in Professional Psychology, 3*(4 Suppl), S5–S26, p. S19.

functional competency of intervention. (The complete list of subcompetencies under Intervention is as follows: A. Knowledge of interventions; B. Intervention planning; C. Skills; D. Intervention implementation; and E. Progress evaluation.)

Although no competency list is perfect or makes the responsibility of evaluation easy (DeMers, 2009), Fouad et al. (2009) offer a significant attempt to operationalize the assessment process. Readers are encouraged to consult this contribution to the professional literature as a model for their own identification and description of criteria that they intend to use for the purposes of evaluation.

Engels et al. (2010) attempt a similar effort to track competencies that parallel the CACREP Standards of the counseling profession. Chapters cover not only generic counseling competencies, but also those specific to distinct CACREP programs (e.g., clinical mental health counseling, school counseling). For each competency listed, performance guidelines are listed along with the relevant CACREP standard(s). The authors also suggest a 5-point Likert scale assessment on each competency from low to high performance.

Despite the efforts of Fouad et al. (2009), Engels et al. (2010), and others, most supervisors assert that it is difficult to operationalize all that is considered in clinical evaluation. Furthermore, although the deconstructions of competency that have been attempted may be exactly the kind of road map that some supervisees need, it may overwhelm or confuse others, at least at first. Individual learning styles veer toward either the concrete or the abstract, and it is up to supervisors to establish a working alliance within the constraints posed by each supervisee. It should also be noted that competencies inform supervisees *what* must be accomplished, but not *how*. Each element of the evaluation process, therefore, must be attended to with care. In short, as helpful as delineations of competencies are, as well as rubrics that track progress, their use is productive only when embedded in a positive supervisory relationship that is sensitive to individual differences of all sorts.

Beyond attending to individual learning styles, supervisors must also make decisions about prioritizing criteria within a particular timeframe (e.g., the first 5 weeks of internship). Although supervisees should always begin a supervision experience with a comprehensive list of evaluation criteria, supervisors may choose a developmental approach in addressing competencies. For example, a supervisor may give a novice supervisee the task of listening carefully and communicating culturally sensitive regard for the client as the first task in supervision. Theory may be "back-burnered" until these important tasks are accomplished. Another supervisor may find this approach anathema to what he or she believes is essential to becoming a competent and theoretically consistent therapist. Despite differences among supervisors, we must stress that supervisees are absolutely vulnerable if their supervisors have not spent some time thinking about how they believe competence is developed and translating this into some framework (which may include a list of competencies) and that takes the individual supervisee and the length of time available for supervision into account.

Finally, the supervision contract includes not only the supervisor's agenda (e.g., a list of required competencies to be mastered) but the supervisee's goals as well. Therefore, establishing criteria for the supervision experience is done in the context of one's profession, but also within the context of the relationship with the individual supervisee. As a result, the beginning of what will become the working alliance is centered on the topic of criteria for evaluation, providing the supervisor with ample opportunities to advance the working alliance or, if not prepared, to stall it.

FAVORABLE CONDITIONS FOR EVALUATION

A major problem with evaluation in the helping professions is that it hits so close to home. Because counseling and therapy draw heavily on interpersonal and intuitive abilities, it can be difficult for supervisees to draw a boundary between their performance as helping professionals and their worth as persons. For this reason, and because of the vulnerability accompanying any evaluation process, it is important that supervisors do all that is possible to create favorable conditions when evaluating. Favorable conditions not only make evaluation more palatable, but directly influence the overall outcome of supervision. As Ekstein and Wallerstein (1972) note, when the context of supervision is favorable, the supervisee stops asking, "How can I avoid criticism?" and starts asking, "How can I make the most of this supervision time?"

Several authors address the conditions that make evaluation a more positive experience. Several of these conditions also ensure that the evaluation process is conducted in an ethical manner. The following list of conditions draws on our own thoughts, as well as the work of others (Borders, Bernard, Dye, Fong, Henderson, & Nance, 1991; Briggs & Miller, 2005; Coffey, 2002; Ekstein & Wallerstein, 1972; Elman & Forrest, 2007; Forrest et al., 1999; Fox, 1983; Fried, Tiegs, & Bellamy, 1992; Jacobs et al., 2011; Kadushin, 1992a; Kaslow et al., 2007; Ladany, 2004; Ladany, Hill, Corbett, & Nutt, 1996; Lopez, 1997; Mathews, 1986; Murphy & Wright, 2005; Olson & Stern, 1990; Ramos-Sanchez et al., 2002):

1. Supervisors must remember that supervision is an unequal relationship. No amount of empathy erases the fact that supervisors' reactions to supervisees have consequences for them, some of which may be negative. Being sensitive to the position of the supervisee makes supervisors more compassionate evaluators.

2. Clarity adds to a positive context. Supervisors must state their administrative as well as their clinical roles clearly. Who is privy to the feedback that supervisors give supervisees? Will the supervisor be making decisions regarding the supervisee's continuation in a graduate program or job? If not, what is the supervisor's relationship to those persons who make these decisions? For example, most graduate programs conduct periodic student reviews, during which the evaluation by the clinical supervisor is often weighed more heavily than other evaluations. Students should be aware, at the very least, that their performance in the clinical component of the program will be discussed by the total faculty at some point in the future.

3. Supervisees' defensiveness should be addressed openly (Coffey, 2002; Costa, 1994). Supervision makes supervisees feel "naked," at least initially. It is natural, if not desirable, that they attempt to defend themselves. Supervisees differ in their coping styles, some exhibiting behaviors that are far more productive than others. Some deal with their feeling of defensiveness by "digging in deeper" and doing all that they can to get on the same page as the supervisor; others defend by trying to outguess the supervisor; still others appear vulnerable and helpless. The truth is that all supervisees are vulnerable, and supervisors must be sensitive to this fact and not hold their vulnerability against them.

Coffey (2002) suggests that supervisors take time at the outset of supervision to teach students how to receive corrective feedback. The source of defensive reactions and how they have served one in the past must be understood by supervisees so that they can process these reactions in light of the present situation. Coffey proposes that the use of awareness-enhancing exercises that focus on early experience with authority figures is well worth the time spent so that supervisees can understand their defensive reactions and process them when they occur; this puts them in a better position to determine the usefulness of the supervisor's corrective feedback.

4. Along with defensiveness, individual differences should be addressed openly. Evaluation may well be affected by differences of cultural background, gender, race, and so forth, particularly if these differences are not understood to be relevant to supervision (Forrest, Elman, & Shen-Miller, 2008). Furthermore, competence in therapy includes the ability to communicate in ways that are culturally flexible. The first cultural context to be addressed, therefore, is the supervision context.

5. Evaluation should be a mutual and continuous process. Beyond foundational competencies, the supervisee should be actively involved in determining what is to be learned (Briggs & Miller, 2005; Ladany, 2004; Lehrman-Waterman & Ladany, 2001). In a sense, the supervisor is there to serve the supervisee, and this contractual dimension should not get lost. Also, the formative aspect of evaluation should be the most active. Although both parties know that they will be taking stock down the road, the process of learning should not feel *pro forma*.

6. Evaluation must occur within a strong administrative structure. Whether in an educational or a work setting, supervisors must know that their evaluations will be taken seriously. Nothing is as frustrating and damaging as when a supervisor risks the consequences of a negative evaluation only to have this overturned by an administrator in the organization. When this happens, more often than not, one of two things has happened: Either due process was not followed, or the supervisor did not have a clear sense of administrative support beforehand—in other words, the supervisor assumed that he or she would be backed up without bothering to see if this was actually so, or the supervisor did not have the political savvy to inform his or her superiors prior to the evaluation, both to warn them and to make sure that the process would be supported. Whether the supervisor is correct in the evaluation can be a moot issue if the supervisee's rights were not protected—or appeared not to be protected—during the evaluation process. It is important that the system be perceived as trustworthy by both supervisor and supervisee. If the history of the system is that evaluation is arbitrary or capricious, supervisees will risk less and be more defensive overall in their interactions with supervisors.

Finally, it is as important that the supervisee be cognizant of a supportive structure, as for the supervisor. Supervisees must know that there is a place to go if they think an evaluation is unfair or incomplete. On university campuses, the grievance committee is usually the administrative body of choice once the head of the department has been consulted; in employment settings, the appropriate person is the supervisor's immediate superior. If there is no such protective body or person, it is up to the supervisor to establish some sort of safeguard for the supervisee (e.g., through a Professional Disclosure Statement that provides pertinent information in this regard). Supervision objectives are greatly handicapped if anyone in the system feels trapped.

7. Premature evaluations of supervisees should be avoided. Whether a supervisor is working with one supervisee or several, it is important to resist overreacting to either the person who shows unusual potential or the person who seems to be faltering. We are not implying that one should withhold feedback or be dishonest; rather, we believe that supervisors can react too quickly and, by evaluating too soon, do serious disservice to talented supervisees, as well as to those who need more grounding to begin their better work. If supervision occurs in a group, morale is hurt when it becomes obvious that early distinctions have been made among supervisees. On the contrary, when the group is challenged to ensure that everyone achieve competence, the atmosphere is energetic, supportive, and competitive in the best sense.

Some supervisees enter supervision expecting to be recognized and treated as stars. It is the supervisor, however, who makes such a designation happen (Murphy & Wright, 2005) by relying on initial impressions and forgetting that some counseling or therapy skills can only be assessed accurately over the long term. Whether a supervisee "wears well" is terribly important to that supervisee's future colleagues, supervisors, and clients. This cannot be determined in a few weeks, regardless of the strength of the supervisee's entry behavior or the intuitive abilities of the supervisor.

8. Supervisees must witness the professional development of their supervisors. As a supervisor, the best way to accomplish this goal is to invite feedback and use it. Supervisees feel empowered if they sense that they have something valuable to offer their supervisors. In addition, a supervisor's involvement and sharing of continuing-education activities models the need for development across the life span of one's career. For supervisors to present new ideas to which they have recently been exposed gives a much more accurate picture of professional growth than for them to play the part of the all-knowing guru. Also, presenting some tentativeness in thinking reminds the supervisor to be tentative about the work of supervisees. Supervisors must constantly remind themselves that they do not deal in a profession of facts, but of concepts; and that humility is an indicator of wisdom, not weakness (Nelson et al., 2008).

9. Supervisors must always keep an eye to the relationship, which influences all aspects of supervision (Barnett, 2007). Evaluation becomes especially difficult when the relationship has become too close or too distant. In fact, it is the reality of evaluation that behooves the supervisor to maintain both a positive and supportive relationship with the supervisee, yet one that is professional, not personal. If relationships are strained for whatever reason, supervisors must ask themselves if they can evaluate objectively enough. (No evaluation is totally objective; the goal is to keep objective standards in mind while considering subjective impressions.) This point was underscored by Ladany et al. (1996), who found that negative reactions to the supervisor, personal issues, clinical mistakes, and evaluation concerns were the top four categories of supervisee nondisclosures in supervision. A weak relationship between supervisor and supervisee, then, can cause the supervisee to withhold essential supervision information. Burkard et al. (2006) found that needed discussions about cultural differences did not take place when favorable conditions were not evident to the supervisee. In short, when supervisees are guarded because the supervision context feels unsafe, it is virtually impossible for the supervisor to get an accurate picture of the supervisee's strengths and areas for growth.

10. No one who does not enjoy supervising should supervise. For this final condition, we go back to the point we made at the beginning of this chapter: Evaluation is difficult, even for those supervisors who love the challenge of supervision. For the supervisor who is supervising for any lesser reason, evaluation may feel like too great a burden. When this is the case, the supervisor shortchanges the supervisee and gives perfunctory evaluations or avoids the task, especially if the evaluation could carry negative consequences. Supervisors always have many other responsibilities to use as rationalizations for keeping a supervisee at arm's length. It is not difficult to find helping professionals who can attest to the frustration of being supervised with unclear expectations, getting little or no constructive feedback, or receiving mostly negative feedback (Magnuson, Wilcoxon, & Norem, 2000; Ramos-Sanchez et al., 2002). It is little wonder that the absence of favorable conditions for evaluation have been found to compromise the working alliance between supervisor and supervisee (Ramos-Sanchez et al., 2002). Whenever a supervisee is denied appropriate supervision and evaluation, the professional community is diminished.

THE PROCESS OF EVALUATION

We discussed the important task of choosing criteria and made brief reference to using some sort of evaluation instrument to communicate a final assessment regarding the supervisee's level of competence. These, respectively, make up the beginning and the end of evaluation. *Process* defines how supervisors conduct supervision between these two markers and how they incorporate the issue of evaluation from the beginning of supervision to its completion. In other words, the process of evaluation is not separate from the process of clinical supervision, but is embedded within it. The evaluation process also includes the means by which supervisors obtain the data that they use to make their assessments. For our discussion here, the process of evaluation is considered to have six elements, most of which interact throughout the supervision experience:

1. Negotiating a supervision–evaluation contract
2. Choosing evaluation methods and supervision interventions
3. Choosing evaluation instrument(s)
4. Communicating formative feedback
5. Encouraging self-assessment
6. Conducting formal summative evaluation sessions

The Supervision–Evaluation Contract

When students register for a course, they receive a syllabus identifying requirements, course objectives, an outline of activities or topics to be discussed, and the instructor's plan for evaluation. Whether or not clinical experience is gained within a course structure, each supervisee should be provided with a plan that parallels a syllabus. Unlike most course syllabi, however, the supervision contract should include individualized components. Described as *goal-directed supervision,* Talen and Schindler (1993) assert that supervisee-initiated goals set the stage for a collaborative relationship with the supervisor. Similarly, Lehrman-Waterman and Ladany (2001) found that goal setting with supervisees was highly correlated with a positive supervisory working alliance and to overall supervisee satisfaction with supervision. Mead (1990) suggests that ample time be given during this process to considering discrepancies between the supervisee's goals and those set for the supervisee by the supervisor. Mead advises that some goals identified by the supervisee may be a residue from past experiences in supervision and may need thorough discussion and modification. This admonition is important in light of new initiatives to communicate required program competencies (e.g., Fouad et al., 2009) as the basis for supervision.

An initial focus on the supervision contract serves a purpose for new supervisees also in that it helps them to understand the difference between clinical supervision and other learning experiences. Although plans can vary, all supervision contracts should establish learning goals, describe criteria and competencies for evaluation, establish supervision methods that to be used, describe the length and frequency of supervision contacts, and establish how a summative evaluation will be achieved. The relationship of formative feedback to summative feedback should also be explained to the supervisee.

A working contract is not only relevant to the beginning of supervision. Rather, like the course syllabus referred to earlier, each supervision session should be of assistance to the supervisee in knowing how one is progressing. Therefore, each conference should begin with an update on progress toward the goals set at the beginning of the supervisory relationship (Briggs & Miller, 2005) and should end with a plan of action for attainment of the next level of skill development. To the extent possible, timelines should also be established for skill development.

A final note about the supervision contract, one confirmed by Talen and Schindler (1993), is the compatibility between this activity and the developmental needs of relatively inexperienced supervisees (Stoltenberg & McNeill, 2010). The structure offered through the process of establishing learning goals and referring to them in each supervision session supplies the supervisee with a concrete anchor to help weather the onslaught of clinical sessions that include many unknowns.

Choosing Supervision Methods for Evaluation

Each method of supervision—process notes, self-report, audio or video recordings of therapy sessions, or live supervision—influences evaluation differently. Some supervisors rely heavily on group supervision, and may even encourage some form of peer evaluation among supervisees. This approach provides markedly different information than that gathered from, for example, a review of video-recorded counseling sessions. When the ultimate responsibility to evaluate is in the forefront of the supervisor's awareness, however, the supervisor seeks supplemental data (if necessary) to arrive at a balanced evaluation.

Supervisees can be at a disadvantage when the form of supervision changes from one setting to the next. For example, Collins and Bogo (1986) observe that early training experiences (on campus) tend to use a good amount of technology, whereas field supervision is more likely to be based on self-reporting and case notes. Therefore, they found that supervision in the field was far more reflective in nature than that on campus, which focused more on skills and their development. Perhaps supervisors need not only to inform their students about the forms of supervision that they use, but also to educate them about the forms that they do not use and how to best take advantage of these alternate forms.

Of paramount importance is that supervisors realize that supervision methods have both instructional and evaluation consequences. A supervisor may favor one form of gathering supervision material (e.g., audio recording), but the supervisor must realize that each method is a lens through which to view the work of the supervisee. Some lenses provide a sharper image of one aspect of the supervisee's work, but on occasion, a wide angle may be desirable to allow the supervisor a different perspective from which to evaluate; therefore, multiple methods are the surest way to get an accurate picture of the supervisee's strengths and weaknesses (Harris, 1994).

Choosing Evaluation Instruments

Despite the advances made in articulating criteria within different mental health professions, we suspect that there are still nearly as many evaluation instruments as there are mental health training programs. Many—if not most—supervisors tend to develop and use Likert-type measures (or borrow such from others) for summative purposes. Depending on how well a measure reflects criteria and competencies that already have been selected and communicated by the supervisor (or negotiated between supervisor and supervisee), the measure may help supervisees appreciate their progress toward learning goals. When evaluation measures have not been integrated into the supervision experience, their use can be superficial or frustrating from the standpoint of the supervisee.

Although our focus in this section is primarily regarding instruments used for summative evaluation, many instruments were constructed for formative feedback and research, such as Olk and Friendlander's (1992) instrument to detect role ambiguity or role conflict in supervision, or Sodowsky, Taffe, Gutkin, and Wise's (1994) inventory of perceived multicultural competence, and afford excellent opportunities for important discussions within supervision.

A scientist–practitioner model calls for summative evaluation measures that are more than unvalidated and home-grown instruments, and yet, to date, most evaluation measures could be described this way. Gonsalvez and Freestone (2007) are critical of the lack of efforts to remedy the situation: "It appears that psychology has applied its considerable expertise in measurement and evaluation more assiduously to a wide array of other domains and disciplines, while neglecting what is arguably the most important component of its professional training" (p. 24). Despite this critical call to action, most evaluation measures of clinical practice continue to lack scientific rigor.

The most common summative evaluation instrument continues to use a Likert scale, perhaps with some open-ended questions as well. Because of the subsequent quantification of evaluations, supervisees may need some assistance in translating the feedback received. For example, the supervisor must decide what is adequate (numerically speaking) for supervisees to be assured that they are receiving a positive evaluation. In addition, it should be clear what level of performance is below standards and what level meets the highest standards. If a supervisee comes into supervision with superior ability in several areas, the Likert-scale ratings should reflect this. Some supervisors use scales differently, deciding that no supervisee should receive a score higher than a certain number (e.g., 5 out of a possible 7) until the supervisory experience is at least half complete. If this is the supervisor's policy, it is important that the supervisee know this. When the supervisor uses a scale in this way, however, the supervisor sidesteps the issue of competence level.

One trend in the development of more useful assessment instruments has been an increasing interest in the development of anchored rubrics (Hanna & Smith, 1998; Hatcher & Lassiter, 2007). Rubrics are an attempt to offer supervisees more information about their professional development and are often viewed favorably by accrediting bodies (e.g., National Council for Accreditation of Teacher Education [NCATE], 2008). Rubrics can be *generic,* in that the rubric can be used for all competencies to be evaluated. Table 2 depicts a generic rubric that describes the relative need for supervision around the (unidentified) skill or skill set, as well as the supervisee's mastery. Generic rubrics add professional language to what otherwise might simply be communicated as "average" or "good." A supervisee is more likely to benefit from knowing that his or her development requires less oversight from the supervisor, or that the supervisee is using the skill, but still with a degree of self-consciousness.

A second kind of rubric is more time consuming to develop but also communicates more information to the supervisee. As is demonstrated in Table 3, this type of rubric deconstructs a particular skill or skill set and attempts to describe more explicitly where the supervisee is performing along a continuum. Because skill-specific rubrics are much more labor intensive for the supervisor, we suggest they be used only when supervisees are struggling around a specific learning goal. In such a case, a clear description of what level of skill is not acceptable for advancement, and a clear description of acceptable behaviors might prove invaluable for a struggling supervisee.

Finally, and congruent with a scientist–practitioner posture, supervisors may seek client input or client outcome data for the sake of formative or summative evaluation of supervisees (Frey, Beesley, & Liang, 2009; Galassi & Brooks,

TABLE 2 Generic Rubric

Rate the supervisee on the competencies described in the supervision contract using this 5-point scale.	
Level 1	Performs inadequately on this skill/skill set. Needs close supervision. Does not appear to have acquired requisite ability to demonstrate this skill/skill set.
Level 2	Performs skill/skill set only in most rudimentary fashion. Needs close supervision. Shows little ability to integrate this skill/skill set with other skills.
Level 3	Performs skill/skill set adequately, although somewhat self-consciously. Has begun to integrate skill/skill set with other skills. Will benefit from continued supervision.
Level 4	Performs skill/skill set with competence. Is comfortable using skill/skill set and can integrate it with other skills to arrive at a more complex approach to counseling. Is able to articulate when supervision is needed regarding this skill/skill set.
Level 5	Demonstrates mastery of this skill/skill set. Is proficient without benefit of supervision; seeks consultation when appropriate.

1992; Reese et al., 2009). As instruments become increasingly validated (e.g., Frey et al., 2009), client input becomes an additional training resource. Reese et al. (2009) found that when comparing trainees who received constant client feedback over a one-year period with a similar group of trainees in the no-feedback condition, those receiving feedback had twice the rate of improved client outcomes. In addition, the authors note that such specific feedback given to both trainees and their supervisors was considered to be a key ingredient in effective supervision.

The choices are expanding for clinical supervisors when selecting evaluation instruments. What each supervisor must determine is whether a particular instrument is consistent with the supervisor's criteria; when and how to introduce the instrument to the supervisee; whether the instruments will be used for formative purposes exclusively, or for both formative and summative

TABLE 3 Rubric for Participation in the Supervision Process

UNACCEPTABLE	ACCEPTABLE	EXEMPLARY
• Is not forthcoming in supervision • Does not plan for supervision sessions • Does not follow-up on agreed-on supervision suggestions • Does not provide recordings of counseling for the purposes of supervision • Is not engaged with supervisor, even when supervisor is supportive • Does not appear to hear or assimilate supervisor input	• Comes to supervision with recordings of counseling sessions • Is prepared to ask questions of supervisor about his or her counseling • Discusses the outcome of attempts to use supervisory suggestions • Is attentive in supervision and willing to discuss areas of concern. • Is realistic about what is being done well and what needs improvement	• Comes to supervision with recordings cued at a particularly fruitful place for discussion • Is prepared to share outcome of using agreed-on supervision suggestions, and can reflect about success or lack of success • Is engaged in supervision and communicates a willingness to be challenged • Is realistic about what is being done well; seeks input to improve performance

assessment; and how to use a summative instrument as an evaluation intervention, rather than simply a completed form to be filed and forgotten.

Communicating Formative Feedback

When supervisees reflect on their supervision, what comes to mind most often is the quality and quantity of the feedback that they received. Giving feedback is a central activity of clinical supervision and the core of evaluation (Barnett, Cornish, Goodyear, & Lichtenberg, 2007; Hahn & Molnar, 1991). Curiously, researchers have given relatively little specific attention to feedback within supervision; one of the first studies to address the issue was that of Friedlander, Siegel, and Brenock (1989), who define *feedback* as a process in which the supervisor verbally shares thoughts and assessment of the supervisee's progress, either explicitly or implicitly. For their study, they did not include questions or nonevaluative observations as feedback. Trained raters examined each speaking turn of one supervisor across nine supervision sessions with one supervisee to determine the presence or absence of feedback. They identified only 14 speaking turns as containing feedback; 8 speaking turns occurred in the final 2 feedback sessions; sessions 3, 4, and 6 had no feedback whatsoever.

The Friedlander et al. (1989) study is an intensive case study; therefore, the results might be idiosyncratic to the particular dyad studied and might not apply to supervision in general. However, Hoffman, Hill, Holmes, and Freitas (2005) also found that giving feedback can be difficult for supervisors when they interviewed 15 supervisors of predoctoral psychology interns and found varying levels of directness, especially if the feedback was perceived as being difficult to deliver or if the situation was a difficult one in which supervisors admitted that they refrained from offering feedback. In general, it seemed that feedback delivered easily had to do with supervisees' work with their clients. Feedback considered more challenging to deliver addressed issues either more personal to the supervisee or about the relationship between the supervisor and the supervisee. Not surprisingly, Hoffman and colleagues (2005) found that conditions such as supervisee openness, a strong positive relationship, a clear need for feedback, and the supervisor feeling competent to impart the feedback worked to facilitate the delivery of feedback. Supervisors reported that timing was also important to them in delivering feedback, as was outside support if difficult feedback was not received well. When asked if they would change anything if they could start the process over, none of the supervisors interviewed stated that they would give less feedback; rather, some supervisors reported that they would operate as they had, whereas others noted that they would give feedback sooner, more directly, and more often regarding supervisees' personal issues.

Phelps, Burkard, Knox, Clarke, and Inman (2009) address the issue of delivering difficult feedback to culturally different supervisees in their qualitative study. Focusing on the issue of racial differences, these authors found that European American supervisors (EASR) tended to express concern to their supervisees about their interpersonal style, whereas supervisors of color (SRC) expressed concern to their supervisees about their lack of understanding of cultural issues. Interestingly, EASRs reported more productive supervision outcomes than SRCs. Therefore, this study could be interpreted as offering support for the assumption that cultural conversations are a challenge in supervision, especially within the context of evaluation.

In light of the challenge in giving and receiving critical feedback, Sobell, Manor, Sobell, and Dum (2008) introduce the use of written self-critiques of audio-recorded sessions for clinical psychology trainees prior to meetings with supervisors as a strategy for minimizing trainee resistance to constructive feedback. The critiques were based on motivational interviewing principles (Miller & Rollnick, 2002) and given a positive assessment by trainees as helping them accept critical feedback from supervisors.

Ironically, as difficult as supervisors find it to deliver critical feedback, other researchers report that supervisees believe they receive far too little feedback (Kadushin, 1992b), and that the lack of feedback negatively affects their feelings about the value of the supervision they received (cf. Ladany, 2004; Lehrman-Waterman & Ladany, 2001; Magnuson, Wilcoxon, & Norem, 2000). In fact, rather than perceiving the delivery of feedback as being detrimental to the supervisory relationship, Lehrman-Waterman and Ladany recommend that supervisors engage in increased goal setting and feedback if they believe their relationship with a supervisee is troubled. Feedback, then, is viewed by these researchers as a corrective measure to put the supervisory relationship back on good footing. Sapyta, Riemer, and Bickman (2005) stress that, in the long run, the key is for feedback, whether positive or negative, be accurate.

The feedback described thus far relies primarily on a linear model, originating from the supervisor to the supervisee. There is also what Claiborn and Lichtenberg (1989) refer to as *interactional feedback,* which allows us to think of feedback as ongoing and constant between the supervisor and the supervisee. Two premises are basic to understanding the interactional or systemic perspective: first, you cannot *not* communicate. This premise was suggested as an axiom of communication by Watzlawick, Beavin, and Jackson (1967). Therefore, offering the supervisee no feedback is likely to be understood by the supervisee to mean *something*, such as, "You're doing fine," or perhaps even, "I don't have time to pull my thoughts together to give you cohesive feedback."

The second premise essential to understanding the interactional perspective is that any communication to another person contains both a message about the relationship between the two parties and a message about some particular content (Watzlawick et al., 1967). For example, within the context of supervision, the content may be about a particular difficult moment in the supervisee's session with a client; the message about the relationship, however, might be, "I enjoy working with you," or, "This relationship is very tenuous." If the feedback about the relationship is negative or more pronounced than the content, it might be more difficult for the supervisee to hear the content in the way that the supervisor would like. Similarly, the message back from the supervisee might be, "I find your feedback very useful," as well as, "I am too intimidated by you to ever tell you otherwise" (the second message being nonverbalized). If cultural differences are pronounced between supervisor and supervisee, dissonance within the relationship may complicate feedback even more. For these reasons, the relationship between supervisor and supervisees receives quite a bit of attention in the professional literature. Finally, it is imperative to remember that the supervisor is not only delivering both levels of feedback, but is also receiving (and reacting to) both levels. The idea of supervisor feedback, therefore, is deceptively simple when compared to the actual interactive process.

There are instances when supervisor and supervisee do not see eye to eye. Ratliff, Wampler, and Morris (2000) studied communication styles using a qualitative design when there was a lack of consensus between supervisor and supervisee. Their findings suggest that supervisors tend to be subtle more often than not in attempting to direct supervisees toward their own position. At the same time, they found that supervisors engaged in a progression of supervision strategies, from low confrontation (e.g., asking leading questions) to high confrontation (e.g., giving explicit direction), when lack of consensus about the direction of therapy emerged. In their discussion, these authors raise the issue of increased autonomy (i.e., accurate self-evaluation) among supervisees as an important goal of supervision. They suggest that supervisors consider the negative consequences when consensus is the goal, especially if they rely on confrontational strategies to accomplish consensus, potentially leading to heightened supervisee dependency in the process.

Despite an acknowledgment that supervision includes give and take, convergence of thinking, and occasional divergence, most supervisors conceptualize feedback per se as communicating to the supervisee an assessment of particular behaviors as either on or off target, as either progressing toward or diverging from competence. The clarity of supervisors' communications for this purpose is of paramount importance. Each message affirms, encourages, challenges, discourages, confuses, or angers a supervisee. If the metamessage is different from the stated message, the result is unclear communication. The most serious communication problem is when the message is dishonest, either intentionally or unintentionally. This typically occurs when the supervisor does not want to deal with the fact that the supervisee is not meeting expectations. As a result, the supervisor is not prepared to address the critical issues at hand (Hoffman et al., 2005; Magnuson et al., 2000).

Several authors offer suggestions for giving formative feedback, including feedback that is critical or corrective in nature (Abbott & Lyter, 1998; Borders, 2006; Borders & Brown, 2005; Chur-Hansen & McLean, 2006; Hawkins & Shohet, 1989; Heckman-Stone, 2003; Jacobs et al., 2011; Lehrman-Waterman & Ladany, 2001; Munson, 2002; Poertner, 1986; Sapyta et al., 2005). Drawing from these various sources as well as our own experience, we have compiled the following:

- Feedback should be based on learning goals (competencies) negotiated between the supervisor and the supervisee or, at the very least, are already established, and communicated to the supervisee early in the supervision experience (Falender, Collins, & Shafranske, 2009).
- Feedback should be offered regularly and, as much as possible, should be based on direct samples of the supervisee's work (Newman, 2010).
- Feedback should be balanced between support/reinforcement and challenge/criticism, because over time, either extreme is eventually rejected by supervisees as disappointing supervision (Gross, 2005).
- Especially when feedback is corrective, it should be timely, specific, nonjudgmental, behaviorally based, and should offer the supervisee direction in how to improve.
- Feedback should address learning goals (competencies) that the supervisee can achieve.
- Because communication is, in part, culturally determined, supervisors should use listening skills to conclude if feedback was received as intended.
- Feedback should be owned by the supervisor as professional perception, not fact or truth. Supervisors must model self-critique, flexibility, and brainstorming in conjunction with formative feedback.
- Supervisors must understand that supervisees want honest feedback, yet are fearful of it.
- The acceptance of feedback is integrally related to the level of trust the supervisee has for the supervisor. Supervisees must trust that formative feedback has a different purpose than summative feedback.
- Feedback should be a two-way street. Supervisors should seek feedback concerning their approach to supervision, and be open to altering their style based on the feedback.
- Feedback should be direct and clear, but never biased, hurtful, threatening, or humiliating.

To help supervisors remember some essential aspect of good formative feedback, Hawkins and Shohet (1989) suggest the use of the mnemonic CORBS, which stands for Clear, Owned, Regular, Balanced, and Specific. It is worthwhile for supervisors to develop a rubric for themselves and assess the quality of their feedback occasionally. This is best accomplished by recording supervision sessions for review.

Encouraging Self-Assessment

An important aspect of supervision is assisting supervisees in the evaluation of their own work (Bernstein & Lecomte, 1979; Borders et al., 1991; Borders & Brown, 2005; Falender et al., 2004; Munson, 2002; Perlesz, Stolk, & Firestone, 1990; Sobell et al., 2008). In a related study, Rønnestad and Skovholt (2003) found that a commitment to ongoing self-reflection is a skill that characterizes good therapists at all points across the professional life span. Kadushin (1992a) asserts the importance of supervisee self-assessment, and notes that supervisory evaluation, in and of itself, makes learning conspicuous to the supervisee and helps set a pattern of self-evaluation. From their seminal psychodynamic text, Ekstein and Wallerstein (1972) are more cautious about the notion of self-evaluation, reminding the supervisor that asking supervisees to self-evaluate stimulates all their past experiences of being selected, rejected, praised, and so on. We challenge the thoughts of Ekstein and Wallerstein in that self-evaluation, we believe, takes away some of the parent-like authority from the supervisor, rather than adding to it. If negative feelings are going to be experienced as a result of evaluation, those feelings are there regardless of whether the supervisee is given an opportunity to contribute to the assessment.

Although the idea of supervisee self-assessment is intuitively appealing and generally endorsed by the professional literature, research has produced mixed results about the ability of the supervisee to engage in self-assessment productively. We review key research on the topic and end this section with recommendations.

An early study by Dowling (1984) found evidence that graduate student supervisees were both accurate self-evaluators and good peer evaluators, a finding consistent with Hillerbrand's (1989) observation. Dennin and Ellis (2003) found mixed results when using self-supervision with four doctoral students to increase distinct skill sets. Although self-supervision appears to have some effect in increasing the students' use of metaphor in counseling, it does not significantly increase the use of empathy. Dennin and Ellis conclude that their research did not support some of the robust effects claimed in the literature regarding self-assessment and self-supervision, and suggest that current literature regarding self-supervision is overly simplistic because mediating variables, such as supervisee developmental level and skill level, are not typically addressed. They conclude that, especially for neophyte supervisees, any use of self-assessment should be paired with feedback from a more advanced supervisor. Indeed, it seems that self-assessment is best perceived as a skill to be developed under supervision (Barnes, 2004) rather than some parallel evaluation activity.

Although the research to date is limited, there is some evidence that supervisors influence the development of their supervisees' self-assessment skills based on distinct factors. Steward, Breland, and Neil (2001) studied supervisee self-evaluation, including *self-efficacy,* defined as counselors knowing what to do and having judgments about their capabilities to respond effectively to upcoming counseling situations. In a study that reports results that initially appear to be counterintuitive, Steward et al. found that accurate self-evaluation on the part of supervisees was negatively associated with supervisor attractiveness. In other words, the more friendly, flexible, supportive, open, positive, and warm the supervisor, the less accurate the novice supervisee's self-evaluation. These authors note that, in general, supervisees tend to underestimate their abilities, and that supervisor attractiveness may reinforce this tendency. Finding one's supervisor as less attractive may stimulate the supervisee's own determination to monitor one's own work, thus resulting in making more accurate self-assessments. Steward et al. do not suggest that supervisors aspire to be unattractive to their supervisees; however, they do state that their study may underscore the importance of supervisors engaging in both supportive and challenging interventions. Steward et al. speculate that consistently supportive supervisors might not expect their supervisees to move beyond their comfort zones. This may, in turn, have negative implications for training, resulting in supervisees whose self-confidence, self-efficacy, and sense of accomplishment are reduced.

In another study with seemingly contradictory results, Daniels and Larson (2001) found that performance feedback from the supervisor influenced supervisee self-efficacy and anxiety in the directions expected (i.e., positive feedback increased self-efficacy and lowered anxiety, whereas negative feedback had the opposite effect). However, unlike the Steward et al. (2001) study, Daniels and Larson used bogus feedback to manipulate supervisee reactions. They caution that their negative feedback in particular may have been too extreme; at the same time, the authors note that the degree of anxiety that a supervisee presents in supervision should modify a supervisor's behavior. In other words, the balance between support and challenge must be tailored for each supervisee to arrive at optimal results.

Finally, as noted earlier, Sobell et al. (2008) found self-critique to lead to more supervisee openness to supervisor critical feedback: "Having supervisees identify their own performance deficiencies prior to their supervisor's evaluation is intended to minimize resistance from trainees" (p. 152). Their goal in incorporating supervisee self-critique into their supervision with clinical psychology trainees, therefore, was to form an alliance with them in tackling target behaviors that needed attention.

Based on limited empirical work on the topic and paired with consistent calls for the practice of self-assessment, we offer the following guidelines:

1. Self-assessment is best viewed as a developmental issue for supervisees rather than a parallel process of evaluation. Supervisees have been known to either over- or underestimate their abilities (Barnes, 2004), either of which can have negative consequences for supervisee development and for client care. Therefore, making self-assessment a goal of supervision rather than an activity for evaluation seems a reasonable approach.

There are several highly productive ways that the supervisee can be involved in self-assessment. The most obvious is for the supervisor to communicate an expectation that the supervisee will do some sort of self-assessment prior to each supervision session. It has been our experience that unless the supervisor follows through on this expectation, however, most supervisees falter in their intentions to self-assess.

A useful self-evaluating activity is to ask the supervisee to review a segment of a counseling session in greater depth periodically for response patterns (Collins & Bogo, 1986; Sobell et al., 2008). If the supervisee can identify nonproductive patterns, this exercise can be instrumental in breaking bad habits.

2. To the extent possible, the supervisor might share how he or she arrives at assessments of the supervisee. This should be done regularly. It is one thing to say, "You're not attending to the client's affect." It is another thing to say, "When I'm assessing a session, I listen for important affect and whether the counselor picks up on it. I thought your client expressed important feelings twice during the session—when he said he felt overwhelmed by life, and when he said that he was disgusted with his son. While you've told me that you reacted to each of these statements internally, you didn't express to your client that you heard him. So, I'd assess the skill of attending to client affect as needing to be improved." The supervisor should be equally explicit when a skill of the supervisee has been assessed positively.

3. Self-assessment should never be a "test." In other words, like other skills that are viewed developmentally, self-assessment should be monitored as a series of approximations toward a goal, not in a dichotomous right/wrong fashion. For this reason, it is perhaps unwise to ask supervisees to complete evaluation forms of their skills using Likert scales. Instead, a supervisor might ask the supervisee to choose items on a form to identify areas in which they are having difficulty self-assessing. This moves the discussion to the area for assessment and the issues making self-assessment difficult, rather than setting up a tug-of-war between the supervisee and the supervisor regarding a particular skill.

4. At the time for summative evaluation, evaluate self-assessment as a skill set rather than asking the supervisee to prepare an alternative final self-evaluation. This method complements the approach to self-assessment throughout the supervisory experience.

In summary, the rationale for emphasizing self-assessment within supervision is that it ultimately may have utility beyond the formal training context, meaning that part of the responsibility of clinical supervisors is to assist supervisees in establishing a habit of self-scrutiny that will follow them into their professional careers. Although supervision is always warranted in the early years of practice, it is not always forthcoming—at least not always at an optimal level. Even though our knowledge about self-assessment is modest, it makes intuitive sense to include self-assessment as part of clinical supervision.

Communicating Summative Evaluations

Although the word *summative* might imply a single final evaluation, summative evaluations usually occur at least twice during a typical supervisory relationship. In academic settings, there is usually a midsemester and a final summative evaluation. For off-campus externships, internships, and work settings, the summative evaluations are typically given at the halfway mark and at the end or as annual reviews, respectively. If all has gone well within supervision, a summative review should contain no surprises for the supervisee—the summative review should be the culmination of evaluation, not the beginning of it. If there is more than one summative review, the initial review is perhaps the more important, because it is at this point that the supervisor learns if the supervisee understood the implications of formative assessments. If so, the summative evaluation provides an opportunity to take stock and plan a productive sequel to the supervision that has transpired to this point—a second supervision contract, so to speak. If formative assessment has been resisted by the supervisee, the first summative evaluation must be specific regarding the progress required for the supervisee to remain in good standing, and must be conducted early enough for the supervisee to have a reasonable opportunity to achieve success. In all cases, summative evaluations should be conducted face to face, and should also be put in writing (Belar, Bieliauskas, Klepac, Larsen, Stigall, & Zimet, 1993).

Even when a correct process has been established for summative evaluations, their ultimate success depends in large part on the communication skill of the supervisor. Unfortunately, supervisor training often gives short shrift to the process of conducting summative evaluation sessions (Jacobs et al., 2011). What follows are two segments taken from actual summative evaluation conferences conducted by supervisors-in-training with counselors-in-training. In each case, both supervisor and counselor are female. In the first segment, the pair begins by reviewing the Evaluation of Counselor Behaviors—Revised form (Bernard, 1997) completed by the supervisor prior to the session. The person referred to as Dr. P. is the counselor's faculty instructor.

S: Uh, I'd put this more here, I think, and more here . . . . And I think, you know, again, I did this here. I may go back and circle . . . if you see anything that you don't agree with, just go ahead and question it. I think you know how I look at it. I see you just having started to work.

C: Oh, I . . .

S: You know, you may not like that. I just think since that one big leap, when you started to consciously try to do things differently . . .

C: I can't even visualize ten years down the line having you say that everything is excellent. I don't know. To me, you're asking for close to perfection.

S: It would be hard for me to get there (*laughs*). I wouldn't want to be evaluated.

C: So much that comes to me comes through experience.

S: Yeah. I suppose, you know, maybe it's the teacher part of me . . . whenever I see the word "always" (*referring to the evaluation form*), I just can't . . . we're in trouble.

C: Yeah.

S: Even for me (*laughs*).

C: I understand. You know, as I look at this, it looks like a positive evaluation because of what you've said so far.

S: Um, well, you have a lot of twos and ones, but "good" to me is good. Letter-grade wise, I don't know. I can't tell you. Part of me says, because of what's gone on the whole semester, you know, and part of me says, "Okay. What are you doing now?" So, you know, I don't assign grades. It won't be an A. I'm not too sure. I'd say probably a C plus to B minus in that area.

C: But there are no pluses or minuses in the grading schedule.

S: That's right.

C: To me, a C is a failure and I'm assuming that you are not . . .

S: I don't think I look at it as a failure. I think that maybe, you know, when you do course work and things like that, maybe you could look at it that way. But I don't look at it as a failure because failure is an F.

C: Um hum.

S: If I were to have to assess a grade by skill level, it probably would be close to a C/D. But in looking from the beginning, you know, you've come a long way. But that isn't for me to assess. That's for Dr. P. to assess and I don't know how he will do it. I definitely think that there has been a lot of improvement.

C: And to me, it seems like it's been such a short time.

S: Yes, a very short time.

It is not difficult to see that there are several communication problems in this example. Actually, four things contribute to the ambiguity presented here: (a) The supervisor's personal style of communication is clouded. She does not finish many of her statements. She is not crisp. She would do well to practice the delivery of her feedback for clarity. (b) The process is ambiguous. Either Dr. P. has not been clear regarding procedures, or neither supervisor nor counselor has attended to these details. The result is that the supervisor does not seem to know her role in the evaluation process. Another possibility is that, because of her discomfort, she is playing down her role and referring the counselor to Dr. P. for the difficult task of final evaluation. From the conversation as it stands, we cannot know which of these is the case. (c) Criteria for evaluation also seem to be ambiguous to the supervisor. She vacillates from references to skill level and references to progress. It is obvious that she is not clear about how Dr. P. will weigh each of these two factors. (d) The supervisor seems to be uncomfortable with the responsibility of evaluation, especially in this case, where the practicum seems to be ending on a down note. We do not know if the supervisor has not prepared adequately for this conference or whether any amount of preparation would have countered her personal discomfort. The result is a series of mixed messages:

1. "You're not a very good counselor."/"'C' isn't a bad grade."
2. "You've come a long way."/"You still aren't very good."
3. "I'm trying to be fair."/"I wouldn't want to be in your shoes."
4. "I'm recommending between a C plus and a B minus."/"I don't assign grades."

It is clear that this evaluation is happening within the context of a weak working alliance. Specifically, there is no relationship bond apparent; in fact, the supervisor often appears insensitive and glib. In addition, there is no sense that formative evaluation has led to an understanding of clear and mutually agreed-on goals that are being used as the yardstick for the summative meeting.

In our second summative session from a different training program, the supervisor and counselor have had a better working relationship. Also, we can assume that organizational matters have been better handled so that the summative discussion is about the learning that has occurred within supervision, not how grades are assigned.

S: In getting ready for our meeting today, I've been thinking about how you've progressed and our working relationship over this period of time.

C: Oh, yes, I am going to miss you! I was wishing today wasn't our last day.

S: You know, it's such a parallel experience. Much like what you've been doing with your clients and how you've been feeling the impact of ending those relationships, it's really hard to end things here as well. I feel like I've gotten to know you really well, and have felt really lucky to be a part of your growth this semester.

C: Oh, thank you! Me too. It has been a really great experience.

S: I wondered if you might be willing to start by giving yourself some feedback on your progress this semester.

C: I'd say that I was able to be creative and willing to try new things. I really feel like I took the time to get to know each client and to understand who they were, and that helped build our relationship. I feel like I formed good therapeutic relationships with all the clients I worked with.

S: I echo what you are saying. Something that really stands out about you is how flexible you are with your clients. I've noticed that when you have ideas of something that might work for a client and you find that it doesn't, you are able to think on your feet instead of trying to push ahead with your original idea. . . . What else have you thought about in terms of feedback for yourself?

C: I know we'll talk about this more when we meet with Dr. S., but I was looking at my midterm evaluation and I think there are some areas where I've improved in terms of my skills. I think in particular I've gotten better about not asking too many questions like I did at the beginning. I was thinking about my first session with [Client] and (*laughs*) I was remembering how I must've asked her like twenty questions in a row without even stopping! (*laughter*)

S: (*laughter*) Oh, I remember that too! The first session, you asked so many questions and then you felt so uncomfortable about it that the second session you hardly said anything! I'm very happy to give you feedback that I think you've found a really good middle ground.

C: Ah, that was really bad. And that was the one I presented to the class! I can't even believe it.

S: It's okay! I think that's the whole purpose, and you were able to get good feedback that you put into practice right away. That's one of the other things that I really have appreciated about you, particularly in our relationship. You've really put yourself into this experience and have put yourself out there to get feedback, even when you were nervous or uncertain. It could be really easy to only show the class or me your very best clips, and I so appreciate that you were always willing to show us the parts you struggled with. I hope you can see that your contribution is part of what made this such a meaningful semester for you.

C: Yeah, I feel like even though it was hard, it was worth it. But, you know, I never felt embarrassed here, even when I knew I hadn't done a great job or had missed an opportunity.

S: I'm really glad to hear you say that, and I'm glad to get that feedback. . . . So, I'm wondering what some of your goals are for yourself moving forward, and what are some areas you'd like to continue to work on?

C: I feel ready for my internship. It's going to be a whole new world; I'm going to be doing all sorts of stuff that I have no experience doing. I feel really nervous, but excited and ready to dive in and get my feet wet. My goals are really to get involved with as many different types of groups as I can so I can get some group experience, and to work on using more challenges and silence in my sessions. Those were things I think I worked on a little bit more the second half of this semester.

S: Those sound like good goals for you. I agree that silence and challenging are two areas that you can continue to work on. I've certainly seen you make improvement in both of those skills, especially challenging.

C: My new supervisor and I have talked about clients and have really put together a group of clients that are very diverse and will give me opportunities to work with lots of different types of clients with different kinds of issues.

S: You know, as I think about you moving onto this new site and working with clients with more complex concerns and with different backgrounds, the part of you that I'd really like to see you continue to nurture is that part of you that's increasingly able to directly and compassionately challenge clients and point out inconsistencies, as well as hold them accountable to what they're saying they want for themselves. I think you were very successful in doing that with [Client A] this semester, and I think he was receptive to that—and that it caught you by surprise!

C: Yeah, I think with [Client A], it really showed me that if the relationship is there, you know, he's going to appreciate what I have to say and be open to some challenge. I'm sure that won't happen with every client, but I felt that with him.

S: I think so, and I think it mattered that he knew you cared and helped him see some things about himself and make some changes. I also think that your clients this semester have been good experiences for you to reflect on when you meet a client who seems to have a tough exterior, or when you meet someone really different from you—whether it's gender, race, culture, religion, socioeconomics—to remind you of the ways you've been successful in crossing those barriers by being compassionate, and being open to learning about their experiences.

C: Yeah, I think you're right. Having this experience with especially like [Client B] or [Client A] when I worried I'd never get through this. It reminds me that it's going to take time, and it's not instantaneous. . . .

S: I'd be appreciative of any feedback you might have for me, or what feels unfinished for you.

C: Oh, wow; well, when you said "feels unfinished," um, I was just feeling wistful, like, I just really enjoyed this so much, and I feel like I don't know what I would have done without it. The way you've given me feedback has been so nurturing but not coddling-like in a way; you've shown me how you can challenge someone in a compassionate way.

S: It means a lot to me to hear you say that. I think our working relationship is an example of how much can happen in a short period of time and what it can feel like to be with somebody and be able to be open, which is what I'd hoped to create here with you. . . . It's even been rewarding for me to watch you struggle at times, because I always believed that you could navigate your way through, with some support.

The most dramatic difference between this pair and the previous pair is the quality of the working alliance. Apparently, this has been a positive experience for both supervisor and counselor. Furthermore, many of the important aspects of good supervision and a good summative evaluation are evident. The supervisor reinforces the important task of self-assessment by asking the supervisee to take stock of her development. It is obvious that both challenge and support (i.e., balanced formative evaluation) have been a part of the supervision over the semester. In addition, the midterm evaluation evidently gave the supervisee direction for her development. The supervisor not only invites feedback about the supervision that has been offered, but addresses some of the parallels between the supervision relationship and therapeutic relationships. In doing so, she underscores the importance of supervision as a relationship-driven activity that requires vulnerability and honesty from the persons involved. Finally, the supervisor puts their time together in context by asking the supervisee to address future goals for her continuing development as a counselor.

A summative evaluation is an important marker for the therapist-in-training; it is also an important moment for the supervisor. Despite the content of the evaluation, delivering a summative statement with integrity, interpersonal and cultural sensitivity, adequate specificity, and appropriate authority advances both the professional development of the supervisee and the profession as a whole. Good summative evaluations are often one of the reasons that a supervisor decides to continue to invest in the supervision process. Like a good termination with a client, it leaves the supervisor feeling empowered for the next journey with yet another supervisee.

SUPERVISEES WITH PROBLEMS OF PROFESSIONAL COMPETENCE

Virtually all training programs in the helping professions admit students with the intention of graduating and ultimately endorsing them. Similarly, mental health agencies hire professionals with optimistic expectations about their performance. The unpleasant idea of dismissal of students or employees is something most supervisors attempt to repress; and yet evaluation of mental health professionals must include the possibility that the person being evaluated has failed to meet competencies at a minimally acceptable level. Although supervisors typically exhibit a high commitment to their supervisees, they must be ever cognizant that "duty to the public and the profession takes precedence" (Pearson & Piazza, 1997, p. 93).

Definitions

Beginning around the mid-1980s, the mental health professions leaned toward the word *impairment* to describe either a troublesome reversal in performance or an inability to meet the requirements of (usually) the clinical component of a training program (Lamb, Cochran, & Jackson, 1991; Lamb, Presser, Pfost, Baum, Jackson, & Jarvis, 1987; Muratori, 2001; Oliver, Bernstein, Anderson, Blashfield, & Roberts, 2004; Vacha-Haase, Davenport, & Kerewsky, 2004). *Impairment* has also been described as affecting several areas of a supervisee's functioning, going beyond problems typically expected of supervisees, and impervious to feedback (Burgess, 1994). Reversals in performance have typically been hypothesized as a consequence of emotional and physical depletion or burnout. Manifestations of such impairment include substance abuse, boundary violations, misuse of power, and diminished clinical judgment (Muratori, 2001). Michaelson, Estrada-Hernández, and Wadsworth (2003) differentiate *unprepared supervisees* from *unqualified supervisees,* suggesting that the former might benefit from additional training, whereas the latter are more likely to be dismissed from training programs. Therefore, these authors seem to equate unqualified supervisees with impaired supervisees.

Falender, Collins, and Shafranske (2005) assert that the Americans with Disabilities Act (ADA) has "preempted" the word *impairment,* and that supervisors are advised to refrain from use of the term lest they be accused of discrimination if they have not followed ADA guidelines. Furthermore, impairment requires a diagnosis of a disability, a role outside of the role of educator or supervisor. Therefore, to avoid legal complications (Falender et al., 2005, 2009; Gilfoyle, 2008), supervisors should avoid diagnosing supervisees and focus on evaluating competencies. The consensus term that follows this line of thinking, therefore, is *professional competence problems (PCC)* or *problems of professional competence (PPC)* (e.g., Elman & Forrest, 2007; Jacobs et al., 2011; Johnson et al., 2008; Shen-Miller et al., 2011). Elman and Forrest suggest that this term "captures the three components essential to defining the issue: (a) the inclusion of the concept that there is a problem with performance, (b) a professional standard, and (c) a focus on competence" (p. 505).

Despite the admonitions to avoid the word *impairment,* it continues to appear in the mental health literature, including in the 2005 American Counseling Association Code of Ethics (i.e., sections C.2.g., F.8.b). Yet, because the term *problems of professional competence (PPC)* establishes a clear boundary between diagnostic roles and supervisory roles, we choose it for our purposes here.

Incidence

Supervisees with PPC are endemic to the supervision process. There is an increasingly robust body of anecdotal and empirical literature attesting to the fact that a small percentage of supervisees are found to be unqualified to practice in the helping professions by their supervisors (e.g., Elman & Forrest, 2004; Forrest et al.,1999; Gaubatz & Vera, 2006; Gizara & Forrest, 2004; Lamb & Swerdlik, 2003; McAdams et al., 2007; Oliver et al., 2004; Rosenberg, Getzelman, Arcinue, & Oren, 2005; Russell & Peterson, 2003; Shen-Miller et al., 2011; Vacha-Haase et al., 2004). In their seminal review of the literature on this topic, Forrest and colleagues (1999) document the consistent incidence of supervisees with PPC and the numerous struggles of supervisors to determine appropriate responses to problematic behaviors.

Not surprisingly, it appears that not only supervisors are aware of supervisees with PPC. In an exploratory study in which researchers interviewed clinical psychology students about what they labeled as *impairment* among their peers (Oliver et al., 2004), students identified a host of observed behaviors—including what they viewed as depression, anxiety disorders, personality disorders, eating disorders, alcohol abuse, and boundary concerns. Another study surveying counseling and clinical psychology students (Rosenberg et al., 2005) reports a similar awareness among peers regarding problems of professional competence, and identify lack of awareness of impact on others, emotional problems, clinical deficiency, and poor interpersonal skills as among the most common problematic behaviors, whereas less frequently reported behaviors include isolative behavior, eating disorders, substance abuse, and anger/aggression. It is interesting to note that the lists of behaviors reported by the researchers of these two studies include both reference to competencies (e.g., poor interpersonal skills) as well as diagnoses (e.g., depression). This kind of boundary blurring has been more the norm than the exception until recent admonitions to separate the two have been more forthcoming (e.g., Falender et al., 2009; Gilfoyle, 2008).

Gaubatz and Vera (2006) surveyed both students and faculty of counselor education programs and found that students reported a higher rate of peer deficiency than did the faculty. One of the interesting outcomes of all of the investigations seeking student perspectives was that students were not aware if or when their training directors or faculty became aware of the troublesome behavior they were observing. As a result, there was some frustration among these students directed at their supervisors and faculty. Student participants in the Gaubatz and Vera study thought that nearly 18 percent of deficient students received no faculty intervention, whereas faculty subjects in the same study estimated their rate of slippage to be under 3 percent. Additional results reported by Gaubatz and Vera included some insight into student posture toward the issue of PPC in relationship to themselves. In general, students reported that they would be open to remediation if they were identified as being deficient; however, 22 percent reported that they would pursue legal action if dismissed from a program, and 43 percent of student respondents noted that they would attempt to be admitted to another counseling program if dismissed from their present program. In short, it seems that at least some students take a consumer approach to their training, and are not open to their supervisors' opinion if it is a negative assessment of their ability to be a successful mental health professional.

Students seem to be unaware of policies and procedures regarding problematic peers or of their roles if they identify a peer with PPC (Oliver et al., 2004; Rosenberg et al., 2005; Shen-Miller et al., 2011). Participants in both the Rosenberg et al. and Shen-Miller et al. studies report that their most common response to such peers was to vent with other peers or to seek consultation with peers and sometimes faculty/supervisors. It seems then that there is a need in educational and supervision contexts for clearer protocol so students know how to address the issue of peers with PPC in a way that is both caring and professional. Shen-Miller et al. stress the importance of preventive and educational interventions with supervisees before issues occur. Foster and McAdams (2009) concur, and emphasize the importance of creating a transparent supervisory culture where policies are developed and communicated, opportunities for top-down and bottom-up communication are established, and a commitment to assistance and remediation are apparent. We add that an additional positive consequence of opening up the lines of communication between supervisors and supervisees about the possibility of encountering a peer who is struggling is that it can also encourage supervisees to reflect on their own coping styles when under stress.

Remediation

In spite of ongoing documentation of incidence, educators and supervisors have struggled in their attempts to respond appropriately to supervisees with PPC (Vacha-Haase et al., 2004). Depending on the severity of the PPC, faculty and supervisors must determine if remediation is possible, in and of itself often a dilemma. Remediation plans must be defensible; therefore, they must be as concrete as possible and must link remediation activities to required skills and attributes (Gilfoyle, 2008). We have found it worthwhile to name deficits (and it is best if these refer to program documents that have been in the possession of all supervisees) and ask the supervisee to work with us to devise the remediation plan. If handled with directness and empathy, this can empower the supervisee to be part of the solution. This process also allows for communication between supervisor(s) and the supervisee with PPC, perhaps in a manner that has not been possible until this point.

Russell, DuPree, Beggs, Peterson, and Anderson (2007) report responses from directors of marriage and family therapy programs include increased supervision, requiring a leave of absence, increased contact with one's academic advisor, and a requirement to repeat coursework, all of which have merit and none of which is a panacea. What is essential for remediation is a plan that, when executed, it provides the data faculty or a supervisor needs to make an informed decision about the readiness of the supervisee to re-engage in training.

We also note that, historically, psychotherapy has been chosen as a sole remediation plan, even though there is little support that such an intervention remediates these supervisees adequately for competent practice (Elman & Forrest, 2004; Vacha-Haase et al., 2004). Furthermore, suggesting a need for therapy blends the supervisory role with a therapeutic one (Russell et al., 2007), which is fraught with issues, including the possibility that a report from a therapist to reinstate the supervisee might inform a training program of a disability that brings ADA protections (Guilfoyle, 2008).

Although the issue of supervisees with PPC has been well exposed in the literature, in general, clinical supervisors report feeling unprepared to respond to supervisees with PPC (Gizara & Forrest, 2004; Jacobs et al., 2011). McCutcheon (2008) addresses the difficulty of assessing a predoctoral internship student as having insufficient competence, knowing not only the high stakes of such an assessment, but being aware of the risk of error when the intern is often in transition from one context and geographic area to another, and the supervisor and intern have little history with one another.

Because the issue of identifying a supervisee as having a PPC is chronic, more clarity has occurred around the role of supervisors with supervisees in training programs. At one time, supervisors were concerned about evaluating what were considered to be *nonacademic traits* of the supervisee. As already noted, it is indeed inappropriate for faculty to take action based on what would be a diagnosis in another context. However, many competencies in the mental health professions (e.g., a willingness to admit errors and accept feedback; Fouad et al., 2009) are outside of what has traditionally been perceived as "academic." Fortunately, a review of court cases (Kerl, Garcia, McCullough, & Maxwell, 2002; Lumadue & Duffey, 1999) reveals that courts view personal attitudes or behaviors necessary for adequate performance within a profession to be academic issues. Therefore, characteristics such as low impulse control, limited empathy for clients, debilitating anxiety, and pronounced cultural insensitivity could be defended as part of an academic dismissal. This is important, because legally, academic dismissals are the right and responsibility of the faculty, whereas disciplinary dismissals require additional documentation and a formal hearing. The due process obligation for the faculty when the issue is an academic one is met simply by notifying the supervisee prior to dismissal regarding his or her failure or impending failure to meet program standards (Kerl et al., 2002). Still, this could get complicated if the student's GPA does not support a negative assessment.

Related to this is the importance of processes that assist supervisors and inform supervisees that there are parameters regarding their interpersonal functioning. Duba, Paez, and Kindsvatter (2010) investigated ways in which CACREP community counseling programs evaluated students to meet what they described as *nonacademic standards* (i.e., forming effective interpersonal relationships and openness to self-examination). The ability of training programs to articulate their evaluation methods meets an important element of the kind of transparency advocated by Foster and McAdams (2009). Although these may not be legally necessary for gatekeeping, the parameters help build a training culture that is perceived as healthy (Gizara & Forrest, 2004), fair, and concerned simultaneously with the professional development of their supervisees and the public they serve. As stated by Kaslow et al. (2007):

> *[S]upervisors must rise to the occasion in terms of creating, communicating, and sustaining, a safe, growth-enhancing climate in which their supervisees can learn optimally to conduct therapy more and more competently. At the same time, supervisors have a very real responsibility to spot serious problems and deficits in their supervisees' performance, to address them overtly toward the goal of remediation, and to serve as professional gatekeepers to protect the public in the event that the supervisee is unable or unwilling to make the necessary improvements in their professional behavior.* (p. 16)

Part of a description of processes that must be in place prior to addressing supervisees with PPC include informed consent and due process. Lumadue and Duffey (1999) outline the six informed consent goals that faculty of one counselor training program agreed on:

1. To identify the qualities and behaviors expected of students
2. To reach faculty consensus on the expectations for student fitness and performance
3. To devise a rating form listing these qualities and behavior
4. To standardize evaluation procedures within the department by using these forms
5. To communicate these expectations to all students in each class
6. To include these expectations in the admissions packets issued to interested students (p. 106)

The rating form developed by this training program was published later (Kerl et al., 2002) and includes five areas of evaluation: counseling skills and abilities, professional responsibility, competence, maturity, and integrity. Students are assessed as meeting, meeting minimally, or not meeting each criterion. Similarly, after reflecting on a long (and unsuccessful) legal challenge from a dismissed student, McAdams et al. (2007) formulated a rubric that assists students in understanding acceptable and unacceptable behaviors across 10 domains. We refer the reader to McAdams et al. (2007) for this valuable evaluation tool.

Finally, Gilfoyle (2008) offers 10 best practice suggestions for risk management in addressing supervisee competence issues. We believe they represent a primer for forming an infrastructure that can not only support training, but can also support the weight of necessary gatekeeping activity.

1. Provide written notice of the standards (training goals and objectives) against which student performance will be measure.
2. Provide written notice of procedures for dealing with competency problems that

provide, at a minimum, notice of performance program and opportunity to respond before any action is taken.

3. Educate and require faculty and administrators to follow procedures and standards established by the program.
4. Apply established standards and procedures consistently to trainees who are similarly situated.
5. Establish internal review and evaluation procedures that respect the confidentiality of opinion about a trainee, and restrict discussion of problems to those with a need to know.
6. When problems emerge, focus on behavior that is problematic in relation to training goals.
7. Design remediation plans to coordinate with program criteria, training goals, and objectives.
8. Consider safety issues for all involved—clients, coworkers, and the trainee.
9. Keep a written record of interactions and decisions.
10. Do not delay in addressing problems. (p. 208)

To this excellent list, we add Wester, Christianson, Fouad, and Santiago-Rivera's (2008) admonitions that faculty/supervisors must be committed to enforcing the remediation plan consistently, and that they spend some time anticipating how the supervisee might react to the intervention of requiring remediation before they begin the process.

In summary, there is no more dreaded evaluation situation than the possible assessment of a supervisee as unable or unfit to practice in the profession that he or she has chosen. At the same time, this task is representative of the gatekeeping function required of all clinical supervisors. Historically, when supervisors avoided this responsibility, they have done so using the nebulousness of the profession as their argument. Stepping up to the challenge of addressing supervisees with competency problems requires more specificity about a range of behaviors, attitudes, and characteristics from acceptable to unacceptable. This specificity assists all supervisees—not only those who struggle, and sometimes fail—in meeting professional standards.

ADDITIONAL EVALUATION ISSUES

At the beginning of this chapter, we mentioned that evaluation is a difficult task because of the personal nature of the skills being evaluated. Relatively clear criteria, good evaluation instruments, and a credible process go far to diminish the difficulty of evaluation. However, the supervision process is not sterile, and neither is the evaluation process. What is called for when supervisors evaluate is a judgment based on as much objective data as possible; yet the judgment still includes a subjective element.

The Subjective Element

Clinical supervisors work hard to be fair and reasonable in their evaluations. Without some awareness of the pitfalls to objective evaluation, however, supervisors are at a disadvantage for attaining this goal. At the same time, supervisors must know that the subjective element of evaluations cannot and should not be eliminated completely. There is something intrinsically intuitive about counseling and psychotherapy, and this is equally true for clinical supervision. Evaluation is a delicate blend of subjective judgment and objective criteria. Yet sometimes our *personal subjectivity* contaminates our *professional subjectivity*, and evaluation becomes less intuitive and more biased (Gonsalvez & Freestone, 2007; Robiner, Saltzman, Hoberman, Semrud-Clikeman, & Schirvar, 1997). No clinical supervisor is above this dilemma. Being aware of the possibility, however, may help the supervisor draft a checklist of personal vulnerabilities and potential blind spots to review when evaluating. Each clinical supervisor has a separate list of subjective obstacles to navigate when facing the task of evaluation. Our list is only a partial one of some of the more common problems from our own personal experience or that have received attention in the professional literature.

Similarity. An assumption that has spawned a good deal of empirical investigation is that attraction (which includes the concept of similarity) influences the therapeutic process and, likewise, the supervision process (Turban & Jones, 1988). Although Kaplan (1983) reports mixed findings, similarity with one's supervisor is probably more of an advantage than a disadvantage. Still, there are times when this is not so. If the supervisor is suffering from a poor self-image, this may spill over to a supervisee perceived as similar. From another vantage point, dissimilarity is an advantage for the supervisee if the lack of similarity gives the supervisee additional influence in the relationship. For example, if the supervisor is young and relatively inexperienced and the supervisee is older and has more life experience, such dissimilarity might translate to a better evaluation than if the supervisor were the same age as the supervisee, especially if the supervisee is male (Granello, 2003). There is evidence also that females rate males higher in competence; therefore, a female supervisor might rate a male supervisee higher than would a male supervisor (Goodyear, 1990). (Goodyear cites several such studies, but in his own study found no evidence of gender bias in supervisee evaluations.)

There is a situation-specific form of similarity that the supervisor should consider. When life has dealt two people the same hand, or at least some of the same cards, this tends to create a bond between them. Both supervisor and supervisee might have recently been through a divorce, have children of the same age, or have a parent who abuses alcohol. Depending on the amount of self-disclosure that occurs in supervision and each person's comfort level about these life situations, such similarity can be an advantage or a disadvantage. Regardless, how these similarities might influence evaluation must be considered.

Liking one's supervisee seems more important than similarity, although the two concepts are related. Turban, Jones, and Rozelle (1990) found that liked supervisees received more psychological support during supervision than disliked supervisees, supervisors extended more effort in working with liked supervisees, and supervisors evaluated liked supervisees more favorably than disliked supervisees. In a related study, Dohrenbusch and Lipka (2006) found that one of the four factors accounting for 56 percent of the variance in supervisors' evaluations was the social competence of the supervisee. (Although somewhat different from liking of the supervisee, we trust that there might be a healthy correlation between the two.) The other three factors in the Dohrenbusch and Lipka study were the degree to which supervisees were goal directed in their therapy; the capacity of supervisees to establish a therapeutic relationship with their clients; and their ability to demonstrate behaviors that motivated and supported their clients.

It is difficult to determine whether liking leads to inflated performance evaluation or if better-performing supervisees are more liked. The fact that liking affects the interactions between supervisor and supervisee long before summative evaluation, however, makes this a variable to which supervisors should be alerted.

Familiarity. "He's difficult to get to know, but he wears well." How many of us have had negative first impressions of people we now hold in high esteem? Not all of a person's qualities are apparent in the short run, and sometimes it takes a significant amount of time (in graduate-training terms) to arrive at what might be described as a balanced view of the trainee's strengths and weaknesses. In conjunction with this, when affection for someone has grown over time, it can become increasingly difficult to evaluate that supervisee objectively (Robiner et al., 1997).

Some empirical evidence supports the case that familiarity affects evaluation. Blodgett, Schmidt, and Scudder (1987) found that supervisors rated the same trainees differently depending on how long they knew the trainees. If a supervisor had the trainee in a class prior to the supervision experience, the supervisor was more likely to evaluate the trainee more positively. Blodgett and colleagues note that the trainees who had received their undergraduate and graduate training at the same institution had a distinct advantage in this particular study. The authors warn that it would be unwise, however, to assume that familiarity always works to the trainee's advantage. Our experience supports this admonition; just as some trainees wear well, others do not.

A corollary to the issue of familiarity is the perseverance of first impressions (Sternitzke, Dixon, & Ponterotto, 1988). Although we stated earlier that our first impressions are not always our last, it is important to mention that first impressions can be long lasting. If supervisors attribute dispositional characteristics to their trainees early in their relationship, it may require an inordinate amount of evidence for the trainee to reverse the supervisor's opinion. In this case, the trainee may be familiar to the supervisor, but the trainee might be far from known.

Priorities and Bias. Each supervisor has an individual set of priorities when judging the skill of a supervisee. For this reason, it is a fruitful exercise to have novice supervisors discuss a list of competencies (e.g., Fouad et al., 2009) that they use to evaluate supervisees and the relative importance they place on some over others. Most often, supervisors are not cognizant that their priorities are partially subjective, and that an equally qualified supervisor might have a somewhat different list of priorities.

This tendency is supported by attribution theory as explained by Sternitzke et al. (1988). Building on Ross's (1977) work, they identify *egocentric bias* as a common problem for supervisors when observing supervisee behavior, and explain the nature of the bias as follows:

> *One's estimate of deviance and normalcy are egocentrically biased in accord with one's own behavioral choices, because observers tend to think about what they would have done in a similar situation and then compare their hypothesized behavior with the actor's actual behavior. If the observers believe they would have acted differently, then there is an increased tendency for them to view the actor's [behavior] as deviant. If the observers believe they would have acted in a similar fashion, then their tendencies are to view the actor's behavior as normal.* (p. 9)

Robiner et al. (1993) addressed idiosyncratic tendencies for individual supervisors to demonstrate a leniency bias, a strictness bias, or a central-tendency bias. In a subsequent study of 62 supervisors, Robiner et al. (1997) found that an acknowledgment of evaluation bias was commonplace (59 percent), with only 10 percent of supervisors believing that their evaluations were free from bias and 31 percent being unsure. Of those supervisors who admitted bias, 40 percent believed that they leaned toward leniency in their ratings of supervisees; 45 percent believed that they leaned toward central tendency; and only 7 percent believed that they exhibited a strictness bias.

According to Robiner et al. (1993), *leniency bias*—that is, the tendency to evaluate more favorably than objective data might warrant—may result from any of four sources: (a) measurement issues, such as a lack of clear criteria; (b) legal and administrative issues, such as a concern about a grievance procedure; (c) interpersonal issues, such as experiencing the anguish about damaging a supervisee's career; or (d) supervisor issues, such as having limited supervision experience. Interestingly, leniency bias within mental health training programs continues to be cited as a reason for failed gatekeeping (Brear & Dorrian, 2010). Table 4 delineates factors described by Robiner and Ristvedt (1993) that may contribute to a leniency bias.

Strictness bias is the tendency to rate supervisees more severely than warranted. This kind of bias seems to be the most difficult for the supervisee. Ward, Friedlander, Schoen, and Klein (1985) suggest that such ratings can lead to excessive defensiveness on the part of the supervisee or to attempts to manipulate the supervisor to gain more positive ratings. Robiner et al. (1993) suggest that consistent critical ratings are likely to suggest problems within the supervisor (e.g., unrealistic standards; displaced personal frustration). In

TABLE 4 Factors Contributing to Leniency or Inflation in Faculty Evaluations of Interns

Definition and Measurement Issues

1. Lack of clear criteria and objective measures of competence or incompetence in psychology
2. Lack of clear criteria and objective measures of impairment or distress in psychology
3. Supervisor awareness of subjectivity inherent in evaluation
4. Apprehension about defending evaluations due to lack of clear criteria and objective measures

Legal and Administrative Issues

5. Concern that negative evaluations may result in administrative inquiry, audit, grievance, or litigation
6. Lack of awareness of internship or institutional policies and procedures involved in negative evaluations
7. Social and political dynamics: feared or perceived lack of support from institutions, directors of training, and colleagues for providing negative evaluations
8. Concern that failing to "pass" an intern may result in loss of future training funds or training slots or the need to find additional funds to extend the intern's training
9. Concern that failing to "pass" an intern may result in adverse publicity that could affect institutional reputation and the number of internship applicants

Interpersonal Issues

10. Fear of diminishing rapport or provoking hostility from supervisees
11. Fear of eliciting backlash from current or future trainees
12. Anguish about damaging a supervisee's career or complicating or terminating his or her graduate training

Supervisor Issues

13. Supervisors' wish to avoid scrutiny of their own behavior, competence, ethics, expectations, or judgment of their clinical and supervisory practices
14. Limited supervisory experiences with impaired or incompetent trainees
15. Inability to impart negative evaluations (e.g., deficit in assertive communication skills)
16. Indifference to personal responsibility for upholding the standards of the profession
17. Discomfort with gatekeeper role
18. Identification with supervisee's problems
19. Inadequate attention to supervisee's performance or problems
20. Supervisors' presumption of supervisee competence (e.g., overreliance on selection procedures)
21. Minimization of incompetence or impairment in supervisees
22. Inappropriate optimism that problems will resolve without intervention
23. Preference to avoid the substantial energy and time commitment necessary to address or remediate deficient trainees

Source: From "Evaluation Difficulties in Supervising Psychology Interns," by W. Robiner, M. Fuhrman, and S. Ristvedt, 1993, *The Clinical Psychologist, 46*(1), 3–13. Copyright ©1993 by the Division of Clinical Psychology, Division 12 of the American Psychological Association, p. 7.

addition, what may be explained as a strictness bias may be applied inconsistently, and may, instead, indicate bias toward, for example, female supervisees (e.g., Chung, Marshall, & Gordon, 2001) or older supervisees (e.g., Granello, 2003).

The *central-tendency bias* is the tendency to rate supervisees uniformly average. In this case, supervisees are denied feedback that would allow them to address deficits seriously or to appreciate when their performance was above average.

Gonsalvez and Freestone (2007) conducted an important follow-up to the Robiner et al. (1997) study that focused on field supervisors rather than faculty. They collected data on 130 field supervisors over 12 years and found that these supervisors indeed reflected a leniency bias. (Their data did not support a central-tendency or strictness bias.) In addition, they found that early field supervisor assessments of supervisees regarding particular competencies did not predict later assessments on the same competencies. As a reflection regarding the documented leniency bias, the authors state:

> *It is possible that the supportive and nurturing role supervisors are called to play in their own therapy with clients, and the formative role they play in building up skills and confidence in an often anxious and sometimes vulnerable trainee, conspire against objective and critical supervisory judgments.* (p. 28)

Bogo, Regehr, Power, and Regehr's (2007) research supports this conclusion. They found that social work field supervisors believed the task of evaluation collided with some highly valued professional values, such as being nonjudgmental and sensitive to individual learning needs. Therefore, although acknowledging the importance of making evaluative judgments, these field supervisors acknowledged that the process of facilitating learning was far more appealing to them than being gatekeepers for the profession.

Their findings led Gonsalvez and Freestone (2007) to state a concern that a leniency bias might translate to a *halo effect* for supervisees, along with negative consequences. In particular, these authors are concerned that supervisees might bypass additional supervision or professional development, thinking they are better than their peers. Referring to processes like the use of outside readers for dissertations, Gonsalvez and Freestone suggest that at least some aspects of supervisee performance should be assessed by persons other than the field supervisors.

We concur with Gonsalvez and Freestone's (2007) recommendation. Although several different types of subjective variables can influence evaluation, a single action may serve to counter their effect: consultation. Supervision is less vulnerable to subjective confounding when others are brought into the process. Supervisors are more likely to involve other opinions when there is a supervision crisis, especially if the situation has ethical or legal implications. The wise supervisor, however, involves others in the evaluation process when things are seemingly at their smoothest. Not only is this good practice, it also affords the supervisor ongoing professional development that assists him or her in becoming a better evaluator.

Consequences of Evaluation

Like most activities of any importance, the process of evaluation contains some risks. There have been both false positives and false negatives in the evaluation experience of most clinical supervisors. Possibly because supervisors all know that they have evaluated incorrectly in the past, the consequences of their evaluations can loom before them like an unforgiving superego. Supervisors know that a positive evaluation may mean that a supervisee will be competitive in the job market or an employee will be promoted, whereas a negative evaluation may result in a student being dropped from a training program or an employee being the first to be let go. Because of supervisors' awareness of the consequences of evaluation, they find themselves doing extra soul-searching over the evaluations of the strongest and weakest supervisees.

Yet even for the average evaluation, there are consequences. Levy (1983) refers to the *costs of evaluation* as the inordinate time it requires of the supervisor, the anxiety it causes the supervisee, and the stress it puts on the supervisory relationship. Burke, Goodyear, and Guzzardo (1998) found that evaluation interventions that resulted in breaches in the supervision working alliance left the supervision relationship vulnerable. Yet, Levy notes that program or agency integrity and the welfare of future clients places the costs and benefits of evaluation in alignment.

In a highly pragmatic discussion, Kadushin (1992a) mentions the administrative consequences for the supervisor when a negative evaluation is necessary. If, in a work environment, an employee is let go because of an evaluation, the supervisor is often the person to feel the brunt of the extra workload until a replacement can be found. In a training program, a negative evaluation typically means more extensive documentation and the possibility of an appeal process or even a court case (McAdams et al., 2007), or, at the very least, lengthy interviews with the supervisee involved. Robiner et al. (1997) notes that, indeed, legal and administrative issues play a role in supervisor leniency bias. It is understandable, although not acceptable, that some supervisors shy away from giving negative evaluations in order to avoid unattractive consequences. Such shortsightedness, however, does not acknowledge the much more significant consequences when evaluations are not conducted properly.

CONCLUSION

Evaluation poses a range of issues for the clinical supervisor. It is at the same time the most disconcerting, the most challenging, and the most important of responsibilities. There are, however, conceptual and structural aids described in this chapter that can increase a supervisor's confidence and competence, and contribute to a productive evaluation process for both the supervisor and the supervisee.

The Supervisor's Toolbox

The Supervisor's Toolbox

This toolbox offers resources to support the research, practice, and teaching of supervision. Its contents are listed in the order in which they are presented.

Documents for Use in Supervision

- Counseling Supervision Contract
- Reciprocal Supervision Agreement
- Example of a Professional Disclosure Statement
- Supervisee's Bill of Rights
- Supervision Agreement
- The Practicum Competencies Outline
- Supervision Record Form (SRF-1)
- Supervision Record Form (SRF-2)

Measures for Supervision Research and Practice

- *Supervisory Satisfaction Questionnaire*
- *Supervisee Needs Index*
- *Group Supervision Scale*
- *Supervisee Levels Questionnaire–Revised*
- *Anticipatory Supervisee Anxiety Scale (ASAS)*
- *Role Conflict and Role Ambiguity Inventory*
- *Multicultural Supervision Competencies Questionnaire*
- *Evaluation Process within Supervision Inventory*
- *Supervisory Working Alliance (SWA)–Supervisor Form*
- *Supervisory Working Alliance (SWA)–Supervisee Form*
- *Supervisory Styles Inventory*
- *Counselor Supervisor Self-Efficacy Scale*

Supervision Ethics Codes

- *The Approved Clinical Supervisor Code of Ethics,* National Board for Certified Counselors
- *Ethical Guidelines for Counseling Supervisors,* Association for Counselor Education and Supervision

From Canadian Psychological Association

- *Guidelines for Ethical Supervision*

COUNSELING SUPERVISION CONTRACT*

This contract serves as verification and a description of the counseling supervision provided by Cynthia J. Osborn, Ph.D., PCC-S ("Supervisor"), to ________________ ("Supervisee"), Clinical Mental Health Counseling (CMHC) Practicum Student enrolled in Practicum I in the CHDS Program at Kent State University for Spring Semester 2012.

I. ***Purpose, Goals, and Objectives***

a. Monitor and ensure welfare of clients seen by Supervisee.
b. Promote development of Supervisee's professional counselor identity and competence.
c. Fulfill academic requirement for Supervisee's Practicum.
d. Fulfill requirements in preparation for Supervisee's pursuit of counselor licensure.

II. ***Context of Services***

a. One (1) clock hour of individual supervision weekly.
b. Individual supervision will be conducted in Supervisor's office in 310 White Hall, Kent State University, on ___________s [day of week], from ______ a.m./p.m. to ______ a.m./p.m. Digital video recordings of Supervisee's counseling sessions will be viewed on Supervisor's laptop computer.
c. A motivational interviewing style, collaborative case conceptualization, interpersonal process recall, and role plays will be used in supervision.
d. Regular review of Supervisee's counseling video recordings and clinical documentation in weekly individual supervision.

III. ***Method of Evaluation***

a. Feedback will be provided by the Supervisor during each session, and a formal evaluation, using the CHDS standard evaluation of student clinical skills, will be conducted at mid-semester and at the conclusion of the Spring Semester. A narrative evaluation also will be provided at mid-semester and at the conclusion of the semester as an addendum to the objective evaluations completed.
b. Specific feedback provided by Supervisor will focus on Supervisee's demonstrated counseling skills and clinical documentation, which will be based on Supervisor's regular observation of Supervisee's counseling sessions (via video recording and live), as well as review of clinical documentation.
c. Supervisee will evaluate Supervisor at mid-semester and at the close of Spring Semester, using the CHDS standard evaluation form for evaluating supervisors. A narrative evaluation also will accompany the objective evaluations.
d. Supervision notes will be shared with Supervisee at Supervisor's discretion and at the request of the Supervisee.

IV. ***Duties and Responsibilities of Supervisor and Supervisee***

a. Supervisor

a. Examine client clinical information (e.g., assessment) and determine appropriate services.
b. Review on a regular basis Supervisee's video recorded counseling sessions.

*Based on C. J. Osborn and T. E. Davis (1996). The Supervision Contract: Making It Perfectly Clear. *The Clinical Supervisor, 14*(2), 121–134.

c. Review, correct, and sign off on all client documentation completed using Titanium Schedule© software program.
d. Challenge Supervisee to justify approach and techniques used.
e. Monitor Supervisee's basic attending skills, specifically those consistent with a motivational interviewing style.
f. Present, describe, and model appropriate directives.
g. Intervene when client welfare is at risk.
h. Model and ensure American Counseling Association (ACA; 2005) *ACA Code of Ethics* are upheld.
i. Maintain professional liability insurance coverage.
j. Maintain weekly supervision notes.
k. Assist Supervisee in developing an appreciation for and demonstrating the "spirit" of motivational interviewing.
l. Assist Supervisee in reviewing various counseling theories, with goal of gaining an appreciation for an integrative practice approach.
m. Assist Supervisee in gaining greater self-awareness during counseling and supervision sessions.

b. Supervisee

a. Uphold ACA (2005) *ACA Code of Ethics.*
b. Maintain professional liability insurance coverage.
c. View counseling session video recordings in preparation for weekly supervision.
d. Complete "Counselor Trainee Self-Critique and Reflection Form" as a result of having viewed counseling session video recordings and have these ready to discuss in Supervision.
e. Be prepared to discuss all client cases—have any client files, current and completed client case notes on Titanium Schedule© software program, and counseling session video recordings ready to review in weekly supervision sessions.
f. Justify client case conceptualizations made and approach and techniques used.
g. Complete client case notes and supervision notes in a timely fashion and place in appropriate file in CHDC.
h. Consult with CHDC staff and Supervisor in cases of emergency.
i. Implement supervisory directives in subsequent sessions.
j. Practice skills consistent with a motivational interviewing style with the goal of developing and demonstrating the "spirit" of motivational interviewing.
k. Practice working from a variety of and appropriate counseling theories.
l. Demonstrate willingness to discuss in supervision supervisee's experiences of professional development.

c. Supervisee's Expressed Learning Objectives for Practicum I

NOTE: What follows are examples of learning objectives taken from individual student contracts. These objectives are based on each supervisee's experiences in the training program thus far, unique career objectives, etc.

a. Learn how to conduct biopsychosocial history, psychological assessments, and mental status exam as part of the intake process.
b. Provide "smoother" paraphrasing in session with clients.
c. Become more comfortable with receiving, processing, and implementing feedback.
d. Becoming more aware of who I am as a counselor, while building on my identity within the profession of counseling. This includes becoming attentive to the structure of counseling

sessions, engaging in person-centered counseling, remaining thoughtful in each session, and attending to issues of immediacy in each session.

e. Learn how to manage and assess suicide risk.

V. ***Procedural Considerations***

a. Supervisee's written case notes (completed using Titanium Schedule© software), treatment plans, and video recordings will be reviewed and evaluated in each session.

b. Issues related to Supervisee's professional development will be discussed in each supervision session.

c. Sessions will be used to discuss issues of conflict and failure of either party to abide by directives outlined here in contract. If concerns of either party are not resolved in supervision, Dr. ___________, CMHC program coordinator, will be consulted.

d. In event of emergency, Supervisee is to contact Supervisor at the office, ( ) ___-____, or on her cell phone, ( ) ___-____.

VI. ***Supervisor's Scope of Competence***

Dr. Osborn earned her Ph.D. in counselor education and supervision from Ohio University in 1996. She is licensed as a Professional Clinical Counselor, with supervisory endorsement (PCC-S; #E2428) by the state of Ohio, and is also licensed in Ohio as a Chemical Dependency Counselor (LCDC-III; #081091). She is currently Professor in the CHDS Program at Kent State University. She has received formal academic training in clinical supervision, has supervised both CHDS doctoral student supervisors and Clinical Mental Health Counseling/Community Counseling Master's students during the course of either their supervision or Practica training at Kent State University, and has taught a section of the doctoral level supervision course in the CHDS program at KSU. She has received training and has practiced as a PCC in the areas of substance abuse counseling and utilizes primarily a solution-focused counseling approach and a motivational interviewing style (she is a member of the Motivational Interviewing Network of Trainers).

VII. ***Terms of the Contract***

This supervision contract is subject to revision at any time, upon the request of either the Supervisor or Supervisee. A formal review of the contract will be made at the mid-term of Spring Semester 2012, and revisions will be made only with consent of Supervisee and approval of the Supervisor.

We agree, to the best of our ability, to uphold the directives specified in this supervision contract and to conduct our professional behavior according to the ethical principles of our professional association.

_________________________/_________ _________________________/__________

Supervisor__________________Date ______**Supervisee**________________Date ________

This contract is effective from ______________________ to ______________________

(start date) (finish date)

(Date of revision or termination) ________________________________

Osborn, C. J. (2012). Unpublished counseling supervision contract. Reprinted with permission.

RECIPROCAL SUPERVISION AGREEMENT
Developed by Christopher R. Smith, Ph.D., and Michelle Pride, Ph.D.

We recognize the importance of safety and mutual awareness to the development and maintenance of multicultural competence and practitioner growth, and we agree to the following:

1. Supervision is a collaborative process.
2. Creating a reciprocal relationship is important to fostering supported growth and higher level thinking about issues of diversity.
3. Diversity dialogues can be difficult, but are a necessary part of supervision.
4. Evaluation is an aspect of supervision and it creates an inherent power differential in the supervisory relationship. This needs to be negotiated in order to foster a working supervisory alliance.
5. Differences in beliefs will not be used as a basis for negative evaluation. Open and honest communication is valued and is a basis for evaluation of competencies.

In my capacity as supervisor I will:

- Work to create a safe atmosphere where learning and growth can occur.
- Take responsibility for initiating discussions of multicultural and diversity issues in supervision.
- Work to bridge cultural differences with my supervisee. As such, it is my responsibility to be aware of myself as a cultural being and aware of how this affects my communication and supervisory style and to make necessary adjustments to meet the needs of my supervisee and foster a healthy working alliance.
- Acknowledge and accept differences between my supervisee's and my beliefs.
- Refrain from making assumptions and take time to assess my supervisee's multicultural knowledge and skills and provide manageable challenge to encourage their growth and development.
- Welcome and encourage feedback from my supervisee that will allow me to see my own blind spots and be open to new learning.
- Refrain from allowing feedback about my blind spots to affect my evaluation of my supervisee in a negative way.

In my capacity as a supervisee, I will:

- Make a commitment to growing and developing as a competent, ethical professional.
- Accept that this process may sometimes be uncomfortable or challenging.
- Take risks regarding my cultural awareness and skills in supervision.
- Be open to my supervisor's help in identifying my own cultural blind spots.
- Endeavor to help my supervisor see their blind spots.
- Acknowledge and accept differences between my supervisor's and my beliefs.
- Share my own unique knowledge and expertise with my supervisor.

We recognize that evaluation is an inherent aspect of supervision. The purpose of evaluation is to provide feedback to aid in the development of ability, knowledge, and skills. While differences in beliefs will not be used in evaluation, competence and ethical practice will be kept in mind throughout supervision. Through this reciprocal supervision process, both the supervisor and the supervisee can benefit and grow as people and as multiculturally competent practitioners.

Supervisor ____________________Date_________Supervisee_______________ Date _______

EXAMPLE OF A PROFESSIONAL DISCLOSURE STATEMENT
Prepared by Course Instructor for Practicum Supervision

As your Practicum instructor, I am responsible for the individual and group supervision you receive this semester. This statement is to be used in conjunction with your syllabus, which spells out all the requirements of Practicum. My purpose in presenting this to you is to acquaint you with some of my goals for supervision, to provide you with an overview of the supervision process, and to outline some of the conditions under which we both must operate.

Prior to addressing the points listed above, I'd like to review my qualifications for conducting supervision (includes degrees in counseling, licenses, and certifications).

I have been engaged in clinical supervision for over (number) years, mostly through my department responsibilities at (name of university[ies]). (List areas of specialization that inform or limit one's supervision. List other activity that qualifies one to supervise, e.g., publications in supervision, workshops conducted.) I adhere to the NBCC Code of Ethics (attach for supervisee) and to the NBCC Clinical Supervision Standards of Practice (attach for supervisee).

Clinical supervision has two goals: the development of the counseling skills of the supervisee (counselor-in-training) and the protection of the client. These are always operating simultaneously when supervision is occurring. Most of the time, it will seem that primary attention is being paid to your developing skills. When this is so, it is because a judgment has been made that your client(s) is receiving adequate counseling services. When there is any question about the adequacy of the counseling your client(s) is receiving, supervision will become more active and, perhaps, more intrusive.

You will work with two supervisors this semester. You will have weekly hour-long individual sessions with a doctoral student supervisor. This weekly session will occur at your mutual convenience. The individual supervisors receive weekly supervision-of-supervision by me. On occasion, I will observe your individual supervision sessions. All supervision sessions will be audiotaped or videotaped. The Practicum class (or group supervision) will be conducted by me and will be a weekly 3-hour session. Group supervision allows you to learn from your peers as well as from your supervisors. Both individual and group supervision are explained in greater detail in your syllabus.

You are required to submit a *minimum* of one audiotaped counseling session per week to your individual supervisor. In addition, you will be required to submit audiotapes as part of group supervision (on average, one every 3 weeks). You will also be required to submit case notes on all individual, family, and group counseling sessions that you conduct each week. It is your responsibility to turn in the required tapes and paperwork. It is my responsibility to coordinate your supervision from me, your individual supervisor, and in some cases, your site supervisor. Your case notes and records of all individual supervision sessions will be maintained by the Department for 7 years.

Your supervisors may draw from different supervision models. You can count on the following, however: You will be encouraged to consider your thoughts, your behaviors, and your feelings as you conduct counseling sessions. Your supervisors will draw from the roles of teacher, consultant, and counselor to assist you in doing this. The supervision you will be offered will be developmentally appropriate (that is, the supervision will be matched to your level of experience and your relative ability). The supervision you receive will include discussions about cultural context—your own, the supervisor's, and the client's—and how these affect the counseling and supervision relationships of which you are a part. The supervision you receive will be sensitive to your personal goals for yourself as a counselor and will be consistent with how you conceptualize client issues theoretically. You will be challenged and supported throughout supervision. You will be treated with respect.

Although one of your supervisors may draw on a counselor role, it is important for you to understand that this is only to help you understand any personal reactions you may be having that are diminishing your positive effect as a counselor. The resolution of personal difficulties cannot be attained through supervision. A referral list of counseling services is available in campus publications and can also be obtained through any Department faculty member. It is not unusual for a student to seek personal counseling while working toward a counseling degree.

You will receive a copy of an Evaluation Instrument on the first day of class. This will be used by me and by your individual supervisor throughout the semester to track your progress and to give you specific, formative feedback. You will receive two formal feedback sessions, one slightly before the midpoint of the semester and one at the end. At this time, you will receive written feedback. If I have any serious concerns about your progress in practicum, I will inform you of these concerns as soon as possible, preferably at the first formal feedback session.

Because you are a student in a counselor training program, I cannot guarantee confidentiality of information gained in supervision if it is relevant to your overall progress in the program. I can, however, commit to honoring and respecting all information I receive in supervision about you and/or your clients and keeping all such information confidential to the degree possible. Occasionally, there are situations that occur that make confidentiality impossible. These include:

1. Threats to harm self or others
2. Reasonable suspicion of abuse of a child or other vulnerable persons
3. When ordered to do so by the court

Confidentiality may also be broken in one's defense against legal action before a court.

Please feel free to call me at home whenever you have any concern about a client for the duration of the practicum. My home number is ________. For regular communications, please call me at the office (________) or e-mail me at [email address]. In case of emergency when I am out of town, you will be advised regarding who is the most appropriate contact person in my absence.

Although it is rare, occasionally a student does not feel that he or she has received adequate supervision or a fair evaluation. If this should occur, your first step is to attempt to resolve the issue with me. If you remain dissatisfied, this course is protected by the same appeal procedure as any other course as is outlined in Department materials and the SOE catalogue. If you believe I have acted unethically in any way, you may report your complaint to:

Although the many parameters of the Practicum course listed in this document may make the experience sound tedious or intimidating, I assure you that on the contrary, this is a most exciting time in your development as a professional counselor. I look forward to working with you and to celebrating your progress as you take the next step in your goal of entering a noble profession.

Please sign, date and return one copy of this form.

______________________________ ______________________________

Practicum Instructor Signature Student Signature

DATE: ______________ DATE: ______________

NBCC Ethics Officer (phone number)

SUPERVISEE'S BILL OF RIGHTS

Introduction

The purpose of the Bill of Rights is to inform supervisees of their rights and responsibilities in the supervisory process.

Nature of the Supervisory Relationship

The supervisory relationship is an experiential learning process that assists the supervisee in developing therapeutic and professional competence. A professional counselor supervisor who has received specific training in supervision facilitates professional growth of the supervisee through

- Monitoring client welfare
- Encouraging compliance with legal, ethical, and professional standards
- Teaching therapeutic skills
- Providing regular feedback and evaluation
- Providing professional experiences and opportunities

Expectations of the Initial Supervisory Session

The supervisee has the right to be informed of the supervisor's expectations of the supervisory relationship. The supervisor shall clearly state expectations of the supervisory relationship that may include

- Supervisee identification of supervision goals for oneself
- Supervisee preparedness for supervisory meetings
- Supervisee determination of areas for professional growth and development
- Supervisor's expectations regarding formal and informal evaluations
- Supervisor's expectations of the supervisee's need to provide formal and informal self-evaluations
- Supervisor's expectations regarding the structure and/or the nature of the supervisory sessions
- Weekly review of case notes until supervisee demonstrates competency in case conceptualization
- The supervisee shall provide input to the supervisor regarding the supervisee's expectations of the relationship.

Expectations of the Supervisory Relationship

A *supervisor* is a professional counselor with appropriate credentials. The supervisee can expect the supervisor to serve as a mentor and a positive role model who assists the supervisee in developing a professional identity. The supervisee has the right to work with a supervisor who is culturally sensitive and is able to openly discuss the influence of race, ethnicity, gender, sexual orientation, religion, and class on the counseling and the supervision process. The supervisor is aware of personal cultural assumptions and constructs and is able to assist the supervisee in developing additional knowledge and skills in working with clients from diverse cultures.

Since a positive rapport between the supervisor and supervisee is critical for successful supervision to occur, the relationship is a priority for both the supervisor and supervisee. In the event that relationship concerns exist, the supervisor or supervisee will discuss concerns with one another and work towards resolving differences. Therapeutic interventions initiated by the supervisor or solicited by the supervisee shall be implemented only in the service of helping the supervisee increase effectiveness with clients. A proper referral for counseling shall be made if appropriate.

The supervisor shall inform the supervisee of an alternative supervisor who will be available in case of crisis situations or known absences.

Ethics and Issues in the Supervisory Relationship

1. *Code of Ethics & Standards of Practice:* The supervisor will insure the supervisee understands the *American Counseling Association Code of Ethics and Standards of Practice* and legal responsibilities. The supervisor and supervisee will discuss sections applicable to the beginning counselor.
2. *Dual Relationships:* Since a power differential exists in the supervisory relationship, the supervisor shall not utilize this differential to their gain. Since dual relationships may affect the objectivity of the supervisor, the supervisee shall not be asked to engage in social interaction that would compromise the professional nature of the supervisory relationship.
3. *Due Process:* During the initial meeting, supervisors provide the supervisee information regarding expectations, goals, and roles of the supervisory process. The supervisee has the right to regular verbal feedback and periodic formal written feedback signed by both individuals.
4. *Evaluation:* During the initial supervisory session, the supervisor provides the supervisee a copy of the evaluation instrument used to assess the counselor's progress.
5. *Informed Consent:* The supervisee informs the client she is in training, is being supervised, and receives written permission from the client to audiotape or videotape.
6. *Confidentiality:* The counseling relationship, assessments, records, and correspondences remain confidential. Failure to keep information confidential is a violation of the ethical code and the counselor is subject to a malpractice suit. The client must sign a written consent prior to counselor's consultation.
7. *Vicarious Liability:* The supervisor is ultimately liable for the welfare of the supervisee's clients. The supervisee is expected to discuss with the supervisor the counseling process and individual concerns of each client.
8. *Isolation:* The supervisor consults with peers regarding supervisory concerns and issues.
9. *Termination of Supervision:* The supervisor discusses termination of the supervisory relationship and helps the supervisee identify areas for continued growth and explore professional goals.

Expectations of the Supervisory Process

The supervisee shall be encouraged to determine a theoretical orientation that can be used for conceptualizing and guiding work with clients.

The supervisee has the right to work with a supervisor who is responsive to the supervisee's theoretical orientation, learning style, and developmental needs.

Since it is probable that the supervisor's theory of counseling will influence the supervision process, the supervisee needs to be informed of the supervisor's counseling theory and how the supervisor's theoretical orientation may influence the supervision process.

Expectations of Supervisory Sessions

The weekly supervisory session shall include a review of all cases, audiotapes, videotapes, and may include live supervision.

The supervisee is expected to meet with the supervisor face-to-face in a professional environment that insures confidentiality.

Expectations of the Evaluation Process

During the initial meeting, the supervisee shall be provided with a copy of the formal evaluation tool(s) that will be used by the supervisor.

The supervisee shall receive verbal feedback and/or informal evaluation during each supervisory session. The supervisee shall receive written feedback or written evaluation on a regular basis during beginning phases of counselor development. Written feedback may be requested by the supervisee during intermediate and advanced phases of counselor development.

The supervisee should be recommended for remedial assistance in a timely manner if the supervisor becomes aware of personal or professional limitations that may impede future professional performance.

Beginning counselors receive written and verbal summative evaluation during the last supervisory meeting. Intermediate and advanced counselors may receive a recommendation for licensure and/or certification.

Maria A. Giordano, Michael K. Altekruse, and Carolyn W. Kern (2000). Unpublished manuscript. Reprinted by the permission of the authors.

SUPERVISION AGREEMENT

Based on the Supervisee's Bill of Rights

The supervisory relationship is an experiential learning process that assists the supervisee in developing therapeutic and professional competence. This contract is designed to assist the supervisor and supervisee in establishing clear expectations about the supervisory process.

Supervisee

Read the *Supervisee's Bill of Rights* and this agreement. Complete the sections on skills, goals, and professional opportunities and bring this agreement to the initial supervisory session.

Prior to the first supervisory session, read the American Counseling Association's *Code of Ethics and Standards of Practice*.

Introduction and Expectations of the Supervisory Experience

Supervisor

1. Introduce yourself: discuss your credentials, licenses, academic background, counseling experience, and your supervisory style.
2. Describe your role as a supervisor: teacher, consultant, counselor, and evaluator.
3. Discuss your responsibilities: monitoring client welfare, teaching therapeutic skills, providing regular verbal and written feedback and evaluation, and insuring compliance with legal, ethical, and professional standards.
4. Ask the supervisee about his or her learning style and developmental needs.

Supervisee

1. Introduce yourself and describe your academic background, clinical experience, and training.
2. Briefly discuss information you want to address during the supervisory meetings.
3. Describe the therapeutic skills you want to enhance and professional development opportunities you want to experience during the next three months.

List three therapeutic skills you would like to further develop.

1. ______________________________
2. ______________________________
3. ______________________________

List three general goals you would like to attain during the supervisory process.

1. ______________________________
2. ______________________________
3. ______________________________

List three specific counseling or professional development experiences you would like to have during the next three months (attending a conference, facilitating a group, presentation, etc.).

1. ______________________________
2. ______________________________
3. ______________________________

Expectations of the Supervisory Relationship

Supervisor and Supervisee

1. Discuss your expectations of the supervisory relationship.
2. Discuss how you will work towards establishing a positive and productive supervisory relationship. Also, discuss how you will address and resolve conflicts.
3. The supervisory experience will increase the supervisee's awareness of feelings, thoughts, behavior, and aspects of self which are stimulated by the client. Discuss the role of the supervisor in assisting with this process.
4. Share your thoughts with one another about the influence of race, ethnicity, gender, sexual orientation, religion, and class on the counseling and the supervision process.

Supervisee

1. Describe how you would like to increase your awareness of personal cultural assumptions, constructs, and ability to work with clients from diverse cultures.

Supervisor

1. If the supervisee needs to consult with you prior to the next supervision session, discuss how you would like to be contacted. Also, if you are unavailable during a period of time, inform the supervisee of an alternate supervisor who will be available in your absence.

Ethics and Issues in the Supervisory Relationship

1. Discuss the *Code of Ethics and Standards of Practice*. Review key issues not listed in this section.
2. A professional relationship is maintained between the supervisor and supervisee. The supervisor and supervisee do not engage in social interaction that interferes with objectivity and professional judgment of the supervisor.
3. After the initial supervisory meeting, the supervisee and supervisor can reestablish goals, expectations, and discuss roles of the supervisory process. The supervisor and supervisee provide one another with regular feedback.
4. During the initial counseling session, the supervisee will inform the client that she/he is in training and is being supervised. If the supervisee wishes to audiotape or videotape, the client needs to give written consent.
5. Discuss confidentiality and the importance of obtaining a written release from the client prior to consultation with other professionals who are serving the client.
6. The supervisor is ultimately responsible for the welfare of the supervisee's clients. During each supervisory session, the supervisee will review each client's progress and relate specific concerns to the supervisor in a timely manner.

Expectations of the Supervisory Process

Supervisor

1. Describe your theory of counseling and how it influences your counseling and supervision style.
2. Discuss your theory or model of supervision.

Supervisee

1. Discuss your learning style and your developmental needs.
2. Discuss your current ideas about your theoretical orientation.

Expectations of Supervisory Sessions

Supervisee

1. Discuss your expectations about the learning process and interest in reviewing audiotapes, videotapes, and case notes.

Supervisor

1. Describe the structure and content of the weekly supervisory sessions.
2. Discuss your expectations regarding supervisee preparedness for supervisory sessions (audiotapes, videotapes, case notes).

CACREP standards require students in their internship experience to receive a minimum 1 hour of individual supervision per week and 90 minutes of group supervision each week.

The weekly supervisory session will take place face-to-face in a professional environment that insures confidentiality. Decide the location, day, and time.

Location ____________ Day _____ Time _____

Expectations Regarding Evaluation

Supervisee

1. Discuss your interest in receiving weekly feedback in areas such as: relationship building, counseling techniques, client conceptualization, and assessment.

Supervisor

1. Discuss your style of providing verbal feedback and evaluation.
2. Provide the supervisee with a copy of the formal evaluation you will use; discuss the evaluation tools and clarify specific items that need additional explanation.
3. Discuss the benefit of self-evaluation; provide a copy of self-evaluation forms, and clarify specific items that need additional explanation.

______________________________Supervisor's Signature Date________

______________________________Supervisee's Signature Date________

THE PRACTICUM COMPETENCIES OUTLINE

Report on Practicum Competencies

A. Baseline Competencies

1. Personality characteristics, intellectual and personal skills students bring to the graduate training experience:
   a. interpersonal skills: encompass both verbal and nonverbal forms of communication, the ability to listen and be empathic and respectful of others, and the ability to be open to feedback.
   b. cognitive skills: includes an attitude of intellectual curiosity and flexibility, and abilities in problem-solving, critical thinking, and organized reasoning.
   c. affective skills: the ability to tolerate affect, to tolerate and understand interpersonal conflict, and to tolerate ambiguity and uncertainty.
   d. personality/attitudes: the desire to help others, openness to new ideas, honesty and integrity, and the valuing of ethical behavior, and personal courage.
   e. expressive skills: the ability to communicate accurately one's ideas, feelings, and information in verbal, nonverbal, and written forms.
   f. reflective skills: the ability to examine and consider one's own motives, attitudes, and behaviors and one's effect on others.
   g. personal skills: personal organization, hygiene, and appropriate dress.
2. Knowledge from graduate classroom experience prior to or concurrent with practicum:
   a. assessment and clinical interviewing
   b. intervention
   c. ethical and legal standards
   d. individual and cultural differences

B. Skills Developed during Practicum

1. Relationship/interpersonal skills
2. Application of research
3. Psychological assessment
4. Intervention
5. Consultation/interprofessional collaboration
6. Diversity: Individual and cultural differences
7. Ethics
8. Leadership
9. Supervisory skills
10. Professional development: Building a foundation for life-long learning
    a. practical skills to maintain effective clinical practice
    b. professional development competencies
11. Metaknowledge/metacompetencies

The following table illustrates how each of the 11 above skills is then elaborated into subskills, with the expected level of attained competence for each. Elaborations of the remaining 10 skills can be found online at www.aptc.org/public_files/Practicum%20Competencies%20FINAL%20(Oct%20'06%20Version).pdf.

B. Description of Skills Leading to Competencies That Are Developed during the Practicum Experience — Completed Practicum

Competence level expected by the completion of practicum is indicated in the column on the right. N = *Novice;* I = *Intermediate;* A = *Advanced.* These competencies are built upon fundamental personality characteristics, intellectual and personal skills (see below for definitions).

1. Relationship/Interpersonal Skills

The ability to form and maintain productive relationships with others is a cornerstone of professional psychology.

Productive relationships are respectful, supportive, professional, and ethical. Professional psychologists should possess these basic competencies when they first begin their clinical training. Although the ability to form such relationships is grounded in basic skills that most students will have developed over the course of their lives to date, helping the student hone and refine these abilities into professional competencies in the clinical setting is a key aim of the practicum.

In particular, the practicum seeks to enhance students' skills in forming relationships:

a) With patients/clients/families:
- i) Ability to take a respectful, helpful professional approach to patients/clients/families. — A
- ii) Ability to form a working alliance. — I
- iii) Ability to deal with conflict, negotiate differences. — I
- iv) Ability to understand and maintain appropriate professional boundaries. — I

b) With colleagues:
- i) Ability to work collegially with fellow professionals. — A
- ii) Ability to support others and their work and to gain support for one's own work. — I
- iii) Ability to provide helpful feedback to peers and receive such feedback nondefensively from peers. — I

c) With supervisors, the ability to make effective use of supervision, including:
- i) Ability to work collaboratively with the supervisor. — A

  Collaboration means understanding, sharing, and working by a set of common goals for supervision. Many of these goals will change as the student gains professional competence, although a core goal, of working cooperatively to enhance the student's skills as a clinician, will remain constant. It is this aspect of collaboration that is expected to be at the "A" level by the end of practicum training. Competencies ii and iii below may be considered aspects of collaboration with the supervisor
- ii) Ability to prepare for supervision. — A
- iii) Ability/willingness to accept supervisory input, including direction; ability to follow through on recommendations; ability to negotiate needs for autonomy from and dependency on supervisors. — A

iv) Ability to self-reflect and self-evaluate regarding clinical skills and use of supervision, including using good judgment as to when supervisory input is necessary.	I
d) With support staff:	
i) Ability to be respectful of support staff roles and persons.	A
e) With teams at clinic:	
i) Ability to participate fully in team's work.	A
ii) Ability to understand and observe team's operating procedures.	I
f) With community professionals:	
i) Ability to communicate professionally and work collaboratively with community professionals.	I
g) For the practicum site itself:	
i) Ability to understand and observe agency's operating procedures.	A
ii) Ability to participate in furthering the work and mission of the practicum site.	A
iii) Ability to contribute in ways that will enrich the site as a practicum experience for future students.	A

1. *Novice (N):* Novices have limited knowledge and understanding of (a) how to analyze problems and (b) intervention skills and the processes and techniques of implementing them. Novices do not yet recognize patterns and do not differentiate well between important and unimportant details; they do not have filled-in cognitive maps of how, for example, a given client may move from where he or she is to a place of better functioning.
2. *Intermediate (I):* Psychology students at the intermediate level of competence have gained enough experience through practice, supervision, and instruction to be able recognize some important recurring domain features and to select appropriate strategies to address the issue at hand. Surface-level analyses of the Novice stage are less prominent, but generalization of diagnostic and intervention skills to new situations and clients is limited, and support is needed to guide performance.
3. *Advanced (A):* At this level, the student has gained deeper, more integrated knowledge of the competency domain in question, including appropriate knowledge of the scholarly/research literature as needed. The student is considerably more fluent in his or her ability to recognize important recurring domain features and to select appropriate strategies to address the issue at hand. In relation to clinical work, recognition of overall patterns, of a set of possible diagnoses, and/or treatment processes and outcomes for a given case are taking shape. Overall plans, based on the more integrated knowledge base and identification of domain features are clearer and more influential in guiding action. At this level, the student is less flexible in these areas than the proficient psychologist [the next level of competence] but does have a feeling of mastery and the ability to cope with and manage many contingencies of clinical work.

From Hatcher, R. L., & Lassiter, K. D. (2007). Initial training in professional psychology: The practicum competencies outline. *Training and Education in Professional Psychology, 1,* 49–63.

Date: ________

SUPERVISION RECORD FORM (SRF-1)

Supervisor: ____________________________ Counselor: ______________________

First name(s) of client(s) discussed: ____

For the names of clients listed, indicate whether you heard/saw a portion of the counseling session:

Pre-session goals for the supervision session:

Extent to which presession goals were met: (Comment)

Major topics that emerged during the supervision session (either supervisor-initiated or supervisee-initiated):

List any supervision interventions (including a rationale for each) having to do with your supervisee's work with a particular client:

List area(s) where your supervisee needs to grow that you attended to in this session:

Note strengths of the supervisee demonstrated in this session:

Goals for next supervision session:

Risk management review. Note any concerns based on review of supervisee's entire caseload. Include (a) first name [or case number] of client, (b) nature of the concern, and (c) supervision intervention at this time.

Signature____

Date: ___________

SUPERVISION RECORD FORM (SRF-2)

Supervisor: ___________________________ Counselor: _______________________

First name(s) (pseudonym) of client(s) discussed: ____

For the names of clients listed, indicate whether you heard/saw a portion of the counseling session:

1. Which developmental model of supervision informed this session and how?
2. Which process model of supervision informed this session and how?
3. To what extent did your counseling—theoretical orientation inform this session and how? Did you use another counseling theory in this session?
4. List supervision interventions (and context) in this session that were consistent with your answers for 1, 2, and 3.
5. To what extent were your presession goals met? (Comment)
6. What are your goals for the next supervision session? (Be sure to use language that reflects your supervisee's development, a process model, and/or your thoughts about counseling theory as it pertains to your supervision. You do not, however, need to address all three, only what is most pertinent.)

Risk management review. Note any concerns based on review of supervisee's entire caseload. Include (a) first name [or case number] of client, (b) nature of the concern, and (c) supervision intervention at this time.

Signature___________________________

MEASURES FOR SUPERVISION RESEARCH AND PRACTICE

SUPERVISORY SATISFACTION QUESTIONNAIRE

1. How would you rate the quality of the supervision you have received?

1	2	3	4
Excellent	*Good*	*Fair*	*Poor*

2. Did you get the kind of supervision you wanted?

1	2	3	4
No, definitely not	*No, not really*	*Yes, generally*	*Yes, definitely*

3. To what extent has this supervision fit your needs?

4	3	2	1
Almost all my needs have been met	*Most of my needs have been met*	*Only a few of my needs have been met*	*None of my needs have been met*

4. If a friend were in need of supervision, would you recommend this supervisor to him or her?

1	2	3	4
No, definitely not	*No, I don't think so*	*Yes, I think so*	*Yes, definitely*

5. How satisfied are you with the amount of supervision you have received?

1	2	3	4
Quite dissatisfied	*Indifferent or mildly dissatisfied*	*Mostly satisfied*	*Very satisfied*

6. Has the supervision you received helped you to deal more effectively in your role as a counselor or therapist?

4	3	2	1
Yes, definitely	*Yes, generally*	*No, not really*	*No, definitely not*

7. In an overall, general sense, how satisfied are you with the supervision you have received?

4	3	2	1
Very satisfied	*Mostly satisfied*	*Indifferent or mildly dissatisfied*	*Quite dissatisfied*

8. If you were to seek supervision again, would you come back to this supervisor?

1	2	3	4
No, definitely not	*No, I don't think so*	*Yes, I think so*	*Yes, definitely*

The score is the sum of the items.

Developed by Ladany, N., Hill, C. E., Corbett, M., & Nutt, E. A. (1996), as a modified version of the Client Satisfaction Questionnaire (Larsen, Attkisson, Hargreaves, & Nguyen, 1979), with permission of the original authors. Unpublished instrument. Reprinted with permission of the authors.

SUPERVISEE NEEDS INDEX

Please rate your current, individual supervisor. Using the following scale as a guide, select a number to indicate how much you agree with each statement.

1 -------------- 2 -------------- 3 -------------- 4 -------------- 5 -------------- 6 ------------- 7

Strongly Disagree *Strongly Agree*

1. My supervisor does not encourage me to grow personally.	1 ---- 2 --- 3 ---- 4 ---- 5 ---- 6 ---- 7
2. Supervision regularly includes opportunities to review recordings of my clinical work.	1 ---- 2 --- 3 ---- 4 ---- 5 ---- 6 ---- 7
3. When faced with a client issue that is new to me, supervision provides little guidance.	1 ---- 2 --- 3 ---- 4 ---- 5 ---- 6 ---- 7
4. I am content with the emphasis placed on learning therapy techniques in supervision.	1 ---- 2 --- 3 ---- 4 ---- 5 ---- 6 ---- 7
5. When ethical issues arise, my supervisor provides meaningful assistance.	1 ---- 2 --- 3 ---- 4 ---- 5 ---- 6 ---- 7
6. Countertransference issues are not discussed as much as I would prefer in supervision.	1 ---- 2 --- 3 ---- 4 ---- 5 ---- 6 ---- 7
7. There are sufficient opportunities to receive formal evaluation of my therapy work during supervision.	1 ---- 2 --- 3 ---- 4 ---- 5 ---- 6 ---- 7
8. I feel my supervision has ample focus on my clients' needs.	1 ---- 2 --- 3 ---- 4 ---- 5 ---- 6 ---- 7
9. I leave supervision feeling that my pressing issues were not addressed.	1 ---- 2 --- 3 ---- 4 ---- 5 ---- 6 ---- 7
10. We have a regularly scheduled time for supervision that my supervisor honors.	1 ---- 2 --- 3 ---- 4 ---- 5 ---- 6 ---- 7
11. My supervisor helps me to feel self-assured in my clinical work.	1 ---- 2 --- 3 ---- 4 ---- 5 ---- 6 ---- 7
12. My supervisor is clearly motivated to help me in supervision.	1 ---- 2 --- 3 ---- 4 ---- 5 ---- 6 ---- 7
13. There are many times when my supervisor does not seem to be listening to me.	1 ---- 2 --- 3 ---- 4 ---- 5 ---- 6 ---- 7
14. I do not receive the mentoring I want in supervision.	1 ---- 2 --- 3 ---- 4 ---- 5 ---- 6 ---- 7
15. My supervisor has helped improve my ability to understand my clients.	1 ---- 2 --- 3 ---- 4 ---- 5 ---- 6 ---- 7
16. My supervisor spends time explaining her or his expectations of me.	1 ---- 2 --- 3 ---- 4 ---- 5 ---- 6 ---- 7
17. My supervisor rarely makes time for me when I need it.	1 ---- 2 --- 3 ---- 4 ---- 5 ---- 6 ---- 7
18. I feel safe in supervision.	1 ---- 2 --- 3 ---- 4 ---- 5 ---- 6 ---- 7
19. I frequently leave supervision feeling I did not learn enough about therapy.	1 ---- 2 --- 3 ---- 4 ---- 5 ---- 6 ---- 7

20. My role as a supervisee is not clear.	1 ---- 2 --- 3 ---- 4 ---- 5 ---- 6 ---- 7
21. I wish my supervisor would suggest literature related to my clinical work when I request it.	1 ---- 2 --- 3 ---- 4 ---- 5 ---- 6 ---- 7
22. My most significant concerns are addressed in supervision.	1 ---- 2 --- 3 ---- 4 ---- 5 ---- 6 ---- 7
23. I feel my supervisor only wants me to utilize her or his theoretical orientation.	1 ---- 2 --- 3 ---- 4 ---- 5 ---- 6 ---- 7
24. My clinical knowledge has expanded through supervision.	1 ---- 2 --- 3 ---- 4 ---- 5 ---- 6 ---- 7
25. I am concerned my clients' well-being is overlooked in supervision.	1 ---- 2 --- 3 ---- 4 ---- 5 ---- 6 ---- 7
26. My supervisor appropriately challenges me to think for myself.	1 ---- 2 --- 3 ---- 4 ---- 5 ---- 6 ---- 7
27. The emphasis in supervision on my personal growth meets my needs.	1 ---- 2 --- 3 ---- 4 ---- 5 ---- 6 ---- 7
28. At times, my supervisor's behavior feels invalidating.	1 ---- 2 --- 3 ---- 4 ---- 5 ---- 6 ---- 7
29. I am dissatisfied with the supervisory relationship.	1 ---- 2 --- 3 ---- 4 ---- 5 ---- 6 ---- 7
30. It would be helpful for my supervisor to give me greater autonomy in clinical decision-making.	1 ---- 2 --- 3 ---- 4 ---- 5 ---- 6 ---- 7
31. I wish my supervisor would directly observe my therapy sessions more often.	1 ---- 2 --- 3 ---- 4 ---- 5 ---- 6 ---- 7
32. I am not able to be myself in supervision.	1 ---- 2 --- 3 ---- 4 ---- 5 ---- 6 ---- 7
33. When I ask for readings on a particular issue, my supervisor provides recommendations.	1 ---- 2 --- 3 ---- 4 ---- 5 ---- 6 ---- 7
34. I would prefer more emphasis be placed on issues of diversity in supervision.	1 ---- 2 --- 3 ---- 4 ---- 5 ---- 6 ---- 7
35. My supervisor encourages me to work from the theoretical approach that fits for me.	1 ---- 2 --- 3 ---- 4 ---- 5 ---- 6 ---- 7
36. Multicultural issues are sufficiently discussed in supervision.	1 ---- 2 --- 3 ---- 4 ---- 5 ---- 6 ---- 7
37. My supervisor's feedback about my therapy skills is insufficient.	1 ---- 2 --- 3 ---- 4 ---- 5 ---- 6 ---- 7
38. I feel the supervisory relationship is supportive.	1 ---- 2 --- 3 ---- 4 ---- 5 ---- 6 ---- 7
39. In supervision, we appropriately discuss my personal issues as they relate to my clinical work.	1 ---- 2 --- 3 ---- 4 ---- 5 ---- 6 ---- 7
40. Conceptualization of my clients during supervision has little impact on my clinical work.	1 ---- 2 --- 3 ---- 4 ---- 5 ---- 6 ---- 7
41. I wish my supervisor would willingly discuss my ethical concerns.	1 ---- 2 --- 3 ---- 4 ---- 5 ---- 6 ---- 7
42. It seems that my supervisor does not give much consideration to my needs.	1 ---- 2 --- 3 ---- 4 ---- 5 ---- 6 ---- 7

43. My supervisor is not trustworthy.	1 ---- 2 --- 3 ---- 4 ---- 5 ---- 6 ---- 7
44. My supervisor serves as a guide in my professional development.	1 ---- 2 --- 3 ---- 4 ---- 5 ---- 6 ---- 7
45. My supervisor makes our relationship a priority.	1 ---- 2 --- 3 ---- 4 ---- 5 ---- 6 ---- 7
46. My supervisor is helpful when I am unfamiliar with a particular clinical issue.	1 ---- 2 --- 3 ---- 4 ---- 5 ---- 6 ---- 7
47. I feel able to disclose my honest reactions to my supervisor.	1 ---- 2 --- 3 ---- 4 ---- 5 ---- 6 ---- 7
48. My supervisor does not focus enough on utilizing different therapy interventions.	1 ---- 2 --- 3 ---- 4 ---- 5 ---- 6 ---- 7

SNI Scoring Procedures

To find a total score for the SNI, reverse score the items listed below. Then, add each Likert-scale score to achieve a Total Score (Range = 48 – 336).

Reverse Scored:

Items: 1, 3, 6, 9, 13, 14, 17, 19, 20, 21, 23, 25, 28, 29, 30, 31, 32, 34, 37, 40, 41, 42, 43, 48

Therefore, for those items, 7 = 1, 6 = 2, 5 = 3, 4 = 4, 3 = 5, 2 = 6, 1 = 7

GROUP SUPERVISION SCALE

For each of the following items, please circle the number that best describes your experience with your group supervisor. Please use a five-point scale where 1 = *strongly disagree* and 5 = *strongly agree*.

1. The supervisor provides useful feedback regarding my skills and interventions.	1	2	3	4	5
2. The supervisor provides helpful suggestions and information related to client treatment.	1	2	3	4	5
3. The supervisor facilitates constructive exploration of ideas and techniques for working with clients.	1	2	3	4	5
4. The supervisor provides helpful information regarding case conceptualization and diagnosis.	1	2	3	4	5
5. The supervisor helps me comprehend and formulate clients' central issues.	1	2	3	4	5
6. The supervisor helps me understand the thoughts, feelings, and behaviors of my clients.	1	2	3	4	5
7. The supervisor encourages supervisee self-exploration appropriately.	1	2	3	4	5
8. The supervisor enables me to express opinions, questions, and concerns about my counseling.	1	2	3	4	5
9. The supervisor creates a safe environment for group supervision.	1	2	3	4	5
10. The supervisor is attentive to group dynamics.	1	2	3	4	5
11. The supervisor effectively sets limits, and establishes norms and boundaries for the group.	1	2	3	4	5
12. The supervisor provides helpful leadership for the group.	1	2	3	4	5
13. The supervisor encourages supervisees to provide each other feedback.	1	2	3	4	5
14. The supervisor redirects the discussion when appropriate.	1	2	3	4	5
15. The supervisor manages time well between all the group members.	1	2	3	4	5
16. The supervisor provides enough structure in the group supervision.	1	2	3	4	5

Scoring: *Group Safety Scale:* Sum items 7, 8, 9, 10, and 13; divide by 5

Skill Development and Case Conceptualization Scale:
Sum items 1, 2, 3, 4, 5, and 6; divide by 6.

Group Management Scale: Sum items 11, 12, 15, and 16

SUPERVISEE LEVELS QUESTIONNAIRE–REVISED

Please answer the following items in terms of your own *current* behavior. In responding to those items, use the following scale:

Never	*Rarely*	*Sometimes*	*Half the Time*	*Often*	*Most of the Time*	*Always*
1	2	3	4	5	6	7

1. I feel genuinely relaxed and comfortable in my counseling/therapy sessions.
   1 2 3 4 5 6 7
2. I am able to critique counseling tapes and gain insights with minimum help from my supervisor.
   1 2 3 4 5 6 7
3. I am able to be spontaneous in counseling/therapy, yet my behavior is relevant.
   1 2 3 4 5 6 7
4. I lack self-confidence in establishing counseling relationships with diverse client types.
   1 2 3 4 5 6 7
5. I am able to apply a consistent personalized rationale of human behavior in working with my clients.
   1 2 3 4 5 6 7
6. I tend to get confused when things don't go according to plan and lack confidence in ability to handle the unexpected.
   1 2 3 4 5 6 7
7. The overall quality of my work fluctuates; on some days I do well, on other days, I do poorly.
   1 2 3 4 5 6 7
8. I depend upon my supervision considerably in figuring out how to deal with my clients.
   1 2 3 4 5 6 7
9. I feel comfortable confronting my clients.
   1 2 3 4 5 6 7
10. Much of the time in counseling/therapy I find myself thinking about my next response instead of fitting my intervention into the overall picture.
    1 2 3 4 5 6 7
11. My motivation fluctuates from day to day.
    1 2 3 4 5 6 7
12. At times, I wish my supervisor could be in the counseling/therapy session to lend a hand.
    1 2 3 4 5 6 7
13. During counseling/therapy sessions, I find it difficult to concentrate because of my concern about my own performance.
    1 2 3 4 5 6 7
14. Although at times I really want advice/feedback from my supervisor, at *other* times I really want to do things my own way.
    1 2 3 4 5 6 7

15. Sometimes the client's situation seems so hopeless. I just don't know what to do.
    1 2 3 4 5 6 7
16. It is important that my supervisor allow me to make my own mistakes.
    1 2 3 4 5 6 7
17. Given my current state of professional development, I believe I know when I need consultation from my supervisor and when I don't.
    1 2 3 4 5 6 7
18. Sometimes I question how suited I am to be a counselor/therapist.
    1 2 3 4 5 6 7
19. Regarding counseling/therapy, I view my supervisor as a teacher/mentor.
    1 2 3 4 5 6 7
20. Sometimes I feel that counseling/therapy is so complex, I never will be able to learn it all.
    1 2 3 4 5 6 7
21. I believe I know my strengths and weaknesses as a counselor sufficiently well to understand my professional potential and limitations.
    1 2 3 4 5 6 7
22. Regarding my counseling/therapy, I view my supervisor as a peer/colleague.
    1 2 3 4 5 6 7
23. I think I know myself well and am able to integrate that into my therapeutic style.
    1 2 3 4 5 6 7
24. I find I am able to understand my clients' view of the world, yet help them objectively evaluate alternatives.
    1 2 3 4 5 6 7
25. At my current level of professional development, my confidence in my abilities is such that my desire to do counseling/therapy doesn't change much from day to day.
    1 2 3 4 5 6 7
26. I find I am able to empathize with my clients' feeling states, but still help them focus on problem resolution.
    1 2 3 4 5 6 7
27. I am able to adequately assess my interpersonal impact on clients and use that knowledge therapeutically.
    1 2 3 4 5 6 7
28. I am adequately able to assess the client's interpersonal impact on me and use that therapeutically.
    1 2 3 4 5 6 7
29. I believe I exhibit a consistent professional objectivity and ability to work within my role as a counselor without *undue overinvolvement* with my clients.
    1 2 3 4 5 6 7
30. I believe I exhibit a consistent professional objectivity and ability to work within my role as a counselor without *excessive distance* from my clients.
    1 2 3 4 5 6 7

Scoring key: *Self and Other Awareness items:* 1, 3, 5, 9, 10*, 13*, 24, 26, 27, 28, 29, 30
Motivation items: 7, 11*, 15*, 18*, 20*, 21, 23, 25
Dependency–Autonomy items: 2, 4*, 6*, 8, 12*, 14, 16, 17, 19*, 22

***Indicates reverse scoring. To score: sum the items in the scale, then divide by the number of items.**

Developed by Stoltenberg, C. D. Unpublished version of Supervisee Levels Questionnaire–Revised. Reprinted by permission of the author.

ANTICIPATORY SUPERVISEE ANXIETY SCALE (ASAS)

Directions: Complete before your supervision session.

Following are a number of statements that describe possible feelings or experiences you may have about your upcoming supervision session. Recall, if you have more than one supervisor or supervision session per week, please choose the supervision session you were asked to rate.

Please indicate your *current* thoughts and/or feelings about your *upcoming* supervision session by responding to the sentence stem: "In anticipation of my upcoming supervision session, I ...." Rate each item on a scale of 1 to 9; 1 meaning "Not at all true of me," 5 meaning "Moderately true of me," and 9 meaning "Completely true of me." It is very important to answer all questions; otherwise your data will not be fully useable.

1	2	3	4	5	6	7	8	9
Not at all true		*Mildly true*		*Moderately true*		*Very true*		*Completely true*

"In anticipation of my upcoming supervision session, I ..."

_____ 1. have difficulty focusing on what I will say to my supervisor
_____ 2. feel my heart pounding
_____ 3. feel anxious about how my supervisor might evaluate me
_____ 4. feel self-conscious
_____ 5. worry about how my peers will see me
_____ 6. think less of myself because of my shortcomings as a therapist
_____ 7. feel fearful that I might receive a negative evaluation from my supervisor
_____ 8. notice I am having a hard time relaxing
_____ 9. feel nervous
_____ 10. feel annoyed with my limitations
_____ 11. am concerned about my skills compared to other therapists
_____ 12. can't help but compare myself to my peers
_____ 13. feel overwhelmed
_____ 14. begin to find fault with my therapy session
_____ 15. feel apprehensive
_____ 16.* feel calm
_____ 17. feel antsy
_____ 18. feel stressed out
_____ 19. feel afraid I might lose face in front of my supervisor
_____ 20. question my abilities as a therapist
_____ 21. think that I won't perform at my best in the supervision session
_____ 22. feel myself getting tense
_____ 23.* feel relaxed
_____ 24. worry that I might not make sense (be coherent in presenting the issues)

_____ 25. wonder what my supervisor might be thinking of me

_____ 26. become concerned about what my supervisor might think of me

_____ 27. worry that I might appear stupid

_____ 28. am uneasy about receiving criticism from my supervisor

*Reverse scored item.

To score the ASAS, reverse score items first, then sum items; higher scores indicate greater anticipatory supervisee anxiety.

From Ellis, M. V., Singh, N. N., Dennin, M. K., & Tosado, M. *The Anticipatory Supervisee Anxiety Scale*. Unpublished measure. University at Albany, SUNY, Albany, NY. Reprinted with permission. Additional supporting data can be found in Ellis et al. (1993), Singh & Ellis (2000), and Tosado (2004).

ROLE CONFLICT AND ROLE AMBIGUITY INVENTORY

Instructions: The following statements describe some problems that therapists-in-training may experience during the course of clinical supervision. Please read each statement and then rate the extent to which you have experienced difficulty in supervision in your most recent clinical training.

For each of the following, circle the most appropriate number, where 1 = *not at all,* and 5 = *very much so*.

I have experienced difficulty in my current or most recent supervision because:

1. I was not certain about what material to present to my supervisor.	1	2	3	4	5
2. I have felt that my supervisor was incompetent or less competent than I. I often felt as though I was supervising him/her.	1	2	3	4	5
3. I have wanted to challenge the appropriateness of my supervisor's recommendations for using a technique with one of my clients, but I have thought it better to keep my opinions to myself.	1	2	3	4	5
4. I wasn't sure how best to use supervision as I became more experienced, although I was aware that I was undecided about whether to confront her/him.	1	2	3	4	5
5. I have believed that my supervisor's behavior in one or more situations was unethical or illegal and I was undecided about whether to confront him/her.	1	2	3	4	5
6. My orientation to therapy was different from that of my supervisor. She or he wanted me to work with clients using her or his framework, and I felt that I should be allowed to use my own approach.	1	2	3	4	5
7. I have wanted to intervene with one of my clients in a particular way and my supervisor has wanted me to approach the client in a very different way. I am expected both to judge what is appropriate for myself and also to do what I am told.	1	2	3	4	5
8. My supervisor expected to me to come prepared for supervision, but I had no idea what or how to prepare.	1	2	3	4	5
9. I wasn't sure how autonomous I should be in my work with clients.	1	2	3	4	5
10. My supervisor told me to do something I perceived to be illegal or unethical and I was expected to comply.	1	2	3	4	5
11. My supervisor's criteria for evaluating my work were not specific.	1	2	3	4	5
12. I was not sure that I had done what the supervisor expected me to do in a session with a client.	1	2	3	4	5
13. The criteria for evaluating my performance in supervision were not clear.	1	2	3	4	5
14. I got mixed signals from my supervisor and I was unsure of which signals to attend to.	1	2	3	4	5
15. When using a new technique, I was unclear about the specific steps involved. As a result, I wasn't sure how my supervisor would evaluate my work.	1	2	3	4	5

16. I disagreed with my supervisor about how to introduce a specific issue to a client, but I also wanted to do what the supervisor recommended.	1	2	3	4	5
17. Part of me wanted to rely on my own instincts with clients, but I always knew that my supervisor would have the last word.	1	2	3	4	5
18. The feedback I got from my supervisor did not help me to know what was expected of me in my day to day work with clients.	1	2	3	4	5
19. I was not comfortable using a technique recommended by my supervisor; however, I felt that I should do what my supervisor recommended.	1	2	3	4	5
20. Everything was new and I wasn't sure what would be expected of me.	1	2	3	4	5
21. I was not sure if I should discuss my professional weaknesses in supervision because I was not sure how I would be evaluated.	1	2	3	4	5
22. I disagreed with my supervisor about implementing a specific technique, but I also waned to do what the supervisor thought best.	1	2	3	4	5
23. My supervisor gave me no feedback and I felt lost.	1	2	3	4	5
24. My supervisor told me what to do with a client, but did not give me very specific ideas about how to do it.	1	2	3	4	5
25. My supervisor wanted me to use an assessment technique that I considered inappropriate for a particular client.	1	2	3	4	5
26. There were no clear guidelines for my behavior in supervision.	1	2	3	4	5
27. The supervisor gave no constructive or negative feedback and as a result, I did not know how to address my weaknesses.	1	2	3	4	5
28. I did not know how I was doing as a therapist and, as a result, I did not know how my supervisor would evaluate me.	1	2	3	4	5
29. I was unsure of what to expect from my supervisor.	1	2	3	4	5

Scoring key: *Role Ambiguity items:* 1, 4, 8, 9, 11, 12, 13, 18, 20, 21, 23, 24, 26, 27, 28, 29
Role Conflict items: 2, 3, 5, 6, 7, 10, 14, 15, 16, 17, 19, 22, 25

From Olk, M., & Friedlander, M. L. (1992). Trainees' experiences of role conflict and role ambiguity in supervisory relationships. *Journal of Counseling Psychology, 39,* 389–397.

MULTICULTURAL SUPERVISION COMPETENCIES QUESTIONNAIRE

This questionnaire is intended to evaluate the quality of multicultural supervision. If you have had a supervisor who is culturally or racially different from you, I would like you to complete this questionnaire with respect to this particular supervisor.

Your ethnic/racial identity ______________________________

Your supervisor's ethnic/racial background ______________________

Your gender ______________________ Your supervisor's gender ______________________

How long ago? __________ How long did you have him/her as supervisor? ________

What was the level of your clinical training during this supervision?

____

What was the nature of the clinical site where this supervision took place?

____

Based on your experiences and observation, please rate the following statements according to the following scale:

1	2	3	4	5
Strongly Disagree	*Disagree*	*Undecided*	*Agree*	*Strongly Agree*

Circle the response code (e.g., 4 for Agree, 2 for Disagree) at the end of each statement that most clearly reflects your opinion about this supervisor. Try to use 3 sparingly.

1. Understands my culture and value systems.	1	2	3	4	5
2. Shows openness and respect for culturally different supervisees.	1	2	3	4	5
3. Actively avoids cultural biases and discriminatory practices in working with minority students.	1	2	3	4	5
4. Understands the worldviews of supervisees and clients from other cultures.	1	2	3	4	5
5. Understands the tendency and the problem of racial stereotyping.	1	2	3	4	5
6. Makes an effort to understand and accommodate culturally different supervisees.	1	2	3	4	5
7. Is able to avoid racial stereotypes by taking into account both the uniqueness of individuals as well as the known characteristics of the culture.	1	2	3	4	5
8. Makes use of every opportunity to increase supervisees' multicultural competence in counseling.	1	2	3	4	5
9. Is able to clarify presenting problems and arrives at culturally relevant case conceptualization with clients from different cultural backgrounds.	1	2	3	4	5
10. Shows an understanding of how culture, ethnicity, and race influence supervision and counseling.	1	2	3	4	5
11. Is able to overcome cultural and language barriers in relating to minority students and clients.	1	2	3	4	5

12. Has never mentioned that race is an important consideration in supervision and counseling.	1	2	3	4	5
13. Demonstrates skills to balance between the generic characteristics of counseling and the unique values of different cultural groups.	1	2	3	4	5
14. Shows sensitivity and skills in supervising culturally different supervisees.	1	2	3	4	5
15. Shows unconditional acceptance of all supervisees, regardless of their race, ethnicity, and culture.	1	2	3	4	5
16. Recognizes the limitations of models and approaches based on Western assumptions in working with culturally different individuals.	1	2	3	4	5
17. Knows how to encourage discussion of cultural and racial issues in counseling and supervision.	1	2	3	4	5
18. Shows interest in learning new skills and enhancing own multicultural competence in supervision and counseling.	1	2	3	4	5
19. Recognizes that what is inappropriate from the standpoint of the majority culture may be appropriate for some minority cultures.	1	2	3	4	5
20. Takes into account cultural biases in assessing supervisees and forming clinical judgments.	1	2	3	4	5
21. Exhibits respect for other cultures without overly identifying self with minority culture or becoming paternalistic.	1	2	3	4	5
22. Is willing to advocate for minorities who experience institutional discrimination.	1	2	3	4	5
23. Understands the cultural reasons why minority students and clients tend to defer to authority figures.	1	2	3	4	5
24. Communicates effectively with culturally different supervisees at both the verbal and nonverbal levels.	1	2	3	4	5
25. Understands cultural differences in help-giving and help-seeking.	1	2	3	4	5
26. Believes that Western models and approaches of counseling are equally generalizable to ethnic minorities.	1	2	3	4	5
27. Gives emotional support and encouragement to minority students.	1	2	3	4	5
28. Is very rigid and dogmatic regarding what constitutes the proper approach of counseling.	1	2	3	4	5
29. Shows an interest in helping minority students overcome systemic and institutional barriers.	1	2	3	4	5
30. Welcomes my input even when I express different views and values.	1	2	3	4	5
31. Knows how to consult or refer to resources available in ethnocultural communities.	1	2	3	4	5
32. Takes into account racial biases and sociopolitical implications in counseling and supervision.	1	2	3	4	5
33. Considers supervisees' cultural and linguistic backgrounds in giving them feedback and evaluation.	1	2	3	4	5

34. Shows a genuine interest in learning about other cultures.	1	2	3	4	5
35. Recognizes individual differences in ethnic/racial identity.	1	2	3	4	5
36. Demonstrates a familiarity with the value systems of diverse cultural groups.	1	2	3	4	5
37. Knows that biases and assumptions of Western counseling models can have a negative effect on culturally different supervisees and clients.	1	2	3	4	5
38. Knows how to adapt knowledge of cultural differences to supervision and counseling.	1	2	3	4	5
39. Does not seem to be aware of own limitations in working with culturally different supervisees or clients.	1	2	3	4	5
40. Does not pay any attention to the demographics of supervisees.	1	2	3	4	5
41. Is able to develop culturally appropriate treatment plans for clients from different cultural backgrounds.	1	2	3	4	5
42. Makes an effort to establish a relationship of trust and acceptance with culturally different supervisees.	1	2	3	4	5
43. Is flexible in adjusting his/her supervisory style to culturally different supervisees.	1	2	3	4	5
44. Assists supervisees in formulating culturally appropriate assessment and treatment plans.	1	2	3	4	5
45. Makes use of the support network of minorities.	1	2	3	4	5
46. Does not seem to be aware of own implicit cultural biases in counseling and supervision.	1	2	3	4	5
47. Acknowledges that his or her own life experiences, values, and biases may influence the supervision process.	1	2	3	4	5
48. Actively interacts with minority students outside of counseling and classroom settings.	1	2	3	4	5
49. Knows something about how gender, socioeconomic status, and religious issues are related to minority status.	1	2	3	4	5
50. Shows some knowledge about the cultural traditions of various ethnic groups.	1	2	3	4	5
51. Is able to integrate own beliefs, knowledge, and skills in forming relationships with culturally different supervisees.	1	2	3	4	5
52. Is able to reduce my defensiveness, suspicions, and anxiety about having a supervisor from a different culture.	1	2	3	4	5
53. Shows no interest in understanding my cultural background and ethnic/racial heritage.	1	2	3	4	5
54. Negatively evaluates supervisees who do not conform to supervisor's own theoretical orientation and approach of counseling.	1	2	3	4	5
55. Has a tendency to abuse supervisory power (e.g., imposes view on supervisees).	1	2	3	4	5

56. Respects the worldview, religious beliefs, and values of culturally different supervisees.	1	2	3	4	5
57. Demonstrates competence in a wide variety of methods of assessment and interventions, including nontraditional ones.	1	2	3	4	5
58. Provides guidance to international students and new immigrants to facilitate their acculturation.	1	2	3	4	5
59. Makes minority supervisees feel safe to share their difficulties and concerns.	1	2	3	4	5
60. Is able to relate to culturally different supervisees, while maintaining own cultural values.	1	2	3	4	5

Scoring: Before scoring, reverse the scoring of the following items: 12, 26, 28, 39, 40, 46, 53, 54, 55

Attitude and beliefs (how the supervisor feels about multicultural issues and culturally different supervisees): 2, 12, 16, 19, 21, 26, 34, 39, 40, 46, 47, 56

Knowledge and understanding (what the supervisor knows about multicultural supervision): 1, 4, 5, 10, 23, 25, 36, 37, 49, 50

Skills and practices (how the supervisor demonstrates multicultural competencies in actual practices of supervision): 7, 8, 9, 13, 14, 17, 18, 20, 24, 28, 31, 32, 33, 35, 38, 41, 43, 44, 45, 52, 54, 57

Relationship (how the supervisor relates to culturally different supervisees): 3, 6, 11, 15, 22, 27, 29, 30, 42, 48, 51, 53, 55, 58, 59, 60

EVALUATION PROCESS WITHIN SUPERVISION INVENTORY

Please indicate the extent to which you agree or disagree with each of the following statements. For each, circle the appropriate number on a 7-point scale, where 1 = *strongly disagree* and 7 = *strongly agree*.

1. The goals my supervisor and I generated for my training seem important.	1	2	3	4	5	6	7
2. My supervisor and I created goals that were easy for me to understand.	1	2	3	4	5	6	7
3. The objectives my supervisor and I created were specific.	1	2	3	4	5	6	7
4. My supervisor and I created goals that were realistic.	1	2	3	4	5	6	7
5. I think my supervisor would have been against my reshaping/changing my learning objectives over the course of our work together.	1	2	3	4	5	6	7
6. My supervisor and I created goals that seemed too easy for me.	1	2	3	4	5	6	7
8. I felt uncertain as to what my most important goals were for this training experience.	1	2	3	4	5	6	7
9. My training objectives were established early in our relationship.	1	2	3	4	5	6	7
10. My supervisor and I never had a discussion about my objectives for my training experience.	1	2	3	4	5	6	7
11. My supervisor told me what he/she wanted me to learn from the experience without inquiring about what I hoped to learn.	1	2	3	4	5	6	7
12. Some of the goals my supervisor and I established were not practical in light of the resources available at my site (e.g., requiring videotaping and not providing equipment).	1	2	3	4	5	6	7
13. My supervisor and I set objectives which seemed practical given the opportunities available at my site, (e.g., if career counseling skills was a goal, I was able to work with people with career concerns).	1	2	3	4	5	6	7
14. My supervisor welcomed comments about his or her style as a supervisor.	1	2	3	4	5	6	7
15. The appraisal I received from my supervisor seemed impartial.	1	2	3	4	5	6	7
16. My supervisor's comments about my work were understandable.	1	2	3	4	5	6	7
17. I did not receive information about how I was doing as a counselor until late in the semester.	1	2	3	4	5	6	7
19. My supervisor balanced his or her feedback between positive and negative statements.	1	2	3	4	5	6	7

20. The feedback I received from my supervisor was based upon his or her direct observation of my work.	1	2	3	4	5	6	7
21. The feedback I received was directly related to the goals we established.	1	2	3	4	5	6	7

Scoring: *First, reverse score the following items:* 5, 6, 8, 10, 11, 12, and 17.

Goal Setting: Sum of items 1–13.

Feedback: Sum of items 14–21.

From Lehrman-Waterman, D., & Ladany, N. (2001). Development and validation of the evaluation process within supervision inventory [Special issue]. *Journal of Counseling Psychology, 48*(2), 168–177.

SUPERVISORY WORKING ALLIANCE (SWA)—SUPERVISOR FORM

Instructions: Please indicate the frequency with which the behavior described in each of the following items seems characteristic of your work with your supervisee. After each item, check (*X*) the space over the number corresponding to the appropriate point of the following 7-point scale:

	1	2	3	4	5	6	7
	Almost Never						*Almost Always*
1. I help my supervisee work within a specific treatment plan with his/her client.	1	2	3	4	5	6	7
2. I help my supervisee stay on track during our meetings.	1	2	3	4	5	6	7
3. My style is to carefully and systematically consider the material that my supervisee brings to supervision.	1	2	3	4	5	6	7
4. My supervisee works with me on specific goals in the supervisory session.	1	2	3	4	5	6	7
5. In supervision, I expect my supervisee to think about or reflect on my comments to him or her.	1	2	3	4	5	6	7
6. I teach my supervisee through direct suggestion.	1	2	3	4	5	6	7
7. In supervision, I place a high priority on our understanding of the client's perspective.	1	2	3	4	5	6	7
8. I encourage my supervisee to take time to understand what the client is saying and doing.	1	2	3	4	5	6	7
9. When correcting my supervisee's errors with a client, I offer alternative ways of intervening.	1	2	3	4	5	6	7
10. I encourage my supervisee to formulate his/her own interventions with his/her clients.	1	2	3	4	5	6	7
11. I encourage my supervisee to talk about the work in ways that are comfortable for him/her.	1	2	3	4	5	6	7
12. I welcome my supervisee's explanations about his/her client's behavior.	1	2	3	4	5	6	7
13. During supervision, my supervisee talks more than I do.	1	2	3	4	5	6	7
14. I make an effort to understand my supervisee.	1	2	3	4	5	6	7
15. I am tactful when commenting about my supervisee's performance.	1	2	3	4	5	6	7
16. I facilitate my supervisee's talking in our sessions.	1	2	3	4	5	6	7
17. In supervision, my supervisee is more curious than anxious when discussing his/her difficulties with me.	1	2	3	4	5	6	7
18. My supervisee appears to be comfortable working with me.	1	2	3	4	5	6	7
19. My supervisee understands client behavior and treatment techniques similar to the way I do.	1	2	3	4	5	6	7

20. During supervision, my supervisee seems able to stand back and reflect on what I am saying to him/her.	1	2	3	4	5	6	7
21. I stay in tune with my supervisee during supervision.	1	2	3	4	5	6	7
22. My supervisee identifies with me in the way he/she thinks and talks about his/her clients.	1	2	3	4	5	6	7
23. My supervisee consistently implements suggestions made in supervision.	1	2	3	4	5	6	7

The Supervisor form of the SWA has three scales, scored as follows:

Rapport: Sum items 10–16, then divide by 7.

Client Focus: Sum items 1–9, then divide by 9.

Identification: Sum items 17–23, then divide by 7.

SUPERVISORY WORKING ALLIANCE (SWA)—SUPERVISEE FORM

Instructions: Please indicate the frequency with which the behavior described in each of the following items seems characteristic of your work with your supervisor. After each item, check (*X*) the space over the number corresponding to the appropriate point of the following 7-point scale:

	1 *Almost Never*	2	3	4	5	6	7 *Almost Always*
1. I feel comfortable working with my supervisor.	1	2	3	4	5	6	7
2. My supervisor welcomes my explanations about the client's behavior.	1	2	3	4	5	6	7
3. My supervisor makes the effort to understand me.	1	2	3	4	5	6	7
4. My supervisor encourages me to talk about my work with clients in ways that are comfortable for me.	1	2	3	4	5	6	7
5. My supervisor is tactful when commenting about my performance.	1	2	3	4	5	6	7
6. My supervisor encourages me to formulate my own interventions with the client.	1	2	3	4	5	6	7
7. My supervisor helps me talk freely in our sessions.	1	2	3	4	5	6	7
8. My supervisor stays in tune with me during supervision.	1	2	3	4	5	6	7
9. I understand client behavior and treatment technique similar to the way my supervisor does.	1	2	3	4	5	6	7
10. I feel free to mention to my supervisor any troublesome feelings I might have about him/her.	1	2	3	4	5	6	7
11. My supervisor treats me like a colleague in our supervisory sessions.	1	2	3	4	5	6	7
12. In supervision, I am more curious than anxious when discussing my difficulties with clients.	1	2	3	4	5	6	7
13. In supervision, my supervisor places a high priority on our understanding the client's perspective.	1	2	3	4	5	6	7
14. My supervisor encourages me to take time to understand what the client is saying and doing.	1	2	3	4	5	6	7
15. My supervisor's style is to carefully and systematically consider the material I bring to supervision.	1	2	3	4	5	6	7
16. When correcting my errors with a client, my supervisor offers alternative ways of intervening with that client.	1	2	3	4	5	6	7
17. My supervisor helps me work within a specific treatment plan with my clients.	1	2	3	4	5	6	7

18. My supervisor helps me stay on track during our meetings.	1	2	3	4	5	6	7
19. I work with my supervisor on specific goals in the supervisory session.	1	2	3	4	5	6	7

The supervisee form of the SWA has two scales, scored as follows:

Rapport: Sum items 1–12, then divide by 12.

Client Focus: Sum items 13–19, then divide by 6.

SUPERVISORY STYLES INVENTORY

For supervisees' form: Please indicate your perception of the style of your current or most recent supervisor of psychotherapy/counseling on each of the following descriptors. Circle the number on the scale, from 1 to 7, which best reflects your view of him or her.
For supervisors' form: Please indicate your perceptions of your style as a supervisor of psychotherapy/counseling on each of the following descriptors. Circle the number on the scale, from 1 to 7, which best reflects your view of yourself.

	1	2	3	4	5	6	7
	Not very						*Very*
1. goal-oriented	1	2	3	4	5	6	7
2. perceptive	1	2	3	4	5	6	7
3. concrete	1	2	3	4	5	6	7
4. explicit	1	2	3	4	5	6	7
5. committed	1	2	3	4	5	6	7
6. affirming	1	2	3	4	5	6	7
7. practical	1	2	3	4	5	6	7
8. sensitive	1	2	3	4	5	6	7
9. collaborative	1	2	3	4	5	6	7
10. intuitive	1	2	3	4	5	6	7
11. reflective	1	2	3	4	5	6	7
12. responsive	1	2	3	4	5	6	7
13. structured	1	2	3	4	5	6	7
14. evaluative	1	2	3	4	5	6	7
15. friendly	1	2	3	4	5	6	7
16. flexible	1	2	3	4	5	6	7
17. prescriptive	1	2	3	4	5	6	7
18. didactic	1	2	3	4	5	6	7
19. thorough	1	2	3	4	5	6	7
20. focused	1	2	3	4	5	6	7
21. creative	1	2	3	4	5	6	7
22. supportive	1	2	3	4	5	6	7
23. open	1	2	3	4	5	6	7
24. realistic	1	2	3	4	5	6	7
25. resourceful	1	2	3	4	5	6	7
26. invested	1	2	3	4	5	6	7
27. facilitative	1	2	3	4	5	6	7
28. therapeutic	1	2	3	4	5	6	7
29. positive	1	2	3	4	5	6	7

30. trusting	1	2	3	4	5	6	7
31. informative	1	2	3	4	5	6	7
32. humorous	1	2	3	4	5	6	7
33. warm	1	2	3	4	5	6	7

Scoring key: *Attractive:* Sum items 15, 16, 22, 23, 29, 30, 33; divide by 7.

Interpersonally sensitive: Sum items 2, 5, 10, 11, 21, 25, 26, 28; divide by 8.

Task oriented: Sum items 1, 3, 4, 7, 13, 14, 17, 18, 19, 20; divide by 10.

Filler items: 6, 8, 9, 12, 24, 27, 31, 32.

From Friedlander, M. L., & Ward, L. G. (1984). Development and validation of the Supervisory Styles Inventory. *Journal of Counseling Psychology, 31,* 542–558.

COUNSELOR SUPERVISOR SELF-EFFICACY SCALE

Directions: Each of the items listed below is related to a task performed in counselor supervision. Please rate your level of confidence for completing each task *right now*. Circle the number that reflects your confidence level. Please answer every question, regardless of whether you have actually performed the corresponding activity.

1	2	3	4	5	6	7	8	9	10
Not confident at all				*Somewhat confident*					*Completely confident*

1. Select supervision interventions congruent with the model/theory being used
   1 2 3 4 5 6 7 8 9 10
2. Articulate to a supervisee the ethical standards regarding client welfare
   1 2 3 4 5 6 7 8 9 10
3. Present procedures for assessing and reporting an occurrence of child abuse
   1 2 3 4 5 6 7 8 9 10
4. Describe the strengths and limitations of the various supervision modalities (e.g., self-report, live observation, audiotape review)
   1 2 3 4 5 6 7 8 9 10
5. Assist a supervisee to deal with termination issues
   1 2 3 4 5 6 7 8 9 10
6. Assist a supervisee to include relevant cultural variables in case conceptualization
   1 2 3 4 5 6 7 8 9 10
7. Model effective decision making when faced with ethical and legal dilemmas
   1 2 3 4 5 6 7 8 9 10
8. Demonstrate knowledge of various counseling theories, systems, and their related methods
   1 2 3 4 5 6 7 8 9 10
9. Structure supervision around a supervisee's learning goals
   1 2 3 4 5 6 7 8 9 10
10. Assist a supervisee to develop working hypotheses about her/his clients
    1 2 3 4 5 6 7 8 9 10
11. Solicit critical feedback on my work as a supervisor from either my peers or an evaluator
    1 2 3 4 5 6 7 8 9 10
12. Understand key research on counselor development and developmental models as they pertain to supervision
    1 2 3 4 5 6 7 8 9 10
13. Assist a supervisee to develop a strategy to address client resistance
    1 2 3 4 5 6 7 8 9 10
14. Encourage a supervisee to share his/her negative feelings about supervision without becoming defensive
    1 2 3 4 5 6 7 8 9 10
15. Listen carefully to concerns presented by a supervisee
    1 2 3 4 5 6 7 8 9 10

16. Identify key ethical and legal issues surrounding client confidentiality
1 2 3 4 5 6 7 8 9 10

17. Address a supervisee's racial or ethnic identity as a counseling process variable
1 2 3 4 5 6 7 8 9 10

18. Understand appropriate supervisor functions of teacher, counselor, and consultant
1 2 3 4 5 6 7 8 9 10

19. Employ interventions appropriate to a supervisee's learning needs
1 2 3 4 5 6 7 8 9 10

20. Describe the legal liabilities involved in counseling minors
1 2 3 4 5 6 7 8 9 10

21. Establish a plan to safeguard a supervisee's due process within supervision
1 2 3 4 5 6 7 8 9 10

22. Help a supervisee assess the compatibility between his/her in-session behaviors and espoused theoretical orientation
1 2 3 4 5 6 7 8 9 10

23. Model strategies that may enhance a supervisee's case conceptualization skills
1 2 3 4 5 6 7 8 9 10

24. Conduct supervision in strict accordance to the ethical standards governing my profession
1 2 3 4 5 6 7 8 9 10

25. Facilitate a supervisee's cultural awareness
1 2 3 4 5 6 7 8 9 10

26. Appear competent in interactions with a supervisee
1 2 3 4 5 6 7 8 9 10

27. Receive critical feedback from a supervisee on my performance as a supervisor without becoming defensive or angry
1 2 3 4 5 6 7 8 9 10

28. State a rationale for choosing a supervision intervention based on theory, client/counselor dynamics, and/or setting
1 2 3 4 5 6 7 8 9 10

29. Recognize possible multiple relationship issues that may arise within supervision
1 2 3 4 5 6 7 8 9 10

30. Demonstrate respect for a supervisee who has a different worldview from myself
1 2 3 4 5 6 7 8 9 10

31. Assess a supervisee's multicultural competencies
1 2 3 4 5 6 7 8 9 10

32. Address parallel processes as they arise within the supervisory relationship
1 2 3 4 5 6 7 8 9 10

33. Communicate due process procedures to a supervisee if he/she is unhappy with the supervision I have provided
1 2 3 4 5 6 7 8 9 10

34. Demonstrate respect for various learning styles and personal characteristics within supervision
    1 2 3 4 5 6 7 8 9 10
35. Facilitate case discussion during group supervision
    1 2 3 4 5 6 7 8 9 10
36. Balance the needs of the group with the individual needs of each supervisee during group supervision
    1 2 3 4 5 6 7 8 9 10
37. Model appropriate responses to affect presented in group supervision
    1 2 3 4 5 6 7 8 9 10
38. Offer adequate support to all members of a group during group supervision
    1 2 3 4 5 6 7 8 9 10
39. Integrate an understanding of supervisees' learning styles into the group supervision process
    1 2 3 4 5 6 7 8 9 10

Scoring key: *Theories and Techniques:* 1, 4, 8, 9, 10, 12, 13, 18, 19, 21, 22, 23, 28, 32
Group Supervision: 35, 36, 37, 38, 39
Supervisory Ethics: 2, 5, 7, 15, 24, 26, 29, 33
Self in Supervision: 11, 14, 27, 30, 34
Multicultural Competence: 6, 17, 25, 31
Knowledge of Legal Issues: 3, 16, 20

SUPERVISION ETHICS CODES

THE APPROVED CLINICAL SUPERVISOR CODE OF ETHICS, NATIONAL BOARD FOR CERTIFIED COUNSELORS

In addition to following your profession's Code of Ethics, clinical supervisors shall:

1. Ensure that supervisees inform clients of their professional status (e.g., intern) and of all conditions of supervision. Supervisors need to ensure that supervisees inform their clients of any status other than being fully qualified for independent practice or licensed. For example, supervisees need to inform their clients if they are a student, intern, supervisee or, if licensed with restrictions, the nature of those restrictions (e.g., associate or conditional). In addition, clients must be informed of the requirements of supervision (e.g., the audiotaping of all counseling sessions for purposes of supervision).
2. Ensure that clients have been informed of their rights to confidentiality and privileged communication when applicable. Clients also should be informed of the limits of confidentiality and privileged communication. The general limits of confidentiality are when harm to self or others is threatened; when the abuse of children, elders, or disabled persons is suspected; and in cases when the court compels the counselor to testify and break confidentiality. These are generally accepted limits to confidentiality and privileged communication, but they may be modified by state or federal statute.
3. Inform supervisees about the process of supervision, including supervision goals, case management procedures, and the supervisor's preferred supervision model(s).
4. Keep and secure supervision records and consider all information gained in supervision as confidential.
5. Avoid all multiple relationships with supervisees that may interfere with the supervisor's professional judgment or exploit the supervisee.

   Although all multiple relationships are not in of themselves inappropriate, any sexual relationship is considered to be a violation. Sexual relationship means sexual contact, sexual harassment, or sexual bias toward a supervisee by a supervisor.
6. Establish procedures with their supervisees for handling crisis situations.
7. Provide supervisees with adequate and timely feedback as part of an established evaluation plan.
8. Render assistance to any supervisee who is unable to provide competent counseling services to clients.
9. Intervene in any situation where the supervisee is impaired and the client is at risk.
10. Refrain from endorsing an impaired supervisee when such impairment deems it unlikely that the supervisee can provide adequate counseling services.
11. Refrain from offering supervision outside of their area(s) of competence.
12. Ensure that supervisees are aware of the current ethical standards related to their professional practice, as well as legal standards that regulate the practice of counseling. Current ethical standards would mean standards published by the National Board for Certified Counselors (NBCC) and other appropriate entities such as the American Counseling Association (ACA). In addition, it is the supervisor's responsibility to ensure that the supervisee is aware that state and federal laws might regulate the practice of counseling and to inform the supervisee of key laws that affect counseling in the supervisee's jurisdiction.
13. Engage supervisees in an examination of cultural issues that might affect supervision and/or counseling.
14. Ensure that both supervisees and clients are aware of their rights and of due process procedures.

ETHICAL GUIDELINES FOR COUNSELING SUPERVISORS, ASSOCIATION FOR CONSELOR EDUCATION AND SUPERVISION

Adopted by ACES Executive Counsel and Delegate Assembly, March 1993

Preamble

The Association for Counselor Education and Supervision (ACES) is composed of people engaged in the professional preparation of counselors and people responsible for the ongoing supervision of counselors. ACES is a founding division of the American Counseling Association (ACA) and as such adheres to ACA's current ethical standards and to general codes of competence adopted throughout the mental health community. ACES believes that counselor educators and counseling supervisors in universities and in applied counseling settings, including the range of education and mental health delivery systems, carry responsibilities unique to their job roles. Such responsibilities may include administrative supervision, clinical supervision, or both. Administrative supervision refers to those supervisory activities which increase the efficiency of the delivery of counseling services; whereas, clinical supervision includes the supportive and educative activities of the supervisor designed to improve the application of counseling theory and technique directly to clients. Counselor educators and counseling supervisors encounter situations which challenge the help given by general ethical standards of the profession at large. These situations require more specific guidelines that provide appropriate guidance in everyday practice. The Ethical Guidelines for Counseling Supervisors are intended to assist professionals by helping them: 1. Observe ethical and legal protection of clients' and supervisees' rights; 2. Meet the training and professional development needs of supervisees in ways consistent with clients' welfare and programmatic requirements; and 3. Establish policies, procedures, and standards for implementing programs.

The specification of ethical guidelines enables ACES members to focus on and to clarify the ethical nature of responsibilities held in common. Such guidelines should be reviewed formally every five years, or more often if needed, to meet the needs of ACES members for guidance. The Ethical Guidelines for Counselor Educators and Counseling Supervisors are meant to help ACES members in conducting supervision. ACES is not currently in a position to hear complaints about alleged non-compliance with these guidelines. Any complaints about the ethical behavior of any ACA member should be measured against the ACA Ethical Standards and a complaint lodged with ACA in accordance with its *procedures* for doing so. One overriding assumption underlying this document is that supervision should be ongoing throughout a counselor's career and not stop when a particular level of education, certification, or membership in a professional organization is attained.

Definitions of Terms

Applied Counseling Settings—Public or private organizations of counselors such as community mental health centers, hospitals, schools, and group or individual private practice settings.

Supervisees—Counselors-in-training in university programs at any level who working with clients in applied settings as part of their university training program, and counselors who have completed their formal education and are employed in an applied counseling setting.

Supervisors—Counselors who have been designated within their university or agency to directly oversee the professional clinical work of counselors. Supervisors also may be persons who offer supervision to counselors seeking state licensure and so provide supervision outside of the administrative aegis of an applied counseling setting.

1. Client Welfare and Rights

1.01 The Primary obligation of supervisors is to train counselors so that they respect the integrity and promote the welfare of their clients. Supervisors should have supervisees inform clients that they are being supervised and that observation and/or recordings of the session may be reviewed by the supervisor.

1.02 Supervisors who are licensed counselors and are conducting supervision to aid a supervisee to become licensed should instruct the supervisee not to communicate or in any way convey to the supervisee's clients or to other parties that the supervisee is himself/herself licensed.

1.03 Supervisors should make supervisees aware of clients' rights, including protecting clients' right to privacy and confidentiality in the counseling relationship and the information resulting from it. Clients also should be informed that their right to privacy and confidentiality will not be violated by the supervisory relationship.

1.04 Records of the counseling relationship, including interview notes, test data, correspondence, the electronic storage of these documents, and audio and videotape recordings, are considered to be confidential professional information. Supervisors should see that these materials are used in counseling, research, and training and supervision of counselors with the full knowledge of the clients and that permission to use these materials is granted by the applied counseling setting offering service to the client. This professional information is to be used for full protection of the client. Written consent from the client (or legal guardian, if a minor) should be secured prior to the use of such information for instructional, supervisory, and/or research purposes. Policies of the applied counseling setting regarding client records also should be followed.

1.05 Supervisors shall adhere to current professional and legal guidelines when conducting research with human participants such as Section D-1 of the ACA Ethical Standards.

1.06 Counseling supervisors are responsible for making every effort to monitor both the professional actions, and failures to take action, of their supervisees.

2. Supervisory Role

Inherent and integral to the role of supervisor are responsibilities for:

a. Monitoring client welfare;
b. Encouraging compliance with relevant legal, ethical, and professional standards for clinical practice;
c. Monitoring clinical performance and professional development of supervisees; and
d. Evaluating and certifying current performance and potential of supervisees for academic, screening, selection, placement, employment, and credentialing purposes.

2.01 Supervisors should have had training in supervision prior to initiating their role as supervisors.

2.02 Supervisors should pursue professional and personal continuing education activities such as advanced courses, seminars, and professional conferences on a regular and ongoing basis. These activities should include both counseling and supervision topics and skills.

2.03 Supervisors should make their supervisees aware of professional and ethical standards and legal responsibilities of the counseling profession.

2.04 Supervisors of post-degree counselors who are seeking state licensure should encourage these counselors to adhere to the standards for practice established by the state licensure board of the state in which they practice.

2.05 Procedures for contacting the supervisor, or an alternative supervisor, to assist in handling crisis situations should be established and communicated to supervisees.

2.06 Actual work samples via audio and/or videotape or live observation in addition to case notes should be reviewed by the supervisor as a regular part of the ongoing supervisory process.

2.07 Supervisors of counselors should meet regularly in face-to-face sessions with their supervisees.

2.08 Supervisors should provide supervisees with ongoing feedback on their performance. This feedback should take a variety of forms, both formal and informal, and should include verbal and written evaluations. It should be formative during the supervisory experience and summative at the conclusion of the experience.

2.09 Supervisors who have multiple roles (e.g., teacher, clinical supervisor, administrative supervisor, etc.) with supervisees should minimize potential conflicts. Where possible, the roles should be divided among several supervisors. Where this is not possible, careful explanation should be conveyed to the supervisee as to the expectations and responsibilities associated with each supervisory role.

2.10 Supervisors should not participate in any form of sexual contact with supervisees. Supervisors should not engage in any form of social contact or interaction which would compromise the supervisor–supervisee relationship. Dual relationships with supervisees that might impair the supervisor's objectivity and professional judgment should be avoided and/or the supervisory relationship terminated.

2.11 Supervisors should not establish a psychotherapeutic relationship as a substitute for supervision. Personal issues should be addressed in supervision only in terms of the impact of these issues on clients and on professional functioning.

2.12 Supervisors, through ongoing supervisee assessment and evaluation, should be aware of any personal or professional limitations of supervisees which are likely to impede future professional performance. Supervisors have the responsibility of recommending remedial assistance to the supervisee and of screening from the training program, applied counseling setting, or state licensure those supervisees who are unable to provide competent professional services. These recommendations should be clearly and professionally explained in writing to the supervisees who are so evaluated.

2.13 Supervisors should not endorse a supervisee for certification, licensure, completion of an academic training program, or continued employment if the supervisor believes the supervisee is impaired in any way that would interfere with the performance of counseling duties. The presence of any such impairment should begin a process of feedback and remediation wherever possible so that the supervisee understands the nature of the impairment and has the opportunity to remedy the problem and continue with his/her professional development.

2.14 Supervisors should incorporate the principles of informed consent and participation; clarity of requirements, expectations, roles and rules; and due process and appeal into the establishment of policies and procedures of their institutions, program, courses, and individual supervisory relationships. Mechanisms for due process appeal of individual supervisory actions should be established and made available to all supervisees.

3. Program Administration Role

3.01 Supervisors should ensure that the programs conducted and experiences provided are in keeping with current guidelines and standards of ACA and its divisions.

3.02 Supervisors should teach courses and/or supervise clinical work only in areas where they are fully competent and experienced.

3.03 To achieve the highest quality of training and supervision, supervisors should be active participants in peer review and peer supervision procedures.

3.04 Supervisors should provide experiences that integrate theoretical knowledge and practical application. Supervisors also should provide opportunities in which supervisees are able to apply the knowledge they have learned and understand the rationale for the skills they have acquired. The knowledge and skills conveyed should reflect current practice, research findings, and available resources.

3.05 Professional competencies, specific courses, and/or required experiences expected of supervisees should be communicated to them in writing prior to admission to the training program or placement/employment by the applied counseling setting, and, in case of continued employment, in a timely manner.

3.06 Supervisors should accept only those persons as supervisees who meet identified entry-level requirements for admission to a program of counselor training or for placement in an applied counseling setting. In the case of private supervision in search of state licensure, supervisees should have completed all necessary prerequisites as determined by the state licensure board.

3.07 Supervisors should inform supervisees of the goals, policies, theoretical orientations toward counseling, training, and supervision model or approach on which the supervision is based.

3.08 Supervisees should be encouraged and assisted to define their own theoretical orientation toward counseling, to establish supervision goals for themselves, and to monitor and evaluate their progress toward meeting these goals.

3.09 Supervisors should assess supervisees' skills and experience in order to establish standards for competent professional behavior. Supervisors should restrict supervisees' activities to those that are commensurate with their current level of skills and experiences.

3.10 Supervisors should obtain practicum and fieldwork sites that meet minimum standards for preparing students to become effective counselors. No practicum or fieldwork setting should be approved unless it truly replicates a counseling work setting.

3.11 Practicum and fieldwork classes would be limited in size according to established professional standards to ensure that each student has ample opportunity for individual supervision and feedback. Supervisors in applied counseling settings should have a limited number of supervisees.

3.12 Supervisors in university settings should establish and communicate specific policies and procedures regarding field placement of students. The respective roles of the student counselor, the university supervisor, and the field supervisor should be clearly differentiated in areas such as evaluation, requirements, and confidentiality.

3.13 Supervisors in training programs should communicate regularly with supervisors in agencies used as practicum and/or fieldwork sites regarding current professional practices, expectations of students, and preferred models and modalities of supervision.

3.14 Supervisors at the university should establish clear lines of communication among themselves, the field supervisors, and the students/supervisees.

3.15 Supervisors should establish and communicate to supervisees and to field supervisors specific procedures regarding consultation, performance review, and evaluation of supervisees.

3.16 Evaluations of supervisee performance in universities and in applied counseling settings should be available to supervisees in ways consistent with the Family Rights and Privacy Act and the Buckley Amendment.

3.17 Forms of training that focus primarily on self-understanding and problem resolution (e.g., personal growth groups or individual counseling) should be voluntary. Those who conduct these forms of training should not serve simultaneously as supervisors of the supervisees involved in the training.

3.18 A supervisor may recommend participation in activities such as personal growth groups or personal counseling when it has been determined that a supervisee has deficits in the areas of self-understanding and problem resolution which impede his/her professional functioning. The supervisors should not be the direct provider of these activities for the supervisee.

3.19 When a training program conducts a personal growth or counseling experience involving relatively intimate self-disclosure, care should be taken to eliminate or minimize potential role conflicts for faculty and/or agency supervisors who may conduct these experiences and who also serve as teachers, group leaders, and clinical directors.

3.20 Supervisors should use the following prioritized sequence in resolving conflicts among the needs of the client, the needs of the supervisee, and the needs of the program or agency. Insofar as the client must be protected, it should be understood that client welfare is usually subsumed in federal and state laws such that these statutes should be the first point of reference. Where laws and ethical standards are not present or are unclear, the good judgment of the supervisor should be guided by the following list.

a. Relevant legal and ethical standards (e.g., duty to warn, state child abuse laws, etc.);
b. Client welfare;
c. Supervisee welfare;
d. Supervisor welfare; and
e. Program and/or agency service and administrative needs.

FROM CANADIAN PSYCHOLOGICAL ASSOCIATION

Ethical Guidelines for Supervision in Psychology: Teaching, Research, Practice, and Administration

GUIDELINES FOR ETHICAL SUPERVISION

Principle I: Respect for the Dignity of Persons

The principle of Respect for the Dignity of Persons requires supervisors and supervisees to demonstrate respect for each other as well as for all other persons with whom they relate in their psychological activities. Respect involves valuing the innate worth of persons and not using them solely as a means to an end. Respect is an essential characteristic in the relationship between supervisors and supervisees. The supervisee shares the responsibility for respect, even though the supervisor has the greater responsibility for modelling and maintaining a respectful relationship and for addressing problems that may arise. The power differential adds to the complexity of the supervisory relationship.

Supervisors and supervisees should:

1. Demonstrate respect, courtesy, and understanding for each other in their respective roles.
2. Be vigilant in all situations to prevent discrimination on the basis of personal characteristics, e.g., ethnicity, race, religion, gender, sex, sexual orientation, gender identity and expression, marital status, age, and socioeconomic status.
3. Share in defining the goals and role expectations for the supervisory relationship.
4. When establishing a supervisory relationship, disclose preferences for theories and practices, as well as strive to disclose personal biases, beliefs, and personal characteristics that may affect the supervisory process.
5. Address professional and interpersonal differences between supervisor and supervisee in as open, amicable, and constructive a way as possible. If appropriate, they should consider third party consultation or mediation.
6. Clearly define the parameters of supervisee and supervisor confidentiality of personal information shared during supervision, including stated limitations relevant to reasonable curricular and educational planning for the enhancement of learning, evaluations of competency for independent practice as required by regulatory bodies, and legal requirements to prevent serious and imminent harm.
7. Make reasonable accommodations for valid crises or unexpected events in the life of the supervisee or supervisor that may temporarily interfere with supervision.

Principle II: Responsible Caring

The principle of Responsible Caring requires supervisors and supervisees to care for the wellbeing and best interests of persons who, and organisations that, benefit directly from their work and, where the benefit is indirect, to take care that their work meets expected standards of performance. Responsible caring also involves self-awareness and self-exploration of personal attitudes and beliefs that may influence how they conduct their psychological activities. Knowledge regarding, and attitudes toward a range of population diversities are especially important. The supervisee shares these responsibilities even though the supervisor has the greater responsibility for maintaining a level of caring that benefits concerned parties.

Supervisors and supervisees should:

1. Share, under the leadership of the supervisor, a clarification and understanding of their respective roles and how to use them to enhance learning and performance in psychology. They should be well prepared, make efficient use of time, and be receptive to mutual learning.

2. Keep up to date with the standards, guidelines, codes, laws, and regulations that are specific to the work undertaken or to the workplace, and which support supervisor-supervisee learning. They should commit themselves to long term continuing-competence activities.
3. Establish their current levels of competence in the relevant areas as a basis for defining supervision goals, procedures, and conditions.
4. Aspire to the same standard of work by supervisees as would be required of competent psychologists not receiving supervision.
5. Keep up to date with current knowledge and competencies in supervision, as appropriate to your role expectations.
6. Be aware of professional and personal limitations that may affect working relationships, be open to and elicit feedback regarding issues, and manage limitations in ways that support a positive supervisory relationship.
7. Maintain records to a standard required by the nature of the psychological activity and setting, and to the extent needed to maintain an effective supervisory relationship.
8. Ensure availability for supervision at all regular times and ensure that there are special arrangements for communication in the event of unanticipated circumstances or emergencies.
9. Ensure that articulated plans are in place to address emergencies or other serious events.
10. Maintain supervision on site where appropriate and possible, and where inappropriate or not possible, maintain the quality of supervision through creative use of distance technology.
11. Seek clarification of the respective responsibilities of supervisees and supervisors when supervision is provided concurrently from more than one supervisor (e.g., university supervisor and field supervisors, supervisors in different specialty areas, cross-disciplinary supervision).

Principle III: Integrity in Relationships

The principle of Integrity in Relationships requires openness, objectivity, honesty, straightforwardness, and avoidance of conflict of interest in keeping with respect and caring for others. Any exceptions need to be justified by the ethical principles of the *Canadian Code of Ethics for Psychologists* and are not permitted only as a matter of convenience. The supervisee shares these responsibilities even though the supervisor has the greater responsibility for maintaining an open trusting relationship and for addressing problems that may arise.

Supervisors and supervisees should:

1. Identify and address conflict in the supervisory relationship in open, honest, and beneficial ways.
2. Explore personal values as they are relevant to maintaining adequate objectivity to the work under supervision or to the supervisory process.
3. Respect each other's substantive contributions to research findings and to publications, give credit as earned, and avoid any distortion of results for personal, political, or other reasons.
4. Avoid all forms of exploitation, or actions that harm the supervisor or supervisee (e.g., financial, sexual, gossip, blackmail, false allegations, and coercion in the supervisory and the work relationships).
5. Strive for the highest level of competence consistent with the supervisee's developmental level, training and experience.
6. On an ongoing basis, be open in sharing information with each other about the supervisee's level of professional development.
7. Avoid dual or multiple relationships that may be harmful to themselves, to others, or that interfere with the learning objectives of the supervisory process.

8. Be aware of professional boundaries in the supervisory relationship, and manage additional roles (e.g., social relationships) in a manner that does not compromise the supervisory relationship. Intimate sexual relationships, however, are prohibited.
9. Ensure that relevant parties (e.g., clients, guardians, and research participants) are informed that the services/activities are being performed by an individual who is under supervision, are discussed with a supervisor, and that these parties if they wish may request a meeting with the supervisor.
10. Present accurate evaluations in providing direct feedback and in providing references.

Principle IV: Responsibility to Society

The principle of Responsibility to Society requires that psychologists have a responsibility to promote the collective wellbeing of society. There are many ways from a foundation of teaching, research, practice, and administration that supervisors and supervisees can contribute to the welfare of society. Psychologists who practice their discipline with high standards serve the public interest, as do those who advocate for change in social policies. There is a wide range of ways in which psychologists may contribute to the greater good of society. The supervisee and supervisor need to be aware of the responsibility to promote the collective wellbeing of society.

Supervisors and supervisees should:

1. Be open to considering appropriate roles for psychologists in promoting social advocacy or social justice.
2. Take into account systemic issues that apply to the particular area of work that is being supervised and in the management of conflicting interests.
3. Ensure that issues of ethics and standards, and the legal and regulatory requirements that apply to the particular area of work are addressed.
4. Strive to achieve the highest quality of learning from the supervisory relationship in order to use their combined competence to serve the public interest.

From *Ethical Guidelines for Supervision in Psychology: Teaching, Research, Practice, and Administration* (pp. 5–8). For complete document, go to www.cpa.ca/cpasite/userfiles/Documents/SupervisionGuidelinesfinal25Jan09.pdf.

References

References

Abadie, P. D. (1985). *A study of interpersonal communication processes in the supervision of counseling.* Unpublished doctoral dissertation, Kansas State University.

Abbass, A., Arthey, S., Elliott, J., Fedak, T., Nowoweiski, D., Markovski, J., & Nowoweiski, S. (2011). Web-conference supervision for advanced psychotherapy training: A practical guide. *Psychotherapy (Chicago, Ill.), 48*(2), 109–118. doi:10.1037/a0022427

Abbott, A. (1988). *The system of professions: An essay on the division of expert labor.* Chicago, IL: The University of Chicago Press.

Abbott, A. A., & Lyter, S. C. (1998). The use of constructive criticism in field supervision. *Clinical Supervisor, 17*(2), 43–57.

Abreu, J. M. (1999). Conscious and nonconscious African American stereotypes: Impact on first impression and diagnostic ratings by therapists. *Journal of Consulting and Clinical Psychology, 67,* 387–393.

Abroms, G. M. (1977). Supervision as metatherapy. In F. W. Kaslow (Ed.), *Supervision, consultation, and staff training in the helping professions* (pp. 81–99). San Francisco: Jossey-Bass.

Acuff, C., Bennett, B. E., Bricklin, P. M., Canter, M. B., Knapp, S. J., Moldawsky, S., & Phelps, R. (1999). Considerations for ethical practice in managed care. *Professional Psychology: Research & Practice, 30,* 563–575.

Adamek, M. S. (1994). Audio-cueing and immediate feedback to improve group leadership skills: A live supervision model. *Journal of Music Therapy, 31,* 135–164.

Adams, J. (1995). Perspectives on live supervision: Working live. *The Supervision Bulletin, 8*(2), 4.

Ægisdottir S., Gerstein L. H., Leung S. A.; Kwan K. K., & Lonner W. J. (2009). Theoretical and methodological issues when studying culture. In L. H. Gerstein, P. P. Heppner, S. Ægisdóttir, S. A. Leung, & K. L. Norsworthy (Eds.), *International Handbook of Cross-Cultural Counseling* (pp. 89–109). Thousand Oaks, CA: Sage Publications.

Ahia, C. E., & Martin, D. (1993). The danger-to-self-or-others exception to confidentiality. In T. P. Remley (Series Ed.), *The ACA legal series* (Vol. 8). Alexandria, VA: American Counseling Association.

Aiello, J. R., & Douthitt, E. A. (2001). Social facilitation from Triplett to electronic performance monitoring. *Group Dynamics: Theory, Research, and Practice, 5,* 163–180.

Albee, G. W. (1970). The uncertain future of clinical psychology. *American Psychologist, 25,* 1071–1080.

Alderfer, C. (1983). *The supervision of the therapeutic system in family therapy.* Unpublished manuscript.

Allen, G. J., Szollos, S. J., & Williams, B. E. (1986). Doctoral students' comparative evaluations of best and worst psychotherapy supervision. *Professional Psychology: Research & Practice, 17,* 91–99.

Allphin, C. (1987). Perplexing or distressing episodes in supervision: How they can help in the teaching and learning of psychotherapy. *Clinical Social Work Journal, 15,* 236–245.

Alonso, A., & Rutan, J. S. (1988). Shame & guilt in supervision. *Psychotherapy, 25,* 576–581.

Alpher, V. S. (1991). Interdependence and parallel processes: A case study of structural analysis of social behavior in supervision and short-term dynamic psychotherapy. *Psychotherapy, 28,* 218–231.

Alvarez, A. N., & Helms, J. E. (2001). Racial identity and reflected appraisals as influences on Asian Americans' racial adjustment. *Cultural Diversity and Ethnic Minority Psychology, 7,* 217–231.

American Association for Marriage and Family Therapy (AAMFT). (2006). Standards of Accreditation, Version 11. Alexandria, VA: Author.

American Counseling Association (ACA). (2005). *Code of ethics* (rev. ed.). Alexandria, VA: Author.

American Psychological Association (APA). (2002). *Ethical principles of psychologists & code of conduct.* Washington, DC: Author. Retrieved January 2, 2008, from www.apa.org/ethics/code2002.html

American Psychological Association (APA). (2008). *Guidelines and principles for accreditation of programs in professional psychology.* Washington, DC: Author.

Amerikaner, M., & Rose, R. (2012). Direct observation of psychology supervisees' clinical work: A snapshot of current practice. *The Clinical Supervisor, 31,* 61–80.

Ancis, J. R., & Ladany, N. (2001). A multicultural framework for counselor supervision. In L. J. Bradley & N. Ladany (Eds.). *Counselor supervision: Principles, process, and practice* (pp. 63–90). Philadelphia, PA: Brunner-Routledge.

Anderson, J. R. (1995). *Cognitive psychology and its implications* (4th ed.). New York, NY: W. H. Freeman & Co.

Anderson, J. R. (1996). ACT: A simple theory of complex cognition. *American Psychologist, 51,* 355–365.

Anderson, S. A., Schlossberg, M., & Rigazio-DiGilio, S. (2000). Family therapy trainees' evaluations of their best and worst supervision experiences. *Journal of Marital & Family Therapy, 26*(1), 79–91.

Anderson, T. (1987). The reflecting team: Dialogue and meta-dialogue in clinical work. *Family Process, 26,* 415–428.

Angus, L., & Kagan, F. (2007). Empathic relational bonds and personal agency in psychotherapy: Implications for psychotherapy supervision, practice, and research. *Psychotherapy: Theory, Research, Practice, Training, 44,* 371–377.

Anonymous. (1991). Sexual harassment: A female counseling student's experience. *Journal of Counseling & Development, 69,* 502–506.

Anonymous. (1995). Perspectives on live supervision: A client's voice. *The Supervision Bulletin, VIII*(2), 5.

Aponte, H. J. (1994). How personal can training get? *Journal of Marital & Family Therapy, 20,* 3–15.

Arcinue, F. (2002). *The development and validation of the Group Supervision Scale.* Unpublished doctoral dissertation, University of Southern California.

Arkowitz, S. W. (2001). Perfectionism in the supervisee. In S. Gill (Ed.), *The supervisory alliance: Facilitating the psychotherapist's learning experience* (pp. 33–66). Northvale, NJ: Jason Aronson, Inc.

Aronson, M. L. (1990). A group therapist's perspectives on the use of supervisory groups in the training of psychotherapists. *Psychoanalysis & Psychotherapy, 8,* 88–94.

Arthur, A. R. (2000). The personality and cognitive–epistemological traits of cognitive behavioural and psychoanalytic psychotherapists. *British Journal of Medical Psychology, 73,* 243–257.

Arthur, G. L., & Gfoerer, K. P. (2002). Training and supervision through the written word: A description and intern feedback. *The Family Journal: Counseling & Therapy for Couples & Families, 10,* 213–219.

Association for Counselor Education and Supervision. (1990). Standards for counseling supervisors. *Journal of Counseling & Development, 69,* 30–32.

Aten, J. D., & Hernandez, B. C. (2004). Addressing religion in clinical supervision: A model. *Psychotherapy: Theory, Research, Practice, Training, 41,* 152–160.

Aten, J. D., Madson, M. B., & Kruse, S. J. (2008). The supervision genogram: A tool for preparing supervisors-in-training. *Psychotherapy: Theory, Research, Practice, Training, 45*(1), 111–116.

Aten, J. D., Strain, J. D., & Gillespie, R. E. (2008). A transtheoretical model of clinical supervision. *Training and Education in Professional Psychology, 2,* 1–9.

Atkinson, D. R., Morten, G., & Sue, D. W. (1998). *Counseling American minorities.* Boston, MA: McGraw-Hill.

Ault-Riche, M. (1988). Teaching an integrated model of family therapy: Women as students, women as supervisors. *Journal of Psychotherapy and the Family, 3,* 175–192.

Aveline, M. (1992). The use of audio and videotape recordings of therapy sessions in the supervision and practice of dynamic psychotherapy. *British Journal of Psychotherapy, 8,* 347–358.

Averitt, J. (1989). Individual versus group supervision of counselor trainees. Doctoral dissertation, University of Tennessee, 1988. *Dissertation Abstracts International, 50,* 624.

Bahrick, A. S. (1990). Role induction for counselor trainees: Effects on the supervisory working alliance. *Dissertation Abstracts International, 51*(3-B), 1484 (Abstract #1991-51645).

Bahrick, A. S., Russell, R. K., & Salmi, S. W. (1991). The effects of role induction on trainees' perceptions of supervision. *Journal of Counseling & Development, 69,* 434–438.

Baker, D. E. (1990). The relationship of the supervisory working alliance to supervisor and supervisee narcissism, gender, and theoretical orientation. *Dissertation Abstracts International, 51*(7-B), 3602–3603 (Abstract #1991-54991).

Baker, S. B., Exum, H. A., & Tyler, R. E. (2002). The developmental process of clinical supervisors in training: An investigation of the supervisor complexity model. *Counselor Education & Supervision, 42,* 15–30.

Bakes, A. S. (2005). The supervisory working alliance: A comparison of dyadic and triadic supervision models. *Dissertation Abstracts International, 66,* (06), 2122A.

Balint, M. (1948). On the psychoanalytic training system. *International Journal of Psychoanalysis, 29,* 163–173.

Balkin, R. S., Schlosser, L. Z., & Levitt, D. H. (2009). Religious identity and cultural diversity: Exploring the relationships between religious identity, sexism, homophobia, and multicultural competence. *Journal of Counseling & Development, 87*(4), 420–427.

Bambling, M., King, R., Raue, P., Schweitzer, R., & Lambert, W. (2006). Clinical supervision: Its influence on client-rated working alliance and client symptom reduction in the brief treatment of major depression. *Psychotherapy Research 16*(3), 317–331.

Bandura, A. (1994). Self-efficacy. In V. S. Ramachaudran (Ed.), *Encyclopedia of human behavior* (Vol. 4, pp. 71–81). Retrieved December 30, 2007, from www.des.emory.edu/mfp/BanEncy.html

Bang, K., & Park, J. (2009). Korean supervisors' experiences in clinical supervision. *The Counseling Psychologist, 37,* 1042–1075.

Bargh, J.A., & Chartrand, T.L. (1999). The unbearable automaticity of being. *American Psychologist, 54,* 462–479.

Barlow, D. H. (Ed.). (2001). *Clinical handbook of psychological disorders: A step-by-step treatment manual* (3rd ed.). New York, NY: Guilford Press.

Barnes, K. L. (2004). Applying self-efficacy theory to counselor training and supervision: A comparison of two approaches. *Counselor Education & Supervision, 44,* 56–69.

Barnes, K. L., & Bernard, J. M. (2003). Women in counseling and psychotherapy supervision. In M. Kopala & M. Keitel (Eds.), *The handbook of counseling women* (pp. 535–545). Thousand Oaks, CA: Sage Publications.

Barnes, K. L., & Moon, S. M. (2006). Factor structure of the psychotherapy supervisor development scale. *Measurement & Evaluation in Counseling & Development, 39,* 130–140.

Barnett, J. E. (2007). Whose boundaries are they anyway? *Professional Psychology: Research & Practice, 38,* 401–405.

Barnett, J. E. (2010). Ask the ethicist: Supervisors need competence too! *Psychotherapy* (Div29), 1.

Barnett, J. E. (2011). Utilizing technological innovations to enhance psychotherapy supervision, training, and outcomes. *Psychotherapy (Chicago, Ill.), 48*(2), 103–108.

Barnett, J. E., Cornish, J. A. E., Goodyear, R. K., & Lichtenberg, J. W. (2007). Commentaries on the ethical and effective practice of clinical supervision. *Professional Psychology: Research & Practice, 38,* 268–275.

Baron, R. M., & Kenny, D. A. (1986). The moderator–mediator variable distinction in social psychological research: Conceptual, strategic, and statistical considerations. *Journal of Personality & Social Psychology, 51*(60), 1173–1182.

Barrett, M. S., & Barber, J. P. (2005). A developmental approach to supervision of therapists in training. *Journal of Contemporary Psychotherapy, 35,* 169–183.

Barretti, M. A. (2009). Ranking desirable field instructor characteristics: Viewing student preferences in context with field & class experience. *The Clinical Supervisor, 28,* 47–71.

Bartell, P. A., & Rubin, L. J. (1990). Dangerous liaisons: Sexual intimacies in supervision. *Professional Psychology: Research & Practice, 21,* 442–450.

Bartholomew, K., & Horowitz, L. M. (1991). Attachment styles among young adults: A test of a four-category model. *Journal of Personality and Social Psychology, 61,* 226–244.

Bartle-Haring, S., Silverthorn, B. C., Meyer, K., & Toviessi, P. (2009) Does live supervision make a difference? A multilevel analysis. *Journal of Marital & Family Therapy, 35,* 406–414.

Bartlett, F. C. (1932). *Remembering: An experimental and social study.* Cambridge: Cambridge University Press.

Bartlett, F. C. (1958). *Thinking.* New York, NY: Basic Books.

Bashe, A., Anderson, S. K., Handelsman, M. M., & Klevansky, R. (2007). An acculturation model for ethics training: The ethics autobiography and beyond. *Professional Psychology: Research & Practice, 38,* 60–67.

Bateson, G. (1958). *Naven.* London: Cambridge University Press. (Original work published 1936.)

Baum, N. (2010). Co-supervisees as siblings: A study of student trainees sharing the same supervisor. *The Clinical Supervisor, 29,* 209–227.

Baum, N. (2011). The supervisory relationship as a triangle. *Families in Society, 92,* 262–268.

Baumeister, R. F., & Leary, M. R. (1995). The need to belong: Desire for interpersonal attachments as a fundamental human motivation. *Psychological Bulletin, 117,* 497–529.

Bava, S., Burchard, C., Ichihashi, K., Irani, A., & Zunker, C. (2002). Conversing and constructing spirituality in a postmodern training context. *Journal of Family Psychotherapy, 13,* 237–258.

Bear, T. M., & Kivlighan, D. M., Jr. (1994). Single–subject examination of the process of supervision of beginning and advanced supervisees. *Professional Psychology: Research & Practice, 25,* 450–457.

Beauchamp, T. L., & Childress, J. F. (2001). *Principles of biomedical ethics* (5th ed.). New York, NY: Oxford University Press.

Beavers, W. R. (1986). Family therapy supervision: An introduction and consumer's guide. *Family Therapy Education & Supervision, 1*(4), 15–24.

Beck, A. T., Rush, A. J., Shaw, B. F., & Emery, G. (1979). *Cognitive therapy of depression.* New York, NY: Guilford.

Beck, J. S., Sarnat, J. E., & Barenstein, V. (2008) Psychotherapy-based approaches to supervision. In C. A. Falender & E. P. Shafranske (Eds.). *Casebook for clinical supervision: A competency-based approach* (pp. 57–96). Washington, DC: American Psychological Association.

Beck, T. D., Yager, G. G., Williams, G. T., Williams, B. R., & Morris, J. R. (1989, March). *Training field supervisors for adult counseling situations.* Paper presented at the annual meeting of the American Association for Counseling & Development, Boston, MA.

Beddoe, L., Ackroyd, J., Chinnery, S., & Appleton, C. (2011). Life supervision of student in field placement: More than just watching. *Social Work Education, 30,* 512–528.

Behan, C. P. (2003). Some ground to stand on: Narrative supervision. *Journal of Systemic Therapies, 22,* 29–42.

Behling, J., Curtis, C., & Foster, S. A. (1988). Impact of sex-role combinations on student performance in field instruction. *The Clinical Supervisor, 6*(3), 161–168.

Behnke, S. H. (2005, May). Ethics rounds: The supervisor as gatekeeper: Reflections on Ethical Standards 7.02, 7.04, 7.05, 7.06, and 10.01. *Monitor on Psychology, 36(5),* 90.

Belar, C. D., Bieliauskas, L. A., Klepac, R. K., Larsen, K. G., Stigall, T. T., & Zimet, C. N. (1993). National conference on postdoctoral training in professional psychology. *American Psychologist, 48,* 1284–1289.

Benedek, T. (1954). Countertransference in the training analyst. *Bulletin of the Menninger Clinic, 18,* 12–16.

Benjamin, L. S. (1974). Structural analysis of social behavior. *Psychological Review, 81,* 392–425.

Bennett, L., & Coe, S. (1998). Social work field instructor satisfaction with faculty field liaisons. *Journal of Social Work Education, 34,* 345–352.

Bennett, S., Mohr, J., Brintzenhofe-Szoc, K., & Saks, L. V. (2008). General and supervision-specific attachment styles: Relations to student perceptions of field supervisors. *Journal of Social Work Education, 44,* 75–94.

Berger, M., & Dammann, C. (1982). Live supervision as context, treatment, and training. *Family Process, 21,* 337–344.

Berkel, L. A., Constantine, M. G., & Olson, E. A. (2007). Supervisor multicultural competence: Addressing religious and spiritual issues with counseling students in supervision. *The Clinical Supervisor, 26*(1/2), 3–15.

Berliner, D. C. (July 10, 2012). Inequality, poverty and school achievement: Relationships too powerful to ignore. Invited presentation, University of Redlands, Redlands, CA.

Berman, M., & Berger, B. (Eds.) (2007). *New York calling: From blackout to Bloomberg.* London: Reaktion Books.

Bernard, J. L., & Jara, C. S. (1986). The failure of clinical psychology graduate students to apply understood ethical principles. *Professional Psychology: Research & Practice, 17,* 313–315.

Bernard, J. M. (1979). Supervisor training: A discrimination model. *Counselor Education & Supervision, 19,* 60–68.

Bernard, J. M. (1981). In-service training for clinical supervisors. *Professional Psychology, 12,* 740–748.

Bernard, J. M. (1989). Training supervisors to examine relationship variables using IPR. *The Clinical Supervisor, 7,* 103–112.

Bernard, J. M. (1992). The challenge of psychotherapy-based supervision: Making the pieces fit. *Counselor Education and Supervision, 31,* 232–237.

Bernard, J. M. (1994a). Multicultural supervision: A reaction to Leong and Wagner, Cook, Priest, and Fukuyama. *Counselor Education and Supervision, 34,* 159–171.

Bernard, J. M. (1994b). Reaction: On-campus training of doctoral-level supervisors. In J. E. Myers (Ed.), *Developing and directing counselor education laboratories.* Alexandria, VA: American Counseling Association.

Bernard, J. M. (1997). The discrimination model. In C. E. Watkins, *Handbook of psychotherapy supervision* (pp. 310–327). New York, NY: Wiley.

Bernard, J. M. (2005). Tracing the development of clinical supervision. *The Clinical Supervisor, 24,* 3–21.

Bernard, J. M., & Goodyear, R. K. (1992). Fundamentals of clinical supervision. Boston, MA: Allyn & Bacon.

Bernstein, B. L. (1993). Promoting gender equity in counselor supervision: Challenges and opportunities. *Counselor Education & Supervision, 32,* 198–202.

Bernstein, B. L., & Lecomte, C. (1979). Self-critique technique training in a competency-based practicum. *Counselor Education & Supervision, 19,* 69–76.

Bernstein, R. M., Brown, E. M., & Ferrier, M. J. (1984). A model for collaborative team processing in brief systemic family therapy. *Journal of Marital & Family Therapy, 10,* 151–156.

Bersoff, D. N., & Koeppl, P. M. (1993). The relation between ethical codes and moral principles. *Ethics & Behavior, 3,* 345–357.

Betan, E. J., & Stanton, A. L. (1999). Fostering ethical willingness integrating emotional and contextual awareness with rational analysis. *Professional Psychology: Research & Practice, 30,* 295–301.

Beutler, L. E., Moleiro, C., & Talebi, H. (2002a). Resistance in psychotherapy: What conclusions are supported by research. *Journal of Clinical Psychology/In Session: Psychotherapy in Practice, 58,* 207–217.

Beutler, L. E., Moleiro, C., & Talebi, H. (2002b). Resistance. In J. C. Norcross (Ed.), *Psychotherapy relationships that work: Therapist contributions and responsiveness to patients* (pp. 129–144). New York, NY: Oxford University Press.

Bhat, C. S., & Davis, T. E. (2007). Counseling supervisors' assessment of race, racial identity, and working alliance in supervisory dyads. *Journal of Multicultural Counseling & Development, 35,* 80–91.

Bilodeau, C., Savard, R., & Lecompte, C. (2012). Trainee shame-proneness and the supervisory process. *Journal of Counselor Preparation & Supervision, 4,* 37–49.

Binder, J. L. (2004). *Key competencies in brief dynamic psychotherapy: Clinical practice beyond the manual.* New York, NY: Guilford Press.

Birk, J. M., & Mahalik, J. R. (1996). The influence of trainee conceptual level, trainee anxiety, and supervision evaluation on counselor developmental level. *The Clinical Supervisor, 14*(1), 123–137.

Bishop, D. R., Avila-Juarbe, E., & Thumme, B. (2003). Recognizing spirituality as an important factor in counselor supervision. *Counseling & Values, 48,* 34–46.

Blackwell, T. L., Strohmer, D. C., Belcas, E. M., & Burton, K. A. (2002). Ethics in rehabilitation counselor supervision. *Rehabilitation Counseling Bulletin, 45,* 240–247.

Blake, R. R., & Mouton, J. S. (1976). *Consultation.* London, UK: Addison-Wesley.

Blocher, D. (1983). Toward a cognitive developmental approach to counseling supervision. *The Counseling Psychologist, 11,* 27–34.

Blocher, D. H. (1987). On the uses and misuses of the term theory. *Journal of Counseling & Development, 66,* 67–68.

Blodgett, E. G., Schmidt, J. F., & Scudder, R. R. (1987). Clinical session evaluation: The effect of familiarity with the supervisee. *The Clinical Supervisor, 5,* 33–43.

Bloom, B. S., Engelhart, M. D., Furst, F. J., Hill, W. H., & Krathwohl, D. R. (1956). *Taxonomy of educational objectives: Cognitive domain.* New York, NY: McKay.

Bob, S. (1999). Narrative approaches to supervision and case formulation. *Psychotherapy: Theory, Research, Practice, Training, 36,* 146–153.

Boëthius, S. B., Sundin, E., & Ögren, M.-L.(2006). Group supervision from a small group perspective. *Nordic Psychology, 58,* 22–42.

Bogo, M. (2005). Field instruction in social work: A review of the research literature. *The Clinical Supervisor, 24*(1/2), 163–193.

Bogo, M., Regehr, C., Power, R., & Regehr, G. (2007). When values collide: Field instructors' experiences of providing feedback and evaluating competence. *The Clinical Supervisor, 26*(1/2), 99–117.

Bonney, W. (1994). Teaching supervision: Some practical issues for beginning supervisors. *The Psychotherapy Bulletin, 29,* 31–36.

Borders, L. D. (1989). A pragmatic agenda for developmental supervision research. *Counselor Education & Supervision, 29,* 16–24.

Borders, L. D. (1990). Developmental changes during supervisees' first practicum. *The Clinical Supervisor, 8*(2), 157–167.

Borders, L. D. (1991). A systemic approach to peer group supervision. *Journal of Counseling & Development, 69,* 248–252.

Borders, L. D. (1992). Learning to think like a supervisor. *The Clinical Supervision, 10*(2), 135–148.

Borders, L. D. (2006, June). *Subtleties in clinical supervision.* Paper presented at the Annual International Interdisciplinary Supervision Conference, Buffalo, NY.

Borders, L. D. (2009). Subtle messages in clinical supervision. *The Clinical Supervisor, 28,* 200–209.

Borders, L. D. (2010). Principles of best practices for clinical supervisor training. In J. R. Culbreth & L. L. Brown (Eds.), *State of the art in clinical supervision*. New York, NY: Routledge.

Borders, L. D., Bernard, J. M., Dye, H. A., Fong, M. L., Henderson, P., & Nance, D. W. (1991). Curriculum guide for training counseling supervisors: Rationale, development, and implementation. *Counselor Education & Supervision, 31,* 58–82.

Borders, L. D., & Brown, L. L. (2005). *The new handbook of counseling supervision.* Mahway, NJ: Lahaska Press.

Borders, L. D., Cashwell, C. S., & Rotter, J. C. (1995). Supervision of counselor licensure applicants: A comparative study. *Counselor Education & Supervision, 35,* 54–69.

Borders, L. D., & Fong, M. L. (1991). Evaluations of supervisees: Brief commentary and research report. *The Clinical Supervisor, 9*(2), 43–51.

Borders, L. D., & Leddick, G. R. (1988). A nationwide survey of supervision training. *Counselor Education & Supervision, 27*(3), 271–283.

Borders, L. D., & Usher, C. H. (1992). Postdegree supervision: Existing and preferred practices. *Journal of Counseling and Development, 70,* 594–599.

Borders, L. D., Welfare, L., Greason, P. B., Paladino, D. A., Mobley, K., Villalba, J. A., & Wester, K. L. (2012). Individual and triadic and group: Supervisee and supervisor perceptions of each modality. *Counselor Education & Supervision, 51,* 281–295.

Bordin, E. S. (1979). The generalizability of the psychodynamic concept of the working alliance. *Psychotherapy: Theory, Research, and Practice, 16,* 252–260.

Bordin, E. S. (1983). A working alliance model of supervision. *The Counseling Psychologist, 11,* 35–42.

Boswell, J. F., Nelson, D. L., Nordberg, S. S., McAleavey, A. A., & Castonguay, L. G. (2010). Competency in integrative psychotherapy: Perspectives on training and supervision. *Psychotherapy Theory, Research, Practice, Training, 47,* 3–11.

Bowen, M. (1978). *Family therapy in clinical practice.* New York, NY: Aronson.

Bowlby, J. (1977). The making and breaking of affectional bonds. I. Aetiology and psychopathology in the light of attachment theory. *British Journal of Psychiatry, 130,* 201–210.

Bowlby, J. (1978). Attachment theory and its therapeutic implications. In S. C. Feinstein & P. L. Giovacchini (Ed.), *Adolescent psychiatry* (Vol. VI: Development and clinical studies, pp. 5–33). Chicago, IL: University of Chicago Press.

Boyd, J. (1978). *Counselor supervision: Approaches, preparation, practices.* Muncie, IN: Accelerated Development, Inc.

Boysen, G. A., & Vogel, D. L. (2008). The relationship between level of training, implicit bias, and multicultural competency among counselor trainees. *Training & Education in Professional Psychology,* 2(2), 103–110.

Bradley, L. J., & Gould, L. J. (1994). *Supervisee resistance.* Greensboro, NC: ERIC Clearinghouse on Counseling and Student Services. (ERIC Document Reproduction Service No. ED372344)

Bradshaw, W. H., Jr. (1982). Supervision in Black and White: Race as a factor in supervision. In M. Blumenfield (Ed.), *Applied supervision in psychotherapy* (pp. 199–220). New York, NY: Grune & Stratton.

Brandell, J. R. (1992). Focal conflict analysis: A method of supervision in psychoanalytic psychotherapy. *The Clinical Supervisor, 10*(1), 51–69.

Brantley, A. P. (2000). A clinical supervision documentation form. In L. VandeCreek & T. L. Jackson (Eds.), *Innovations in clinical practice: A sourcebook* (Vol. 18, pp. 301–307). Sarasota, FL: Professional Resource Press.

Brashears, F. (1995). Supervision as social work practice: A reconceptualization. *Social Work, 40,* 692–699.

Brawer, P. A., Handal, P. J., Fabricatore, A. N., Roberts, R., & Wajda-Johnston, V. A. (2002). Training and education in religion/spirituality within APA-accredited clinical psychology programs. *Professional Psychology: Research & Practice, 33,* 203–206.

Brear, P., & Dorrian, J. (2010). Gatekeeping or gate slippage? A national survey of counseling educators in Australian undergraduate and postgraduate academic training programs. *Training & Education in Professional Psychology, 4,* 264–273.

Brehm, J. (1966). *A theory of psychological reactance.* New York, NY: Academic Press.

Breunlin, D., Karrer, B., McGuire, D., & Cimmarusti, R. (1988). Cybernetics of videotape supervision. In H. Liddle, D. Breunlin, & R. Schwartz (Eds.), *Handbook of family therapy training and supervision* (pp. 194–206). New York, NY: Guilford.

Brewer, M. B., & Gardner, W. (1996). Who is this "we"? Levels of collective identity and self representations. *Journal of Personality & Social Psychology, 71,* 83–93.

Bridges, N. A. (1999). The role of supervision in managing intense affect and constructing boundaries in therapeutic relationships. *Journal of Sex Education & Therapy, 24*(4), 218–225.

Bridges, N. A., & Wohlberg, J. W. (1999). Sexual excitement in therapeutic relationships: Clinical and supervisory management. *The Clinical Supervisor, 18*(2), 123–141.

Briggs, J. R., & Miller, G. (2005). Success enhancing supervision. *Journal of Family Psychotherapy, 16,* 199–222.

British Association for Counselling and Psychotherapy (BACP). (2007). Ethical framework for good practice in counselling & psychotherapy. Leicestershire, UK: Author. Retrieved December 28, 2007, from www.bacp.co.uk/ethical_framework

Brown, L. M., & Gilligan, C. (1990, August). *Listening for self and relational voices: A responsive/resisting reader's guide.* Paper presented at the annual meeting of the American Psychological Association, Boston, MA.

Brown, R. W., & Otto, M. L. (1986). Field supervision: A collaborative model. *Michigan Journal of Counseling & Development, 17*(2), 48–51.

Bruss, K. V., Brack, C. J., Brack, G., Glickauf-Hughes, C., & O'Leary, M. (1997). A developmental model for supervising therapists treating gay, lesbian, and bisexual clients. *The Clinical Supervisor, 15*(1), 61–73.

Bryant-Jefferies, R. (2005). *Person-centred counselling supervision; personal and professional.* Abingdon, UK: Radcliffe Publishing.

Bubenzer, D. L., Mahrle, C., & West, J. D. (1987). *Live counselor supervision: Trainee acculturation and supervisor interventions.* Paper presented at the American Association for Counseling and Development Annual Convention, New Orleans.

Bubenzer, D. L., West, J. D., & Gold, J. M. (1991). Use of live supervision in counselor preparation. *Counselor Education & Supervision, 30,* 301–308.

Bucky, S. F., Marques, S., Daly, J., Alley, J., & Karp, A. (2010). Supervision characteristics related to the supervisory working alliance as rated by doctoral-level supervisees. *The Clinical Supervisor*, *29,* 149–163.

Buhrke, R. A. (1989). Incorporating lesbian and gay issues into counselor training: A resource guide. *Journal of Counseling & Development, 68,* 77–80.

Buhrke, R. A., & Douce, L. A. (1991). Training issues for counseling psychologists in working with lesbian women and gay men. *The Counseling Psychologist, 19,* 216–234.

Burgess, S. L. (1994). *The impaired clinical and counseling psychology doctoral student.* Unpublished doctoral dissertation, The California School of Professional Psychology, Alameda, CA.

Burkard, A. W., Johnson, A. J., Madson, M. B., Pruitt, N. T., Contreras-Tadych, D. A., Kozlowski, J. M., . . . & Knox, S. (2006). Supervisor cultural responsiveness and unresponsiveness in cross-cultural supervision. *Journal of Counseling Psychology, 53,* 288–301.

Burkard, A. W., Knox, S., Hess, S. A., & Schultz, J. (2009). Lesbian, gay, and bisexual supervisees' experiences of LGB-affirmative and nonaffirmative supervision. *Journal of Counseling Psychology, 56,* 176–188.

Burke, W., Goodyear, R. K., & Guzzardo, C. (1998). A multiple-case study of weakenings and repairs in supervisory alliances. *American Journal of Psychotherapy, 52,* 450–462.

Burnes, T. R., Wood, J., Inman, J., & Welikson, G. (in press). An investigation of process variables in feminist group clinical supervision. *The Counseling Psychologist.*

Burns, C. I., & Holloway, E. L. (1990). Therapy in supervision: An unresolved issue. *The Clinical Supervisor, 7*(4), 47–60.

Butler-Byrd, N. (2010). An African American supervisor's reflections on multicultural supervision. *Training & Education in Professional Psychology, 4*(1), 29–35.

Byng-Hall, J. (1982). The use of the earphone in supervision. In R. Whiffen & J. Byng-Hall (Eds.), *Family therapy supervision: Recent developments in practice* (pp. 47–56). London, UK: Academic Press.

Cade, B. W., Speed, B., & Seligman, P. (1986). Working in teams: The pros and cons. *The Clinical Supervisor, 4,* 105–117.

Caligor, L. (1984). Parallel and reciprocal processes in psychoanalytic supervision. In L. Caligor, P. M. Bromberg, & J. D. Meltzer (Eds.), *Clinical perspectives on the supervision of psychoanalysis and psychotherapy* (pp. 1–28). New York, NY: Plenum.

Callaghan, G. M. (2006). Functional analytic psychotherapy and supervision. *International Journal of Behavioral and Consultation Therapy, 2,* 416–431.

Callahan, J. L., Almstrom, C. M., Swift, J. K., Borja, S. E., & Heath, C. J. (2009). Exploring the contribution of supervisors to intervention outcomes. *Training & Education in Professional Psychology, 3*(2), 72–77.

Campbell, T. W. (1994). Psychotherapy and malpractice exposure. *American Journal of Forensic Psychology, 12,* 5–41.

Candy, P. C. (1991). *Self-direction for life-long learning*. San Francisco, CA: Jossey-Bass.

Caplan, G. (1970). *The theory and practice of mental health consultation*. New York, NY: Basic Books.

Caplan, G., & Caplan, R. (2000). Principles of community psychiatry. *Community Mental Health Journal, 36,* 7–24.

Caplow, T. (1968). *Two against one: Coalitions in triads*. Englewood Cliffs, NJ: Prentice-Hall.

Carkhuff, R. R., & Truax, C. B. (1965). Training in counseling and psychotherapy: An evaluation of an integrated didactic and experiential approach. *Journal of Consulting Psychology, 29,* 333–336.

Carlozzi, A. F., Romans, J. S. C., Boswell, D. L., Ferguson, D. B., & Whisenhunt, B. J. (1997). Training and supervision practices in counseling and marriage and family therapy programs. *Clinical Supervisor, 15*(1), 51–60.

Carroll, M. (1996). *Counseling supervision: Theory, skills, and practice*. London, UK: Cassell.

Carroll, M. (2001). The spirituality of supervision. In M. Carroll & M. Tholstrup (Eds.), *Integrative approaches to supervision* (pp. 76–89). London, UK: Jessica Kingsley.

Carroll, M. (2007). One more time: What is supervision? *Psychotherapy in Australia, 13,* 34–40.

Carroll, M., & Gilbert, M. C. (2005). *On being a supervisee: Creating learning partnerships.* London, UK: Vukani Publishing.

Carson, R. C. (1969). *Interaction concepts of personality.* Chicago: Aldine.

Carter, J. W., Enyedy, K. C., Goodyear, R. K., Arcinue, F., & Puri, N. N. (2009). Concept mapping of the events supervisees find helpful in group supervision. *Training & Education in Professional Psychology, 3*(1), 1–9.

Cashwell, C. S., Looby, E. J., & Housley, W. F. (1997). Appreciating cultural diversity through clinical supervision. *The Clinical Supervisor, 15*(1), 75–85.

Cass, V. C. (1979). Homosexual identity formation: A theoretical model. *Journal of Homosexuality, 4,* 219–235.

Cass, V. C. (1984). Homosexual identity formation: Testing a theoretical model. *Journal of Sex Research, 20,* 143–167.

Castonguay, L. G., Constantino, M. J., & Holtforth, M. G. (2006). The working alliance: Where are we and where should we go? *Psychotherapy, 43,* 271–279.

Celano, M. P., Smith, C. O., & Kaslow, N. J. (2010). A competency-based approach to couple and family therapy supervision. *Psychotherapy Theory, Research, Practice, Training, 47,* 35–44.

Center for Credentialing and Education (CCE). (2001). *Approved clinical supervisor.* Greensboro, NC: Author.

Chaiklin, H., & Munson, C. E. (1983). Peer consultation in social work. *The Clinical Supervisor, 1,* 21–34.

Chaimowitz, G. A., Glancy, G. D., & Blackburn, J. (2000). The duty to warn and protect: Impact on practice. *Canadian Journal of Psychiatry, 45,* 899–904.

Chambless, D. L., & Ollendick, T. H. (2001). Empirically supported psychological interventions: Controversies and evidence. *Annual Review of Psychology, 52,* 685–716.

Champe, J., & Kleist, D. M. (2003). Live supervision: A review of the literature. *Family Journal: Counseling & Therapy for Couples & Families, 11,* 268–275.

Chang, C. Y., Hays, D. G., & Milliken, T. F. (2009). Addressing social justice issues in supervision: A call for client and professional advocacy. *The Clinical Supervisor, 28,* 20–35.

Chang, C. Y., Hays, D. G., & Shoffner, M. F. (2003). Cross-racial supervision: A developmental approach for White supervisors working with supervisees of color. *The Clinical Supervisor, 22,* 121–138.

Chang, J. (2010). The reflecting team: A training method for family counselors. *The Family Journal: Counseling & Therapy for Couples & Families, 18,* 36–44.

Chapin, J., & Ellis, M. V. (2002). *Effects of role induction workshops on supervisee anxiety.* Paper presented at the annual meeting of the American Psychological Association, Chicago, IL.

Chapman, R. A., Baker, S. B., Nassar-McMillan, S. C., & Gerler, E. R., Jr. (2011). Cybersupervision: Further examination of synchronous and asynchronous modalities in counseling practicum supervision. *Counselor Education & Supervision, 50,* 298–313.

Chen, E. C., & Bernstein, B. L. (2000). Relations of complementarity and supervisory issues to supervisory working alliance: A comparative analysis of two cases. *Journal of Counseling Psychology, 47,* 485–497.

Chickering, A. W. (1969). *Education and identity.* San Francisco, CA: Jossey–Bass.

Chung, R. G., Kim, B. S. K., & Abreu, J. M. (2004). Asian American Multidimensional Acculturation Scale: Development, factor analysis, reliability, and validity. *Cultural Diversity & Ethnic Minority Psychology, 10,* 66–80.

Chung, Y. B., Marshall, J. A., & Gordon, L. L. (2001). Racial and gender biases in supervisory evaluation and feedback [Special issue]. *The Clinical Supervisor, 20*(1), 99–111.

Chur-Hansen, A., & McLean, S. (2006). On being a supervisor: The importance of feedback and how to give it. *Australasian Psychiatry, 14,* 67–71.

Cikanek, K., McCarthy Veach, P., & Braun, C. (2004). Advanced doctoral students' knowledge and understanding of clinical supervisor ethical responsibilities: A brief report. *The Clinical Supervisor, 23*(1), 191–196.

Claiborn, C. D., Etringer, B. D., & Hillerbrand, E. T. (1995). Influence processes in supervision. *Counselor Education & Supervision, 35,* 43–53.

Claiborn, C. D., Goodyear, R. K., & Horner, P. A. (2002). In J. C. Norcross (Ed.), *Psychotherapy relationships that work: Therapist contributions and responsiveness to patients* (pp. 217–234). New York, NY: Oxford University Press.

Claiborn, C. D., & Lichtenberg, J. W. (1989). Interactional counseling. *The Counseling Psychologist, 17,* 355–453.

Clarke, G., & Rowan, A. (2009). Looking again at the team dimension in systemic psychotherapy: Is attending to group process a critical context for practice? *Journal of Family Therapy, 31,* 85–107.

Clarkson, P. (1994). In recognition of dual relationships. *Transactional Analysis Journal, 24,* 32–38.

Clingerman, T. L., & Bernard, J. M. (2004). An investigation of the use of e-mail as a supplemental modality for clinical supervision. *Counselor Education & Supervision, 44,* 82–95.

Cobia, D. C., & Boes, S. R. (2000). Professional disclosure statements and formal plans for supervision: Two strategies for minimizing the risk of ethical conflicts in post-master's supervision. *Journal of Counseling & Development, 78,* 293–296.

Cobia, D. C., & Pipes, R. B. (2002). Mandated supervision: An intervention for disciplined professionals. *Journal of Counseling & Development, 80,* 140–144.

Coffey, D. (2002). Receiving corrective feedback: A special set of skills. Presentation at the Association for Counselor Education and Supervision Convention. Park City, UT.

Cohen, J. (1992). A power primer. *Psychological Bulletin, 112,* 155–159.

Cohen, R. J. (1979). *Malpractice: A guide for mental health professionals.* New York, NY: Free Press.

Coll, K. M. (1995). Clinical supervision of community college counselors: Current and preferred practices. *Counselor Education & Supervision, 35,* 111–117.

Collins, D., & Bogo, M. (1986). Competency-based field instruction: Bridging the gap between laboratory and field learning. *The Clinical Supervisor, 4*(3), 39–52.

Committee on Professional Practice and Standards. (2003). Legal issues in the professional practice of psychology. *Professional Psychology: Research & Practice, 34,* 595–600.

Congress, E. P. (1992). Ethical decision making of social work supervisors. *The Clinical Supervisor, 10*(1), 157–169.

Conn, S. R., Roberts, R. L., & Powell, B. M. (2009). Attitudes and satisfaction with a hybrid model of counseling supervision. *Educational Technology & Society, 12,* 298–306.

Constantine, J. A., Piercy, F. P., & Sprenkle, D. H. (1984). Live supervision-of-supervision in family therapy. *Journal of Marital & Family Therapy, 10,* 95–97.

Constantine, M. G. (1997). Facilitating multicultural competency in counseling supervision: Operationalizing a practical framework. In D. B. Pope-Davis & H. L. K. Coleman (Eds.), *Multicultural counseling competencies: Assessment, education and training, and supervision* (pp. 310–324). Thousand Oaks, CA: Sage Publications.

Constantine, M. G., & Sue, D. W. (2007). Perceptions of racial microaggressions among Black supervisees in cross-racial dyads. *Journal of Counseling Psychology, 54,* 142–153.

Constantine, M. G., Warren, A. K., & Miville, M. L. (2005). White racial identity dyadic interactions in supervision: Implications for supervisees' multicultural counseling competence. *Journal of Counseling Psychology, 52,* 490–496.

Cook, D. A. (1994). Racial identity in supervision. *Counselor Education & Supervision, 34,* 132–141.

Cook, D. A., & Helms, J. E. (1988). Visible racial/ethnic group supervisees' satisfaction with cross-cultural supervision as predicted by relationship characteristics. *Journal of Counseling Psychology, 35,* 268–274.

Cooley, C. H. (1902). *Human nature and the social order.* New York, NY: Scribner's.

Cooper, J. B., & Ng, K.-M. (2009). Trait emotional intelligence and perceived supervisory working alliance of counseling trainees and their supervisors in agency settings. *International Journal for the Advancement of Counselling, 31,* 145–157.

Copeland, S. (1998). Counselling supervision in organizational contexts: New challenges and perspectives [Special issue]. *British Journal of Guidance & Counselling, 26*, 377–386.

Corey, G., Corey, M. S., & Callanan, P. (1993). *Issues and ethics in the helping professions* (4th ed.). Pacific Grove, CA: Brooks/Cole.

Cormier, L. S., & Bernard, J. M. (1982). Ethical and legal responsibilities of clinical supervisors. *The Personnel & Guidance Journal, 60,* 486–491.

Cornell, W. F. (1994). Dual relationships in transactional analysis: Training, supervision, and therapy. *Transactional Analysis Journal, 24,* 21–30.

Corrigan, J. D., Dell, D. M., Lewis, K. N., & Schmidt, L. D. (1980). Counseling as a social influence process: A review [Monograph]. *Journal of Counseling Psychology, 27,* 395–441.

Costa, L. (1994). Reducing anxiety in live supervision. *Counselor Education & Supervision, 34,* 30–40.

Cottone, R. R., & Claus, R. E. (2000). Ethical decision-making models: A review of the literature. *Journal of Counseling & Development, 78*, 275–283.

Couchon, W. D., & Bernard, J. M. (1984). Effects of timing of supervision on supervisor and counselor performance. *The Clinical Supervisor, 2*(3), 3–20.

Council for Accreditation of Counseling and Related Educational Programs. (CACREP). (2001). *The 2001 standards*. Alexandria, VA: Author. www.counseling.org/cacrep/2001standards700.htm

Council for the Accreditation of Counseling and Related Education Programs (CACREP). (2009). *2009 Standards*. Author.

Counselman, E. F., & Weber, R. L. (2004). Organizing and maintaining peer supervision groups. *International Journal of Group Psychotherapy, 54,* 125–143.

Court, J. H., & Winwood, P. (2005). Seeing the light in cyberspace: A cautionary tale of developing a practical model for cybercounseling and cyber supervision within the University of South Australia. *Journal of Technology in Counseling, 4*(1), 1–17.

Covey, S. R., Merrill, A. R., & Merrill, R. R. (1994). *First things first*. New York, NY: Simon & Schuster.

Covner, B. J. (1942a). Studies in phonographic recordings of verbal material: I. The use of phonographic recordings in counseling practice and research. *Journal of Consulting Psychology, 6,* 105–113.

Covner, B. J. (1942b). Studies in phonographic recordings of verbal material: II. A device for transcribing phonographic recordings of verbal material. *Journal of Consulting Psychology, 6,* 149–151.

Crocket, K., Cahill, F., Flanagan, P., Franklin, J. McGill, R., Stewart, A., Whalan, M., & Mulcah, D. (2009). Possibilities and limits of cross-disciplinary supervision: An exploratory study. *New Zealand Journal of Counselling, 29,* 25–41.

Cronbach, L. J., & Snow, R. E. (1977). *Aptitudes and instructional methods*. New York, NY: Halstead Press.

Croteau, J. M., Talbot, D. M., Lance, T. S., & Evans, N. J. (2002). A qualitative study of the interplay between privilege and oppression. *Journal of Multicultural Counseling & Development, 30*, 239–258.

Csikszentmihalyi, M. (1990). *Flow: The psychology of optimal experience*. New York, NY: Harper.

Culloty, T., Milne, D. L., & Sheikh, A. I. (2010). Evaluating the training of clinical supervisors: A pilot study using the fidelity framework. *The Cognitive Behaviour Therapist, 3*, 132–144.

Cummings, A. L., Hallberg, E. T., Martin, J., Slemon, A., & Hiebert, B. (1990). Implications of counselor conceptualizations for counselor education. *Counselor Education and Supervision, 30,* 120–134.

Cummings, P. (2002). Cybervision: Virtual peer group counselling supervision—Hindrance or help? *Counselling and Psychotherapy Research, 2,* 223–229.

D'Andrea, M., & Daniels, J. (1997). Multicultural counseling supervision: Central issues, theoretical considerations, and practical strategies. In D. Pope-Davis & H. Coleman (Eds.), *Multicultural counseling competencies: Assessment, education and training, and supervision. Multicultural aspect of counseling series* (Vol. 7, pp. 290–309). Thousand Oaks, CA: Sage.

D'Andrea, M., & Daniels, J. (2001). Respectful counseling: An integrative multidimensional model for counselors. In D. B. Pope-Davis & H. L. K. Coleman (Eds.), *The intersection of race, class, and gender in multicultural counseling* (pp. 417–466). Thousand Oaks, CA: Sage.

Daniels, J. A., & Larson, L. M. (2001). The impact of performance feedback on counseling self-efficacy and counselor anxiety. *Counselor Education & Supervision, 41*, 120–130.

Dawes, R. M. (1994). *House of cards: Psychology and psychotherapy built on myth*. New York, NY: The Free Press.

Day, S. X., & Schneider, P. L. (2002). Psychotherapy using distance technology: A comparison of face-to-face, video, and audio treatment. *Journal of Counseling Psychology, 49,* 499–503.

Deacon, S. A. (2000). Using divergent thinking exercises within supervision to enhance therapist creativity. *Journal of Family Psychotherapy, 11*(2), 67–73.

Deal, K. H. (2003). The relationship between critical thinking and interpersonal skills: Guidelines for clinical supervision. *The Clinical Supervisor, 22*(2), 3–19.

Dean, J. E. (2001). Sandtray consultation: A method of supervision applied to couple's therapy. *The Arts in Psychotherapy, 28,* 175–180.

Deist, F. D. L., & Winterton, J. (2005). What is competence? *Human Resource Development International, 8,* 27–46.

Delaney, H. D., Miller, W. R., & Bisonó, A. M. (2007). Religiosity and spirituality among psychologists: A survey of clinician members of the American Psychological Association. *Professional Psychology: Research and Practice, 38,* 538–546.

deMayo, R. A. (2000). Patients' sexual behavior and sexual harassment: A survey of clinical supervisors. *Professional Psychology: Research & Practice, 31,* 706–709.

DeMers, S. T. (2009). Real progress with significant challenges ahead: Advancing competency assessment in psychology. *Training & Education in Professional Psychology, 3*(4, Suppl), S66–S69. doi: 10.1037/a0017534

Dennin, M. K., & Ellis, M. V. (2003). Effects of a method of self-supervision for counselor trainees. *Journal of Counseling Psychology, 50,* 69–83.

Denton, W. A., Nakonezny, P. A., & Burwell, S. R. (2011). The effects of meeting a family therapy supervision team on client satisfaction in an initial session. *Journal of Family Therapy, 33,* 85–97.

Desmond, K. J., & Kindsvatter, A. (2010). Intentional practices in supervision of family counseling: The use of supervisory letters. *The Family Journal: Counseling & Therapy for Couples & Families, 18,* 31–35.

DeStefano, J., D'Iuso, N., Blake, E., Fitzpatrick, M., Drapeau, M., & Chamodraka, M. (2007). Trainees' experiences of impasses in counselling and the impact of group supervision on their resolution: A pilot study. *Counselling & Psychotherapy Research, 7,* 42–47.

Dewey, J. (1933). *How we think.* New York, NY: D. C. Heath.

Dickens, A. D. H. (2011). Satisfaction of supervisory working alliance: Distance versus face-to-face. *Dissertation Abstracts International, 71* (3-A), 827.

Dickey, K. D., Housley, W. F., & Guest, C. (1993). Ethics in supervision of rehabilitation counselor trainees: A survey. *Rehabilitation Education, 7,* 195–201.

Dickson, J. M., Moberly, N. J., Marshall, Y., & Reilly, J. (2011). Attachment style and its relationship to working alliance in the supervision of British clinical psychology trainees. *Clinical Psychology & Psychotherapy, 18,* 322–30.

Disney, M. J., & Stephens, A. M. (1994). *Legal issues in clinical supervision.* Alexandria, VA: ACA Press.

Dixon, D. N., & Claiborn, C. D. (1987). A social influence approach to counselor supervision. In J. E. Maddux, C. D. Stoltenberg, & R. Rosenwein (Eds.). *Social processes in clinical and counseling psychology* (pp. 83–93). New York, NY: Springer-Verlag.

Dodds, J. B. (1986). Supervision of psychology trainees in field placements. *Professional Psychology: Research & Practice, 17,* 296–300.

Dodenhoff, J. T. (1981). Interpersonal attraction and direct–indirect supervisor influence as predictors of counselor trainee effectiveness. *Journal of Counseling Psychology, 28,* 47–52.

Doehrman, M. (1976). Parallel processes in supervision and psychotherapy. *Bulletin of the Menninger Clinic, 40,* 3–104.

Dohrenbusch, R., & Lipka, S. (2006). Assessing and predicting supervisors' evaluations of psychotherapists—an empirical study. *Counselling Psychology Quarterly, 19,* 395–414.

Dombeck, M. T., & Brody, S. L. (1995). Clinical supervision: A three-way mirror. *Archives of Psychiatric Nursing, 9,* 3–10.

Dowd, E. T. (1989). Stasis and change in cognitive psychotherapy: Client resistance and reactance as mediating variables. In W. Dryden & P. Trower (Eds.), *Cognitive psychotherapy: Stasis and change* (pp. 139–158). New York, NY: Springer.

Dowling, S. (1984). Clinical evaluation: A comparison of self, self with videotape, peers, and supervisors. *The Clinical Supervisor, 2*(3), 71–78.

Downing, N., & Roush, K. (1985). From passive acceptance to active commitment: A model of feminist identity development for women. *The Counseling Psychologist, 13,* 695–709.

Dressel, J. L., Consoli, A. J., Kim, B. S. K., & Atkinson, D. R. (2007). Successful and unsuccessful multicultural supervisory behaviors: A Delphi poll. *Journal of Multicultural Counseling & Development, 35,* 51–64.

Driscoll, J. (2000). *Practicing clinical supervision: A reflective approach.* London, UK: Bailliere Tindall.

Duan, C., & Roehlke, H. (2001). A descriptive "snapshot" of cross-racial supervision in university counseling center internships [Special issue]. *Journal of Multicultural Counseling & Development, 29*(2), 131–146.

Duba, J. D., Paez, S. B., & Kindsvatter, A. (2010). Criteria of nonacademic characteristics used to evaluate and retain community counseling students. *Journal of Counseling & Development, 88,* 154–162.

Dubin, S. (1972). Obsolescence or lifelong learning: A choice for the professional. *American Psychologist, 27,* 486–498.

Dudding, C. C., & Justice, L. M. (2004). An E-supervision model: Videoconferencing as a clinical training tool. *Communication Disorders Quarterly, 25,* 145–151.

Duys, D. K., & Hedstrom, S. M. (2000). Basic counselor skills training and counselor cognitive complexity. *Counselor Education & Supervision, 40,* 8–18.

Dye, A. (1994). Training doctoral student supervisors at Purdue University. In J. E. Myers (Ed.), *Developing and directing counselor education laboratories* (pp. 121–130). Alexandria, VA: ACA Press.

Dykas, M. J., & Cassidy, J. (2011). Attachment and the processing of social information across the life span: Theory and evidence. *Psychological Bulletin, 137,* 19–46.

Edelstein, L. (1943). *The Hippocratic Oath.* Baltimore, MD: Johns Hopkins Press.

Edwards, J. K., & Chen, M. W. (1999). Strength-based supervision: Frameworks, current practice, and future directions: A Wu Wei method. *The Family Journal, 7,* 349–357.

Edwards, T. M., & Hashmati, A. (2003). A guide for beginning family therapy group supervisors. *The American Journal of Family Therapy, 31,* 295–304.

Efstation, J. F., Patton, M. J., & Kardash, C. M. (1990). Measuring the working alliance in counselor supervision. *Journal of Counseling Psychology, 37,* 322–329.

Eisenberg, D., Hunt, J., Speer, N., & Zivin, K. (2011). Mental health service utilization among college students in the United States. *The Journal of Nervous & Mental Disease, 199,* 301–308.

Eisenberg, S. (1956). *Supervision in the changing field of social work.* Philadelphia, PA: The Jewish Family Service of Philadelphia.

Ekstein, R., & Wallerstein, R. S. (1972). *The teaching and learning of psychotherapy* (2nd ed.). New York, NY: International Universities Press, Inc.

Elizur, J. (1990). "Stuckness" in live supervision: Expanding the therapist's style. *Journal of Family Therapy, 12,* 267–280.

Ellis, A. (1974). *The techniques of Disputing Irrational Beliefs (DIBs).* New York, NY: Institute for Rational Living.

Ellis, M. V. (1991a). Critical incidents in clinical supervision & in supervisor supervision: Assessing supervisory issues. *Journal of Counseling Psychology, 38,* 342–349.

Ellis, M. V. (1991b). Research in clinical supervision: Revitalizing a scientific agenda. *Counselor Education & Supervision, 30,* 238–251.

Ellis, M. V. (2001). Harmful supervision, a cause for alarm: Commentary on Nelson & Friedlander (2001) & Gray et al. (2001). *Journal of Counseling Psychology, 48,* 401–406.

Ellis, M. V. (2010). Bridging the science and practice of clinical supervision: Some discoveries, some misconceptions. *The Clinical Supervisor, 29,* 95–116.

Ellis, M. V., Anderson-Hanley, C. M., Dennin, M. K., Anderson, J. J., Chapin, J. L., & Polstri, S. M. (1994, August). *Congruence of expectation in clinical supervision: Scale development and validity data.* Paper presented at the annual meeting of the American Psychological Association, Los Angeles, CA.

Ellis, M. V., Berger, L. R., Ring, E., Swords, B., Hanus, A., Siembor, M., & Wallis, A. (2010, August). *Construct validity of harmful and inadequate clinical supervision.* Paper presented at the 118th Annual Convention of the American Psychological Association, San Diego, CA.

Ellis, M. V., Chapin, J. L., Dennin, M. K., & Anderson-Hanley, C. (August, 1996). *Role induction for clinical supervision: Impact on neophyte supervisees.* Paper presented at the annual meeting of the American Psychological Association, Toronto.

Ellis, M. V., & Dell, D. M. (1986). Dimensionality of supervisor roles: Supervisors' perceptions of supervision. *Journal of Counseling Psychology, 33,* 282–291.

Ellis, M. V., Dell, D. M., & Good, G. E. (1988). Counselor trainees' perceptions of supervisor roles: Two studies testing the dimensionality of supervision. *Journal of Counseling Psychology, 35,* 315–322.

Ellis, M. V., & Douce, L. A. (1994). Group supervision of novice clinical supervisors: Eight recurring issues. *Journal of Counseling & Development, 72,* 520–525.

Ellis, M. V., Krengel, M., & Beck, M. (2002). Testing self-focused attention theory in clinical supervision:

Effects of supervisee anxiety and performance. *Journal of Counseling Psychology, 49,* 101–116.

Ellis, M. V., & Ladany, N. (1997). Inferences concerning supervisees and clients in clinical supervision: An integrative review. In C. E. Watkins, Jr. (Ed.), *Handbook of psychotherapy supervision* (pp. 467–507). New York, NY: Wiley.

Ellis, M. V., Ladany, N., Krengel, M., & Schult, D. (1996). Clinical supervision research from 1981 to 1993: A methodological critique. *Journal of Counseling Psychology, 43,* 35–50.

Ellis, M. V., & Robbins, E. S. (1993). Voices of care and justice in clinical supervision: Issues and interventions. *Counselor Education & Supervision, 32,* 203–212.

Ellis, M. V., Siembor, M. J., Swords, B. A., Morere, L., & Blanco, S. (June 2008). Prevalence and characteristics of harmful and inadequate clinical supervision. Paper presented at the 4th annual International Interdisciplinary Clinical Supervision Conference, Buffalo, NY.

Elman, N. S., & Forrest, L. (2004). Psychotherapy in the remediation of psychology trainees: Exploratory interviews with training directors. *Professional Psychology: Research & Practice, 49,* 123–130.

Elman, N. S., & Forrest, L. (2007). From trainee impairment to professional competence problems: Seeking new terminology that facilitates effective action. *Professional Psychology: Research and Practice, 38,* 501–509.

Elman, N., Forrest, L., Vacha-Haase, T., & Gizara, S. (1999). A systems perspective on trainee impairment: Continuing the dialogue. *The Counseling Psychologist, 27,* 712–721.

Emmons, L. (2011). *The relationship with academic training programs: Communication and supervision.* American Psychological Association National Conference, Washington, DC.

Engels, D. W., Minton, C. A. B., Ray, D. C., et al. (2010). *The professional counselor: Portfolio, competencies, performance guidelines, and assessment* (4th ed.). Alexandria, VA: American Counseling Association Press.

Enyedy, K. C., Arcinue, F., Puri, N. N., Carter, J. W., Goodyear, R. K., & Getzelman, M. A. (2003). Hindering phenomena in group supervision: Implications for practice. *Professional Psychology: Research & Practice, 34,* 312–317.

Epstein, L. (1986). Collusive selective inattention to the negative impact of the supervisory interaction. *Contemporary Psychoanalysis, 22,* 389–408.

Epstein, L. (2001). Collusive selection inattention to the negative impact of the supervisory interaction. In S. Gill (Ed.), *The supervisory alliance: Facilitating the psychotherapist's learning experience* (pp. 139–163). Northvale, NJ: Jason Aronson, Inc.

Epstein, R. M., & Hundert, E. M. (2002). Defining and assessing professional competence. *Journal of the American Medical Association, 287,* 226–235.

Erera, I. P., & Lazar, A. (1994). The administrative and educational functions in supervision: Indications of incompatibility. *The Clinical Supervisor, 12*(2), 39–55.

Ericcson, K. A., & Lehmann, A. C. (1996). Expert and exceptional performance: Evidence of maximal adaptation to task constraints. *Annual Review of Psychology, 47,* 273–305.

Eriksen, K., Marston, G., & Korte, T. (2002). Working with God: Managing conservative Christian beliefs that may interfere with counseling. *Counseling & Values, 47,* 48–72.

Erwin, W. J. (2000). Supervisor moral sensitivity. *Counseling Education & Supervision, 40,* 115–127.

Eshach, H., & Bitterman, H. (2003). From case-based reasoning to problem-based learning. *Academic Medicine, 5,* 491–496.

Estrada, D., Frame, M. W., & Williams, C. B. (2004). Cross-cultural supervision: Guiding the conversation toward race and ethnicity. *Journal of Multicultural Counseling & Development, 32,* 307–319.

Evans, D. (1987). Live supervision in the same room: A practice teaching method. *Social Work Education, 6*(3), 13–17.

Falender, C. A. (2009). Relationship and accountability: Tensions in feminist supervision. *Women & Therapy, 33,* 22–41.

Falender, C. A., Collins, C., & Shafranske, E. P. (2005, June). *Impairment in psychology training.* International Interdisciplinary Conference on Clinical Supervision, Buffalo, NY.

Falender, C. A., Collins, C. J., & Shafranske, E. P. (2009). "Impairment" and performance issues in clinical supervision: After the 2008 ADA amendments act. *Training & Education in Professional Psychology, 3,* 240–249.

Falender, C. A., Cornish, J. A. E., Goodyear, R. K., Hatcher, R., Kaslow, N. J., Leventhal, G., . . . , & Grus, C. (2004). Defining competencies in psychology supervision: A consensus statement. *Journal of Clinical Psychology, 60,* 771–785.

Falender, C. A., & Shafranske, E. P. (2004). *Clinical supervision: A competency-based approach.* Washington, DC: APA.

Falender, C. A., & Shafranske, E. P. (2007). Competence in competency-based supervision practice: Construct and application. *Professional Psychology: Research & Practice, 38,* 232–240.

Fall, M., & Sutton, J. M., Jr. (2004). *Clinical supervision: A handbook for practitioners.* Boston, MA: Allyn & Bacon.

Fall, M. & Sutton, J. M. Jr. (2006). Sandtray: A new tool for peer supervision groups for play therapists. Unpublished manuscript.

Falvey, J. E. (1987). *Handbook of administrative supervision.* Alexandria, VA: Association for Counselor Education & Supervision.

Falvey, J. E. (2002). *Managing clinical supervision: Ethical practice and legal risk management.* Pacific Grove, CA: Brooks/Cole.

Falvey, J. E., Caldwell, C. F., & Cohen, C. R. (2002). *Documentation in supervision: The focused risk management supervision system.* Pacific Grove, CA: Brooks/Cole.

Falvey, J. E., & Cohen, C. R. (2003). The buck stops here: Documenting clinical supervision. *The Clinical Supervisor, 22*(2), 63–80.

Farber, E. W. (2010). Humanistic–existential psychotherapy competencies and the supervisory process. *Psychotherapy Theory, Research, Practice, Training, 47,* 28–34.

Farber, E. W. (2012). Supervising humanistic–existential psychotherapy: Needs, possibilities. *Journal of Contemporary Psychotherapy, 42,* 173–182.

Feindler, E. L., & Padrone, J. J. (2009). Self-disclosure in clinical supervision. In A. Bloomgarden & R. B. Mennuti (Eds.), *Psychotherapist revealed: Therapists speak about self-disclosure in psychotherapy* (pp. 287–310). New York, NY: Taylor & Francis.

Feiner, A. H. (1994). Comments on contradictions in the supervisory process. *Contemporary Psychoanalysis, 30,* 57–75.

Fernando, D. M., & Hulse-Killacky, D. (2005). The relationship of supervisory styles to satisfaction with supervision and the perceived self-efficacy of master's level counseling students. *Counselor Education & Supervision, 44,* 293–304.

Field, L. D., Chavez-Korell, S., & Rodriguez, M. M. D. (2010). No hay rosas sin Espinas: Conceptualizing Latina–Latina supervision from a multicultural developmental supervisory model. *Training and Education in Professional Psychology, 4,* 47–54.

Fine, M. (2003). Reflections on the intersection of power and competition in reflecting teams as applied to academic settings. *Journal of Marital & Family Therapy, 29,* 339–351.

Fiscalini, J. (1985). On supervisory parataxis and dialogue. *Contemporary Psychoanalysis, 21,* 591–608.

Fiscalini, J. (1997). On supervisory parataxis and dialogue. In M. H. Rock (Ed.), *Psychodynamic supervision: Perspectives of the supervisor and the supervisee* (pp. 29–58). Northvale, NJ: Aronson.

Fisher, B. (1989). Differences between supervision of beginning and advanced therapists: Hogan's hypothesis empirically revisited. *The Clinical Supervisor, 7*(1), 57–74.

Fitch, J. C., Pistole, M. C., & Gunn, J. E. (2010). The bonds of development: An attachment–caregiving model of supervision. *The Clinical Supervisor,* 29, 20–34.

Fleming, J. (1953). The role of supervision in psychiatric training. *Bulletin of the Menninger Clinic, 17,* 157–159.

Fleming, L. M., Glass, J. A., Fujisaki, S., & Toner, S. L. (2010). Group process and learning: A grounded theory model of group supervision. *Training & Education in Professional Psychology, 4,* 194–203.

Fly, B. J., van Bark, W. P., Weinman, L., Kitchener, K. S., & Lang, P. R. (1997). Ethical transgressions of psychology graduate students: Critical incidents with implications for training. *Professional Psychology: Research & Practice, 28,* 492–495.

Fong, M. L., Borders, L. D., Ethington, C. A., & Pitts, J. H. (1997). Becoming a counselor: A longitudinal study of student cognitive development. *Counselor Education and Supervision, 37,* 100–114.

Fong, M. L., & Lease, S. H. (1997). Cross-cultural supervision: Issues for the White supervisor. In D. B. Pope-Davis & H. L. K. Coleman (Eds.), *Multicultural counseling competencies: Assessment, education and training, and supervision* (pp. 387–405). Thousand Oaks, CA: Sage Publications.

Ford, S. J. W., & Britton, P. J. (2002). *Multicultural supervision: What's really going on?* Presentation at the American Counselor Education and Supervision Conference, Park City, UT.

Forrest, L., Elman, N. S., & Shen-Miller, D. S. (2008). Psychology trainees with competence problems: From individual to ecological conceptualizations. *Training & Education in Professional Psychology* 2(4), 183–192.

Forrest, L., Elman, N., Gizara, S., & Vacha-Haase, T. (1999). Trainee impairment: A review of identification, remediation, dismissal, and legal issues. *Counseling Psychologist, 27*(5), 627–686.

Foster, J. T., Heinen, A. D., Lichtenberg, J. W., & Gomez, A. D. (2006). Supervisor attachment as a predictor of developmental ratings of supervisees. *American Journal of Psychological Research, 2,* 28–39.

Foster, J. T., Lichtenberg, J. W., & Peyton, V. (2007). The supervisory attachment relationship as a predictor of the professional development of the supervisee. *Psychotherapy Research, 17,* 343–350.

Foster, V. A., & McAdams, C. R., III. (2009). A framework for creating a climate of transparency for professional performance assessment: Fostering student investment in gatekeeping. *Counselor Education & Supervision, 48,* 271–284.

Fouad, N., Grus, C. L., Hatcher, R. L., Kaslow, N. J., Hutchings, P. S., Madson, M. B., . . . , & Crossman, R. E. (2009). Competency benchmarks: A model for understanding and measuring competence in professional psychology across training levels. *Training & Education in Professional Psychology, 3*(4, Suppl), S5–S26.

Fox, R. (1983). Contracting in supervision: A goal oriented process. *The Clinical Supervisor, 1*(l), 37–49.

Foy, C. W., & Breunlin, D. C. (2001) Integrative supervision: A metaframework perspective. In S. H. McDaniel, D. D. Lusterman, & C. L. Philpot (Eds.), *Casebook for integrating family therapy: An ecosystemic approach* (pp. 387–394). Washington, DC: American Psychological Association.

Fraenkel, P., & Pinsof, W. M. (2001). Teaching family therapy–centered integration: Assimilation and beyond. *Journal of Psychotherapy Integration, 11,* 59–85.

Frame, M. W. (2001). The spiritual genogram in training and supervision. *Family Journal–Counseling & Therapy for Couples & Families, 9*(2), 109–115.

Frame, M. W., & Stevens-Smith, P. (1995). Out of harm's way: Enhancing monitoring and dismissal processes in counselor education programs. *Counselor Education & Supervision, 35,* 118–129.

Frank, A. D. (1961). *Persuasion and healing.* Baltimore, MD: Johns Hopkins University Press.

Frankel, B. R. (1990). Process of family therapy live supervision: A brief report. *The Commission on Supervision Bulletin, III*(1), 5–6.

Frankel, B. R., & Piercy, F. P. (1990). The relationship among selected supervisor, therapist, and client behaviors. *Journal of Marital & Family Therapy, 16,* 407–421.

Frawley-O'Dea, M. G., & Sarnat, J. E. (2001). *The supervisory relationship: A contemporary psychodynamic approach.* New York, NY: Guilford Press.

Frayn, D. H. (1991). Supervising the supervisors: The evolution of a psychotherapy supervisors' group. *American Journal of Psychotherapy, 45,* 31–42.

Frazier, P. A., Tix, A. P., & Barron, K. E. (2004). Testing moderator and mediator effects in counseling psychology research. *Journal of Counseling Psychology, 51,* 115–134.

Freeman, S. C. (1993). Reiterations on client-centered supervision. *Counselor Education and Supervision, 32,* 213–215.

Freitas, G. J. (2002). The impact of psychotherapy supervision on client outcome: A critical examination of two decades of research. *Psychotherapy: Theory, Research, Practice, Training, 39,* 354–367.

French, J. R. P., Jr., & Raven, B. (1959). The bases of social power. In D. Cartwright (Ed.), *Studies in social power* (pp. 150–167). Ann Arbor, MI: Institute for Social Research.

Freud, S. (1986). On the history of the psychoanalytic movement. In *Historical and expository works on psychoanalysis.* Harmondsworth, UK: Penguin. (Original work published 1914.)

Frey, L. L., Beesley, D., & Liang, Y. (2009). The client evaluation of counseling inventory: Initial validation of an instrument measuring counseling effectiveness. *Training & Education in Professional Psychology, 3,* 28–36.

Frick, D. E., McCartney, C. I., & Lazarus, J. A. (1995). Supervision of sexually exploitative psychiatrists: APA district branch experience. *Psychiatric Annuals, 25,* 113–117.

Fried, L. (1991). Becoming a psychotherapist. *Journal of College Student Psychotherapy, 5,* 71–79.

Fried, Y., Tiegs, R. B. & Bellany, A. R. (1992). Personal and interpersonal predictors of supervisors' avoidance of evaluating subordinates. *Journal of Applied Psychology, 77,* 462–468.

Friedlander, M. L., Keller, K. E., Peca-Baker, T. A., & Olk, M. E. (1986). Effects of role conflict on counselor trainees' self-statements, anxiety level, and performance. *Journal of Counseling Psychology, 33,* 73–77.

Friedlander, M. L., & Schwartz, G. S. (1985). Toward a theory of strategic self-presentation in counseling and psychotherapy. *Journal of Counseling Psychology, 32,* 483–501.

Friedlander, M. L., Siegel, S. M., & Brenock, K. (1989). Parallel process in counseling and supervision: A case study. *Journal of Counseling Psychology, 36,* 149–157.

Friedlander, M. L., & Snyder, J. (1983). Trainees' expectations for the supervisory process: Testing a developmental model. *Counselor Education and Supervision, 22,* 342–348.

Friedlander, M. L., & Ward, L. G. (1984). Development and validation of the Supervisory Styles Inventory. *Journal of Counseling Psychology, 31,* 542–558.

Friedman, R. (1983). Aspects of the parallel process and counter-transference issues in student supervision. *School Social Work Journal, 8*(1), 3–15.

Frohman, A. L. (1998). Building a culture for innovation. *Research Technology Management, 41,* 9–12.

Frølund, L., & Nielsen, J. (2009). The reflective meta-dialogue in psychodynamic supervision. *Nordic Psychology, 61*(4), 85–105.

Fukuyama, M. A. (1994). Critical incidents in multicultural counseling supervision: A phenomenological approach to supervision. *Counselor Education & Supervision, 34,* 142–151.

Fulero, S. M. (1988). Tarasoff: 10 years later. *Professional Psychology: Research & Practice, 19,* 184–190.

Gabbard, G. O. (2005). How not to teach psychotherapy. *Academic Psychiatry, 29,* 332–338.

Gabbard, G. O., & Crisp-Han, H. (2010). Teaching professional boundaries to psychiatric residents. *Academic Psychiatry, 34,* 369–372.

Galassi, J. P., & Brooks, L. (1992). Integrating scientist and practitioner training in counseling psychology: Practicum is the key. *Counselling Psychology Quarterly, 5,* 57–65.

Gallant, J. P., & Thyer, B. A. (1989). The "bug-in-the-ear" in clinical supervision: A review. *The Clinical Supervisor, 7*(2), 43–58.

Gallant, J. P., Thyer, B. A., & Bailey, J. S. (1991). Using bug-in-the-ear feedback in clinical supervision: *Research on Social Work Practice, 1,* 175–187.

Gallessich, J., & Olmstead, K. M. (1987). Training in counseling psychology: Issues & trends in 1986. *The Counseling Psychologist, 15,* 596–600.

Garcia, M., Kosutic, I., McDowell, T., & Anderson, S. A. (2009). Raising critical consciousness in family therapy supervision. *Journal of Feminist Family Therapy, 21,* 18–38.

Garfield, S. L. (1983). Effectiveness of psychotherapy: The perennial controversy. *Professional Psychology: Theory, Research, & Practice, 14,* 35–43.

Garfield, S. L. (1986). Research on client variables in psychotherapy. In S. L. Garfield & A. E. Bergin (Eds.), *Handbook of psychotherapy and behavior change* (3rd ed., pp. 190–228). New York, NY: John Wiley & Sons.

Garfield, S. L. (2006). *Therapies—modern and popular: PsycCRITIQUES 2006.* Washington, DC: American Psychological Association.

Gatmon, D., Jackson, D., Koshkarian, L., Martos-Perry, N., Molina, A., Patel, N., & Rodolfa, E. (2001). Exploring ethnic, gender, and sexual orientation in supervision: Do they really matter? *Journal of Multicultural Counseling & Development, 29,* 102–113.

Gaubatz, M. D., & Vera, E. M. (2002). Do formalized gatekeeping procedures increase programs' follow-up with deficient trainees? *Counselor Education & Supervision, 41,* 294–305.

Gaubatz, M. D., & Vera, E. M. (2006). Trainee competence in master's-level counseling programs: A comparison of counselor educators' and students' views. *Counselor Education & Supervision, 46*(1), 32–43.

Gautney, K. (1994). What if they ask me if I am married? *The Supervisor Bulletin, VII*(1), 3, 7.

Gediman, H. K., & Wolkenfeld, F. (1980). The parallelism phenomenon in psychoanalysis and supervision: Its reconsideration as a triadic system. *Psychoanalytic Quarterly, 49,* 234–255.

Geller, J. D., Farber, B. A., & Schaffer, C. E. (2010). Representations of the supervisory dialogue and the development of psychotherapists. *Psychotherapy: Theory, Research, & Practice, 47,* 211–220.

Gelso, C. A., & Carter, A. (1985). The relationship in counseling and psychotherapy. *The Counseling Psychologist, 13,* 155–243.

Gershenson, J., & Cohen, M. (1978). Through the looking glass: The experiences of two family therapy trainees with live supervision. *Family Process, 17,* 225–230.

Getz, H. G., & Agnew, D. (1999). A supervision model for public agency clinicians. *The Clinical Supervisor, 18,* 51–61.

Getzelman, M. A. (2004). Development and validation of the Group Supervision Impact Scale. *Dissertation Abstracts International: Section B: The Sciences and Engineering, 65*(5-B), 2625.

Gibbons, M. B. C., Rothbard, A., Farris, K. D., Stirman, S. W., Thompson, S. M., Scott, K., . . . & Crits-Christoph, P. (2011). Changes in psychotherapy utilization among consumers of services for major depressive disorder in the community. *Administration*

& Policy in Mental Health & Mental Health Services Research, 38, 495–503.

Giddings, M. M., Cleveland, P. H., & Smith, C. H. (2006). Responding to inadequate supervision: A model promoting integration for post-MSW practitioners. *The Clinical Supervisor, 25*(1/2), 105–126.

Giddings, M. M., Vodde, R., & Cleveland, P. (2003). Examining student–field instructor problems in practicum: Beyond student satisfaction measures. *The Clinical Supervisor, 22*(2), 191–214.

Gilbert, P. (1998). What is shame: Some core issues and controversies. In P. Gilbert & B. Andrews (Eds.), *Shame: Interpersonal behavior, psychopathology, and culture* (pp. 3–38). New York, NY: Oxford University Press.

Gilfoyle, N. (2008). The legal exosystem: Risk management in addressing student competence problems in professional psychology training. *Training & Education in Professional Psychology, 2,* 202–209.

Gill, S. (Ed.). (2001). *The supervisory alliance: Facilitating the psychotherapist's learning experience.* Northvale, NJ: Jason Aronson, Inc.

Gilligan, C. (1982). *In a different voice.* Cambridge, MA: Harvard University Press.

Gilovich, T., & Griffin, D. (2002). Heuristics and biases: Then and now. In T. Gilovich, D. Griffin, & D. Kahneman (Eds.). *Heuristics and biases: The psychology of intuitive judgment.* Cambridge: Cambridge University Press.

Giordano, M. A., Altekruse, M. K., & Kern, C. W. (2000). *Supervisee's bill of rights.* Unpublished manuscript.

Gizara, S. S., & Forrest, L. (2004). Supervisors' experiences of trainee impairment and incompetence at APA-accredited internship sites. *Professional Psychology: Research & Practice, 35,* 131–140.

Glaser, R. D., & Thorpe, J. S. (1986). Unethical intimacy. *American Psychologist, 41,* 43–51.

Glidden, C. E., & Tracey, T. J. (1992). A multidimensional scaling analysis of supervisory dimensions and their perceived relevance across trainee experience levels. *Professional Psychology: Research & Practice, 23,* 151–157.

Globerman, J., & Bogo, M. (2003). Changing times: Understanding social workers' motivation to be field instructors. *Social Work, 48,* 65–73.

Gloria, A. M., Hird, J. S., & Tao, K. W. (2008). Self-reported multicultural supervision competence of White predoctoral intern supervisors. *Training & Education in Professional Psychology, 2,* 129–136.

Gnilka, P., & Chang, C. (2012). The relationship between supervisee stress, coping resources, the working alliance, and the supervisory working alliance. *Journal of Counseling & Development, 90,* 63–70.

Goldberg, D. A. (1985). Process notes, audio, and videotape: Modes of presentation in psychotherapy training. *The Clinical Supervisor, 3,* 3–13.

Goldstein, A. P., Heller, K., & Sechrest, L. B. (1966). *Psychotherapy and the psychology of behavior change.* New York: John Wiley & Sons.

Gonsalvez, C. & Freestone, J. (2007). Field supervisors' assessments of trainee performance: Are they reliable and valid? *Australian Psychologist, 42,* 23–32.

Gonsalvez, C. J., & Milne, D. L. (2010). Clinical supervisor training in Australia: A review of current problems and possible solutions. *Australian Psychologist, 45,* 233–242.

Gonzalez, R. C. (1997). Postmodern supervision: A multicultural perspective. In D. B. Pope-Davis & H. L. K. Coleman (Eds.), *Multicultural counseling competencies: Assessment, education and training, and supervision* (pp. 350–386). Thousand Oaks, CA: Sage Publications.

Goodyear, R. K. (1990). Gender configurations in supervisory dyads: Their relation to supervisee influence strategies and to skill evaluations of the supervisee. *The Clinical Supervisor, 8*(2), 67–79.

Goodyear, R. K. (2006, June). Supervision to foster reflective practice. Presentation at the 2nd International Interdisciplinary Conference on Clinical Supervision, Buffalo, NY.

Goodyear, R. K., Abadie, P. D., & Efros, F. (1984). Supervisory theory into practice: Differential perceptions of supervision by Ekstein, Ellis, Polster, and Rogers. *Journal of Counseling Psychology, 31,* 228–237.

Goodyear, R. K., Bunch, K., & Claiborn, C. D. (2005). Current supervision scholarship in psychology: A five year review. *The Clinical Supervisor, 24,* 137–147.

Goodyear, R. K., & Guzzardo, C. R. (2000). Psychotherapy supervision and training. In S. D. Brown & R. W. Lent (Eds.), *Handbook of counseling psychology* (3rd ed., pp. 83–108). New York, NY: John Wiley & Sons.

Goodyear, R. K., Murdock, N., Lichtenberg, J. W., McPherson, R., Petren, S., & O'Byrne, K. K. (2008). Stability and change in counseling psychologists' identities, roles, functions, and career satisfaction across fifteen years. *The Counseling Psychologist, 36,* 220–249.

Goodyear, R. K., & Nelson, M. L. (1997). The major supervision formats. In C. E. Watkins, *Handbook of psychotherapy supervision* (pp. 328–344). New York, NY: Wiley.

Goodyear, R. K., & Robyak, J. E. (1982). Supervisors theory and experience in supervisory focus. *Psychological Reports, 51,* 978.

Goodyear, R. K., & Rodolfa, E. (2012). Negotiating the complex ethical terrain of clinical supervision. In L. D. Knapp, S. J. Gottlieb, M. C. Handelsman, & M. M. VandeCreek (Eds.), *APA handbook of ethics in psychology, Vol. 2: Practice, teaching, and research* (pp. 261–276). Washington, DC: American Psychological Association.

Goodyear, R. K., & Sinnett, E. D. (1984). Current and emerging ethical issues for counseling psychologists. *Counseling Psychologist, 12*(3), 87–98.

Goodyear, R. K., Wertheimer, A., Cypers, S., & Rosemond, M. (2003). Refining the map of the counselor development journey: Response to Rønnestad and Skovholt. *Journal of Career Development, 30,* 73–80.

Gordon, S. P. (1990). Developmental supervision: An exploratory study of a promising model. *Journal of Curriculum and Supervision, 5,* 293–307.

Gottlieb, M. C. (1993). Avoiding exploitive dual relationships: A decision-making model. *Psychotherapy, 30,* 41–48.

Gottlieb, M. C., Robinson, K., & Younggren, J. N. (2007). Multiple relations in supervision: Guidance for administrators, supervisors, and students. *Professional Psychology: Research & Practice, 38,* 241–247.

Graf, N. M., & Stebnicki, M. A. (2002). Using E-mail for clinical supervision in practicum: A qualitative analysis. *Journal of Rehabilitation, 68*(3), 41–49.

Granello, D. H. (1996). Gender and power in the supervisory dyad. *The Clinical Supervisor, 14*(2), 53–67.

Granello, D. H. (2002). Assessing the cognitive development of counseling students: Changes in epistemological assumptions. *Counselor Education and Supervision, 41,* 279–293.

Granello, D. H. (2003). Influence strategies in the supervisory dyad: An investigation into the effects of gender and age. *Counselor Education & Supervision, 42,* 189–202.

Granello, D. H., Beamish, P. M., & Davis, T. E. (1997). Supervisee empowerment: Does gender make a difference? *Counselor Education & Supervision, 36,* 305–317.

Grant, J., & Schofield, M. (2007). Career-long supervision: Patterns and perspectives. *Counselling and Psychotherapy Research, 7*(1), 3–11.

Gray, J. (1992). *Men are from Mars, women are from Venus.* New York, NY: Harper Collins.

Gray, L. A., Ladany, N., Walker, J. A., & Ancis, J. R. (2001). Psychotherapy trainees' experience of counterproductive events in supervision. *Journal of Counseling Psychology, 48,* 371–383.

Gray, S. W., & Smith, M. S. (2009). The influence of diversity in clinical supervision: A framework for reflective conversations and questioning. *The Clinical Supervisor, 28*(2), 155–179.

Green, D., & Dye, L. (2002). How should we best train clinical psychology supervisors? A Delphi survey. *Psychology Learning & Teaching, 2,* 108–115.

Green, M. S., & Dekkers, T. D. (2010). Attending to power and diversity in supervision: An exploration of supervisee learning outcomes and satisfaction with supervision. *Journal of Feminist Family Therapy, 22,* 293–312.

Green, S. L., & Hansen, J. C. (1986). Ethical dilemmas in family therapy. *Journal of Marital & Family Therapy, 12,* 225–230.

Greenberg, L. S. (1984). Task analysis: The general approach. In L. N. Rice & L. S. Greenberg (Eds.), *Patterns of change: Intensive analysis of psychotherapy process* (pp. 124–148). New York, NY: Guilford.

Greenwald, A. G., McGhee, D. E., & Schwartz, J. L. K. (1998). Measuring individual differences in implicit cognition: The Implicit Association Test. *Journal of Personality & Social Psychology, 74,* 1464–1480.

Grey, A. L., & Fiscalini, J. (1987). Parallel process as transference–countertransference interaction. *Psychoanalytic Psychology, 4,* 131–144.

Griffith, B. A., & Frieden, G. (2000). Facilitating reflective thinking in counselor education. *Counselor Education & Supervision, 40,* 82–93.

Grigg, G. (2006). Designs and discriminations for clinical group supervision in counselling psychology: An analysis. *Canadian Journal of Counselling, 40*(2), 110–122.

Gross, S. M. (2005). Student perspectives on clinical and counseling psychology practica. *Professional Psychology: Research & Practice, 36,* 299–306.

Gubi, P. M. (2007). Exploring the supervision experience of some mainstream counsellors who integrate prayer in counseling. *Counselling & Psychotherapy Research, 7,* 114–121.

Guest, C. L., Jr., & Dooley, K. (1999). Supervisor malpractice: Liability to the supervisee in clinical supervision. *Counselor Education & Supervision, 38,* 269–279.

Guest, P. D., & Beutler, L. E. (1988). Impact of psychotherapy supervision on therapist orientation and values. *Journal of Consulting and Clinical Psychology, 56,* 653–658.

Guiffrida, D. A. (2005). The emergence model: An alternative pedagogy for facilitating self-reflection and theoretical fit in counseling students. *Counselor Education & Supervision, 44,* 201–213.

Guiffrida, D. A., Jordan, R., Saiz, S., & Barnes, K. L. (2007). The use of metaphor in clinical supervision. *Journal of Counseling & Development, 85,* 393–400.

Guth, L. J., & Dandeneau, C. J. (2007, June). *Nonlinear supervision process model (NSPM): Augmenting existing supervision theories.* Paper presented at the Annual International Interdisciplinary Supervision Conference, Buffalo, NY.

Gutheil, T. G., & Gabbard, G. O. (1993). The concept of boundaries in clinical practice: Theoretical and risk-management dimensions. *American Journal of Psychiatry, 150,* 188–196.

Haas, L. J., & Cummings, N. A. (1991). Managed outpatient mental health plans: Clinical, ethical and practical guidelines for participation. *Professional Psychology: Research & Practice, 22,* 45–51.

Haas, L. J., Malouf, J. L., & Mayerson, N. H. (1986). Ethical dilemmas in psychological practice: Results of a national survey. *Professional Psychology: Research & Practice, 17,* 316–321.

Haber, R., Marshall, D., Cowan, K., Vanlandingham, A., Gerson, M., & Fitch, J. (2009). "Live" supervision of supervision: "Perpendicular" interventions in parallel processes. *The Clinical Supervisor, 28,* 72–90.

Hackney, H. L., & Goodyear, R. K. (1984). Carl Rogers' client-centered supervision. In R. F. Levant & J. M. Schlien (Eds.), *Client-centered therapy and the person-centered approach* (pp. 278–296). New York: Praeger.

Hadjistavropoulos, H., Kelher, M., & Hadjistavropoulos, T. (2010). Training graduate students to be clinical supervisors: A survey of Canadian professional psychology programmes. *Canadian Psychology, 51,* 206–212.

Hadjistavropoulos, T., & Malloy, D. C. (2000). Making ethical choices: A comprehensive decision-making model for Canadian psychologists. *Canadian Psychology, 41,* 104–115.

Haggerty, G., & Hilsenroth, M. J. (2011). The use of video in psychotherapy supervision. *British Journal of Psychotherapy, 27,* 193–210.

Hahn, W. K. (2002). The experience of shame in psychotherapy supervision. *Psychotherapy, 38,* 272–284.

Hahn, W. K., & Molnar, S. (1991). Intern evaluation in university counseling centers: Process, problems, and recommendations. *The Counseling Psychologist, 19,* 414–430.

Haidt, J. (2001). The emotional dog and its rational tail: A social intuitionist approach to more judgment. *Psychological Review, 108,* 814–834.

Haidt, J. (2008). Morality. *Psychological Science, 3,* 65–72.

Haj-Yahia, M. M., & Roer-Strier, D. (1999). On the encounter between Jewish supervisors and Arab supervisees in Israel. *Clinical Supervisor, 18*(2), 17–37.

Haley, J. (1976). *Problem solving therapy.* San Francisco, CA: Jossey-Bass.

Haley, J. (1987). *Problem solving therapy* (2nd ed.). San Francisco, CA: Jossey-Bass.

Hall, J. E. (1988a). Protection in supervision. *Register Report, 14*(4), 3–4.

Hall, J. E. (1988b). Dual relationships in supervision. *Register Report, 15*(1), 5–6.

Hall, R. C. W., Macvaugh, III, G. S., Merideth, P., & Montgomery, J. (2007). Commentary: Delving further into liability for psychotherapy supervision. *The Journal of the American Academy of Psychiatry & the Law, 35,* 196–199.

Halpert, S. C., & Pfaller, J. (2001). Sexual orientation and supervision: Theory and practice. *Journal of Gay & Lesbian Social Services: Issues in Practice, Policy & Research, 13*(3), 23–40.

Halverson, R. (2004). Accessing, documenting, and communicating practical wisdom: The phronesis of school leadership practice. *American Journal of Education, 111,* 90–121.

Hamilton, J. C., & Spruill, J. (1999). Identifying and reducing risk factors related to trainee–client sexual misconduct. *Professional Psychology: Research & Practice, 30,* 318–327.

Hamlin, E. R., II, & Timberlake, E. M. (1982). Peer group supervision for supervisors. *Social Casework, 67,* 82–87.

Handelsman, M. M., Gottlieb, M. C., & Knapp, S. (2005). Training ethical psychologists: An acculturation model. *Professional Psychology: Research & Practice, 36,* 59–65.

Hanna, M. A., & Smith, J. (1998). Using rubrics for documentation of clinical work supervision. *Counselor Education & Supervision, 37,* 269–278.

Hansen, J. C., Pound, R., & Petro, C. (1976). Review of research on practicum supervision. *Counselor Education & Supervision, 16,* 107–116.

Hansen, N. D., & Goldberg, S. G. (1999). Navigating the nuances: A matrix of considerations for ethical–legal dilemmas. *Professional Psychology: Research & Practice, 30,* 495–503.

Hansen, N. D., Randazzo, K. V., Schwartz, A., Marshall, M., Kalis, D., Frazier, R., et al. (2006). Do we practice what we preach? An exploratory survey of multicultural psychotherapy competencies. *Professional Psychology: Research & Practice, 37,* 66–74.

Hardcastle, D. A. (1991). Toward a model for supervision: A peer supervision pilot project. *The Clinical Supervisor, 9*(2), 63–76.

Hardiman, R. (1982) White identity development: A process-oriented model for describing the racial consciousness of White Americans. Unpublished doctoral dissertation, University of Massachusetts, Amherst.

Hardy, K. V. (1993). Live supervision in the postmodern era of family therapy: Issues, reflections, and questions. *Contemporary Family Therapy: An International Journal, 15,* 9–20.

Harkness, D., & Poertner, A. (1989). Research and social work supervision: A conceptual review. *Social Work, 34,* 115–119.

Harrar, W. R., VandeCreek, L., & Knapp, S. (1990). Ethical and legal aspects of clinical supervision. *Professional Psychology: Research & Practice, 21,* 37–41.

Harris, M. B. C. (1994). Supervisory evaluation & feedback. In L. D. Borders (Ed.), *Supervision: Exploring the effective components.* Greensboro, NC: ERIC/CASS.

Hart, G. M., & Nance, D. (2003). Styles of counselor supervision as perceived by supervisors and supervisees. *Counselor Education and Supervision, 43,* 146–158.

Harvey, C., & Katz, C. (1985). *If I'm so successful, why do I feel like a fake? The impostor phenomenon.* New York, NY: St. Martin's Press.

Harvey, O. J., Hunt, D. E., & Schroeder, H. M. (1961). *Conceptual systems and personality organization.* New York, NY: Holt, Rinehart, & Winston.

Hatcher, R. L., & Lassiter, K. D. (2007). Initial training in professional psychology: The practicum competencies outline. *Training & Education in Professional Psychology, 1,* 49–63.

Hawkins, P., & Shohet, R. (1989). *Supervision in the helping professions.* Milton Keynes, UK: Open University Press.

Hawkins, P., & Shohet, R. (2000). *Supervision in the helping professions: An individual, group and organizational approach* (2nd ed.). Philadelphia, PA: Open University Press.

Hawkins, P., & Shohet, R. (2006). *Supervision in the helping professions: An individual, group and organization approach* (3rd ed.). Philadelphia, PA: Open University Press.

Hayes, J. R. (1981). *The complete problem solver.* Philadelphia, PA: Franklin Institute Press.

Hayes, R. L. (1989). Group supervision. In L. J. Bradley & J. D. Boyd (Eds.), *Counselor supervision* (2nd ed., pp. 399–421). Muncie, IN: Accelerated Development Inc.

Hays, D. G., & Chang, C. Y. (2003). White privilege, oppression, and racial identity development: Implications for supervision. *Counselor Education & Supervision, 43,* 134–145.

Heath, A. (1982). Team family therapy training: Conceptual and pragmatic considerations. *Family Process, 21,* 187–194.

Heckman-Stone, C. (2003). Trainee preferences for feedback and evaluation in clinical supervision. *The Clinical Supervisor, 22*(1), 21–33.

Heid, L. (1997). Supervisor development across the professional lifespan. *The Clinical Supervisor, 16,* 139–152.

Hein, S., & Lawson, G. (2008). Triadic supervision and its impact on the role of the supervisor: A qualitative examination of supervisors' perspectives. *Counselor Education & Supervision, 48,* 16–31.

Hein, S. F., & Lawson, G. (2009). A qualitative examination of supervisors' experiences of the process of triadic supervision. *The Clinical Supervisor, 28,* 91–108.

Hein, S. F., Lawson, G., & Rodriguez, C. P. (2011). Supervisee incompatibility and its influence on triadic supervision: An examination of doctoral student supervisors' perspectives. *Counselor Education & Supervision, 50,* 422–436.

Helms, J. (1985). Toward a theoretical explanation of the effects of race on counseling: A Black and White model. *The Counseling Psychologist, 12,* 153–165.

Helms, J. E. (1995). An update on Helms' White and people of color racial identity models. In J. G. Ponterrotto, J. M. Casas, L. A. Suzuki, & C. M. Alexander (Eds.), *Handbook of multicultural counseling* (pp. 181–198). Thousand Oaks, CA: Sage.

Helms, J. E., & Cook, D. A. (1999). *Using race and culture in counseling and psychotherapy: Theory and process.* Boston, MA: Allyn & Bacon.

Helms, J. E., Jernigan, M., & Mascher, J. (2005). The meaning of race in psychology and how to change it. *American Psychologist, 60,* 27–36.

Helms, J. E., & Piper, R. E. (1994). Implications of racial identity theory for vocational psychology. *Journal of Vocational Behavior, 44,* 124–138.

Henderson, P. (1994). Administrative skills in counseling supervision. In L. D. Borders (Ed.), *Supervision: Exploring the effective components.* Greensboro, NC: ERIC/CASS. (ERIC Document Reproduction Services No. EDOCG9425.)

Henggeler, S. W., Schoenwald, S. K., Liao, J. G., Letourneau, E. J., & Edwards, D. L. (2008). Transporting efficacious treatments to field settings: The link between supervisory practices and therapist fidelity in MST programs. *Journal of Clinical Child and Adolescent Psychology 31,* 155–167.

Henry, W. P., Strupp, H. H., Butler, S. F., Schact, T. E., & Binder, J. L. (1993). Effects of training in time-limited dynamic psychotherapy: Changes in therapist behavior. *Journal of Consulting & Clinical Psychology, 61,* 434–440.

Heppner, P. P., & Claiborn, C. D. (1989). Social influence research in counseling: A review and critique [Monograph]. *Journal of Counseling Psychology, 36,* 365–387.

Heppner, P. P., & Dixon, D. N. (1981). A review of the interpersonal influence process in counseling. *Personnel and Guidance Journal, 59,* 542–550.

Heppner, P. P., & Handley, P. G. (1982). A study of the interpersonal influence process in supervision. *Journal of Counseling Psychologist, 28,* 437–444.

Heppner, P. P., Kivlighan, D. M., Burnett, J. W., Berry, T. R., Goedinhaus, M., Doxsee, D. J., . . . & Wallace, D. L. (1994). Dimensions that characterize supervisor interventions delivered in the context of live supervision of practicum counselors. *Journal of Counseling Psychology, 41,* 227–235.

Heppner, P. P., & Roehlke, H. J. (1984). Differences among supervisees at different levels of training: Implications for a developmental model of supervision. *Journal of Counseling Psychology, 31,* 76–90.

Herman, K. C. (1993). Reassessing predictors of therapist competence. *Journal of Counseling & Development, 72,* 29–32.

Hernández, P. (2008). The cultural context model in clinical supervision. *Training & Education in Professional Psychology, 2,* 10–17.

Hernández, P., & McDowell, T. (2010). Intersectionality, power, and relational safety in context: Key concepts in clinical supervision. *Training & Education in Professional Psychology, 4,* 29–35.

Heron, J. (1989). *Six-category intervention analysis* (3rd Ed.). Surrey, UK: Human Potential Resource Group, University of Surrey.

Heru, A. M., Strong, D. R., Price, M., & Recupero, P. R. (2004). Boundaries in psychotherapy supervision. *American Journal of Psychotherapy, 58,* 76–89.

Heru, A. M., Strong, D. R., Price, M., & Recupero, P. R. (2006). Self-disclosure in psychotherapy supervisors: Gender differences. *American Journal of Psychotherapy, 60,* 323–334.

Hess, A. K. (1986). Growth in supervision: Stages of supervisee and supervisor development. *The Clinical Supervisor, 4*(1–2), 51–67.

Hess, A. K. (1987). Psychotherapy supervision: Stages, Buber, and a theory of relationship. *Professional Psychology: Research & Practice, 18,* 251–259.

Hess, A. K., & Hess, K. A. (1983). Psychotherapy supervision: A survey of internship training practices. *Professional Psychology, 14,* 504–513.

Hess, S. A., Knox, S., Schultz, J. M., Hill, C. E., Sloan, L., Brandt, S., . . . , & Hoffman, M. A. (2008). Predoctoral interns' nondisclosure in supervision. *Psychotherapy Research, 18,* 400–411.

Hewson, J. (1999). Training supervisors to contract in supervision. In E. Holloway & M. Carroll (Eds.), *Training counselling supervisors* (pp. 67–91). London, UK: Sage Publications.

Hildebrand, M. W., Host, H. H., Binder, E. F., Carpenter, B., Freedland, K. E., Morrow-Howell, N., Baum, C. M., et al. (2012). Measuring treatment fidelity in a rehabilitation intervention study. *American Journal of Physical Medicine & Rehabilitation, 91,* 1–10.

Hill, C. E., Charles, D., & Reed, K. G. (1981). A longitudinal analysis of changes in counseling skills during doctoral training in counseling psychology. *Journal of Counseling Psychology, 28,* 428–436.

Hill, C. E., & Knox, S. (2002). Self-disclosure. In J. C. Norcross (Ed.), *Psychotherapy relationships that work: Therapist contributions and responsiveness to patients* (pp. 255–266). New York, NY: Oxford University Press.

Hill, C. E., & Knox, S. (2013). Training and supervision in psychotherapy: Evidence for effective practice. In M. Lambert (Ed.), *Bergin and Garfield's handbook of psychotherapy and behavior change* (6th ed.). New York, NY: Wiley.

Hill, C. E., O'Grady, K. E., Balenger, V., Busse, W., Falk, D. R., Hill, M., . . . , & Taffe, R. (1994). Methodological examination of videotape-assisted reviews in brief therapy: Helpfulness ratings, therapist intentions, client reactions, mood, and session evaluation. *Journal of Counseling Psychology, 41,* 236–247.

Hillerbrand, E. T. (1989). Cognitive differences between experts and novices: Implications for group supervision. *Journal of Counseling & Development, 67,* 293–296.

Hillman, S. L., McPherson, R. H., Swank, P. R., & Watkins, C. E., Jr. (1998). Further validation of the Psychotherapy Supervisor Development Scale. *The Clinical Supervisor, 17,* 17–32.

Hilmes, T. S., Payne, K. T., Anderson, E. K., Casanova, C. C., Woods, S. W., & Cardin, S. A. (August, 2011). *Case study in predoctoral peer supervision: Our own robbers cave.* American Psychological Association 2011 Convention Presentation, Washington, DC.

Hilsenroth, M., Ackerman, S., Clemence, A., Strassle, C., & Handler, L. (2002). Effects of structured clinical training on patient and therapist perspectives of alliance early in psychotherapy. *Psychotherapy: Theory, Research, Practice, Training, 39,* 309–323.

Hilton, D. B., Russell, R. K., & Salmi, S. W. (1995). The effects of supervisor's race and level of support on perceptions of supervision. *Journal of Counseling & Development, 73,* 559–563.

Hinett, K. (2002). *Developing reflective practice in legal education.* Warwick, UK: UK Centre for Legal Education, University of Warwick.

Hird, J. S., Tao, K. W., & Gloria, A. M. (2004). Examining supervisors' multicultural competence in racially similar and different supervision dyads. *The Clinical Supervisor, 23*(2), 107–120.

Hoffman, L. W. (1990). *Old scapes, new maps: A training program for psychotherapy supervisors.* Cambridge, MA: Milusik Press.

Hoffman, L. W. (1994). The training of psychotherapy supervisors: A barren scape. *Psychotherapy in Private Practice, 13,* 23–42.

Hoffman, M. A., Hill, C. E., Holmes, S. E., & Freitas, G. F. (2005). Supervisor perspective on the process and outcome of giving easy, difficult, or no feedback to supervisees. *Journal of Counseling Psychology, 52,* 3–13.

Hogan, R. (1964). Issues and approaches in supervision. *Psychotherapy: Theory, Research, & Practice, 1,* 139–141.

Holloway, E. L. (1987). Developmental models of supervision: Is it supervision? *Professional Psychology: Research and Practice, 18,* 209–216.

Holloway, E. L. (1988). Instruction beyond the facilitative conditions: A response to Biggs. *Counselor Education & Supervision, 27,* 252–258.

Holloway, E. L. (1992). Supervision: A way of teaching and learning. In S. D. Brown & R. W. Lent (Eds.), *Handbook of counseling psychology* (pp. 177–214). New York, NY: John Wiley.

Holloway, E. L. (1995). *Clinical supervision: A systems approach.* Thousand Oaks, CA: Sage Publications, Inc.

Holloway, E. L. (1997). Structures for the analysis and teaching of psychotherapy. In C. E. Watkins, Jr. (Ed.), *Handbook of psychotherapy supervision* (pp. 249–276). New York, NY: Wiley.

Holloway, E. L., & Carroll, M. (1996). Reaction to the special section on supervision research: Comment on Ellis et al. (1996), Ladany et al. (1996), Neufeldt et al. (1996), & Worthen & McNeill (1996). *Journal of Counseling Psychology, 43,* 51–55.

Holloway, E. L., Freund, R. D., Gardner, S. L., Nelson, M. L., & Walker, B. R. (1989). Relation of power and involvement to theoretical orientation in supervision: An analysis of discourse. *Journal of Counseling Psychology, 36,* 88–102.

Holloway, E. L., & Neufeldt, S. A. (1995). Supervision: Its contributions to treatment efficacy. *Journal of Consulting and Clinical Psychology, 63,* 207–213.

Holloway, E. L., & Roehlke, H. J. (1987). Internship: The applied training of a counseling psychologist. *The Counseling Psychologist, 15,* 205–260.

Holloway, E. L., & Wampold, B. E. (1983). Patterns of verbal behavior and judgments of satisfaction in the supervision interview. *Journal of Counseling Psychology, 30,* 227–234.

Holtzman, R. F., & Raskin, M. S. (1988). Why field placements fail: Study results. *The Clinical Supervisor, 6*(3), 123–136.

Horvath, A. O., & Greenburg, L. S. (1989). Development and validation of the working alliance inventory. *Journal of Counseling Psychology, 36,* 223–233.

Horvath, A. O., & Symonds, B. D. (1991). Relation between working alliance and outcome in psychotherapy: A meta-analysis. *Journal of Counseling Psychology, 38,* 139–149.

Hotelling, K., & Forrest, L. (1985). Gilligan's theory of sex-role development: A perspective for counseling. *Journal of Counseling & Development, 64,* 183–186.

Howard, F. (2008). Managing stress or enhancing well-being? Positive psychology's contributions to clinical supervision. *Australian Psychologist, 43*(2), 105–113.

Hoyt, M. F., & Goulding, R. (1989). Resolution of a transference–countertransference impasse: Using Gestalt techniques in supervision. *Transactional Analysis Journal, 19,* 201–211.

Hsu, W. (2009). The components of solution-focused supervision. *Bulletin of Education Psychology, 41,* 475–496.

Huhra, R.L., Yamokoski-Maynhart, C.A., & Prieto, L.R. (2008). Reviewing videotape in supervision: A developmental approach. *Journal of Counseling & Development, 86,* 412–418.

Hunt, C. & Sharpe, L. (2008). Within-session supervision communication in the training of clinical psychologists. *Australian Psychologist, 43,* 121–126.

Hyrkäs, K. (2005). Clinical supervision, burnout, and job satisfaction among mental health and psychiatric nurses in Finland. *Issues in Mental Health Nursing, 26,* 531–556.

Hyrkäs, K., Appelqvist-Schmidlechner, K., & Oksa, L. (2003). Validating an instrument for clinical supervision using an expert panel. *International Journal of Nursing Studies, 40,* 619–625.

Igartua, K. J. (2000). The impact of impaired supervisors on residents. *Academic Psychiatry, 24*(4), 188–194.

Illfelder-Kaye, J. (2002). Tips for trainers: Implications of the new ethical principles of psychologists and code of conduct on internship and pre-doctoral training programs. *Association of Psychology Postdoctoral & Internship Centers Newsletter* (November), 25.

Improving Access to Psychological Therapies (IAPT). (2011). Retrieved from www.iapt.nhs.uk/silo/files/guidance-for-commissioning-iapt-training-201213.pdf

Inman, A. G. (2008). *Race and culture in supervision: Challenges and opportunities.* Paper presented at the American Psychological Association Annual Conference. Boston.

Inskipp, F., & Proctor, B. (2001). *Becoming a supervisor* (2nd ed.). Twickenham, UK: Cascade.

Itzhaky, H., & Sztern, L. (1999). The takeover of parent–child dynamics in a supervisory relationship: Identifying the role transformation. *Clinical Social Work Journal, 27,* 247–258.

Jacobs, D., David, P., & Meyer, D. J. (1995). *The supervisory encounter: A guide for teachers of psychodynamic psychotherapy and analysis.* New Haven, CT: Yale University Press.

Jacobs, E. E., Masson, R. L. L., Harvill, R. L., & Schimmel, C. J. (2012). *Group counseling: Strategies and skills,* 7th ed. Independence, KY: Brooks/Cole.

Jacobs, S. C., Huprich, S. K., Grus, C. L., et al. (2011). Trainees with professional competency problems: Preparing trainers for difficult but necessary conversations. *Training & Education in Professional Psychology, 5*(3), 175–184.

Jacobsen, C. H. (2007). A qualitative single case study of parallel process. *Counselling & Psychotherapy Research, 7,* 26–33.

Jacobsen, C. H., & Tanggaard, L. (2009). Beginning therapists' experiences of what constitutes good and bad psychotherapy supervision with a special focus on individual differences. *Nordic Psychology, 61*(4), 59–84.

James, I. A., Milne, D., Marie–Blackburn, I., & Armstrong, P. (2006). Conducting successful supervision: Novel elements towards an integrative approach. *Behavioural & Cognitive Psychotherapy, 35,* 191–200.

Jaschik, S. (January 30, 2012). Anti-gay student's suit revived. *Inside Higher Education.* Retrieved on March 17, 2012, from www.insidehighered.com/news/2012/01/30/appeals-court-revives-suit-dismissal-anti-gay-psychology-student#ixzz1pLzK1dCC

Jennings, L., Goh, M., Skovholt, T. M., Hanson, M., & Banerjee-Stevens, D. (2003). Multiple factors in the development of the expert counselor and therapist. *Journal of Career Development, 30,* 59–72.

Jernigan, M. M., Green, C. E., Helms, J. E., Perez-Gualdron, L., & Henze, K. (2010). An examination of people of color supervision dyads: Racial identity matters as much as race. *Training & Education in Professional Psychology, 4*(1), 62–73.

Jerome, L. W., DeLeon, P. H., James, L. C., Folen, R., Earles, J., & Gedney, J. J. (2000). The coming age of telecommunications in psychological research and practice. *American Psychologist, 55,* 407–421.

Johnson, E. A., & Stewart, D. W. (2008). Perceived competence in supervisory roles: A social cognitive analysis. *Training & Education in Professional Psychology, 2*(4), 229–236.

Johnson, E., & Moses, N. C. (1988, August). *The dynamic developmental model of supervision.* Paper presented at the annual convention of the American Psychological Association, Atlanta.

Johnson, W. B., Elman, N. S., Forrest, L., Rodolfa, E., Schaffer, J. B., & Robiner, W. (2008). Addressing professional competence problems in trainees: Some ethical considerations . *Professional Psychology, Research & Practice, 39,* 589–599.

Jordan, K. (1999). Live supervision for beginning therapists in practicum: Crucial for quality counseling and avoiding litigation. *Family Therapy, 26*(2), 81–86.

Jordan, K. (2006). Beginning supervisees' identity: The importance of relationship variables and experience versus gender matches in the supervisee/supervisor interplay. *The Clinical Supervisor, 25*(1/2), 43–51.

Juhnke, G. A. (1996). Solution-focused supervision: Promoting supervisee skills and confidence through successful solutions. *Counselor Education and Supervision, 36,* 48–57.

Kadushin, A. (1968). Games people play in supervision. *Social Work, 13,* 23–32.

Kadushin, A. (1974). Supervisor–supervisee survey. *Social Work, 19,* 288–297.

Kadushin, A. (1985). *Supervision in social work* (2nd ed.). New York, NY: Columbia University Press.

Kadushin, A. (1992a). *Supervision in social work* (3rd ed.). New York, NY: Columbia University Press.

Kadushin, A. (1992b). What's wrong, what's right with social work supervision. *The Clinical Supervisor, 10*(1), 3–19.

Kadushin, A. (1992c). Social work supervision: An updated survey. *The Clinical Supervisor, 10*(2), 9–27.

Kadushin, A., & Harkness, D. (2002). *Supervision in social work* (4th ed.). New York, NY: Columbia University Press.

Kaduvettoor, A., O'Shaughnessy, T., Mori, Y., Beverly, C., III, Weatherford, R. D., & Ladany, N. (2009). Helpful and hindering multicultural events in group supervision: Climate and multicultural competence. *The Counseling Psychologist, 37,* 786–820.

Kagan, H. K., & Kagan, N. I. (1997). Interpersonal process recall: Influencing human interaction. In C. E. Watkins, Jr. (Ed.), *Handbook of psychotherapy supervision* (pp. 296–309). New York: Wiley.

Kagan, N. (1976). *Influencing human interaction.* Mason, MI: Mason Media, Inc. or Washington, DC: American Association for Counseling & Development.

Kagan, N. (1980). Influencing human interaction—eighteen years with IPR. In A. K. Hess (Ed.), *Psychotherapy supervision: Theory, research & practice* (pp. 262–286). New York, NY: Wiley.

Kagan, N., & Krathwohl, D. R. (1967). *Studies in human interaction: Interpersonal process recall stimulated by videotape.* East Lansing, MI: Michigan State University.

Kagan, N., Krathwohl, D. R., & Farquahar, W. W. (1965). *IPR—Interpersonal process recall by videotape: Stimulated recall by videotape.* East Lansing, MI: Michigan State University.

Kagan, N., Krathwohl, D. R., & Miller, R. (1963). Stimulated recall in therapy using videotape—a case study. *Journal of Counseling Psychology, 10,* 237–243.

Kahn, B. (1999). Priorities and practices in field supervision of school counseling students. *Professional School Counseling, 3*(2), 128–136.

Kahneman, D. (2011). *Thinking, fast and slow.* New York, NY: Farrar, Straus & Giroux.

Kanz, J. E. (2001). Clinical-supervision.com: Issues in the provision of online supervision. *Professional Psychology: Research & Practice, 32,* 415–420.

Kaplan, D. M., Rothrock, D., & Culkin, M. (1999). The infusion of counseling observations into a graduate counseling program. *Counselor Education & Supervision, 39,* 66–75.

Kaplan, M. (1983). A woman's view of *DSM-III. American Psychologist, 38,* 786–792.

Kaplan, R. (1987). The current use of live supervision within marriage and family therapy training programs. *The Clinical Supervisor, 5*(3), 43–52.

Kaslow, N. J., & Rice, D. G. (1985). Developmental stresses of psychology internship training: What training staff can do to help. *Professional Psychology: Research & Practice, 16,* 253–261.

Kaslow, N. J., Borden, K. A., Collins, F. L., Forrest, L., Illfelder-Kaye, J., Nelson, P. D., et al. (2004). Competencies Conference: Future directions in education and credentialing in professional psychology. *Journal of Clinical Psychology, 80,* 699–712.

Kaslow, N. J., Celano, M. P., & Stanton, M. (2005). Training in family psychology: A competencies-based approach. *Family Process, 44,* 337–353.

Kaslow, N. J., Grus, C. L., Campbell, L. F., Fouad, N. A., Hatcher, R. L., & Rodolfa, E. R. (2009). Competency assessment toolkit for professional psychology. *Training and Education in Professional Psychology, 3,* S27–S45.

Kaslow, N. J., Rubin, N. J., Forrest, L., et al. (2007). Recognizing, assessing, and intervening with problems of professional competence. *Professional Psychology: Research & Practice, 38,* 479–492.

Katz, J. H. (1985). The sociopolitical nature of counseling. *The Counseling Psychologist, 13,* 615–624.

Kavanagh, D. J., Spence, S. H., Strong, J., Wilson, J., Sturk, H., & Crow, N. (2003). Supervision practices in allied mental health: Relationships of supervision characteristics to perceived impact and job satisfaction. *Mental Health Services Research, 5,* 187–195.

Keith, D. V., Connell, G., & Whitaker, C. A. (1992). Group supervision in symbolic experiential family therapy. *Journal of Family Psychotherapy, 3*(1), 93–109.

Kell, B. L., & Burow, J. M. (1970). *Developmental counseling and therapy.* Boston, MA: Houghton Mifflin.

Kell, B. L., & Mueller, W. J. (1966). *Impact and change: A study of counseling relationships.* New York, NY: Appleton-Century-Crofts.

Kelly, G. A. (1955). *The psychology of personal constructs* (2 vols.). New York, NY: Norton.

Kerl, S. B., Garcia, J. L., McCullough, C. S., & Maxwell, M. E. (2002). Systematic evaluation of professional performance: Legally supported procedure and process. *Counselor Education & Supervision, 41,* 321–334.

Kerr, B. A., Claiborn, C. D., & Dixon, D. N. (1982). Training counselors in persuasion. *Counselor Education and Supervision, 22,* 138–148.

Kiesler, D. J. (1983). The 1982 Interpersonal Circle: A taxonomy for complementarity in human transactions. *Psychological Review, 90,* 185–214.

Killian, K. D. (2001). Differences making a difference: Cross-cultural interactions in supervisory relationships. *Journal of Feminist Family Therapy, 12*(2–3), 61–103.

Kim, B. S. K., Li, L. C., & Liang, C. T. H. (2002). Effects of Asian American client adherence to Asian cultural values, session goal, and counselor emphasis of client expression on career counseling process. *Journal of Counseling Psychology, 49,* 342–354.

Kim, B. S. K., & Omizo, M. M. (2003). American client adherence to Asian cultural values, session goal, and counselor emphasis of client expression on career counseling process. *Journal of Counseling Psychology, 49,* 342–354.

King, D., & Wheeler, S. (1999). The responsibilities of counsellor supervisors: A qualitative study. *British Journal of Guidance & Counselling, 27*(2), 215–229.

Kirschner, P. A., Sweller, J., & Clark, R. (2006). Why minimal guidance during instruction does not work: An analysis of the failure of constructivist, discovery, problem-based, experiential and inquiry-based teaching. *Educational Psychologist,* 41, 75–86.

Kitchener, K. S. (1984). Intuition, critical evaluation and ethical principles: The foundation for ethical decisions in counseling psychology. *The Counseling Psychologist, 12,* 43–55.

Kitchener, K. S. (1988). Dual role relationships: What makes them so problematic? *Journal of Counseling & Development, 67,* 217–221.

Kivlighan, D. M., Angelone, E. O., & Swafford, K. G. (1991). Live supervision in individual psychotherapy: Effects on therapist's intention use and client's evaluation of session effect and working alliance. *Journal of Counseling Psychology, 22,* 489–495.

Klein, G. A. (2003). *Intuition at work: Why developing your gut instincts will make you better at what you do.* New York, NY: Currency/Doubleday.

Kleintjes, S., & Swartz, L. (1996). Black clinical psychology trainees at a "White" South African university: Issues for clinical supervision. *The Clinical Supervisor, 14*(1), 87–109.

Klitzke, M. J., & Lombardo, T. W. (1991). A "bug-in-the-eye" can be better than a "bug-in-the-ear": A teleprompter technique for on-line therapy skills training. *Behavior Modification, 15,* 113–117.

Knapp, S., Gottlieb, M., Berman, J., & Handelsman, M. M. (2007). When laws and ethics collide: What should psychologists do? *Professional Psychology: Research & Practice, 38,* 54–59.

Knapp, S. J., & VandeCreek, L. D. (2006). *Practical ethics for psychologists: A positive approach.* Washington, DC: American Psychological Association.

Knapp, S., & VandeCreek, L. (1997). Ethical and legal aspects of clinical supervision. In C. E. Watkins, Jr. (Ed.), *Handbook of Psychotherapy Supervision* (pp. 589–602). New York, NY: Wiley.

Knoff, H. M., & Prout, H. T. (1985). Terminating students from professional psychology programs: Criteria, procedures and legal issues. *Professional Psychology: Research & Practice, 16,* 789–797.

Knowles, Z., Gilbourne, D. Tomlinson, V., & Anderson, A. G. (2007). Reflections on the application of reflective practice for supervision in applied sport psychology. *The Sport Psychologist, 21,* 109–122.

Knox, S., Burkard, A., Edwards, L., Smith, J. J. & Schlosser, L. Z. (2008). Supervisors' reports of the effects of supervisor self-disclosure on supervisees. *Psychotherapy Research, 18,* 543–559.

Knox, S., Edwards, L. M., Hess, S. A, & Hill, C. E. (2011). Supervisor self-disclosure: Supervisees' experiences and perspectives. *Psychotherapy, 48,* 336–341.

Knudsen, H. K., Ducharme, L. J., & Roman, P. M. (2008). Clinical supervision, emotional exhaustion, and turnover intention: A study of substance abuse treatment counselors in NIDA's Clinical Trials Network. *Journal of Substance Abuse Treatment, 35,* 387–395.

Koch, L. C., Arhar, J. M., & Wells, L. M. (2000). Educating rehabilitation counseling students in reflective practice. *Rehabilitation Education, 14,* 255–268.

Koenig, T. L., & Spano, R. N. (2003). Sex, supervision, and boundary violations: Pressing challenges and possible solutions. *The Clinical Supervisor, 22*(1), 3–19.

Kolbert, J. B., Morgan, B., & Brendel, J. M. (2002). Faculty and student perceptions of dual relationships within counselor education: A qualitative analysis. *Counselor Education & Supervision, 41,* 193–206.

Kollock, P., Blumstein, P., & Schwartz, P. (1985). Sex and power in interaction: Conversational privileges and duties. *American Sociological Review, 50,* 34–46.

Kolodinsky, P., Lindsey, C. V., Young, M. Lund, N., Edgerly, B., & Zlatev, M. (2011). An analysis of supervision modalities utilized in CACREP on-campus clinical training programs: Results of a national survey. *Professional Issues in Counseling,* Online journal. Retrieved June 14, 2012, from www.shsu.edu/~piic/documents/AnAnalysisofSupervisionModalitiesUtilizedinCACREPOn-CampusClinicalTraining.pdf

Koocher, G. P., & Keith-Spiegel, P. (2008). *Ethics in psychology and the mental health professions: Standards and cases* (3rd ed.). New York, NY: Oxford University Press.

Kopp, R. R., & Robles, L. (1989). A single-session, therapist-focused model of supervision of resistance based on Adlerian psychology. *Individual Psychology, 45,* 212–219.

Kozlowska, K., Nunn, K., & Cousins, P. (1997). Adverse experiences in psychiatric training. Part 2. *Australian & New Zealand Journal of Psychiatry, 31,* 641–652.

Krause, A. A., & Allen, G. J. (1988). Perceptions of counselor supervision: An examination of Stoltenberg's model from the perspectives of supervisor and supervisee. *Journal of Counseling Psychology, 35,* 77–80.

Kruse, T. D., & Leddick, G. R. (2005, October). *A comparison of reflecting team techniques and live supervision.* Paper presented at the Association for Counselor Education and Supervision Conference, Pittsburgh, PA: Landis & Young.

Kuechler, C. F. (2006). Practitioners' voices: Group supervisors reflect on their practice. *The Clinical Supervisor, 25*(1/2), 83–103.

Kugler, P. (1995). *Jungian perspectives on clinical supervision.* Einsiedeln, Switzerland: Daimon.

Kurpius, D., Gibson, G., Lewis, J., & Corbet, M. (1991). Ethical issues in supervising counseling practitioners. *Counselor Education & Supervision, 31,* 48–57.

Ladany, N. (2004). Psychotherapy supervision: What lies beneath. *Psychotherapy Research, 14,* 1–19.

Ladany, N. (2007). Does psychotherapy training matter? Maybe not. *Psychotherapy: Theory, Research, Practice, Training, 44,* 392–396.

Ladany, N., Brittan-Powell, C. S., & Pannu, R. K. (1997). The influence of supervisory racial identity interaction and racial matching on the supervisory working alliance and supervisee multicultural competence. *Counselor Education & Supervision, 36,* 284–304.

Ladany, N., Constantine, M. G., Miller, K., Erickson, C. D., & Muse-Burke, J. L. (2000). Supervisor countertransference: A qualitative investigation into its identification and description. *Journal of Counseling Psychology, 47,* 102–115.

Ladany, N., Ellis, M. V., & Friedlander, M. L. (1999). The supervisory working alliance, trainee self-efficacy, and satisfaction. *Journal of Counseling & Development, 77,* 447–455.

Ladany, N., & Friedlander, M. L. (1995). The relationship between the supervisory working alliance and trainees' experience of role conflict and role ambiguity. *Counselor Education & Supervision, 34,* 220–231.

Ladany, N., Friedlander, M. L., & Nelson, M. L. (2005). *Critical events in psychotherapy supervision: An interpersonal approach.* Washington, DC: American Psychological Association.

Ladany, N., Hill, C. E., Corbett, M. M., & Nutt, E. A. (1996). Nature, extent, and importance of what psychotherapy trainees do not disclose to their supervisors. *Journal of Counseling Psychology, 43,* 10–24.

Ladany, N., & Inman, A. G. (2008). Developments in counseling skills training and supervision. In S. D. Brown & R. W. Lent (Eds.), *Handbook of counseling psychology* (4th ed.). Hoboken, NJ: John Wiley.

Ladany, N., Inman, A. G., Constantine, M. G., & Hofheinz, E. W. (1997). Supervisee multicultural case conceptualization ability and self-reported multicultural competence as functions of supervisee racial identity and supervisor focus. *Journal of Counseling Psychology, 44,* 284–293.

Ladany, N., Lehrman-Waterman, D., Molinaro, M., & Wolgast, B. (1999). Psychotherapy supervisor ethical practices: Adherence to guidelines, the supervisory working alliance, and supervisee satisfaction. *The Counseling Psychologist, 27,* 443–475.

Ladany, N., & Lehrman-Waterman, D. E. (1999). The content and frequency of supervisor self-disclosures and their relationship to supervisor style and the supervisory working alliance. *Counselor Education & Supervision, 38,* 143–160.

Ladany, N., Marotta, S., & Muse-Burke, J. L. (2001). Counselor experience related to complexity of case conceptualization and supervision preference [Special issue]. *Counselor Education & Supervision, 40*(3), 203–219.

Ladany, N., & Melnicoff, D. S. (1999). The nature of counselor supervisor nondisclosure. *Counselor Education & Supervision, 38,* 161–176.

Ladany, N., O'Brien, K. M., Hill, C. E., Melincoff, D. S., Knox, S., & Petersen, D. A. (1997). Sexual attraction toward clients, use of supervision, and prior training: A qualitative study of predoctoral psychology interns. *Journal of Counseling Psychology, 44,* 413–424.

Ladany, N., Walker, J. A., & Melincoff, D. S. (2001). Supervisory style: Its relation to the supervisory working-alliance and supervisor self-disclosure. *Counselor Education & Supervision, 40,* 263–275.

LaFleur, N. K., Rowe, W., & Leach, M. M. (2002). Reconceptualizing White racial consciousness. *Journal of Multicultural Counseling & Development, 30,* 148–152.

Lamb, D. H., & Catanzaro, S. J. (1998). Sexual and nonsexual boundary violations involving psychologists, clients, supervisees, and students: Implications for professional practice. *Professional Psychology: Research & Practice, 29,* 498–503.

Lamb, D. H., Catanzaro, S. J., & Moorman, A. S. (2003). Psychologists reflect on their sexual relationships with clients, supervisees, and students: Occurrence, impact, rationales and collegial intervention. *Professional Psychology: Research & Practice, 34,* 102–107.

Lamb, D. H., Catanzaro, S. J., & Moorman, A. S. (2004). A preliminary look at how psychologists identify, evaluate, and proceed when faced with possible multiple relationship dilemmas. *Professional Psychology: Research & Practice, 35,* 248–254.

Lamb, D. H., Cochran, D. J., & Jackson, V. R. (1991). Training and organizational issues associated with identifying and responding to intern impairment. *Professional Psychology: Research & Practice, 22,* 291–296.

Lamb, D. H., Presser, N., Pfost, K., Baum, M., Jackson, R., & Jarvis, P. (1987). Confronting professional impairment during the internship: Identification, due process, and remediation. *Professional Psychology: Research & Practice, 18,* 597–603.

Lamb, D. H., & Swerdlik, M. E. (2003). Identifying and responding to problematic school psychology supervisees: The evaluation process and issues of impairment. *The Clinical Supervisor, 22*(1), 87–110.

Lambers, E. (2007). A person-centered perspective on supervision. In M. Cooper, M. O'Hara, P. F. Schmid, & G. Wyatt (Eds.), *The handbook of person-centered psychotherapy and counseling* (pp. 366–378). New York, NY: Palgrave Macmillan.

Lambert, M. J., & Arnold, R. C. (1987). Research and the supervision process. *Professional Psychology: Research and Practice, 18,* 217–224.

Lambert, M. J., & Hawkins, E. J. (2001). Using information about patient progress in supervision: Are outcomes enhanced? *Australian Psychologist, 36*(2), 131–138.

Lambert, M. J., & Ogles, B. M. (1997). The effectiveness of psychotherapy supervision. In C. E. Watkins, Jr. (Ed.), *Handbook of psychotherapy supervision* (pp. 421–446). New York, NY: Wiley.

Lampropoulos, G. K. (2002). A common factors view of counseling supervision process. *The Clinical Supervisor, 21,* 77–94.

Lane, R. C. (1986). The recalcitrant supervisee: The negative supervisory reaction. *Current Issues in Psychoanalytic Practice, 2,* 65–81.

Lanning, W. (1986). Development of the supervisor emphasis rating form. *Counselor Education & Supervision, 25,* 191–196.

Lanning, W. L. (1971). A study of the relation between group and individual counseling supervision and three relationship measures. *Journal of Counseling Psychology, 18,* 401–406.

Larson, L. M., & Daniels, J. A. (1998). Review of the counseling self-efficacy literature. *The Counseling Psychologist, 26,* 179–218.

Larson, L. M., Suzuki, L. A., Gillespie, K. N., Potenza, M. T., Bechtel, M. A., & Toulouse, A. (1992). Development and validation of the Counseling Self-Estimate Inventory. *Journal of Counseling Psychology, 39,* 105–120.

Lassiter, P. S., Napolitano, L., Culbreth, J. R., & Ng, K.-M. (2008). Developing multicultural competence using the structured peer group supervision model. *Counselor Education & Supervision, 47,* 164–178.

Lawson, D. M. (1993). Supervision methods for addressing triangulation issues with counselors-in-training. *The Family Journal, 1,* 260–268.

Lawson, G., Hein, S. F., & Getz, H. (2009). A model for using triadic supervision in counselor preparation programs. *Counselor Education & Supervision, 48,* 257–270.

Lawson, G., Hein, S. F., & Stuart, C. L. (2009). A qualitative investigation of supervisees' experiences of triadic supervision. *Journal of Counseling & Development, 87,* 449–457.

Lazar, L., & Eisikovits, Z. (1997). Social work students' preferences regarding supervisory styles and supervisor's behaviour. *The Clinical Supervisor, 16,* 25–37.

Lazovsky, R., & Shimoni, A. (2007). The on-site mentor of counseling interns: Perceptions of ideal role and actual role performance. *Journal of Counseling and Development, 85,* 303–314.

Leary, M. R., & Kowalski, R. M. (1990). Impression management: A literature review and two-component model. *Psychological Bulletin, 107,* 34–47.

Leary, T. (1957). *Interpersonal diagnosis of personality: A theory and a methodology for personality evaluation.* New York, NY: Ronald Press.

Leddick, G. R. (1994). Counselor education clinics as community resources. In J. E. Myers (Ed.), *Developing and directing counselor education laboratories* (pp. 147–152). Alexandria, VA: ACA Press.

Leddick, G. R., & Bernard, J. M. (1980). The history of supervision: A critical review. *Counselor Education and Supervision, 19,* 186–196.

Lee, R. E., & Everett, C. A. (2004). *The integrative family therapy supervisor: A primer.* New York, NY: Brunner-Routledge.

Lee, R. E., Nichols, D. P., Nichols, W. C., & Odom, T. (2004). Trends in family therapy supervision: The past 25 years and into the future. *Journal of Marital & Family Therapy, 30,* 61–69.

Lee, R. W., & Cashwell, C. S. (2001). Ethical issues in counseling supervision: A comparison of university and site supervisors. *The Clinical Supervisor, 20*(2), 91–100.

Lee, R. W., & Gillam, S. L. (2000). Legal and ethical issues involving the duty to warn: Implications for supervisors. *The Clinical Supervisor, 19*(1), 123–136.

Lehrman-Waterman, D., & Ladany, N. (2001). Development and validation of the evaluation process within supervision inventory [Special issue]. *Journal of Counseling Psychology, 48*(2), 168–177.

Leonardelli, C. A., & Gratz, R. R. (1985). Roles and responsibilities in fieldwork experience: A social systems approach. *The Clinical Supervisor, 3*(3), 15–24.

Leong, F. T. L., & Wagner, N. S. (1994). Cross-cultural counseling supervision: What do we know? What do we need to know? *Counselor Education & Supervision, 34,* 117–131.

Lesser, R. M. (1983). Supervision: Illusions, anxieties, and questions. *Contemporary Psychoanalysis, 19,* 120–129.

Levenson, E. A. (1984). Follow the fox. In L. Caligor, P. M. Bromberg, & J. D. Meltzer (Eds.), *Clinical perspectives on the supervision of psychoanalysis and psychotherapy* (pp. 153–167). New York: Plenum Press.

Levinson, D. J. (1978). *The seasons of a man's life.* New York, NY: Alfred A. Knopf, Inc.

Levy, L. H. (1983). Evaluation of students in clinical psychology programs: A program evaluation perspective. *Professional Practice: Research & Practice, 14,* 497–503.

Lewis, B. L., Hatcher, R. L., & Pate, W. E., II. (2005). The practicum experience: A survey of practicum site coordinators. *Professional Psychology: Research & Practice, 36,* 291–298.

Lewis, G. J., Greenburg, S. L., & Hatch, D. B. (1988). Peer consultation groups for psychologists in private practice: A national survey. *Professional Psychology: Research & Practice, 9,* 81–86.

Lewis, H. B. (1971). *Shame and guilt in neurosis.* New York, NY: International University Press.

Lewis, W. (1988). A supervision model for public agencies. *The Clinical Supervisor, 6*(2), 85–91.

Lewis, W. C. (2001). Transference in analysis and in supervision. In S. Gill (Ed.), *The supervisory alliance: Facilitating the psychotherapist's learning experience* (pp. 75–80). Northvale, NJ: Jason Aronson, Inc.

Lewis, W., & Rohrbaugh, M. (1989). Live supervision by family therapists: A Virginia survey. *Journal of Marital & Family Therapy, 15,* 323–326.

Lichtenberg, J. W., & Goodyear, R. K. (2012). Informal learning, incidental learning, and deliberate continuing education: Preparing psychologists to be effective lifelong learners. In G. J. Neimeyer & J. M. Taylor (Eds.), *Continuing education: Types, roles, and societal impacts* (pp. 71–80). Hauppauge, NY: Nova Science Publishers.

Lichtenberg, J. W., Goodyear, R. K., & McCormick, K. (2000). The structure of supervisor–supervisee interactions. *The Clinical Supervisor, 19,* 1–24.

Liddle, B. (1986). Resistance in supervision: A response to perceived threat. *Counselor Education and Supervision, 26,* 117–127.

Liddle, H. A. (1988). Systemic supervision: Conceptual overlays and pragmatic guidelines. In H. A. Liddle, D. C. Breunlin, & R. C. Schwartz (Eds.), *Handbook of family therapy training and supervision* (pp. 153–171). New York, NY: Guilford.

Liddle, H. A., Breunlin, D. C., Schwartz, R. C., & Constantine, J. A. (1984). Training family therapy supervisors: Issues of content, form and context. *Journal of Marital and Family Therapy, 10,* 139–150.

Liddle, H. A., Davidson, G., & Barrett, J. (1988). Outcome in live supervision: Trainee perspectives. In H. Liddle, D. Breunlin, & R. Schwartz (Eds.), *Handbook of family therapy training and supervision* (pp. 183–193). New York, NY: Guilford Press.

Liddle, H. A., & Halpern, R. J. (1978). Family therapy training and supervision literature: Comparative review. *Journal of Marriage & Family Counseling, 4,* 77–98.

Liddle, H. A., & Saba, G. W. (1983). On context replication: The isomorphic relationship of family therapy and family therapy training. *Journal of Strategic and Systemic Therapies, 2*(2), 3–11

Liddle, H. A., & Schwartz, R. C. (1983). Live supervision/consultation: Conceptual and pragmatic guidelines for family therapy trainers. *Family Process, 22,* 477–490.

Lidmila, A. (1997). Shame, knowledge and modes of enquiry in supervision. In G. Shipton (Ed.), *Supervision of psychotherapy and counselling: Making a place to think.* Buckingham: Open University Press.

Liese, B. S., & Beck, J. S. (1997). Cognitive therapy supervision. In C. E. Watkins, Jr. (Ed.), *Handbook of psychotherapy supervision* (pp. 114–133). New York, NY: Wiley.

Lilienfeld, S. O., & Norcross, J. C. (2003, October 23). Colloquy live: The safety and efficacy of psychotherapy. *Chronicle of Higher Education.*

Linton, J., & Hedstrom, S. (2006). An exploratory qualitative investigation of group processes in group supervision: Perceptions of master's-level practicum students. *Journal for Specialists in Group Work, 31,* 51–72.

Lipshitz, R., & Strauss, O. (1997). Coping with uncertainty: A naturalistic decision-making analysis. *Organizational Behavior & Human Decision Processes, 69,* 149–163.

Littrell, J. M., Lee-Borden, N., & Lorenz, J. A. (1979). A developmental framework for counseling supervision. *Counselor Education and Supervision, 19,* 119–136.

Lizzio, A., Wilson, K., & Que, J. (2009). Relationship dimensions in the professional supervision of psychology graduates: supervisee perceptions of processes and outcome. *Studies in Continuing Education, 3,* 127–140.

Lloyd, A. P. (1992). Dual relationship problems in counselor education. In B. Herlihy & G. Corey (Eds.), *Dual relationships in counseling* (pp. 59–64). Alexandria, VA: AACD.

Locke, L. D., & McCollum, E. E. (2001). Clients' views of live supervision and satisfaction with therapy. *Journal of Marital & Family Therapy, 27,* 129–133.

Loganbill, C., Hardy, E., & Delworth, U. (1982). Supervision: A conceptual model. *The Counseling Psychologist, 10,* 3–42.

Lopez, S. R. (1997). Cultural competence in psychotherapy: A guide for clinicians and their supervisors. In C. E. Watkins, Jr. (Ed.), *Handbook of psychotherapy supervision* (pp. 570–588). New York, NY: John Wiley & Sons.

Lovell, C. (1999). Supervisee cognitive complexity and the Integrated Developmental Model. *The Clinical Supervisor, 18*(1), 191–201.

Lowe, R., Hunt, C., & Simmons, P. (2008). Towards multi-positioned live supervision in family therapy:

Combining treatment and observation teams with first- and second-order perspectives. *Contemporary Family Therapy, 30,* 3–14.

Lower, R. B. (1972). Countertransference resistances in the supervisory relationship. *American Journal of Psychiatry, 129,* 156–160.

Luepker, E. T. (2003). *Record keeping in psychotherapy and counseling: Protecting confidentiality and the professional relationship.* East Sussex, UK: Brunner-Routledge.

Luke, M., & Goodrich, K. M. (2012). LGBTQ responsive school counseling supervision. *The Clinical Supervisor, 31,* 81–102.

Luke, M., & Gordon, C. (2012). Supervisors' use of reinforcement, reframing, and advice to re-author the supervisory narrative through email supervision. *The Clinical Supervisor, 31*(2), 159–177.

Luke, M., Ellis, M. V., & Bernard, J. M. (2011). School counselor supervisors' perceptions of the discrimination model of supervision. *Counselor Education and Supervision, 50,* 328–343.

Lumadue, C. A., & Duffey, T. H. (1999). The role of graduate programs as gatekeepers: A model for evaluating student counselor competence. *Counselor Education & Supervision, 39,* 101–109.

Lyon, R. C., Heppler, A., Leavitt, L., & Fisher, L. (2008). Supervisory training experiences and overall supervisory development in predoctoral interns. *The Clinical Supervisor, 27,* 268–284.

MacIntyre, A. C. (1998). *A short history of ethics: A history of moral philosophy from the Homeric Age to the Twentieth Century* (2nd ed.). Notre Dame, IN: University of Notre Dame Press.

MacKinnon, C. J., Bhatia, M., Sunderani, S., Affleck, W., & Smith, N. G. (2011). Opening the dialogue: Implications of feminist supervision theory with male supervisees. *Professional Psychology: Research & Practice, 42,* 130–136.

Magnuson, S. (1995). *Supervision of prelicensed counselors: A study of educators, supervisors, and supervisees.* Unpublished doctoral dissertation. University of Alabama.

Magnuson, S., Norem, K., & Wilcoxon, A. (2000). Clinical supervision of prelicensed counselors: Recommendations for consideration and practice. *Journal of Mental Health Counseling, 22,* 176–188.

Magnuson, S., Wilcoxon, S. A., & Norem, K. (2000). A profile of lousy supervision: Experienced counselors' perspectives. *Counselor Education & Supervision, 39,* 189–202.

Maher, A. R. (2005). *Supervision of psychotherapists: The discovery-oriented approach.* London: Whurr Publishers.

Maheu, M. M., & Gordon, B. L. (2000). Counseling and therapy on the Internet. *Professional Psychology: Research & Practice, 31,* 484–489.

Mahoney, M. (1974). *Cognition and behavior modification.* Cambridge, MA: Ballinger.

Mahoney, M. J. (1977). Reflections on the cognitive-learning trend in psychotherapy. *American Psychologist, 32,* 5–13.

Maione, P. V. (2011). Help me help you: Suggested guidelines for case presentation. *Contemporary Family Therapy, 33,* 17–24.

Majcher, J.-A., & Daniluk, J. C. (2009). The process of becoming a supervisor for students in a doctoral supervision training course. *Training and Education in Professional Psychology, 3,* 63-71.

Maki, D. R., & Bernard, J. M. (2007). The ethics of clinical supervision. In R. R. Cottone & V. M. Tarvydas (Eds.), *Ethical & professional issues in counseling* (3rd ed.; pp. 347–368). Columbus, OH: Pearson Merrill Prentice Hall.

Mallinckrodt, B., & Nelson, M. L. (1991). Counselor training level and the formation of the psychotherapeutic working alliance. *Journal of Counseling Psychology, 38,* 133–138.

Malouf, J. L., Haas, L. J., & Farah, M. J. (1983). Issues in the preparation of interns: Views of trainers and trainees. *Professional Psychology: Research & Practice, 14,* 624–631.

Mangione, L. (2011). *Practicum coordinators: What keeps them going, and what do they need to continue?* American Psychological Association National Conference, Washington, DC.

Manzanares, M. G., O'Halloran, T. M., McCartney, T. J., Filer, R. D., Varhely, S. C., & Calhoun, K. (2004). CD-ROM technology for education and support of site supervisors. *Counselor Education & Supervision, 43,* 220–231.

Markey, P. M., Funder, D. C., & Ozer, D. J. (2003). Complementarity of interpersonal behaviors in dyadic interactions. *Personality & Social Psychological Bulletin, 29,* 1082–1090.

Marks, J. L., & Hixon, D. F. (1986). Training agency staff through peer group supervision. *Social Casework, 67,* 418–423.

Markus, H. (1977). Self-schemata and processing information about the self. *Journal of Personality & Social Psychology, 35,* 63–78.

Martin, J. M. (1988). A proposal for researching possible relationships between scientific theories and the personal theories of counselors and clients. *Journal of Counseling & Development, 66,* 261–265.

Martin, J. M., Slemon, A. G., Hiebert, B., Hallberg, E. T., & Cummings, A. L. (1989). Conceptualizations of novice and experienced counselors. *Journal of Counseling Psychology, 36,* 395–400.

Martin, J. S., Goodyear, R. K., & Newton, F. B. (1987). Clinical supervision: An intensive case study. *Professional Psychology: Research and Practice, 18,* 225–235.

Martino, C. (2001, August). Secrets of successful supervision: Graduate students' preferences and experiences with effective and ineffective supervision. In J. E. Barnett (Chair), *Secrets of successful supervision—Clinical and ethical issues.* Symposium conducted at the 109th Annual Convention of the American Psychological Association, San Francisco, CA.

Marx, R. (2011). Relational supervision: Drawing on cognitive–analytic frameworks. *Psychology & Psychotherapy: Theory, Research, & Practice, 84,* 406–424.

Mastoras, S. M., & Andrews, J. J. W. (2011). The supervisee experience of group supervision: Implications for research and practice. *Training & Education in Professional Psychology, 5,* 102–111.

Mathews, G. (1986). Performance appraisal in the human services: A survey. *The Clinical Supervisor, 3*(4), 47–61.

Matthews, G., Davies, D. R., & Lees, J. L. (1990). Arousal, extraversion, and individual differences in resource availability. *Journal of Personality and Social Psychology, 59,* 150–168.

Mauzey, E., & Erdman, P. (1997). Trainee perceptions of live supervision phone-ins: A phenomenological inquiry. *Clinical Supervisor, 15*(2), 115–128.

Mauzey, E., Harris, M. B. C., & Trusty, J. (2000). Comparing the effects of live supervision interventions on novice trainee anxiety and anger [Special issue]. *Clinical Supervisor, 19*(2), 109–122.

McAdams, C. R., & Wyatt, K.L, (2010). The regulation of technology-assisted distance counseling and supervision in the United States: An analysis of current extent, trends, and implications. *Counselor Education & Supervision, 49,* 179–192.

McAdams, C. R., III, Foster, V. A., & Ward, T. J. (2007). Remediation and dismissal policies in counselor education: Lessons learned from a challenge in federal court. *Counselor Education & Supervision, 46,* 212–229.

McCarn, S. & Fassinger, R. F. (1996). Revisioning sexual minority identity formation: A new model of lesbian identity and its implications for counseling and research. *The Counseling Psychologist, 24,* 508–534.

McCarthy, P., Kulakowski, D., & Kenfield, J. A. (1994). Clinical supervision practices of licensed psychologists. *Professional Psychology: Research & Practice, 25,* 177–181.

McCarthy, P., Sugden, S., Koker, M., Lamendola, F., Maurer, S., & Renninger, S. (1995). A practical guide to informed consent in clinical supervision. *Counselor Education & Supervision, 35,* 130–138.

McColley, S. H., & Baker, E. L. (1982). Training activities and styles of beginning supervisors: A survey. *Professional Psychology, 13,* 283–292.

McCollum (1995). Perspectives on live supervision: The supervisor's view. *Supervision Bulletin, 8*(2), 4.

McCutcheon, S. R. (2008). Addressing problems of insufficient competence during the internship year. *Training & Education in Professional Psychology, 2,* 210–214.

McDaniel, S., Weber, T., & McKeever, J. (1983). Multiple theoretical approaches to supervision: Choices in family therapy training. *Family Process, 22,* 491–500.

McKenzie, P. N., Atkinson, B. J., Quinn, W. H., & Heath, A. W. (1986). Training and supervision in marriage and family therapy: A national survey. *American Journal of Family Therapy, 14,* 293–303.

McMahon, M. (2002) Peer networks: Support or supervision or both? *Connections, 19*(3), 15–17.

McNamee, C. M., & McWey, L. M. (2004). Using bilateral art to facilitate clinical supervision. *The Arts in Psychotherapy, 31,* 229–243.

McNeill, B. W., Stoltenberg, C. D., & Pierce, R. A. (1985). Supervisee's perceptions of their development: A test of the counselor complexity model. *Journal of Counseling Psychology, 32,* 630–633.

McNeill, B. W., Stoltenberg, C. D., & Romans, J. S. (1992). The Integrated Developmental Model of supervision: Scale development and validation procedures. *Professional Psychology: Research & Practice, 23,* 504–508.

McNeill, B. W., & Worthen, V. (1989). The parallel process in psychotherapy supervision. *Professional Psychology: Research & Practice, 20,* 329–333.

McWilliams, N. (1994). *Psychoanalytic diagnosis: Understanding personality structure in the clinical process*. New York, NY: The Guilford Press.

McWilliams, N. (2004). Some observations about supervision/consultation groups. *New Jersey Psychologist, Winter,* 16–18.

Mead, D. E. (1990). *Effective supervision: A task-oriented model for the mental health professions*. New York, NY: Brunner/Mazel.

Mead, G. H. (1962). *Mind, self, and society.* Chicago, IL: University of Chicago Press.

Mehr, K. E., Ladany, N., & Caskie, G. I. L. (2010). Trainee nondisclosure in supervision: What are they not telling you? *Counselling and Psychotherapy Research, 10,* 103–113.

Meichenbaum, D. (1977). *Cognitive–behavior modification*. New York, NY: Plenum Press.

Melnick, J., & Fall, M. (2008). A gestalt approach to group supervision. *Counselor Education & Supervision, 48,* 48–60.

Merriam-Webster online dictionary (n.d.). Retrieved August 20, 2011, at www.merriam-webster.com/dictionary/supervision

Messinger, L. (2004). Out in the field: Gay and lesbian social work students' experiences in field placement. *Journal of Social Work Education, 40,* 187–204.

Messinger, L. (2007). Supervision of lesbian, gay, and bisexual social work students by heterosexual field instructors: A qualitative dyad analysis. *The Clinical Supervisor, 26*(1.2), 195–222.

Meyer, R. G. (1980). Legal and procedural issues in the evaluation of clinical graduate students. *The Clinical Psychologist, 33,* 15–17.

Meyer, R. G., Landis, E. R., & Hays, J. R. (1988). *Law for the psychotherapist*. New York, NY: W. W. Norton & Co.

Miars, R. D., Tracey, T. J., Ray, P. B., Cornfeld, L., O'Farrell, M., & Gelso, C. J. (1983). Variation in supervision process across trainee experience levels. *Journal of Counseling Psychology, 30,* 403–412.

Michaelson, S. D., Estrada-Hernández, & Wadsworth, J. S. (2003). A competency-based evaluation model for supervising novice counselors-in-training. *Rehabilitation Education, 17,* 215–223.

Michalski, D., & Mulvey, T. (August 2010). *Psychology's researchers and educators: What's on our workforce horizon?* Paper presented at the annual meeting of the American Psychological Association, San Diego, CA. Retrieved online on April 7, 2012, from www.apa.org/workforce/presentations/future psychology-workforce.pdf

Miller, G. M., & Larrabee, M. J. (1995). Sexual intimacy in counselor education and supervision: A national survey. *Counselor Education & Supervision, 34,* 332–343.

Miller, K. L., Miller, S. M., & Evans, W. J. (2002). Computer-assisted live supervision in college counseling centers. *Journal of College Counseling, 5,* 187–192.

Miller, M. M., & Ivey, D. C. (2006). Spirituality, gender, and supervisory style in supervision. *Contemporary Family Therapy, 28,* 323–337.

Miller, W. R., & Rollnick, S. (2002). *Motivational interviewing: Preparing people for change* (2nd ed.). New York, NY: Guilford Press.

Milne, D. (2006). Developing clinical supervision research through reasoned analogies with therapy. *Clinical Psychology and Psychotherapy, 13,* 215–222.

Milne, D. (2007). An empirical definition of clinical supervision. *British Journal of Clinical Psychology, 46,* 437–447.

Milne, D. (2008). CBT Supervision: From reflexivity to specialization. *Behavioural & Cognitive Psychotherapy, 36,* 779–786.

Milne, D. (2009). *Evidence-based clinical supervision: Principles and practice.* Chicester, UK: Wiley-Blackwell.

Milne, D., Aylott, H., Fitzpatrick, H., & Ellis, M. V. (2008). How does clinical supervision work? Using a "best evidence synthesis" approach to construct a basic model of supervision. *The Clinical Supervisor, 27*(2), 170–190.

Milne, D. L., & James, I. A. (2002). The observed impact of training on competence in clinical supervision. *British Journal of Clinical Psychology, 41*(1), 55–72.

Milne, D. L., & James, I. A. (2005). Clinical supervision: Ten tests of the tandem model. *Clinical Psychology Forum, 151,* 6–9.

Milne, D., & Reiser, R. P. (2012). A rationale for evidence-based clinical supervision. *Journal of Contemporary Psychotherapy, 42*(3), 139–149.

Milne, D., Sheikh, A., Pattison, S., & Wilkinson, A. (2011). Evidence-based training for clinical supervisors: A systematic review of 11 controlled studies. *The Clinical Supervisor, 30,* 53–71.

Milne, D., & Westerman, C. (2001). Evidence-based clinical supervision: Rationale and illustration. *Clinical Psychology & Psychotherapy, 8,* 444–457.

Minuchin, S., & Fishman, C. (1981). *Family therapy techniques*. Cambridge, MA: Harvard Press.

Miyake, A., & Priti, S. (Eds.). (1999). *Working memory: Mechanisms of executive maintenance and active control*. Cambridge, UK: Cambridge University Press.

Moffett, L.A. (2009). Directed self-reflection protocols in supervision. *Training & Education in Professional Psychology, 3,* 78–83.

Molnar, A., & de Shazer, S. (1987). Solution-focused therapy: Toward the identification of therapeutic tasks. *Journal of Marital & Family Therapy, 13,* 349–358.

Monks, G. M. (1996). A meta-analysis of role induction studies. *Dissertation Abstracts International: Section B: The Sciences & Engineering, 56*(12-B), Jun 1996, 7051.

Montalvo, B. (1973). Aspects of live supervision. *Family Process, 12,* 343–359.

Montgomery, L. M., Cupit, B. E., & Wimberley, T. K. (1999). Complaints, malpractice, and risk management: Professional issues and personal experiences. *Professional Psychology: Research & Practice, 30,* 402–410.

Montgomery, M. L., Hendricks, C. B., & Bradley, L. J. (2001). Using systems perspectives in supervision. *The Family Journal: Counseling & Therapy for Couples and Families, 9,* 305–313.

Moorhouse, A., & Carr, A. (2001). A study of live supervisory phone-ins in collaborative family therapy: Correlates of client cooperation [Special issue]. *Journal of Marital & Family Therapy, 27,* 241–249.

Moorhouse, A., & Carr, A. (2002). Gender and conversational behavior in family therapy and life supervision. *Journal of Family Therapy, 24,* 46–56.

Moradi, B., & Subich, L. M. (2002a). Perceived sexist events and feminist identity development attitudes. *The Counseling Psychologist, 30,* 44–65.

Moradi, B., & Subich, L. M. (2002b). Feminist identity development measures: Comparing the psychometrics of three instruments. *The Counseling Psychologist, 30,* 66–86.

Moradi, B., Subich, L. M., & Phillips, J. C. (2002). Revisiting feminist identity development: Theory, research, & practice. *The Counseling Psychologist, 30,* 6–43.

Morgan, M. M., & Sprenkle, D. H. (2007). Toward a common-factors approach to supervision. *Journal of Marital & Family Therapy, 33,* 1–17.

Mori, Y., Inman, A. G., & Caskie, G. I. L. (2009). Supervising international students: Relationship between acculturation, supervisor multicultural competence, cultural discussions, and supervision satisfaction. *Training & Education in Professional Psychology, 3,* 10–18.

Moskowitz, D. S. (2009). Coming full circle: Conceptualizing the study of interpersonal behaviour. *Canadian Psychology, 50,* 33–41.

Mothersole, G. (1999). Parallel process: A review. *The Clinical Supervisor, 18,* 107–122.

Mueller, W. J. (1982). Issues in the application of "Supervision: A conceptual model" to dynamically oriented supervision: A reaction paper. *The Counseling Psychologist, 10,* 43–46.

Mueller, W. J., & Kell, B. L. (1972). *Coping with conflict: Supervising counselors and therapists*. New York, NY: Appleton-Century-Crofts.

Mullen, J. A., Luke, M., & Drewes, A. (2007). Supervision can be playful too: Play therapy techniques that enhance supervision. *International Journal of Play Therapy, 16,* 69–85.

Munson, C. E. (1983). *An introduction to clinical social work supervision*. New York, NY: Haworth Press.

Munson, C. E. (2002). *Handbook of clinical social work supervision* (3rd ed.). Binghamton, NY: Haworth Press, Inc.

Muratori, M. C. (2001). Examining supervisor impairment from the counselor trainee's perspective. *Counselor Education & Supervision, 41,* 41–56.

Murphy-Shigematsu, S. (2010). Microaggressions by supervisors of color. *Training & Education in Professional Psychology, 4*(1), 16–18.

Murphy, J. A., Rawlings, E. I., & Howe, S. R. (2002). A survey of clinical psychologists on treating lesbian, gay, and bisexual clients. *Professional Psychology: Research & Practice, 33,* 183–189.

Murphy, J. W., & Pardeck, J. T. (1986). The "burnout syndrome" and management style. *Clinical Supervisor, 4,* 35–44.

Murphy, M. J., & Wright, D. W. (2005). Supervisees' perspectives of power use in supervision. *Journal of Marital & Family Therapy, 31,* 283–295.

Murray, G. C., Portman, T., & Maki, D. R. (2003). Clinical supervision: Developmental differences during pre-service training. *Rehabilitation Education, 17,* 19–32.

Muslin, H. L., Thurnblad, R. J., & Meschel, G. (1981). The fate of the clinical interview: An observational study. *American Journal of Psychiatry, 138,* 822–825.

Myers, J. E. (Ed.). (1994). *Developing and directing counselor education laboratories*. Alexandria, VA: ACA Press.

Myers, J. E., & Hutchinson, G. H. (1994). Dual role or conflict of interest? Clinics as mental health providers. In J. E. Myers (Ed.), *Developing and directing counselor education laboratories* (pp. 161–167). Alexandria, VA: ACA Press.

Narvaez, D. (2010). Moral complexity: The fatal attraction of truthiness and the importance of mature moral functioning. *Perspectives on Psychological Science, 5,* 163–181.

Narvaez, D., & Lapsley, D. K. (2005). The psychological foundations of everyday morality and moral expertise. In C. Lapsley, D., Power (Ed.), *Character psychology and character education* (pp. 140–165). Notre Dame, IN: University of Notre Dame Press.

Nathanson, D. L. (1992). *Shame and pride: Affect, sex, and the birth of the self.* New York, NY: W.W. Norton.

National Council for Accreditation of Teacher Education (NCATE). (2008). *Professional Standards for the Accreditation of Teacher Preparation Institution.* Washington, DC: Author.

Navin, S., Beamish, P., & Johanson, G. (1995). Ethical practices of field-based mental health counselor supervisors. *Journal of Mental Health Counseling, 17,* 243–253.

Neiss, R. (1988). Reconceptualizing arousal: Psychobiological states in motor performance. *Psychological Bulletin, 103,* 345–366.

Nelson, J. A., Nichter, M., & Henriksen, R. (2010). On-line supervision and face-to-face supervision in the counseling internship: An exploratory study of similarities and differences. Retrieved from counselingoutfitters.com/vistas/vistas10/Article_46.pdf

Nelson, M. L. (2002, October). *How to be a lousy supervisor: Lessons from the research.* Paper presented at the annual meeting of the Association for Counselor Education and Supervision, Park City, UT.

Nelson, M. L., Barnes, K. L., Evans, A. L., & Triggiano, P. J. (2008). Working with conflict in clinical supervision: Wise supervisors' perspectives. *Journal of Counseling Psychology, 55,* 172–184.

Nelson, M. L., & Friedlander, M. L. (2001). A close look at conflictual supervisory relationships: The trainee's perspective. *Journal of Counseling Psychology, 48,* 384–395.

Nelson, M. L., Gizara, S., Hope, A. C., Phelps, R., Steward, R., & Weitzman, L. (2006). A feminist multicultural perspective on supervision. *Journal of Multicultural Counseling & Development, 34,* 105–116.

Nelson, M. L., Gray, L. A., Friedlander, M. L., Ladany, N., & Walker, J. A. (2001). Toward relationship-centered supervision: Reply to Veach (2001) and Ellis (2001). *Journal of Counseling Psychology, 48,* 407–409.

Nelson, M. L., & Holloway, E. L. (1990). Relation of gender to power and involvement in supervision. *Journal of Counseling Psychology, 37,* 473–481.

Nelson, M. L., & Neufeldt, S. A. (1998). The pedagogy of counseling: A critical examination. *Counselor Education & Supervision, 38,* 70–88.

Nelson, T. S. (1991). Gender in family therapy supervision. *Contemporary Family Therapy: An International Journal, 13,* 357–369.

Neufeldt, S. (1994). Use of a manual to train supervisors. *Counselor Education & Supervision, 33,* 327–333.

Neufeldt, S. A. (1999). Training in reflective processes in supervision. In M. Carroll & E. L. Holloway (Eds.), *Education of clinical supervisors* (pp. 92–105). London: Sage.

Neufeldt, S. A., Iverson, J. N., & Juntunen, C. L. (1995). *Supervision strategies for the first practicum.* Alexandria, VA: American Counseling Association.

Neufeldt, S. A., Karno, M. P., & Nelson, M. L. (1996). A qualitative analysis of experts' conceptualization of supervisee reflectivity. *Journal of Counseling Psychology, 43,* 3–9.

Neufeldt, S. A., & Nelson, M. L. (1999). When is counseling an appropriate and ethical supervision function? *The Clinical Supervisor, 18,* 125–135.

Neukrug, E., Milliken, T., & Walden, S. (2001). Ethical complaints made against credentialed counselors: An updated survey of state licensing boards. *Counselor Education & Supervision, 41,* 57–70.

Neukrug, E. S. (1991). Computer-assisted live supervision in counselor skills training. *Counselor Education & Supervision, 31,* 132–138.

Newman, C. F. (2010). Competency in conducting cognitive–behavioral therapy: Foundational, functional, and supervisory aspects. *Psychotherapy Theory, Research, Practice, Training, 47,* 12–19.

Nguyen, H. D. & Ryan, A. M. (2008). Does stereotype threat affect test performance of minorities and women? A meta-analysis of experimental evidence. *Journal of Applied Psychology, 93,* 1314–1334.

Nguyen, T. V. (2004). A comparison of individual supervision and triadic supervision. *Dissertation Abstracts International, 64*(9), 3204A.

Nicholas, M. W. (1989). A systemic perspective of group therapy supervision: Use of energy in the supervisor-therapist-group system. *Journal of Independent Social Work, 3*(4), 27–39.

Nichols, M. (1984). *Family therapy: Concepts and methods*. New York, NY: Gardner Press.

Nichols, W. C., Nichols, D. P., & Hardy, K. V. (1990). Supervision in family therapy: A decade restudy. *Journal of Marital & Family Therapy, 16,* 275–285.

Nielsen, G. H., Skjerve, J., Jacobsen, C. H., Gullestad, S. E., Hansen, B. R., Reichelt, S., . . . , & Torgerson, A. M. (2009). Mutual assumptions and facts about nondisclosure among clinical supervisors and students in group supervision: A comparative analysis. *Nordic Psychology, 61*(4), 49–58.

Nigam, T., Cameron, P. M., & Leverette, J. S. (1997). Impasses in the supervisory process: A resident's perspective. *American Journal of Psychotherapy, 51,* 252–272.

Nilsson, J. E. (2007). International students in supervision: Course self-efficacy, stress, and cultural discussions in supervision. *The Clinical Supervisor, 16*(1/2), 35–47.

Nilsson, J. E., & Anderson, M. Z. (2004). Supervising international students: The role of acculturation, role ambiguity, and multicultural discussions. *Professional Psychology: Research & Practice, 35,* 306–312.

Nilsson, J. E., & Dodds, A. K. (2006). A pilot phase in the development of the international student supervision scale. *Journal of Multicultural Counseling & Development, 34,* 50–62.

Noelle, M. (2002). Self-report in supervision: Positive and negative slants. *The Clinical Supervisor, 21,* 125–134.

Norcross, J. C., & Halgin, R. P. (1997). Integrative approaches to psychotherapy supervision. In J. C. E. Watkins (Ed.), *Handbook of psychotherapy supervision*. New York, NY: Wiley.

Norcross, J. C., & Halgin, R. P. (2005). Training in psychotherapy integration. In J. C. Norcross and M. R. Goldfried (Eds.), *Handbook of psychotherapy integration* (2nd ed.). Oxford series in clinical psychology (pp. 439–458). New York, NY: Oxford University Press.

Norcross, J. C., Hedges, M., & Castle, P. H. (2002). Psychologists conducting psychotherapy in 2001: A study of the division 29 membership. *Psychotherapy: Theory, Research, Practice, Training, 39,* 97–102.

Norcross, J. C., & Wampold, B. E. (2011). Evidence-based therapy relationships: Research conclusions and clinical practices. *Psychotherapy, 48,* 98–102.

Nyman, S. J., Nafziger, M. A., & Smith, T. B. (2010). Client outcomes across counselor training level within a multitiered supervision model. *Journal of Counseling & Development, 88,* 204–209.

O'Connor, T. S. J., Davis, A., Meakes, E., Pickering, R., & Schuman, M. (2004). Narrative therapy using a reflecting team: An ethnographic study of therapists' experiences. *Contemporary Family Therapy: An International Journal, 26,* 23–39.

O'Neil, J. M. (2008). Summarizing 25 years of research on men's gender role conflict using the Gender Role Conflict Scale: New research paradigms and clinical implications. *The Counseling Psychologist, 36,* 358–445.

O'Neil, J. M., Good, G. E., & Holmes, S. (1995). Fifteen years of theory and research on men's gender role conflict. In R. F. Levant & W. S. Pollack (Eds.), *The new psychology of men* (pp. 164–206). New York, NY: Basic Books.

O'Neil, J. M., Helms, B., Gable, R., David, L., & Wrightsman, L. (1986). Gender Role Conflict Scale: College men's fear of femininity. *Sex Roles, 14,* 335–350.

Ober, A. M., Granello, D. H., & Henfield, M. S. (2009). A synergistic model to enhance multicultural competence in supervision. *Counselor Education & Supervision, 48,* 204–221.

Ogbu, J. U. (1992). Understanding cultural diversity and learning. *Educational Researcher, 21,* 5–14, 24.

Ogloff, J. R. P., & Olley, M. C. (1998). The interaction between ethics and the law. The ongoing refinement of ethical standards for psychologists in Canada. *Professional Psychology: Research & Practice, 39,* 221–230.

Ögren, M. L., Boëthius, S. B., & Sundin, E. C. (2008). From psychotherapist to supervisor: The significance of group format and supervisors' function as role models in supervisor training. *Nordic Psychology, 60,* 3–23.

Ögren, M. L., Jonsson, C. O., & Sundin, E. (2005). Group supervision in psychotherapy. The relationship between focus, group climate and perceived attained skill. *Journal of Clinical Psychology, 61*(4), 373–389.

Oliver, M., Nelson, K., & Ybañez, K. (2010). Systemic processes in triadic supervision. *The Clinical Supervisor, 29,* 51–67.

Oliver, M. N. I., Bernstein, J. H., Anderson, K. G., Blashfield, R. K., & Roberts, M. C. (2004). An exploratory examination of student attitudes toward "impaired" peers in clinical psychology training programs. *Professional Psychology: Research & Practice, 35,* 141–147.

Olk, M., & Friedlander, M. L. (1992). Trainees' experiences of role conflict and role ambiguity in supervisory relationships. *Journal of Counseling Psychology, 39,* 389–397.

Olsen, D. C., & Stern, S. B. (1990). Issues in the development of a family therapy supervision model. *The Clinical Supervisor, 8*(2), 49–65.

Olson, M. M., Russell, C. S., & White, M. B. (2001). Technological implications for clinical supervision and practice. *The Clinical Supervisor, 20*(2), 201–215.

Orchowski, L., Evangelista, N.M., & Probst, D.R. (2010). Enhancing supervisee reflectivity in clinical supervision: A case study illustration. *Psychotherapy Theory, Research, Practice, Training, 47,* 51–67.

Orlinsky, D. E., Botermans, J. F., & Rønnestad, M. H. (2001). Towards an empirically grounded model of psychotherapy training: Four thousand therapists rate influences on their development. *Australian Psychologist, 36,* 139–148.

Orlinsky, D. E., Grawe, K., & Parks, B. K. (1994). Process and outcome in psychotherapy: Noch einmal. In A. E. Bergin & S. L. Garfield (Eds.), *Handbook of psychotherapy and behavior change* (3rd ed., pp. 270–376). New York, NY: Wiley.

Osborn, C. J. (2004). Seven salutary suggestions for counselor stamina. *Journal of Counseling & Development, 82,* 319–328.

Osborn, C. J., & Davis, T. E. (1996). The supervision contract: Making it perfectly clear. *The Clinical Supervisor, 14*(2), 121–134.

Osborn, C. J., & Davis, T. E. (2009). Ethical issues in the clinical supervision of evidence-based practices. In N. Pelling, J. Barlette, & P. Armstrong (Eds.), *The practice of clinical supervision* (pp. 56–80). Bowen Hills, Queensland, Australia: Australian Academic Press.

Osborn, C. J., Paez, S. B., & Carrabean, C. L. (2007). Reflections on shared practices in a supervisory lineage. *The Clinical Supervisor, 26*(1/2), 119–139.

Osterberg, M. J. (1996). Gender in supervision: Exaggerating the differences between men and women. *The Clinical Supervisor, 14*(2), 69–83.

Pack-Brown, S. P., & William, C. B. (2003). *Ethics in a multicultural context.* Thousand Oaks, CA: Sage Publications.

Page, S., & Woskett, V. (2001). *Supervising the counsellor: A cyclical model* (2nd ed.). London, UK: Brunner-Routledge.

Panos, P. T. (2005). A model for using videoconferencing technology to support international social work field practicum students. *International Social Work, 48,* 834–841.

Panos, P. T., Roby, J. L., Panos, A., Matheson, K. W., & Cox, S. E. (2002). Ethical issues concerning the use of videoconferencing to supervise international social work field practicum students. *Journal of Social Work Education, 38,* 421–437.

Parry, A., & Doan, R. E. (1994). *Story re-visions: Narrative therapy in the postmodern world.* New York, NY: Guilford.

Patrick, K. D. (1989). Unique ethical dilemmas in counselor training. *Counselor Education & Supervision, 28,* 337–341.

Patterson, C. H. (1964). Supervising students in the counseling practicum. *Journal of Counseling Psychology, 11,* 47–53.

Patterson, C. H. (1983). Supervision in counseling: II. Contemporary models of supervision: A client-centered approach to supervision. *The Counseling Psychologist, 11,* 21–25.

Patterson, C. H. (1997). Client-centered supervision. In C. E. Watkins (Ed.), *Handbook of psychotherapy supervision* (pp. 134–146). New York, NY: John Wiley.

Patton, M. J., & Kivlighan, Jr., D. M. (1997). Relevance of the supervisory alliance to the counseling alliance and to treatment adherence in counselor training. *Journal of Counseling Psychology, 44,* 108–115.

Pearson, B., & Piazza, N. (1997). Classification of dual relationships in the helping professions. *Counselor Education & Supervision, 37,* 89–99.

Pearson, Q. M. (2000). Opportunities and challenges in the supervisory relationship: Implications for counselor supervision. *Journal of Mental Health Counseling, 22,* 283–294.

Pearson, Q. M. (2006). Psychotherapy-driven supervision: Integrating counseling theories into role-based supervision. *Journal of Mental Health Counseling, 28,* 241–252.

Peleg-Oren, N. & Even-Zahav, R. (2004). Why do field supervisors drop out of student supervision? *The Clinical Supervisor, 23*(2), 15–30.

Pelling, N. (2008). The relationship of supervisory experience, counseling experience, and training in supervision to supervisory identity development. *International Journal for the Advancement of Counselling, 30,* 235–248.

Penman, R. (1980). *Communication processes and relationships.* London, UK: Academic Press.

Perkins, J. M., & Mercaitis, P. A. (1995). A guide for supervisors and students in clinical practicum. *The Clinical Supervisor, 13,* 67–78.

Perlesz, A. J., Stolk, Y., & Firestone, A. F. (1990). Patterns of learning in family therapy training. *Family Process, 29,* 29–44.

Perry, W. G., Jr. (1970). *Forms of intellectual and ethical development in the college years.* New York, NY: Holt, Rinehart, & Winston.

Perry, W. G., Jr. (1981). Cognitive and ethical growth: The making of meaning. In A. W. Chickering (Ed.), *The modern American college* (pp. 76–116). New York, NY: Jossey–Bass.

Peterson, M. (1993). Covert agendas in supervision. *The Supervision Bulletin, VI* (1), 1, 7–8.

Peterson, R. (2002, November 7). Discussant. Panel discussion: Landscapes (M. Willmuth, Chair). APPIC Competencies Conference, Scottsdale, AZ.

Peterson, R. L., Peterson, D. R., Abrams, J. C., & Stricker, G. (1997). The National Council of Schools and Programs of Professional Psychology educational model. *Professional Psychology: Research and Practice, 28,* 373–386.

Pettifor, J. L., & Sawchuk, T. R. (2006). Psychologists' perceptions of ethically troubling incidents across international borders. *International Journal of Psychology, 41*(3), 216–225.

Petty, R. E., & Cacioppo, J. T. (1986). *Communication and persuasion: Central and peripheral routes to attitude change.* New York, NY: Springer-Verlag.

Pfohl, A. H. (2004). The intersection of personal and professional identity: The heterosexual supervisor's role in fostering the development of sexual minority supervisees. *The Clinical Supervisor, 23*(1), 139–164.

Phelps, D., Burkard, A., Knox, S., Clarke, R., & Inman, A. G. (2009). *Difficult feedback in cross-cultural supervision.* American Psychological Association Convention, Washington, DC.

Philp, K. M., Guy, G. E., & Lowe, R. D. (2007). Social constructionist supervision or supervision as social construction? Some dilemmas. *Journal of Systemic Therapies, 26,* 51–62.

Phinney, J. S., & Ong, A. D. (2007). Conceptualization and measurement of ethnic identity: Current status and future directions. *Journal of Counseling Psychology, 54,* 271–281.

Pierce, R. M., & Schauble, P. G. (1970). Graduate training of facilitative counselors: The effects of individual supervision. *Journal of Counseling Psychology, 17,* 210–215.

Piercy, F. P., Sprenkle, D. H., & Constantine, J. A. (1986). Family members' perceptions of live, observation/supervision: An exploratory study. *Contemporary Family Therapy, 8,* 171–187.

Pilkington, N. W., & Cantor, J. M. (1996). Perceptions of heterosexual bias in professional psychology programs. *Professional Psychology: Research & Practice, 27,* 604–612.

Pinsof, W. M., & Wynne, L. C. (1995). The efficacy of marital and family therapy: An empirical overview, conclusions, and recommendations. *Journal of Marital & Family Therapy, 21,* 585–613.

Pistole, M. C., & Watkins, C. E. (1995). Attachment theory, counseling process, and supervision. *The Counseling Psychologist, 23,* 457–478.

Plante, T. G. (1995). Training child clinical predoctoral intern and post-doctoral fellows in ethics and professional issues: An experiential model. *Professional Psychology: Research & Practice, 26,* 616–619.

Poertner, J. (1986). The use of client feedback to improve practice: Defining the supervisor's role. *The Clinical Supervisor, 4*(4), 57–67.

Polanski, P. J. (2003). Spirituality in supervision. *Counseling & Values, 47,* 131–141.

Polkinghorne, D. (1988). *Narrative knowing and the human sciences.* Albany, NY: State University of New York Press.

Ponterotto, J. G. (1988). Racial consciousness development among White counselor trainees: A stage model. *Journal of Multicultural Counseling & Development, 16,* 146–156.

Ponterotto, J. G., Utsey, S. O., & Pederson, P. B. (2006). Preventing prejudice: A guide for counselors, educators, and parents. In J. G. Ponterotto, S. O. Utsey, & P. B. Pederson (Eds.), *Identity* (2nd ed.). Thousand Oaks, CA: SAGE Publications.

Pope, K. S., & Bajt, T. R. (1988). When laws and values conflict: A dilemma for psychologists. *American Psychologist, 45,* 1066–1070.

Pope, K. S., & Vasquez, M. J. T. (2011). *Ethics in psychotherapy and counseling: A practical guide* (4th ed.). Hoboken, NJ: Wiley.

Pope, K. S., & Vetter, V. A. (1992). Ethical dilemmas encountered by members of the American Psychological Association: A national survey. *American Psychologist, 47,* 397–411.

Pope, K. S., Levenson, H., & Schover, L. R. (1979). Sexual intimacy in psychology training: Results and implications of a national survey. *American Psychologist, 34,* 682–689.

Pope, K. S., Tabachnik, B. G., & Spiegel, P. K. (1987). Ethics of practice: The beliefs and behaviors of psychologists and therapists. *American Psychologist, 42,* 993–1006.

Porter, N. (1994). Empowering supervisees to empower others: A culturally responsive supervision model. *Hispanic Journal of Behavioral Sciences, 16,* 43–56.

Porter, N., & Vasquez, M. (1997). Covision: Feminist supervision, process, and collaboration. In J. Worell & N. G. Johnson (Eds.), *Shaping the future of feminist psychology: Education, research, and practice.* Washington, DC: American Psychological Association.

Powell, D., & Migdole, S. (June, 2012). *Can you hear me now? New frontiers of clinical supervision.* Presentation at the International Interdisciplinary Conference of Clinical Supervision. Garden City, NY.

Presbury, J., Echterling, L. G., & McKee, J. E. (1999). Supervision for inner-vision: Solution-focused strategies. *Counselor Education and Supervision, 39,* 146–155.

Prest, L. A., Russel, R., & D'Souza, H. (1999). Spirituality and religion in training, practice, and personal development. *Journal of Family Therapy, 21,* 60–78.

Pretorius, W. M. (2006). Cognitive–behavioural therapy supervision: Recommended practice. *Behavioural & Cognitive Psychotherapy, 34,* 413–420.

Prochaska, J. O., & Norcross, J. C. (2007). *Systems of psychotherapy: A transtheoretical analysis* (6th ed.). Belmont, CA: Wadsworth.

Proctor, B. (1986). Supervision: A co-operative exercise in accountability. In A. Marken & M. Payne (Eds.), *Enabling and ensuring: Supervision in practice.* Leicester National Youth Bureau/Council for Education and Training in Youth and Community Work.

Proctor, B. (1991). On being a trainer. In W. Dryden & B. Thorne (Eds.), *Training and supervision for counselling in action* (pp. 49–73). London, UK: Sage Publications.

Proctor, B. (2000). *Group supervision: A guide to creative practice.* London, UK: Sage Publications.

Proctor, B., & Inskipp, F. (1988). *Skills for supervising and being supervised.* Sussex, UK: Alexia Publications.

Proctor, B., & Inskipp, F. (2001). Group supervision. In J. Scaife (Ed.), *Supervision in the mental health professions: A practitioner's guide* (pp. 99–121). London: Routledge.

Prouty, A. (2001). Experiencing feminist family therapy supervision. *Journal of Feminist Family Therapy, 12,* 171–203.

Prouty, A. M., Thomas, V., Johnson, S., & Long, J. K. (2001). Methods of feminist family therapy supervision. *Journal of Marital & Family Therapy, 27,* 85–97.

Putney, M. W., Worthington, E. L., & McCulloughy, M. E. (1992). Effects of supervisor and supervisee theoretical orientation and supervisor–supervisee matching on interns' perceptions of supervision. *Journal of Counseling Psychology, 39,* 258–265.

Quarto, C. J. (2002). Supervisors' and supervisees' perceptions of control and conflict in counseling supervision. *The Clinical Supervisor, 21,* 21–37.

Quinn, W. H., Atkinson, B. J., & Hood, C. J. (1985). The stuck-case clinic as a group supervision model. *Journal of Marital & Family Therapy, 11,* 67–73.

Rabinowitz, F. E., Heppner, P. P., & Roehlke, H. J. (1986). Descriptive study of process and outcome variables of supervision over time. *Journal of Counseling Psychology, 33,* 292–300.

Raichelson, S. H., Herron, W. G., Pimavera, L. H., & Ramirez, S. M. (1997). Incidence and effects of parallel process in psychotherapy supervision. *The Clinical Supervisor, 15,* 37–48.

Raiger, J. (2005). Applying a cultural lens to the concept of burnout. *Journal of Transcultural Nursing, 16,* 71–76.

Ramos-Sanchez, L., Esnil, E., Goodwin, A., Riggs, S., Touster, L. O., Wright, L. K., . . . , & Rodolfa, E. (2002). Negative supervisory events: Effects on supervision and supervisory alliance. *Professional Psychology: Research & Practice, 33,* 197–202.

Ratliff, D. A., Wampler, K. S., & Morris, G. H. B. (2000). Lack of consensus in supervision. *Journal of Marital & Family Therapy, 26,* 373–384.

Ray, D., & Altekruse, M. (2000). Effectiveness of group supervision versus combined group and individual supervision. *Counselor Education & Supervision, 40,* 19–30.

Recupero, P. R., & Rainey, S. E. (2007). Liability and risk management in outpatient psychotherapy supervision. *The Journal of the American Academy of Psychiatry & the Law, 35*(2), 188–195. Retrieved January 2, 2012, from www.jaapl.org/content/35/2/188.full.pdf+html

Reese, R. J., Usher, E. L., Bowman, D. C., Norsworthy, L. A., Halstead, J. L., Rowlands, S. R., & Chisholm, R. R. (2009). Using client feedback in psychotherapy training: An analysis of its influence on supervision and counselor self-efficacy. *Training & Education in Professional Psychology, 3*(3), 157–168.

Reichelt, S., Gullestad, S.E., Hansen, BR Rønnestad, M. H., Torgersen, A. M., Jacobsen, C. H., . . . , & Skjerve, J. (2009). Nondisclosure in psychotherapy group supervision: The supervisee perspective. *Nordic Psychology, 61*(4), 5–27.

Reid, E., McDaniel, S., Donaldson, C., & Tollers, M. (1987). Taking it personally: Issues of personal authority and competence for the female in family therapy training. *Journal of Marital & Family Therapy, 13,* 157–165.

Reiser, R. P., & Milne, D. (2012). Supervising cognitive–behavioral psychotherapy: Pressing needs, impressing possibility. *Journal of Contemporary Psychotherapy, 42,* 161–171.

Reising, G. N., & Daniels, M. H. (1983). A study of Hogan's model of counselor development and supervision. *Journal of Counseling Psychology, 30,* 235–244.

Remley, T. R., Jr., & Herlihy, B. (2001). *Ethical, legal, and professional issues in counseling.* Upper Saddle River, NJ: Prentice-Hall.

Renfro-Michel, E. L. (2006). *The relationship between counseling supervisee attachment orientation and supervision working alliance.* Unpublished doctoral dissertation, Mississippi State University.

Resnick, R. F., & Estrup, L. (2000). Supervision: A collaborative endeavor. *Gestalt Review, 4,* 121–137.

Retzinger, S. M. (1998). Shame in the therapeutic relationship. In P. Gilbert & B. Andrews (Eds.), *Shame: Interpersonal behavior, psychopathology, and culture* (pp. 206–222). New York, NY: Oxford University Press.

Rice, L. N. (1980). A client-centered approach to the supervision of psychotherapy. In A. K. Hess (Ed.), *Psychotherapy supervision: Theory, research and practice* (pp. 136–147). New York, NY: Wiley.

Richman, J. M., Aitken, D., & Prather, D. L. (1990). Intherapy consultation: A supervisory and therapeutic experience from practice. *The Clinical Supervisor, 8*(2), 81–89.

Rickert, V. L., & Turner, J. E. (1978). Through the looking glass: Supervision in family therapy. *Social Casework, 59,* 131–137.

Rigazio-DiGilio, S. A. (1995). The four SCDS cognitive–developmental orientations. Unpublished document.

Rigazio-DiGilio, S. A. (1997). Integrative supervision: Pathways to tailoring the supervisory process. In T. C. Todd & C. L. Storm (Eds.), *The complete systemic supervisor: Context, philosophy, and pragmatics* (pp. 195–216). Needham Heights, MA: Allyn & Bacon.

Rigazio-DiGilio, S. A., & Anderson, S. A. (1994). A cognitive–developmental model for marital and family therapy supervision. *The Clinical Supervisor, 12*(2), 93–118.

Rigazio-DiGilio, S. A., Daniels, T. G., & Ivey, A. E. (1997). Systemic Cognitive–Developmental Supervision: A developmental–integrative approach to psychotherapy supervision. In C. E. Watkins, Jr. (Ed.), *Handbook of psychotherapy supervision* (pp. 223–249). New York, NY: John Wiley & Sons, Inc.

Riggs, S. A., & Bretz, K. M. (2006). Attachment processes in the supervisory relationship: An exploratory investigation. *Professional Psychology: Research and Practice, 37,* 558–566.

Rings, J., Genuchi, M. C., Hall, M. D., Angelo, M.-A., & Cornish, J. E. (2009). Is there consensus among predoctoral internship training directors regarding clinical supervision competencies? A descriptive analysis. *Training and Education in Professional Psychology, 3*(3), 140–147.

Rioch, M. J., Coulter, W. R., & Weinberger, D. M. (1976). *Dialogues for therapists: Dynamics of learning and supervision.* San Francisco, CA: Jossey-Bass.

Rita, E. S. (1998). Solution-focused supervision. *The Clinical Supervisor, 17*(2), 127–139.

Riva, M. T., & Cornish, J. A. E. (1995). Group supervision practices at psychology predoctoral internship programs: A national survey. *Professional Psychology: Research & Practice, 26,* 523–525.

Riva, M. T., & Cornish, J. A. E. (2008). Group supervision practices at psychology predoctoral internship programs: 15 years later. *Training & Education in Professional Psychology, 2,* 18–25.

Roberts, J. (1997). Reflecting processes and "supervision": Looking at ourselves as we work with others. In T. C. Todd & C. L. Storm (Eds.), *The complete systemic supervisor: Context, philosophy, and pragmatics* (pp. 334–348). Boston: Allyn & Bacon.

Roberts, W. B., Morotti, A. A., Herrick, C., & Tilbury, R. (2001). Site supervisors of professional school counseling interns: Suggested guidelines. *Professional School Counseling, 4,* 208–215.

Robiner, W. N. (2008) Addressing professional competence problems in trainees: Managing hot potatoes with heightened ethical awareness. *Professional Psychology: Research & Practice, 39,* 589–599.

Robiner, W. N., Fuhrman, M., & Ristvedt, S. (1993). Evaluation difficulties in supervising psychology interns. *The Clinical Psychologist, 46,* 3–13.

Robiner, W. N., Fuhrman, M., Ristvedt, S. L., Bobbit, B., & Schirvar, J. (1994). The Minnesota Supervisory Inventory (MSI): Development, psychometric characteristics, and supervisory evaluation issues. *The Clinical Psychologist, 47,* 4–17.

Robiner, W. N., Saltzman, S. R., Hoberman, H. M., Semrud-Clikeman, M., & Schirvar, J. A. (1997). Psychology supervisors' bias in evaluations and letters of recommendation. *The Clinical Supervisor, 16*(2), 49–72.

Robinson, W. L., & Reid, P. T. (1985). Sexual intimacies in psychology revisited. *Professional Psychology: Research & Practice, 16,* 512–520.

Robyak, J. E., Goodyear, R. K., & Prange, M. (1987). Effects of supervisors' sex, focus, and experience on preferences for interpersonal power bases. *Counselor Education & Supervision, 26,* 299–309.

Rock, M. L. (1997). Effective supervision. In M. R. Rock (Ed.), *Psychodynamic supervision: Perspectives of the supervisor and supervisee* (pp. 107–132). Northvale, NJ: Jason Aronson, Inc.

Rodenhauser, P. (1994). Toward a multidimensional model for psychotherapy supervision based on developmental stages. *Journal of Psychotherapy Practice & Research, 3,* 1–15.

Rodenhauser, P. (1996). On the future of psychotherapy supervision in psychiatry. *Academic Psychiatry, 20,* 82–91.

Rodenhauser, P. (1997). Psychotherapy supervision: Prerequisites and problems in the process. In C. E. Watkins (Ed.), *Handbook of psychotherapy supervision* (pp. 527–548). New York, NY: John Wiley.

Rodolfa, E., Bent, R., Eisman, E., Nelson, P., Rehm, L., & Ritchie, P. (2005). A cube model for competency development: Implications for psychology educators and regulators. *Professional Psychology: Research and Practice, 36,* 347–354.

Rodolfa, E., Rowen, H., Steier, D., Nicassio, T., & Gordon, J. (1994). Sexual dilemmas in internship training: What's a good training director to do? *APPIC Newsletter, 19*(2), 1, 22–24.

Rodway, M. R. (1991). Motivation and team building of supervisors in a multi-service setting. *The Clinical Supervisor, 9*(2), 161–169.

Rogers, C. R. (1942). The use of electrically recorded interviews in improving psychotherapeutic techniques. *American Journal of Orthopsychiatry, 12,* 429–434.

Rogers, C. R. (1951). *Client-centered therapy.* Boston, MA: Houghton-Mifflin.

Rogers, C. R. (1957). Training individuals to engage in the therapeutic process. In C. R. Strother (Ed.), *Psychology and mental health* (pp. 76–92). Washington, DC: American Psychological Association.

Rogers, C. R., Gendlin, E. T., Kiesler, D. J., & Truax, C. B. (Eds.). (1967). *The therapeutic relationship and its impact: A study of psychotherapy with schizophrenics.* Madison, WI: University of Wisconsin Press.

Rogers, G., & McDonald, P. L. (1995). Expedience over education: Teaching methods used by field instructors. *The Clinical Supervisor, 13*(2), 41–65.

Romans, J. S. C., Boswell, D. L., Carlozzi, A. F., & Ferguson, D. B. (1995). Training and supervision practices in clinical, counseling, and school psychology programs. *Professional Psychology: Research & Practice, 26,* 407–412.

Rønnestad, M. H., & Lundquist, K. (2009).The Brief Supervisory Alliance Scale—Trainee Form. Unpublished manuscript. Department of Psychology, University of Oslo.

Rønnestad, M. H., & Skovholt, T. M. (1993). Supervision of beginning and advanced graduate students of counseling and psychotherapy. *Journal of Counseling and Development, 71,* 396–405.

Rønnestad, M. H., & Skovholt, T. M. (2003). The journey of the counselor and therapist: Research findings and perspectives on professional development. *Journal of Career Development, 30,* 5–44.

Rønnestad, M. H., Orlinsky, D. E., Parks, B. K., & Davis, J. D. (1997). Supervisors of psychotherapy: Mapping experience level and supervisory confidence. *European Psychologist, 2,* 191–201.

Rosen-Galvin, C. M. (2005). Values, spirituality, and religious topics discussed in counseling supervision. *Dissertation Abstracts International Section A: Humanities and Social Sciences,* 65(9-A).

Rosenbaum, M., & Ronen, T. (1998). Clinical supervision from the standpoint of cognitive–behavior therapy. *Psychotherapy: Theory, Research, Practice, Training, 35,* 220–230.

Rosenberg, J. I. (2006). Real-time training: Transfer of knowledge through computer-mediated, real-time feedback. *Professional Psychology: Research & Practice, 37,* 539–546.

Rosenberg, J. I., Getzelman, M. A., Arcinue, F., & Oren, C. Z. (2005). An exploratory look at students' experiences of problematic peers in academic professional psychology programs. *Professional Psychology: Research & Practice, 36,* 665–673.

Rosenblum, A. F., & Raphael, F. B. (1987). Students at risk in the field practicum and implications for field teaching. *The Clinical Supervisor, 5*(3), 53–63.

Rosenthal, L. (1999). Group supervision of groups: A modern analytic perspective. *International Journal of Group Psychotherapy, 49,* 197–213.

Ross, L. (1977). The intuitive psychologist and his shortcomings: Distortions in the attribution process. In L. Berkowitz (Ed.), *Advances in experimental social psychology* (Vol. 10). New York, NY: Academic Press.

Ross, W. D. (1930). *The right and the good.* Oxford: Oxford University Press.

Roth, A. D., & Pilling, S. (2008). *The competence framework for the supervision of psychological therapies.* Unpublished document. Retrieved online January 25, 2012, from www.ucl.ac.uk/clinical-psychology/CORE/core_homepage.htm

Roth, A. D., & Pilling, S. (2008). *The competence framework for the supervision of psychological therapies.* Unpublished document. Retrieved January 25, 2011, from www.ucl.ac.uk/clinical-psychology/CORE/core_homepage.htm

Roth, A. D., Pilling, S., & Turner, J. (2010). Therapist training and supervision in clinical trials: implications for clinical practice. *Behavioural and cognitive psychotherapy, 38,* 291–302.

Rousmaniere, T., & Frederickson, J. (2012). *Internet-based one-way-mirror supervision for advanced, post-graduate training.* Unpublished manuscript.

Rubin, L. J., Hampton, B. R., McManus, P. W. (1997). Sexual harassment of students by professional psychology educators: A national survey. *Sex Roles, 37,* 753–771.

Rubin, N. J., Bebeau, M., Leigh, I. W., Lichtenberg, J. W., Nelson, P. D., Portnoy, S., Smith, I. L., & Kaslow, N. (2007). The competency movement within psychology: An historical perspective. *Professional Psychology: Research and Practice, 38*(5), 452–462. doi:10.1037/0735-7028.38.5.452

Rubinstein, M., & Hammond, D. (1982). The use of videotape in psychotherapy supervision. In M. Blumenfield (Ed.), *Applied supervision in psychotherapy* (pp. 143–164). New York, NY: Grune & Stratton.

Rumsfeld, D. (2002, June 6). News transcript: Secretary Rumsfeld Press Conference at NATO Headquarters, Brussels, Belgium. Retrieved from www.defense.gov/transcripts/transcript.aspx?transcriptid=3490

Russell, C. S., DuPree, W. J., Beggs, M. A., Peterson, C. M., & Anderson, M. P. (2007). Responding to remediation and gatekeeping challenges in supervision. *Journal of Marital & Family Therapy, 33,* 227–244.

Russell, G. M., & Greenhouse, E. M. (1997). Homophobia in the supervisory relationship: An invisible intruder. *Psychoanalytic Review, 84*(1), 27–42.

Russell, C. S., & Peterson, C. M. (2003). Student impairment and remediations in accredited marriage and family therapy programs. *Journal of Marital & Family Therapy, 29,* 329–337.

Russell, R. K., Crimmings, A. M., & Lent, R. W. (1984). Counselor training and supervision: Theory and research. In S. D. Brown & R. W. Lent (Eds.), *Handbook of counseling psychology* (pp. 625–681). New York, NY: John Wiley & Sons.

Russell, R. K., & Petrie, T. (1994). Issues in training effective supervisors. *Applied & Preventive Psychology, 3,* 27–42.

Ryde, J. (2000). Supervising across difference. *International Journal of Psychotherapy, 5*(1), 37–48.

Ryde, J. (2011). Culturally sensitive supervision. In C. Lago (Ed.), *The handbook of transcultural counselling and psychotherapy.* (pp. 94–104). New York, NY: Open University Press.

Ryder, R., & Hepworth, J. (1990). AAMFT ethical code: "Dual relationships." *Journal of Marital & Family Therapy, 16,* 127–132.

Saba, G. W. (1999). Live supervision: Lessons learned from behind the mirror. *Academic Medicine: Journal of the Association of American Medical Colleges, 74,* 856–858.

Sabnani, H. B., Ponterotto, J. G., & Borodovsky, L. G. (1991). White racial identity development and cross-cultural counselor training: A stage model. *The Counseling Psychologist, 19,* 76–102.

Safran, J. D., & Muran, J. C. (1996). The resolution of ruptures in the therapeutic alliance. *Journal of Consulting & Clinical Psychology, 64,* 447–458.

Safran, J. D., & Muran, J. C. (2000). Resolving therapeutic alliance ruptures: Diversity and integration. *Journal of Clinical Psychology: In Session: Psychotherapy in Practice, 56,* 233–243.

Safran, J. D., Muran, J. C., & Eubanks-Carter, C. (2011). Repairing alliance ruptures. *Psychotherapy, 48,* 80–87.

Sagrestano, L. M. (1992). Power strategies in interpersonal relationships. *Psychology of Women Quarterly, 16,* 439–447.

Sakinofsky, I. (1979). Evaluating the competence of psychotherapists. *Canadian Journal of Psychiatry, 24,* 193–205.

Saltzburg, S., Greene, G. J., & Drew, H. (2010). Using live supervision in field education: Preparing social work students for clinical practice. *Family in Society: The Journal of Contemporary Social Services, 91,* 293–299.

Samuel, S. E., & Gorton, G. E. (1998). National survey of psychology internship directors regarding education for prevention of psychologist–patient sexual exploitation. *Professional Psychology: Research & Practice, 29,* 86–90.

Sansbury, D. L. (1982). Developmental supervision from a skill perspective. *The Counseling Psychologist, 10*(1), 53–57.

Sapyta, J., Riemer, M., & Bickman, L. (2005). Feedback to clinicians: Theory, research, and practice. *Journal of Clinical Psychology, 61,* 145–153.

Sarnat, J. E. (2010). Key competencies of the psychodynamic psychotherapist and how to teach them in supervision. *Psychotherapy: Theory, Research, Practice, Training, 47,* 20–27.

Sarnat, J. E. (2012). Supervising psychoanalytic psychotherapy: Present knowledge, pressing needs, future possibilities. *Journal of Contemporary Psychotherapy, 42,* 151–160.

Sarnat, J. E., & Frawley-O'Dea, M. G. (2001, April). *Supervisory relationship: Contemporary psychodynamic approach.* Discussion hour (S. A. Pizer, moderator) at the 21st Annual Spring meeting of the APA Division of Psychoanalysis, Sante Fe, NM.

Saxe, J. D. (1865). The blind men and the elephant. In *Clever stories of many nations.* Boston, MA: Ticknor & Fields. Retrieved January 1, 2008, from www.noogenesis.com/pineapple/blind_men_elephant.html

Scaife, J. (2001). *Supervision in the mental health professions: A practitioner's guide.* Philadelphia, PA: Taylor & Francis.

Scanlon, C. R., & Gold, J. M. (1996). The balance between the missions of training and service at a university counseling center. *The Clinical Supervisor, 14*(1), 163–173.

Scarborough, J. L., Bernard, J. M., & Morse, R. E. (2006). Boundary considerations between doctoral students and master's students. *Counseling & Values, 51,* 53–65.

Scaturo, D. J. (2012). Supervising integrative psychotherapy in the 21st century: Pressing needs, impressing possibilities. *Journal of Contemporary Psychotherapy, 42,* 183–192.

Schein, E. (1973). *Professional education.* New York, NY: McGraw-Hill.

Schimel, J. L. (1984). In pursuit of truth: An essay on an epistemological approach to psychoanalytic supervision. In L. Caligor, P. M. Bromberg, & J. D. Meltzer (Eds.), *Clinical perspectives on the supervision of psychoanalysis and psychotherapy* (pp. 231–241). New York, NY: Plenum Press.

Schlenker, B. R. (1980). *Impression management: The self-concept, social identity, and interpersonal relations.* Monterey, CA: Brooks/Cole.

Schlenker, B. R., & Leary, M. R. (1982). Social anxiety and self-presentation: A conceptualization and model. *Psychological Bulletin, 92,* 641–669.

Schneider, S. (1992). Transference, counter-transference, projective identification and role responsiveness in the supervisory process. *The Clinical Supervisor, 10*(2), 71–84.

Schön, D. (1983). *The reflective practitioner: How professionals think in action.* New York, NY: Basic Books.

Schön, D. A. (1987). *Educating a reflective practitioner.* San Francisco, CA: Jossey–Bass.

Schrag, K. (1994). Disclosing homosexuality. *The Supervisor Bulletin, VII*(1), 3, 7.

Schreiber, P., & Frank, E. (1983). The use of a peer supervision group by social work clinicians. *The Clinical Supervisor, 1*(1), 29–36.

Schroll, J. T., & Walton, R. N. (1991). The interaction of supervision needs with technique and context in the practice of live supervision. *The Clinical Supervisor, 9*(1), 1–14.

Schuck, K. D., & Liddle, B. J. (2001). Religious conflicts experienced by lesbian, gay and bisexual individuals. *Journal of Gay & Lesbian Psychotherapy, 5,* 63–82.

Schultz, J. C., & Finger, C. (2003). Distance-based clinical supervision: Suggestions for technology utilization. *Rehabilitation Education, 17,* 95–99.

Schultz, J. C., Ososkie, J. N., Fried, J. H., Nelson, R. E., & Bardos, A. N. (2002). Clinical supervision in public rehabilitation counseling settings. *Rehabilitation Counseling Bulletin, 45,* 213–222.

Schutz, B. M. (1982). *Legal liability in psychotherapy.* San Francisco, CA: Jossey-Bass.

Schwartz, R. C., Liddle, H. A., & Breunlin, D. C. (1988). Muddles in live supervision. In A. A. Liddle, D. C. Breunlin, & R. C. Schwartz (Eds.), *Handbook of family therapy training and supervision* (pp. 183–193). New York, NY: The Guilford Press.

Schwartz, S. J., Unger, J. B., Zamboanga, B. L., & Szapocznik, J. (2010). Rethinking the concept of acculturation: Implications for theory and research. *American Psychologist, 65,* 237–251.

Scott, K. J., Ingram, K. M., Vitanza, S. A., & Smith, N. G. (2000). Training in supervision: A survey of current practices. *The Counseling Psychologist, 28,* 403–422.

Searles, H. (1955). The informational value of the supervisor's emotional experiences. *Psychiatry, 18;* 135–146.

Sechrest, L., Brewer, M. B., Garfield, S. L., Jackson, J. S., Kurz, R. B., Messick, S. J., . . . , & Thompson, R. F. (1982). *Report of the task force on the evaluation of education, training, and service in psychology.* Washington, DC: American Psychological Association.

Sells, J. N., Goodyear, R. K., Lichtenberg, J. W., & Polkinghorne, D. E. (1997). Relationship of supervisor and trainee gender to in-session verbal behavior and ratings of trainee skills. *Journal of Counseling Psychology, 44,* 1–7.

Sen, A. (2009). *The idea of justice.* Cambridge, MA: Belknap Press of Harvard University Press.

Seo, Y. S. (2010). Individualism, collectivism, client expression, and counselor effectiveness among South Korean international students. *The Counseling Psychologist, 38*(6), 824–847.

Shapiro, C. H. (1988). Burnout in social work field instructors. *The Clinical Supervisor, 6*(4), 237–248.

Shaw, B. F., & Dobson, K. S. (1988). Competency judgments in the training and evaluation of psychotherapists. *Journal of Consulting & Clinical Psychology, 56,* 666–672.

Shechtman, Z., & Wirzberger, A. (1999). Need and preferred style of supervision among Israeli school counselors at different stages of professional development. *Journal of Counseling & Development, 77,* 456–464.

Shelton, K., & Delgado-Romero, E. A. (2011). Sexual orientation microaggressions: The experience of lesbian, gay, bisexual, and queer clients in psychotherapy. *Journal of Counseling Psychology, 58,* 210–221.

Shen-Miller, D. S., Grus, C. L., Van Sickle, K.S., Schwartz-Mette, R., Cage, E. A., Elman, N. S., . . . , & Kaslow, N.J. (2011). Trainees' experiences with peers having competence problems: A national survey. *Training & Education in Professional Psychology, 5,* 112–121.

Sherry, P. (1991). Ethical issues in the conduct of supervision. *The Counseling Psychologist, 19,* 566–584.

Shilts, L., Rudes, J., & Madigan, S. (1993). The use of a solution-focused interview with a reflecting team format: Evolving thoughts from clinical practice. *Journal of Systemic Therapies, 12*(1), 1–10.

Shoben, E. J. (1962). The counselor's theory as personal trait. *Personnel and Guidance Journal, 40,* 617–621.

Shulman, L. (2010). *Interactional supervision* (3rd ed.) Washington, DC: NASW Press.

Shulman, L. S. (2005a, February 6–8). The signature pedagogies of the professions of law, medicine, engineering, and the clergy: potential lessons for the education of teachers. Presentation at the math science partnerships (msp) workshop: Teacher education for effective teaching and learning. Hosted by the national research council's center for education, Irvine, CA. Retrieved December 28, 2007, from www.taylorprograms.com/images/Shulman_Signature_Pedagogies.pdf

Shulman, L. S. (2005b). Signature pedagogies in the professions. *Daedalus, 134,* 52–59.

Siegel, M. (1979). Privacy, ethics and confidentiality. *Professional Psychology, 10,* 249–258.

Simon, R. (1982). Beyond the one-way mirror. *Family Therapy Networker, 26*(5), 19, 28–29, 58–59.

Singh, A., & Chun, K. Y. S. (2010). "From the margins to the center": Moving towards a resilience-based model of supervision for queer people of color supervisors. *Training & Education in Professional Psychology, 4*(1), 36–46.

Skjerve, J., Nielsen, G., Jacobsen, C. H., Gullestad, S. E., Hansen, B. R., Reichelt, S., . . . , & Torgersen, A. M. (2009). Nondisclosure in psychotherapy group supervision: The supervisor perspective. *Nordic Psychology, 61*(4), 28–48.

Skovholt, T. (2012). *Becoming a therapist: On the path to mastery.* New York, NY: John Wiley & Sons.

Skovholt, T. M., & Rønnestad, M. H. (1992a). *The evolving professional self: Stages and themes in therapist and counselor development.* Chichester, UK: Wiley.

Skovholt, T. M., & Rønnestad, M. H. (1992b). Themes in therapist and counselor development. *Journal of Counseling and Development, 70,* 505–515.

Skovholt, T. M., & Rønnestad, M. H. (1995). *The evolving professional self: Stages and themes in therapist and counselor development.* Chichester, UK: Wiley.

Slater, L. (2003, January 26). Full disclosure. *New York Times.* Retrieved February 2003 from www.nytimes.com/2003/01/26/magazine/26WWLN.html

Slavin, J. H. (1994). On making rules: Toward a reformulation of the dynamics of transference in psychoanalytic treatment. *Psychoanalytic Dialogues, 4,* 253–274.

Sloan, G., & Watson, H. (2001). John Heron's six-category intervention analysis: Towards understanding interpersonal relations and progressing the delivery of clinical supervision for mental health nursing in the United Kingdom. *Journal of Advanced Nursing, 36,* 206–214.

Smadi, A. A., & Landreth, G. G. (1988). Reality therapy supervision with a counselor from a different theoretical orientation. *Journal of Reality Therapy, 7*(2), 18–26.

Smith, C. R., & Pride, M. (2011). *Reciprocal Supervision Agreement: Development and uses.* American Psychological Association National Conference, Washington, DC.

Smith, J. L., Amrhein, P. C., Brooks, A. C., Carpenter, K. M., Levin, D., Schreiber, E. A., . . . , & Nunes, E. V. (2007). Providing live supervision via teleconferencing improves acquisition of motivational interviewing skills after workshop attendance. *American Journal of Drug & Alcohol Abuse, 22,* 163–168.

Smith, R. C., Mead, D. E., & Kinsella, J. A. (1998). Direct supervision: Adding computer-assisted feedback & data capture to live supervision. *Journal of Marital & Family Therapy, 24,* 113–125.

Smith, T. B., Constantine, M. G., Dunn, T. W, Dinehart, J. M., & Montoya, J. A. (2006). Multicultural education in the mental health professions: A meta-analytic review. *Journal of Counseling Psychology, 53,* 132–145.

Smith, T. E., Yoshioka, M., & Winton, M. (1993). A qualitative understanding of reflecting teams: I. Client perspectives. *Journal of Systemic Therapies, 12,* 28–43.

Snider, P. D. (1985). The duty to warn: A potential issue of litigation for the counseling supervisor. *Counselor Education & Supervision, 25,* 66–73.

Snider, P. D. (1987). Client records: Inexpensive liability protection for mental health counselors. *Journal of Mental Health Counseling, 9,* 134–141.

Sobell, L. C., Manor, H. L, Sobell, M. B., & Dum, M. (2008). Self-critiques of audiotaped therapy sessions: A motivational procedure for facilitating feedback during supervision. *Training & Education in Professional Psychology, 3,* 151–155.

Sodowsky, G. R., Taffe, R. C., Gutkin, T. B., & Wise, S. L. (1994). Development of the Multicultural Counseling Inventory: A self-report measure of multicultural competencies. *Journal of Counseling Psychology, 41,* 137–148.

Soisson, E. L., Vandecreek, L., & Knapp, S. (1987). Thorough record keeping: A good defense in a litigious era. *Professional Psychology: Research & Practice, 18,* 498–502.

Sommer, C. A., & Cox, J. A. (2003). Using Greek mythology as a metaphor to enhance supervision. *Counselor Education & Supervision, 42,* 326–335.

Sommer, C. A., & Cox, J. A. (2005). Elements of supervision in sexual violence counselors' narratives: A qualitative analysis. *Counselor Education & Supervision, 45,* 119–134.

Sommer, C. A., & Cox, J. A. (2006). Sexual violence counselors' reflections on supervision: Using stories to mitigate vicarious traumatization. *Journal of Poetry Therapy, 19*(1), 3–16.

Son, E. J., Ellis, M. V., & Yoo, S. (in press). Clinical supervision in South Korea and the U.S.: A comparative descriptive study. *The Counseling Psychologist, 40.*

Son, E. J., Ellis, M. V., & Yoo, S. K. (2007). The relations among supervisory working alliance, role difficulties, and supervision satisfaction: A cross-cultural comparison. *Korean Journal of Psychology, 26,* 161–162.

Sparks, D., & Loucks-Horsley, S. (1989). Five models of staff development for teachers. *Journal of Staff Development, 10*(4), 40–57.

Speed, B., Seligman, P. M., Kingston, P., & Cade, B. W. (1982). A team approach to therapy. *Journal of Family Therapy, 4,* 271–284.

Speight, S. L., & Vera, E. M. (2004). A social justice agenda: Ready, or not? *The Counseling Psychologist, 32,* 109–118.

Spelliscy, D., Chen, E. C., & Zusho, A. (2007, August). *Predicting supervisee role conflict and ambiguity: A path analytic model.* Paper presented at the annual meeting of the American Psychological Association, San Francisco, CA.

Sperling, M. B., Pirrotta, S., Handen, B. L., Simons, L. A., Miller, D., Lysiak, G., . . . , & Terry, L. (1986). The collaborative team as a training and therapeutic tool. *Counselor Education & Supervision, 25,* 183–190.

Spotnitz, H. (1969). *Modern psychoanalysis of the schizophrenic patient.* New York, NY: Grune & Stratton.

Steele, C. M. & Aronson, J. (1995). Stereotype threat and the intellectual test performance of African-Americans. *Journal of Personality & Social Psychology, 69,* 797–811.

Stein, D. M., & Lambert, M. J. (1995). Graduate training in psychotherapy: Are therapy outcomes enhanced? *Journal of Consulting and Clinical Psychology, 63,* 182–196.

Stenack, R. J., & Dye, H. A. (1982). Behavioral descriptions of counseling supervision roles. *Counselor Education and Supervision, 22,* 295–304.

Sterling, M. M., & Bugental, J. F. (1993). The meld experience in psychotherapy supervision. *Journal of Humanistic Psychology, 33,* 38–48.

Sterner, W. (2009). Influence of the supervisory working alliance on supervisee work satisfaction and work-related stress. *Journal of Mental Health Counseling, 31,* 249–263.

Sternitzke, M. E., Dixon, D. N., & Ponterotto, J. G. (1988). An attributional approach to counselor supervision. *Counselor Education & Supervision, 28,* 5–14.

Stevens-Smith, P. (1995). Gender issues in counselor education: Current status ad challenges. *Counselor Education & Supervision, 34,* 283–293.

Stevens, D. T., Goodyear, R. K., & Robertson, P. (1997). Supervisor development: An exploratory study in changes in stance and emphasis. *The Clinical Supervisor, 16,* 73–88.

Steward, R. J., Breland, A., & Neil, D. M. (2001). Novice supervisees' self-evaluations and their perceptions of supervisor style. *Counselor Education & Supervision, 41,* 131–141.

Stiles, W. B., Shapiro, D. A., & Firth-Cozens, J. A. (1988). Do sessions of different treatments have different impacts? *Journal of Counseling Psychology, 35,* 391–396.

Stinchfield, T. A., Hill, N. R., & Kleist, D. M. (2007). The reflective model of triadic supervision: Defining an emerging modality. *Counselor Education & Supervision, 46,* 172–183.

Stinchfield, T. A., Hill, N. R., & Kleist, D. M. (2010). Counselor trainees' experiences in triadic supervision: A qualitative exploration of transcendent themes. *International Journal for the Advancement of Counselling, 32,* 225–239.

Stoltenberg, C. (1981). Approaching supervision from a developmental perspective: The counselor–complexity model. *Journal of Counseling Psychology, 28,* 59–65.

Stoltenberg, C., & Delworth, U. (1987). *Supervising counselors and therapists.* San Francisco, CA: Jossey-Bass.

Stoltenberg, C. D., & McNeill, B. W. (2010). *IDM Supervision: An integrative developmental model for supervising counselors & therapists* (3rd ed.). New York, NY: Routledge.

Stoltenberg, C. D., McNeill, B. W., & Crethar, H. C. (1994). Changes in supervision as counselors and therapists gain experience: A review. *Professional Psychology: Research & Practice, 25,* 416–449.

Stoltenberg, C. D., McNeill, B. W., & Crethar, H. C. (1995). Persuasion and development in counselor supervision. *The Counseling Psychologist, 23,* 633–648.

Stoltenberg, C. D., McNeill, B. W., & Delworth, U. (1998). *IDM: An Integrated Developmental Model for supervising counselors and therapists.* San Francisco, CA: Jossey-Bass.

Stoltenberg, C. D., Pierce, R. A., & McNeill, B. W. (1987). Effects of experience on counselors needs. *The Clinical Supervisor, 5,* 23–32.

Stoppard, J. M., & Miller, A. (1985). Conceptual level matching in therapy: A review. *Current Psychological Research & Reviews, 4,* 47–68.

Storm, C. L., & Haug, I. E. (1997). Ethical issues: Where do you draw the line? In T. C. Todd & C. L. Storm (Eds.), *The complete systemic supervisor: Context, philosophy, and pragmatics* (pp. 26–40). Boston, MA: Allyn & Bacon.

Storm, C. L., McDowell, T., & Long, J. K. (2003). The metamorphosis of training and supervision. In T. L. Sexton, G. R. Weeks, & M. S. Robbins (Eds.), *Handbook of family therapy: The science and practice of working with families and couples* (pp. 431–446). New York: Brunner-Routledge.

Storm, C. L., Todd, T. C., & Sprenkle, D. H. (2001). Gaps between MFT supervision assumptions and common practice: Suggested best practices. *Journal of Marital and Family Therapy, 27,* 227–239.

Storm, H. A. (1994). *Enhancing the acquisition of psychotherapy skills through live supervision.* Paper presented at the annual meeting of the American Psychological Association, Los Angeles.

Stout, C. E. (1987). The role of ethical standards in the supervision of psychotherapy. *The Clinical Supervisor, 5*(1), 89–97.

Strassle, C. G., Borckardt, J. J., Handler, L., Nash, M. (2011). Video-tape role induction for psychotherapy: Moving forward. *Psychotherapy, 48,* 170–178.

Stratton, J. S., & Smith, R. D. (2006). Supervision of couples cases. *Psychotherapy: Theory, Research, Practice, Training, 43,* 337–348.

Strean, H. S. (2000). Resolving therapeutic impasses by using the supervisor's countertransference. *Clinical Social Work Journal, 28,* 263–279.

Strein, W., & Hershenson, D. B. (1991). Confidentiality in nondyadic counseling situations. *Journal of Counseling & Development, 69,* 312–316.

Strong, S. R. (1968). Counseling: An interpersonal influence process. *Journal of Counseling Psychology, 15,* 215–224.

Strong, S. R., & Hills, H. (1986). *Interpersonal Communication Rating Scale.* Richmond, VA: Virginia Commonwealth University.

Strong, S. R., Hills, H., & Nelson, B. (1988). *Interpersonal communication rating scale* (rev. ed.). Richmond, VA: Virginia Commonwealth University.

Strupp, H. H., & Binder, J. (1984). *Psychotherapy in a new key: A guide to time-limited dynamic psychotherapy.* New York: Basic Books.

Studer, J. R. (2005). Supervising school counselors-in-training: A guide for field supervisors. *Professional School Counseling, 8,* 353–359.

Sue, D. W., Arredondo, P., & McDavis, R. J. (1992). Multicultural counseling competencies and standards: A call to the profession. *Journal of Counseling & Development, 70,* 477–486.

Sue, D. W., Capodilupo, C. M., Torino, G. C., Bucceri, J. M., Holder, A. M. B., Nadal, K. L., & Esquilin, M. (2007). Racial microaggressions in everyday life: Implications for clinical practice. *American Psychologist, 62,* 271–286. Retrieved from www.olc.edu/local_links/socialwork/OnlineLibrary/microaggression%20article.pdf

Sue, D. W., Lin, A. I., Torino, G. C., Capodilupo, C. M., & Rivera, D. P. (2009). Racial microaggressions and difficult dialogues on race in the classroom. *Cultural Diversity & Ethnic Minority Psychology, 15,* 183–190.

Sullivan, H. S. (1953). *The interpersonal theory of psychiatry.* New York: Norton.

Sumerel, M. B., & Borders, L. D. (1996). Addressing personal issues in supervision: Impact of counselor's experience level on various aspects of the supervisory relationship. *Counselor Education and Supervision, 35,* 268–286.

Sundin, E. C., Ogren, M. L., & Boëthius, S. B. (2008). Supervisor trainees' and their supervisors' perceptions of attainment of knowledge and skills: An empirical evaluation of a psychotherapy supervisor training programme. *British Journal of Clinical Psychology, 47,* 381–396.

Supervision Interest Network, Association for Counselor Education and Supervision. (1993, Summer). ACES ethical guidelines for counseling supervisors. *ACES Spectrum, 53*(4), 5–8.

Sussman, T., Bogo, M., & Globerman, J. (2007). Field instructor perceptions in group supervision: Establishing trust through managing group dynamics. *The Clinical Supervisor, 26*(1/2), 61–80.

Sutter, E., McPherson, R. H., & Geeseman, R. (2002). Contracting for supervision. *Professional Psychology: Research & Practice, 33,* 495–498.

Sutton, J. M., Jr. (2000). Counselor licensure. In H. Hackney (Ed.), *Practice issues for the beginning counselor* (pp. 55–78). Boston, MA: Allyn & Bacon.

Swanson, J. L., & O'Saben, C. L. (1993). Differences in supervisory needs and expectations by trainee experience, cognitive style, and program membership. *Journal of Counseling & Development, 71,* 457–464.

Swenson, L. S. (1997). *Psychology and law for the helping professions* (2nd ed.). Pacific Grove, CA: Brooks/Cole.

Symons, C., Khele, S., Rogers, J., Turner, J., & Wheeler, S. (2011). Allegations of serious professional misconduct: An analysis of the British Association for Counselling and Psychotherapy's Article 4.6 cases, 1998–2007. *Counselling & Psychotherapy Research, 11,* 257–265.

Szymanski, D. M. (2003). The Feminist Supervision Scale (FSS): A rational/theoretical approach. *Psychology of Women Quarterly, 27,* 221–232.

Szymanski, D. M. (2005). Feminist identity and theories as correlates of feminist supervision practices. *The Counseling Psychologist, 33,* 729–747.

Szymanski, D. M., Carr, E. R., & Moffitt, L. B. (2010). Sexual objectification of women: Clinical implications and training considerations. *The Counseling Psychologist, 39,* 107–126.

Tabachnick, B. G., Keith-Spiegel, P., & Pope, K. S. (1991). Ethics of teaching: Beliefs and behaviors of psychologists as educators. *American Psychologist, 46,* 506–515.

Talen, M. R., & Schindler, N. (1993). Goal-directed supervision plans: A model for trainee supervision and evaluation. *The Clinical Supervisor, 11*(2), 77–88.

Tangney, J. P., Wagner, P., Fletcher, C., & Gramzow, R. (1992). Shamed into anger? The relation of shame and guilt to anger and self-reported aggression. *Journal of Personality & Social Psychology, 62,* 669–675.

Tarvydas, V. M. (1995). Ethics and the practice of rehabilitation counselor supervision. *Rehabilitation Counseling Bulletin, 38,* 294–306.

Taylor, S. E. (1991). The interface of cognitive and social psychology. In J. H. Harvey (Ed.), *Cognition, social behavior, and the environment* (pp. 189–211). Hillsdale, NJ: Erlbaum.

Tebb, S., Manning, D. W., & Klaumann, T. K. (1996). A renaissance of group supervision in practicum. *The Clinical Supervisor, 14*(2), 39–51.

Tebes, J. K., Matlin, S. L., Migdole, S. J., Farkas, M. S., Money, R. W., Shulman, L., & Hoge, M. A. (2011). Providing competency training to clinical supervisors through an interactional supervision approach. *Research on Social Work Practice, 21,* 190–199.

Teitelbaum, S. H. (1990). Supertransference: The role of the supervisor's blind spots. *Psychoanalytic Psychology, 7,* 243–258.

Tennen, H. (1988). Supervision of integrative psychotherapy: A critique. *Journal of Integrative and Eclectic Psychotherapy, 7,* 167–175.

Thomas, F. N. (1996). Solution-focused supervision: The coaxing of expertise. In S. D. Miller, M. A. Hubble, & B. L. Duncan (Eds.), *Handbook of solution-focused therapy* (pp. 128–151). San Francisco, CA: Jossey-Bass.

Thomas, J. T. (2007). Informed consent through contracting for supervision: Minimizing risks, enhancing benefits. *Professional Psychology: Research & Practice, 38,* 221–231.

Thomas, J. T. (2010). *The ethics of supervision and consultation: Practical guidance for mental health professionals.* Washington, DC: American Psychological Association.

Thorell, K. M. (2003). Spirituality and religion in supervision: Supervisors' and supervisees' perceptions. *Dissertation Abstract International, 64*(5), 1543.

Thoreson, R., Morrow, K., Frazier, P., & Kerstner, P. (1991, April). *Needs and concerns of women in AACD: Preliminary results.* Paper presented at the annual meeting of the American Association of Counseling and Development, Reno, NV.

Thyer, B. A., Sowers-Hoag, K., & Love, J. P. (1988). The influence of field instructor–student gender combinations on student perceptions of field instruction quality. *The Clinical Supervisor, 6*(3), 169–179.

Tichenor, Y, & Hill, C. E. (1989). A comparison of six measures of working alliance. *Psychotherapy, 26,* 195–199.

Topolinski, S., & Hertel, G. (2007). The role of personality in psychotherapists' careers: Relationships between personality traits, therapeutic schools, and job satisfaction. *Psychotherapy Research, 17,* 365–375.

Tracey, T. J. (1993). An interpersonal stage model of the therapeutic process. *Journal of Counseling Psychology, 40,* 396–409.

Tracey, T. J. (2002). Stages of counseling and therapy: An examination of complementarity and the working alliance. In G. S. Tryon (Ed.), *Counseling based on process research: Applying what we know* (pp. 265–297). Boston, MA: Allyn & Bacon.

Tracey, T. J. G., Bludworth, J., & Glidden-Tracey, C. E. (2012). Are there parallel processes in psychotherapy supervision? An empirical examination. *Psychotherapy, 49,* 330–343.

Tracey, T. J., Ellickson, J. L., & Sherry, P. (1989). Reactance in relation to different supervisory environments and counselor development. *Journal of Counseling Psychology, 36,* 336–344.

Tracey, T. J., Hays, K. A., Malone, J., & Herman, B. (1988). Changes in counselor response as a function of experience. *Journal of Counseling Psychology, 35,* 119–126.

Tracey, T. J., Ryan, J. M., & Jaschik-Herman, B. (2001). Complementarity of interpersonal circumplex traits. *Personality and Social Psychology Bulletin, 27,* 786–797.

Tracey, T. J., & Sherry, P. (1993). Complementary interaction over time in successful and less successful supervision. *Professional Psychology: Research & Practice, 24,* 304–311.

Triantafillou, N. (1997). A solution-focused approach to mental health supervision. *Journal of Systemic Therapies, 16,* 305–328.

Tromski-Klingshirn, D. (2006). Should the clinical supervisor be the administrative supervisor? The ethics versus the reality. *The Clinical Supervisor, 25*(1/2), 53–67.

Tromski-Klingshirn, D. M., & Davis, T. E. (2007). Supervisees' perceptions of their clinical supervision: A study of the dual role of clinical and administrative supervisor. *Counselor Education & Supervision, 46,* 294–304.

Tuckett, T. D. (2005). Does anything go? Toward a framework for the more transparent assessment of psychoanalytic competence. *International Journal of Psychoanalysis, 86,* 31–49.

Tuckman, B. W. (1965). Developmental sequence in small groups. *Psychological Bulletin, 63,* 384–399.

Tuckman, B. W., & Jensen, M. A. C. (1977). Stages of small group development revisited. *Group & Organizational Studies, 2,* 419–427.

Tudor, K., & Worrall, M. (2004). *Freedom to practise: Person-centered approaches to supervision.* Ross-on-Wye, UK: PCCS Books.

Tudor, K., & Worrall, M. (2007). *Freedom to practise: Volume II: Developing person-centered approaches to supervision.* Ross-on-Wye, UK: PCCS Books.

Turban, D. B., & Jones, A. P. (1988). Supervisor–subordinate similarity: Types, effects, and mechanisms. *Journal of Applied Psychology, 73,* 228–234.

Turban, D. B., Jones, A. P., & Rozelle, R. M. (1990). Influences of supervisor liking of a subordinate and the reward context on the treatment and evaluation of that subordinate. *Motivation & Emotion, 14,* 215–233.

Turner, J. (1993). Males supervising females: The risk of gender-power blindness. *The Supervisor Bulletin, VI,* 4, 6.

Turner, R. A., & Schabram, K. F. (2012). The bases of power revisited: An interpersonal perceptions perspective. *Journal of Organizational Psychology, 12,* 9-18.

Tversky, A., & Kahneman, D. (1974). Judgment under uncertainty: Heuristics and biases. *Science, 185,* 1124–1131.

Twohey, D., & Volker, J. (1993). Listening for the voices of care and justice in counselor supervision. *Counselor Education & Supervision, 32,* 189–197.

Usher, C. H., & Borders, L. D. (1993). Practicing counselors' preferences for supervisory style and supervisory emphasis. *Counselor Education and Supervision, 33,* 66–79.

Utsey, S. O., Gernat, C. A., & Hammar, L. (2005). Examining white counselor trainees' reactions to racial issues in counseling and supervision dyads. *The Counseling Psychologist, 33,* 449–478.

Utsey, S. O., Ponterotto, J. G., & Porter, J. S. (2008). Prejudice and racism, Year 2008—still going strong: Research on reducing prejudice with recommended methodological advances. *Journal of Counseling & Development, 86,* 339–347.

Vaccaro, A. (2010). Still chilly in 2010: Campus climates for women. *On Campus with Women, 39*(2). Online publication by the American Association of Colleges and Universities. Retrieved March 25, 2012, from www.aacu.org/ocww/volume39_2/feature.cfm?section=1

Vaccaro, N., & Lambie, G. W. (2007). Computer-based counseling-in-training supervision: Ethical and practical implications for counselor educators and supervisors. *Counselor Education & Supervision, 47,* 46–57.

Vacha-Haase, T., Davenport, D. S., & Kerewsky, S. D. (2004). Problematic students: Gatekeeping practices of academic professional psychology programs. *Professional Psychology: Research & Practice, 35,* 115–122.

Van Horne, B. A. (2004). Psychology Licensing Board disciplinary actions: The realities. *Practice, 35,* 170–178.

Vandecreek, L., Knapp, S., & Brace, K. (1990). Mandatory continuing education for licensed psychologists: Its rationale and current implementation. *Professional Psychology: Research & Practice, 21,* 135–140.

Vander Kolk, C. (1974). The relationship of personality, values, and race to anticipation of the supervisory relationship. *Rehabilitation Counseling Bulletin, 18,* 41–46.

Vandiver, B. J., Fhagen-Smith, P. E., Cokley, K., Cross, W. E., Jr., & Worrell, F. C. (2001). Cross' nigrescence model: From theory to scale to theory. *Journal of Multicultural Counseling & Development, 29,* 174–200.

Vargas, L. A. (1989, August). *Training psychologists to be culturally responsive: Issues in supervision.* Paper presented at the Annual Convention of the American Psychological Association, New Orleans, LA.

Vasquez, M. J. T. (1992). Psychologist as clinical supervisor: Promoting ethical practice. *Professional Psychology: Research & Practice, 23,* 196–202.

Vasquez, M. J. T. (2007). Sometimes a taco is just a taco! In Barnett, J. E., Lazarus, A. E., Vasquez, M. J. T., Moorehead-Slaughter, O., & Johnson, W. B.: Boundary issues and multiple relationships: Fantasy and reality. *Professional Psychology: Research & Practice, 38,* 401–410.

Vera, E. M., & Speight, S. L. (2003). Multicultural competence, social justice, and counseling psychology: Expanding our roles. *The Counseling Psychologist, 31,* 253–272.

Vespia, K. M., Heckman-Stone, C., & Delworth, U. (2002). Describing and facilitating effective supervision behavior in counseling trainees. *Psychotherapy: Theory, Research, Practice, Training, 39,* 56–65.

Vygotsky, L. S. (1978). *Mind in society: The development of higher psychological processes* (M. Cole, V. John–Steiner, S. Scribner, & E. Souberman, Eds. and Trans.). Cambridge, MA: Harvard University Press.

Walker, D. F., Gorsuch, R. L., Tan, S., & Otis, K. E. (2008). Use of religious and spiritual interventions by trainees in APA-accredited Christian clinical psychology programs. *Mental Health, Religion & Culture, 11,* 623–633.

Walker, J. A., & Gray, L. A. (2002, June). *Categorizing supervisor countertransference.* Paper presented at the annual meeting of the Society for Psychotherapy Research International Conference, Santa Barbara, CA.

Walker, J. A., Ladany, N., & Pate-Carolan, L. M. (2007). Gender-related events in psychotherapy supervision: Female trainee perspectives. *Counselling & Psychotherapy Research: Linking Research with Practice, 7,* 12–18.

Walker, R., & Clark, J. J. (1999). Heading off boundary problems: Clinical supervision as risk management. *Psychiatric Services, 50,* 1435–1439.

Walzer, R. S., & Miltimore, S. (1993). Mandated supervision: Monitoring and therapy of disciplined health care professionals. *The Journal of Legal Medicine, 14,* 565–596.

Wampold, B. E. (2001). *The great psychotherapy debate: Models, methods, and findings.* Mahwah, NJ: Lawrence Erlbaum Associates.

Wampold, B. E., Goodheart, C. D., & Levant, R. F. (2007). Clarification and elaboration on evidence-based practice in psychology. *American Psychologist, 62,* 616–618.

Warburton, J. R., Newberry, A., & Alexander, J. (1989). Women as therapists, trainees, and supervisors. In M. McGoldrick, C. Anderson, & F. Walsh (Eds.), *Women in families: A framework for family therapy* (pp. 152–165). New York, NY: Norton.

Ward, C. C., & House, R. M. (1998). Counseling supervision: A reflective model. *Counselor Education & Supervision, 38,* 23–33.

Ward, J., & Sommer, C. A., (2006). Using stories in supervision to facilitate counselor development. *Journal of Poetry Therapy, 19*(2), 1–7.

Ward, L. G., Friendlander, M. L., Schoen, L. G., & Klein, J. G. (1985). Strategic self-presentation in supervision. *Journal of Counseling Psychology, 32,* 111–118.

Wark, L. (2000). Research: Trainees talk about effective live supervision. *Readings in family therapy supervision* (p. 119). Washington, DC: American Association for Marriage & Family Therapy.

Waskett, C. (2006). The pluses of solution-focused supervision. *Healthcare Counseling and Psychotherapy Journal, 6*(1), 9–11.

Watkins, C. E. (2011). Does psychotherapy supervision contribute to patient outcomes? Considering thirty years of research. *The Clinical Supervisor, 30,* 235–256.

Watkins, C. E., Lopez, F. G., Campbell, V. L., & Himmell, C. D. (1986). Contemporary counseling psychology: Results of a national survey. *Journal of Counseling Psychology, 33,* 301–309.

Watkins, C. E., Jr. (1990a). Development of the psychotherapy supervisor. *Psychotherapy, 27,* 553–560.

Watkins, C. E., Jr. (1990b). The separation–individuation process in psychotherapy supervision. *Psychotherapy, 27,* 202–209.

Watkins, C. E., Jr. (1993a). Development of psychotherapy supervisors. *Journal of Clinical Psychology, 47,* 145–147

Watkins, C. E., Jr. (1993b). Development of the psychotherapy supervisor: Concepts, assumptions, and hypotheses of the supervisor complexity model. *American Journal of Psychotherapy, 47,* 58–74.

Watkins, C. E., Jr. (1994). The supervision of psychotherapy supervisor trainees. *American Journal of Psychotherapy, 48,* 417–431.

Watkins, C. E., Jr. (1995a). Considering psychotherapy supervisor development: A status report. *The Psychotherapy Bulletin, 29*(4), 32–34.

Watkins, C. E., Jr. (1995b). Psychotherapy supervisor & supervisee: Developmental models & research nine years later. *Clinical Psychology Review, 15,* 647–680.

Watkins, C. E., Jr. (1995c). Psychotherapy supervisor development: On musings, models, & metaphor.

Journal of Psychotherapy Practice & Research, 4, 150–158.

Watkins, C. E., Jr. (1995d). Researching psychotherapy supervisor development: Four key considerations. *The Clinical Supervisor, 13*(2), 111–118.

Watkins, C. E., Jr. (2012). On demoralization, therapist identity development, and persuasion and healing in psychotherapy supervision. *Journal of Psychotherapy Integration, 22,* 187–205.

Watkins, C. E., Jr., Schneider, L. J., Hayes, J., & Nieberding, R. (1995). Measuring psychotherapy supervisor development: An initial effort at scale development and validation. *The Clinical Supervisor, 13,* 77–90.

Watson, J. C. (2003). Computer-based supervision: Implementing computer technology into the delivery of counseling supervision. *Journal of Technology in Counseling, 3*(1).

Watson, M. F. (1993). Supervising the person of the therapist: Issues, challenges and dilemmas. Special Issue: Critical issues in marital and family therapy education. *Contemporary Family Therapy: An International Journal, 15,* 21–31.

Watzlawick, P., & Beavin, J. (1976). Some formal aspects of communication. In P. Watzlawick & J. H. Weakland (Eds.), *The interactional view* (pp. 56–67). New York, NY: Norton.

Watzlawick, P., Beavin, J. H., & Jackson, D. D. (1967). *Pragmatics of human communication: A study of interactional patterns, pathologies, and paradoxes.* New York, NY: Norton.

Webb, A., & Wheeler, S. (1998). How honest do counsellors dare to be in the supervisory relationship? An exploratory study. *British Journal of Guidance & Counselling, 26,* 509–524.

Weinstein (2007, October 15). If it's legal, it's ethical—right? *BusinessWeek.* Retrieved online, October 28, 2012, from www.businessweek.com/stories/2007-10-15/if-its-legal-its-ethical-right-businessweek-business-news-stock-market-and-financial-advice

Welfare, L. E., & Borders, L. D. (2010a). The counselor cognitions questionnaire: Development and validation. *The Clinical Supervisor, 29,* 188–208.

Welfare, L. E., & Borders, L. D. (2010b). Counselor cognitions: General and domain-specific complexity. *Counselor Education & Supervision, 49,* 162–178.

Wendorf, D. J. (1984). A model for training practicing professionals in family therapy. *Journal of Marital & Family Therapy, 10,* 31–41.

Wendorf, D. J., Wendorf, R. J., & Bond, O. (1985). Growth behind the mirror: The family therapy consortiums' group process. *Journal of Marriage & Family Therapy, 11,* 245–255.

West, J. D., Bubenzer, D. L., Pinsoneault, T., & Holeman, V. (1993). Three supervision modalities for training marital and family counselors. Special Section: Marriage and family counselor training. *Counselor Education & Supervision, 33,* 127–138.

West, J. D., Bubenzer, D. L., & Zarski, J. J. (1989). Live supervision in family therapy: An interview with Barbara Oken and Fred Piercy. *Counselor Education & Supervision, 29,* 25–34.

West, W. (2003). The culture of psychotherapy supervision. *Counselling and Psychotherapy Research, 3,* 123–127.

Wester, S. R., Christianson, H. F., Fouad, N. A., & Santiago-Rivera, A. L. (2008). Information processing as problem solving: A collaborative approach to dealing with students exhibiting insufficient competence. *Training and Education in Professional Psychology, 2*(4), 193–201.

Wester, S. R., & Vogel, D. L. (2002). Working with the masculine mystique: Male gender role conflict, counseling self-efficacy, and the training of male psychologists. *Professional Psychology: Research & Practice, 33,* 370–376.

Wester, S. R., Vogel, D. L., & Archer, J., Jr. (2004). Male restricted emotionality and counseling supervision. *Journal of Counseling & Development, 82,* 91–98.

Wetchler, J. L. (1989). Supervisors' and supervisees' perceptions of the effectiveness of family therapy supervisor interpersonal skills. *American Journal of Family Therapy, 17,* 244–256.

Wetchler, J. L., Piercy, F. P., & Sprenkle, D. H. (1989). Supervisors' and supervisees' perceptions of the effectiveness of family therapy supervisory techniques. *The American Journal of Family Therapy, 17,* 35–47.

Wetchler, J. L., & Vaughn, K. A. (1992). Perceptions of primary family therapy supervisory techniques: A critical incident analysis. *Contemporary Family Therapy: An International Journal, 14,* 127–136.

Wheeler, S., Aveline, M., & Barkham, M. (2011). Counselling and psychotherapy research practice–based supervision research: A network of researchers using a common toolkit. *Counselling & Psychotherapy Research, 11,* 88–96.

Wheeler, S., & King, D. (2000). Do counselling supervisors want or need to have their supervision supervised? An exploratory study. *British Journal of Guidance & Counselling, 28*(2), 279–290.

Wheeler, S., & Richards, K. (2007). The impact of clinical supervision on counselors and therapists, their practice and their clients. A systematic review of the literature. *Counselling & Psychotherapy Research, 7,* 54–65.

Whiston, S. C., & Emerson, S. (1989). Ethical implications for supervisors in counseling of trainees. *Counselor Education & Supervision, 28,* 318–325.

White, H. D., & Rudolph, B. A. (2000). A pilot investigation of the reliability and validity of the Group Supervisory Behavior Scale (GBS). *The Clinical Supervisor, 19,* 161–171.

White, M. B., & Russell, C. S. (1997). Examining the multifaceted notion of isomorphism in marriage and family therapy supervision: A quest for conceptual clarity. *Journal of Marital and Family Therapy, 23,* 315–333.

White, V. E., & Queener, J. (2003). Supervisor and supervisee attachments and social provisions related to the supervisory working alliance. *Counselor Education and Supervision, 42,* 203–218.

Whiting, J. B. (2007). Authors, artists, and social constructionism: A case study of narrative supervision. *The American Journal of Family Therapy, 35,* 139–150.

Whitman, S. M., Ryan, B., Rubenstein, D. F. (2001). Psychotherapy supervisor training: Differences between psychiatry and other mental health disciplines. *Academic Psychiatry, 25,* 156–161. Retrieved online on May 18, 2012, from ap.psychiatryonline.org/article.aspx?articleID=47460

Whittaker, S. M. (2004). *A multi-vocal synthesis of supervisees' anxiety and self-efficacy during clinical supervision: Meta-analysis and interviews.* Unpublished dissertation, Virginia Polytechnic Institute and State University. Retrieved December 20, 2007, from http://scholar.lib.vt.edu/theses/available/etd-09152004-151749

Wiggins, J. S. (1985). Interpersonal circumplex models: 1948–1983. *Journal of Personality Assessment, 49,* 626–631.

Wilbur, M. P., & Roberts-Wilbur, J. (1983). Schemata of the steps of the SGS model. Unpublished table.

Wilbur, M. P., Roberts-Wilbur, J. M., Hart, G., Morris, J. R., & Betz, R. L. (1994). Structured Group Supervision (SGS): A pilot study. *Counselor Education & Supervision, 33,* 262–279.

Wilcoxon, S. A. (1992). Videotape review of supervision-of-supervision in concurrent training: Allowing trainees to peer through the door. *Family Therapy, 19,* 143–153.

Wiley, M. O. (1994, August). *Supervising oneself in independent practice: From student to solo practitioner.* Paper presented at the American Psychological Association, Los Angeles, CA.

Wiley, M., & Ray, P. (1986). Counseling supervision by developmental level. *Journal of Counseling Psychology, 33,* 439–445.

Wilkerson, K. (2006). Peer supervision for the professional development of school counselors: Toward an understanding of terms and findings. *Counselor Education and Supervision, 46,* 59–67.

Williams, A. (1995). *Visual and active supervision: Roles, focus, technique.* New York: W. W. Norton.

Williams, A. B. (2000). Contribution of supervisors' covert communication to the parallel process. *Dissertation Abstracts International Section A: Humanities & Social Sciences Vol. 61*(3-A), 1165.

Williams, E. N., Judge, A. B., Hill, C. E., & Hoffman, M. A. (1997). Experiences of novice therapists in prepracticum: Trainees', clients', and supervisors' perceptions of therapists' personal reactions and management strategies. *Journal of Counseling Psychology, 44,* 390–399.

Winstanley, J., & White, E. (2011). The MCSS-26: Revision of the Manchester Clinical Supervision Scale using the Rasch measurement model. *Journal of Nursing Measurement, 19,* 160–178.

Winter, M., & Holloway, E. L. (1991). Relation of trainee experience, conceptual level, and supervisor approach to selection of audiotaped counseling passages. *The Clinical Supervisor, 9*(2), 87–103.

Wise, P. S., Lowery, S., & Silverglade, L. (1989). Personal counseling for counselors in training: Guidelines for supervisors. *Counselor Education & Supervision, 28,* 326–336.

Wong, Y.-L. S. (1997). Live supervision in family therapy: Trainee perspectives. *The Clinical Supervisor, 15*(1), 145–157.

Wood, B., Klein, S., Cross, H., Lammers, C., & Elliot, J. (1985). Impaired practitioners: Psychologists' opinions about prevalence, and proposals for intervention. *Professional Psychology: Research & Practice, 16,* 843–850.

Woodside, D. B. (1994). Reverse live supervision: Leveling the supervisory playing field. *The Supervision Bulletin, VII*(2), 6.

Woodworth, C. B. (2000). Legal issues in counseling practice. In H. Hackney (Ed.), *Practice issues for the beginning counselor* (pp. 119–136). Boston, MA: Allyn & Bacon.

Woody, R. H. & Associates. (1984). *The law and the practice of human services*. San Francisco, CA: Jossey-Bass.

Woolley, G. (1991). Beware the well-intentioned therapist. *The Family Therapy Networker*, 15 (Jan./Feb.), 30.

Worthen, V., & McNeill, B. W. (1996). A phenomenological investigation of "good" supervision events. *Journal of Counseling Psychology, 43*, 25–34.

Worthen, V. E., & Lambert, M. J. (2007). Outcome oriented supervision: Advantages of adding systematic client tracking to supportive consultations. *Psychotherapy, 7*(March), 48–53.

Worthington, E. L. (1984). Empirical investigation of supervision of counselors as they gain experience. *Journal of Counseling Psychology, 31*, 63–75.

Worthington, E. L., Jr. (1987). Changes in supervision as counselors and supervisors gain experience: A review. *Professional Psychology: Research and Practice, 18*, 189–208.

Worthington, E. L., Jr., & Roehlke, H. J. (1979). Effective supervision as perceived by beginning counselors-in-training. *Journal of Counseling Psychology, 26*, 64–73.

Worthington, R. L., Savoy, H. B., Dillon, F. R., & Vernaglia, E. R. (2002). Heterosexual identity development: A multidimensional model of individual and social identity. *The Counseling Psychologist, 30*, 496–531.

Worthington, E. L., Jr., & Stern, A. (1985). Effects of supervisor and supervisee degree level and gender on the supervisory relationship. *Journal of Counseling Psychology, 32*, 252–262.

Worthington, R. L., Tan, J. A., & Poulin, K. (2002). Ethically questionable behaviors among supervisees: An exploratory investigation. *Ethics & Behavior, 12*, 323–351.

Woskett, V., & Page, S. (2001). *The cyclical model of supervision: A container for creativity and chaos*. In M. Carroll & M. Tholstrup (Eds.), *Integrative approaches to supervision* (pp. 13–31). London: Jessica Kingsley Publishers.

Wright, L. M. (1986). An analysis of live supervision "phone-ins" in family therapy. *Journal of Marital & Family Therapy, 12*, 187–191.

Wulf, J., & Nelson, M. L. (2001). Experienced psychologists' recollections of internship supervision and its contributions to their development. *The Clinical Supervisor, 19*, 123–145.

Wynne, M. E., Susman, M., Ries, S., Birringer, J., & Katz, L. (1994). A method for assessing therapists' recall of in-session events. *Journal of Counseling Psychology, 41*, 53–57.

Yabusaki, A. S. (2010). Reflections on the importance of place. *Training & Education in Professional Psychology, 4*, 3–6.

Yager, G. G., Wilson, F. R., Brewer, D., & Kinnetz, P. (1989). *The development and validation of an instrument to measure counseling supervisor focus and style*. Paper presented at the American Educational Research Association, San Francisco.

Yalom, I. D. (1985). *The theory and practice of group psychotherapy* (3rd ed.). New York: Basic Books.

Yeh, C. J., Chang, T., Chiang, L., Drost, C. M., Spelliscy, D., Carter, R. T., & Chang, Y. (2008). Development, content, process and outcomes of an online peer supervision group for counselor trainees. *Computers in Human Behavior, 24*, 2889–2903.

Yerkes, R. M., & Dodson, J. D. (1908). The relation of strength of stimulus to rapidity of habit formation. *Journal of Comparative Neurology and Psychology, 18*, 459–482.

Yerushalmi, H. (1999). The roles of group supervision of supervision. *Psychoanalytic Psychology, 16*, 426–447.

Yeung, K. T., & Martin, L. (2003). The looking glass self: An empirical test and elaboration. *Social Forces, 81*, 843–879.

Yogev, S. (1982). An eclectic model of supervision: A developmental sequence of beginning psychotherapy students. *Professional Psychology, 13*, 236–243.

Yoon, E., Langrehr, K., & Ong, L. Z. (2011). Content analysis of acculturation research in counseling and counseling psychology: A 22-year review. *Journal of Counseling Psychology, 58*, 83–96.

Young, J., Perlesz, A., Paterson, R., O'Hanlon, B., Newbold, A., Chaplin, R., & Bridge, S. (1989). The reflecting team process in training. *Australia & New Zealand Journal of Family Therapy, 10*, 69–74.

Young, T. L., Lambie, G. W., Hutchinson, T., & Thurston-Dyer, J. (2011). The integration of reflectivity in developmental supervision: Implications for clinical supervisors. *The Clinical Supervisor, 30*, 1–18.

Yourman, D. B. (2003). Trainee disclosure in psychotherapy supervision: The impact of shame. *Journal of Clinical Psychology, 59,* 601–609.

Yourman, D. B., & Farber, B. A. (1996). Nondisclosure and distortion in psychotherapy supervision. *Psychotherapy: Theory, Research, Practice, Training, 33,* 567-575.

Yozwiak, J. A., Robiner, W. N., Victor, A. M., & Durmusoglu, G. (2010). Videoconferencing at psychology internships: Interns' perceptions of interactive television experiences and prospects. *The Journal of Clinical Psychology in Medical Settings, 17*(3), 238–248.

Yu, A. (2012). *iSupe: An innovation in live supervision.* The Eighth International Interdisciplinary Conference on Clinical Supervision, Garden City, NY, June 13–15.

Yum, J. O. (1988). The impact of Confucianism on interpersonal relationships and communication patterns in East Asia. *Communication Monographs, 55,* 374–388.

Zajonc, R. B. (1965). Social facilitation. *Science, 149,* 269–274.

Zakrzewski, R.F. (2006). A national survey of America Psychology Association Student affiliates' involvement and ethical training in psychology educator-student sexual relationships. *Professional Psychology: Research & Practice, 6,* 724–730.

Zarski, J. J., Sand-Pringle, C., Pannell, L., & Lindon, C. (1995). Critical issues in supervision: Marital and family violence. *The Family Journal: Counseling and Therapy for Couples and Families, 3,* 18–26.

Žorga, S. Dekleva, B., & Kobolt, A. (2001). The process of internal evaluation as a tool for improving peer supervision. *International Journal for the Advancement of Counseling, 23,* 151–162.

Index

Page references followed by "f" indicate illustrated figures or photographs; followed by "t" indicates a table.

D

Q

R

U

V

W

Z